Visual Languages for Interactive Computing:
Definitions and Formalizations

Fernando Ferri
Istituto di Ricerca sulla Popolazione e le Politiche Sociali
Consiglio Nazionale delle Ricerche, Italy

INFORMATION SCIENCE REFERENCE

Hershey · New York

Acquisitions Editor:	Kristin Klinger
Development Editor:	Kristin Roth
Senior Managing Editor:	Jennifer Neidig
Managing Editor:	Sara Reed
Assistant Managing Editor:	
Copy Editor:	Larissa Vinci
Typesetter:	Michael Brehm
Cover Design:	Lisa Tosheff
Printed at:	Yurchak Printing Inc.

Published in the United States of America by
Information Science Reference (an imprint of IGI Global)
701 E. Chocolate Avenue, Suite 200
Hershey PA 17033
Tel: 717-533-8845
Fax: 717-533-8661
E-mail: cust@igi-pub.com
Web site: http://www.igi-pub.com/reference

and in the United Kingdom by
Information Science Reference (an imprint of IGI Global)
3 Henrietta Street
Covent Garden
London WC2E 8LU
Tel: 44 20 7240 0856
Fax: 44 20 7379 0609
Web site: http://www.eurospanonline.com

Library of Congress Cataloging-in-Publication Data

Visual languages for interactive computing : definitions and formalizations / Fernando Ferri, editor.

p. cm.

Summary: "This book presents problems and methodologies related to the syntax, semantics, and ambiguities of visual languages. It defines and formalizes visual languages for interactive computing, as well as visual notation interpretation"--Provided by publisher.

Includes bibliographical references and index.

ISBN 978-1-59904-534-4 (hardcover) -- ISBN 978-1-59904-536-8 (ebook)

1. Interactive computer systems. 2. Visual programming languages (Computer science) 3. Visual programming (Computer science) I. Ferri, Fernando.

QA76.9.I58V59 2007

005.1'18--dc22

2007007281

British Cataloguing in Publication Data
A Cataloguing in Publication record for this book is available from the British Library.

All work contributed to this book set is new, previously-unpublished material. The views expressed in this book are those of the authors, but not necessarily of the publisher.

Table of Contents

Section I
Visual Languages Theory

Section IV
Visual Interfaces for Standard Languages

Section V
Visualization, Aesthetic Computing, and Usability

Detailed Table of Contents

Section I
Visual Languages Theory

*This chapter introduces the theory of visual languages providing characteristics of interactive processes
and the modelling of visual transformations by visual rewriting systems. The dynamics of visual sentences
are discussed considering the enabling and disabling mechanisms and coordination of transformations.
Finally the chapter gives, before concluding, some elements for the integration of the theory's components
to provide a framework for the design of interactive visual systems.*

*This chapter discusses visual and diagrammatic languages in logic perspective. The grammatical
approach to visual language specification, highlighting its shortcomings as a basis for this research
plan, is presented. The different logic approaches to diagrammatic languages and advantages and
disadvantages of the different types of logic formalization are discussed too. An original approach, that
is based on linear logic and completely subsumes the grammatical approach, is proposed to avoid most
of these shortcomings.*

*This chapter proposes an abstract view of the semantic of visual elements with respect to a transforma-
tion-based metamodel approach. It introduces and discusses an integrated framework and interactive*

environment, which uses a collection of metamodels to express both syntactical characterisations and semantic interpretations of diagrammatic sentences.

Chapter IV

The chapter presents an approach for the definition of multi-view visual languages (MVVLs). It introduces two techniques to define MVVL environments: meta-modelling and graph transformation. The former is used to describe the syntax of the language as a whole. Consistency between views is ensured by translating each one into a unique repository model, which conforms to the meta-model of the language as a whole. The translation is performed by automatically generated graph transformation rules.

Chapter V

This chapter gives an overview of extended positional grammars (XPG), an extension of context-free grammars used for modelling visual notations. The chapter describes the XpLR parsing algorithm (Costagliola, Deufemia, & Polese, 2004) based on the well-known LR parsing technique. The benefits of the formalism of a visual language include easier customisation and modification as well as maintenance and debugging, code and report generation by definition of suitable semantic productions, implementation of visual and textual languages within a common framework.

Chapter VI

This chapter classifies ambiguities that can arise in visual sentences into lexical and syntactic ambiguities. When an image associated with a visual sentence is unable to exactly express (be completely faithful to) the user's intentions, the system may produce an erroneous interpretation. In particular, a visual sentence can assume more than one meaning, or incorrect/imprecise user's drawing actions does not permit an unequivocal interpretation of the image produced by the.

Chapter VII

This chapter proposes a classification of methods to resolve ambiguities that can arise in visual sentences related to the system's interpretation function. These methods are grouped in three classes: prevention of ambiguities, a-posteriori resolution, and approximation resolution methods. Prevention methods are based on a predefined set of possible system's configurations. A-posteriori resolution methods are based on mediation techniques. Approximation resolution methods are based on theories such as Fuzzy Logic, Markov Random Field, and Bayesian Networks.

Section II
Approaches and Methods for Specific Domains

This chapter discusses the main characteristics of VQLs analysing visual languages to query conventional relational databases and information systems with a less rigid structure such as Web resources storing XML documents. It classifies VQLs according to the adopted visual representation technique (e.g., based on forms and tables, diagrams, icons, sketches, or combinations thereof) and the underlying data model, (e.g., visual languages to query relational databases, object-oriented databases, collections of XML documents, and languages specifically designed for particular data such as geographic and multidimensional data).

This chapter focuses on visual query languages for spatio-temporal databases. It presents a spatio-temporal visual query environment (S-TVQE) and a VQS that allows the formulation of conventional, spatial, temporal, and spatio-temporal database queries in an integrated environment. With S-TVQE, the user, instead of querying the database by textual query languages, interacts with the system by visual operators to state the query conditions.

This chapter presents a multi-facet design of interactive systems considering that the knowledge relevant to the design of an interactive system is distributed among domain experts, software engineers, and human-computer interaction experts. Each community describes an interactive system through visual sentences of a visual language (VL). Each VL permits user-system interaction processes to be specified from a different point of view and for a different audience.

The chapter presents a framework for creating visual languages to represent interactions using human movement as a source for the language's core concepts. It starts from the assumption that interaction is the core of interactive computing, but poorly understood.

This chapter presents a state of the art sketch of understanding techniques and tools. Sketch recognition is a particularly difficult task as the symbols of a sketched diagram can be drawn with different stroke orders, numbers, and directions.

Section III
Visual Languages for the Semantic Web

This chapter discusses user-interface formalisation in visual data mining and provides an approach for the formalisation of the visual interface of a core data mining system. The description of the system properties is given without touching on implementation details, and enables fundamental design issues to be detected before they are manifested in the implementation.

This chapter discusses the visualisation of defeasible logic rules in the semantic Web domain. Logic plays an important role in the development of the semantic Web and defeasible reasoning seems a very suitable tool. The proposed approach uses direct graphs to assist the user. It appears highly applicable to the representation of rule attacks and superiorities in defeasible reasoning.

This chapter discusses of the knowledge representation for AI planning problems, especially those related to semantic Web service composition. It discusses current approaches in encoding planning problems and presents ViTAPlan, a user-friendly visual tool for planning.

Section IV
Visual Interfaces for Standard Languages

Chapter XVI

This chapter shows UML diagrams for describing the user interfaces introducing the user-interaction, user-interface, and GUI-class diagrams. It also examines code generation to implement the system's user interfaces through GUI-class diagrams and user-interaction diagrams. A case study of an Internet book shopping system is introduced to test and illustrate the proposed user interaction and interface design technique.

Chapter XVII

This chapter describes XQBE, a visual framework for XML data management, enabling the visualisation of XML documents, query formulation, the representation and specification of document schemata, the definition of integrity constraints, the formulation of updates, and the expression of reactive behaviours in response to data modifications.

Section V
Visualization, Aesthetic Computing, and Usability

Chapter XVIII

This chapter analyses the relationships among geovisualisation, human computer interaction (HCI), geographic information systems (GIS), and cartography as a means of supporting decision making. It discusses the importance of data modelling and associated visualisations in terms of what the user can do by way of analysis and the methods by which he can undertake the analysis.

Chapter IXX

This chapter presents an algorithm for the generic representation of biochemical graphs in which users can present knowledge about how to draw graphs in accordance with the biochemical semantics. The visualisation tools must be able to cope with graphs and take account of the particular semantics of all kinds of biochemical subgraphs.

Preface

INTRODUCTION FROM THE EDITOR

This book gathers the contributions of authors working in the area of visual languages from countries as diverse as Spain, Italy, United Kingdom, Australia, Greece, Canada, Brazil, and the USA.

It consists of 22 chapters written by a total of 54 different authors to provide an in-depth investigation of new approaches and methods for visual language theory, visualisation techniques, aesthetic computing, and usability.

I hope that academics, researchers, technicians, and students in computer science will find this book a valuable contribution to their knowledge of this important research area.

In normal life, people organise a complex structure of signs to communicate with the world around them. The brain acts as an interface between the sign system and the environment, orienting the individual in space. Visual languages systemise the visual representation of concepts in a formalised language using visual objects such as images or pictorial objects and possibly formal visual expressions. They are based on simple visual elements, which construct symbols that can be grouped to form structured visual sentences.

THE OVERALL OBJECTIVE OF THIS BOOK

The main objective and mission of this book is to present problems and methodologies concerning the syntax, semantics, and ambiguities of visual languages. Various syntactic techniques can be used to define visual languages, which differ significantly in the way they conceptualise a visual notation and describe its syntactic structure. From the semantic point of view, the precise meaning of a visual language is required in order to use it effectively. Finally, ambiguity is one of the main problems of visual languages. A visual configuration expressing a sentence or a visual action may be interpreted in a number of ways producing ambiguity. Visual languages offer an intuitive and incremental view of sentences, but may give different interpretations of the same sentence.

ORGANISATION

The book contains 22 chapters split into five sections. Section I examines the theory underlying visual languages. Section II discusses different approaches to and methods for visual languages on specific domains. Section III describes visual languages for the semantic Web. Section IV examines visual interfaces for standard languages. Finally, Section V considers several topics closely related to visual languages such as visualisation, aesthetic computing, and usability.

Section I. Visual Languages Theory

Section I opens with a chapter by Bottoni, Costabile, Levialdi, and Mussio, introducing the *Theory of Visual Sentences* by highlighting their main concepts, presenting some problems central to the definition of a theory of visual languages, and describing current developments. After an informal overview of the main components of the theory, the authors explore the characteristics of interactive processes and the modelling of visual transformations by visual rewriting systems. They go on to examine the dynamics of visual sentences, focusing on the relationship between constancy and variability in visual sentences, enabling and disabling mechanisms and coordination of transformations. The chapter ends with a discussion of how the theory's components can be integrated to provide a framework for the design of interactive visual systems before drawing some conclusions.

Chapter II, by Meyer and Bottoni, traces progress in *Visual and Diagrammatic Languages: The Logic Perspective*. The chapter starts by outlining the grammatical approach to visual language specification highlighting its shortcomings as a basis for this research plan. It then revisits the history of logic approaches to diagrammatic languages and details the comparative advantages and disadvantages of the different types of logic formalisation. Finally, it develops a new approach based on linear logic, which avoids most of these shortcomings and completely subsumes the grammatical approach.

Chapter III, by Bottoni, Frediani, Quattrocchi, Rende, Sarajlic, and Ventriglia, proposes a *Transformation-Based Metamodel Approach,* which enables an abstract view of the semantic roles that visual elements can play with respect to the process being described. More specifically, the chapter proposes an integrated framework and interactive environment based on a collection of metamodels in which it is possible to express both syntactical characterisations of diagrammatic sentences and their semantic interpretations.

Chapter IV, by de Lara and Guerra, presents an approach for the definition of *Multi-View Visual Languages (MVVLs)*. These are made up of a set of different diagram types, which are used to specify the different aspects of a system. The chapter introduces two techniques to define MVVL environments: Meta modelling and graph transformation. The former is used to describe the syntax of the language as a whole. A meta-model for each of the language's diagram types (*viewpoints*) is defined as a restriction of the complete MVVL meta-model. Consistency between views is ensured by translating each one into a unique *repository* model, which conforms to the meta-model of the language as a whole. The translation is performed by automatically generated graph transformation rules.

Chapter V, by Costagliola, Deufemia, and Polese, presents an overview of *eXtended positional grammars* (XPG), a grammar formalism for modelling visual notations, which represents an extension of context-free grammars and describes the XpLR parsing methodology. XPG and XpLR extend positional grammars (PG) and the associated pLR parsing methodology. These extensions have enabled the modelling and efficient parsing of a wide class of notations. The associated parsing algorithm is the XpLR parser based on the well-known LR parsing technique. The benefits of the formalism of a visual language include easier customisation and modification as well as maintenance and debugging, code and report generation by definition of suitable semantic productions, and implementation of visual and textual languages within a common framework.

Chapter VI, by D'Ulizia, Grifoni, and Rafanelli, classifies the *Different Kinds of Ambiguities* that can arise in visual sentences, distinguishing between lexical and syntactic ambiguities. When an image associated with a visual sentence is unable to express exactly (be completely faithful to) the user's intentions, the system may produce an erroneous interpretation. Ambiguities are generally produced by (1) the language, which can produce such one-to-many relationships, (2) imprecision introduced by the interaction behaviour producing the visual sentence. In the first case, an image can assume more than one meaning. The second case is connected with incorrect/imprecise information that does not permit an unequivocal interpretation of the image produced by the drawing actions.

The final chapter in this section, by Caschera, Ferri, and Grifoni, proposes *Different Kinds of Solutions to Ambiguities* that can arise in visual sentences. This chapter deals with ambiguities related to the system's interpretation function and methods to resolve them. These methods can be grouped in three classes: prevention of ambiguities, a-posteriori resolution, and approximation resolution methods. Prevention methods consider only a predefined set of possible system configurations, avoiding ambiguous configurations. A-posteriori resolution methods are based on mediation techniques, which enable the user to disambiguate his or her intention by dialogue. In contrast, approximation resolution methods are based on theories such as Fuzzy Logic, Markov Random Field, and Bayesian Networks and do not require user disambiguation.

Section II. Approaches and Methods for Specific Domains

Section II opens with the chapter by Caschera, D'Ulizia, and Tininini, which analyses the main characteristics of VQLs, concentrating on *visual languages to Query Conventional Relational Databases* but also examining information systems with a less rigid structure such as Web resources storing XML documents. It considers two main VQL classifications: the adopted visual representation technique (e.g., based on forms and tables, diagrams, icons, sketches, or combinations thereof) and the underlying data model (e.g., visual languages to query relational databases, object-oriented databases, collections of XML documents, and languages specifically designed for particular data such as geographic and multidimensional data).

Chapter IX, by Cavalcanti, Schiel, and de Souza Baptista, focuses on the specific category of *Visual Query Languages for Spatio-Temporal Databases,* which enable formulation of queries involving both spatial and temporal dimensions. Current papers treat these dimensions separately with only a few integrated proposals. This chapter presents a VQS called spatio-temporal visual query environment (S-TVQE), which allows the formulation of conventional, spatial, temporal, and spatio-temporal database queries in an integrated environment. With S-TVQE, the user, instead of querying the database by textual query languages, interacts with the system by visual operators to state the query conditions.

Chapter X, by Fogli, Marcante, Mussio, Provenza, and Piccinno, considers that the knowledge relevant to the design of an interactive system is distributed among several stakeholders: domain experts, software engineers, and human-computer interaction experts, and presents a *Multi-facet Design of Interactive Systems*. Each community describes an interactive system through visual sentences of a visual language (VL). This view results in an approach to VIS design based on the definition and use of three visual languages. Each VL permits user-system interaction process to be specified from a different point of view and for a different audience.

The chapter by Deray and Simoff starts from the assumption that although interaction is the core of interactive computing, its mechanisms remain poorly understood. The tendency has been to examine interactions in terms of the results they produce rather than to provide mechanisms explaining how interactions unfold in time. The authors present a framework for creating visual languages to represent interactions using human movement as a source for the language's core concepts. The approach is motivated and supported by evidence from research on kinaesthetic thinking that constructs based on human movement support higher-level cognitive processes and can be intuitively recognised by humans.

The final chapter of Section II, by Deufemia, considers *Sketch Understanding*. This is a particularly difficult task as the symbols of a sketched diagram can be drawn with different stroke orders, numbers, and directions. The recognition process is often made even harder by lack of precision and ambiguities in messy, hand-drawn sketches. The chapter presents a brief survey of sketch understanding techniques and tools.

Section III. Visual Languages for the Semantic Web

Chapter XIII, by Catarci, Kimani, and Lodi, examines *User-Interface Formalisation in Visual Data Mining*. A formal specification facilitates the description of the system properties without touching on implementation details, and enables fundamental design issues to be detected before they are manifested in the implementation. An approach for the formalisation of the visual interface of a core data mining system is given.

Chapter XIV, by Kontopoulos, Bassiliades, and Antoniou, discusses the *Visualisation of Defeasible Logic Rules* in the semantic Web domain. Logic plays an important role in the development of the semantic Web and defeasible reasoning seems a very suitable tool. However, it is too complex for end users who often need graphical traces and explanation mechanisms for the derived conclusions. The chapter proposes an approach that uses directed graphs to assist the user by offering the notion of direction, which appears highly applicable to the representation of rule attacks and superiorities in defeasible reasoning.

The last chapter in the section, by Vrakas, Hatzi, Bassiliades, Anagnostopoulos, and Vlahavas, is concerned with *Knowledge Representation for AI Planning Problems*, especially those related to semantic Web service composition. It discusses current approaches in encoding planning problems and presents ViTAPlan, a user-friendly visual tool for planning.

Section IV. Visual Interfaces for Standard Languages

Chapter XVI, by Almendros-Jimenez and Iribarne, shows how to use and specialise *UML Diagrams for Describing the User Interfaces* of a software system considering three specialised UML diagrams called user-interaction, user-interface, and GUI-class diagrams. It also examines code generation to implement the system's user interfaces through GUI-class diagrams and user-interaction diagrams. A case study of an Internet book shopping system is introduced to test and illustrate the proposed user interaction and interface design technique.

Chapter XVII, by Campi, Martinenghi, and Raffio, describes a visual framework, XQBE that covers the most important aspects of *XML Data Management*, spanning the visualisation of XML documents, query formulation, the representation, and specification of document schemata, the definition of integrity constraints, the formulation of updates, and the expression of reactive behaviours in response to data modifications.

Section V. Visualisation Aesthetic Computing, and Usability

Chapter XVIII, by Voudouris and Marsh, discusses how cartography, GIS, and HCI shape aspects of *Geovisualisation* can support decision-making. The chapter analyses the relationships among geovisualisation, human computer interaction (HCI), geographic information systems (GIS), and cartography as a means of supporting decision-making. It emphasises the importance of data modelling and associated visualisations in terms of what the user can do by way of analysis and the methods by which he or she can undertake the analysis.

The following chapter, by Skhiri and Zimanyi, presents a *Graph Layout Algorithm for Drawing Biochemical Networks*. Due to the huge amount of information available in biochemical databases, biologists need sophisticated tools to accurately extract the information from such databases and interpret it correctly. Those tools must be able to dynamically generate any kind of biochemical subgraph (i.e., metabolic pathways, genetic regulation, signal transduction, etc.) in a single graph. The visualisation tools must be able to cope with such graphs and take account of the particular semantics of all kinds of biochemical subgraphs. The chapter presents an algorithm designed for the generic representation of biochemical graphs, in which users can present knowledge about how to draw graphs in accordance with the biochemical semantics.

Fishwick discusses the *Aesthetic Computing Method*. The purpose of aesthetic computing is to apply the theory and practice of art and design to the field of computing. The range of aesthetics within the arts is broader than in mathematics and computing where aesthetics is often synonymous with optimality criteria. This chapter introduces aesthetic computing for the multimedia representation of formal structures.

Chapter 21, by Costa, Grings, and Santos, presents *Documentation Methods for Visual Languages*. Visual programming languages (VPL) are generally self-documenting; this chapter analyses their use for the design and documentation of real world applications. Finally, the chapter proposes new tools and approaches for the documentation of data flow for VPL.

The book ends with the chapter by Padula and Reggiori, discussing *Usability*. This does not propose a specific viewpoint on usability but rather examines numerous concepts, aspects, and potentialities, which must nowadays be taken into consideration when detailing usability and design suited systems. This topic is currently of great interest in the field of human-computer interaction as it is highly dependent on the user interface. Systems must be used by a community of users in their working activity as a whole to process material or information, modifying not only rough material but also the working environment and methods. This requires them to be considered as tools in a social context, which expects ever-greater technological progress.

Section I
Visual Languages Theory

Chapter I
The Theory of Visual Sentences to Formalize Interactive Visual Messages

Paolo Bottoni
Università "La Sapienza" di Roma, Italy

Maria Francesca Costabile
Università di Bari, Italy

Stefano Levialdi
Università "La Sapienza" di Roma, Italy

Piero Mussio
Università di Milano

ABSTRACT

This chapter introduces an approach to the theory of visual languages based on the notion of visual sentence as defined by the integration of pictures and descriptions. The chapter proceeds firstly by tracking the history of the ideas that stemmed from the initial IEEE Workshop held at Hiroshima (Japan) during 1984 and then gradually progressing toward the formalisms that build up the theory of visual languages. The theory of visual sentences allows a coherent view of both static and dynamic aspects of human-computer interaction, as well as of the relations between the user and the machine during the interaction.

INTRODUCTION

The official inception of visual languages as an independent research field can be dated to the First International Workshop on Visual Languages (IEEE, 1984) held in Hiroshima in 1984, where a number of researchers subscribed to the idea that graphical and pictorial information (as opposed to simple textual information) could better represent both data and computations. This was motivated by the development of the first computers with a visual user interface based on the desktop metaphor, which in the 80s started to be commercially available after years of developing prototypes in research laboratories. Shneiderman coined the term "direct-manipulation" to refer to the way users were interacting with the elements of a computer system including data and functions operating on such data (Shneiderman, 1983). The key elements of direct manipulation interface are: (a) visibility of objects of interest, (b) substitution of textual commands by physical actions and button clicks, and (c) rapid and reversible incremental actions with immediate feedback.

The workshop in Hiroshima was the first of a series that continued in the following years, sponsored by IEEE, and held annually since 1988; it is now called *IEEE Symposium on Visual Languages and Human-Centric Computing* to indicate a broader spectrum of interest. The scientific research areas of the participants at the Hiroshima workshop were image processing and pattern recognition, database querying, and program visualization (especially in the form of structured flowcharts, data and control flow diagrams, etc.), thus showing a vast field of applications. Formal tools were available from pattern recognition, where systems based on rewriting of strings or even of non-linear structures such as pictures or graphs, had become in current use already in the 70's. Hence, a mix of practice and theory set the scene for the following developments. Several formalisms for visual languages have been proposed in the literature ever since.

The so-called *theory of visual sentences* has been developed with the goal to formalize *visual languages* used in human-computer interaction (HCI), also called *interaction visual languages*. Since the 80's, the availability on the market of graphical workstations has placed more and more emphasis on human-computer interaction (HCI) via pictorial representations including images, sketches, diagrams, and forms, as well as text. Pictorial representations play two fundamental roles: communication between humans and programs and communication among humans through computers. In both cases, pictorial representations are the exchanged messages. Such messages may be

regarded as images in that they are represented on a computer screen, which is structured as a rectangular array of pixels; the concept of image is thus generalized to any arrangement of signs appearing on the whole screen. Humans act on these images to steer the computation and/or the communication. Computer systems act on them to respond to human requests and to synthesise the state of the interactive computation.

The *theory of visual sentences* formalizes the way the computer associates a computational meaning with an image shown on the computer screen and, conversely, the way it generates an image on the screen from a computation. The visual sentence is defined as an interpreted image and a visual language is viewed as a set of visual sentences in a user-computer dialogue. This theory emphasizes the algebraic structure of visual languages, characterised by the relations between the structures present in the images on the computer screen, by the formal description of each image (its meaning) managed by the computer or held by the user, and by the relationships between image and description. The theory models the semantic level of visual interaction, pointing out the existence of two semantics, one of the user and one of the computer, which can explain many of the difficulties of human-computer interaction. It also provides a formalism to model the transformations of the visual sentences that occur during the interaction between a human and a computer, through a visual interface (i.e., a visual language).

In this chapter, we summarize the *theory of visual sentences* by highlighting its main concepts, how it models interaction visual languages of current WIMP (Window, Icon, Menu, Pointer) interfaces (Dix, Finlay, Abowd, & Beale, 1998), and briefly describe its current developments. The chapter has the following organization. We first present some problems central to the definition of a theory of visual languages, and which provide the starting impulse for our work. After an informal overview of the main components of the theory, we explore characteristics of interactive processes, and the modeling of visual transformations by visual rewriting systems. In the following three sections, we deal with dynamics of visual sentences, focusing, respectively, on the relation between constancy and variability in visual sentences, with mechanisms of enabling and disabling, and with coordination of transformations. We then discuss how the components of the theory can be integrated to provide a framework for designing interactive visual systems before drawing conclusions.

PROBLEMS IN THE THEORY OF VISUAL LANGUAGES

The foundation of a theory of visual languages presents specific problems that only to a point can be faced with traditional tools from the theory of formal, programming, or natural languages. While we can still employ the traditional distinction between syntax, semantics, and pragmatics defined by studies on natural languages, the availability of a second dimension marks a substantial difference from the one-dimensional setting in which most frequently studied languages have traditionally been formalized. In particular, in absence of a predefined order in generating or interpreting the actual deployment of 2-D symbols in the 2-D plane a wealth of spatial relations can be arbitrarily imposed on any arrangement of bidimensional elements, so that the identification of those semantically significant must be carefully conducted. Finally, visual languages have an aspect of *concreteness* (Goldberg, Burnett, & Lewis, 1995), so that different arrangements of the same elements can be interpreted in different ways, even when restricted to lie on a single strip. Consider, for example, a linear representation of a highway where nodes represent its exits. Nodes can be shown at the same distance from one another or at distances proportional to the actual distance on the highway, or clustered according

to the provinces to which they belong. This also implies that any visual specification of a visual language must be interpreted so as to identify which parts of its concrete specification can be abstracted from and which retained. Of course, this wide scope of problems is doubled by the fact that any visual sentence, besides having to be managed by some programmed tool, is ultimately designed for being interpreted, and possibly interacted with, by some human user. Hence, the relations between the interpretation designed into the tool by its programmer and those of the possible users of the visual sentence, must be considered. This involves cognitive aspects which are remote from the studies on formal languages, which the first approaches to the theory of visual languages had turned to.

The theory of visual sentences tries to provide a reference framework to account for the many aspects of visual languages, in particular those exploited for interaction between human and computer. Along this line, it starts by studying three fundamental aspects: the algebraic structure underlying the possibility of bidimensional arrangements of structures in an image, the relation between these pictorial structures and their interpretation, and the notion of visual alphabet as a system of visual types abstracting from, but constraining, the admissible concrete representations of instances of the type.

AN INFORMAL OVERVIEW OF THE THEORY OF VISUAL SENTENCES

Starting from the previous considerations, the *theory of visual sentences* has been developed with the goal to formalize visual languages used in human-computer interaction (HCI), also called interaction visual languages. The first paper that gives the definition of *visual sentence* is Bottoni, Costabile, Levialdi, and Mussio (1995). That paper was the initial seed of the theory; it formalized the way the computer associates a computational meaning with an image (including the whole screen image) and, conversely, the way it generates an image on the screen from a computation. The visual sentence is defined as an interpreted image and a visual language is viewed as a set of visual sentences in a user-computer dialogue. The notion of interpretation supports the possibility of having different descriptions associated with the same image, or of relating different structures to a same symbol, or, vice versa, of reading a same structure in different ways. Several situations are thus modelled, which can arise during an interaction process, and which may either be the cause of errors and misunderstandings or support complex cognitive processes, or allow the use of multiple representations for visualising a given set of data as shown through various examples provided in that paper.

More specifically, a *visual sentence* is defined as a three-component structure consisting of the *image* on the screen, its *meaning* (i.e., its description with respect to the computational process defining the interaction), and the *relations* between program and image components. In Chang and Mussio (1996) and Bottoni, Costabile, Levialdi, and Mussio (1997), a set of visual sentences in a human-computer interaction is defined as *visual language* and it is shown how such a language may be constructed from a finite generator set. This provides the framework to formalize the relations between images and meanings. Meaning description was first given in the form of strings of attributed symbols (Tsai & Fu, 1980), generalizing the seminal work of Fu in pattern recognition, and following a then widespread approach to description formalization, fundamentally aimed at generalizing parsing techniques from context-free string grammars to the bi-dimensional world of images and structures therein. It was soon recognized that the absence of any privileged reading order in bi-dimensional structure makes it difficult to deal with visual processes other than parsing by imposing on the picture the linear order inherent to strings. A more adequate definition

of descriptions as multisets of attributed symbols was therefore soon adopted. Operations on visual sentences were defined, which preserve the structure of operations on the separate components. As a consequence, pictorial and visual alphabets were defined.

In order to allow users to interact with a computer system and to correctly perform their tasks, it is crucial that: (1) both humans and computers assign the same meaning to each message (i.e., to the displayed image, and (2) possible human errors be trapped before they cause any undesired consequence. The objective of the theory of visual sentences is to provide a formal framework and an approach for designing and implementing visual interactive systems, which guarantee these properties. The formal definition of visual sentence emphasizes the fact that in visual interactive systems a complex relation exists between images and descriptions. Within the computer, such descriptions result into structured sets of data or program code. The definition of visual sentence allows the dual and coordinated specification and management of images and underlying computational specifications. Moreover, it allows a systematic study of the characteristics of current visual interactive systems and the specification of the requirements for the design of such systems. In particular, by adopting this point of view, it becomes possible to study visual sentences and visual languages with respect to some basic requirements for interaction, namely that users cannot cause unexpected events and should not become disoriented by the system behaviour (Shneiderman, 1992). Hence, a visual interaction process is seen as a sequence of visual sentences in which, for each visual sentence, only a limited set of legal user actions is possible (Bottoni, Costabile, Levialdi, & Mussio, 1997; Bottoni, Costabile, & Mussio, 1999). In particular, visual sentences within an interaction process are not produced arbitrarily. Each image is generated on the computer screen from the previous one as the result of a system computation, performed either in reaction to a user action or autonomously by the system.

This process of visual sentence transformation is modelled through visual conditional attributed rewriting systems (vCARWs), which are seen as a general tool for the formal description of visual languages (Bottoni, Costabile, Levialdi, & Mussio, 1996; Mussio, Pietrogrande, & Protti, 1991). Compared to other formalisms for specifying visual languages, vCARWs are characterised by dealing directly with elements of visual alphabets. That is to say that they do not involve the use of non-terminal symbols, and that they simultaneously rewrite both the pictorial and the description components of visual sentences. A typical vCARW rule states that if a (multi)set of visual elements are present, they will be replaced by a different (multi)set, provided some condition holds. Some elements can be present both in the antecedent and in the consequent of a rule, thus indicating that they will be modified in some way, or that they simply provide context for the rule application. In Bottoni, Costabile, and Mussio (1999) it was shown how vCARWs have at least the same expressive power of conditional set rewriting systems (Najork & Kaplan, 1993) (the underlying algebra being one of multisets rather than of sets). However, the absence of non-terminals requires specific techniques to embody some constraints on the desired language in the rewriting systems. These constraints can be made explicit by considering a visual language as defined by a pair (vCARW, VALID), where VALID defines a predicate to be satisfied by the visual sentences in the language. It is also possible to introduce different kinds of constraints on the form or on the application of rules in order to achieve specific effects, for example by imposing a certain sequence on rule application, or preventing the execution of some rules in certain configurations of a visual sentence.

In particular, the specification of interactive visual languages must consider that, while vCARWs define the whole set of generatable

visual sentences, some transformations are actually activated by user actions, and only certain actions can be considered legal. Within the theory of vCARWs, mechanisms have therefore been defined to constrain the possible actions. In particular, control automata have been defined whose automatic generation insures that only correct interactions can occur, leading to the generation of visual sentences in the language defined by a vCARW. Moreover, vCARWs can be enriched with enabling mechanisms to prevent the user to try and activate rules, which are not coherent with the current state. This leads to the definition of a new family of vCARWs, called enabling visual Conditional Attributed ReWriting systems (evCARWs) (Bottoni, Chang, Costabile, Levialdi, & Mussio, 2002).

Finally, the antecedent-consequent model of vCARW rules only allows the expression of local effects through a rule application. In order to achieve the effect of global actions, forms of coordination among rules have been defined, so that different rules can be applied concurrently on different matches, leading to the definition of group evCARWs (gevCARWs) (Bottoni et al., 2002).

A moving force in the definition of the theory of vCARWs was the possibility of reflecting these concepts in the implementation of effective visual environments. Hence, attention was placed on the possibility of automatically generating parts of the interaction control, starting from their formal description in terms of vCARWs.

INTERACTION VIA VISUAL LANGUAGES

When a user interacts with a WIMP interface of a computer system, a set of visual sentences belonging to the interaction visual language of that system is produced. In the theory of visual sentences, the interaction between users and computer systems is modelled as a cyclic process in which users and systems communicate by materializing and interpreting a sequence of messages at successive times. These messages are subject to two interpretations: one performed by the user, depending on his or her role in the task, as well as on his or her culture, experience, and skills, and the second, internal to the system, associating the message with a computational meaning, as determined by the programs implemented in the system. In the case of WIMP interfaces, the messages exchanged between user and system are the whole images represented on the screen display, formed by texts, pictures, icons, etc. As shown in Figure 1, the human user and the computer visual interactive system communicate by materialising and interpreting images $i(t_i)$ visible on the computer screen at successive times $t_1,...,t_n$.

The image on the screen is the materialisation of the meaning intended by the sender (human or computer) and must be interpreted by the receiver (computer or human), which associates with it a (possibly different) meaning. The screen is the communication surface between human and computer, thus acting as a bi-directional channel in the transmission of messages. The interaction process is modelled as the generation of a sequence of images, each interpreted by both the human and the computer. Each image derives from the transformation of the previous one, according to the user's actions and/or the computer's activities.

The fundamental cognitive process, which enables the whole visual interaction activity is that of recognising sets of pixels on the screen as functional or perceptual units (Bottoni et al., 1997; Bottoni et al., 2002). Examples of css (*characteristic structures*) are letters in an alphabet, symbols, icons, etc. Users associate each cs with a meaning. This association depends on the capability of the user to interpret the implicit information conveyed by the image on the screen. For example, a radiologist looking at an x-ray image shown on a Web page recognizes and correctly interprets it but, if not acquainted with Web tools, may not understand how to interact with it. On the other hand, a Web surfer looking at the same page may understand how to operate on the shown buttons and menus, but will not be able to interpret the x-ray image. Users recognize complex css formed by simpler ones (words formed by letters, plant maps formed by icons, etc.) and attribute a meaning to them, which stems from the meaning of the component css.

The visual interactive system, on its side, captures every gesture of the user, and interprets it with respect to the image i(t) using a description d of it. The system updates the description

Figure 1. The model of visual interaction at the basis of the theory of visual sentences. The image i(t) materialises the meaning intended by the sender (either the human H or the computer C) and must be interpreted by the receiver (either H or C).

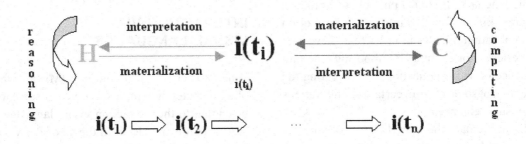

and the image and accordingly changes the set of pixels in the screen.

In the theory of visual sentences, a *characteristic structure* is a set of pixels to which either the human or the computer associates a meaning. In the adopted model, such a meaning is expressed as an attributed symbol. The association of a characteristic structure with a description forms a *characteristic pattern*, which is modelled as a triple formed by the *characteristic structure* itself (the pictorial component), an attributed symbol (description component), and a *relation* between the two. The characteristic structure is the *materialisation* of the attributed symbol and the attributed symbol is the *interpretation* of the characteristic structure.

In an image, many structures can be simultaneously identified. The set of characteristic patterns formed by such structures, their meaning, and the relations between them uniquely characterise the message and its meaning. The set of attributed symbols associated with the characteristic structures in an image, form the image *description*.

A *visual sentence* is thus defined as a triple vs = <i,d,<int,mat>> where i is an *image*, d is a *description* (i.e., a set of attributed symbols), int a function mapping a structure of i into a symbol describing it, and mat a function mapping a symbol in d into a structure in i. i and d are called pictorial and description component of the visual sentence, respectively.

In general, a visual sentence is built from a finite set of generator elements, called the visual alphabet K (Bottoni, Costabile, & Mussio, 1999). Given a characteristic pattern k, a set $\Theta_k = \{\theta_1 ..., \theta_n\}$ of transformations can be associated with it, such that the application of a transformation $\theta_i \in \Theta_k$ to k results into a new characteristic pattern which maintains the same type as k. A typical transformation θ_i may change attribute values in the description component, assigning new values in the corresponding domains; or it may change the pictorial component, by defining a characteristic structure, which maintains some topological or

geometrical invariant of the original one; accordingly, it may change the int and mat functions.

This view allows the identification of visual languages as sets of visual sentences without taking into account the possible relations between them. Their definition can thus be expressed in terms of visual rewriting systems, by considering the whole set of visual sentences that such a system can generate.

Moreover, interest in the so-called *interaction VL* leads to considering not only the set of all the visual sentences, which can be produced during user interaction with a visual interactive system, but also the process itself by which visual sentences are produced according to some admissible sequence. Hence, the interaction between user and computer is formalised as a transformation process of these visual sentences. As vCARWs are *pure* rewriting systems (i.e., without the distinction between terminals and non-terminals), the derivation process of a sentence must be restricted, so as to reflect the sequences of interactive steps through which the sentence was produced.

VISUAL TRANSFORMATIONS

Within an interaction process, every visual sentence produced during an interaction derives from a direct parent and all the visual sentences in the interaction process are derived from a common predecessor, the initial visual sentence, characterising the *initial* state of the visual interactive system. The pictorial component of this initial visual sentence is the image appearing on the screen when the user starts the interactive session.

As visual sentences are finite objects, a visual sentence produced during the interaction and its parent differ for a finite set of characteristic patterns, while maintaining a finite set of common characteristic patterns. Either set can be possibly empty. To the user, this is reflected by the observation that some characteristic structures were created in the image, some were deleted, some changed in various ways (e.g., changing colour, size, orientation, location) and some remained unchanged. The identification of what changes and what remains constant in the process is the key to its understanding from the cognitive point of view. The conception of a visual interactive system consists of the design of the set of visual sentences, which can be produced during an interaction and of the algebraic structure to be imposed on it, taking into account what changes and in which way.

The rule-based approach adopted in the theory of visual sentences and realised through the definition of vCARWs, stresses both *locality* aspects—by prescribing what has to be changed—and *coordination* aspects—by indicating which related transformations must be simultaneously executed. Hence, the definition of the admissible sequences of rules' applications is a way to specify the dynamics of the visual sentence as determined by the interaction. In particular, the designer can specify pairs of sets of characteristic patterns, in the form of *before-after* rules, to indicate what is required to change as a consequence of the interaction. The components of rules are sets of characteristic patterns built on a common alphabet.

This approach has its first realisation in the definition of *visual conditional attributed rewriting system* (vCARW). A vCARW is a triple $<K,P, \Rightarrow_c>$, where K is a visual alphabet; P is a set of rewrite rules, which are pairs of visual sentences (*antecedent* and *consequent*) on K, guarded by a *condition* on the antecedent that must be satisfied for the rule to be applicable (a rule is written in the form $r=(ant,cons,cond)$); and $\Rightarrow_c$ is the rewriting relation specifying how rules in P are applied to visual sentences. We say that vs_1 *directly generates* vs_2 ($vs_1 \Rightarrow_c vs_2$) if and only if $\exists\ r=(ant,cons,cond)\in P$ such that: (a) vs_1 contains an instance A of ant; (b) the condition cond evaluates to true on A; (c) vs_2 contains an instance C of cons such that its attribute values are equal to those computed from A according to specifications in cons; (d) all other

characteristic patterns in vs_1 are found unchanged in vs_2; (e) no other characteristic pattern is in vs_2. We say that vs_0 *generates* vs_n ($vs_0 \Rightarrow_c^* vs_n$) if a sequence of visual sentences, vs_0, vs_1,..., vs_{n-1}, vs_n, exists such that $vs_i \Rightarrow_c vs_{i+1}$ by some rule in P, for $i=0,...,n-1$. Given a vCARW = $<K,P, \Rightarrow_c>$ and a set of visual sentences Ax, called the set of axioms, the generated language is the set of visual sentences $L(vCARW, Ax) = \{vs \mid \exists vs_0 \in Ax, vs_0 \Rightarrow_c^* vs\}$ (Bottoni et al., 1999).

Different subtypes of vCARWs have been introduced with different goals. For example, k-increasing vCARWs are such that they admit rules whose effect can only be the insertion of some new characteristic pattern and the modification of some already existing one, but not the deletion of any pattern already present in the visual sentence. For the 1-increasing case, this allows the automatic construction of a control automaton driving the interaction, so that the user is guided to produce sentences in an incremental way. The automaton can be extended with states and transitions to manage user errors. The construction of the automaton can be readily generalised to the increasing case by associating special transitions with the request to apply a rule.

In order to illustrate the transformation process of the visual sentences during user interaction with a visual interactive system, let us consider the visual interface of the Corporate Digital Library (CDL), a prototype of a visual interactive system developed at the University of Bari (Costabile, Esposito, Semeraro, & Fanizzi, 1999). The WWW interface of CDL visualizes in a window opened by a Web browser the topics of the documents stored in the digital library through a "geographic" metaphor where cities, representing topics of the CDL thesaurus, are connected by roads, representing links between topics, and a region represents a set of topics (i.e., the topics in a certain class). We abstract from interaction with the browser and focus on the CDL visual interface. A colour-based technique codes a topic relevance depending on the number of documents

Figure 2. Topic map giving the overview of the topics in a library of CDL

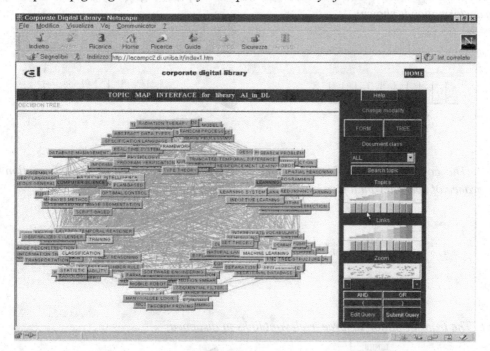

the topic has been assigned to. Therefore, the rectangle used to represent a topic (city on the map) is drawn in an appropriate color (appearing in the grey level figures of this chapter as different shades of grey). Figure 2 gives an overview of all topics in the current CDL prototype by showing the *topic map*. A rectangle representing a topic may be partially overlapped by other rectangles. A mouse click on a visible part of an overlapped rectangle will bring it in the foreground making it completely visible.

Topics are visualised in ten colours ranging from light blue to red, where light blue is used to represent the less relevant topics, and red the most relevant ones. The user can interact with the widget with the colour scale and with label Topics, appearing on the right of the topic map, to quickly filter the information on the map by

clicking on a coloured rectangle, thus eliminating less relevant topics (and all their links) in order to obtain a less cluttered map (Costabile, Esposito, Semeraro, & Fanizzi, 1999).

For example, the transformation of the relevance columns in the Topics widget determined by the user selecting the third rectangle can be represented by a pair such as the one in Figure 3. The arrow below the third rectangle does not appear in the actual visual sentence, but is here used to indicate that this transformation occurs as effect of the user's action of selecting this rectangle, abstracting from the concrete realization of this action.

This transformation must be coordinated with the one depicted in Figure 4b to set the appearance of less relevant topics to "not visible" as stated by the condition indicated under the

Figure 3. The transformation of the relevance columns in the Topics widget (only the pictorial component of the transformation is shown)

Figure 4. The coordinated transformation for disappearance of non-relevant topics

Figure 5. The coordinated transformation forces links to disappear

Figure 6. The transformation to force irrelevant links to disappear

arrow. At the same time, this transformation is also coordinated with the one depicted in Figure 5b, which also makes links connected to non relevant topics disappear. In these specifications, a reminder of the transformation, which starts the set of coordinated actions, is placed close to each pair (in parts a) of Figures 4 and 5. In the figures, only some attributes of the characteristic pattern are shown, namely those significant for the transformation.

All these transformations must concurrently occur in parallel when the user performs the action of filtering the topics whose relevance is less than three. Note that this set of transformations is different from the one causing link disappearance when links are filtered according to their own relevance. The specification of such a transformation is shown instead in Figure 5, where the occurrence of the transformation is conditioned to the relevance of the link being below a given threshold. In this case, a transformation such as the one in Figure 6 would be synchronized with transformations of the characteristic pattern relative to the LINKS relevance columns and the associated selection rectangle.

CONSTANCY ASPECTS DURING INTERACTION

The transformation from a visual sentence into the subsequent one during human-computer interaction must be visible in the sense that the variation of the image component of the visual sentence must indicate to the user what has changed, thus providing both syntactic and semantic feedback to the user. Moreover, the context must be identifiable. These requirements extend the requirement of visibility (Dix, Finlay, Abowd, & Beale, 1998) to the dynamic case, which can be restated in our terminology by saying that the characteristic structure present on the screen must indicate to the user which is the current state of the interaction. Moreover, those characteristic structures must be preserved allowing users to keep their bearings in the interaction space. These considerations lead to the formulation of the notion of *frame* to define the emergent property of remaining constant in a sequence of steps, and to the proposal of the notion of *scaffold* as a set of characteristic patterns, which the designer exploits to communicate to the users the context in which they are operating.

When considering interaction, it may happen that a visual sentence in an interaction VL is produced several times as a consequence of different actions performed on different visual sentences. In particular, sequences of actions may produce a closed path between two visual sentences (e.g., a sequence of *undo* and *redo* actions). In general, some characteristic structures in the image component of a visual sentence remain unchanged or change according to a limited set of transformations, thus identifying the frame of reference for the interaction. Moreover, it is usually required that the interpretation of these characteristic structures remains consistent throughout the visual sentences so that two occurrences of a same symbol are associated, via int and mat, to identical characteristic structures appearing in the frame in different visual sentences.

As a consequence, the pictorial component of a visual sentence is made of a frame and a variable part. The frame is a set of characteristic structures, which maintain a constant support in all the visual sentences generated during the interaction. The variable part is a set of characteristic structures, which are generated, disappear, or change their support according to the performed user actions or computer activities. The frame identifies the context in which a user action or a computer activity is performed for the user; the variable part identifies the results of any action/activity, as well as the indication of the current state of the computation. The whole interaction results

into several sequences of visual sentences with a common frame in which each visual sentence is derived from the previous one according to the current instruction fed by the user. When a user switches to a new environment, for example from Word to Netscape™, the previous frame is cancelled and substituted by the frame of the VL for the new environment.

An example of frame is the menu bar in a Macintosh application. In Microsoft Word™, the frame can also include the external icon bar if it is positioned at the right end of the screen and the document window is not moved during the interaction. Hence, this icon bar is not part of the frame for the whole dynamic visual language defined by Word™ since in some cases it may not be visible, but it can be part of the frame for the set of visual sentences generated during a specific interaction.

The designer must provide a way for the system to communicate the state of the interaction and the available functionality to the user. Moreover, the formal definition of the set of sequences of visual sentences and of user actions that must be allowed and those that must be forbidden, requires the identification of the inter-dependencies between local states of individual characteristic patterns and the global state of the interaction process.

The scaffold is informally defined as a set of characteristic patterns in a visual sentence facilitating the understanding of the overall strategy for performing a task and for recording the history of the interaction. It consists of a set of icons, text lines, and other widgets used to denote:

1. The *activities* that can be performed such as select a characteristic structure launch a program, terminate the current activity, save current results;
2. The *cornerstones*, which allow users to establish orientation during the task execution.

Examples of cornerstones are window titles, status bar, etc.

In general, the characteristic structures in a scaffold must belong to the frame for some sequence of visual sentences in an interaction process. More precisely, each state of the scaffold defines a sub-visual language for the visual interactive system. All the visual sentences in such a sub-visual language refer to a common context, and the user can recognise this context by the persistence of the appearance of the characteristic patterns in the scaffold.

MODELING INTERACTION DYNAMICS

The sentences of an interaction VL are derived in sequence starting from an initial visual sentence x_1. Each visual sentence x_i in this sequence is generated from a sentence x_{i-1} by the computer performing a computation or interpreting the user input and the description part of x_{i-1}. This transformation is described as a derivation in a proper visual rewriting system.

By devising a rule, the designer expresses what may change in an atomic transaction concerning a given set of characteristic patterns without making assumptions on how this transaction is going to be realised, provided that its atomicity is guaranteed. The user action is thus seen as a trigger for rule application. The local character of rule application is such that it may not affect arbitrary sets of characteristic patterns. Dependencies among sets of characteristic patterns must therefore be identified and made explicit as rule dependencies, by the designer, who has to define models of coordination to prescribe simultaneous application of different rules, or of the same rule to several instances of the antecedent.

The considerations above are at the basis of the proposal of a specific family of rewriting systems, called evCARWs, which take into consideration dependencies among rules and the role of triggering in the rewriting process.

An *enabling visual conditional attributed rewriting system* (evCARW) is a construct $D=<K,P,\Rightarrow_e,Ac,\varepsilon,\phi,\mu>$ where K is a visual alphabet, P is a set of visual conditional rewriting rules, Ac is a set of *actions*, ε and ϕ are two mappings ε,ϕ: $P \rightarrow \wp(Ac)$, called *enabling* and *forbidding* mapping respectively, μ is a mapping $\mu:Ac \rightarrow \wp(P)$. The rewriting relation $\Rightarrow_e \subset (DVL \times \wp(Ac))^2$ is defined on a pair (visual sentence, set of enabled actions) as follows: $(vs,en) \Rightarrow_e (vs',en')$ if and only if $\exists p \in P$, $\exists$ $ac \in en \subset Ac$, such that $p \in \mu(ac)$, $vs \Rightarrow_c vs'$, where $en'=((en-\phi(p))-ac) \cup \varepsilon(p)$.

In words, every rule can enable or forbid the subsequent application of rules from some set. The pictorial representation of these rules may also indicate the associated enabled and disabled rules, as in Figure 7. The fact that a rule is enabled does not imply that it will be applied, or that it can be applied at all. In particular, it is possible that no set of characteristic patterns in the current visual sentence matches the antecedent of a currently enabled rule. Conversely, the fact that a rule is currently not enabled implies that it cannot be applied, even if an instance of its antecedent can be found in the current visual sentence.

The language generated by an evCARW D from a set of axioms Ax with initial enabled actions A is:

$$L(D,Ax,A) = \{vs \mid \exists ax \in Ax, \exists en \in \wp(Ac), (ax,A) \Rightarrow^*_C (vs,en)\}$$

Note that in this case we implicitly indicate the set of sequences of (enabled) actions, which may cause the transition from a sentence in the language to any other reachable sentence in the language. In order to model an actual interaction, it is necessary to couple the evCARW with a process able to provide correct sentences in a language of actions. Hence, we assume that the user produces actions in accordance with their enabling, and that incorrect actions are captured and rejected by the system.

Figure 7. A rule for composing queries out of topics and logical operators. The pictorial representation also specifies the enabling and disabling of some components according to the ε and φ mappings.

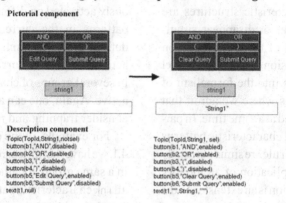

As an example, consider the rule sketched in Figure 7, which is part of the specification of a visual system for query composition integrated within the prototype CDL. The identifier attribute is reported for all characteristic patterns as the first element in the tuple, either as a constant or as a variable, with capitalised initial (e.g., TopId for topic, b1 for a button, etc.). For a topic characteristic pattern, only two more attributes have been considered: nameOfTopic and selection. Each occurrence of the variable String1 in the rule must be unified with a corresponding value found in the visual sentence for attribute nameOfTopic for a match of the antecedent. For the button characteristic pattern, the attributes nameOfButton and enabling are considered. For the text characteristic pattern, designating the query string, the value of the attribute contentOfQuery changes from the constant null to the current value of nameOfTopic written between quotes. This rule is associated with the action "select topic." The set of rules associated with this action also comprises a rule for the case in which the query is already partially formed, so that the buttons for operators and clearing are enabled. These rules specify the way in which the CDL prototype allows users to request documents by direct manipulation of the map shown on the screen. The reader may refer to Bottoni (2002) for more details.

The evCARWs previously presented allow the specification of VLs produced as the reaction to sequences of correct actions (i.e., enabled ones, since disabled ones cannot contribute to a derivation). In most cases, however, it is of interest in visual interaction to trap user incorrect actions and produce warning messages. To model such situations, we augment the previous specification by a VL Trap, whose visual sentences can be composed via superimposition on the current visual sentence. The reader may refer to Bottoni (1997) for the formal definition of superimposition and to Bottoni (2002) for more detail on VL Trap.

COORDINATION IN RULE APPLICATION

It is often the case that a user action provokes effects that are not only local, but extend over several characteristic patterns. For examples, several windows can be linked to react in a consistent way to a single zoom command, or to opening or closing a window (Bianchi, Bottoni, Mussio, & Protti, 1993). Even in a same dynamic VL, it can often occur that simultaneous modifications of several characteristic patterns are started by the same action. For example, when using radio buttons in a dialogue window or selecting a textual item from a menu, the selection of an item disables any previously selected item. Moreover, the corresponding characteristic structures are also constrained to appear or disappear simultaneously. The definition of these coordination aspects requires an extension to the basic model of evCARWs bringing us into the formalism of parallel rewriting systems where we admit that several rules can be applied at a same time. In particular, we assume that all characteristic patterns not explicitly affected by a rule are simultaneously rewritten through the application of an identity rule. The following definition is an extension to the case of visual rewriting systems of the concept of group rewriting for attributed 0L-systems, which was applied to coordination problems in Bottoni, Mauri, and Mussio (1998a).

Let $\Pi(K)$ define the set of characteristic patterns that can be generated from the elements of an alphabet K. An evCARW with groups, or gevCARW, is a construct $gD=<K,P,\Rightarrow_g,Ac,\varepsilon,\phi,\mu,\rho,\nu>$, where K, P, Ac, ε, ϕ, μ are the same as in evCARWs, ρ is a symmetrical predicate of the form $\rho:\wp(\Pi(K))\rightarrow$ {true, false} assessing whether a set of characteristic patterns form a group, ν a mapping $\nu:$ $\Pi\backslash Iden\rightarrow\wp(P)$, where $Iden$ is the set of identity rules, with the property that if $p_i\in\nu(p_j)$, $p_j\notin Iden$, then $p_j\in\nu(p_i)$. Moreover, the rules in $\nu(p)$ are such that they are all associated with the same action. If ν is extended to $Iden$, the property holds also in $Iden$. To sum up, ρ defines group formation, ν defines for each non-identical rule the associated set of rules.

The direct generation relation is as follows, under the constraint imposed by the set of enabled actions, acting as before. $vs\Rightarrow_g vs'$ iff vs is characterised by the union of sets of characteristic patterns $\{\alpha_1, \alpha_2, ..., \alpha_n\}$, vs' is characterised by the union of sets of characteristic patterns $\{\beta_1, \beta_2, ..., \beta_n\}$, $\alpha_i=\beta_i$ or $\alpha_i\rightarrow\beta_i\in P$ for each $i=1,...,n$, and if $\rho(\alpha_i\cup\alpha_j)=$true, and a rule $\alpha_j\rightarrow\beta_j\in P$ in the domain of ν has been applied, a rule $\alpha_i\rightarrow\beta_i\in P$ has also been applied, where $\alpha_i\rightarrow\beta_i\in\nu(\alpha_j\rightarrow\beta_j)$.

In other words, this means that several rules, all associated with a same action, can be simultaneously activated on different sets of characteristic patterns in the current visual sentence. This definition also accounts for the case when several actions can be concurrently activated, resulting in several groups of characteristic patterns being active. Again, one can augment this definition to consider trapping and recovery actions.

For example, in the case presented in Section 4.1, we have that all topic characteristic patterns are in a same group, together with the Topics widget, all link characteristic patterns are in a same group together with the Links widget, and a topic and a link characteristic patterns are in a same group if the link is connected to the topic. Formally, let $\alpha_i =$ link(IdL,(Top1,Top2)) and $\alpha_j =$ topic(IdT,LinkList), where we have presented only the attributes relevant for group assessment. Then $\rho(\{\alpha_i,\alpha_j\}) =$ true if and only if IdL$\in$LinkList $\wedge$ (IdT=Top1 $\vee$ IdT=Top2).

DESIGNING VISUAL ENVIRONMENTS

The formal specification of the intended behaviours expressed in terms of vCARWs allow the automatic generation of significant parts of interactive environments, in particular as regards dialogue management and coordination of behaviours. Such specifications are typically platform-independent and must therefore be adapted to the specific intended realisations, which may involve use of different interaction devices, platforms, and programming languages. Hence, Bottoni, Costabile, Fogli, Levialdi, & Mussio (2001) propose the adoption of a design space, depicted in Figure 8, in which each dimension represents types of languages: (1) *user activity languages* to specify users activities; (2) *programming languages* to specify system computations; (3) *pictorial languages* to specify the images appearing on the computer screen. The coordinates of this space indicate the

Figure 8. The 3-D interaction modeling space. Each point in the space identifies the abstraction levels of the system model.

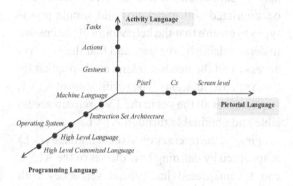

level of abstraction for each dimension and each point represents a virtual interaction machine (i.e., a hypothetical interactive system defined by the user activity language, the programming language, and the pictorial language).

The consistent design of an interactive system requires that precise mappings be defined both intra- and inter-dimensions. For example, a complex user action must be reducible to a sequence of elementary gestures issuing commands to the computer (intra-dimension mapping). On the other hand, a user gesture must be managed through appropriate sequences of instructions and must result into the modification of identified sets of pixels (inter-dimension mapping).

To design an interactive computer application, the set of admissible user activities, as well as the set of rules, which determine the modelled interaction process, have to be specified. This specification process starts from the construction of the set of the css and the set of computational constructs used to build the rules, and arrives at the definition of: (1) a language to specify user activities; (2) a language to specify css; and (3) a language to specify computational constructs. These specifications may occur at different levels of abstraction. The choice of the abstraction level is determined by the tools available to the designer

(i.e., which programming languages, toolkits, I/O devices, are available).

For example, a system specification may be composed of programs in some high-level language for the computational axis, references to icons for the pictorial axis, and an alphabet of actions such as "select icon" without considering the gestures by which they are performed as activity language. A mapping to concrete realisations of these activities as sequences of gestures will have to be constructed in order to construct such a system.

In general, the design of a concrete system is detailed as the design of the interaction visual language, which will allow users to interact with the system. In this process, the designer moves back and forth along the different axes to define several visual languages at different levels of abstraction and with increasing levels of complexity.

In particular, starting from user and task analysis and from the observation of the produced documents, an explicit but informal characterisation of the domain is produced in the form of a visual alphabet and a set of rules expressed in the user language, defining a first task visual language TVLo. The adequacy of TVLo with respect to the user significant constructs requires a *verification* phase to demonstrate that all the sentences in the TVLo can be produced and that no sentence violating the constraints required by the users can be created. Moreover, a *validation* phase is also necessary to check that the visual alphabet and the rules can be properly understood and managed by the user.

From the observation of the produced documents and of the users' activities, we abstract the definition of the task visual language (TVL) (i.e., we identify the visual alphabet and rules implicitly used by experts in building and transforming their documents). This process can go through the definition of several tentative generalisations of the TVLo before an agreement is reached. In particular, it is possible that the typical graphical constructs employed by the users are not sufficiently expressive or non-ambiguous to build a formal notation. Several steps are then required to reach a form adequate to be formalised by eliminating the identified ambiguities and inconsistencies.

Once an agreement is achieved on what has to belong to the TVL, a formal definition of this language is needed. In Bottoni, Chang, Costabile, Levialdi, and Mussio (1998b), details on this are provided. A semi-formal verification is possible by checking that every observed document can be produced with the use of the rewriting system that specifies the language, that incorrect documents cannot be composed, and that the legal sentences correspond to acceptable intermediate steps during document construction and transformation. The formal notation thus obtained must be evaluated with respect to the user semantics. In particular, it is necessary to verify that the users correctly understand the definition of the derived TVL and of its use.

The TVL thus defined is then augmented to take a communicational advantage from the interactive capabilities of the system. Indeed, the sequences of TVL vss describe the development of experts' activity. The TVL is an intermediate step in the design of IVL, which proceeds by enriching the TVL with the definition of the cps through which the visual system communicates to the user the state of the interaction and provides access to its functionalities. Moreover, the TVL itself can be augmented to exploit the possibilities of interaction and animation available in a computer system. The designer may augment TVL by introducing new css to make the vss in the language more compact and expressive. The designer can also use attention holders, feedback mechanisms, animation effects, detail exhibition, and focus modification. The notation must also be adapted--hence often changed and approximated--to the digital technologies by which the image on the screen is generated as well as to the fixed, limited dimensions of the screen.

The validation of the augmented TVL (ATVL) requires a partial implementation or mock-up of the system so that the consistency of the dynamics can be checked with the one expected by the user. In particular, the interaction dynamics can be simulated with mock-ups and simple prototypes to ensure that the behaviours of the cps are understandable by the user and that the user has access to all the needed details made implicit by the synthetic notations. The verification of ATVL requires that all the vss in the TVL remain accessible and obtainable through ATVL.

Finally, the interaction visual language (IVL) is specified by defining how the vss of the ATVL can be integrated into visual sentences with additional support for the interaction, such as frames and scaffolds providing context for user orientation in the interaction, or giving access to the system functionalities, tools to operate on the vss themselves, etc. The definition of the IVL also encompasses the constraints posed by the strategies of document construction identified during the task analysis. These may imply sequences of actions to be performed in the production of the document, checklists, levels of access to functionalities, etc.

Hence, each step of the IVL design consists of: (1) design and implementation of abstract or concrete tools; (2) verification of their soundness, completeness, and consistency; and (3) validation of their adequacy with respect to human-computer communication, using tools according to the technique chosen with respect to the users' semantics.

During this process, each step or sequence of steps may be iterated several times if the verification or the validation of the results of some steps in the procedure so requires. Each step in the IVL design requires the preliminary choice of tools necessary to execute the step and of a technique of assessment of the obtained results: new tools or new sets of data. In the tool choice and use, problems arise from the existence of the two semantics, the user, and the program ones. Evaluation of the results must be performed with respect to both semantics and require verification and validation through experimental evaluation.

CONCLUSION

This chapter has illustrated the theory of visual sentence developed with the aim of formally specifying visual interactive system. Sets of visual sentences are specified through the use of visual rewriting systems called vCARWs. Other families of vCARWs have been defined whose visual rewriting rules, augmented with regulation mechanisms, coordinate transformations of sets of visual elements so that the complete dynamic behaviour of a visual interface can be specified.

An important aspect of the interpretation process is that it is not simply compositional, as context can play a role, and often emergent phenomena lead to revisions or enrichments of the current description and of the interpretation function itself. Hence, the process by which the description and the interaction process itself are created can only partially be modelled through a local analysis of the image. The theory takes this into account by allowing the definition of attributed symbols associated with the whole image and by allowing the possibility of defining structures of arbitrary complexity.

From this theoretical core, different lines of development have been pursued. In a first line, some works by Bottoni and Levialdi have seen characteristic patterns as visual resources, consumed and produced during visual transformations. The WIPPOG language (Bottoni, Mussio, Olivieri, & Protti, 1998) has therefore been adopted as a way to specify resource transformations, and uniformly employed to define both visual rewriting systems and interactive control mechanisms (Bottoni, De Marsico, Di Tommaso, Levialdi, & Ventriglia, 2004). The adoption of a resource-based perspective also supports modeling of interaction errors

as related to a mismatch between the perceived and real absence or presence of resources during the interaction process (Bottoni & Levialdi, 2005, 2006). The notion of resource has also been related to an abstract view of visual languages as defined by the existence of spatial relations between identifiable elements with semantic relevance (Bottoni & Costagliola, 2002; Bottoni & Grau, 2004). This approach, considering both syntactical and semantical aspects of the definition of visual languages can be specified through the identification of the specific roles, played by concrete instances with respect to the metamodels defining a syntactic family or a semantic variety (Bottoni, Frediani, Quattrocchi, Rende, Sarajlic, & Ventriglia, 2006a; Bottoni, Quattrocchi, & Ventriglia, 2006b). A metamodel for interaction can also be defined so that abstract actions can be associated with different syntactic or semantic roles (Bottoni, de Lara, & Guerra, 2006c).

A second line of research was motivated by the use of visual expressions as boundary objects (Arias, Eden, Fischer, Gorman, & Scharff, 2000) (i.e., shared objects to talk about and think with in Web-based collaborative activities and in end-user development (EUD)) (Carrara, Fogli, Fresta, & Mussio, 2002; Costabile, Fogli, Mussio, & Piccinno, 2006a; Sutcliffe & Mehandjiev, 2004). Visual interactive systems for collaborative activities allow users that have different stances on the problems at hand to cooperate to a common activity interacting among them and with systems via visual sentences (which are at this level the boundary objects) (Mussio, 2003). The design and development of such systems is recognised as a complex activity, which requires collaborative and participatory approaches that include representatives of users in the design team, thus performing activities of EUD (Costabile, Fogli, Fresta, Mussio, & Piccinno, 2003; Costabile, Fogli, Lanzilotti, Mussio, & Piccinno, 2006c). The visual interactive systems, the widgets, and the other visual entities are described as open virtual systems called *virtual entities* (Costabile,

Fogli, Fresta, Mussio, & Piccinno, 2003; Fogli, Mussio, Celentano, & Pittarello, 2002;), whose dynamics are described starting from the tools introduced by the theoretical core described in this chapter.

Finally, the interaction model at the basis of the theory of visual sentences has been recently extended by considering an important phenomenon occurring during the use of interactive systems, which is called *co-evolution of users and systems* (Costabile, Fogli, Marcante, & Piccinno, 2006b). It is based on the following two observations: (1) once people gain proficiency in system usage, they would like to use the system in different ways and need different interfaces than those they required when they were novice users (*user evolution*) (Nielsen, 1993; Norman, 2005); and (2) designers are then forced to evolve the system to meet the new users' needs (*system evolution*) (Arondi, Baroni, Fogli, & Mussio, 2002; Bourguin, Derycke, & Tarby, 2001; Carroll & Rosson, 1992; Costabile, Fogli, Mussio, & Piccinno, 2006a). In Costabile, Fogli, Marcante, and Piccinno (2006b) and Costabile, Fogli, Marcante, Mussio, and Piccinno (2006d), a model of the interaction and co-evolution processes (ICE model) occurring between users and system is discussed. It leads to re-examine the way interactive system are designed and to define new theoretical foundations on which new design approaches should be based.

REFERENCES

Arias, E., Eden, H., Fischer, G., Gorman, A., & Scharff, E. (2000). Transcending the individual human mind--creative shared understanding through collaborative design. *ACM Trans on CHI, 7*(1), 84-113.

Arondi, S., Baroni, P., Fogli, D., & Mussio, P. (2002). Supporting co-evolution of users and systems by the recognition of Interaction Patterns.

Proceedings of the International Conference on Advanced Visual Interfaces (AVI 2002) (pp. 177-189). Trento, Italy: ACM Press.

Bianchi, N., Bottoni, P., Mussio, P., & Protti, M. (1993). Cooperative visual environments for the design of effective visual systems. *Journal of Visual Languages and Computing, 4*(4), 357-381.

Bottoni, P., Costabile, M.F., Levialdi, S., & Mussio, P. (1995). Formalising Visual Languages. In *Proceedings of Visual Language '95*, (pp. 45-52). IEEE Computer Society Press.

Bottoni, P., & Costagliola, G. (2002). On the definition of visual languages and their editors. In M. Hegarty, B. Meyer, & N. Hari Narayanan (Eds.), *Diagrammatic representation and inference: Second International Conference, Diagrams 2002, Proceedings, LNAI 2317* (pp. 305-319). Berlin, Germany: Springer.

Bottoni, P., & Grau, A. (2004). A suite of meta-models as a basis for a classification of visual languages. In P. Bottoni, C. Hundhausen, S. Levialdi, & G. Tortora (Eds.), *Proceedings of VL/HCC 2004*, (pp. 83-90). Roma, Italy: IEEE CS Press.

Bottoni, P., & Levialdi, S. (2005). Resource-based models of visual interaction: Learning from errors. *Proceedings of the VL/HCC 2005* (pp. 137-144). Dallas, USA: IEEE Computer Society Press.

Bottoni, P., & Levialdi, S. (2006). Entities, substances, and time: Resources for interaction. In *Proceedings of VL/HCC 2006* (pp. 121-124). Brighton, UK: IEEE Computer Society Press.

Bottoni, P., Chang, S. K., Costabile, M. F., Levialdi, S., & Mussio, P. (1998b). On the specification of dynamic visual languages. In *Proceedings of IEEE Symposium Visual Languages* (pp. 14-21). Halifax, Canada: IEEE Computer Society Press.

Bottoni, P., Chang, S. K., Costabile, M. F., Levialdi, S., & Mussio, P. (2002). Modeling visual interactive systems through dynamic visual languages.

IEEE Trans. on Systems, Man, and Cybernetics--Part A, 32(6), 654-669.

Bottoni, P., Costabile, M. F., Fogli, D., Levialdi, S., & Mussio, P. (2001). Multilevel modeling and design of visual interactive systems. In *Proceedings of HCC 2001* (pp. 256-263). Stresa, Italy: IEEE Computer Society Press.

Bottoni, P., Costabile, M. F., & Mussio, P. (1999). Specification and dialogue control of visual interaction through visual rewriting systems. *ACM Trans. on Programming Languages and Systems (TOPLAS), 21*(6), 1077-1136.

Bottoni, P., Costabile, M. F., Levialdi, S., & Mussio, P. (1996). Visual conditional attributed rewriting systems in visual language specification. *Proceedings of VL 1996* (pp. 156-163). Boulder: IEEE Computer Society Press.

Bottoni, P., Costabile, M. F., Levialdi, S., & Mussio, P. (1997). Defining visual languages for interactive computing. *IEEE Trans. on Systems, Man, and Cybernetics--Part A, 27*(6), 773-783.

Bottoni, P., de Lara, J., & Guerra, E. (2006c). Metamodel-based definition of interaction with visual environments. *Proceedings of MDDAUI 2006*. In press.

Bottoni, P., De Marsico, M., Di Tommaso, P., Levialdi, S., & Ventriglia, D. (2004). Definition of visual processes in a language for expressing transitions. *Journal of Visual Languages and Computing, 15*(3), 211-242.

Bottoni, P., Frediani, D., Quattrocchi, P., Rende, L., Sarajlic, G., & Ventriglia, D. (2006a). A transformation-based metamodel approach to the definition of syntax and semantics of diagrammatic languages. *In this volume.*

Bottoni, P., Mariotto, M., Mussio, P., & Biella, G. (1995). The design of anthropocentric cooperative visual environments. *Proceedings of VL 1995* (pp. 334-341). Darmstadt, Germany: IEEE Computer Society Press.

Bottoni, P., Mauri, G., & Mussio, P. (1998a). Coordination through group rewriting. In A. Salomaa & G. Paun (Eds.), *Grammatical models of multi agent systems* (pp. 226-246). IEEE Computer Society Press: Gordon & Breach.

Bottoni, P., Mussio, P., Olivieri, B., & Protti, M. (1998). A completely visual environment for agent-based computing. In T. Catarci, M. F. Costabile, G. Santucci, & L. Tarantino (Eds.), *Proceedings of AVI'98* (pp. 261-263). L'Aquila, Italy: ACM Press.

Bottoni, P., Quattrocchi, P., & Ventriglia, D. (2006b). Constraining concrete syntax via metamodel information. *Proceedings of VL/HCC 2006* (pp. 85-88). Città, stato: IEEE Computer Society Press.

Bourguin, G., Derycke, A., & Tarby, J. C. (2001). Beyond the interface: Co-evolution inside interactive systems: A proposal founded on the Activity theory. In Blandford, A., Vanderdonckt, J., & Gray, P.H. (Eds), *Proceedings of the of IHM-HCI 2001 Conference* (pp. 297-310). Lille, France, People and computer XV – Interactions without Frontiers: Springer Verlag.

Carrara, P., Fogli, D., Fresta, G., & Mussio, P. (2002). Toward overcoming culture, skill, and situation hurdles in human-computer interaction. *International Journal Universal Access in the Information Society, 1*(4), 288-304.

Carroll, J. M., & Rosson, M. B. (1992). Deliberated evolution: Stalking the view matcher in design space. *Human-Computer Interaction, 6*(3 and 4), 281-318.

Chang, S. K., & Mussio, P. (1996). Customized visual language design. *Proceedings of International Conference on Software Engineering and Knowledge Engineering (SEKE 96)* (pp. 553-562). Lake Tahoe, NV: IEEE Computer Society Press.

Costabile, M. F., Esposito, F., Semeraro, G., & Fanizzi, N. (1999). An adaptive visual environment for digital libraries. *International Journal on Digital Libraries*, *2*(2 and 3), 124-143.

Costabile, M. F., Fogli, D., Fresta, G., Mussio, P., & Piccinno, A. (2003). Building environments for end-user development and tailoring. In *Proceedings of the 2003 IEEE Symposia on Human Centric Computing Languages and Environments (HCC' 03)* (pp. 31-38). Auckland, New Zealand: IEEE Computer Society Press.

Costabile, M., Fogli, D., Lanzilotti, R., Mussio, P., & Piccinno, A. (2006c). Supporting work practice through end-user development environments. *Journal of Organizational and End User Computing, 18*(4), 43-65.

Costabile, M. F., Fogli, D., Marcante, A., Mussio, P., & Piccinno, A. (2006d). Interactive environments supporting user and system co-evolution. In C. Hochberger & R. Liskowsky (Eds.), *Lecture Notes in Informatics (LNI). Proceedings of Informatik 2006: Vol. P93* (pp. 588-591). Dresden, Germany: Köllen Druck+Verlag GmbH.

Costabile, M. F., Fogli, D., Marcante, A., & Piccinno, A. (2006b). Supporting interaction and co-evolution of users and systems. *Proceedings of AVI 2006* (pp. 143-150). Venezia, Italy: ACM Press.

Costabile, M. F., Fogli, D., Mussio, P., & Piccinno, A. (2006a). End-user development: the software shaping workshop approach. In H. Lieberman, F. Paternò, & V. Wulf (Eds.), *End user development* (pp. 183-205). Dordrecht, The Netherlands: Springer.

Dix, A., Finlay, J., Abowd, G., & Beale, R. (1998). *Human computer interaction*. London: Prentice Hall.

Fogli, D., Mussio, P., Celentano, A., & Pittarello, F. (2002). Toward a model-based approach to the

specification of virtual reality environments. *Proceedings of the Multimedia Software Engineering (MSE2002)* (pp. 148-155). Newport Beach, CA: IEEE Computer Society Press.

Goldberg, A., Burnett, M., & Lewis, T. (1995). What is visual object-oriented programming? In M. M. Burnett, A. Goldberg, & T. G. Lewis (Eds.), *Visual object-oriented programming: Concepts and environments* (pp. 3-20). Greenwich, CT: Manning Publications Co.

Ichikawa, T., Chang, S.K. (eds.) (1984). IEEE Computer Society Workshop on Visual Languages. Hiroshima, Silver Spring, USA: IEEE Computer Society Press.

Mussio, P., Pietrogrande, M., & Protti, M. (1991). Simulation of hepatological models: A study in visual interactive exploration of scientific problems. *Journal of Visual Languages and Computing, 2*(1), 75-95.

Mussio, P. (2003). E-documents as tools for the humanized management of community knowledge. In H. Linger et al. (Eds.), *Constructing the infrastructure for the knowledge economy: Methods and tools; theory and practice. Keynote Address, ISD 2003*. Melbourne, Australia: Kluwer.

Najork, M., & Kaplan, S. M. (1993). Specifying visual languages with conditional set rewrite systems. *Proceedings of the 1993 IEEE Workshop on Visual Languages* (pp. 12-18). Bergen, Norway: IEEE Computer Society Press.

Nielsen, J. (1993). *Usability engineering*. San Diego: Academic Press.

Norman, D. A. (2005). Human-centered design considered harmful. *Interactions of ACM, 12*(4), 14-19.

Shneiderman, B. (1983). Direct manipulation: A step beyond programming languages. *IEEE Computer, 16*(8), 57-69.

Shneiderman, B. (1992). Direct manipulation. In *Designing the User Interface*. Reading, MA: Addison-Wesley.

Sutcliffe, A., & Mehandjiev, M. (2004). End-user development. *Communications of the ACM, 47*(9), 31-32.

Tsai, W. H., & Fu, K. S. (1980). Attributed grammar: A tool for combining syntatic and statistical approaches to pattern recognition. *IEEE Trans. on Systems, Man, and Cybernetics, 10*(12), 873-885.

Chapter II
Visual and Diagrammatic Languages:
The Logic Perspective

Bernd Meyer
Monash University, Australia

Paolo Bottoni
University of Rome "La Sapienza", Italy

ABSTRACT

In this chapter we investigate a new approach to formalizing interpretation of and reasoning with visual languages based on linear logic. We argue that an approach based on logic makes it possible to deal with different computational tasks in the usage of visual notations, from parsing and animation to reasoning about diagrams. However, classical first order logic, being monotonic, is not a suitable basis for such an approach. The chapter therefore explores linear logic as an alternative. We demonstrate how parsing corresponds to linear proofs and prove the soundness and correctness of this mapping. As our mapping of grammars is into a subset of a linear logic programming language, we also demonstrate how multi-dimensional parsing can be understood as automated linear deduction. We proceed to discuss how the same framework can be used as the foundation of more complex forms of reasoning with and about diagrams.

INTRODUCTION

Like written textual languages and their spoken equivalents, many other types of symbolic notations, for example musical scores, can be regarded as languages. By "languages" we mean that they constitute communication systems based on symbol combinations and that they are, at least in principle, formalizable. Where such systems are visual or graphical in nature, it is thus justified to speak of "visual languages." However, this term is ambiguous: we often speak of the "visual language" of an artist to describe the artist's particular way of expressing himself or herself. This almost never means that we could define a formal system of expression that the artist uses and through which we could mechanically derive an "interpretation" of a work. In contrast, the syntax and semantics of more technical visual languages such as organizational charts, dance notation, electrical circuit diagrams, and mathematical notations can often be formalized rigorously. A whole spectrum of semi-formal visual languages exists between these two extremes, ranging from draft sketches in architectural design over maps to sign languages such as ASL or Auslan.

In general, visual languages do not only differ in the degree to which they are strict and can be formalized, but also in the degree to which they use distinct symbols as their fundamental means of expression. For example, a valve in a mechanical diagram is clearly a distinct symbol, whereas it is not so clear whether shading in a map can or should always be understood in the same way. For the sake of clarity, we will use the term "diagrammatic languages" for visual languages that are based on individual symbols and form expressions through spatial arrangement of these symbols. As is evident from the previous examples, such diagrammatic languages are central in almost all technical domains, and they are also relevant to many aspects of everyday life.

The research field of "diagrammatic reasoning" investigates such languages from the perspective of computer science and cognitive science. The central questions for this field are how we understand such languages and how we employ them as tools in reasoning processes. To investigate these questions in a rigorous way, we need formal frameworks that allow us to define diagrammatic languages and to reason about them. From the perspective of computer science, we are particularly interested in how interpretation and reasoning can be performed automatically on the basis of formal specifications of diagrammatic languages. It seems obvious that the treatment of diagrammatic languages should distinguish between syntax and semantics, just as we do for textual languages, and that a general framework needs to bridge between these two aspects.

The treatment of diagram syntax has been investigated for close to three decades and is now reasonably well understood. The vast majority of methods that are employed are essentially generalizations of approaches from computational linguistics for textual languages, mostly grammar

frameworks. However, as diagrammatic notations are inherently two- or three-dimensional rather than linear (as textual languages are), these grammar frameworks have to be extended. This has given rise to the field of multi-dimensional grammars. The various forms of multi-dimensional grammars, such as relational grammars, multiset grammars, and constraint multiset grammars, are now relatively mature formalisms that are widely used to specify diagram syntax and to build computational tools for diagrammatic languages.

The majority of computational methods for the automatic interpretation of diagrams take a syntax-based two-step approach consisting of parsing and interpretation proper, and multi-dimensional grammar frameworks are well suited to cover the first phase. However, when it comes to the interpretation proper (i.e., the treatment of semantics) they provide little support. Thus, this phase is most often covered by ad-hoc approaches defined on a case-by-case basis for individual diagram languages.

Grammar-based methods also have some other shortcomings: Firstly, it is important to acknowledge that diagrams are rarely used in isolation, but rather in combination with textual language. Thus, the interpretation of diagrammatic languages needs to take into account non-diagrammatic contextual information, for example for disambiguation. In a grammatical framework, the integration of such contextual information is difficult. Secondly, while multi-dimensional grammars are relatively mature computational tools, their theory is not well developed, meaning that it is difficult, for instance, to prove formal properties such as the equivalence of grammars.

In the light of these shortcomings, logic approaches present themselves as a valuable alternative to grammatical frameworks. Logic approaches, by their very nature, are semantic. A logic calculus for reasoning with and about diagrammatic languages is thus a more adequate approach to treating semantics. Interestingly, the increased power of a logic specification over a grammatical one does not come at a price, as a well-designed logic approach can fully subsume the grammatical approach.

The remainder of the chapter will trace out the progress that the last two decades of research have made in this direction. In the next section, we briefly outline the grammatical approach to visual language specification and highlight its shortcomings as a basis for this research plan. We will then revisit the question: Why do we want reasoning with diagram languages? to motivate an alternative approach, and outline what forms of reasoning will be required. Following this, we will outline the history of logic approaches to diagrammatic languages and detail the comparative advantages and disadvantages of the different types of logic formalization. Based on this, the core of this chapter will develop a new approach based on linear logic, which avoids most of the shortcomings and completely subsumes the grammatical approach. We will show this subsumption formally. We will then briefly outline existent software systems based on this approach. The concluding section reflects on what has been achieved so far and gives recommendations for future research direction.

THE CLASSICAL APPROACH: GRAMMAR SPECIFICATION

The vast majority of approaches to visual language specification interpretation are based on various forms of multi-dimensional grammars, which are essentially either extensions of string grammars or graph grammars.[1] The main differences between grammars for diagrammatic languages and grammars for textual languages is that the former must allow us to capture the multi-dimensional (usually 2-dimensional) spatial arrangement of symbols instead of just a sequential (1-dimensional) concatenation. We therefore call such grammars multi-dimensional grammars. A full review of the many different forms of multi-dimensional grammars that have been presented in the literature is beyond the scope of this article, but the interested reader can find a comprehensive survey in Marriott et al. (1998), which also contains the "fossil record" of visual language specification.[2]

For the purpose of this chapter, it will suffice to divide the class of multi-dimensional grammars broadly into two categories: relation-based grammars and attribute-based grammars.

We will briefly sketch an example of relation-based grammars to highlight the basic characteristics of this approach and point out why this approach is insufficient as a basis of more general forms of diagrammatic reasoning. We will then turn our attention to attribute-based formalisms, which provide a better basis for this, and discuss these in more detail.

Relation-Based Grammars

Almost all specification formalisms model a diagram as a set of primitive graphical objects (tokens) that are classified into primitive types. The terms terminal (or primitive) and non-terminal (or derived) are used analogously to the case of textual languages. The only difference lies in the fact that terminal types in diagrams refer to graphic primitives such as line and circle, instead of textual tokens. A symbol is an instance of a symbol type.

As a running example, consider the language of state transition diagrams such as the one shown in Figure 1. To represent such a diagram, we would use sets of symbols with types such as circle, line, arrow, and text label. Such a set structure by itself does, of course, not reflect the exact appearance of the diagram or the spatial relations between these symbols. The relation-based approach dispenses with representing the exact geometry and instead just represents the spatial relations between individual symbols that are essential to the interpretation.

Figure 1. State transition diagram

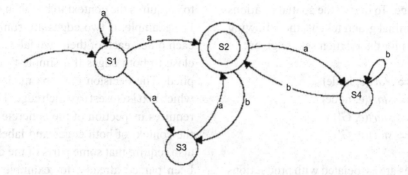

Consider the state chart: for the interpretation of such a state chart, we would need to model whether a text label is inside a circle or attached_to an arrow, whether an arrow starts_at or ends_at a circle, etc. For example, the diagram fragment in Figure 2 could be represented with the token set:

$$T = \{circle_1, circle_2, text_1, text_2, text_3, arrow_1\}$$

and the relation set:

$$R = \{arrow_1, \text{starts\_at } circle_1, arrow_1, \text{ends\_at}$$
$$circle_2, text_1 \text{ inside } circle_1, text_2, \text{ inside}$$
$$circle_2, text_3 \text{ attached\_to } arrow_1\}$$

In principle, the relation-based approach thus models a diagram as a set of graphical tokens and as a set of primitive spatial relations between these tokens.[3]

The relations between the primitive tokens can be extracted at the time of tokenization. In

Figure 2. Fragment of an NFA diagram

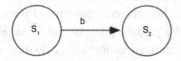

principle, tokenization is the only phase during which the actual geometry of the diagram needs to be inspected. After this, the explicitly modeled spatial relations are processed only in symbolic form. The obvious question is, how are relations between derived (non-terminal) symbols computed in this approach? The key to this is to explicitly re-write not only the set of tokens, but also the set of spatial relations, so that derived spatial relations are computed in parallel with non-terminal symbols.

We outline Relation Grammars (Crimi et al., 1990) as a simple example of the relational approach. Consider the following grammar from Crimi et al. (1990), which essentially describes diagrams that are directed graphs. There are two terminal token types: nodes (n), and edges (e), and one non-terminal token type: graph (G). Only two types of relations are used: start, which holds if a node (or graph) is at the start of an edge and end, if it is at the end of an edge. The productions for the token set are:

1: $G \rightarrow \{n\}$
2: $G \rightarrow \{n, G'\}$
3: $G \rightarrow \{n, G'\} \{start\ (e, G'),\ end\ (e, G')\}$

which formalize that a primitive graph consists of a single node, and that a graph can be augmented by either adding an unconnected node to it or by adding a node that is connected to the rest of the graph by an edge. To derive the spatial relations for the non-terminal graph tokens, the following derivation rules for the relation set are given:

$start(e, G)$ [1] $\Rightarrow$ $start(e, \text{node})$
$start(e, G)$ [2] $\Rightarrow$ $start(e, \text{node})$
$start(e, G)$ [2] $\Rightarrow$ $start(e, G')$
$start(e, G)$ [3] $\Rightarrow$ $start(e, G')$

Evaluation rules are associated with productions (the number of the production is shown in brackets) and indicate how the relations have to be rewritten when this production is applied. Thus for example, the first evaluation rule states that, whenever a node is reduced to a non-terminal graph G by production 1, all edges that start at this node have to be rewritten to start at G. The evaluation rules for end are analogous to those for start.

Pure graph-grammars, which were among the earliest methods for diagram specification, also fall into the relation-based category. Here, the embedding function takes over the explicit rewriting of symbolic spatial relations. The interested reader is referred to Marriott et al. (1998), Tucci, Vitiello, and Pacini (1992), and Tucci, Vitiello, and Costagliola (1994) for a detailed discussion of this aspect.[4]

The clear advantage of the relation-based approach is that it allows reasonably efficient parsing in the context-free case.[5] However, there are a couple of conceptual as well as technical disadvantages to this seemingly simple approach: Firstly, all spatial relations are purely symbolic. This makes it very hard to model vague relations such as "close to" in a meaningful way. Consider the case of a text labeling an arrow in a transition diagram. The correspondence of the arrow and the text is established by writing the text close to the arrow. However, it is hard (and in general impossible) to reduce this spatial relationship to a binary symbolic relation that can be determined locally (by only inspecting the edge and the text

during the tokenization phase). This is because the disambiguation of the vague concept "close to" requires the context to be taken into account. For example, if two edges are running close to each other, each of their two labels may well be close to both edges if a simple threshold is applied. The decision must be made by deciding which text is closest to which edge. This, however, requires inspection of the concrete geometry in the context of both edges and labels. As it may also require that some parts of the diagram have been parsed already, for example if the edges themselves are derived tokens, it is impossible to determine these relations before parsing. Instead, to perform such disambiguation effectively, inspection of the concrete geometry during the parsing process is required. This is not possible in a purely symbolic approach.

The second problem stems from the requirement to write the production rules for relations. Consider a production for a final state (depicted by two concentric circles) in this approach:

1: final $\rightarrow$ {$circle_1$, $circle_2$} {$inside(circle_1, circle_2)$}
   $inside$ ($circle_1$, text)[1] $\Rightarrow$ $inside$ (final, text)

Effectively, these rules do nothing but emulate the natural laws of geometry: If the text is in a circle that is inside another circle and we consider the two circles as a final state token, the text is obviously inside it. As we are generally dealing with a concrete, drawable geometry, the whole task of these rules usually is to model (some part of) basic geometric inference. However, since these rules are tied in with the grammar for the symbols, we cannot state them once for all as the axioms of our geometry, but we have to tailor them to every new grammar. Writing such rules is complex, tedious and error prone at the best of times.

Both problems can be overcome if we have access to the concrete geometry of the diagram during the parsing process and if we allow to compute derived geometric attributes, such as bounding boxes, explicitly during parsing. This is where the attribute-based approach comes in.

Attribute-Based Grammars

The attribute-based approach, in contrast to the relation-based approach, does not ignore the details of the spatial information during the parsing process. Instead of just using un-attributed tokens[6], it attributes all tokens with their concrete geometry. The parsing formalism based on this approach uses calculations embedded into the grammar productions to compute derived attributes of non-terminal symbols. For example, assume that an arrow in the state diagram is not modeled as a primitive token, and instead we only have line and triangle as primitives. A production for an arrow would specify that it is composed of a line and a triangle attached to it, and it would calculate the coordinates etc. of the arrow from the spatial attributes of the line and the triangle. The attribute-based approach thus deals with concrete geometries explicitly. This allows it to dispense with rewriting a set of relations and to just rewrite a set of attributed tokens instead.

Arguably the most advanced attribute-based grammar approach to visual language specification is constraint multiset grammars (Helm et al., 1991), which have been used by a number of researchers for reasonably complex tasks such as the interpretation of state diagrams and mathematical equations. We will review CMGs in more formal detail than the relation-based approach, as we will later use CMGs to formally demonstrate how the logical approach to diagram specification subsumes the grammatical approach. Full detail, in particular parsing algorithms for CMGs are given in Marriott (1994), and an in-depth analysis of the relation between CMGs and other multidimensional grammar frameworks is given in Marriott and Meyer (1998).

A diagrammatic sentence to be parsed by a CMG is just an attributed multiset of graphical tokens. CMG productions rewrite multisets of attributed symbols and have the form:

$$U ::= U_1, ..., U_n \; exists \; U_{n+1}, ..., U_m \; where \; (C) \; \{E\} \qquad (1)$$

This specifies that the symbols $U_1, ..., U_n$ can be rewritten into the symbol U using this production if and only if the context symbols $U_{n+1}, ..., U_m$ exist in the current multiset and the constraint expression C holds. The symbols U_i can be attributed and C is a predicate on the attributes of $U_1, ..., U_m$. During rewriting, the attributes of U are computed from the attributes of $U_1, ..., U_m$ using the assignment expression E. Including the attributes in the formal definition, a CMG production takes the form:

$$U(\vec{x}) ::= U_1(\vec{x}_1), ..., U_n(\vec{x}_n) \; exists \; U_{n+1}(\vec{x}_{n+1}), ..., U_m(\vec{x}_m) \; where \; C(\vec{x}_1, ..., \vec{x}_m) \; \{\vec{x} = E(\vec{x}_1, ..., \vec{x}_m)\} \qquad (2)$$

In each grammar, there is a distinguished non-terminal symbol type called the start type. Attributes can be associated with tokens and are typically used to describe their geometric properties, but they can also be used to capture the semantics of the interpretation, similar to the way textual grammars process semantic attributes. As productions are applied in the parsing process, semantic functions in E can compute the attribute values for the generated non-terminal, up to the construction of a global interpretation in a designated attribute of the start symbol.

We show a production for recognizing a final state in a state transition diagram. This is made up of two circles *C1* and *C2* and a text *T* satisfying three geometric relationships: the mid-points of the circle *C1* and the circle *C2* are the same; the mid-points of the circle *C1* and the text *T* are the same; and *C2* is the outermost circle. Note the additional attributes kind and label used to construct an "interpretation." The production is:

S: state ::= C1: circle, C2: circle, T:text where (
C1.mid = C2.mid and C1.mid = T.mid and
C1.radius ≤ C2.radius){
S.mid = C1.mid and S.radius = C2.radius and
S.label = T.label and S.kind = final}

We are using the dot notation to refer to named attributes (e.g., *C1.mid* refers to the attribute named *mid* of the token *C1*). Written in the form of Equation 2 the previous production is therefore equivalent to:

state $(S_{mid}, S_{radius}, S_{label}, S_{kind})$ ::=
circle $(C1_{mid}, C1_{radius})$, *circle*$(C2_{mid}, C2_{radius})$,
text (T_{mid}, T_{label}) *where* (
$C1_{mid} = C2_{mid} \wedge C1_{mid} = T_{mid} \wedge C1_{radius} \le C2_{radius}$) {
$(S_{mid}, S_{radius}, S_{label}, S_{kind}) = (C1_{mid}, C2_{radius}, T_{label},$
final)}

It is now easy to see that we do not need to write extra rules to emulate the laws of geometry as in the relation-based approach. All that we do is to transfer the relevant spatial attributes to the derived symbol using semantic rules. CMGs also allow us to use context-sensitive productions. As indicated in the general form (1) of a production above, context symbols are denoted by existential quantification. For example, the following context-sensitive production recognizes a transition:

T:transition ::= *A:arc exists S1:state, S2:state
where* (
OnCircle (*A.start, S1.mid, S1.radius*) $\wedge$
OnCircle (*A.end, S2.mid, S2.radius*))
{*T.start = S1.label $\wedge$ T.tran = A.label $\wedge$ T.end = S2.label*}

where an arc is simply a labeled arrow

R:arc ::= *A:arrow, T:text where* (*A.mid = T.mid*)
      {*R.start = A.start $\wedge$ R.end = A.end $\wedge$ R.mid = A.mid $\wedge$ R.label = T.label*}

Note that this existentially quantified form is equivalent to using the more conventional (but lengthier) notation, which puts context symbols on both sides of the production:

T:transition, S1:state, S2:state ::= *A: arc, S1:state,
      S2:state where* (
      OnCircle (*A.start, S1.mid, S1.radius*) $\wedge$

OnCircle(A.end, S2.mid, S2.radius)) {*T.start = S1.label $\wedge$ T.tran = A.label $\wedge$ T.end = S2.label*}

The unrestricted form of CMG productions (type 0) allows us to rewrite an arbitrary number of symbols simultaneously and is thus given by:

$$U_1(\vec{x}_1), ..., U_n(\vec{x}_n) ::= V_1(\vec{y}_1), ..., V_m(\vec{y}_m)$$
$$\text{where } C(\vec{y}_1, ..., \vec{y}_m) \{(\vec{x}_1, ..., \vec{x}_n) = E(\vec{y}_1, ..., \vec{y}_m)\} \qquad (3)$$

Corresponding to the standard structural classification of string grammars, we define a CMG production as shown in Equation 3 to be context-sensitive if $1 \le n \le m$ and context-free if additionally $n = 1$. For a detailed analysis of the expressiveness of the different classes of CMGs, see Marriott and Meyer (1997).

THE GRAND CHALLENGE: REASONING WITH AND ABOUT DIAGRAMS

Grammar formalisms like CMGs provide us with a powerful method for parsing and interpretation of diagrammatic notations, but are grammars an adequate framework for all aspects of diagram specification? The answer is that they are not, we believe. Syntax-directed interpretation of diagrams is often straightforward enough: it is, for example, not difficult to define a grammar that extracts the regular expression described by the NFA in Figure 1. But syntax-directed interpretation (by means of parsing) is only a small part of the reasoning tasks that we would like to perform with diagrams, and grammars are ill-suited for other kinds of reasoning.

Arguably the most striking examples of complex formal reasoning with diagrams arise from the "diagrammatic calculus" movement that is rooted in the pioneering works of Shin (1995) and Hammer (1996) and subsequent extensions of these by other authors, in particular Howse,

Figure 3. A diagrammatic proof of $n^2 = \sum_{i=1}^{n} (2i-1)$

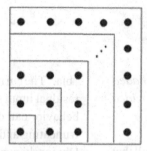

Molina, Taylor, Kent, and Gil (2001). Diagrams have long been used as a tool of thought in mathematical investigations, and examples of elegant diagrammatic proofs are plentiful (see Nelsen, 1993, for an inspiring collection).

Consider, for example, Figure 3, which gives a simple and elegant argument for $n^2 = \sum_{i=1}^{n} (2i-1)$. However, such diagrammatic reasoning contains dangerous pitfalls. The question, whether these "diagrammatic proofs" actually constitute valid proofs or mere illustration had been a matter of a long-standing debate. The core problem is that the inference rules in such proofs are not clearly formalized. For example, it is not unambiguous what the ellipsis in Figure 3 means. To further clarify this point let us look at the classic example of the proof of Pythagoras' theorem in Figure 4.

This sequence of diagrams appears to be a clear and unambiguous proof of Pythagoras' theorem $a^2 + b^2 = c^2$.[7] The white area in the left diagram clearly is $a^2 + b^2$ and the corresponding surface

Figure 4. Pythagoras' theorem

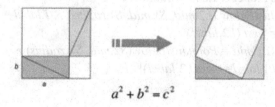

$$a^2 + b^2 = c^2$$

in the right diagram clearly is c^2. As we have treated the objects in the diagram as rigid (i.e., only translation and rotation were applied), this might be considered as a proper proof. However, there are several kinds of problems with this type of reasoning. Firstly, this "proof" uses only one particular diagram. It is not clear or explicit for which other instances the proof would remain valid (i.e., what we quantify over): all right triangles, all triangles, or even all polygons? The second problem is that the inference rules that have been used to derive the second diagram from the first one are not formalized. They have just been informally derived from the analogy to physical objects. This is neither rigorous enough nor sufficient for more abstract types of reasoning. These considerations have led many researchers to question whether visual formalisms can ever be valid tools for formal mathematical reasoning.

Luckily this debate has (at least in principle) been settled by the ground-breaking work of Shin, who fully formalized the system of (extended) Venn Diagrams into a visual set calculus with clearly stated inference rules. Others, in particular Howse (2001) have followed this lead and have later established similarly rigorous visual calculi. As an illustration of how such calculi work, consider the following inference rule from Shin's calculus:

Figure 5. Reasoning with a Venn Diagram

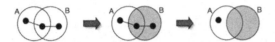

Figure 6. Transition in an NFA Diagram

If an element of a chain is located in a shaded region, this element may be removed provided that the chain is reconnected.

To clarify the meaning of this rule we recall that shaded regions in Venn Diagrams denote empty sets and that chains of elements postulate the existence of an element in at least one of the regions in which the chain's elements are located.

Consider the diagram in Figure 5. The complete translation of the leftmost Venn Diagram in this figure is the proposition $\exists x: x \in A \cap B \vee x \in A - B \vee x \in B - A$ (from the chain). Now imagine adding shading to the right set B (middle Venn Diagram). This is equivalent to adding the proposition $B = \varnothing$ to the interpretation of the diagram. Repeated application of the above transformation rule now allows us to reduce the diagram to the form given on the right-hand side, which is equivalent to inferring the proposition $x \in A - B$.

It should have become clear that a diagrammatic calculus, such as Shin's Venn calculus, can rightfully be given the same status as a reasoning device that a syntactic calculus for a textual logic has. As in the latter case, its basic ingredients are syntactic transformations, but in this case, the transformations act on a multi-dimensional visual notation.

It is interesting to note that this form of syntactic calculus closely corresponds to a more "natural" form of reasoning with diagrams, namely the idea that the animation of diagrams (again, syntactic transformation) can be used as a simple form of reasoning. For example, Figure 6 provides an illustration of a single step in the animation of an NFA that is processing the string

"bla." The current state is identified by placing the residual input string under it and the automaton's behavior can diagrammatically be simulated by truncating and moving this residual input string. Obviously, such animation can be used as a simple form of diagrammatic reasoning, for example to test whether a certain input is accepted by a given automaton. Diagram notations that can be used in this form have therefore been termed "executable graphics" (Lakin, 1986).

The crucial issue with the syntactic transformations used in both examples is that they must be formally well defined. Unfortunately, the inference rules of Shin's system and other syntactic calculi for diagrammatic notations (Shin, 1996; Hammer, 1996; Howse et al., 2001) have been stated only in natural language.[8] What is required to fully specify these calculi is a formal meta-language that allows us to specify diagram transformations on the level of the actual visual tokens.

In the case of executable graphics, this seems straightforward enough: If we move from context-free to context sensitive multi-dimensional grammars, we can directly write down such animation rules.[9] For example, using the CMG formalism, the rule that is the basis for the transformation step illustrated in Figure 6 is:

L1:text, S1:state, S2:state, T:transition ::= L2:text, S1:state, S2:state, T:transition where T.start = S1.label $\wedge$ T.end = S2.label $\wedge$ JustBelow (L2.mid, S1.mid, S1.radius) $\wedge$ T.label = first (L2.label))
{L1.mid = PointJustBelow(S2.mid, S2.radius) $\wedge$ L1.label = rest(L2.label)}

Note that the production in this example is context-sensitive. It is straightforward to give the remaining rules that complete the specification for the visual execution of a state automaton such as the one for ε-transitions. Thus, unrestricted CMGs allow us to formalize the concept of "executable graphics."[10] Such specifications will allow us, for example, to prove that a concrete word w (say, w = ababa) is accepted by a given automaton or to extract the regular expression that describes this automaton, say $L = a^+ (ba \mid ab^+)^*$. However, we must always reason using a finite sequence of animation steps and we must actually execute the animation to perform any inference. This constitutes a very weak mechanism for reasoning. It would, for example, by no means be straightforward to devise an animation to prove that two automata are equivalent (in particular, in the presence of attributed transitions). Such reasoning would require a general calculus for grammars, which does not exist for CMGs or for any other type of multi-dimensional grammar. We can execute a grammar specification and parse with it, but we cannot mechanically reason about a grammar specification.

The need to identify a framework that supports this kind of automatic (deductive) reasoning with and about diagram specifications is the main rationale behind the logic approach to diagram specification.

A WAY FORWARD: LOGIC SPECIFICATION OF DIAGRAMS

Logic formalisms for the specification of visual and diagrammatic languages have been investigated before, but only for first-order logic and for logic programming based on first-order logic. An overview of the different techniques can be found in Marriott et al. (1998). For the context of this chapter, it will suffice to summarize the fundamental properties of these methods, which can be

grouped into two distinct main categories: term-based models and predicate-based models.

The first approach encodes a diagram as a single term modeling a hierarchical collection of the graphical objects in the diagram. This is closely related to the way linear sentences are modeled in DCGs (Pereira & Warren, 1980) and other computational logic grammars. In fact, one of the first approaches to use this modeling was a straightforward extension of DCGs by set structures called definite clause set grammars or DCSGs (Tanaka, 1991). Various other forms of such encodings have been demonstrated (Marriott et al., 1998), some modeling a diagram as a hierarchical term (Helm et al., 1991), others using a term to represent a graph-based model of the diagram (Meyer, 1992, 1997).

The key idea is the same in both cases, namely to model a diagram as a single term. The key predicate is *reduce*(D, D'), which holds if diagram D can be reduced to D' using one of the productions in the grammar. To handle spatial conditions, we assume a first-order theory C, which models the relevant aspects of geometry. C is assumed to be an additional set of axioms in our inferences.

For the state transition diagram grammar we can define *reduce*(D, D'), which holds if D' can be obtained from D by recognizing a final state:

$$
\begin{aligned}
reduce_{fs}\,(D, D') &\leftrightarrow \overline{\exists \{D, D'\}} \\
&circle(C^1_{mid}, C^1_{radius}) \in D \\
&\wedge\, circle(C^2_{mid}, C^2_{radius}) \in D \,\wedge \\
&text(T_{mid}, T_{label}) \in D \,\wedge \\
&C^1_{mid} = C^2_{mid} \wedge C^1_{mid} = T_{mid} \wedge C^1_{radius} \le C^2_{radius} \,\wedge \\
&S_{mid} = C^1_{mid} \wedge S_{radius} = C^2_{radius} \wedge S_{label} = T_{label} \,\wedge \\
&S_{kind} = final \,\wedge \\
&D' = D \setminus \{circle(C^1_{mid}, C^1_{radius}), \\
&circle(C^2_{mid}, C^2_{radius}), text(T_{mid}, T_{label})\} \\
&\uplus \{state(S_{mid}, S_{radius}, S_{label}, S_{kind})\}
\end{aligned}
$$

where we use the Prolog convention of using identifiers starting with an upper-case letter for variables and those starting with a lowercase letter for predicates and functions, the functions $\uplus, \setminus, \in$ work on multisets, and $\tilde{\exists}\{D, D'\}$ indicates existential closure over all variables but D and D'. This encoding, of course, allows a faithful modeling of diagram parsing—it exactly captures rewriting with a CMG production. However, it hardly leverages from first-order logic.

In contrast, the second approach encodes the graphical objects directly as predicates, rather than terms. Based on classical first-order logic this approach has been demonstrated in Helm and Marriott (1991), Marriott (1994), and Meyer (2000).

In such an embedding, we map, for example, the production for the (final) state type from the state transition diagram grammar to the predicate state:

$$state(\underline{S_{mid}}, S_{radius}, S_{label}, S_{kind}) \leftrightarrow \tilde{\exists}\overline{\{S_{mid}, S_{radius}, S_{label}, S_{kind}\}}.$$
$$circle(C1_{mid}, C1_{radius}) \wedge circle(C2_{mid}, C2_{radius})$$
$$\wedge \; text(T_{mid}, T_{label}) \wedge$$
$$C1_{mid} = C2_{mid} \wedge C1_{mid} = T_{mid} \wedge C1_{radius} \leq C2_{radius}$$
$$\wedge$$
$$S_{mid} = C1_{mid} \wedge S_{radius} = C2_{radius} \wedge S_{label} = T_{label}$$
$$\wedge \; S_{kind} = final$$

where $\tilde{\exists}\overline{\{x_1, ..., x_n\}}$ is the existential closure over all variables but $x_1, ..., x_n$.

The advantage of this embedding is that implication directly corresponds to reduction. The disadvantage is that there is a fundamental mismatch between implication in first-order logic and grammatical reduction: Because first-order logic is monotonic there is no way of determining if an element in the diagram has already been reduced; in particular there is no way to determine whether all elements in the original diagram have been reduced to the start symbol. Thus parsing cannot truthfully be captured in such a modeling if it is based on classical first-order logic. It also means that it is impossible to fully model negative constraints. In the first-order logic encoding not exists X means that the symbol X can never be recognized during parsing while the CMG reading is that the symbol X is currently not recognized (i.e., in the CMG reading the negative context is required not to be present in the current sentential form).

It should be pointed out that not all approaches to logical specification of visual and diagrammatic languages were designed to support parsing (Haarslev, 1998; Janneck & Esser; 2001; Marriott et al., 1998). Notably, the description-logic based approach (Haarslev, 1998) is oriented toward more general reasoning tasks. For example, this formalism allows us to deduce which additional elements are needed to complete a partial diagram into a syntactically valid form (Haarslev, 1994). In such approaches, diagram interpretation is viewed as an instance of more general reasoning about visual representations. While this could (and should!) be viewed as a conceptual advantage, a severe computational penalty has to be paid: Even in simple cases, the interpretation of a diagram requires powerful general inference mechanisms with the associated high computational costs. This is problematic as simple syntax-directed interpretation is arguably one of the most common tasks in diagram processing and should be supported efficiently.

It is for these reasons that alternative frameworks for the logical specification of diagram languages are investigated. Ideally, such a framework should fulfill at least the following requirements:

1. It should be based on a form of logic that is not narrowly targeted toward visual representations but rather supports general forms of reasoning. In particular, it should at least be as powerful as classical first order logic. This provides a sound basis to integrate diagrammatic reasoning with domain reasoning, as the same logic can be used to reason about diagrams as well as about the domain of discourse represented in the diagram.

2. It should be based on a computational logic, so that effective methods for computational reasoning about these specifications exist and so that directly executable specifications can be obtained (e.g., by mapping to logic programs).

3. It should be able to support reasoning about geometries in a generic way, without the need to "re-implement geometry" for every new diagram specification.

4. Simple parsing should be supported with low computational overhead (i.e., the framework should combine the advantage of grammars (more efficient parsing) with the power of a general logic formalism (more general reasoning)).

HARNESSING NON-CLASSICAL LOGIC: A LINEAR LOGIC FRAMEWORK

In the quest to design such a framework, non-standard logics have been explored in recent years as an alternative to classical first order logic. In particular, linear logic has emerged as a candidate for a framework that can unify the treatment of syntax and semantics of diagrammatic languages while still providing the basis for effective computational interpretation. Linear logic (Girard, 1987), which was originally conceived as a logic of resources and actions, relaxes the monotonicity constraint of classical logic, and thus overcomes the core problem of the predicate-based encoding of classical first order logic. While this is also true for many other non-classical logics such as certain modal logics and default logic, linear logic does this in a particularly controlled way that makes it very suitable for our application.

We cannot give a full introduction to linear logic here, so that we just provide some intuition. Linear logic has been widely used in computer science to formalize such diverse things as Petri

nets and functional language implementation. Linear implication $X \multimap Y$ is used to indicate that resource X can be consumed to produce Y. As an example, if A is "$20" and B is "a bottle of wine" then $A \multimap B$ captures the rule that we can purchase a bottle of wine for $20, but once we do so the money is gone. The linear connective $X \otimes Y$ is used to indicate that we have both the resource X and the resource Y. If C is a main dish then $A \otimes A \multimap B \otimes C$ states that for 2*$20 we can buy both a main dish and a bottle of wine.[11] Clearly, linear implication provides a natural way of formalizing reduction in grammars: the resource-oriented nature of linear logic allows us to map grammatical frameworks directly to linear logic. At the same time, linear logic provides us with a semantic approach. Thus, it has the potential to serve as a unifying framework for the formalization of diagrammatic languages.

The inference rules for two linear calculi used in this chapter are given in the appendix. For a full introduction, the interested reader is referred to Girard (1987).

The specific merits of the linear logic approach that we introduce here are that it fulfils the requirements for a logical diagram framework that were outlined at the end of the last section: (1) Linear logic supports general forms of reasoning. It subsumes classical first-order logic and was particularly designed to overcome its deficiencies when reasoning about actions and events. (2) Our framework is well suited for computational reasoning as it maps directly to a fragment of linear logic that is the basis for linear logic programming. (3) Reasoning about geometries can be performed in a generic way by arithmetic reasoning about spatial attributes. (4) Our linear framework fully subsumes a powerful multi-dimensional grammar framework, constraint multiset grammars (CMGs). The translation of CMGs to linear specifications is sound and complete, and there is a strong equivalence between a grammar and the corresponding logic program in the following sense: For a given grammar G and the language

$\mathcal{L}(G)$ defined by G, the grammatical reduction of a word $w \in \mathcal{L}(G)$ corresponds step by step to the logical deduction executed by the logic specification derived from G when proving $w \in \mathcal{L}(G)$. This strong equivalence of the grammar reduction and the corresponding logic program is an important result, because it proves that we do not have to pay a performance penalty for parsing, even though we have switched to a more powerful formalism.

To the best of our knowledge this is the first framework for diagram specification and reasoning in linear logic.[12] The remainder of this section will detail how grammatical specifications can be mapped to the linear logic framework and prove the properties of this embedding.

Mapping Multiset Grammars to Linear Logic

As we want to be able to perform diagrammatic reasoning mechanically, it is crucial that our framework is suitable for automated deduction. Deduction in full linear logic is extremely complex and it would seem desirable to have a simpler fragment of linear logic that still is expressive enough to model diagrammatic parsing and transformation. We can find such a fragment in the calculi that are used for linear logic programming languages (Miller, 1995).

Our embedding uses a subset of the calculus that is behind the linear logic programming language Lygon (Harland, Pym, & Winikoff, 1996, Winikoff, 1996). Alternatively, the fragment that we are using can be viewed as a minor extension of the fragment underlying the linear logic programming language LO (Andreoli & Pareschi, 1991).[13] The CMG embedding into this fragment uses linear disjunction to concatenate tokens and additive conjunction to express (spatial) constraints that limit the applicability of a rule. The linear mapping $\tau(p)$ of a (possibly unrestricted) CMG production p:

$$U_1, ..., U_n ::= V_1, ..., V_m \; where \; (C)\{E\}$$

is an exponential universal closure

$$! \; \tilde{\forall} \; \tau(V_1) \,\mathbin{\rotatebox[origin=c]{180}{\&}}\, ... \,\mathbin{\rotatebox[origin=c]{180}{\&}}\, \tau(V_m) \multimap \tau_\&(C) \& \tau_\&(E) \& \tau(U_1) \,\mathbin{\rotatebox[origin=c]{180}{\&}}\, ... \,\mathbin{\rotatebox[origin=c]{180}{\&}}\, \tau(U_n)$$

The complete translation of a grammar is the set of all rules obtained from the individual mappings of all its productions. In the case of a context-free CMG we have $n = 1$ for all productions. Note that the exponential is required to make the rule a resource that can be applied arbitrarily often.

We use τ to map each CMG terminal and non-terminal symbol u_i in the production to a first order term $\tau(u_i)$, which has the token type of u_i as the main functor and contains the attributes in some fixed order. $\tau(u_i)$ Thus is a complete and unique representation of a symbol including all its attributes. We extend τ in the obvious way to map a single constraint or assignment to a first order term and use $\tau_\&$ to map a classical conjunction of constraints to an additive conjunction (&) of linear first order terms. For convenience, we extend the mapping function τ canonically to the encoding of full productions. More exactly, $\tau(U_1, ..., U_n)$ denotes $\tau(U_1) \,\mathbin{\rotatebox[origin=c]{180}{\&}}\, ... \,\mathbin{\rotatebox[origin=c]{180}{\&}}\, \tau(U_n)$. In the same way, $\tau(p)$, for a CMG production p, denotes its mapping to a linear rule as previous. $\tau(G) = \{\tau(p) \mid p \in P\}$, where P is the production set of G, denotes the mapping of a complete CMG G to a linear program.

As a concrete example consider the CMG production for a transition given above and the definition of the token types it uses. The linear mapping of this production is:

$! \; \tilde{\forall} \; state(mid_{s1}, radius_{s1}, label_{s1}, kind_{s1}) \,\mathbin{\rotatebox[origin=c]{180}{\&}}\, state(mid_{s2}, radius_{s2}, label_{s2}, kind_{s2}) \,\mathbin{\rotatebox[origin=c]{180}{\&}}\, arc(start_a, mid_a, end_a, label_t) \multimap$
$OnCircle(start_a, mid_{s1}, radius_{s1}) \, \& \,$
$OnCircle(end_a, mid_{s2}, radius_{s2}) \, \& \,$
$start_t = label_{s1} \& tran_t = label_a \&$

$end_t = label_{s2} \&$
$state(mid_{s1}, radius_{s1}, label_{s1}, kind_{s1}) \bindnasrepma$
$state(mid_{s2}, radius_{s2}, label_{s2}, kind_{s2}) \bindnasrepma$
$transition\ (start_t, tran_t, end_t)$

To provide some intuition for why additive disjunction is used to connect the tokens, we note that additive disjunction has strong conjunctive properties, despite being technically classified as a disjunctive operator. The reader is referred to Appendix A for the proof rules for additive disjunction and is encouraged to compare them with those for multiplicative disjunction. To quote the father of linear logic, Girard, "$\bindnasrepma$ [...] is technically a disjunction, but has prominent conjunctive features [...] The meaning of $\bindnasrepma$ is not that easy [...]; in some sense $\bindnasrepma$ is the constructive content of classical disjunction" (Girard, 1995).

The use of additive conjunction for the constraints and attribute computations is motivated by the application of the theory of focusing proofs to linear logic programming (Andreoli, 1992). Intuitively, it can be thought of as "spawning off" an additional branch in the proof which tests the condition *C&E*.

To evaluate the constraints in the grammar and to compute the attribute assignments we assume that the geometric (arithmetic) theory is available as a first-order theory Γ_g in linear logic.

Each rule $\tau(p)$ emulates exactly one production p. To emulate parsing fully, we also need a rule which declares that a parse is successful if and only if the initial diagram is reduced to the start symbol and no other symbols are left. For a CMG G with start symbol s, we can do this in linear logic by adding $\tau(s) \circ\!\!-1$ as an axiom to $\tau(G)$ using the linear goal **1**, which succeeds if and only if the linear proof context is empty. The complete set of linear rules that implement a grammar G is: $\Pi = \tau(G) \cup \{\tau(s) \circ\!\!-1\}$. A successful parse of a diagram D now corresponds to a proof of

$$\Gamma_g, \Pi \vdash \tau(D)$$

This embedding maps positive CMGs (i.e., grammars without negative contexts) to proper linear logic programs so that we directly obtain an executable deductive theory for diagram parsing. In general, however, positive grammars are not strong enough. There are a large number of visual languages that can only be defined using negative conditions (Marriott et al., 1997). Therefore, many diagram specification frameworks, such as constraint multiset grammars or description-logic based methods (Haarslev, 1998) have adopted negative contexts (Marriott et al., 1998). Likewise, many graph grammar formalisms used to specify visual languages (Bardohl, Minas, Schürr, & Taentzer, 1999) such as the single push-out approach (Ehrig et al., 1997) allow rule designers to express negative application conditions.

An example of a CMG production with negative context is that for recognizing a start state in an NFA. A start state is composed of a labeled circle C and a text T with an arrow A pointing to it. Of course, A should not have a label, otherwise it would be a transition and this would be a normal (or final) state not a start state (see Figure 1). Therefore, to avoid ambiguity between the production for a start state and the production for a final state, negative context is required.

S:*state* ::= C:*circle*, T:*text*, A:*arrow where* (
    $T.mid == C.mid \wedge OnCircle\ (A.end, C.mid,$
    $C.radius) \wedge$
    not exist $T1$:*text where* ($T1.mid = A.mid$)
    ){
    $S.mid = C.mid \wedge S.radius = C.radius \wedge$
    $S.label = T.label \wedge S.kind = start$}

In a logic-based approach, handling negative application conditions is comparatively easy. Instead of using a negative context ($\neg\exists x : \phi(x)$) we can model the application condition as ($\forall x: \neg\phi(x)$). The linear approach even allows us to emulate this type of application condition in rules that do not explicitly use universal quantification. This is achieved by looping over all symbols of type *x*, checking the condition ¬φ(·), and using the **1** connective to ensure that all symbols of type *x* have been checked.[14] Full details of negative application conditions are given elsewhere (Meyer, Bottoni, & Marriott, 2006).

Properties of the Linear Embedding

In the following section, we will discuss the most important formal properties of the embedding of CMGs into linear logic as presented in the previous section. We start by proving the most fundamental property: the equivalence of the embedding in linear logic with the original grammar (i.e., the correctness of the embedding). This result is constructive and demonstrates that the equivalence is strong in the sense that the linear proof tree is isomorphic to the parse tree. This is an important result as it demonstrates that we can move from the grammatical formalism to a more powerful logical formalism without having to pay a performance penalty when implementing simple grammatical tasks such as parsing. We conclude by demonstrating that our embedding in combination with a linear sequent calculus gives us an effective decision procedure for the membership problem for a given CMG *G*.

Preliminaries

We will use standard formal language theory terminology when using CMGs. Thus, we call the language of a CMG the set of all sets of attributed symbols that can be derived from the start symbol. Let $a \doteq b$ denote that the symbols *a*, *b* have the same type (i.e., attribute values are disregarded). A CMG is a quadruple $G = (V_T, V_{NT}, S, P)$, where V_T is the set of terminal token types, V_{NT} is the set of non-terminal token types, S is the designated start symbol and P is the set of productions. The language $\mathcal{L}(G)$ of the CMG $G = (V_T, V_{NT}, S, P)$ is the set of sentences $\alpha \in V_T^*$ such that for some $S' \doteq S$, $S' \to_G^* \alpha$ where $\beta \to_G \gamma$ holds if the multiset of symbols β can be rewritten into γ by applying

one of the productions in G and $\to^*$ is the transitive closure of $\to$.

Since CMGs may perform computation with their attributes, parsing even with context-free CMGs may not terminate. A decidable parsing algorithm for attributed multiset grammars was presented in Marriott (1994). This restricts the CMG to be context-sensitive and cycle-free. We usually also require the rules to be safe.

Definition 1: *A CMG* $G = (V_T, V_{NT}, S, P)$ *is called cycle-free iff*
$$\forall a, b \in V_{NT}. \ \forall \alpha \in (V_T \cup V_{NT})^*. \ (a\alpha \to_G^+ b\alpha) \Rightarrow \neg (a \doteq b)$$

Definition 2: *A grammar rule H ::= B where (C){F} is safe iff all attributes in H are either attributes in B or set by an assignment in F, and C is a constraint on the attributes of B only.*

We assume that there is a first-order language L_g consisting of the predicates $g_1, ..., g_n$ (including equality) used in C and the functions $f_1, ..., f_m$ used in *E* and *C* and that there is an associated first-order predicate logic theory *g* that captures the geometric interpretation of these symbols. We will denote the encoding of *g* in linear logic as Γ_g.

A CMG production is positive if the constraint $C(\bar{y})$ is a first-order formula $\phi(\bar{y})$ in L_g. Note that $f(\bar{y})$ may include negated predicates.

Correctness

The transformation of a cycle-free grammar generates a linear program that is in the LinLog fragment of linear logic (cf. Andreoli, 1992, p. 16). In LinLog, the proof would be immediate using the LinLog calculus, which replaces free application of contraction by progression, such that a contraction is only applied if a LinLog rule is applicable. However, in order to encode Γ_g we need full linear logic and it is not obvious how the application of contraction can be restricted

Box 1.

$$\frac{\vdash \hat{\Pi} : \hat{\Gamma}, \Delta_1, \tau(u)\Theta, \tau(u_{n+1})\Theta, \ldots, \tau(u_m)\Theta \Uparrow}{\vdash \hat{\Pi} : \hat{\Gamma}, \Delta_1 \Uparrow \tau(u)\Theta, \tau(u_{n+1})\Theta, \ldots, \tau(u_m)\Theta} \; (R \Uparrow)^*$$

$$\frac{\vdash \hat{\Pi} : \hat{\Gamma}, \Delta_1 \Uparrow F\Theta \qquad \vdash \hat{\Pi} : \hat{\Gamma}, \Delta_1 \Uparrow H\Theta}{\vdash \hat{\Pi} : \hat{\Gamma}, \Delta_1 \Uparrow (F\&H)\Theta} \; (\&) \qquad (\otimes)^*$$

$$\frac{\vdash \hat{\Pi} : \hat{\Gamma}, \Delta_1 \Downarrow (F\&H)\Theta}{\vdash \hat{\Pi} : \hat{\Gamma}, \Delta_1, \Delta_2 \Downarrow (B^\perp \otimes F\&H)\Theta} \; (R \Downarrow) \qquad *_1 \; (\otimes)$$

$$\frac{\vdash \hat{\Pi} : \hat{\Gamma}, \Delta_1, \Delta_2 \Downarrow \tilde{\exists}(B^\perp \otimes F\&H)}{\vdash \hat{\Pi} : \hat{\Gamma}, \Delta_1, \Delta_2 \Uparrow} \; (\exists) \; (D_2)$$

with

$$\frac{\vdash \hat{\Pi} : \tau(u_1)\Theta \Downarrow \tau(u_1)^\perp\Theta}{} \; (I_1) \quad \ldots \quad \frac{\vdash \hat{\Pi} : \tau(u_m)\Theta \Downarrow \tau(u_m)^\perp\Theta}{\vdash \hat{\Pi} : \Delta_2 \Downarrow B^\perp\Theta} \; (I_1) \qquad (\otimes)^*$$
$$*_1$$

in an appropriate way in the full calculus. Fortunately, focusing proofs (Andreoli, 1992) give us a handle on this problem: focusing allows us to (i) restrict the application of contraction adequately and (ii) to cleanly separate the parts of the proof that are concerned with computations in Γ_g from the parts that are concerned with grammatical derivations.

We therefore use the triadic focusing calculus Σ_3 in Andreoli (1992), which handles full linear logic. The relevant rules are shown in Appendix B. We show that the equivalent of the contraction rule in Σ_3, the Decision rule D_2, can be restricted in the same way as progression in the LinLog Σ_3 calculus, if the formula concerned stems from a grammar rule.

We start by showing that an individual production application is mimicked exactly in the linear logic derivation.

Theorem 1: *Let G be a positive, context-sensitive grammar CMG and let p be a production in G.* $(D \to_p D') \Leftrightarrow (\Gamma_g, \Pi \vdash \Gamma_g, \Pi, \tau(D)\!\circ\!\!-\tau(D'))$, *where* $\Pi = \tau(G) \cup \{(\tau(s)\!\circ\!\!-\mathbf{1})\}$

Proof: We give the linear inference steps corresponding to $D \to_p D'$. Let $\tau(D) = \Delta_1, \Delta_2$ and $\tau(D') = \Delta_1, \tau(u)\Theta, \tau(u_{n+i})\Theta, \ldots, \tau(u_m)\Theta$ and $\Delta_2 = \tau(u_1)\Theta, \ldots, \tau(u_m)\Theta$. As Σ_3 is single-sided, we need to analyze the proof of $\vdash \Gamma_g^\perp, \Pi^\perp, \Delta_1, \Delta_2$.

The translated production rules in Π have the form $!\tilde{\forall}(B\!\circ\!\!-F\&H)$, where H is the translation of the LHS of the production rule, B is the translation of the RHS and F is the combination of the constraints and its attribute computations. $\Pi^\perp$ thus consists of rules of the form $?\tilde{\exists}(B\!\circ\!\!-F\&H)^\perp$.

Let $\hat{\Gamma} = \Gamma_g^\perp$ and $\hat{\Pi} = \tilde{\exists}\pi_1^\perp, \ldots, \tilde{\exists}\pi_n^\perp$ for $\Pi^\perp = ?\tilde{\exists}\pi_1^\perp, \ldots, ?\tilde{\exists}\pi_n^\perp$. By Theorem 1 and Theorem 2 of (Andreoli, 1992) the sequent $\vdash \Gamma_g^\perp, \Pi^\perp, \Delta_1, \Delta_2$ can be proven if and only if $\vdash \hat{\Pi} : \hat{\Gamma}, \Delta_1, \Delta_2 \Uparrow$ can be derived in the triadic calculus.[15]

Let the functor sets of $\hat{\Gamma}$ and of $\hat{\Pi}$ be $\mathcal{F}_\Gamma$ and $\mathcal{F}_\Pi$, respectively. Observe that $\mathcal{F}_\Gamma$ does not contain any functors belonging to terminals or non-terminals in G.

We start by showing the "if" direction. For this we construct an inference chain that mimics the production application. It must start by focusing on the production rule $\tau(p) \in \hat{\Pi}$ which has the form $\tilde{\exists}(B\!\circ\!\!-F\&H)^\perp$ or $\tilde{\exists}(B^\perp \otimes F\&H)$.

We analyze how the proof must unfold from this application of (D_2). Let $\Theta = [t_1 / x_1, ..., t_n / x_n]$ be a substitution. The proof sequence is given in Box 1.

We can make the following observations:

1. The proof of the leftmost top sequent focuses on a formula that contains only functors in $\mathcal{F}_\Gamma$ and G is safe, so this branch terminates successfully if the grammar rule is applicable.
2. The rightmost proof branch $(*_1)$ is provable if Δ_2 contains exactly the elements of $B\Theta$.

Therefore, if $D \rightarrow_p D'$, a valid inference chain can be constructed. Previously we have only illustrated the context-free case, but the extension to unrestricted grammars is straightforward.

To show the "only-if" direction, it is sufficient to analyze all possible proof segments that change the part of the linear context, which models the diagram symbols. A change to the linear context modeling the diagram can only occur if the derivation focuses on functors in $\mathcal{F}_\Pi$. As $\tau(D)$ contains only positive atoms, inference rule (D_1) cannot be applied to $\tau(D)$. Therefore, the only rule that allows us to focus on a formula $\mathcal{F}$ containing functors in $\mathcal{F}_\Pi$ is (D_2). In this case $\mathcal{F}$ must be the translation of a production rule p_i.

After focusing on a given production rule, the proof segment must unfold exactly as given in Box 1. At every step, the inference figure applied in the proof is the only applicable inference figure. The only choices in the construction of the proof schema are the tokens Δ_2 to which it is applied if there are multiple possible applications. For the top leftmost branch of the proof segment to be successful, $F\Theta$ must be provable from Γ_g. From this we know that the constraints of the production on which the proof segment focuses are true for the tokens Δ_2 so that the production p is applicable to Δ_2. Thus $D \rightarrow_p D'$. $\qquad\square$

Theorem 2: The linear logic embedding of cycle-free, safe, positive, context-sensitive CMGs is sound and complete: $(D \in \mathcal{L}(G)) \Leftrightarrow (\Gamma_g, \Pi \vdash \tau(D))$.

Proof: An accepting derivation in G has the structure $D \rightarrow_{p1} D_1 \rightarrow_{p2} ... \rightarrow_{pn} \{s\}$ where $\rightarrow_{pj}$ indicates the application of production p_j in step j. The theorem follows immediately from Theorem 1 by induction on j. $\qquad\square$

An important corollary is that no proof search has to be performed to emulate parsing in linear logic. The previous essentially demonstrates that the deduction for rules derived from the grammar can be limited to the progression rule of the Lin-Log Σ_3 calculus, even though we need the context of full linear logic to embed Γ_g.

Theorem 1 has an interesting implication for the encoding of diagram transformations with unrestricted CMGs. The argument of Theorem 1 can be used without requiring termination. From this we see that if the transformation of a diagram is viewed as a (not necessarily terminating) process, any transformation encoded with an unrestricted production can be captured directly in a linear implication. However, in such a procedural view we must be careful about the order in which the proof branches are processed. If the branch focused on $H\Theta$ is continued before the branch focused on $F\Theta$ is completed, the production has effectively been applied though its applicability check may be delayed indefinitely. This cannot occur if we restrict the deduction mechanism so that the proof branch focused on $F\Theta$ is always completed before the "main" branch is continued.

Decidability

We can now show that the encoding of G into linear logic gives us an effective decision procedure for the membership problem for CMGs.

Theorem 3: For a cycle-free, safe, positive, context-sensitive grammar G, linear deduction is an effective decision procedure for the membership problem $D \in \mathcal{L}(G)$ if the arithmetic constraints in G are decidable under the arithmetic theory Γ_g and the attribute computations in G terminate.

Proof: We show that the total number of possible proof constructions is finite and that every unsuccessful proof construction for $\Gamma_g, \Pi \vdash \tau(D)$ finitely fails.

The core observation is that every derivation corresponding to a grammar rewriting consists of a main inference chain corresponding to production applications which only spawns off side chains for attribute computations. The main chain must terminate because the size of the linear context monotonically decreases along it. The side chains must terminate because G is safe.

We inspect the inference chain constructed in the proof of Theorem 1 and observe the following:

1. Every time a principal formula F is selected for focusing, F must either contain only functors from $\mathcal{F}_\Gamma$ or F must be the translation of a production rule or grammar symbol. If F is an attribute computation in Γ_g the sub-proof of F must terminate as G is safe. This applies to the leftmost top sequent.

2. If the CMG production p_i is context-sensitive the application of $\tau(p_i)$ does not increase the size of the linear context: The sequent at the top of the middle proof branch is either shorter than the sequent at the bottom of the proof segment or it has the same length. If it has the same length only finitely many such proof segments can be concatenated as G is cycle-free.

3. The rightmost proof branch $(*_1)$ can only be successful if Δ_2 contains exactly the elements of $B\Theta$. As we can choose the order in which the proof branches are executed,

we are free to choose this branch first. This gives us an immediate "guard" condition on the application of a production rule: p_i can be used (copied) in the proof only if the current sequent contains the elements of $B\Theta$ for some Θ. This also gives us a terminating procedure to constructively decide whether such a Θ exists (limited to the variables in B). This is by inspection of Δ_1, Δ_2.

4. As G is safe, Θ can only substitute variables in B and those that are bound by computations in F. From this, argument (3), and the fact that the assignment computations in F terminate, it follows that Θ can be completely determined by a terminating procedure.

5. The only choices in the construction of this proof schema are the production rule p_i to be applied and the tokens Δ_2 to which it is applied. For a finite grammar G and a finite diagram D there are only a finite number of choices for each, so the total number of possible proof constructions is finite.

We conclude from (1-4) that all branches in the proof attempt terminate and from (5) that all possible proof sequences can be finitely enumerated. Thus, the search for a proof of $D \in \mathcal{L}(G)$ must either succeed or finitely fail. □

SOFTWARE SUPPORT

In the previous sections, we have presented a formal computational framework for diagram interpretation and reasoning with diagrams. However, the skeptical reader may be wondering how this framework can be applied in software systems that implement advanced diagrammatic interfaces. We are particularly interested in a class of systems that has been termed "smart diagram environments" (SDEs) (Meyer, Marriott, & Allwein, 2002).

SDEs behave as if they "understand" the diagram, for example by providing direct manipulation facilities that take into account the diagram's structure and its intended semantics. SDEs are useful in a wide variety of applications such as high-level query languages for spatial information systems, CAD systems, diagrammatic theorem provers, and online education. They are particularly useful in domains where well-established diagrammatic notations are in use such as UML in software engineering or circuit diagrams in electronic engineering.

Unfortunately, SDEs are not easy to build. The central tasks that every SDE has to provide are modelling of the diagram components, interpretation of diagrams, structure preserving manipulation, visual transformation, and layout. Support for structured interaction with the various other software components is also required. A common approach is to build generic SDE systems, which provide these capabilities but which are then customized for a particular diagrammatic language based on a formal high-level specification of that language. We have developed a component-based

toolkit to support SDE development. This toolkit, CIDER, supports all aspects of drawing, interpreting, and manipulating structured diagrams and provides component-based software support for the implementation of applications that integrate smart diagrammatic communication (Jansen, Marriott, & Meyer, 2003). Cider[16] is based on constraint-multiset grammars and thus its semantics is given by the framework described in this chapter.

CIDER supports all aspects of drawing, interpreting, and manipulating a diagram based on high-level CMG specification. It consists of generic diagramming support components that can easily be embedded in Java applications. The components that make up the CIDER toolkit are shown in Figure 7, which also indicates how these components are used in creating an application. The double-headed arrows indicate interaction between components. The white boxes indicate components of CIDER. The application developer provides the diagram specification in an XML file

Figure 7. The components of the CIDER toolkit

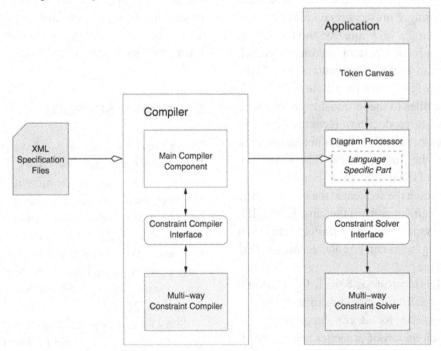

that is compiled into executable code for a diagram processor tailored to the particular diagram notation. The constraint solver and constraint compiler can optionally be tailored to extend the capabilities of the toolkit itself.

In a CIDER-based system, the editing takes place on a token canvas, which is part of the application GUI and is coupled to the diagram processor. The token canvas allows the modeling and rendering of diagrams based on primitive graphical objects, such as circles, lines, and text with additional semantic attributes.

The diagram processor runs transparently in the background and provides incremental parsing and interpretation of the diagram as it is edited on the token canvas according to a CMG specification of the diagram notation used. After each update in the diagram, the diagram processor incrementally modifies the parse forest so that is consistent with the diagram at all times. The CMG specification is translated into an executable component by the CIDER Compiler, which also performs compile time checking of the grammar structure. CIDER can work with unrestricted (type 0) CMGs, but for interpretation cycle-free context-sensitive rules are sufficient in almost all cases.

After compiling the grammar and the transformation specification with CIDER, the only extension to an application that is required to support smart diagrams is to add a token canvas to the user interface. An application can use the diagram interpretation in two ways: Either it reads the semantic representation of the diagram constructed by the diagram processor or it uses an event-based model in which it registers itself as a listener for canvas or processor events that are triggered by some change in the diagram, such as recognition or deletion of non-terminals of a specified type.

CIDER also supports diagram transformations like those discussed for "executable graphics." Syntactically we deviate from the idea of simply using unrestricted CMG productions. Instead,

CIDER uses transformation rules that are based on explicit modification actions. We will see, however, that both approaches to transformation rules ultimately amount to the same when used in the context of incremental parsing.

Transformations are carried out by the diagram processor upon a request by the user or the application program. The basic form of a transformation is:

$$name: S_1, ..., S_n \text{ where } C \Rightarrow apply (A_1, ..., A_m)$$

Transformations are named and complex transactions can be defined in terms of regular expressions on the alphabet of transformation names. When a transformation is triggered it starts by testing if for a given multiset of input symbols $\{S_1, ..., S_n\}$ the attributes of these satisfy the condition C. Transformation conditions can use existentially quantified symbols and negative context. If C is true, the LHS symbols are removed from the parse forest. Additionally, the transitive closure of all symbols that were generated by a production application involving any of these LHS symbols is removed. The next step is to apply the actions $A_1, ..., A_m$. There are three types of actions: adding a new terminal symbol to the parse forest (and providing initial values for all of its attributes), changing the attributes of a symbol, and applying a particular production to a specified set of symbols. For example, consider again the case of a transformation that involves the creation of a NormalState symbol. The action list would look like the following:

```
NTS  ->> nc:Circle(20, <<45,30>>)
NTS  ->> nt:Text("S4", <<45,30>>)
Ap   ->> NormalStateProducion using
(nc  ->> cl, nt ->>t)
```

The first line creates a new terminal symbol (NTS) which is a Circle called *nc* with its initial radius and mid-point defined between the parentheses. The second line creates a new Text symbol called *nt*, with its initial label and mid-point also specified. The last line (AP) applies the Normal-State production:

```
n:NormalState ::= c1:Circle,
t:Text
    where ( c1.mid == t.mid &&
      not exists c2:Circle where
            (c2.mid == c1.mid)
) {n.mid := c1.mid; n.radius :=
c1.radius; n.label := t.label; }
```

The AP action also specifies that the production should only be attempted with the newly created circle symbol *nc* mapped to the RHS symbol *c1* in the production, while the newly created text symbol *nt* is mapped to the RHS symbol *t*. The actions on the right-hand side thus create a parse tree that is to be inserted into the parse forest. Note that it is possible to create multi-level parse trees.

We can now see that the action-based specification of a transformation rule is in effect only a shortcut that allows us rewriting not only on the level of terminal tokens, but also on the level of non-terminal tokens. A transformation that only inserts terminal symbols is obviously directly equivalent to a type 0 CMG production. As the actions only allow us to construct non-terminal symbols on the RHS that conform to the CMG specification and as the incremental parser automatically keeps the parse tree consistent, the effect of a rule inserting non-terminals on the RHS is equivalent to that of a rule inserting only terminals followed by a sequence of recognizing CMG production applications. In either case, the incremental parser works fully interleaved with the transformation rules (i.e., after each transformation the parse forest will be updated so that it is completely consistent with the modified state of the diagram).

As a proof of concept, we have used CIDER to build several diagramming tools, among them

an FSA editor that provides interpretation and execution of hand-sketched automaton diagrams, as well as graphical transformation of regular expressions into FSAs. Incremental interpretation and structure-preserving manipulation was added to the basic GUI implementation with only 10% additional code. This required 11 production rules, with another 13 transformation rules needed to implement the FSA animation and generation from regular expressions (Jansen et al., 2003).

PAST, PRESENT, AND FUTURE: SUGGESTIONS FOR RESEARCH

The linear logic framework that we have presented has the potential to provide the basis for a unified treatment of diagram syntax and semantics. We have proven that it strictly subsumes the grammatical framework for diagram languages and supersedes its expressive power. The linear logic specifications are directly executable, as they map to linear logic programs, but where the specifications are used for parsing only they can be executed with the same efficiency as a grammar. In contrast to grammars, the linear specifications have a proper logical semantic and are cleanly embedded into the general framework of linear reasoning, thus giving us the reasoning capabilities not only of classical first order logic, but also for reasoning about events and actions. This can provide an elegant basis for formalizing diagrammatic calculi that are based on syntactic diagram manipulation. Thus, the linear logic approach successfully merges several previous streams of research in the specification of diagrammatic languages.

Of course, the work discussed here merely represents the first small step into this direction. What, then, are directions for future research? This question should not be answered narrowly from the perspective of the logic-based approach, but from a more general perspective, and it is worthwhile to reflect on the history of the field.

In the past, formal approaches to visual language specification were almost exclusively based on grammatical frameworks, and most of the relevant research was conducted in the "visual language" community. The fact that these methods inherited the limitation to parsing from the grammatical approach was of no (or minor) concern, as parsing and syntax-directed interpretation were the main requirements in the context of visual languages. Grammatical specification of visual languages had its heyday in the early and mid 1990s and made substantial progress during this phase. It can by now be considered as a mature technique.

From an application perspective, this means that it is time to demonstrate the usefulness of this approach. Primarily this requires a move from small and artificial academic examples to real and practically relevant applications. Furthermore, if we believe that diagram parsing is truly useful in a wide range of applications we have the obligation to make these methods available as standard technologies. This would be best achieved by deploying them as part of widely-used standard software platforms for GUI building, such as Java/Swing, Tk, etc. These goals present some serious software engineering challenges.

From a theoretical perspective, on the other hand, the research on grammatical specification of visual languages is basically stagnant, and a different, non-grammatical mindset is required for further fundamental progress with research on visual notations. Future research should focus on goals that are beyond the reach of grammars and should orient itself toward more complex reasoning tasks. Such research has previously been pursued in the "diagrammatic reasoning" community and, for a long time, had little overlap with "visual language" research. These two communities only merged in the mid-1990s[17] by which time the mainstream in both communities had locked into different types of formal approaches: grammars for visual language parsing and implementations, logics for diagrammatic reasoning. We hope that

an integration of a grammatical framework into a general logic framework such as we have presented, may have the ability to bridge between these areas and to foster collaboration.

Such a collaboration will bring together expertise on reasoning and "intelligent" systems with expertise on the implementation of advanced visual interfaces, so that it can make the dream of smart diagrammatic environments (Meyer et al., 2002) come true and can deliver realistic visual applications that incorporate non-trivial reasoning capabilities.

We believe that it is crucial for the joint fields to agree on "touchstone" tasks that allow us to gauge progress over, say, the next decade and that can give shared focus to this endeavor.

The implementation of interactive diagrammatic theorem provers would be a first worthwhile goal: Shin (1995) has convincingly and beyond doubt demonstrated that purely diagrammatic calculi based on syntactic manipulation can be valid tools of formal reasoning. What is missing are real diagrammatic theorem provers based on these ideas. In the ideal case, such a prover would be implemented within a general theorem prover framework, such as Isabelle (Paulson, 1994), and a formalization of Shin's rules in the linear framework could provide the basis for this.

Creating an interactive theorem prover for a diagrammatic calculus would also force us to turn our attention to issues that are all too easily ignored in a theoretical treatment of diagram manipulation. This is in particular the automatic dynamic layout of complex diagram notations, which is absolutely fundamental for any real application. The issue is that the rules for the syntactic manipulation of a diagram only handle the abstract syntax of the diagram, but not its concrete geometry. A rule for a Petri net transition may, for example, tell us that a token has to be moved out of one circle and into another circle, but it does not tell us the exact locations.[18] Likewise, a rule in Shin's calculus may tell us that a contour has to be inserted such that it overlaps all other contours, but it will not tell us how to draw this contour. We thus need to create a concrete layout from the abstract syntax and we need to do so in a way that the manipulation of the abstract syntax changes the concrete layout as little as possible, in order to avoid confusion on the part of the viewer. This problem of dynamic, stable layout is by no means trivial, as even static layout for complex diagrams is basically an open problem. Unfortunately, any SDE that interacts with a user has to address this issue in some form. As far removed as dynamic layout seems to be from a formal treatment of diagrammatic logic calculi, only a combined research effort in these areas can ultimately produce interactive diagrammatic theorem provers. We believe that such a theorem prover is a realistic goal for the next decade of diagrammatic reasoning research.

Let us be optimistic and speculate on a bolder goal for the next decade of diagrammatic reasoning. This could be found in the departure from strictly formal diagrammatic reasoning to flexible "common sense" reasoning about diagrammatic representations--in a move away from artificial diagrammatic notations and toward notations that are practically relevant and commonly used. For initial research, it will of course be important to choose notations that, while not being fully formal, are reasonably close to having a formal semantics. We suggest that diagrams of data structure manipulations, such as the ones that are commonly used in introductory computer science texts for teaching the manipulation of linked lists, would be a good example. We thus propose as a more ambitious touchstone task a system that can interpret such diagrams and automatically generate appropriate programs for the manipulation of these data structure from their pictorial descriptions.[19]

An important real-world application of diagrammatic reasoning is software engineering with visual notations, such as UML. This is particularly interesting in the context of the current move to model-driven architecture, in which systems are initially designed on the level of abstract platform independent models that are subsequently transformed to include platform specific implementation details. These transformations require a significant level of reasoning about the specification and constitute an excellent test case for advanced diagrammatic reasoning. If we succeed in developing a general framework that allows us to perform formal software engineering directly on the diagrammatic level, we will not only have a firm proof of the feasibility of diagrammatic reasoning, but also of its relevance.

Ultimately, diagrammatic notations hold a special interest, because the nature of their representation seems to enable different and potentially more powerful modes of reasoning. The reduction of diagrammatic notations to logic (in the widest sense) is necessary as a basis for handling them computationally, but by itself, it is unlikely to teach us much about this aspect. To learn about this, we need to model human reasoning with diagrams. We need to understand how computers can reason with diagrams, but we need to investigate this in conjunction with how people use diagrams for reasoning. The pursuit of the tasks previously suggested can help us to focus on these goals.

ACKNOWLEDGMENT

BM would like to thank Kim Marriott for many years of collaboration and countless inspiring discussions, which have contributed to ideas presented in this chapter. The opinions expressed here are, however, the authors' individual point of view.

REFERENCES

Andreoli, J. M. (1992). Logic programming with focusing proofs in linear logic. *Journal of Logic and Computation, 2*(3), 297-347.

Andreoli, J. M., & Pareschi, R. (1991). Linear objects: Logical processes with built-in inheritance. *New Generation Computing, 9,* 445-473.

Bardohl, R., Minas, M., Schürr, A., & Taentzer, G. (1999). Application of graph transformation to visual languages. In H. Ehrig, G. Engels, H. J. Kreowski, & G. Rozenberg (Eds.), *Handbook of graph grammars and computing by graph transformation* (Vol. 2, pp. 105-18). Singapore: World Scientific.

Betz, H., & Frühwirth, T. (2005). A linear-logic semantics for constraint handling rules. *International Conference on Principles and Practice of Constraint Programming* (pp. 137-151). Barcelona, Spain.

Christiansen, H. (2005). CHR grammars. *Theory and Practice of Logic Programming, 5,* 467-501.

Crimi, C., Guercio, A., Nota, G., Pacini, G., Tortora, G., & Tucci, M. (1990). Relation grammars for modelling multi-dimensional structures. *IEEE Symposium on Visual Languages* (pp. 168-173). IEEE Computer Society Press.

Ehrig, H., Heckel, R., Korff, M., Löwe, M., Ribeiro, L., Wagner, A., & Corradini, A. (1997). Algebraic approaches to graph transformation II: Single pushout approach and comparison with double pushout approach. In G. Rozenberg (Ed.), *Handbook of graph grammars and computing by graph transformation* (Vol. 1: Foundations, Chapter 4, pp. 247-312). Singapore: World Scientific.

Erwig, M., & Meyer, B. (1995). Heterogeneous visual languages--integrating textual and visual programming. *International IEEE Workshop on Visual Languages (VL'95)* (pp. 318-325). Darmstadt, Germany.

Frühwirth, T. (1998). Theory and practice of constraint handling rules. *Journal of Logic Programming, 37,* 95-138.

Girard, J. Y. (1995). Linear logic, its syntax, and semantics. In Girard & R. Lafont (Ed.), *Advances in linear logic, London Mathematical Society Lecture Notes Series 222.* Cambridge University Press.

Girard, J. Y. (1987). Linear logic. *Theoretical Computer Science, 50,* 1-102.

Göttler, H. (1986a). Graph grammars, a new paradigm for implementing visual languages. EUROGRAPHICS, 89, 505-516. Elsevier Science publishers (North-Holland).

Göttler, H. (1986b). Graph grammars and diagram editing. *Graph-Grammars and Their Application to Computer Science,* LNCS 291 (pp. 211-231). New York: Springer-Verlag.

Haarslev, V. (1998). A fully formalized theory for describing visual notations. In K. Marriott, & B. Meyer (Eds.), *Visual language theory* (pp. 261-292). New York: Springer.

Haarslev, V. (1994). Personal communication.

Hammer, E. (1996). Representing relations diagrammatically. In G. Allwein & J. Barwise (Eds.), *Logical reasoning with diagrams.* New York: Oxford University Press.

Harland, J., & Pym, D. (1994). A uniform proof-theoretic investigation of linear logic programming. *Journal of Logic and Computation, 4*(2), 175-207.

Harland, J., Pym, D., & Winikoff, M. (1996). Programming in Lygon: An overview. *Algebraic methodology and software technology, LNCS 1101* (pp. 391-405). Springer.

Helm, R., & Marriott, K. (1991). A declarative specification and semantics for visual languages. *Journal of Visual Languages and Computing, 2,* 311-331.

Helm, R., Marriott, K., & Odersky, M. (1991). Building visual language parsers. *ACM Conference Human Factors in Computing* (pp. 118-125).

Howse, J., Molina, F., Taylor, J., Kent, S., & Gil, J. (2001). Spider diagrams: A diagrammatic reasoning system. *Journal of Visual Languages and Computing*, *12*(3), 299-324.

Janneck, J., & Esser, R. (2001). A predicate-based approach to defining visual language syntax. *IEEE Symposium on Visual Languages and Formal Methods* (pp. 40-47). IEEE Computer Society.

Jansen, A., Marriott, K., & Meyer, B. (2003). CIDER: A component-based toolkit for creating smart diagram environments. The *9th International Conference on Distributed Multimedia Systems (DMS 2003)*, Miami, Florida.

Lakin, F. (1986). Spatial parsing for visual languages. In S. K. Chang, T. Ichikawa, & P. A. Ligomenides (Eds.), *Visual languages* (pp. 35-85). New York: Plenum Press.

Marriott, K. (1994). Constraint multiset grammars. *IEEE Symposium on Visual Languages* (pp. 118-125). IEEE Computer Society Press.

Marriott, K., & Meyer, B. (1997). On the classification of visual languages by grammar hierarchies. *Journal of Visual Languages and Computing*, *8*(4), 374-402.

Marriott, K., & Meyer, B. (1998). The CCMG visual language hierarchy. In K. Marriott & B. Meyer (Eds.), *Visual language theory* (pp. 129-169). New York: Springer.

Marriott, K., Meyer, B., & Wittenburg, K. (1998). A survey of visual language specification and recognition. In K. Marriott & B. Meyer (Eds.), *Visual language theory* (pp. 5-85). New York: Springer.

Meyer, B. (2000). A constraint-based framework for diagrammatic reasoning. *Applied Artificial Intelligence. Special Issue on Constraint Handling Rules, 4*(14), 327-344.

Meyer, B. (1999). Constraint diagram reasoning. *CP'99: Principles and Practice of Constraint Programming*, LNCS 1713. Alexandria, VA: Springer.

Meyer, B. (1997). Formalization of visual mathematical notations. In M. Anderson (Ed.), *AAAI Symposium on Diagrammatic Reasoning (DR-II)* (pp. 58-68). Boston: AAAI Press.

Meyer, B. (1992). Pictures depicting pictures: On the specification of visual languages by visual grammars. *IEEE Symposium on Visual Languages (VL'92)* (pp. 41-47). Seattle, WA.

Meyer, B., Bottoni, P., & Marriott, K. (2006). Formalizing interpretation of and reasoning with diagrams using linear logic. *Language and Computation*. submitted.

Meyer, B., Marriott, K., & Allwein, G. (2002). Intelligent diagrammatic interfaces: State of the art. In P. Olivier, M. Anderson, & B. Meyer (Eds.), *Diagrammatic representation and reasoning*. London: Springer.

Miller, D. (1995). A survey of linear logic programming. *Computational Logic, 2*(2), 63-67.

Nelsen, R. (1993). *Proofs without words*. The Mathematical Association of America, Washington, DC.

Paulson, L. (1994). *Isabelle*. London: Springer Verlag.

Pereira, F., & Warren, D. H. (1980). Definite clause grammars for language analysis: A survey of the formalism and a comparison with augmented transition networks. *Artificial Intelligence, 13*, 231-278.

Shin, S. J. (1996). A situation theoretic account of valid reasoning with Venn diagrams. In G. Allwein & J. Barwise (Eds.), *Logical reasoning with diagrams* (pp. 81-108). New York: Oxford University Press.

Shin, S. J. (1995). *The logical status of diagrams*. Cambridge: Cambridge University Press.

Swoboda, N. (2002). Implementing Euler/Venn reasoning systems. In P. Olivier, M. Anderson, & B. Meyer (Eds.), *Diagrammatic representation and reasoning*. London: Springer.

Tanaka, T. (1991). Definite clause set grammars: A formalism for problem solving. *Journal of Logic Programming, 10*, 1-17.

Tucci, M., Vitiello, G., & Costagliola, G. (1994). Parsing nonlinear languages. *IEEE Transactions on Software Engineering, 20*, 720-739.

Tucci, M., Vitiello, G., Pacini, G., & Tortora, G. (1992). Graphs and visual languages for visual interface. *Avanced Visual Interfaces (AVI 92)* (pp. 304-318). Singapore: World Scientific.

Winikoff, M. (1996). Hitch Hiker's Guide to Lygon 0.7. Technical Report TR 96/36, University of Melbourne, Dept. of Computer Science.

ENDNOTES

[1] Exceptions are some approaches that are not aimed at parsing, but just at specifying the (syntactical) correctness of a diagram, as for example in Janneck et al. (2001). The important difference is that parsing allows us to decide the syntactical correctness, but additionally provides a parse tree, which can be used to guide a syntax-directed interpretation of the diagram. As we are mainly interested in interpretation of and reasoning with diagrams, we focus on specification methods that allow us to parse a diagram.

[2] General familiarity with grammatical specification formalism is assumed throughout the remainder of this chapter.

[3] Note that these tokens need to have some attributes, for example, the text tokens need to have the exact text that they carry as an attribute. However, in the relation-based approach they do not carry geometric attributes. The geometry is in principle only used during the tokenization phase to extract the relation set.

[4] However, this only applies to pure graph grammars such as edNLC grammars or the ones in (Göttler, 1986a, 1986b). Due to the inflexibility of the pure approach, most modern graph-grammar-based methods for diagram specification use attributed programmed graph grammars and thus fall into the attribute-based category.

[5] Unfortunately, many properties of practically relevant diagram languages are context-sensitive (Marriott et al., 1997, 1998).

[6] or tokens with only non-spatial attributes

[7] Note that you can also deduce $(a + b)^2 = a^2 + 2ab + b^2$ simply by looking at the left diagram only.

[8] To the best of our knowledge, there is only one more technical formalization of Shin's calculus on the level of the actual graphical tokens in the diagram. This formalization uses graph transformations (Swoboda, 2002).

[9] In fact, in a later section we discuss a software system that supports executable graphics specified in this way.

[10] It must be noted, however, that parsing and transformation cannot easily be mixed in the same specification without destroying the declarative meaning of the grammar. Parsing (or interpretation) and transformation are separate tasks and must be specified separately.

[11] Note that A is not the same as $A \otimes A$.

[12] In an earlier work (Meyer, 1999, 2000) we introduced a mapping of constraint relational grammars to constraint handling rules (Frühwirth, 1998). This work was based on the (early) semantics of CHR in terms of classical first-order logic given in (Frühwirth, 1998). Recently a linear logic semantics for CHR has been presented in Betz and Frühwirth (2005), and it may be possible to

re-interpret the approach of (Meyer, 1999, 2000) in the context of this linear semantics. The close connection between CHR, grammatical frameworks and linear logic has also been noted in Christiansen (2005).

[13] The extension to LO is that we allow limited use of the linear goal **1**, which succeeds if and only if the linear proof context is empty.

[14] Note that this is not possible in classical logic where the monotonicity prevents us from ensuring that we have tested $\neg \varphi (\cdot)$ for all symbols.

[15] Note that this requires all formulas to be asynchronous, which can easily be achieved by adding a logically redundant asynchronous top-level connective.

[16] CIDER is freely available from the first author under GNU public licence.

[17] This change is marked by the arrival of the inter-disciplinary "Diagrams" conference series.

[18] Note that previously we have given an NFA transition rule that handles the concrete geometry. However, this was only possible because the rule described a very simple case. In the more general case, the geometry transformation can often not be computed locally in the transformation rule because it depends on the context. For example, the target position of a Petri net token will depend on how many other tokens are already in the same place.

[19] BM would like to acknowledge that this idea was conceived in common work with Martin Erwig and lead to the joint work on heterogeneous visual programming languages (Erwig & Meyer, 1995), which addressed the same type of diagrams but did intentionally not attempt intelligent interpretation of these notations.

APPENDIX A: LINEAR SEQUENT CALCULUS

This appendix shows the relevant rules of the sequent calculus as presented in Harland and Pym (1994).

$$\frac{}{\phi \vdash \phi} \; (ax) \qquad\qquad \frac{\Gamma \vdash \phi, \Delta \quad \Gamma', \phi \vdash \Delta'}{\Gamma, \Gamma' \vdash \Delta, \Delta'} \; (cut)$$

$$\frac{\Gamma, \phi, \psi, \Gamma' \vdash \Delta}{\Gamma, \psi, \phi, \Gamma' \vdash \Delta} \; (X-L) \qquad\qquad \frac{\Gamma \vdash \Delta, \phi, \psi, \Delta'}{\Gamma \vdash \Delta, \psi, \phi, \Delta'} \; (X-R)$$

$$\frac{\Gamma, \phi \vdash \Delta}{\Gamma, \psi \& \phi \vdash \Delta} \qquad \frac{\Gamma, \psi \vdash \Delta}{\Gamma, \psi \& \phi \vdash \Delta} \; (\&-L) \qquad \frac{\Gamma \vdash \phi, \Delta \quad \Gamma \vdash \psi, \Delta}{\Gamma \vdash \phi \& \psi, \Delta} \; (\&-R)$$

$$\frac{\Gamma, \phi \vdash \Delta \quad \Gamma', \psi \vdash \Delta'}{\Gamma, \Gamma', \psi \invamp \phi \vdash \Delta, \Delta'} \; (\invamp - L) \qquad \frac{\Gamma \vdash \phi, \psi, \Delta}{\Gamma \vdash \phi \invamp \psi, \Delta} \; (\invamp - R)$$

$$\frac{\Gamma \vdash \phi, \Delta \quad \Gamma', \psi \vdash \Delta'}{\Gamma, \Gamma', \phi \multimap \psi \vdash \Delta, \Delta'} \; (\multimap - L) \qquad \frac{\Gamma, \phi[t/x] \vdash \Delta}{\Gamma, \forall x. \phi \vdash \Delta} \; (\forall - L)$$

$$\frac{\Gamma \vdash \Delta}{\Gamma, !\phi \vdash \Delta} \; (W! - L) \qquad\qquad \frac{\Gamma, !\phi, !\phi \vdash \Delta}{\Gamma, !\phi \vdash \Delta} \; (C! - L)$$

$$\frac{\Gamma, \phi \vdash \Delta}{\Gamma, !\phi \vdash \Delta} \; (! - L) \qquad\qquad \frac{}{\vdash 1} \; (1 - R)$$

$$\frac{\Gamma, \phi \vdash \Delta \quad \Gamma, \psi \vdash \Delta}{\Gamma, \phi \oplus \psi \vdash \Delta} \; (\oplus - L) \qquad \frac{\Gamma \vdash \phi, \Delta}{\Gamma \vdash \phi \oplus \psi, \Delta} \qquad \frac{\Gamma \vdash \psi, \Delta}{\Gamma \vdash \phi \oplus \psi, \Delta} \; (\oplus - R)$$

APPENDIX B: THE TRIADIC SEQUENT SYSTEM Σ_3

This appendix shows the relevant rules of the sequent calculus as presented in Andreoli (1992).

- Logical Inference Rules

$$\frac{\vdash \Theta : \Gamma \Uparrow L}{\vdash \Theta : \Gamma \Uparrow L, \bot} \ (\bot) \qquad \frac{\vdash \Theta : \Gamma \Uparrow L, F, G}{\vdash \Theta : \Gamma \Uparrow L, F \mathbin{\rotatebox[origin=c]{180}{\&}} G} \ (\mathbin{\rotatebox[origin=c]{180}{\&}}) \qquad \frac{\vdash \Theta, F : \Gamma \Uparrow L}{\vdash \Theta : \Gamma \Uparrow L, ?F} \ (?)$$

$$\frac{}{\vdash \Theta : \Gamma \Uparrow L, \top} \ (\top) \qquad \frac{\vdash \Theta : \Gamma \Uparrow L, F \quad \vdash \Theta : \Gamma \Uparrow L, G}{\vdash \Theta : \Gamma \Uparrow L, F \& G} \ (\&) \qquad \frac{\vdash \Theta : \Gamma \Uparrow L, F[c/x]}{\vdash \Theta : \Gamma \Uparrow L, \forall x \ F} \ (\forall)$$

$$\frac{}{\vdash \Theta : \Downarrow 1} \ (1) \qquad \frac{\vdash \Theta : \Gamma \Downarrow F \quad \vdash \Theta : \Delta \Downarrow G}{\vdash \Theta : \Gamma, \Delta \Downarrow F \otimes G} \ (\otimes) \qquad \frac{\vdash \Theta : \Uparrow F}{\vdash \Theta : \Downarrow !F} \ (!)$$

$$\frac{\vdash \Theta : \Gamma \Downarrow F}{\vdash \Theta : \Gamma \Downarrow F \oplus G} \ (\oplus_l) \qquad \frac{\vdash \Theta : \Gamma \Downarrow G}{\vdash \Theta : \Gamma \Downarrow F \oplus G} \ (\oplus_r) \qquad \frac{\vdash \Theta : \Gamma \Downarrow F[t/x]}{\vdash \Theta : \Gamma \Downarrow \exists x \ F} \ (\exists)$$

- Reaction $\Uparrow$: if F is not asynchronous

$$\frac{\vdash \Theta : \Gamma, F \Uparrow L}{\vdash \Theta : \Gamma \Uparrow L, F} \ (R \Uparrow)$$

- Reaction $\Downarrow$: if F is neither synchronous nor a negative atom

$$\frac{\vdash \Theta : \Gamma \Uparrow F}{\vdash \Theta : \Gamma \Downarrow F} \ (R \Downarrow)$$

- Identities

$$\frac{}{\vdash \Theta : X \Downarrow X^{\perp}} \ (I_1) \qquad \frac{}{\vdash \Theta, X : \Downarrow X^{\perp}} \ (I_2)$$

- Decision: if F is not a positive atom

$$\frac{\vdash \Theta : \Gamma \Downarrow F}{\vdash \Theta : \Gamma, F \Uparrow} \ (D_1) \qquad \frac{\vdash \Theta, F : \Gamma \Downarrow F}{\vdash \Theta, F : \Gamma \Uparrow} \ (D_2)$$

Chapter III
A Transformation–Based Metamodel Approach to the Definition of Syntax and Semantics of Diagrammatic Languages

Paolo Bottoni
University of Rome "La Sapienza", Italy

Dino Frediani
University of Rome "La Sapienza", Italy

Paolo Quattrocchi
University of Rome "La Sapienza", Italy

Luigi Rende
University of Rome "La Sapienza", Italy

Goran Sarajlic
Araneum Srl, Italy

Domenico Ventriglia
Elemedia Spa, Italy

ABSTRACT

The definition of visual languages, of their semantics, and of the interactions with them can all be referred to a notion of transformation of multisets of resources. Moreover, the concrete syntax for a particular language can be obtained in a semi-automatic way, by declaring the conformity of the language to some family of languages, specified by a metamodel. In a similar way, the generation of the associated semantics can take advantage of the identification of the variety of the semantics being expressed. According to the associated metamodel, one can obtain an abstract view of the semantic roles that visual elements can play with respect to the process being described. We propose here an integrated framework and interactive environment based on a collection of metamodels, in which to express both syntactical characterizations of diagrammatic sentences and their semantic interpretations.

INTRODUCTION

Metamodeling frameworks for the definition and management of diagrammatic languages allow the implementation of visual environments based on some abstract notion of visual entities and of relations among them. Such diagrammatic languages, and the associated environments, are typically exploited to model structural or behavioral aspects of systems ranging from formal devices such as finite state automata to biological entities through mechanical plants or communication networks.

The spatial relations between the entities depicted in a diagram express constraints on the possible evolutions of the system being modeled (e.g., state transitions, communication protocols, or activation of computations). In this view, the dynamics expressible with such diagrammatic languages are typically discrete ones. Conversely, a diagram can undergo different types of transformations. Examples are diagram evolution due to user editing activities, animation to reflect the progress of some symbolic execution of the computation specified by the diagram, or representation of the transformations in a real system to which the diagram is causally connected. Moreover, animation can be used to integrate the transition from a diagram configuration to another, offering a smooth visualization of the underlying discrete transformation.

When integrated in a graphical user interface, such diagrammatic sentences can also be used as support for user interactions, typically aimed at composing or editing correct visual sentences, querying the state of the system or process components depicted by diagrammatic elements, or activating local or global processes on these components or on the diagram as such. In this chapter, we consider that the admissible transformations of the diagram, independently of their origin, can be specified through some formal device. In particular, we consider the integration of the syntactic definition of a language with the specification of its associated (operational) semantics and of the admissible interactions with it. We discuss two types of semantics: one in which the diagram models a discrete system and describes its possible evolutions, and one in which the diagram defines the structure of a communication network, over which messages can be delivered according to some well defined protocol.

We argue that for a significant class of diagrammatic languages all these aspects (i.e., the definition of the language itself, of its semantics, and of the interactions with them) can be expressed by resorting to a notion of transformation of multisets of resources. In particular, the characterization of the correct sentences in a diagrammatic language is given in terms of a rewriting system based on an alphabet of visual resources. These multisets are then transformed under the effect of rewriting rules modeling the dynamics of the depicted system, while user interaction is modeled within the same framework by considering user actions as special types of resources, either providing data for parameterized transformations, or triggering specific transformations of the underlying visual resources.

Moreover, the definition of a rewriting system—defining the concrete syntax for a particular language—is obtained in a semi-automatic way, by declaring the conformity of the language under definition to some family of languages, specified by a metamodel. In a similar way, the generation of the associated semantics can take advantage of the identification of the variety of the semantics being expressed. According to the metamodel definition of such a variety, one can obtain an abstract view of the semantic roles that visual elements can play with respect to the process being described.

We propose here an integrated framework and interactive environment, based on a collection of metamodels, in which to express both syntactical characterizations of diagrammatic sentences and their semantic interpretations. This is based on a general model of visual transformation relying on an abstract notion of transition, seen as production/consumption of resources.

In particular, we show the use of metamodels to describe syntactic families of languages--by progressively refining the abstract expression of the significant relations in the diagrams--as well as to characterize the most usual semantic varieties in their interpretations. We show mechanisms to constrain the construction of a visual rewriting system defining a visual language so that only admissible relations, with respect to the family to which the language under definition belongs, can be established. A construction is given such that a certain class of constraints is satisfied at each step of the construction of a correct visual sentence. Semantic interpretations of such sentences are also constructed in an incremental way according to the semantic variety under which a sentence of the language is interpreted.

These interpretations may also be associated with the definition of visual dynamics, by considering the latter as a sequence of transformation steps, where each step is composed by the structured application of a collection of visual transformations, as defined by some application policy.

Finally, we show how user interactions can also be accommodated in this framework by modeling user actions as resources provided to the interaction process.

An integrated implementation of the approach is given based on the reduction of all the types of transformations involved (evolution of visual sentences in a syntax-directed editor, execution of visually specified process, and user steering of visual transformations) to a common model of resource transformation. A visual interface guides the user to the interactive definition of the different components of a visual environment, giving access to the specification of both visual alphabets and visual rules. The discussion is illustrated by examples relative to the specification of simple typical visual languages such as finite state automata or network schemas.

The rest of the chapter develops as follows. After presenting related work in Section 2, we illustrate the notions of syntactic family and semantic variety in Section 3, before proceeding to show the approach to the interactive definition of syntax and semantics in Sections 4 and 5, respectively. Section 6 dwells on the association of basic interaction facilities with visual elements based on their roles with respect to the metamodel, while Section 7 sketches the overall architecture of the proposed environment. Finally, Section 8 discusses conclusions and future developments.

RELATED WORK

Most approaches to visual environment construction from formal specifications derive from rewriting techniques—typically extensions of linear grammars to manage visual aspects (Costagliola, Deufemia, & Polese, 2004), constrained multiset grammars (Jansen, Marriott, & Meyer, 2004), or graph transformations (Ermel & Bardohl, 2004; Minas, 2003)—or, more recently, from metamodel definitions (Celms, Kalnins, & Lace, 2003; de Lara & Vangheluwe, 2004; Nianping, Grundy, J., & Hosking, et al., 2004).

Costagliola et al. (2004) propose positional grammars, in which a string of attributed terminal symbols describes the entities present in the visual sentence and special symbols describe binary relations between them. Relation symbols allow the parsing process to proceed in a different order than that dictated by the linear structure of the string. Alphabet elements can be constructed and attachment zones defined for them. Rules have a context-free form, but allow the insertion of pseudo-terminals in the string to be parsed.

Graph transformations rely on graphs as internal models for visual sentences: each element is a node of a graph and each relevant spatial relation is defined by a type of (hyper)edge. In particular, several approaches have taken advantage of the versatility of graph-based formalisms to define transformations from an abstract representation of the spatial relationships among visual elements to an abstract view of the semantics associated with them, to executing the transformations implied by the semantics. The fundamental contributions in this line come from the distinction between spatial relation graphs and abstract relation graphs (Rekers & Schürr, 1997), and from the notion of abstract visual syntax (Erwig, 1998), exploiting different types of graph transformation as enabling technology to realize the required transformations (Bardohl, Minas, Taentzer, & Schürr, 1999).

Diagen (Minas, 2003, 2006) adopts hypergraphs as internal models for diagrammatic languages. It allows both visual and textual interactive specification of the different components of a visual language specification. Specific code is generated to allow both syntax-directed and free hand editing of visual sentences in the specified language.

This same liberty is offered by the GenGED environment (Bardohl, 2002), exploiting attributed graph transformation in an algebraic setting (Taentzer, 1999). In GenGED, syntax and semantics of a visual language are specified via graph transformations, and each visual language is based on the definition of the associated type graph. Recent extensions include the exploitation of inheritance relations between types of elements (Ehrig, 2005a) and integration with the *ATOM³* environment for the management of model transformation (de Lara & Taentzer, 2004).

ATOM³ (de Lara et al., 2004) allows the definition of a visual language from its metamodel (abstract syntax plus constraints), and interaction control relies on the language constraints. Visual sentences can be transformed in various ways (e.g., translated to other formalisms, or to generate or optimize code). Event-driven grammars are used to associate events with elements in the concrete syntax (Guerra & de Lara, 2004). This requires

the management of two metamodels for concrete and abstract syntax, respectively. Triple graph grammars (Schürr, Winter, & Zundorf, 1995), in which special graphs constitute an intermediate layer between the concrete and abstract syntax graphs, are exploited to reflect the effect of concrete events on the abstract syntax. This provides the advantage, common to several metamodel-based environments, to allow free-order editing without having to set an explicit modality to work on the elements in the visual sentence.

Within GME (Generic Modeling Environment) (Lédeczi et al., 2001), a specific version, GME-UDM (Magyari et al., 2003), allows the definition of domain-specific languages. With GME-UDM, the language writer specifies the data model in UML and relates it to the visual aspects. It also integrates an OCL evaluator for complete management of the metamodel. Behavior definition is based on visual rewriting, involving the definition of visual patterns, implicitly representing sets of visual rules. This facilitates the specification of complex transformations at the cost of having to deal with possible ambiguities.

Design of domain-specific languages is also addressed by the GMT (generic metamodeling tool) environment (Celms et al., 2003). Different types of presentation can be defined for the same domain with different packages for any concrete domain and presentation. A separate graphical diagramming engine supports the graphical operations for diagrams, which can be expressed in terms of extended directed graphs, also incorporating sophisticated diagram layout algorithms. This approach, however, requires the construction of a specific metamodel for each language, with limited possibilities of reuse.

Pounamu (Nianping et al., 2004) allows the construction of different views for a same metamodel, from which the information model for a specific application is derived. Models are expressed as extended entity-relationship diagrams. Visual elements can be decomposed into subelements, which are however accessible only through their main element. Hence, only connection-based languages can be defined without support for the abstract notion of spatial relation. Connections are defined with respect to the types of elements they can connect, so that no real matching of the visual antecedent of a rule has to occur.

Other approaches try to rely on the definition of the admissible interactions during the construction of a visual sentence so that the definition of the language is implicitly derivable from the set of compositions enabled by the system. An example of this approach is provided in Penna, Intrigila, and Orefice (2004), where an environment is presented in which designers can specify a visual automaton in the form of a transition graph, then exploited to drive legal interactions, without defining a concrete or abstract syntax for the language. Interaction control is formally specified in Berstel, Crespi-Reghizzi, Roussel, & San Pietro (2005) via visual event grammars leading to the definition of verifiable finite state systems.

With reference to the possibility of generating concrete syntax from metamodels, work by Ehrig, Küster, Taentzer, and Winkelmann (2005b) aims at producing a layered graph grammar from a complete metamodel definition of a visual language including OCL constraints. This approach looks dual to ours, as they consider metamodels of individual languages, not of families, so that the language designer has to specify many aspects of concrete syntax with OCL constraints, rather than through direct manipulation of rule constituents.

METAMODELS FOR SYNTAX AND SEMANTICS

We capitalize on the notions of syntactic and semantic metamodel presented in Bottoni and Costagliola (2002), Bottoni (2003), Bottoni, De Marsico, Di Tommaso, Levialdi, and Ventriglia (2004b), Bottoni and Grau (2004a), of visual rewriting system (Bottoni, Costabile, & Mussio, 1999), and on the WIPPOG language (Bottoni et al., 2004b), and propose the integrated metamodel of Figure 1, which is at the basis of the definition of syntactic families and semantic variety of visual languages.

In a diagrammatic language, significant spatial relations exist among identifiable elements. An instance *ie* of `IdentifiableElement` is a recognizable entity in the language, to which a semantic role can be associated, and which is univocally materialized by means of a complex graphic element. Each `ComplexGraphicElement` is composed in turn of one or more instances of `GraphicElements`, each possessing one or more attach zone, defining its availability to participate in different spatial relations. The existence of a significant spatial relation between a set of elements is assessed via the predicate `isAttached()` implemented by each realization of `AttachZone`.

Visual transformations are specified by means of visual conditional attributed rewriting systems (vCARW) (Bottoni et al., 1999). A vCARW is a construct $rw = (\Sigma, A, \Delta_A, P, \Rightarrow_P)$, where Σ is a visual alphabet (i.e., a finite set of visual patterns), each corresponding to a distinguished subclass of `IdentifiableElement`, P is a set of rules of the form $p:L[\phi] \rightarrow R, \Theta$, with L (antecedent) and R (consequent) visual sentences on Σ ($L, R \in VS(\Sigma)$), and ϕ a boolean predicate defining an application condition on the antecedent. Θ (not represented in Figure 1) is a set of assignments for variables of elements in R. In the following, we sometimes omit the parts of the rule definition, which are not relevant in the context. Moreover, we represent visual sentences by simply listing the elements in it, in cases where we are not interested in specifying the associated geometry. The rewriting relation $\Rightarrow_P$ stipulates that rules are applied sequentially, by replacing, for each rule p, a match for L with a match for R coherent with Θ, provided that ϕ is satisfied. Given a visual sentence $ax \in VS(\Sigma)$ and a vCARW rw, the language $L(rw, ax) = \{\omega \mid ax \Rightarrow_P$

Figure 1. A synthetic and integrated view of the involved metamodels

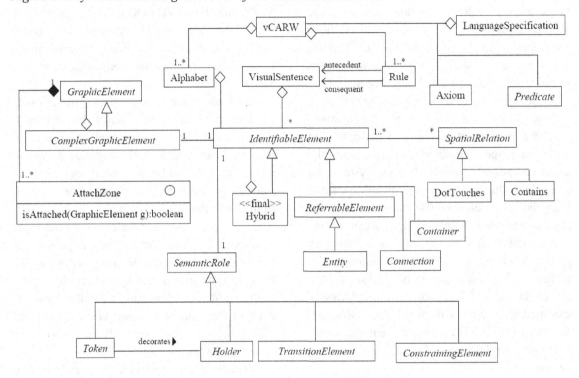

ω} is defined. The definition of a visual language *L* usually involves the use of a set of axioms *Ax Ax* and of a global predicate VALID such that *L* = $\bigcup_{ax \in AX} L(rw, ax) \cap L(VALID)$.

Families of Visual Languages

A family of diagrammatic languages is defined through the specialization of the abstract classes of Figure 1 and the possible addition of specific constraints. For example, in connection-based languages, `ReferableElements` may act as endroles for concretely represented connections, while the significant relation is `DotTouches`, so that `Connections`, typically lines or arrows, are attached by their two extremal points to the attaching area of the referable element. As some languages make connections referable in turn, the class `Entity` models referable elements, which can only act as endroles. Containment-based

languages exploit the composite pattern, whereby an element can contain several elements including containers in turn. In this case, the pattern is mediated by instances of the contains relation.

Further specializations of identifiable elements and spatial relations define more and more refined families. In the case of connection-based languages, graph-like languages are defined by having entities with borders as attaching zones, while in entities of a plex language (Feder, 1971) (e.g., flowcharts), only a fixed number of dots is available to be touched by a connection. The specialization process can go on indefinitely by adding new classes or constraints. For example, bipartite graphs are graph-like languages in which a complete hierarchy of entities composed of two specializations is defined, and connections are constrained to have endroles belonging to different classes. Given two classes *A* and *B* in a metamodel, we indicate by *A* ◀ *B* the existence of an inheritance relation from *A* to *B*, calling *A* a specialization of *B* and *B* a generalization of *A*.

Hybrid languages can also be defined in which a same element can assume different roles in different types of spatial relation. An example is any version of Statecharts where connections are used to indicate transitions, and containment is used to indicate the relation between a composite state and its substates. A thorough analysis of the most common families of diagrammatic languages and of the notion of hybrid language is given in Bottoni et al. (2004a).

The definition of families of diagrammatic languages in terms of progressively refined metamodels is at the basis of the construction of a meta-environment for the design of new languages and the semi-automatic construction of environments for constructing sentences in these languages and interacting with them as discussed later.

Transformations

The definition of a semantics for a diagrammatic sentence is based on the attribution of semantic roles to identifiable elements. In Figure 1, this is depicted through the association of a `Seman-ticRole` with an identifiable element. We call semantic variety of a diagrammatic language the overall type of interpretation to be applied to sentences in the language. Typical varieties correspond to specifications of discrete event systems, communication networks, or diagrammatic reasoning. In general, for each semantic variety, the operational or denotational semantics associated with the language can be defined by a suitable interpretation of the roles that the elements of its visual alphabet can assume and of the reciprocal constraints induced by the spatial relationships.

In this chapter, we restrict ourselves to the study of operational semantics interpreted as specifications of the behavioral aspects of the process or system depicted by a visual sentence. For example, in several visual languages, tran-sitions are explicitly represented as `Transi-tionElements`, while other languages define communication structures by exploiting roles such as `CommunicationElement` or `Com-municator`.

The specification of the operational semantics for a diagrammatic language is here modeled as rewriting of multisets of terms defining the resources available to the system and exchanged with other systems. In particular, we exploit the WIPPOG language, which specifies a modi-fication of the system configuration through six components (Bottoni et al., 2004b). These components define pre- and post-conditions for rule application, distinguishing between internal and external resources. Resources are modeled as flat typed terms (i.e., a term can contain only variables or constant values and variables range on a basic set of domains, including the set of resource identifiers); each resource is equipped with a unique identifier, which can be used as value for attributes of other references, but which can never be modified. The WHEN and GETS components define the resources which are con-sumed by the rule application, internally owned by the system or provided by the environment, respectively. Conversely, the PRODUCES and OUTS components respectively describe the re-sources produced and internally maintained and those sent outside. The IF component contains the condition to be satisfied by the attributes of the consumed resources, while the computational activities associated with the rule application, typically to compute the value of the attributes of the produced resources, are described in the PROCESSES component.

The application of a WIPPOG rule in a WIP-POG Machine (WM) goes through a sequence of steps: (a) resources in the WHEN and GETS components are matched with those from the (internal and input) resource pools of WM; (b) for a match also satisfying the conditions in the IF component, it: (b1) removes the matched re-sources; (b2) executes the activities specified in

PROCESSES; and (b3) produces the resources specified in the PRODUCES and OUTS components, placing them in the internal and output resource pools, respectively.

As both vCARW and WIPPOG are based on multiset rewriting, a simple coding transforms vCARW rules into WIPPOG transitions.

INTERACTIVE DEFINITION OF SYNTAXES

Visual languages are sets of visual sentences constructed on some alphabet according to some formal specification. If a language belongs to a given family, the types of elements composing its alphabet will be specializations of the abstract classes characterizing the identifiable elements for that family. Hence, an occurrence of such an element will be constrained to participate in some spatial relationships and not in others. As an example, by defining Place and Transition as specializations of the two types of entities present in bipartite graphs, and P2TArrow and T2PArrow as types of connections, one is automatically endowed with the specification of all the admissible place-transition Petri nets. Further constraints may require that nets form a connected graph, or, for workflow nets, that unique initial (i.e., without incoming arrows) and final (without outgoing edges) places exist. For condition-event nets, constraints will indicate that a condition cannot act as both pre- and post-condition for the same transition. These constraints may be expressed by specific rules defining the concrete syntax for the intended language. The approach presented here is at the core of the construction of SYNM (syntactic manager), a tool for the creation of new visual languages, providing support to the interactive definition of new alphabets and creation of vCARW rules in such a way that rules defining the concrete syntax of the language are guaranteed to comply with the overall constraints induced by the family the language belongs to.

In particular, an alphabet element is defined by a model, which contains at least the attributes *name*, *identifier*, *shape*, *icon*, and *role*. A name is a unique string within the alphabet and is used as type name for all the instances of the element in visual sentences, thus specifying the attributes they will possess. The identifier does not receive a value in SYNM, but is used during construction of visual sentences to uniquely refer to their visual resources. The icon is defined through the URI of an image file, providing a unique visual representation for the element type to be used as a button for generating instances of it in visual sentences. The shape identifies a specialization of ComplexGraphicElement managing the materialization of the element instances. Finally, the attribute role is used to indicate a set of specializations of IdentifiableElement, giving the syntactic roles the elements can play in the context of the language family. Every role must implement the Role interface (see Figure 2) and is associated with an AttributedSymbolModel defining the attributes needed for that role.

Figure 2. The hierarchy for role definition

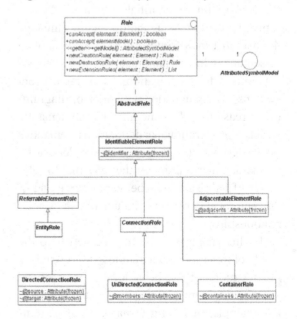

An element can play a syntactic role only if it contains all the required attributes correctly named and typed. For example, supporting the `DirectedConnection` role requires the possession of the attributes *source* and *target*, while the `UnDirectedConnection` role is supported by the attribute *members*, and the `Container` role by *containees*. All these attributes are of type `IdentifierList`.

Language designers can also define other attributes relevant to the use of the element, but which do not have an associated specialized semantics inside the editor. For this reason, SYNM provides a generic interface for attribute definition allowing the user to define the attribute name, type, and default value, possibly null. Figure 3 shows a situation in which the user is inserting a new

attribute for the transition element of Statecharts. SYNM possesses a collection of checkers, each activated as parts of the syntax get defined. For example, an `AttributeChecker` ensures that an attribute name is a valid alphanumeric string, a `TypeChecker` that the type is a valid one (i.e., one mentioned in the list of types defined within SYNM), and an `ExpressionChecker` that the default value is compatible with the type.

The construction of the concrete syntax proceeds by expressing rules as pairs of visual sentences, constituting the antecedent and the consequent of a vCARW rule. The language of antecedents is defined by allowing each configuration of alphabet elements such that they satisfy the constraints associated with their roles in the family the language being defined belongs to. We

Figure 3. The interface for attribute definition

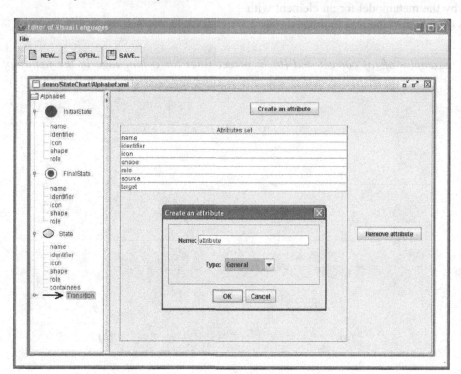

first introduce the case in which every alphabet element can play a single role. Let $\Sigma = \{\sigma_1,\ldots,\sigma_n\}$ be a visual alphabet for a visual language L in a family F and $Roles = \{r_1,\ldots,r_m\}$ the set of roles for the elements of Σ, as defined by the abstract classes in the metamodel for F. We indicate with $\sigma_i.role$ the role played by an element σ_i so that $\forall\sigma_i \in\Sigma$, $\exists! \rho_j \in Roles$, with $\sigma_i.role = \rho_j$. The set HS of antecedents and consequents is defined as $HS = \{x \mid \varnothing \Rightarrow_p x\}$, where $\Rightarrow_p$ is the rewriting relation for a vCARW constructed on Σ, such that $P = P_{ind} \cup P_{dep}$. $P_{ind} = \{\varnothing \rightarrow \sigma_i \mid \sigma_i.role = \rho_k \wedge \rho_k \in Ind\}$, where $Ind \subset \Sigma$ is the set of roles for which the metamodel does not require the presence of other elements. $P_{dep} = \{\tau \rightarrow \tau \oplus \{\sigma_i.role\} \mid \sigma_i.role = \rho_k \wedge \rho_k \in Dep\}$, where $Dep = \Sigma \setminus Ind$ is the set of roles, which cannot exist without the presence of other elements (a typical example is a connection requiring the presence of referable elements). In this case, τ is a multiset composed of the elements required by the metamodel for an element with role ρ_k to exist, and $\oplus$ denotes multiset union[1].

SᴙɴM is equipped with a collection of basic rules, directly generated from the declaration of the roles to which the alphabet elements have to comply. When a new rule for a vCARW is to be created, the visual language designer applies these basic rules to add elements into the antecedent or consequent of the rule under definition. This way, antecedent and consequent are guaranteed to belong in the language of all visual sentences built on top of the selected alphabet, and all the condition and attribute updates related to constraints imposed by the role of the added elements are automatically inserted to complement the ϕ and Θ components of the new rule.

As an example, in the family of connection based languages, $\forall\sigma_i, \sigma_i.role = \rho_k$ ◀Entity $\Rightarrow \exists p_{\sigma i}: \varnothing \rightarrow \{\sigma_i\} \in P$. Conversely, $\forall\sigma_j, \sigma_j.role = \rho_k$ ◀ Connection $\Rightarrow\exists \sigma_i, \sigma_k,\sigma_l$ ◀ ReferableElement such that $p_{\sigma i\sigma l}: \{\sigma_i\}\rightarrow\{\sigma_i,\sigma_i\}$ and $p_{\sigma k\sigma l\sigma j}:\{\sigma_k,\sigma_l\}\rightarrow\{\sigma_k,\sigma_l,\sigma_j\}\in P$.

Figure 4. Examples of (a) correct and (b) incorrect rules for a language in the family of bipartite graphs

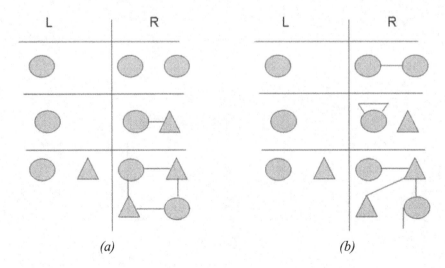

(a)   (b)

Indeed entities are considered independent elements for this family, so that they can be freely added to the antecedents and consequents of the rules being defined, while connections are dependent elements, so that they can be inserted only in the forms of loops on any referable element (rules $p_{\sigma_i\sigma_i}$), or between any two referable elements (rules $p_{\sigma_k\sigma_l\sigma_j}$).

In a similar way, in the family of containment based languages, an element σ_j playing a role of identifiable element can appear in rules of type $\{\sigma_j\}\rightarrow\{\sigma_j,\sigma_i\}$ $\forall\sigma_j$ such that $\sigma_i.role = \rho_k \blacktriangleleft$ Container. This process can be defined for all levels of the hierarchy. For example, if we want to define rules for a language of bipartite graphs, the sentences in the antecedent and in the consequent can contain instances of connections only if they touch entities of different type at their source and target. Figure 4(a) describes some correct antecedent-consequent pairs, while Figure 4(b) describes some incorrect ones. In particular, dangling edges are a typical cause for non-correctness. SYNM is guaranteed never to produce rules such as those in Figure 4(b).

For the case of hybrid languages, the condition that an element can play a single role is relaxed to consider that the element can play the required role (i.e., $\sigma_j.role \supseteq \{\rho_k\}$). It is considered, however, that $\forall(\rho_k, \rho_l)$, $\forall\sigma_j\in\Sigma$, such that $\{\rho_k,\rho_l\}\subseteq \sigma_j.role$, $\neg(\rho_{kl}\blacktriangleleft\rho_l)$ (i.e., no two roles for one same element can be on a same path in the inheritance hierarchy rooted in IdentifiableElement).

The rules for defining a specific visual language are usually given by considering only a restricted subset of pairs of sentences in HS. Typically, only some of the available basic rules will be selected, while some additional rules will be expressed by more complex patterns. Such patterns can be defined by simply adding more elements in the antecedent or the consequent. In any case, any construction of a relation must ensure that the attributes necessary to indicate the existence of the relation are updated. Hence, SYNM provides facilities for the management of the attributes pertaining to the roles related to the created relation. As an example, for rules of type:

$\{entity(id1), entity(id2)\} \rightarrow \{entity(id1), entity(id2), connection(id3)\}$

the Θ component is automatically equipped with the assignments

$Out1 = id3;\ In2 = id3;\ Src = id1;\ Tgt = id3,$

such that the complete rule is[2]

$\{entity(id1,\ outgoing=O1),\ entity(id2,\ incoming = I1!)\} \rightarrow \{entity(id1,\ outgoing=O1\cup Out1),\ entity(id2, incoming = I1! \cup In2), connection(id3,\ source = Src, target = Tgt)\}$

INTERACTIVE DEFINITION OF SEMANTICS

The specification of the semantics for a visual language L is developed with respect to the metamodel defining the adopted variety. In what follows we consider that each language is defined to support only one variety in which elements of a given type from Σ can play only one semantic role and spatial relations support a semantic interpretation coherent with the variety. In particular, we first examine the transition variety and subsequently the communication one.

In any case, the SEMM (semantic manager) environment allows the interactive definition of the semantics for a visual language L, through a sequence of steps, in which a visual language designer D associates elements of Σ with their semantic roles, and specifies the semantics to be associated with visual rewriting rules and axioms. This process exploits a definition of the concrete syntax for L in the form of a visual rewriting system $rw =(\Sigma, P, \Rightarrow_p)$. We assume that each rule $p \in P$ prescribes the creation of some collection *vc* of visual elements, the removal of a collection *vr* and the update of attributes of elements in a collection *vu*.

In particular, *D* has to define:

1. For each $\sigma \in \Sigma$, the role that instances of σ can assume with respect to the semantics of the process described by a visual sentence $vs \in VS$;
2. For each $p \in P$, a semantic rule p_m, constrained by the semantic roles of the elements in *vc*, *vr*, and *vu*.

During the construction of a visual sentence $vs \in L(rw)$, a set of semantic rules $P_m = \{p_m \mid p \in P\}$ is exploited to incrementally specify the semantics described by *vs*. At each application of *p*, *vs* will be transformed by insertion, removal and update of elements in *vc*, *vr*, and *vu*, respectively.

Its overall semantics will be accordingly updated as prescribed by p_m.

The following discussion is based on the overall architecture in Figure 5.

Languages Defining Transitions

The transition semantics variety collects all uses of visual languages to describe transformation processes defined as some form of discrete state transitions. We consider that in general a diagram depicts an instantaneous configuration of a system and that it evolves under some well defined law, which can be inherent to the form of the diagram, or described externally. In any case, we model the evolution law as a collection of WIPPOG rules contained in a *WM* whose internal pool contains a collection of resources related to the identifiable elements in the diagram. Different types of

Figure 5. The overall architecture of SEMM

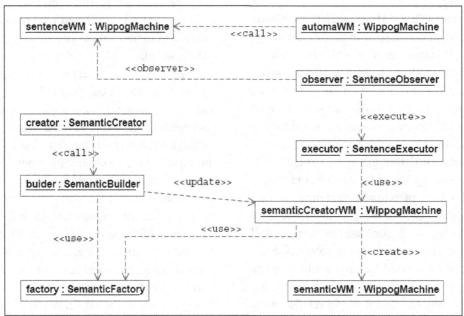

correspondences between identifiable elements and WIPPOG resources can be established and managed in SEMM.

With reference to the metamodel of Figure 1, the representation of the system dynamics can be directly supported by some form of canonical animation, in which instances of the `token` abstract class, may appear or disappear, or move from one instance of a `holder` to another. A visual configuration is actually determined by how tokens decorate holders. Some `ConstrainingElement` can be used to indicate particular conditions on the occurrence of a transition, or reading conventions.

Considering the transition variety, one can devise three types of WIPPOG coding of a visual configuration, namely token-, holder- and graphics-based. Each WIPPOG resource related

to an identifiable element is equipped with two default attributes: `name` and `identifier`. In the token-based coding, only tokens are represented as resources and an attribute specifies the holders to which they belong. Conversely, in the holder-based coding, holders are coded as resources and the presence or absence of tokens in them is represented via attributes. If holder-based coding was adopted, but some tokens contain additional semantic attributes, SEMM automatically switches to a graphics-based coding where both tokens and holders are represented as resources. Such codings are all suitable for diagrammatic languages expressing transitions via specific visual elements. Graphics-based coding is instead typically used for visual transformations expressed in terms of before-after rules, for which each visual element is coded as a resource.

Figure 6. Definition of semantic roles for visual elements

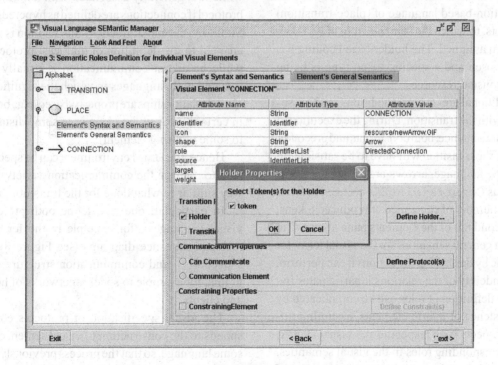

Figure 6 shows the SEMM interface for defining the semantic roles of the visual elements. The Alphabet pane on the left presents the elements from Σ. For each σ∈Σ, the elements pane on the right displays a series of tabs derived from the specific type of `IdentifiableElement` describing its role in the syntactic family. The upper part of the elements pane contains its syntax model, represented by a set of attributes, while the lower part allows *D* to associate semantic roles with the selected element. According to the metamodel of Figure 1, each element can be defined as an explicit representation of a transition (e.g., arrows in finite state machines), as a holder (defining the associated tokens) or as a constraining element. In this latter case, *D* has to specify the expressions that describe its effect on the related transition. Expressions have also to be specified when a holder is put in relation with a transition. In Figure 6, the `Place` element in Σ has been selected. This is a subclass of `Entity` in the connection-based language of (place-transition) Petri nets, to which the semantic role of `Holder` has been assigned. The holder-based coding has been chosen and a specific token type is being used as visual resource.

Additional pre- or post-conditions can be associated with the transition. During the execution of the visual sentence, both constraints and preconditions of the transition will have to be satisfied. In the same language, arrows are `Connections` acting as `ConstrainingElements`, indicating the number of consumed or produced tokens. The second tab of the elements pane allows *D* to define a general semantics for the visual term, for example by describing the actions it can perform, independently of the relations it participates in.

The definition of roles can be complicated by the existence of hybrid elements, assuming different aspects with respect to the visual syntax, and corresponding roles in the visual semantics. A discussion of this case is beyond the scope of this chapter.

Languages Defining Communication

The definition of the communication semantics variety follows the lines discussed in Section 2, and proceeds in accordance with the metamodel described in Figure 7.

In particular, communication occurs among communicators associated with communication elements, which are responsible for receiving and sending legitimate messages according to some protocol. Two communication elements can exchange messages only if they enjoy some matching property.

In a diagrammatic language endowed with a communication semantics, different representations lend themselves to support different protocols. For example, a connection-based diagrammatic language can be suited to the definition of a point-to-point communication protocol, if connections are simple lines, possibly oriented, while it is generally associated with a multicast protocol if connections are defined as hyperedges. Similarly, the containment spatial relation is well adapted to the definition of multicast protocols, while broadcast communication is usually associated with languages in which the significant spatial relationships are property-based (e.g., being in certain areas of the plane or at some distance to some emitting element).

Hence, the SEMM environment can be specialized to manage the communication variety in a way similar to what done for the transition one.

In particular, one can define both protocol visual languages—for example in the form of message sequence diagrams (see Figure 8), or statecharts—and communication structure diagrams, for example to specify networks of hosts and clients.

The visual specification of protocols corresponds to the construction of visual sentences in some language, so that the process previously described for construction of a transition semantics

Figure 7. The metamodel for the communication semantics variety

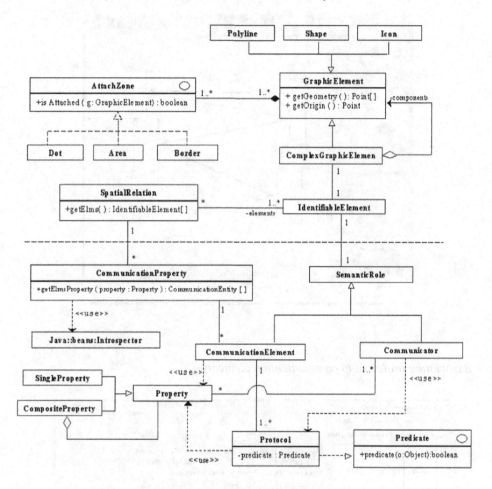

can occur. Hence, defining a protocol corresponds to constructing a system of transitions, possibly distributed among the protocol participants.

Protocol definitions are associated with communication elements and define the states in which these or the associated communicators can be. The construction of the complete semantics derives therefore from the composition of the protocol state transitions with the definition of communication events occurring on the network. State transi-

tions and communication events can in turn be associated with animations of the communication elements or of the communicators.

Figure 9 shows the association of a protocol, in this case the token ring one, with the rule for creating a cable. The protocol rules will then be associated with instances of cables during the construction of a visual sentence.

Figure 8. A sentence defining a point-to-point communication protocol

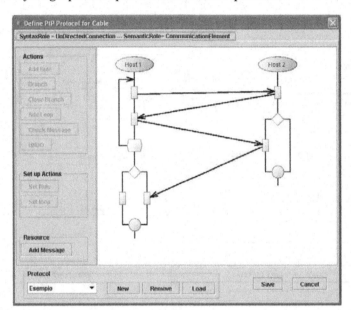

Figure 9. Associating protocols to communication elements

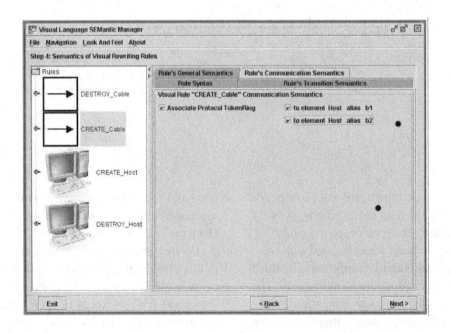

DEFINING INTERACTION WITH VISUAL SENTENCES

The construction of visual sentences defined through SYNM and SEMM, and the interaction with them, occurs in the GEVS (generation and execution of visual sentences) environment.

The definition of the interaction with identifiable elements used in the SYNM, GEVS, and SEMM environments—and in those which can be generated from them—proceeds from the definition of some abstract interaction actions. These actions are defined with reference to the types of identifiable elements present in the alphabet Σ and may be related by complex patterns in the context of the language family under consideration.

We consider that for each element, the abstract actions of creation, deletion, selection and deselection, movement, and querying of the attribute values can be defined.

Formally, let *Act* denote the set of distinct interactive actions a user can perform in a visual environment. *Act* is so defined that $\forall \sigma \in \Sigma$, Act $\supseteq$ {**create(σ)**, **select(σ)**, **deselect(σ)** **delete(σ)**, **move(σ)**, **query(σ)**}.

During interaction, actions are available to the user according to some family-specific constraints. For example, in connection-based languages, **delete(σ)** can be activated only for instances of $\sigma \blacktriangleleft$ ReferableElement which are not related to any connection. Conversely, **move(σ)**, when $\sigma \blacktriangleleft$ Connection, is allowed only if triggered by the movement of some connected element and cannot be activated by direct interaction on the connection. On the other hand, for $\sigma \blacktriangleleft$ ReferableElement, the execution of **move(σ)** triggers the movement of all associated connections. In a similar way, containers can only be destroyed if they are empty and moving one container triggers the movement of all the contained elements. Contained elements can perform two types of movements: one constrained to remain within the container, and one to move them from a container to another. At the time of an element definition, the appropriate constraints on interaction with them are generated by SYNM and subsequently associated with each created instance by usage within the GEVS system.

Actions can be executed in a coordinated way to achieve some task. We do not deal here with this level, which is usually specified through dedicated formalisms such as task action grammars (Howes & Young, 1991) or concur task trees (Mori, Paternò, & Santoro, 2002), as well as by general purpose ones such as hierarchical state machines (Blanch et al., 2005), or statecharts (Harel, 1987).

Actions are defined as compositions of elementary events from an alphabet E, usually concluded by a confirmation event (e.g., the selection of an element can involve several mouse movements concluded by a click when the mouse is within the area occupied by the element), so that a language of events is associated with each action through a mapping $\alpha : Act \to \wp(E^*)$. A language of events for the action act is a language $L(Act) \subseteq E^*$ such that $L(act) = \alpha\,(act)$ (Bottoni, Costabile, Fogli, Levialdi, & Mussio, 2001). If e is a confirmation event for an action *act*, then words of $L(Act)$ have the form $\omega \cdot e$.

A notion of interaction support, analogous to attach zone for spatial relationships, can be associated with identifiable elements once they are placed within an interactive context so that an action *act* is said to be performed on an instance *x* of type σ when a confirmation event *e* for *act* is performed with reference to a position in the interaction support for *x*.

The language designer can also define the sequences of interactions leading to an activity on an element (i.e., the mapping α), by choosing from a set of basic events. Default associations are provided by SYNM. For example, the generation of an instance of σ is performed by clicking on the icon denoted by ω .*icon* or by triggering a rule creating the element. Similarly, instance deletion can be obtained by clicking on its support and then on a destroy icon, while element query by right clicking on it and accessing a pop-up window. A toggle behaviour is prescribed for selection/deselection activities, typically triggered by a left-click. In any case, the language designer can access facilities to modify the α mapping.

Finally, the definition of a rule allows the automatic construction of the control dialogue structure for its activation, along the lines described in Bottoni et al. (1998, 1999). Typically, a control automaton can be derived by a rule p: L[φ]→ R, Θ in such a way that p is enabled if and only if the set of current selections matches L. In this case activating p, for example by clicking on the corresponding icon, causes the evaluation of φ, and, if the condition is satisfied, the construction of all elements present in R but not in L, the destruction of all elements present in L but not in R , the update of all the attributes for the elements matching R, according to Θ and the deselection of all elements remaining from those matching L.

The definition of the automaton depends on two variables:

- The paradigm of interaction (e.g., point and click, grasp and stretch, drag and drop).
- The order of execution (e.g., infix, prefix, or postfix), according to one categorization, or verb-action vs. action-verb according to another one.

All these mechanisms lead to a metamodel definition of the relation between interactive events and identifiable elements as described in Figure 10.

BRINGING IT ALL TOGETHER

The complete process from specification of a visual language L to construction of a visual sentence in vs∈L to the execution of the semantics associated with vs can be recapitulated as follows.

The construction of a vCARW rw in the SᴜɴM environment proceeds by defining the elements of the alphabet Σ and of the rules in *P*, exploiting the basic rules associated with elements in Σ. The axioms and the validation predicates for a specific language L built on rw are defined.

The mapping between sequences of events and high-level activities can be defined with respect to a basic set of activities performable on instances of elements in Σ, or activating rules in *P*.

The semantics for *L* can then be constructed in SᴇᴍM by defining the semantic roles of the elements in Σ and the actions for incremental construction of semantics of visual sentences associated with rules in *P*.

The GEVS environment is loaded, which incorporates an editor *E* for *L*, which is automatically generated from the specification of Σ and *P*.

Figure 10. A metamodel for the definition of user interactive activities on identifiable elements

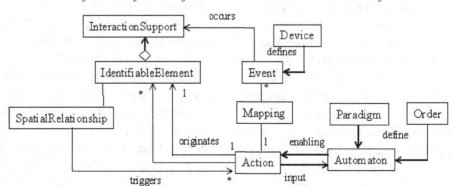

E allows the construction of sentences in *L*(*rw*) and the activation of the validation predicate. The interaction with *E* is constrained by the definition of the mapping between events and high-level activities, which constitute the symbolic input to the control automaton realizing the dialogue control.

The user interacts with *E* to construct a visual sentence *vs*. the semantics for *vs* is contextually built.

The user interacts with *vs* (i.e., initializes it by decorating holders with tokens, activates portions of its semantics, and observes the resulting evolution).

In particular, the semantics generation process for sentences in a language *L* is controlled by a `SemanticCreator`, which invokes the available `SemanticBuilders`. This produces the specification for a *WM* called `SemanticCreatorWM`, which manages the overall semantics for *L*. `SemanticCreatorWM` contains one transition for each rewriting rule *p* and defines a resource with the same name as *p*. The attributes for this resource describe the visual elements involved and that are necessary for the application of the semantic rule, thus determining the preconditions for the transition associated with *p*. During the generation of a visual sentence *vs*∈*L*, `SemanticCreatorWM` will incrementally create the semantics of *vs*, resulting in the specification

of `SemanticWM`. At each application of p, the visual sentence execution environment sends the associated resource to `SemanticCreatorWM`, which will update `SemanticWM` accordingly (see Figure 5). A similar construction is associated with the definition of an axiom and its selection as starting point of the generation process for a visual sentence.

The creation of a visual sentence results in the creation of the set of transitions defining its execution semantics and associated with the `SemanticWM` machine, so that its execution can start. As execution proceeds, the *GEVS* observer devoted to the representation of the visual sentences is notified and its updating produces some animation effect.

Similarly, user interaction during creation and execution of visual sentences is modeled as a sequence of discrete actions, managed in a control WM. User-generated events are mapped to WIPPOG resources, imported into WMs and mentioned in the GETS components.

In the generation phase, typical user actions are: (1) (de)selection of elements forming the antecedent of a visual rule, or (2) requests to apply a rule. As the user selects and deselects elements, `automaWM` performs transitions, which result in the enabling or disabling of rules as the set of selected elements comes to form (or ceases to form) a match for the corresponding antecedents.

Figure 11. Applying a rule

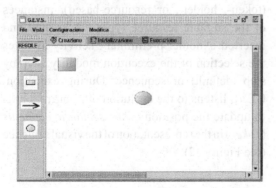
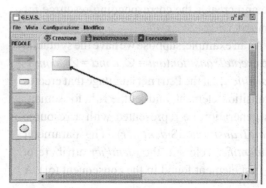

Figure 12. Execution of a computational step of one visual sentence

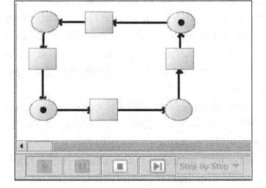

Rule application generally results in the generation or deletion of elements, but may also simply produce a modification in some attributes of existing elements.

For each request to apply a rule, `automaWM` communicates with `sentenceWM`, which checks the applicability of the rule, depending on the values of the attributes of the elements in the selection. `sentenceWM` notifies the `Observer` if the rule has been correctly applied. `Observer` will accordingly produce or destroy the involved visual elements (see Figure 11). For each applied rule, `executor` controls if a corresponding rule exists for the generation of the semantics. Associations of syntactic and semantic rules are represented as resources of `semanticCreatorWM`. The method `addResourceSemanticMachine` of `SentenceExecutor` takes as parameter the name of the applied syntactic rule and creates the corresponding resource for `semanticCreatorWM`.

As an example, suppose we have the syntactic rule *createTransition(ant = ∅, cond = ∅ , cons = {transition}*, of the Petri net language that creates a transition element, and let the rule for semantics generation be represented with a resource *createTransition*(c1$*identifier*). The parameter c1$*identifier* refers to the *identifier* attribute of the first element found in the consequent (c1). A

call `addResourceSemanticMachine`("createTransition") is performed on application of the syntactic rule, to check if a resource of type *createTransition* exists in `semanticCreatorWM`. If this is the case, the element identified by c1$*identifier* is inspected, to retrieve from the corresponding just created *transition* (the first element of the consequent), the attributes mentioned in the semantic rule. After attribute identification, an instance of the resource is created by setting its parameters, and inserted in the specification for `semanticWM`.

The execution of a visual sentence exploiting `semanticWM` (i.e., consuming and producing resources in its pools), requires its initialization by U with the insertion of resources in its *InternalPool*. To do so, *U* selects the holders to which the initial *token* resources must be assigned. According to the adopted type of translation (token-, holder-, or resource-based), instances of the suitable resource types are created and inserted. Another preliminary activity involves the selection of the execution modality: step by step (default) or sequence. During execution, GEVS listens to the evolution of `semanticWM` to update the position of the *semantic elements* (*Token*) in the representation of the visual sentence (see Figure 12).

CONCLUSION AND FUTURE WORK

Formal specification of visual languages is currently achieved following two, up to now distinct, approaches: one based on metamodels and one, which can be called symbolic-oriented, and which primarily exploits formalisms related to rewriting system.

This chapter represents an attempt to overcome such a dichotomy by combining advantages of the two approaches. In particular, we constrain the generation of concrete syntaxes based on information about the language elements derived from their syntactic metamodel. Moreover, a semantic metamodel is also exploited to associate semantic roles with syntactic elements so that the overall semantics of a visual sentence can be incrementally constructed as the interactive definition of the visual sentence proceeds.

Thirdly, the definition of the interactive activities that a user can perform in the construction of visual sentences and in order to execute them can also be based on the syntactic and semantic roles associated with the identifiable elements in the sentence.

The proposed framework can also accommodate hybrid languages, both from the syntactic and semantic points of view. In the first case, a visual element can play different roles in the same sentence, with respect to different types of spatial relationship. In the second case, different transition systems can be associated with the same element, for example to illustrate the communication protocol followed by an element which also undergoes an internal evolution modeled as a Petri net.

Several aspects of visual dynamics still need to be tackled, while progress is also required to define more refined metamodels. In particular, more complex forms of interaction such as continuous interaction have to be modeled within the framework, arriving at a complete metamodel

for styles of interaction. Notions of refinement and of hierarchical specification of complex behaviors have to be accommodated within the formal framework and properly supported by the implementations. Primitives for controlling the activation of transitions have to be defined to provide an efficient management of some interactive situations in which the non-deterministic execution model of WIPPOG is inadequate. The coverage of syntactic families and semantic varieties must be extended, so as to provide a significant library of services to support the creation of new languages. In particular, the diagrammatic reasoning variety of semantics deserves a deep study. A systematic study on the compatibility between syntactic and semantic specifications must be undertaken. This should assist designers in answering questions such as: which is the best representation for this semantic construct? is this representation adequate to express this form of communication?

ACKNOWLEDGMENT

Partially supported by the EC under Research and Training Network SeGraVis and by European Network of Execellence Interop.

REFERENCES

Bardohl, R. (2002). A visual environment for visual languages. *Science of Computer Programming, 44*(2), 181-203.

Bardohl, R., Minas, M., Taentzer, G., & Schürr, A. (1999). Application of graph transformation to visual languages. In G. Rozenberg (Ed.), *Handbook of graph grammars and computing by graph transformation: Volume 2: Applications, languages, and tools* (pp. 105-180). Singapore: World Scientific Publishing.

Berstel, J., Crespi-Reghizzi, S., Roussel, G., & San Pietro, P. (2005). A scalable formal method for design and automatic checking of user interfaces. *ACM Transaction on Software Engineering and Methodology, 14*(2), 124-167.

Blanch, R., Conversy, S., Baudel, T., Zhao, Y., Jestin, Y., & Beaudouin-Lafon, M. (2005). Indigo: une architecture pour la conception d'applications graphiques interactives distribuées. In *Actes des dix-septièmes journées francophones sur l'Interaction Homme-Machine (IHM 2005)*, 139–146.

Bottoni, P. (2003). Dynamic aspects of visual modelling languages. In R. Bardohl & H. Ehrig (Eds.), UNIGRA 2003, *Electronic Notes on Theoretical Computer Science, 7*(82), 131-145.

Bottoni, P., & Costagliola, G. (2002). On the definition of visual languages and their editors. In M. Hegarty, B. Meyer, & N. H. Narayanan (Eds.), *Proceedings Diagrams 2002* (pp. 305-319). Berlin: Springer.

Bottoni, P., & Grau, A. (2004a). A suite of metamodels as a basis for a classification of visual languages. In P. Bottoni, C. Hundhausen, S. Levialdi, & G. Tortora (Eds.), *Proceedings of Visual Languages/Human Centric Computing 2004* (pp. 83-90). IEEE CS Press.

Bottoni, P., Costabile, M. F., & Mussio, P. (1999). Specification and dialogue control of visual interaction through visual rewriting systems. *ACM Transactions on Programming Languages and Systems, 21*(6), 1077-1136.

Bottoni, P., Costabile, M. F., Fogli, D., Levialdi, S., & Mussio, P. (2001). Multilevel modelling and design of visual interactive systems. *Proceedings Human Centric Computing 2001* (pp. 256-263).

Bottoni, P., Costabile, M. F., Levialdi, S., & Mussio, P. (1998). Specifying dialog control in visual interactive systems. *Journal of Visual Languages and Computing, 9*(5), 535-564.

Bottoni, P., De Marsico, M., Di Tommaso, P., Levialdi, S., & Ventriglia, D. (2004b). Definition of visual processes in a language for expressing transitions. *Journal of Visual Languages and Computing, 15*(3), 211-242.

Celms, E., Kalnins, A., & Lace, L. (2003). Diagram definition facilities based on metamodel mappings. *Proceedings OOPSLA 2003 Workshop on Domain Specific Modeling*.

Costagliola, G., Deufemia, V., & Polese, G. (2004). A framework for modeling and implementing visual notations with applications to software engineering. *ACM Transactions on Software Engineering and Methodology, 13*(4), 431-487.

de Lara, J., & Taentzer, G. (2004). Automated model transformation and its validation using AToM³ and AGG. *Proceedings Diagrams 2004* (pp. 182-198). Berlin: Springer.

de Lara, J., & Vangheluwe, H. (2004). Defining visual notations and their manipulation through meta-modelling and graph transformation. *Journal of Visual Languages and Computing, 15*(3-4), 309-330.

Ehrig, H., Ehrig, K., Prange, U., & Taentzer, G. (2005a). Formal integration of inheritance with typed attributed graph transformation for efficient VL definition and model manipulation. *Proceedings of Visual Languages/Human Centric Computing 2005* (pp. 71-78).

Ehrig, K., Küster, J., Taentzer, G., & Winkelmann, J. (2005b). *Automatically generating instances of meta models* (Tech. Rep. No. 2005-09). Berlin, Germany: Technische Universität Berlin.

Ermel, C., & Bardohl, R. (2004). Scenario animation for visual behavior models: A generic approach. *Journal of Software and Systems Modeling, 3*(2), 164-177.

Erwig, M. (1998). Abstract syntax and semantics of visual languages. *Journal of Visual Languages and Computing, 9*(5), 461-483.

Feder, J. (1971). Plex languages. *Information Science, 3*, 225-241.

Guerra, E., & de Lara, J. (2004). Event-driven grammars: Towards the integration of meta-modelling and graph transformation. *Proceedings International Conference on Graph Transformation 2004* (pp. 54-69). Berlin: Springer.

Harel, D. (1987). Statecharts: A visual formalism for complex systems. *Science of Computer. Programming, 8*(3), 231-274.

Howes, A., & Young, R. M. (1991). Predicting the learnability of task-action mappings. *Proceedings SIGCHI Conference on Human Factors in Computing Systems* (pp. 113-118). New York: ACM Press.

Jansen, A. R., Marriott, K., & Meyer, B. (2004). Cider: A component-based toolkit for creating smart diagram environments. *Diagrams 2004* (pp. 415-419). Berlin: Springer.

Lédeczi, A., Bakay, A., Maróti, M., Vülgyesi, P., Nordstrom, G., Sprinkle, J., & Karsai, G. (2001). Composing domain-specific design environments. *IEEE Computer, 34*(11), 44-51.

Magyari, E., Bakay, A., Lang, A., Paka, T., Vizhanyo, A., Agarwal, A., & Karsai, G. (2003). UDM: An infrastructure for implementing domain-specific modeling languages. *Proceedings OOPSLA2003 Workshop on Domain Specific Modeling.*

Minas, M. (2006). VisualDiaGen--A tool for visually specifying and generating visual editors. *In Proceedings of Application of Graph Transformations with Industrial Relevance 2003* (pp. 398-412). Berlin: Springer.

Minas, M. (2003). Syntax definition with graphs. In Proceedings of the School on Foundations of Visual Modelling Techniques (FoVMT 2004) (ENTCS 148-1, pp. 19-40).

Mori, G., Paternò, F., & Santoro, C. (2002). CTTE: Support for developing and analyzing task models for interactive system design. *IEEE Transactions on Software Engineering, 28*(8), 797-813.

Nianping, Z., Grundy, J., & Hosking, J. (2004). Pounamu: A meta-tool for multi-view visual language environment construction. In *VL/HCC 2004* (pp. 254-256).

Penna, G. D., Intrigila, B., & Orefice, S. (2004). An environment for the design and implementation of visual applications. *Journal of Visual Languages and Computing, 15*(6), 439-461.

Rekers, J., & Schürr, A. (1997). Defining and parsing visual languages with layered graph grammars. *Journal of Visual Languages and Computing, 8*(1), 27-55.

Schürr, A., Winter, A., & Zundorf, A. (1995). Graph grammar engineering with PROGRES. *Proceedings of the 5th European Software Engineering Conference ESEC*, LNCS 989 (pp. 219-234). Springer.

Taentzer, G. (1999). AGG: A tool environment for algebraic graph transformation. *Proceedings of Application of Graph Transformations with Industrial Relevance 1999* (pp. 481-488). Berlin: Springer.

ENDNOTES

[1] The presence of unique identifiers actually guarantees that we deal with sets in any case, but we only demand that the algebraic structures on which vCARWs and sentences are constructed satisfy the axioms for multisets.

[2] We are abusing a bit vCARW notation in order to keep the description synthetic.

Chapter IV
Meta–Modelling and Graph Transformation for the Definition of Multi–View Visual Languages

Esther Guerra
Universidad Carlos III, Spain

Juan de Lara
Universidad Autónoma de Madrid, Spain

ABSTRACT

In this chapter, we present our approach for the definition of multi-view visual languages (MVVLs). These are languages made of a set of different diagram types, which are used to specify the different aspects of a system. A prominent example of this kind of languages is UML, which defines a set of diagrams for the description of the static and dynamic elements of software systems. In the multi-view approach, consistency checking is essential to verify that the combination of the various system views yields a consistent description of the system. We use two techniques to define environments for MVVLs: meta-modelling and graph transformation. The former is used to describe the syntax of the whole language. In addition, we define a meta-model for each diagram type of the language (that we call viewpoint) as a restriction of the complete MVVL meta-model. From this high-level description, we can generate a customized environment supporting the definition of multiple system views. Consistency between views is ensured by translating each one of them into a unique repository model, which is conformant to the meta-model of the whole language. The translation is performed by automatically generated graph transformation rules. Whenever a change is performed in a view, some rules are triggered to update the repository. These updates may trigger other rules to propagate the changes from the repository to the rest of the views. In our approach, graph transformation techniques are also used for other purposes such as model simulation, optimisation, and transformation into other formalisms. In this chapter, we also discuss the integration of these concepts in the AToM³ tool, and show some illustrative examples by generating an environment for a small subset of UML.

INTRODUCTION

Visual languages (VLs) play a central role in many computer science activities. For example, in software engineering, diagrams are widely used in most of the phases of software construction. They provide intuitive and powerful domain-specific constructs and allow the abstraction from low-level, *accidental* details. The term *domain specific visual language* (DSVL) (Pohjonen & Tolvanen, 2002) was coined to refer to languages that are especially oriented to a certain domain, limited but extremely efficient for the task to be performed.

Meta-modelling (Atkinson & Kühne, 2002) is a common approach to describe and generate environments for DSVLs. This technique consists on building a model (the meta-model), which describes the set of all valid models of the language. The meta-model is usually built using visual notations such as class or entity relationship diagrams, plus additional restrictions expressed in textual constraint languages such as OCL (Warmer & Kleppe, 2003).

The increasing complexity of software systems makes a common practice its specification by means of a set of smaller diagrams (that we call *system views*) instead of including this information in a single, monolithic one. Each one of these smaller models is more comprehensible and cohesive, describing some feature of the system from a specific *viewpoint*. Thus, ever more frequently, visual notations offer different diagram types in order to describe the various aspects of the system. These notations are known as multi-view visual languages (MVVLs) (Guerra, Díaz, & de Lara, 2005). For example, the UML notation (UML, 2006) proposes a set of diagram types to describe the static and dynamic aspects of the application. Note how MVVLs are not described in a separate way, but the language is described through a common meta-model, which includes the meta-models of the different diagram types and their relation. The meta-models of the differ-

ent diagram types can overlap, and these common elements indicate how the different diagrams are related to each other. For example, in the UML, classes are defined in class diagrams, but can be referenced afterwards in object and sequence diagrams.

An important aspect in the definition of environments for MVVLs is the support for consistency between their different system views. In this way, when the user modifies some system view, these changes may affect other views, which may have to be changed in their turn. For example, if the same class is present in several views of a UML environment, then changing the type of a class attribute in one view has to be reflected in the other views. Additional syntactic checkings (sometimes known as *static semantics*) can be defined by means of OCL (Warmer et al., 2003) or graph constrains. Besides syntactic consistency, the environment should also support semantic consistency. This can be achieved in several ways. For example, one may define an operational semantics for the different diagram types, which allow testing the behaviour of the system. Another possibility is to translate the diagrams into a semantic domain for analysis. We called the result of this translation *semantic view*. For example, in the case of UML, it is possible to define a translation from the different Statecharts into Petri nets for analysis or simulation.

As models and meta-models can be described as attributed typed graphs, they can be visually manipulated by means of graph transformation techniques (Ehrig, Engels, Kreowski, & Rozenberg, 1997; Ehrig, Ehrig, Prange, & Taentzer, 2006). This is a declarative, visual, and formal approach to manipulate graphs. Its formal basis, developed in the last 30 years, makes it possible to demonstrate properties of the transformations. A graph grammar is made of a set of rules and a starting graph. Graph grammar rules are made of a left and a right hand side (LHS and RHS), each one having graphs. When applying a rule to a graph (called *host graph*), an occurrence of the

LHS should be found in the graph and then it can be replaced by the RHS. A special kind of graph grammars are triple graph grammars (Schürr, 1994) that rewrite triple graphs instead of simple graphs. In our work, we use graph transformation techniques to implement consistency checkings and to define model simulation, optimisation, and transformations.

In today's current practice, most meta-modelling approaches and tools concentrate on generating environments for single view VLs. Moreover, as in multi-view systems, one may need to change and manipulate different views at a time, rewriting of more complex structures is needed (i.e., structures able to relate several graphs). Thus, in the present chapter we address the problem of how to extend current techniques to define MV-VLs. Moreover, these techniques should support syntactic and semantic view consistency checking. For these problems, we propose a solution based on meta-modelling and graph transformation.

The rest of the chapter is organized as follows. First, we give an overview of graph transformation techniques. Later, we describe the main approaches for the definition of DSVLs. Then, we show how these techniques can be used to define single view VLs using the AToM³ tool (de Lara & Vangheluwe, 2002). We use as an example a small subset of the UML language. Next, we give an overview of our approach to specify MVVLs and use these concepts to extend the previous example to make it multi-view. Later, we show how graph transformation can be used for model simulation, model optimisation, and model transformation. Finally, we compare with related research and present the conclusions and future work.

GRAPH TRANSFORMATION

In this section, we first give an informal overview of graph transformation. For an extensive presentation see for example Ehrig et al. (2006). Then,

we present triple graph grammars (Schürr, 1994) as a way to rewrite triple graphs. A triple graph is a structure that will be used in this chapter as a way to relate two different system views through a correspondence graph.

Similarly to Chomsky grammars for strings, graph transformation systems are made of rules. In order to apply a rule to a graph (called *host graph*), a matching morphism (an occurrence) should be found between the rule's left hand side (LHS) and the host graph. If such morphism is found, the rule's right hand side (RHS) can substitute the identified part in the host graph. The process ends when no rule in the graph transformation system is applicable. A *graph grammar* is made of a graph transformation system plus an initial graph. The semantics of the graph grammar are all the possible graphs than can be built applying the rules of the grammar, starting from the initial graph.

There are two main sources of non-determinism when applying a graph grammar. First, a rule can be applicable at different matches (i.e., it is possible to find different occurrences of the LHS in the host graph). In this case, a match can be selected at random, can be chosen by the user in an interactive way, or the rule can be applied at all matches in parallel if they are disjoint. In addition, two or more different rules can be applicable at a certain moment.

In principle, the order in which the rules of a graph grammar are applied is arbitrary. However, it is possible to specify a control flow for rule execution by using a control language (Fischer, Niere, Torunski, & Zuendorf, 1998; Karsai, Agrawal, Shi, & Sprinkle, 2003; Kreowski & Kuske, 1999), or by equipping rules with either a priority or a layer. In the case of priorities, rules with higher priorities are tried first (i.e., have higher precedence). In the case of layers, rules in the first layer are applied as long as possible. Then, the following layers are consecutively executed in ascending order.

Figure 1. Application of a rule to a graph

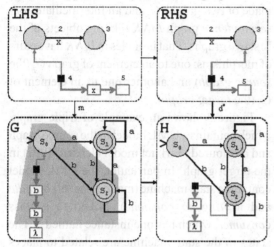

Figure 1 shows a derivation example where a rule specifying a step in the simulation of a state automaton is applied to a host graph G. The LHS shows two states of the automaton (labelled as 1 and 3) connected through a transition (labelled as 2). Node 4 has an edge that points to the current state and a connection to a sequence of inputs. The value of the first element of the input sequence has to be equal to the value of the transition (variable x). The rule describes the consumption of the first input and the change of current state. Throughout the chapter, we will use the following notation for graph grammar rules: the elements preserved by the rule application are labelled with the same numbers in the LHS and RHS; the elements that are deleted are not labelled in the LHS; finally, the elements that are added are not labelled in the RHS. Figure 1 shows the application of the rule to a host graph containing three states. The occurrence of the LHS has been marked in dark colour. In the derivation, variable x in the rule is instantiated to value "b" and the current state is moved from s_0 to s_2. The rule application results in graph H. Note how, in graph H, the rule can be applied again with a non-injective morphism, where nodes 1 and 3 in the LHS are mapped to state s_2.

In addition, rules can be equipped with application conditions (Ehrig, Ehrig, Habel, & Penemann, 2004) constraining their application. One of the most used application conditions is the so-called negative application condition (NAC). A NAC consists of a graph related to the LHS of the rule through a morphism. Finding the NAC in the host graph forbids the rule application. Figure 2 shows a derivation example for a rule with a NAC. The morphism between the LHS and the NAC is given by the elements labelled with the same numbers (i.e., node labelled 1). The rule creates a pointer to the initial state if the pointer has not been created yet (this is controlled by the NAC). In this way, we ensure that the rule is applied once at the beginning of the simulation of the automaton. The figure shows the application of the rule to host graph G. The occurrence of the LHS has been marked in dark colour. Since the NAC is not found in G for such occurrence (i.e., there is no pointer in the graph), the rule is applied yielding graph H. Again, the same occurrence of the LHS is found in H; however, this time the NAC is also found (i.e., a pointer exists), therefore the rule can not be applied. Throughout the paper, we will use a shortcut notation for NACs. In this way, the elements that are already present in the LHS are not shown in the NAC, but only the additional context. In Figure 2, the shortcut notation would

Figure 2. Application of a rule with a negative application condition to a graph

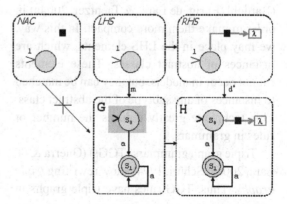

not show node labelled as 1 in the NAC, but it is implicit because it is in the LHS.

There are several formalisations of graph grammars (Ehrig et al., 1997). One the most popular ones is based on category theory (Mac Lane, 1972) and is called *double pushout* (DPO) (Ehrig et al., 2006). This is the formalisation we follow in this chapter. When applying a rule to a host graph at a certain match, the DPO approach requires two conditions in order for the rule to be applicable. The first one is called *dangling edge* condition and states that a rule cannot be applied at a certain match if it deletes a node that makes some edge become dangling. That is, if a node is deleted, all their incoming and outgoing edges should be deleted by the rule as well (i.e., the complete context of a deleted node should be considered by the rule). The other condition is called *identification condition*. It states that if two nodes (resp. edges) of a rule are identified through a non-injective match into the same node (resp. edge), then the rule cannot be applied if one of them has to be deleted and the other preserved.

Graph transformation can be used for model manipulation. This includes parser and creation grammars for VL definition (see next section) and also grammars for simulation, transformation into other formalisms and optimisation (de Lara & Vangheluwe, 2004b). Our approach is to define a VL using meta-modelling, and then use graph transformation systems to manipulate the models. Moreover, we can use the meta-model information in the graph transformation rules (Bardohl, Ehrig, de Lara, & Taentzer, 2004a) in order to make them more compact. In this way, we may place in the LHS elements, which are instances of abstract classes. These elements cannot occur in models, but they can be matched to instances of any subtype of the abstract class. This technique greatly reduces the number of rules in grammars.

Triple graph grammars (TGGs) (Guerra & de Lara, 2006a; Schürr, 1994) allow rewriting *triple graphs*. Thus, TGG rules have triple graphs in their LHS, RHS, and NACs. Triple graphs are made of two graphs G_i and an intermediate *correspondence* graph *LINK* relating objects of the first two graphs. That is, nodes in *LINK* have pairs of morphisms: one to an element of graph G_1 (the *source graph*) and another one to an element of G_2 (the *target graph*).

Figure 3 shows an example of triple graph, which contains a UML model in the source graph and a coloured Petri net model (Jensen, 1992) in the target graph. In particular, the UML model contains a state machine (made of states *con_idle* and *waiting_to_consume*), linked to a class *consumer*, which has one instance named *c*. The states in the state machine are related to places in the coloured Petri net while the transition in the state machine is related to the coloured Petri net transition. Thanks to the extensions for triple graphs and grammars, we proposed in Guerra et al. (2006a), the correspondence graph nodes may relate nodes of one graph with edges of the other or even to be undefined.

In this chapter, focussed on MVVLs, we are interested in graph triples made of a view model and a so-called *repository* model. The *repository* is made of the gluing of all the system views defined by the user. Therefore, each system view is related to the repository through a correspondence graph that relates each element in the view with its respective element in the repository. Automatically generated TGGs are used to specify how this gluing is performed, with the purpose of keeping the views consistent.

DEFINING VISUAL LANGUAGES

In this section, we give an overview of the basic concepts in the definition of VLs, as well as the main techniques: meta-modelling and graph transformation.

In the definition of a VL, one usually differentiates between abstract and concrete syntax. The former includes the concepts of the language and

Figure 3. A triple graph

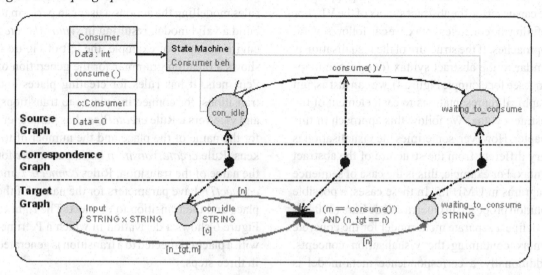

their relations. The concrete syntax specifies how the abstract syntax concepts are visualized. The bottom of Figure 4 shows an example where a simple state automaton is represented using concrete syntax (left) and abstract syntax (right). Note how a rendering function is needed in order to assign visualisations to the abstract syntax elements. In the case of the example, states are represented as circles with additional decorations depending on the value of attributes *isInitial* (an arrow head is attached to the state) and *isFinal* (a double circle is drawn). Transitions are represented as arrows adorned with a symbol. Boxes are used for inputs and the current state pointer.

In addition, it is usual to work with typed graphs. In Figure 4, graph *G'* is conformant to a type graph *TG* (in the upper part of the figure). This simply means that it is possible to find a morphism from the graph *G'* to the type graph *TG*. The concept of type graph is similar to the concept of meta-model, which is one of the techniques for the definition of VLs and the one we follow in this chapter. In this case, a meta-model is used to describe all the admissible models of the language (i.e., those models conformant to the

meta-model). Typically, this is specified by means of class or entity-relationship diagrams.

Figure 5 shows a meta-modelling architecture for the definition of Petri nets. The Petri nets meta-model is shown as an element in the set of all possible UML class diagram models. Note how one of the models describes in fact the set of all class diagrams. This is shown by means of an arrow from the element (the meta-model) to the set. The Petri nets meta-model describes the set of all Petri net models. Obviously, the set of class diagrams and the set of Petri nets are disjoint. The picture shows one element of the Petri nets set, which in its turn defines a set of execution traces. While the figure shows three meta-modelling levels, the UML has been defined by a four meta-level architecture, as the language used to define class diagrams (the MOF, meta object facility (MOF, 2006)) is placed in a different level.

Frequently, meta-models are provided with additional constraints, possibly expressed in some textual constraint language (such as OCL (Warmer et al., 2003)). Thus, the specification of the VL relies in a purely declarative approach (the meta-model), combined with a procedural part based on constraint checking.

Note how, with the meta-modelling approach, we can describe the abstract syntax of the VL. For defining the concrete syntax, we can follow several approaches. If the structure of the visualisation is similar to the abstract syntax (one-to-one mapping, see for example Figure 4), we can just assign graphical representations to each element of the abstract syntax. We follow this approach in this chapter. However, sometimes the visualisation is very different from the structure of the abstract syntax. For example, this is the case of sequence diagrams in UML 1.5. In these cases, a possible solution proposed in Guerra and de Lara (2004) is to define a separate meta-model for the concrete syntax containing the visualisation concepts. Additionally, a correspondence meta-model is used to relate the concrete and abstract syntax elements. Note how in this case, the use of triple graphs becomes very useful.

The second technique for VL definition is based on the use of a parsing or a creation grammar to specify the VL syntax. The former allows the user to build the diagram and then the grammar verifies its validity. The latter contains rules modelling the actions a user can perform to build a valid model, resulting in *syntax directed* environments. For example, the left of Figure 6 shows a creation grammar for the generation of Petri nets. It has rules for creating places and transitions, for connecting places to transitions, and vice versa. Rule *createPlace* has parameters for the name of the place and the number of tokens. Rule *createTransition* has a parameter for the name of the transition. Rules *connectPT* and *connectTP* have parameters for the names of the place and the transition to connect. The right of Figure 6 shows a derivation in which a Petri net with a place connected to a transition is generated in three steps.

Syntax directed environments can be restrictive because the user may have to choose between many possible similar editing actions (e.g., two rules deleting arcs from places to transitions and the other way round). On the other hand, it is possible to model a sequence of complex editing actions through rule sequences, simplifying the in-

Figure 4. Type graph, concrete and abstract syntax

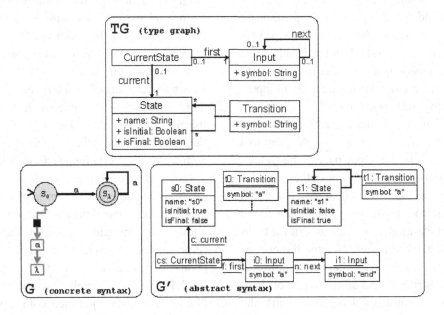

Figure 5. Definition of Petri nets by means of meta-modelling

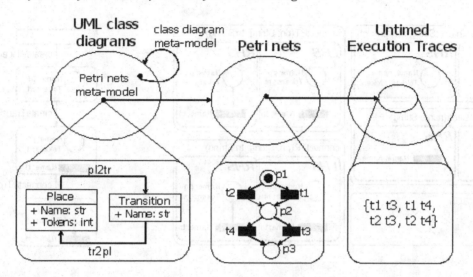

teraction of the user with the environment. Please note that we have used concrete syntax in the rules, as we have assumed a one-to-one mapping between abstract and concrete syntax elements. For more complex cases, a possible solution is to use TGG rules where the source graph contains the concrete syntax, the target graph contains the abstract syntax and the correspondence graph the relations between them.

DESCRIBING SINGLE-VIEW VISUAL LANGUAGES WITH AToM³

In this section, we present an example showing the definition of a simple VL using AToM³ (de Lara et al., 2002). This tool allows defining VLs by means of meta-modelling. The meta-model is built using either a class or an entity relationship diagram and includes information about the abstract and concrete syntax of the VL. Figure 7 shows a snapshot of AToM³ being used to define a very small subset of UML for illustrative pur-

poses. The subset contains classes (*SU_Class*, which have a name, a list of attributes, and a list of methods), binary associations (*SU_Assoc*, which have a name and a list of attributes), inheritance relations between classes (*SU_parent*), objects (*SU_Object*, which have a name, a classifier, and a list of attribute values), binary links between objects (*SU_Link*, which have a name, a classifier, and a list of attribute values), state machines (*SU_StateMachine*, which have a name and should be associated to some class), and states (*SU_State*) and transitions (*SU_Transition*) for state machines. In addition, the VL is also provided with additional helper elements used only for simulation purposes (as we will show later in this chapter), and not for system specification. In this way, objects can receive method calls (*SU_MethodCall*, which have a name) through a *SU_Input* element, and have a pointer (*SU_current*) to the current state in their classifier's state machine.

AToM³ allows specifying constraints for the meta-model in Python. In this way, we have included constraints for ensuring that in each

Figure 6. Creation graph grammar for Petri nets (left) and derivation (right)

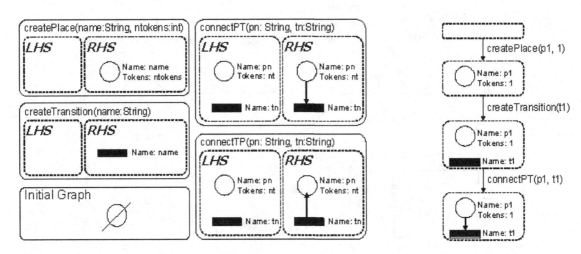

transition, the triggering event is a method of the owning class, and the action is well-formed. Each constraint should define the user event(s) (e.g., creating an element, deleting an element, saving a model, etc.) that cause(s) its evaluation, and whether it should be evaluated before (*pre-con-straint*) or after (*post-constraint*) the event action. If the constraint is evaluated to true, then the event is performed; otherwise, the event is disabled (or undone in the case of a post-constraint).

For the definition of the concrete syntax, each element of the meta-model is assigned a visual appearance. Figure 8 shows the definition of the visualisation for a class. Note how, we can include in the visualisation references to the value of attributes (*name, attr,* and *methods* in this case). In this example, the concrete syntax is very simple and each visualisation element is in one-to-one correspondence with an abstract syntax element. That is, each class of the meta-model is assigned an icon-like visualisation element and each association an arrow-like presentation element.

The environment in Figure 9 was generated by AToM[3] from the meta-model in Figure 7. The environment contains a simple producer-consumer

example with a buffer of capacity one. The model is made of three main classes: *producer, consumer,* and *buffer*. Classes *producer* and *consumer* inherit from class *BufferedProcess*, which provides them with method *buffer_ready()*. The buffer uses this method to signal when it is ready to be read or written. The main classes are assigned a state machine specifying their behaviour. Basically, the producer/consumer has to wait until it is ready to produce/consume (i.e., until it receives the invocation of method *produce()* or *consume()*, respectively) and the buffer is ready (method *buffer_ready()*). Then, it can put/get data from the buffer. In addition, one instance of each one of the three main classes has been included in the model: *p* with classifier *Producer, b* with classifier *Buffer*, and *c* with classifier *Consumer*.

Note however, that we have mixed in a single diagram information about different aspects of the system (static and dynamic). This is neither comprehensible nor maintainable. It would be more suitable to have separate diagrams for the different aspects. This could be done by generating

Figure 7. Definition of a small subset of UML with AToM³

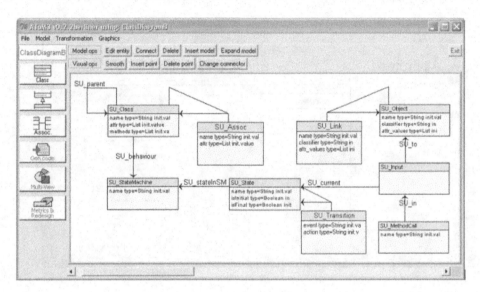

separate tools for the class and object diagrams as well as the state machines. Nonetheless, this solution is not optimal as it would be difficult to assess consistency between the diagrams in the different tools, especially if an element appears in different views (e.g., a class in different class diagrams). Moreover, the user would have to change between tools in order to construct the different diagrams. Therefore, we propose a solution based on identifying the different views on the complete VL meta-model and generating a unique tool for handling all of them. In this tool, the user can create different system views and syntactical view consistency is automatically ensured. The VL designer can specify additional domain specific syntactic constraints (also known as static semantics constraints). The approach is first explained in the next section, and then, we will modify this example to create a multi-view environment in the following one.

OUR APPROACH FOR MULTI-VIEW VISUAL LANGUAGES

Some VLs are composed of a set of diagram types. In the meta-modelling approach, the definition of each one of them can be based on a unique meta-model, which relates their abstract syntax concepts. For example, this is the case of UML2.0. The different diagram definitions, that we call *viewpoints*, may have some overlapping parts in this unique meta-model. If we identify the overlapping elements for each pair of viewpoints, the structure shown in the upper part of Figure 10 is obtained. In the figure, we have a meta-model that comprises three viewpoints. Two of them overlap with the third (represented as patterned rectangles), but not between them. This structure can be described using category theory (Mac Lane, 1972), where all the squares formed by two viewpoints, their overlapping elements, and the complete VL meta-model are *pullbacks* (thus, the squares commute $f_1 \circ v_{12} = f_2 \circ v_{21}$, $f_2 \circ v_{23} = f_3 \circ v_{32}$ and $f_1 \circ v_{13} = f_3 \circ v_{31}$). In the actual implementa-

Figure 8. Definition of the concrete syntax of a class in AToM³

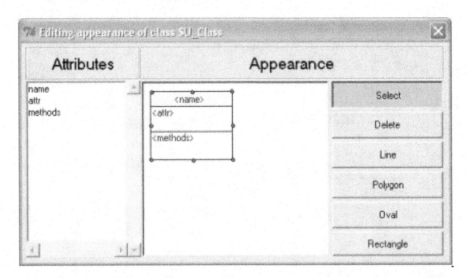

Figure 9. The generated environment for the example

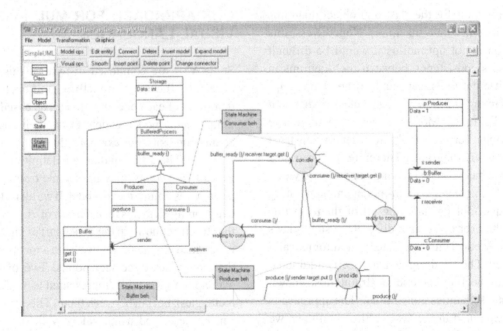

tion of this approach in AToM³ (see next section), the morphisms between each viewpoint and the complete VL meta-model are inclusions, but in general, they can be any function.

At the model level, this structure also holds for *system views*. The lower part of the figure shows two instances of viewpoint 1 and one instance of viewpoint 2. The dotted arrows between models and meta-models denote an *"instance-of"* relationship. The two instances of viewpoint 1 overlap. Note that the overlapping between a viewpoint and itself is not explicitly shown at the meta-model level, but it is implicit.

In order to guarantee syntactic consistency at the model level, we build a unique model (called *repository*) by gluing all the system views built by the user. The resulting model is an instance of the complete VL meta-model. This gluing operation is performed by automatically generated TGG rules derived from the meta-model information. Updating the repository as a result of a system view modification may leave some other system views in an inconsistent state. At this point, other automatically generated triple rules update the necessary system views. In this way, we have TGGs that propagate changes from the system views to the repository and the other way round. This is shown in Figure 11. This mechanism is similar to the model-view-controller (MVC) framework. In the figure, each model has in its upper-right corner the viewpoint it is compliant with. Step 1 is usually performed by the user; steps 2, 3 and 4 are automatically performed by the tool. Note how this mechanism could have been hard coded in the generated environment; however, we decided to explicitly generate TGG rules for it. The advantage is that their graphical nature allows the user to easily understand and modify them. Moreover, it is possible to generate different sets of rules to model different behaviours for the environment (see next section).

For additional domain specific syntactic constraints (also known as static semantics constraints), the MVVL designer may provide

additional TGG rules. In this way, syntax can be checked in a uniform way. For dynamic semantics consistency, the VL designer must provide the necessary mechanisms. Usually, these will involve checkings at the repository level, probably performing a model transformation into another domain for analysis, but other specific checkings can be provided as well. Note how, transformation into another domain can also be expressed as graph transformation (de Lara et al., 2004a). We call the result of such transformation a *semantic view* of the original system.

DESCRIBING MULTI-VIEW VISUAL LANGUAGES IN AToM³

In this section we use our approach for defining MVVLs to extend the previous example. We have created four viewpoints to separate different aspects of the language. The first one is used to define the classes (with attributes and methods) and their associations. The second one is used to define the inheritance hierarchy. In this viewpoint we do not show the information about class attributes and methods. The third viewpoint is used to instantiate objects and links. Finally, the fourth viewpoint is used to specify the state machines. Note how elements that will be used for simulation (such as classes *SU_Input* and *SU_MethodCall*) are not included in any viewpoint, since they do not take part in the system specification. This possibility is very interesting, as it allows the MVVL designer to hide auxiliary elements to the final users.

We have extended AToM³ with a tool (called *views*) for the definition of multi-view environments. The tool allows creating a number of viewpoints by selecting different parts of the complete VL meta-model. Figure 12 shows a moment in the definition of the multi-view environment for the example. The complete VL definition is shown in the background window to the left. Next, the *views* tool is opened, showing the four viewpoints

Figure 10. Meta-model and model levels in a multi-view visual language

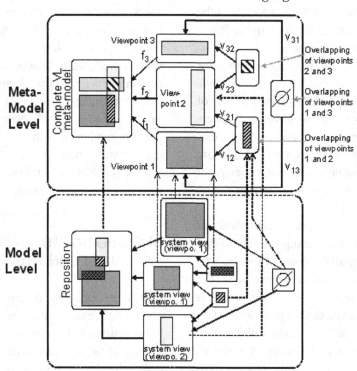

Figure 11. Change propagation

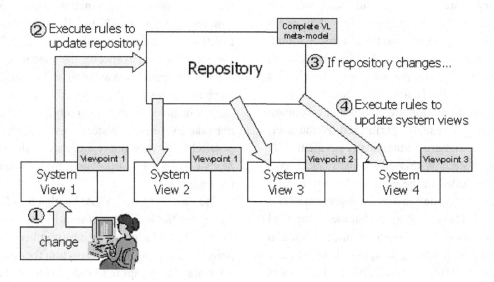

and the repository. They are visually represented as squares with the name of the viewpoint inside. The repository is always present (its definition is read-only) and contains the full meta-model of the VL. The other viewpoints are defined by the VL designer. They also contain the complete VL meta-model by default, which can be modified afterwards. To the right of the views tool, the figure shows a dialog box with additional data about the state machines viewpoint. The data include the viewpoint name, its graphical appearance, its properties, the minimum and maximum number of diagrams of this type the final user can create and its meta-model. The latter is shown in the window to the right. Note how, in this viewpoint, we have left only the relevant information for state machines (states, transitions and state machines). In addition, in order to associate the state machine to its class, we also need *SU_Class* in the viewpoint. However, we are only interested in identifying the class, therefore only the attribute *name* of the class is relevant. In addition, the concrete syntax of each element is specific for each viewpoint. That is, the MVVL designer can show an element in a different way depending on the viewpoint where it appears.

The MVVL designer can define consistency relations (depicted as arrows) between couples of viewpoints. These allow specifying consistency constraints by using TGGs. In the final generated environment, when the user modifies a system view, all the TGGs defined in the outgoing consistency relations of its viewpoint are executed. In its turn, if a view is modified by the action of a consistency grammar, the process is repeated to propagate the changes.

For most multi-view environments, it is not necessary to create by hand the consistency relations between individual viewpoints. The reason is that AToM[3] automatically generates a consistency relation between each view and the repository, and the other way round, as it can be seen in the *views* tool in Figure 12. They contain TGGs that implement the change propagation scheme of

Figure 11. Therefore, a direct consistency relation between two viewpoints is seldom necessary. The purpose of the grammars from the viewpoints to the repository is building the latter by merging the formers. These grammars contain the rules shown in Figure 13 for each element defined in the viewpoint meta-model, although here we only present the ones generated for class *SU_Class*. The first creation rule adds a class to the repository if it does not exist in the repository yet (NAC1). NAC2 prevents creating a new class in the repository when changing the name of a class in a view that already has an associated class in the repository. The second creation rule relates a new class in a view with the same class in the repository. This means that the class was added to the repository by a previous execution of the first creation rule; therefore, the same class is being used in another view. Attribute *refcount* counts how many times a class appears in different views. The first time a class is added to the repository, the counter is set to 1; each time the same class is added to some view, the counter is incremented. The first deletion rule detects when a class is removed from a view, and decrements the *refcount* attribute one unit. When the counter reaches zero, this means that the class does not appear in any view, so it is removed from the repository by means of the second deletion rule. Finally, the edition rule propagates changes in the value of the attributes from the classes in the views to the associated classes in the repository.

The changes performed in the repository are propagated in its turn by the TGGs contained in the consistency relations going from the repository to each view. These grammars contain a rule (as the one shown in Figure 14 for class *SU_Class*) for each element defined in the view meta-model. In this way, we have TGGs that propagate changes from a view to the repository and from there to the rest of the views, providing the required syntactic consistency between views. Note how, in the generated environment the user decides when to perform consistency checking by executing

Figure 12. Defining a multi-view environment for the example

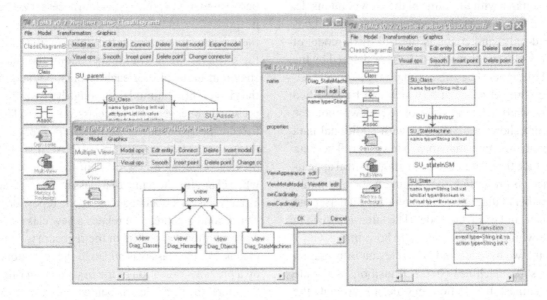

these rules, as sometimes it is neither possible nor adequate to maintain all views consistent at all times.

As stated before, the MVVL designer can define his own consistency relations with additional domain specific syntactic checkings, or enhance the ones generated by the tool. For example, the triple rule in Figure 15 has been added to the consistency relation going from the *Diag_Objects* viewpoint to the repository. The rule checks whether a link has as classifier an association between two classes that are the classifiers of the source and target objects of the link. If such association does not exist in the repository (NAC), then the link is deleted and an error message is shown to the user.

The window to the left in the background of Figure 16 shows the environment automatically generated from the MVVL definition in Figure 12. The interface contains a button for each viewpoint, and another one to show the repository. Users can add a new system view of a certain kind by clicking the corresponding button and then on

the canvas. The newly created view is shown in the canvas as an icon. In the figure, a class diagram, a hierarchy diagram, an object diagram, and three state machines have been created. If the user clicks on a view icon, a control dialog allows editing its attributes (i.e., its name in the example) as well as the model. The latter is edited in a new AToM[3] window. The figure shows to the right the edition of the model corresponding to the state machine for the producer behaviour. The environment verifies that the models are valid instances of the viewpoint. Moreover, when the user finishes the modification of a model, he can decide whether executing the consistency TGGs or not. If the TGG is executed, the changes are automatically propagated to the repository and from there to the other system views.

The TGGs included in the consistency relations determine the behaviour of the generated modelling environment. For example, the rules we have shown generate environments where the deletion of elements from a system view is conservative (i.e., the deletion is not propagated

Figure 13. Triple graph rules for building the repository from the system views

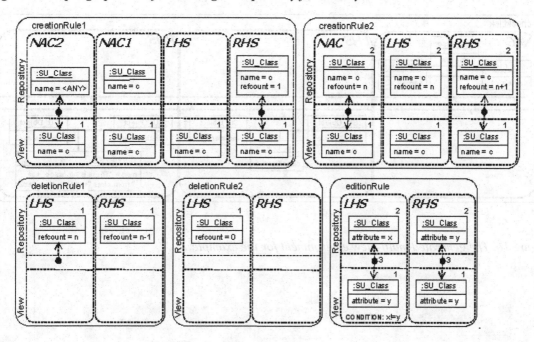

to the other views; instead, the element in the repository is only removed when there is no element in any view referencing it). However, there are occasions when a different behaviour is required (e.g., a cascading deletion where removing an element from a view implies removing the element from any other view and the repository). For this reason, the MVVL designer is provided with a catalogue of different behavioural patterns that allow changing or completing the behaviour given by default by the previous rules. The selection of different behavioural patterns results in different sets of triple rules in the consistency relations. For example, if a "cascading deletion" behavioural pattern is selected, then the deletion rules in Figure 13 are not generated, but the ones shown in Figure 17 are. The first two rules belong to the TGGs in the consistency relations going from each view to the repository. The first one detects when a class has been removed from a view, and then removes the related class from

the repository. The dangling condition of DPO graph grammar rules (see section *graph transformation*) forbids applying the rule if the class has some incoming or outgoing relation. The second

Figure 14. Triple graph rules for propagating changes from the repository to the system views

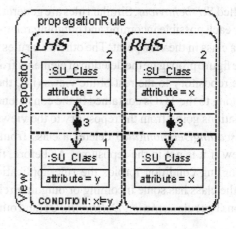

Figure 15. Triple graph rule for additional syntactic consistency checking

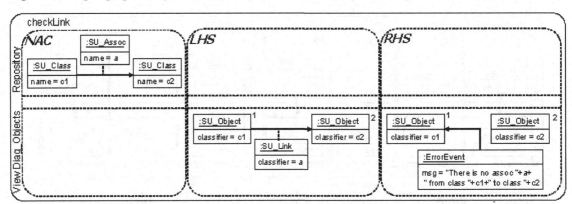

Figure 16. The generated multi-view environment for the example

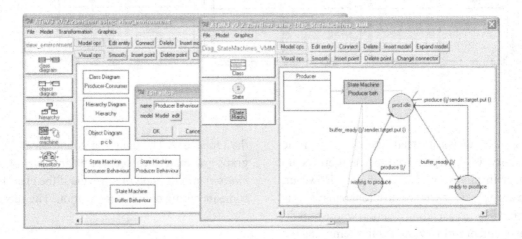

rule handles the deletion of one of such relations called *SU_behaviour*. Similar rules are generated for each possible incoming and outgoing relation to a class in the viewpoint. The other two rules in the figure propagate the deletion of elements from the repository to the rest of the views (i.e., they belong to the TGGs contained in the consistency relations going from the repository to the views). *cascadingDeletionRule3* deletes a class from a view if it is not in the repository. As before, the dangling condition forbids the rule application if the class has some incoming or outgoing relation. The rule *cascadingDeletionRule4* (and other

similar ones for each possible type of relation) handles this deletion of edges.

The consistency grammars are asynchronous because they are executed when the user finishes the edition of a system view and validates changes all at once. In addition, other behavioural patterns are synchronously applied (i.e., they are executed in response to user actions, such as creations or editions). For example, rules as the one shown in Figure 18 provide a modelling environment with intelligent creation behaviour. These rules are immediately executed after creating a new element (a class for the rule shown) in a system

Figure 17. Triple graph rules for the behavioural pattern "cascading deletion"

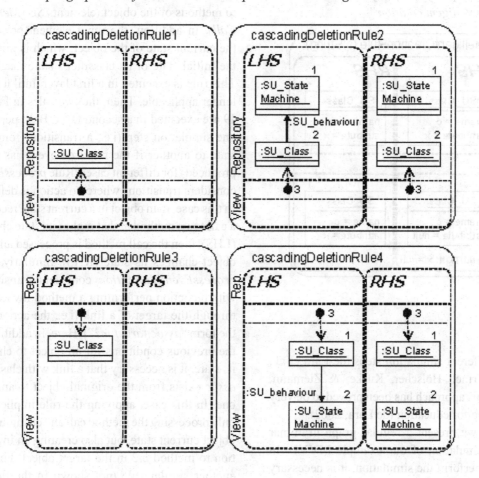

view. The rules copy the value of the attributes from the same element in the repository (if exists) to the element in the view.

MANIPULATING THE MULTI-VIEW VISUAL LANGUAGE

This section presents an overview of our approach for the manipulation of MVVLs using graph transformation. In particular, we show some examples of typical manipulations: simulation, optimisation, and transformation into other se-

mantic domains. In general, we will use regular graph grammars for those manipulations that involve only one system view (or the repository), and TGGs for manipulations where two system views (or one view and the repository) are simultaneously handled.

Model Simulation

By using graph transformation, it is possible to model the operational semantics of a VL (i.e., specify a simulator) with rules. In this way, the execution of the rules results in the visualisation

Figure 18. Triple graph rule for the behavioural pattern "intelligent creation"

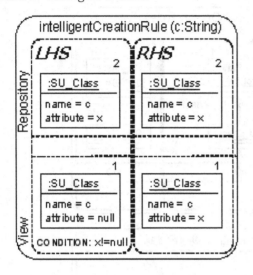

of the different simulation steps (de Lara et al., 2004b; Ermel, Hölscher, Kuske, & Ziemann, 2005). This approach has been proved to be very interesting for education (de Lara, 2002).

Next, we present a regular graph grammar for the simulation of our example MVVL. In order to perform the simulation, it is necessary to take into account not only the system dynamic information (i.e., the state machines) but also the static one (i.e., the object and class diagrams). Thus, the simulation is performed in the repository because it is the only view of the system that contains all the required information. Note that, indeed, it would be more adequate performing the simulation on a view derived from the repository and containing only the necessary elements, but nothing else (Guerra & de Lara, 2006b; QVT, 2006). The simulation graph grammar makes use of some helper elements that were included in the repository meta-model, but not in any of its viewpoints (i.e., classes *SU_Input*, *SU_MethodCall* and its relationships). The first rule in this grammar (not shown) assigns a *SU_Input* element to each

object. The input element stores the invocations to methods of the object (elements *SU_Method-Call*). In addition, the input element points to the current state of the object, which is initially the initial state of its classifier's state machine. This rule is executed in a first layer until it is no longer applicable. Then, the two rules in Figure 19 are executed in a second layer. Both perform one simulation step (i.e., a transition from one state to another if the required event has been produced) for different cases. Rule *processEvent* considers transitions where no action is defined. In this case, if an object in a current state receives a call to its method *m* that makes its state change (LHS), then the call method is processed and the object changes its state (RHS). Similarly, rule *processEventWithAction* considers transitions with an action performing a method invocation through the target of a link (i.e., the action has the form "*assoc.target.m2*"). Here, in addition to the previous conditions for an object to change its state, it is necessary that a link with classifier *assoc* exists from the original object to another one. In this case, applying the rule implies not only processing the method call and changing the object current state, but also creating an invocation to method *m2* in the target object. Finally, another similar rule (not shown in the figure) considers transitions with an action of the form "*assoc.source.m2*."

Model Optimisation

Graph transformation has been widely used for model optimisation (de Lara et al., 2004b; Fahmy & Holt, 2000). A particular kind of optimisation is refactoring (Fowler, 1999), which allows improving the quality of system designs without changing the behaviour. If they are applied in the early phases of the development (i.e., design and analysis), deficiencies can be detected and fixed by performing redesigns before the cost of fixing these defects becomes higher.

Figure 19. Graph grammar for simulation

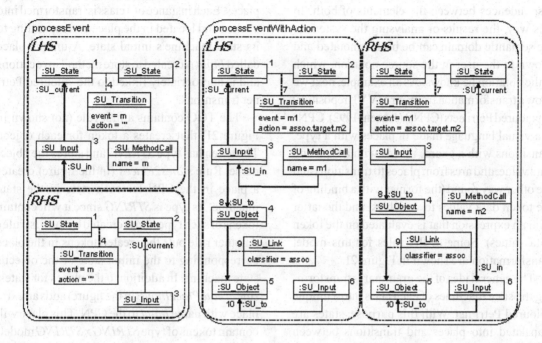

Redesigns can be expressed in a natural way by using graph transformation (Mens, Demeyer, & Janssens, 2002). For example, the first graph grammar rule in Figure 20 implements refactoring *collapseHierarchy* (Fowler, 1999), which is used to merge together a class and its parent when they are not very different. The rule has as parameters the names of the classes to collapse. It copies the attributes and methods from the child class to its parent, deleting the child class. Note that the dangling condition forbids the rule application if the class to delete has incoming or outgoing relations. For this reason, other rules are provided in order to move the incoming and outgoing relations from the child class to its parent. Some of these rules are *pullUpAssociation* and *pullUpChild*, shown in the same figure. They move outgoing *SU_Assoc* and incoming *SU_parent* relations from the child class to its parent, respectively. Note that these are in fact particularisations of the well-known refactorings *PullUpField* and *PullUpMethod* (Fowler, 1999). Due to the fact

that the presented optimisation rules make use of elements from different viewpoints (i.e., class and hierarchy diagrams), they must be applied on the repository. Afterwards, the consistency rules automatically propagate the changes performed in the repository to the rest of the system views.

Model Transformation

By using graph transformation, it is also possible to specify model transformations (de Lara et al., 2004a; Ehrig et al. 2005; Taentzer et al., 2005). These manipulations transform a source model conformant to a meta-model into a target model conformant to a different meta-model. Model transformation can be very useful when dealing with MVVLs since transforming the repository (or some of its views) into another formalism can help us to analyse the system, simulate it, or check its dynamic semantics. With this purpose, the MVVL designer can define TGGs in order to generate the target model (that we call *semantic view*) from the source model, and maintain correspondences between the elements of both. In this way, the results of analysing the system in the semantic domain can be back annotated and shown to the user in the source notation, which is the notation he knows. As an example, next we show a transformation from our MVVL repository to coloured Petri nets (CPNs) (Jensen, 1992). CPNs is a visual language made of places with a type, transitions with a guard, tokens with a type and data value, and arcs from places to transitions and the other way round (the former with a binding of the token data values to variables, and the latter with an expression that is evaluated on the token data values). Some of the rules for this model transformation are shown in Figure 21.

The general idea of the grammar is transforming the state machines of each class into a unique coloured Petri net. With this purpose, states are translated into places and transitions between states are translated into transitions between places. Each instance of a class is transformed into a token and located in the place corresponding to its state machine's initial state. A unique place called *Input* is created to store method invocations and is appropriately linked to the coloured Petri net transitions.

The TGG contains a first rule (not shown in Figure 21) that creates a token for each object. The token has type *STRING* and stores the object name. Rule *states2Places* (in the figure) creates a place in the CPN for each state in the state machine. Its type is *STRING* since it will contain tokens of such type (those created by the first rule). Another rule puts the created tokens in the place corresponding to the initial state of the object's state machine. In addition to the places for states, rule *createPlaceInput* (in the figure) adds an extra place with name *input* to the CPN. This place will contain tokens of type *STRING x STRING* model-

Figure 20. Graph grammar for optimisation

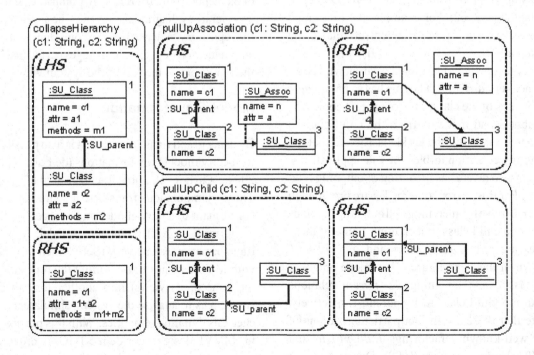

ling method calls. The first component of the data value is the name of the object that receives the method call, and the second one is the name of the method. Rule *transitions2Transitions* (in the figure) translates each transition without an action between two states into a transition between the places that correspond to the states. There are two incoming arcs to the newly created transition: the first one comes from the place associated to the source state in the state machine and binds the data value of tokens (i.e., the object name) to variable n; the second one comes from place *input*, and binds the data value of tokens (i.e., the name of the object that receives a method call, and the method name) to variables n_tgt and m. The

transition has a guard that allows the firing only if a call to a method with the event name exists and, in addition, it is invoked on an object that is in the place associated to the source state (i.e., n and n_tgt have to be equal). The value of n does not change when the transition is fired. A similar rule is necessary to handle transitions with an associated action. This rule creates in addition an outgoing arc from the transition to place *input*. This arc adds a token that models an invocation to the object method specified by the action.

Figure 22 shows the resulting CPN after applying our transformation TGG to the UML producer-consumer model. Once the CPN model is generated, it is possible to export the net into

Figure 21. Triple graph grammar rules for model transformation

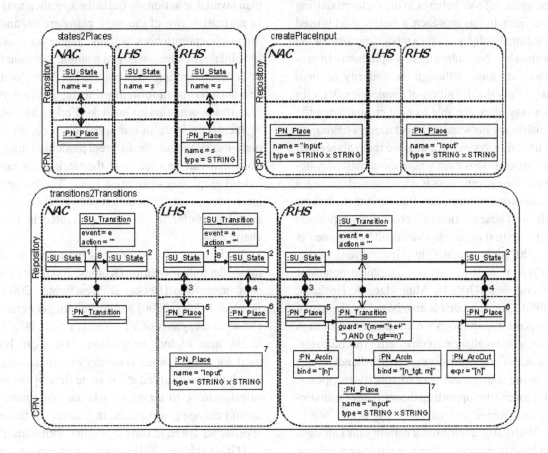

the Petri net markup language (PNML) (Billington et al., 2003) for simulation or analysis in other tools. The simulation of the CPN is a way of validating the state machines, as it can reveal undesired behaviour. The analysis techniques based on the reachability graph (Jensen, 1992) allow checking for deadlocks and test if a certain state can be reached, providing the sequence of method invocations in the state machines that produces it.

RELATED WORK

According to section *Defining Visual Languages*, visual modelling tools can be classified in two main groups, depending on the way the syntax of the VL is specified: a meta-model or a graph grammar. AToM[3] belongs to the meta-modelling paradigm. In this approach, a meta-model is used to automatically generate a modelling tool for the defined VL. Nowadays there is a plethora of meta-modelling tools, although the majority of them only allow the definition of single-view VLs. In that way, they are able to neither guarantee the consistency between different models belonging to the same system, nor analyse them altogether. Some exceptions exist where the consistency between the system views is implemented through a common repository where the views are somehow related. These relations are commonly expressed using textual notations (MetaEdit+ (Pohjonen et al., 2002) or Pounamu (Zhu, Grundy, & Hosking, 2004)), as well as partially graphical notations (JComposer (Grundy, Mugridge, & Hosking, 1998)). Our approach is also based on the use of a repository, although we are interested in high level, graphical, formal consistency mechanisms. The use of graph transformation has the advantage of being a graphical way to specify mappings. Moreover, the supporting theory makes transformations subject to analysis (Ehrig et al., 2006).

With the graph grammar paradigm, VL designers have to provide either a creation or a parsing grammar to specify the VL syntax. The former contains rules modelling the actions that a user can perform to build a valid model. The latter results in less restrictive environments. Users are allowed to perform any action when editing their diagrams, and then a parsing grammar checks their validity. Examples of graph grammars based tools are GenGed (Bardohl, 2002) and DiaGen (Minas, 2003). None of them support the generation of multi-view environments.

The *ViewPoints* approach was defined in Finkelstein, Kramer, Nuseibeh, Finkelstein, and Goedicke (1992) as method for the integration of multiple perspectives in system development. As originally formulated, a viewpoint is an agent with partial knowledge about the system and has a style (the used notation), a domain (the area of concern), the actual specification, and the work plan (available actions to build the specification). In particular, two of the work plans are *In-* and *Inter-* viewpoint check actions. These are used to validate the consistency of a single viewpoint or between multiple viewpoints. The ViewPoint approach has been formalized using distributed graph transformation in Goedicke, Enders, Meyer, & Taentzer (1999). In our approach, a common meta-model relates the different modelling notations that can be used, and the work plans are indeed graph transformation rules. The In- and Inter- viewpoint check actions can be expressed as rules similar to the ones presented in this chapter.

With respect to TGGs, they have been used for model transformation (Königs, 2005) for tool data integration (Becker & Westfechtel, 2003; Jakob & Schürr, 2006) and for relating concrete and abstract syntax of VLs (Guerra et al., 2004). In the area of tool integration, TGGs can be used for synchronous coupling of two models (i.e., both are modified at the same time by triple rules), source-to-target translation and incremental change propagation. In general, all these approaches are based on the original formulation of TGGs (Schürr, 1994), which is less expressive

Figure 22. Coloured Petri net resulting from the model transformation

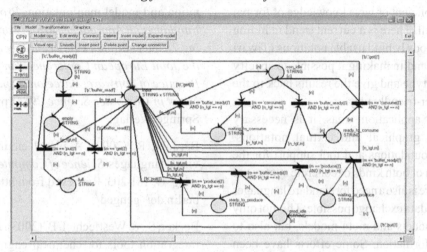

than our formalisation of TGGs (Guerra et al., 2006a). With respect to view handling in Jakob et al. (2006) TGGs are proposed for view creation in the area of tool integration. They work with views that can be considered model transformations similar to our semantic views. They do not consider system views; however, their views are non-materialized, which means that data is not replicated.

CONCLUSION AND FUTURE TRENDS

In this chapter, we have presented our approach for the definition of MVVLs and its implementation in the meta-modelling tool AToM^3. The complete VL is described using a meta-model, and each diagram type is a subset of the complete meta-model. In the generated environment, syntactic consistency is achieved by building a unique model—the repository—from the different system views by using automatically generated TGGs. Additional manipulations such as simulation, optimisation,

and model transformation can also be specified with graph grammars. These concepts have been illustrated defining an environment for a small subset of UML.

We are currently applying these concepts to a design notation in the hypermedia domain. We are also working in automating the verification of the repository models by translating them into other formal semantic domains, and then giving back the results of the verification in the context of the source language.

Future Trends

It is our belief that future practice will tend to provide environments for VLs and MVVLs, which are not just simple drawing tools, but also provide some extra added value (e.g., analysis capabilities) to the user. That is, VLs should come equipped not only with appropriate concrete syntax and usable environments, but also with precise semantics. This allows for example to analyse and simulate the models, checking consistency between system views or performing metrics on models.

This of course does not mean that the final user has to be proficient or have knowledge of formal methods at all. There is a current trend in hiding formal methods behind usable notations (Tiwari et al., 2003) and in making it possible to specify the analysis type and give the results back to the user in a user-friendly way.

In many application areas, it is necessary to combine graphical and textual notations. Therefore, foundations and tool support for the combination of both kinds of concrete syntax are needed. There is also a need for standard languages making tool data exchange possible. This not only applies to models and meta-models, but also to graph transformation. Some efforts have been already taken, such as the MOF (Meta-Object Facility) (MOF, 2006) for meta-modelling, XMI for MOF-models exchange in XML format (XMI, 2006), and GTXL for graph transformation data exchange in XML (Lambers, 2004). However, for graph transformation, the great variety of approaches makes tool integration very difficult. The recent standardisation effort of OMG for model transformation languages QVT (query/views/transformation) (QVT, 2006) can be an important step in this direction.

ACKNOWLEDGMENT

This work has been sponsored by the Spanish Ministry of Science and Education, projects TSI2005-08225-C07-06 and TSI2004-03394.

REFERENCES

Atkinson, C., & Kühne, T. (2002). Rearchitecting the UML infrastructure. *ACM Transactions on Modeling and Computer Simulation, 12*(4), 290-321.

Bardohl, B., Ehrig, H., de Lara, J., & Taentzer, G. (2004). Integrating meta modelling with graph transformation for efficient visual language definition and model manipulation. *Proceedings of Fundamental Approaches to Software Engineering 7th International Conference, held as part of the Joint European Conferences on Theory and Practice of Software, Barcelona, Spain. Lecture Notes in Computer Science 2984* (pp. 214-228). Springer-Verlag.

Bardohl, R. (2002). A visual environment for visual languages. *Science of Computer Programming 44,* 181-203. Retrieved from http://tfs.cs.tu-berlin.de/~genged/

Becker, S., & Westfechtel, B. (2003). Incremental integration tools for chemical engineering: An industrial application of triple graph grammars. *Proceedings of 29th International Workshop on Graph-Theoretic Concepts in Computer Science, Elspeet, the Netherlands. Lecture Notes in Computer Science 2880* (pp. 46-57). Springer-Verlag.

Billington, J., Soren, C., van Hee, K., Kindler, E., Kummer, O., Petrucci, L., Post, R., Stehno, C., & Weber, M. (2003). The Petri net markup language: Concepts, technology, and tools. *Proceedings of the 24th International Conference on Applications and Theory of Petri Nets, Eindhoven, The Netherlands. Lecture Notes in Computer Science 2679* (pp. 483-505). Springer-Verlag.

de Lara, J. (2002). Simulación Educativa mediante Meta-Modelado y Gramáticas de Grafos. *Revista de Enseñanza y Tecnología* nº 23, Mayo-Agosto 2002.

de Lara, J., & Taentzer, G. (2004a). Automated model transformation and its validation with AToM³ and AGG. *Lecture Notes in Artificial Intelligence* 2980 (pp. 182-198). Springer-Verlag.

de Lara, J., & Vangheluwe, H. (2002). AToM³: Atool for multi-formalism modelling and meta-modelling. *Proceedings of Fundamental Approaches to Software Engineering 5th International Conference, held as part of the Joint European Conferences on Theory and Practice of Software,*

Grenoble, France. *Lecture Notes in Computer Science 2306* (pp. 174-188). Springer-Verlag. Retrieved from http://atom3.cs.mcgill.ca

de Lara, J., & Vangheluwe, H. (2004b). Defining visual notations and their manipulation through meta-modelling and graph transformation. *Journal of Visual Languages and Computing. Special issue on "Domain-Specific Modeling with Visual Languages" 15*(3-4), 309-330.

Ehrig, H., Ehrig, K., de Lara, J., Taentzer, G., Varró, D., & Varró-Gyapay, S. (2005). Termination criteria for model transformation. *Proceedings of Fundamental Approaches to Software Engineering 8th International Conference, held as part of the Joint European Conferences on Theory and Practice of Software,* Edinburgh, Scotland. LNCS 3442 (pp. 49-63). Springer-Verlag.

Ehrig, H., Ehrig, K., Habel, A., & Penemann, K.-H. (2004). Constraints and application conditions: From graphs to high-level structures. *Proceedings of 2nd International Conference on Graph Transformation,* Rome, Italy. LNCS 3256 (pp. 287-303). Springer-Verlag.

Ehrig, H., Ehrig, K., Prange, U., & Taentzer, G. (2006). *Fundamentals of Algebraic graph transformation.* Monographs in Theoretical Computer Science. Springer.

Ehrig, H., Engels, G., Kreowski, H. J., & Rozenberg, G. (1997). *Handbook of graph grammars and computing by graph transformation. Vol 1.* World Scientific.

Ermel, C., Hölscher, K., Kuske, S., & Ziemann, P. (2005). Animated simulation of integrated UML behavioural models based on graph transformation. *Proceedings of the 2005 IEEE Symposium on Visual Languages and Human-Centric Computing* (pp. 125-133). Dallas, Texas, USA.

Fahmy, H., & Holt, R. C. (2000). Software architecture transformations. *Proceedings of the 16th IEEE International Conference on Software Maintenance* (pp. 88-96).

Finkelstein, A., Kramer, J., Nuseibeh, B., Finkelstein, L., & Goedicke, M. (1992). ViewPoints: A framework for integrating multiple perspectives in system development. *International Journal of Software Engineering and Knowledge Engineering, 2*(1), 31-57.

Fischer, T., Niere, J., Torunski, L., & Zuendorf, A. (1998). Story diagrams: A new graph rewrite language based on the unified modeling language. *Proceedings of Theory and Application of Graph Transformations 6th International Workshop,* Paderborn, Germany. LNCS1764 (pp. 296-309). Springer-Verlag. Retrieved from http://www.fujaba.de

Fowler, M. (1999). *Refactoring: Improving the design of existing code.* Addison Wesley.

Goedicke, M., Enders, B. E., Meyer, T., & Taentzer, G. (1999). Towards integrating multiple perspectives by distributed graph transformation. *Proceedings of the 1st International Workshop on Applications of Graph Transformation with Industrial Relevance.* LNCS 1779 (pp. 369-377). Springer-Verlag.

Grundy, J. C., Mugridge, W. B., & Hosking, J. G. (1998). Visual specification of multiview visual environments. *Proceedings of the 1998 IEEE Symposium on Visual Languages* (pp. 236-243). Nova Scotia, Canada.

Guerra, E., & de Lara, J. (2004). Event-driven grammars: Towards the integration of meta-modelling and graph transformation. *Proceedings of the 2nd International Conference on Graph Transformation,* Rome, Italy. LNCS 3256 (pp. 54-69). Springer-Verlag.

Guerra, E., & de Lara, J. (2006a). *Typed attributed triple graph trasformation with inheritance in the double pushout approach* (Tech. Rep. UC3M-TR-CS-06-01). Madrid, Spain: Universidad

Carlos III. Retrieved from http://www.ii.uam.es/~jlara/articles

Guerra, E., & de Lara, J. (2006b). Graph transformation vs. OCL for view definition. *Proceedings of the 1ˢᵗ International Workshop on Algebraic Foundations for OCL and Applications*, Valencia, Spain.

Guerra, E., Díaz, P., & de Lara, J. (2005). A formal approach to the generation of visual language environments supporting multiple views. *Proceedings of the 2005 IEEE Symposium on Visual Languages and Human-Centric Computing* (pp. 284-286). Dallas, Texas, USA.

Jakob, J., & Schürr, A. (2006). Creation of meta models by using modified triple graph grammars. *Proceedings of the 5ᵗʰ International Workshop on Graph Transformation and Visual Modelling Techniques. To appear in Electronic Notes in Theoretical Computer Science* (Elsevier).

Jensen, K. (1992). *Coloured Petri nets. Basic concepts, analysis methods, and practical use* (Vol. 1). EATCS Monographs in Theoretical Computer Science. Springer-Verlag.

Karsai, G., Agrawal, A., Shi, F., & Sprinkle, J. (2003). On the use of graph transformation in the formal specification of model interpreters. *Journal of Universal Computer Science 9*(11), 1296-1321.

Königs, A. (2005). Model transformation with triple graph grammars. *Proceedings of the International Workshop on Model Transformation in Practice, satellite event of the ACM/IEEE 8ᵗʰ International Conference on Model Driven Engineering Languages and Systems*, Montego Bay, Jamaica.

Kreowski, H. J., & Kuske, S. (1999). *Graph transformation units and modules.* Handbook of graph grammars and computing by graph transformation: Vol. 2: Applications, languages, and tools (pp. 607-63). River Edge, NJ: World Scientific Publishing Co.

Lambers, L. (2004). *A new version of GTXL: An exchange format for graph transformation systems.* Paper presented at the International Workshop on Graph-Based Tools, a Satellite Event of the 2ⁿᵈ International Conference on Graph Transformation, Rome, Italy.

Lèdczi, A., Bakay, A., Maròi, M., Vögyesi, P., Nordstrom, G., Sprinkle, J., & Karsai, G. (2001). Composing domain-specific design environments. *IEEE Computer*, Nov. 2001 (pp. 44-51). Retrieved from http://www.isis.vanderbilt.edu/Projects/gme/default.html

Mac Lane, S. (1972). *Categories for the working mathematician.* Volume 5 of Graduate Texts in Mathematics. Springer-Verlag, Berlin, 2nd. Edition (1st ed., 1971).

Mens, T., Demeyer, S., & Janssens, D. (2002). Formalising behaviour preserving program transformation. *Proceedings of the 1ˢᵗ International Conference on Graph Transformation.* LNCS 2505 (pp. 286-301). Barcelona, Spain: Springer-Verlag.

Minas, M. (2003). VisualDiaGen: A tool for visually specifying and generating visual editors. *Proceedings of the 2ⁿᵈ International Workshop on Applications of Graph Transformation with Industrial Relevance.* LNCS 3062 (pp. 398-412). Charlottesville, VA: Springer-Verlag. Retrieved from http://www2.informatik.uni-erlangen.de/DiaGen/

MOF 2.0 specification at the OMG home page (2006). http://www.omg.org/docs/formal/06-01-01.pdf.

Pohjonen, R., & Tolvanen, J. P. (2002). Automated production of family members: Lessons learned. *Proceedings of the International Workshop on Product Line Engineering the Early Steps: Planning, Modeling, and Managing* (pp. 49-57), Seattle, USA.

QVT specification at the OMG home page (2006). http://www.omg.org/docs/ptc/05-11-01.pdf

Schürr, A. (1994). *Specification of graph translators with triple graph grammars.* LNCS 903 (pp. 151-163). Springer-Verlag.

Taentzer, G., Ehrig, K., Guerra, E., de Lara, J., Lengyel, L., Levendovszky, T., Prange, U., Varro, D., & Varro-Gyapay, S. (2005). Model transformation by graph transformation: A comparative study. *Proceedings of the International Workshop on Model Transformation in Practice, satellite event of the ACM/IEEE 8th International Conference on Model Driven Engineering Languages and Systems*, Montego Bay, Jamaica.

Tiwari, A., Shankar, N., & Rushby, J. (2003). Invisible formal methods for embedded control systems, In *Proceedings of the IEEE, 91*(1), 29-39.

UML 2.0 specification at the OMG home page (2006). http://www.omg.org/UML

Warmer, J., & Kleppe, A. (2003). *The object constraint language: Getting your models ready for MDA* (2nd ed.). Boston: Pearson Education.

XMI specification at the OMG home page (2006). http://www.omg.org/docs/formal/05-09-01.pdf

Zhu, N., Grundy, J. C., & Hosking, J. G. (2004). Pounamu: A meta-tool for multi-view visual language environment construction. *Proceedings of the 2005 IEEE Symposium on Visual Languages and Human-Centric Computing* (pp. 254-256). Dallas, Texas, USA.

Chapter V
Extended Positional Grammars:
A Formalism for Describing and Parsing Visual Languages

Gennaro Costagliola
Università di Salerno, Italy

Vincenzo Deufemia
Università di Salerno, Italy

Giuseppe Polese
Università di Salerno, Italy

ABSTRACT

Much recent research is focusing on formal methods for the definition and implementation of visual programming environments. Extended positional grammars (XPGs) naturally extend context-free grammars for string languages to grammars for visual languages by considering new relations in addition to string concatenation. Thanks to this analogy, most results from LR parsing can be extended to XPGs while preserving their well-known efficiency. XPGs include mechanisms for handling contextual information enabling us to model a broader class of visual languages, which includes the diagrammatic notations used in software engineering. Moreover, the XPG grammar formalism can be effectively used for modeling both visual and textual notations in a seamless way. The XPG model is the underlying formalism of the VLDesk system for the automatic generation of visual programming environments. VLDesk inherits and extends to the visual field, concepts, and techniques of compiler generation tools like YACC.

INTRODUCTION

In the 80's, visual languages have been introduced in computers as a means to facilitate human-machine interaction for non-expert users. The availability of powerful personal computers motivated the development of visual iconic languages for operating systems, which led to two successful implementations: MacOs and Windows. These results encouraged the development of more sophisticated visual languages, using the concept of spatial relation among icons, which led to the development of syntactic and semantic frameworks for them (Marriott & Meyer, 1998). The aim was to extend the use of visual languages to new application domains such as database definition and manipulation, programming, etc. However, it has been long debated whether visual languages could enhance the activities in many of these application fields. Especially in programming tasks, experienced users would find the visual language cluttering and of no relief. Nevertheless, some years later visual languages have been successfully applied to many other application fields such multimedia databases and software design methodologies. The latter could hardly be exploited in the past because of the complexity of the many diagrammatic notations to be sketched on paper, and to be continuously revised along the development process.

During the last years, formal methods are achieving increasing importance in the context of visual languages. Indeed, much effort is presently put to develop formal techniques for specifying, designing, and implementing visual (programming or modeling) languages (Marriott et al., 1998; Minas, 2002; Rekers & Schürr, 1997). In general, the broader the class of languages to be treated is, the less efficient the parsing algorithm is. Due to this, big efforts are being made to characterize a class, which is expressive enough and, at the same time, efficient to parse. In addition, some efforts are being made in order to classify grammar models according to characteristics such as their expressive power, the way they represent the input, and the parser technology they support.

The research on this topic has been heavily influenced by the work in the formal language theory. The main motivation of this is the aim of exploiting the well-established theoretical background and techniques developed for string languages in the setting of visual languages. As a result, most of the methods proposed for visual language specification are grammar-based, even if in the last years other different approaches have been proposed and investigated such as logic-based (Helm & Marriott, 1990) and algebraic approaches (Uskudarli & Dinesh, 1997).

In this chapter, we present an overview of extended positional grammars (XPG, for short), a grammar formalism for modeling visual notations, which represents an extension of context-free grammars, and we describe the XpLR parsing methodology (Costagliola, Deufemia, & Polese, 2004). XPG and XpLR extend positional grammars (PG) (Costagliola, De Lucia, Orefice, & Tortora, 1997) and the associated pLR parsing methodology. The extensions have enabled us to model a wide class of notations and to efficiently parse them. The associated parsing algorithm is the XpLR parser, which is based on the well-known LR parsing technique. The benefits that can be derived from providing a specification of a visual language in terms of such formalism include facility of customization and modifications, as well as the maintenance and the debugging of the language, generation of code and reports by defining suitable semantic productions, implementation of visual and textual languages within a common framework.

The extended positional grammar model is the underlying formalism of the visual language desk (VLDesk) system (Costagliola et al., 2004) for the automatic generation of visual programming environments. VLDesk uses XPG to define a visual language and XpLR-based methodology to generate visual language compilers. It adopts concepts and techniques of compiler generation tools like YACC (Johnson, 1978) and extends these to the visual field. The final result of the generation process consists of an integrated environment comprising a visual editor and a compiler for the defined visual language.

DESCRIBING VISUAL LANGUAGES

In this section, we present an approach to formally describe visual notations, which can be used to describe many different classes of visual languages (Costagliola, De Lucia, Orefice, & Polese, 2002).

Basically, a visual language is formed by a set of visual sentences over a set of visual symbols from an alphabet. A visual sentence of a language *L* is a set of visual symbols whose spatial arrangement obeys to the syntax of *L*.

A *visual symbol type* is characterized by a set of syntactic attributes and a rule called *visual pattern*. Syntactic attributes are used to relate a visual symbol to others, and their values store the "position" of the visual symbol in the sentence. The visual pattern describes the set of graphical objects with the same visual symbol type, similarly to what happens in traditional string languages (Aho, Sethi, & Ullman, 1985) (in this case, the graphical objects play the role of the lexemes).

A *visual symbol* (*vsymbol*, for short) of type *X* is a graphical object satisfying the visual pattern of *X* and its syntactic attributes are completely instantiated. As an example, let us consider the vsymbol type *DECISION* representing the decision elements of flowcharts. In this case, as usual, the visual pattern describes elements such as rhombuses, whereas the syntactic attributes keep track of the links connected to the attaching points of the rhombuses. The decision element of the flowchart in Figure 1(a) is a vsymbol of type *DECISION*.

A *visual alphabet* Σ is a set of vsymbol types. A *visual sentence* (*vsentence*, for short) on Σ is a set of vsymbols $\{x_1, x_2, ..., x_n\}$ whose types are in Σ. Examples of vsentences are given in Figure 1. In Figure 1(a), the vsymbols are the blocks of the "flowchart." The syntactic attributes of each block correspond to its attaching points and keep track of the connections among the blocks. In the vsentence of Figure 1(b), some of the vsymbols are characterized by syntactic attributes corresponding to attaching lines visualized, in the figure, by thicker lines. Notice that the text in the vsentences may be considered as part of the graphical appearance of a vsymbol (such as a STOP sign), as simple vsymbols (see Figure 1(a)) or as sentences of string languages, such as C++ code fragments, UML labels (see Figure 1(b)), and so forth.

In general, the different types of syntactic attributes can be used to identify several classes of syntactic relations, which yield corresponding ways of modeling visual languages. Two main classes of syntactic relations are *connection* and *geometric* (Costagliola et al., 2002):

1.   A *connection* relation is specified between vsymbols whose syntactic attributes correspond to *attaching points* or *lines*, or more generally *regions*. In this case, visual sentences can be built by making the attaching regions of vsymbols touch each other or by connecting them through links explicitly

Figure 1. A flowchart (a), and a statechart diagram (b)

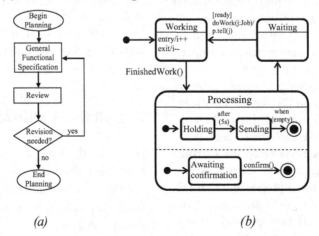

(a)   *(b)*

represented as lines, circles, arrows, and so forth. The values of the syntactic attributes store the connections linked to the corresponding attaching regions. One or more vsymbols can be connected to an attaching region. As an example, the vsymbol *Waiting* in Figure 1(b), representing a simple state in a statechart (Harel, 1988), has one attaching region represented by its border line, and two arrow vsymbols touching it through one of their attaching points.

2. A *geometric* relation between vsymbols is specified on the coordinates of the upper-left and the lower-right vertices of their bounding boxes. Sentences can be built by composing vsymbols through relations such as *containment, sibling, right-to*, etc. As an example, the vsymbol *Processing* in Figure 1(b) is related to the vsymbol *Sending* in its bounding box through the *containment* relation. As another example, the vsymbol *a* in the string *bacb* is related to the vsymbol *c* through the *right-to* relation. In this case, *right-to* is a visual counterpart of the string *concatenation* relation. As a consequence, it is possible to model string languages as a special case of visual languages.

Depending on the abstraction level of the visual language representation, syntactic relations may have an explicit visual representation. In this case, we call them *explicit relations*. As an example, the arrows in the flowchart of Figure 1(a) can be modeled either as vsymbols with two attaching points connected each to a different block or condition vsymbol, or as a connection relation linking the attaching regions of two vsymbols.

EXTENDED POSITIONAL GRAMMARS

The literature offers a variety of grammatical formalisms for the specification of visual languages,

which differ one from another under several aspects (Golin, 1991; Marriott, 1994; Minas, 2002; Rekers et al., 1997). In general, such formalisms extend traditional string grammars in that they rewrite sets or multisets of symbols rather than sequences, and specify several relationships between objects rather than the only concatenation relationship. As a consequence, the analysis of visual languages is much harder due to the high cost of parsing. Indeed, while strings naturally drive a sequential scanning of the symbols, no precise scanning order is implicit in multi-dimensional structures. Thus, parsing efficiency issue is a very relevant topic that has been widely investigated in the literature. Several methods have been proposed, which impose some restrictions to the form of the grammars balancing the ability to express visual languages and the efficiency of parsing techniques (Marriott et al., 1998).

The definition of *positional grammars* has been strongly influenced by the need of having an efficient parser able to process the generated languages (Costagliola et al., 1997). They were conceived as a simple extension of context-free string grammars to the case of two-dimensional symbolic languages. As a consequence, the use of LR parsing techniques has been natural. The result was the definition of the *positional LR* (or *pLR*) parsing methodology. This methodology has evolved in parallel with the grammar formalism.

However, positional grammars were not suitable to model some critical visual languages such as those belonging to the class *Graph[1]* since it does not provide mechanisms to cope with context, which are necessary for modeling many of the notations in this class. This was a considerable limitation, preventing, in part, the application of PGs to some important application fields such as software engineering. XPG overcomes this limitation thanks to the introduction of mechanisms for handling contextual information (Costagliola et al., 2004).

An *extended positional grammar* is a particular type of context-free[2] string attributed grammar (N, T ∪ POS, S, P) where:

- N is a finite nonempty set of *nonterminal* vsymbol types;
- T is a finite nonempty set of *terminal* vsymbol types, with $N \cap T = \varnothing$ and $T = T_T \cup T_F$ where T_T are *true terminals* and T_F are *false terminals*;
- POS is a finite set of binary relation identifiers, with $POS \cap N = \varnothing$ and $POS \cap T = \varnothing$;
- $S \in N$ denotes the starting vsymbol type;
- P is a finite nonempty set of productions having the following format:

$$A \rightarrow x_1 \mathbf{R}_1 x_2 \mathbf{R}_2 \ldots x_{m-1} \mathbf{R}_{m-1} x_m, \Delta, \Gamma$$

where A is a nonterminal vsymbol type, $x_1 \mathbf{R}_1 x_2 \mathbf{R}_2 \ldots x_{m-1} \mathbf{R}_{m-1} x_m$ is a linear representation with respect to POS where each x_i is a vsymbol type in $N \cup T$ and each R_j is partitioned in two sub-sequences

$$(<REL_1{}^{h_1}, \ldots, REL_k{}^{h_k}>, <REL_{k+1}{}^{h_{k+1}}, \ldots, REL_n{}^{h_n}>) \text{ with } 1 \le k \le n$$

The relation identifiers in the first sub-sequence of an $\mathbf{R}_j$ are called *driver relations*, whereas the ones in the second sub-sequence are called *tester relations*. During syntax analysis, driver relations are used to determine the next vsymbol to be scanned, whereas tester relations are used to check whether the last scanned vsymbol (terminal or nonterminal) is properly related to some previously scanned vsymbols.

Without loss of generality, we assume that there are no useless vsymbol types, and no unit and empty productions[1]:

- Δ is a set of rules used to synthesize the values of the syntactic attributes of A from those of $x_1, x_2, \ldots, x_m$;
- Γ is a set of triples $\{(T_j, Cond_j, \Delta_j)\}_{j=1,\ldots,t}$, $t \ge 0$, used to dynamically insert new terminal vsymbols in the input visual sentence during the parsing process. In particular:

  ○ T_j is the terminal vsymbol type of the vsymbol to be inserted in the input visual sentence;
  ○ $Cond_j$ is a pre-condition to be verified in order to insert T_j;
  ○ Δ_j is the rule used to compute the values of the syntactic attributes of T_j from those of $x_1, \ldots, x_m$.

In the following, we characterize the languages described by an extended positional grammar $XPG = (N, T \cup POS, S, P)$. We write $\alpha \Leftarrow \beta$ and say that β reduces to α in one step, if there exist δ, γ, A, η such that:

1. $A \rightarrow \eta, \Delta, \Gamma$ is a production in P;
2. $\beta = \delta \eta \gamma$;
3. $\alpha = \delta A' \pi \gamma$, where A' is a nonterminal whose attributes are set according to the rule Δ and π results from the application of the rule Γ.

We also write $\alpha \Leftarrow_i \beta$ to indicate that the reduction has been achieved by applying production *i*. Moreover, we write $\alpha \Leftarrow^* \beta$ and say that β reduces to α, if there exist $\alpha_0, \alpha_1, \ldots, \alpha_m$ ($m \ge 0$) such that:

$$\alpha = \alpha_0 \Leftarrow \alpha 1 \Leftarrow \ldots \Leftarrow \alpha_m = \beta$$

The sequence $\alpha_m, \alpha_{m-1}, \ldots, \alpha_0$ is called a *derivation* of α from β.

- A positional sentential form from S is a string β such that $S \Leftarrow^* \beta$;
- A positional sentence from S is a string β containing no nonterminals and no false terminals, and such that $S \Leftarrow^* \beta$.

A visual sentence is obtained by instantiating the physical appearance and the syntactic attributes of the true terminal vsymbol types of a positional sentence from *S* (this is meant to be realized by a *materialization function* PE [6]).

The *language described by an XPG*, $L(XPG)$, is the set of the visual sentences obtained from the starting vsymbol type S of *XPG*.

In the following, we define the notion of *reachability* between two vsymbols, which will be used in the description of the parsing technique.

Given the two pairs (x, k) and (y, j), where $x \in N \cup T, y \in T, k$ is a syntactic attribute of x, and j is a syntactic attribute of y, we say that (y, j) is reachable from (x, k) iff one of the following situations occurs:

1. $x = y$;
2. There exists a production $x \rightarrow x_1 R_1 x_2 \ldots x_i \ldots R_{m-1} x_m, \Delta, \Gamma$ in P such that attribute k of x is synthesized from attribute h of x_1 by means of Δ, and (y, j) is reachable from (x_1, h).

If (y, j) is reachable from (x, k), we also say that y is *reachable* from x.

In the following we show two examples of XPG grammars, the first describing a context-sensitive string language, and the second modeling a state transition diagram language.

Example 1: Let us consider the context-sensitive language $L = \{a^n b^n c^n \mid n \geq 1\}$. It is generated by the string grammar with the following productions:

1. $S \rightarrow a\,B\,S\,c$
2. $S \rightarrow a\,B\,c$
3. $B\,c \rightarrow b\,c$
4. $B\,a \rightarrow a\,B$
5. $B\,b \rightarrow b\,b$

where the nonterminals are S and B, and the terminals are a, b, and c. As a matter of fact, the sentence $a^2 b^2 c^2$ is obtained through the following derivation: $S \Leftarrow_1 aBSc \Leftarrow_2 aBaBcc \Leftarrow_3 aBabcc \Leftarrow_4 aaBbcc \Leftarrow_5 aabbcc$.

The extended positional grammar, which generates L can be obtained modifying this string grammar accordingly. In particular, the set of nonterminals is given by $N = \{S, B\}$ where each vsymbol type has two syntactic attributes, called head and tail, both specifying a position in the

plane. The set of terminals is given by $T = T_T = \{a, b, c\}$ ($T_F = \varnothing$) and have one syntactic attribute (the pair of coordinates of their centroid), referred to as head or tail interchangeably. As previously described, the right-to relation is the visual counterpart of the string concatenation relation. Thus, the set of relations is given by $POS = \{\textbf{\textit{right-to}}\}$ and the right-to relation can be defined as:

$u <\textbf{\textit{right-to}}> v$ if and only if $\exists! \; v \mid v_{headx} = u_{tailx} + 1$ and $v_{heady} = u_{taily}$

where $u, v \in N \cup T$. The set of productions P is described below.

(1') $S \rightarrow a <\textbf{\textit{right-to}}> B <\textbf{\textit{right-to}}> S <\text{right-to}> c$
   $\Delta: (S_{head} = a_{head}; S_{tail} = c_{tail})$
(2') $S \rightarrow a <\textbf{\textit{right-to}}> B <\textbf{\textit{right-to}}> c$
   $\Delta: (S_{head} = a_{head}; S_{tail} = c_{tail})$
(3') $B \rightarrow b <\textbf{\textit{right-to}}> c$
   $\Delta: (B_{head} = b_{head}; B_{tail} = b_{tail})$
   $\Gamma: \{(c'; \text{true}; c'_{head} = c_{head}, c'_{tail} = c_{tail})\}$
(4') $B \rightarrow a <\textbf{\textit{right-to}}> B'$
   $\Delta: (B_{head} = a_{head}; B_{tail} = a_{tail})$
   $\Gamma: \{(a'; \text{true}; a'_{head} = B'_{head}, a'_{tail} = B'_{tail})\}$
(5') $B \rightarrow b <\textbf{\textit{right-to}}> b'$
   $\Delta: (B_{head} = b_{head}; B_{tail} = b_{tail})$
   $\Gamma: \{(b''; \text{true}; b''_{head} = b'_{head}, b''_{tail} = b'_{tail})\}$

Notice that the prime marks are used to distinguish different occurrences of the same vsymbol type and the terminals in the left-hand side of the string grammar productions are moved in the Γ rules of the XPG productions.

Example 2: In this example, we introduce an XPG modeling state transition diagrams that recognize sentences on a and b. Let STD = $(N, T \cup POS, S, P)$ be the XPG for state transition diagrams characterized as follows. The set of nonterminals is given by $N = \{Graph, Node, Edge, NLabel, ELabel\}$ where the first two vsymbol types have one attaching region as a syntactic attribute, *Edge* has two attaching points as their syntactic attributes, the last two vsymbol types have two

Figure 2. A typical visual representation of nonterminals and terminals for the grammar STD

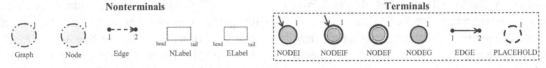

syntactic attributes, called *head* and *tail*, both specifying a position in the plane. *Graph* is the starting vsymbol type (i.e., $S = Graph$). The set of terminals is given by TT = {NODEI, NODEIF, NODEF, NODEG, EDGE, *a*, *b*, DIGIT} and TF = {PLACEHOLD}. The true terminals NODEI, NODEIF, NODEF, and NODEG represent the initial, the initial and final, the final, and the generic node, respectively, of a state transition diagram. As syntactic attributes, they have one attaching region corresponding to the borderline of the node, and one containment area corresponding to the circle area representing the node. The true terminal EDGE has two attaching points as their syntactic attributes corresponding to the start and end points of the edge. PLACEHOLD is a false terminal to be dynamically inserted in the input sentence during the parsing process. It has one attaching region as syntactic attribute. The vsymbol types *a* and *b* represent the labels of the edges and have two syntactic attributes, called *head* and *tail*, both specifying a position in the plane. Finally, DIGIT is a vsymbol type whose visual pattern matches the decimal digits 0 through 9. It is used to compose each nodes' label, and has two syntactic attributes, called *head* and *tail*, both specifying a position in the plane.

Typical instances of vsymbols for this language are graphically depicted in Figure 2. Here, each attaching region is represented by a bold line and each is identified by a number, each containment area is represented by a light gray area, while the attaching points are represented by bullets. In the following, the notation $Vsym_i$ denotes the attaching point *i* of the vsymbol *Vsym*.

The set of relations is given by POS = {$LINK_{i,j}$, *any*, *contains*, *edge-labelling*}, where:

- $LINK_{i,j}$ is defined as follows: a vsymbol *x* is in relation $LINK_{i,j}$ with a vsymbol *y* iff attaching point (or region) *i* of *x* is connected to attaching point (or region) *j* of *y*, and will be denoted as *i_j* to simplify the notation. Moreover, we use the notation *i_j* when describing the absence of a connection between two attaching areas *i* and *j*;

- The relation identifier *any* denotes a relation that is always satisfied between any pair of vsymbols;

- Contains is a containment geometric relation. In particular, if A is a vsymbol with a containment area as syntactic attribute and B is a vsymbol then A contains B if and only if B is inside the containment area of A. As an example from Figure 3(a) NODEI contains the digit 1 in its containment area;

- Edge-labelling is a geometric relation. In particular, if A is a vsymbol of type EDGE and B is a vsymbol representing a string label then A edge-labelling B if and only if B is close to A with respect to their syntactic attributes. As an example from Figure 3(a) the string labels a and b are close to the edges of the diagram.

Next, we provide the set of productions for describing state transition diagrams.

1. Graph → NODEI <*contains*> NLabel
    Δ: (Graph$_1$ = NODEI$_1$)
2. Graph → NODEIF <*contains*> NLabel
    Δ: (Graph$_1$ = NODEIF$_1$)
3. Graph → Graph' <<**1_1**>, <**1_2**>> Edge **2_1** Node
    Δ: (Graph$_1$ = Graph'$_1$ - Edge$_1$)

Γ: {(PLACEHOLD; $|Node_1| > 1$; PLACEHOLD$_1$ = Node$_1$ − Edge$_2$)}

4. Graph → Graph' <<**1_1**>, <**1_2**>> Edge
   Δ: (Graph1 = (Graph'$_1$ - Edge$_1$) - Edge$_2$)

5. Graph → Graph' <<**1_2**>, <**1_1**>> Edge **1_1** Node
   Δ: (Graph1 = Graph'$_1$ - Edge$_2$)
   Γ: {(PLACEHOLD; $|Node_1| > 1$; PLACEHOLD$_1$ = Node$_1$ − Edge$_1$)}

6. Graph → Graph' <*any*> PLACEHOLD
   Δ: (Graph$_1$ = Graph'$_1$ + PLACEHOLD$_1$)

7. Node → NODEG <*contains*> NLabel
   Δ: (Node$_1$ = NODEG$_1$)

8. Node → NODEF <*contains*> NLabel
   Δ: (Node$_1$ = NODEF$_1$)

9. Node → PLACEHOLD
   Δ: (Node$_1$ = PLACEHOLD$_1$)

10. Edge → EDGE <*edge-labelling*> ELabel
    Δ: (Edge$_1$ = EDGE$_1$, Edge$_2$ = EDGE$_2$)

11. NLabel → DIGIT
    Δ: (NLabel$_{head}$ = DIGIT$_{head}$, NLabel$_{tail}$ = DIGIT$_{tail}$)

12. NLabel → NLabel ' <*right-to*> DIGIT
    Δ: (NLabel$_{head}$ = NLabel'$_{head}$, NLabel$_{tail}$ = DIGIT$_{tail}$)

13. ELabel → a
    Δ: (ELabel$_{head}$ = a_{head}, ELabel$_{tail}$ = a_{tail})

14. ELabel → b
    Δ: (ELabel$_{head}$ = b_{head}, ELabel$_{tail}$ = b_{tail})

Notice that $Graph_1 = Graph'_1 − EDGE_1$ indicates set difference and is to be interpreted as follows: "the attaching area 1 of *Graph* has to be connected to whatever is attached to the attaching area 1 of *Graph'* except for the attaching point 1 of EDGE." Moreover, the notation $|Node_1|$ indicates the number of connections to the attaching area 1 of *Node*.

According to these rules, a state transition diagram is described by a graph defined as:

- An initial node containing a label (production 1) or as
- An initial-final node containing a label (production 2) or, recursively, as

- A graph connected to a node through an outgoing (production 3) or incoming (production 5) edge, or as
- A graph with a loop edge (production 4).

A node can be either a generic node containing a label (production 7) or a final node containing a label (production 8). An edge is labeled (production 10) by *a* (production 13) or *b* (production 14). A node label is the string concatenation of decimal digits (productions 11 and 12).

During the reduction process, the introduction of the PLACEHOLD false terminals (productions 3 and 5) and their successive processing (productions 6 and 9) allow us to keep knowledge of the source and the target node of each reduced edge. The same result could be achieved by using the terminal NODEG instead of PLACEHOLD. However, this would let the grammar describe also unconnected graph structures.

Figures 3(a-i) show the steps to reduce a state transition diagram for the language a^+b through the extended positional grammar *STD* previously shown. In particular, dashed ovals indicate the handles to be reduced and their labels indicate the productions to be used. The reduction process starts by applying production 11 to the digit inside the initial state, which is reduced to the nonterminal *NLabel*. Then, production 1 reduces the initial state and *NLabel* to the nonterminal *Graph*. Due to the Δ rule of production 1, *Graph* inherits all the connections of NODEI. Similarly, the application of productions 11 and 7 replace the unique NODEG and the digit of Figure 3(a) with the nonterminal *Node*. Figure 3(b) shows the resulting sentential form, and highlights the handle for the application of productions 13 and 10. The first reduces the edge label to the nonterminal *ELabel*, the latter reduces the terminal EDGE and *ELabel* to the nonterminal *Edge*. Due to the Δ rule of production 10, *Edge* inherits all the connections of EDGE. Figure 3(c) shows the resulting sentential form, and highlights the handle for the application of production 3. The vsymbol types *Graph*, *Edge*, and *Node* are then reduced to the new nonterminal *Graph*. Due to the Δ rule of

Figure 3. Reduction process for a state transition diagram

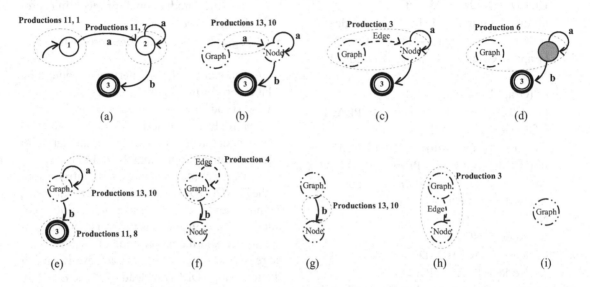

production 3, the new *Graph* is connected to all the remaining edges attached to the old *Graph*. Moreover, due to the Γ rule, since |*Node*| = 4 > 1, a new node PLACEHOLD is inserted in the input, and it is connected to all the remaining edges attached to the old *Node*. Figure 3(d) shows the resulting sentential form. Production 6 reduces the nonterminals *Graph* and PLACEHOLD to a new nonterminal *Graph*. By applying the Δ rule of production 6, the new *Graph* inherits all the connections to PLACEHOLD (see Figure 3(e)). After the application of productions 13, 10, 11, and 8 the sentential form reduces to the one shown in Figure 3(f). The subsequent application of productions 4, 9, 13, 10 and 3 reduces the original state transition diagram to the starting nonterminal in Figure 3(i), confirming that the visual sentence associated to the initial state transition diagram belongs to the visual language L(*STD*).

XpLR PARSING OF VISUAL LANGUAGES

The XpLR methodology is a framework for implementing visual systems based upon XPGs and LR parsing (Costagliola et al., 2004). An XpLR parser scans the input in a non-sequential way driven by the relations used in the grammar.

Lexical Analysis

The role of a lexical analyzer in the parsing of visual languages is to preprocess the input visual sentence in order to put it in a format suitable for the syntax analysis phase. In particular, the lexical analyzer associates each graphical object to a proper vsymbol type and instantiates its syntactic attributes. In the case of string languages, this means giving a value to the attribute *position*, which is the only attribute characterizing vsymbols in this language, and represents the position index of the vsymbol in a string. In the case of *Plex* visual languages (Feder, 1971), the attributes of vsymbols are attaching points numbered and represented by an array $ap[1],...,ap[n]$. Instantiating them for a vsymbol v means giving a value to each $ap[i]$, representing a unique label assigned to the link plugged into attaching point i of v. Similarly, in the case of *Graph* visual languages the attributes are attaching regions numbered and represented by an array $aps[1],..., aps[n]$ of sets. The value of $aps[i]$ for a vsymbol v is the set of

Figure 4. The lexical analysis of an activity diagram

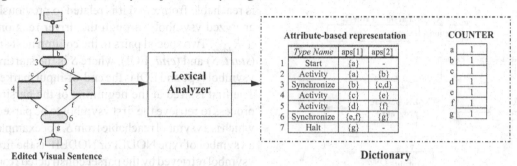

Edited Visual Sentence

	Attribute-based representation			COUNTER	
	Type Name	aps[1]	aps[2]	a	1
1	Start	{a}	-	b	1
2	Activity	{a}	{b}	c	1
3	Synchronize	{b}	{c,d}	d	1
4	Activity	{c}	{e}	e	1
5	Activity	{d}	{f}	f	1
6	Synchronize	{e,f}	{g}	g	1
7	Halt	{g}	-		

Dictionary

labels of the links plugged into attaching region *i* of *v*. If the input picture contains explicit relations (i.e., the relations have a graphical representation), its attribute-based representation is augmented with an array COUNTER containing an entry for each explicit relation. The entry COUNTER(r) for an explicit relation labeled *r* with degree *n* contains the value $n - 1$. This value indicates the number of binary relations describing *r* in any relative representation of the picture.

Figure 4 shows the attribute-based representation produced by the lexical analyzer on the input activity diagram. Here node and edge labels have been explicitly represented only to better describe the corresponding attribute-based representation. Since all the binary relations in the flowchart are explicit the output dictionary also includes an array COUNTER. Obviously, the task of identification of the vsymbols in a picture strongly depends on the visual editor used to compose the vsentence. In our approach, we assume that the editor includes a palette with the graphical appearance of the language vsymbols. Thus, each graphical object in the edited sentence has associated detailed information about the vsymbol it represents, which simplifies the creation of a dictionary during the scanning of the input picture.

The XpLR Parser

The components of an XpLR parser are shown in Figure 5 and are detailed in the following. The input to the parser is the dictionary, called D_p, stores the attribute-based representation of a picture as produced by the lexical analyzer. No parsing order is defined on the vsymbols in the dictionary. The parser retrieves the vsymbols in the dictionary through a find operation, driven by the relations in the grammar. The parser implicitly builds and parses a linear representation from the input attribute-based representation. During the parsing phase, all the visited vsymbols, and the traversed explicit binary relations, are marked in order to guarantee that each vsymbol and each explicit relation be considered at most once. The marking of an explicit binary relation *REL* labeled *r* is done by decreasing the entry COUNTER(r) by 1. The 0-entry of the dictionary always refers to the end-of-input symbol EOI. Similarly, to the usual end-of-string marker, the end-of-input symbol EOI is returned to the parser if and only if the input has been completely visited (i.e., all the input vsymbols have been parsed), and all the explicit relations have been traversed. These conditions are signaled by having all the vsymbols marked and COUNTER(r) = 0 for each explicit relation *r*, respectively.

Figure 5. The architecture of an XpLR parser

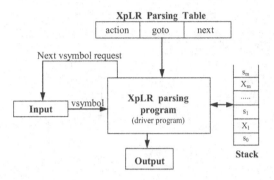

An instance of the stack has the general format $s_0 X_1 s_1 X_2 s_2 ... X_m s_m$, where s_m is the stack top, X_i is a vsymbol, and s_i is a generic state of the parsing table. The parsing algorithm uses the state on the top of the stack, and the vsymbol currently under examination, to access a specific entry of the parsing table in order to decide the next action to execute.

An XpLR parsing table is composed of a set of rows and is divided in three main sections: *action*, *goto*, and *next*. The *action* and *goto* sections are similar to the ones used in LR parsing tables for string languages (Aho et al., 1985), whereas the *next* section is used by the parser to select the next vsymbol to be processed. An entry *next*[k] for a state s_k contains a pair (R_{driver}, x), which drives the parser in selecting the next vsymbol y such that it is reachable from x and it is related to previously analyzed vsymbols through the driver relations in R_{driver}. Two special pairs in the column next are (**start**, S) and (**end**, EOI), where S is the starting vsymbol type and EOI is the end-of-input marker. The first is used at the beginning of the parsing process to retrieve the first vsymbol to be parsed, which is a vsymbol reachable from S. For example, a vsymbol of type NODEI or NODEIF is the first vsymbol retrieved by the parser constructed from the grammar *STD*. The latter is used to check whether the whole input sentence has been parsed. If all the vsymbols have been analyzed and all the explicit relations have been considered, then the query returns the EOI marker. Figure 6 shows a simple example of parsing table for a reduced version of the grammar *STD* of example 2.2 by considering only productions 1, 2, 4, 10, 13, and 14, and disregarding node labels.

An *action* entry has one of the following four values:

1. "R_{tester}: *shift s*" where R_{tester} is a possibly empty sequence of tester relations and s is a state;

2. *Reduce* by a grammar production (*i*) A → β, shown in the table as *r i*;

3. *Accept*;

Figure 6. An XpLR parsing table

State	ACTION						GOTO		NEXT
	NODEI	NODEIF	EDGE	a	b	EOI	Graph	Edge	
0	:sh2	:sh3					:1		(start, Graph)
1			:sh5			acc		1_2: sh4	(1_1, Edge) (end, EOI)
2	r1	r1	r1	r1	r1	r1			-
3	r2	r2	r2	r2	r2	r2			-
4	r4	r4	r4	r4	r4	r4			-
5	r4	r4	r4	r4	r4	r4			-
6				:sh7	:sh8				(edge-labeling, ELabel)
7	r13	r13	r13	r13	r13	r13			-
8	r14	r14	r14	r14	r14	r14			-

4. *Error* shown as an empty entry.

A *goto* entry contains "R_{tester}: s" where R_{tester} is a possibly empty sequence of tester relations and s is a state.

A *shift* or *goto* action is executed only if all the relations in the corresponding R_{tester} are true, or if R_{tester} is empty. As an example, let us consider the XpLR(0) parsing table in Figure 6. If the current state corresponds to row 1, and the vsymbol obtained from a reduction is *Edge*, then the parser executes the goto **1_2**: 4, that is, if the tester relation **1_2** holds between *Edge* and the vsymbol on the stack top, then the parser goes to state 4.

A *configuration* of an XpLR parser is a pair $(s_0 X_1 s_1 X_2 \ldots X_m s_m, t_1 \ldots t_n)$ where the first component is the stack contents and the second component represents the input unmarked vsymbols.

The XpLR parsing program uses two functions *Fetch_Vsymbol* and *Test* to retrieve the row index in the dictionary of the next vsymbol to be

parsed and to validate the tester relations between vsymbols (see Box 1).

Let us suppose that the parser is in the configuration $(s_0 X_1 s_1 X_2 \ldots X_m s_m, t_1 \ldots t_n)$. The XpLR parsing program checks the entries *next*$[s_m]$ of the parsing table. If *Fetch_Vsymbol*(*next*$[s_m]$) is not *null*, then the resulting pointer *ip* points to the next vsymbol t_j to be processed, with $1 \leq j \leq n$, which is used to consult the parsing action table entry *action*$[s_m, T_j]$ where T_j is the type of t_j. The configurations resulting after each of the three types of moves are as follows:

1. If *action*$[s_m, t_j]$ = "R_{tester}: *shift s*," the parser executes a shift move if all the relations in the corresponding R_{tester} are true, entering the configuration $(s_0 X_1 s_1 X_2 \ldots X_m s_m t_j s, t_1 \ldots t_{j-1} t_{j+1} \ldots t_n)$;

2. If *action*$[s_m, t_j]$ = "*accept*," parsing is completed;

Box 1. XpLR parsing program

```
Algorithm: The XpLR parsing algorithm.
Input: A visual sentence in attribute-based representation and an XpLR parsing table.
Output: A bottom-up analysis of the visual sentence if this is syntactically correct, an error message otherwise.
Method: Start with the state s₀ on the top of the stack.
repeat forever
    let s be the state on the stack top
    set ip = Fetch_Vsymbol(next[s])
    if ip is not null then
    let b the vsymbol pointed by ip
    if action[s, b] = "accept" then "success" and exit;
    if action[s, b] is a conditioned shift of type "Rₜ: shift s'" then
        if Rₜ is empty or Test(RELₕ, b) is true for each RELₕ ∈ Rₜ
            then push b and then s' on the stack;
            else emit "syntax error" and exit;
        else emit "syntax error" and exit;
    else if action[s, c] = reduce A → x₁R₁x₂R₂…Rₘ₋ₓₘ, Δ, Γ with c any terminal vsymbol type then
        compute the syntactic attributes of A according to the synthesis rule Δ
        apply rule Γ, if present, and pop 2 * m elements from the stack
        let s' be the new state on the stack top
        if goto[s', A] is a conditioned goto of type "Rₜ: s" then
            if Rₜ is empty or Test(RELₕ, A) is true for each RELₕ ∈ Rₜ then
                push A and then s'' on the stack and
                output the production A → x₁R₁x₂R₂…Rₘ₋ₓₘ, Δ, Γ
            else emit "syntax error" and exit;
        else emit "syntax error" and exit;
    else emit "syntax error" and exit;
endrepeat
```

3. If $action[s_m, t_j] = $ "*error*," the parser has discovered an error.

Otherwise, if $next[s_m]$ is empty, then a reduce action is required. The reduction $action[s_m, t_j]$ = "*reduce* $A \rightarrow x_1 R_1 x_2 R_2 ... R_{m-1} x_m, \Delta, \Gamma$," with t_j terminal vsymbol, is accomplished by calculating the syntactic attributes of A as specified by Δ, possibly introducing vsymbols according to the Γ rule, popping $2 * m$ elements out of the stack, and pushing A on the stack top. If s' is the state on the stack top after popping the $2 * m$ elements, then the next state s'' of the parser is given by the entry $goto[s', A]$. Also in this case, the *goto* action may be triggered by an action condition to be verified between objects below the stack top and the object A.

VLDesk

In this section, we briefly summarize the visual language desk (VLDesk) (Costagliola et al., 2004), a system for the automatic generation of visual programming environments supporting the definition and construction of visual notations modeled through XPGs. VLDesk provides a "desk" where a developer can find an integrated set of tools supporting the whole process for modeling and implementing visual languages. The main components of VLDesk are the *symbol editor*, the *visual grammar editor*, the *textual production editor,* and the *language inspector*.

The *symbol editor* supports the language developer in the complete definition of vsymbols. Basically, for each vsymbol, it allows us to draw its physical aspect, to associate the syntactic attributes, and to "attach" a visual or a textual annotation to it (in order to define hierarchical visual languages). Once defined, each vsymbol is then inserted into a terminals palette.

The *visual grammar editor* is a visual component supporting the language designer in the specification of an XPG grammar and semantic routines. This specification is translated into a YACC-like definition of the visual language. The designer can further refine it through the *textual grammar editor*.

The *language inspector* makes it possible for VLDesk to directly support the hierarchical visual notations. It allows the language designer/implementer to easily navigate through the specifications of the visual notations composing the hierarchy.

Once the visual notation has been completely specified, VLDesk automatically generates an integrated visual programming environment (VPE). In particular, VLDesk generates a VPE composed of a visual sentence editor based on the *terminals palette* built with the *symbol editor* and the visual language XpLR-based compiler generated from the XPG grammar and semantic routines. A final user can then use the VPE to compose and process visual sentences from the implemented language.

FUTURE TRENDS

In the future, we intend to extend the XpLR parsing methodology to enhance the functionalities of the graphical editors generated with the VLDesk system. A first attempt in this direction is represented by the introduction of syntax-directed scanning capabilities within the generated visual editors (Costagliola & Deufemia, 2003). This is achieved by combining the LR-based visual language parsing techniques with the incremental generalized LR parsing techniques developed for string languages (Tomita, 1991). In particular, the generated editors support the editing of visual sentences in a free-order style, whereas the underlying parsers incrementally analyze the visual sentences during their construction, providing an immediate feedback to the user. Another interesting issue to be investigated is an error handling strategy for the XpLR parsing algorithm, that is, a technique that should enable the parser to detect and report as many syntax errors as possible in one parsing step. This also means that the parser should be able to guess recovery actions for detected syntactic errors and apply them in order to be able to continue parsing the rest of the input sentence. Error handling becomes of vital importance in unconstrained free-order editors. In fact, if an editor allows incomplete sketches to be drawn, the parser should be able to report as many errors as possible. Moreover, an effective error handling technique is absolutely necessary for any visual language parser used to facilitate edit-and-compile style visual programming. Incremental parsing and analysis is one possible way to address error-handling issues (Chok & Marriott, 2003). However, another fundamental issue in error handling is the adoption of proper interaction paradigms to communicate error-related information. In fact, the visual programming environment of a visual language should provide informative and highly interactive error reporting facilities.

CONCLUSION

In this chapter, we have presented an overview of the extended positional grammars and the XpLR parsing methodology. Extended positional grammars follow the attributed based approach in the representation of the input and the predictive parsing approach for processing visual languages. XPGs can be used as basis for the implementation of visual languages in the same way as context-free string grammars are for traditional programming languages. So far, this approach has been successfully used to define and implement visual languages for software design methodologies, emerging multimedia and Web development methodologies, workflow management systems, E-business specification tools, document layouts, and many others.

Other tools for the automatic generation of visual language compilers from grammar specifications have also been recently proposed. The main differences are related to the underlying grammar formalisms, which are able to specify different classes of visual languages, and have parsing algorithms with different performances. For instance, the *Penguins* system generates visual editors that support the intelligent diagram metaphor (Chok et al., 2003). Those editors allow the diagrams to be constructed in free form and in any order, and the parsers underlying the editors analyze the diagrams as it is being constructed, performing error correction, and collecting geometric constraints. The *Penguins* system uses constraint multiset grammars (CMGs) for the specification of the visual language. *VisPro* is a set of visual programming tools, which employs the formalism of the reserved graph grammars (RGG) to specify the language grammar (Zhang, Zhang, & Cao, 2001). *GenGEd* is a system for generating visual language editors, which comes with a visual specification tool that allows users to specify the visual language's pictorial objects as well as its syntax rules in the same notation as used in the generated editor (Bardhol, 2002). Finally, *DiaGen* is a rapid-prototyping tool based on hypergraph transformation for generating diagram editors, which support both free hand editing and syntax-directed editing (Minas, 2002). A visual language is specified by a hypergraph language and a mapping from hypergraphs to their visual representation as diagrams.

REFERENCES

Aho, A. V., Sethi, R., & Ullman, J. D. (1985). *Compilers, principles, techniques, and tools*. New York: Addison-Wesley.

Bardhol, R. (2002). A visual environment for visual languages. *Science of Computer Programming, 44*(2), 181-203.

Chok, S. S., & Marriott, K. (2003). Automatic generation of intelligent diagram editors. *ACM Transactions on Computer-Human Interaction, 10*(3), 244-276.

Costagliola, G., & Deufemia, V. (2003). Visual language editors based on LR parsing techniques. *Proceeding of SIGPARSE/ACL 8th International Workshop in Parsing Technologies* (pp. 79-90).

Costagliola, G., De Lucia, A., Orefice, S., & Polese, G. (2002). A classification framework to support the design of visual languages. *Journal of Visual Languages and Computing, 13*(6), 573-600.

Costagliola, G., De Lucia, A., Orefice, S., & Tortora, G. (1997). A parsing methodology for the implementation of visual systems. *IEEE Transactions on Software Engineering, 23*(12), 777-799.

Costagliola, G., Deufemia, V., & Polese, G. (2004). A framework for modeling and implementing visual notations with applications to software engineering. *ACM Transactions on Software Engineering and Methodology, 13*(4), 431-487.

Feder, J. (1971). Plex languages. *Information Science, 3,* 225-241.

Golin, E. J. (1991). Parsing visual languages with picture layout grammars. *Journal of Visual Languages and Computing, 2*(4), 1-23.

Harel, D. (1988). On visual formalisms. *Communications of the ACM, 31*(5), 514-530.

Helm, R., & Marriott, K. (1990). Declarative specification of visual languages. *Proceedings of the IEEE Workshop on Visual Languages* (pp. 98-103). IEEE Press.

Johnson, S. C. (1978). *YACC: Yet another compiler compiler.* Murray Hills, NJ: Bell Laboratories.

Marriott, K. (1994). Constraint multiset grammars. *Proceedings of the IEEE Symposium on Visual Languages* (pp. 118-125). IEEE Press.

Marriott, K., & Meyer, B. (1998). *Visual language theory.* Springer-Verlag.

Minas, M. (2002). Concepts and realization of a diagram editor generator based on hypergraph transformation. *Science of Computer Programming, 44*(2), 157-180.

Rekers, J., & Schürr, A. (1997). Defining and parsing visual languages with layered graph grammars. *Journal of Visual Languages and Computing, 8*(1), 27-55.

Tomita, M. (1991). *Generalized LR parsing.* Kluwer Academic Publishers.

Uskudarli, S. M., & Dinesh, T. B. (1995). Towards a visual programming environment generator for algebraic specifications. *Proceedings of the IEEE Symp. Visual Languages* (pp. 234-241). IEEE Press.

Zhang, K., Zhang, D. Q., & Cao, J. (2001). Design, construction, and application of a generic visual language generation environment. *IEEE Transactions on Software Engineering, 27*(4), 289-307.

ENDNOTES

[1] Graph languages are a generalization of Plex languages since the relations act on attaching regions of the vsymbols they connect. Graph languages are suitable for modeling general graph-structured visual languages whose vsymbols can have any number of connections.

[2] Here "context-free" means that the grammar productions are in "context-free" format and does not refer to the computational power of the formalism.

Chapter VI
Visual Notation Interpretation and Ambiguities

Arianna D'Ulizia
IRPPS-CNR, Italy

Patrizia Grifoni
IRPPS-CNR, Italy

Maurizio Rafanelli
IASI-CNR, Italy

ABSTRACT

This chapter introduces a classification of ambiguities in visual languages and discusses the ambiguities that occur in spatial visual query languages. It has adopted the definition of visual language given in Bottoni, Costabile, Levialdi, and Mussio (1995) as a set of visual sentences, each formed by an image, a description, an interpretation function, and a materialization function. It proposed a distinction between ambiguities produced by 1-n relationship between an image and its description, and ambiguities due to imprecision produced by the user's behavior during the interaction. Furthermore, the authors hope that this comprehensive classification of ambiguities may assist in the definition of visual languages in order to allow the user to communicate through visual notations by avoiding having to formulate sentences that have multiple interpretations.

INTRODUCTION

The use of visual notations in computer science has been having a significant and growing interest in recent years. People usually integrate different images, icons, sketches, and written words, organizing them in complex structures in order to communicate. People have a tendency to intuitively adopt visual communication approaches. Visual information is largely used in the human computer interaction also. However, the intuitive use of visual information presents some problems such as its intrinsic ambiguity. For example, scientific and engineering artifacts must be precisely represented through visual notations so the unambiguous definition of these notations is an important issue. Icons, diagrams, sketches, and visual representations are used to model objects, express the relationships between them, and formulate sentences. Communication through visual elements has led to the definition of visual languages. A visual language (VL) is based on simple visual elements (glyphs, graphemes) to construct characteristic structures (CSs) (Bottoni, Costabile, & Mussio, 1999) that can be grouped to form the visual sentence. A characteristic structure is a set "of image pixels, which form functional or perceptual units" for the user (Bottoni et al., 1999), and can be grouped to form structured visual sentences. According to the definition provided in Bottoni Costabile, Levialdi, and Mussio (1995), a visual language is a set of visual sentences, and a visual sentence is given by an image, its description, its interpretation function, and its materialization function.

Different definitions of ambiguity in visual languages are provided in literature. Among them, Futrelle distinguishes between lexical and syntactic ambiguities (Futrelle, 1999): when a characteristic structure or an image associated with a visual sentence is unable to exactly express the user's intentions, the system may produce an erroneous interpretation (i.e., 1-n associations between the image produced by the user and its description). Ambiguities are generally produced by: (1) the language, which can produce such one-to-many relationships, and (2) imprecision introduced by interaction behaviors producing visual sentences. In the first case, a characteristic structure or an image can assume more than one meaning. The second case is connected with incorrect/imprecise information, which does not permit an unequivocal interpretation of the image produced by the drawing actions.

This chapter proposes a classification of ambiguities in visual languages from the perspective of human-computer interaction and discusses a specific example of such languages—spatial query languages—and their ambiguities.

CLASSIFICATION OF AMBIGUITIES IN VISUAL LANGUAGES

This chapter analyzes ambiguities in visual languages to support different functions such as designing, browsing, and/or querying, from the perspective of human-computer interaction.

The notion of visual language introduced in Bottoni, Costabile, Levialdi and Mussio (1995) is used to discuss ambiguities in interpretation.

Bottoni, Costabile, Levialdi and Mussio (1995) define a visual language as a set of visual sentences. A visual sentence is a triplet $<i,d,<int, mat>>$ where i is an image, d is a description, int is an interpretation function, and mat a materialization function. Several *images* can *materialize* the same *description* and one image can have n interpretations that produce descriptions of the visual sentence.

This analysis is carried out considering both: (1) the ambiguities of the language produced by a 1-n relationship between the image and its description, and (2) ambiguities due to imprecision produced by a 1-m relationship between the user's drawing (the sketch produced by the user's actions and their imprecision) and the description produced by its interpretation.

Ambiguity arises when the interpretation and materialization functions (Bottoni et al., 1995) are unable to univocally associate one image with its description, and vice-versa. In this chapter, we only consider ambiguities produced by the interpretation function on the system side. Favetta and Aufaure-Portier (2000) propose a taxonomy of ambiguities for visual GIS (geographical information system) query languages based on the previous definition of visual language.

Each of the user's actions (or commands) produces a visual representation (image), which has to be interpreted by the system. Likewise, any materialization produced by the system must be interpreted by the user (Figure 1).

Figure 1. The human-computer interaction process

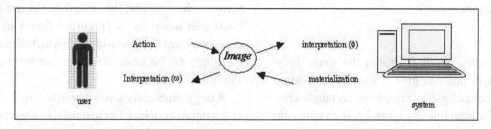

Each of the ambiguities connected with the system's interpretation function can be classified as a case of "recognition ambiguity," introduced in Mankoff, Hudson, and Abowd (2000). A "recognition ambiguity results when a recognizer returns more than one possible interpretation of the user's input."

Language Ambiguities Produced by a 1-n Relationship between an Image and its Description

The classification of ambiguities as lexical or syntactic (Futrelle, 1999) is generally valid for all visual languages. From the perspective of interaction, they can be considered as connected with the interpretation function.

Lexical Ambiguity

Lexical ambiguity is also known as *semantic ambiguity* and involves alternative meanings of simple items. It arises when (1) a characteristic structure has more than one generally accepted meaning, (2) a relationship between two characteristic structures has more than one generally accepted meaning, or (3) the user's intention for the image associated with a visual sentence is unclear. The latter is the case of *target ambiguity,* introduced in Mankoff, Hudson and Abowd (2000).

Three examples of these sub-classes of lexical ambiguities are given next.

As an example of a characteristic structure with more than one generally accepted meaning, we consider a rectangular shape. It can (for example) have the following accepted meanings:

Figure 2. Example of a characteristic structure with more than one generally accepted meaning

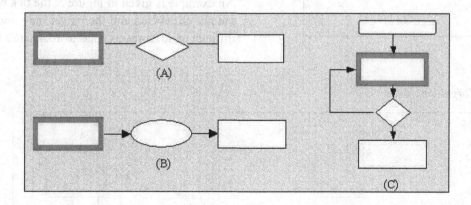

- Entity
- External agent
- Action

It therefore needs to match the shape in a grammar in order to give it a unique meaning within a restricted context. So the rectangle created by the bold line in Figure 2A is an entity in the context of an entity-relationship model, an "external agent" in the data flow diagram context (Figure 2B), and an "action" in the flowchart context (Figure 2C).

As another example of language ambiguity, let us consider the interpretation of a relationship between characteristic structures with more than one generally accepted meaning. The image associated to the visual sentence in Figure 3 involves three characteristic structures: a line, a rectangle, and an oval. If the visual sentence has to specify that the line crosses the rectangle, the rectangle

Figure 3. Ambiguity due to not required spatial relationships between two of the three characteristic structures forced in a two-dimensional space

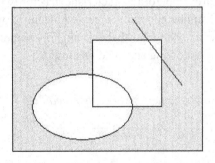

overlaps the oval, and no relationships are given between the oval and the line, then the use of a two-dimensional image (Figure 3) forces an unnecessary spatial relationship with which different meanings can be associated. In other words, an ambiguity is created.

A target ambiguity arises when the target of the user's input is unclear. For instance, in Figure 4A, it is not clear on which characteristic structure the user is focusing his or her attention. The system may thus give an ambiguous interpretation of the user's information goal. It may therefore be necessary to make the information goal explicit by (for example) specifying it with an arrow pointing to the target (Figure 4B).

This chapter uses this notion for visual spatial query languages, defining a target ambiguity as the ambiguity introduced when: (1) the target of the user's input is unclear and/or (2) the target of the user's query is unclear.

Syntactic Ambiguity

Syntactic ambiguity is also known as *structural ambiguity* and arises when the role played by a language element in a sentence is unclear. There are three subclasses of syntactic ambiguity: *gap, attachment,* and *analytical ambiguity.*

The first (gap ambiguity) arises when an element of the sentence is omitted, producing a gap. An example is given in Figure 5: the tick marks are not all labeled and the parser may find this difficult to interpret, as it has to associate a value

Figure 4. Target ambiguity

and a meaning to every tick mark, whether the value is given implicitly or explicitly.

The second subclass comprises attachment ambiguities. This is the ambiguity that arises in matching a characteristic structure to the text item labeling it. For instance, the parser could have the same difficulties in associating text labels and characteristic structures in Figure 6. The "A" label might refer to the line or the region identified by

Figure 5. Gap ambiguity

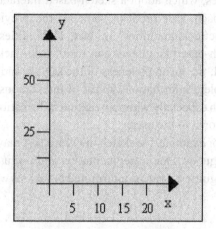

Figure 6. Attachment ambiguity

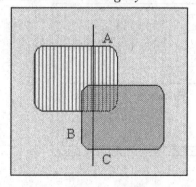

the striped texture; the "B" label might refer to the region identified by the striped texture or the region identified by the dotted texture; while the "C" label might refer to the region identified by the dotted texture or to the line.

The third class comprises analytical ambiguities. These arise when the categorization of a structure is itself in doubt. For instance in Figure 7, the analytical ambiguity is due to the fact that the oval shape labeled "Relation node" in the lower left corner looks like an element of the diagram, but doesn't belong to it because it is actually an element of the key.

Segmentation and Occlusion Ambiguities

This section introduces the concepts of *segmentation ambiguity* and *occlusion ambiguity* (Futrelle, 1999; Mankoff et al., 2000). The first can be considered as a kind of syntactic ambiguity, more specifically a kind of analytical ambiguity. Segmentation ambiguity is more clearly observed when diagram notations are used. Diagrams are replete with a variety of ambiguities, as detailed in Futrelle (1999). Many of these ambiguities are subtle and difficult to resolve.

As any image can be formed by a number of subparts (characteristic structures), segmentation ambiguity arises when a portion of the image can be interpreted as a characteristic structure or its part.

Figure 7. Analytical ambiguity

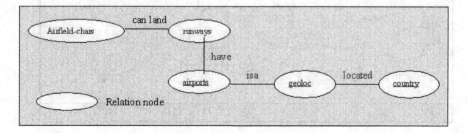

Figure 8. Segmentation ambiguity

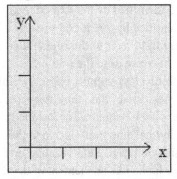

Figure 8 gives an example of segmentation ambiguity. The short lines in the lower left corner could represent two tick marks or the ends of the x- and y-axis lines.

The parser may find it difficult to understand if these short lines are entities themselves or part of the long axis lines.

Let us now introduce the occlusion ambiguity. This arises from the overlap of different elements, causing problems in understanding if the elements are used separately or are the components of only one characteristic structure.

For instance, a simple way to create a table with a box containing its name as shown in Figure 9, is to create two different rectangular shapes with one overlying the other so that only the small visible rectangle containing the table name is relevant.

Two rectangles could therefore be interpreted as a unique characteristic structure. Visual languages, which adopt a sketch-based interaction approach, can produce some of the previous syntactic ambiguities. In fact, ambiguities in sketch-based languages can result from lack of detail, the incompleteness of the sketch, and incomplete information typical of interactions by sketch especially when contextual information is unknown to the user.

For example, the sketch in Figure 10A may be ambiguous. Due to segmentation and occlusion ambiguities, it can be interpreted in various ways

Figure 9. Occlusion ambiguity

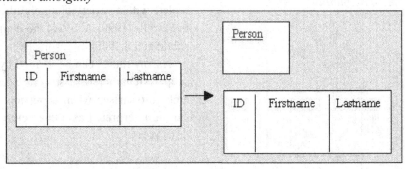

Figure 10. A sketch and some possible interpretations

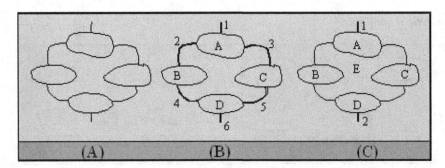

depending on the parsed symbols; two of these interpretations produce Figures 10B and 10C. Figure 10B considers the sketch as formed by four closed shapes (A, B, C, D) and six polylines (1-6). Figure 10C considers the sketch as formed by five closed shapes (A, B, C, D, E) and just two polylines (1-2). Obviously, because the sketch is a diagram, the correct interpretation will produce Figure 10B. However, changing the application domain can lead to changes in determining the correct interpretation. So if Figure 10A is not a diagram but a map, Figure 10C could be the correct interpretation.

Ambiguities Due to Imprecision Produced by Human Computer-Interaction Behavior

Imprecision and noise are introduced by users in their interaction behavior (drawing) and/or by tools and sensors. For this reason, signs in the sketch may not be parsed univocally. The information provided by the sketch may thus be insufficient to identify a unique interpretation.

Imprecision resulting from the user's interaction behavior can produce difficulties in recognizing features that identify characteristic structures of the visual sentence. For example, when a user sketches a rectangle with insufficient precision, the system could interpret it as an ellipse. This example introduces the shape ambiguity class.

Figure 12. The constraints ambiguity

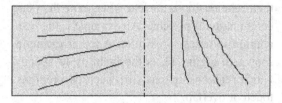

Figure 13. Relationship ambiguity

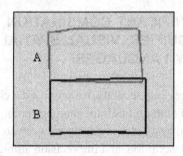

An example of ambiguity due to imprecision in the user's sketch behavior is shown in Figure 11A. This might represent (1) a rectangle (Figure 11B) or (2) an oval (Figure 11C).

Another class of ambiguity caused by imprecise interaction behavior is the constraint (properties) ambiguity. This concerns the evaluation of unary predicates that inspect shape properties. An example is given by the classification of a line into vertical, oblique, or horizontal line. Considering the lines shown in Figure 12, the question is to identify which of these the system will classify as horizontal, vertical, or oblique.

The third class of ambiguities caused by imprecision is relationship ambiguity. This arises when

Figure 11. A shape-ambiguous sketch and some possible interpretations

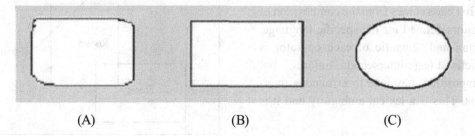

(A)   (B)   (C)

a number of shapes are in close proximity and their relationship is unclear when more than one combination is possible. An example is the *near* relation to assess proximity. Another example, shown in Figure 13, is the inability to specify which relationship exists between two regions: touch or overlap.

A SIGNIFICANT COMBINATION OF AMBIGUITIES: VISUAL SPATIAL QUERY LANGUAGES

In the previous sections, we proposed a classification of ambiguities into: language ambiguities produced by a 1:n relationship between an image and its description, and imprecision ambiguities produced by human-computer interaction behavior. In Carpentier and Mainguenaud (2002), a similar classification was proposed for visual spatial query languages. This classification distinguishes two ambiguity types: visual and selection ambiguities. The first arises when a given visual representation of a query may correspond with several interpretations and descriptions, and can be likened to the language ambiguity described in the previous sections. In Carpentier and Mainguenaud. (2002), this class is referred to as "interpretation ambiguity." The second type arises when several metaphors may correspond to a given selection, and can be considered similar to materialization ambiguity.

Calcinelli and Mainguenaud (1991) classified ambiguities for visual spatial query languages into three classes: visual semantic, level of abstraction, and query label.

The first class comes from the composition of the operators defined for the specific language. The syntax and semantic of each operator is clearly defined (e.g., intersection, union...), but their composition may lead to erroneous interpretations. This is a lexical ambiguity and it is caused by a relationship between two characteristic structures with more than one generally accepted meaning.

The second ambiguity class (level of abstraction) can be divided into two subclasses: the different semantic level and the logical link between the operators. The first concerns the difference in defining and representing the same operator in two different languages, which will thus produce a different result for the same query. The second arises when different operators cannot be logically linked so the query can lead to incorrect interpretations. These are similar to lexical ambiguities.

The third class (query label ambiguity) can be likened to the attachment ambiguity.

Some examples of ambiguities in visual spatial query languages are given next. First, let us introduce the concept of *user's mental query model* (Calcinelli et al., 1991): this affects the semantic that the user gives to the information. This model and how it influences correct query formulation is considered herein. The user's mental query model is the semantic of the query from the user's point of view (in his or her mind). Consider two examples of lexical ambiguities for spatial query languages. The user has in mind the query with the following textual expression:

Figure 14. Ambiguity due to a not required spatial relationship between two of the three characteristic structures in a visual query

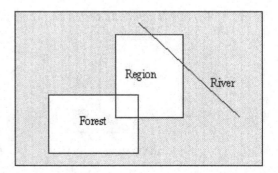

Figure 15. Visual queries for the same NL query

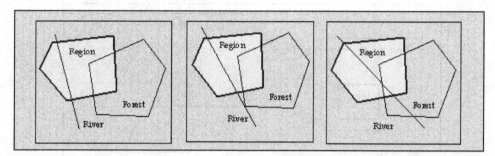

Find all the regions passed through by a river and partially overlapping a forest

Let us suppose the user is not interested in the relationship between the river and forest and there are no explicit relationships between them. Therefore, in the user's mind there are no specific relationships between any river and any forest (i.e., any relationship is good). Drawing the pictorial query as in Figure 14, the pictorial query language interprets it as "Find all the regions, which are passed through by a river and partially overlap a forest, with the river disjoined from the forest."

The user's mental query model, whose textual description is "Find all the regions passed through by a river and partially overlap a forest," could be completely expressed visually considering the visual sentences containing all the possible spatial relationships between river and forest (Figure 15).

The complete expression of the query in natural language without any ambiguity is "Find all the regions, which are passed through by a river and partially overlap a forest, irrespective of the topological relationships between the river and the forest."

However, when the user draws the characteristic structure representing a forest and another representing a river, he or she cannot avoid representing at least one topological relationship between them. This ambiguity is due to the fact that the two-dimensional space used for the image associated with the query's visual sentence forces

at least one of the possible relationships between river and forest to be represented. The ambiguity in Figure 14 can be viewed as the visual semantic ambiguity defined in Calcinelli and Mainguenaud (1991). Furthermore, an attachment ambiguity can also be observed.

A second example of lexical ambiguity, which frequently characterizes the visual spatial query languages, is target ambiguity.

Let us suppose the user has in mind the query with the following textual description:

Find all the provinces that have inside a lake

The image associated with the visual sentence expressing this query is shown in Figure 16A.

Let us now suppose that the user's "mental query model" is coherent with the following query:

Find all the regions with an overlapping forest

The image associated with the visual sentence for this query is shown in Figure 16B.

In the first case, the user can select the target by clicking on the province away from the lake, or by clicking on the province over the lake. Similarly, in the second case the user can select the target clicking on the region in its part separate from or in common with (overlapping) the forest.

In both cases, if the user clicks on the part in common between the two features, the language can result in an ambiguity, and the user must

Figure 16. Examples of target specification

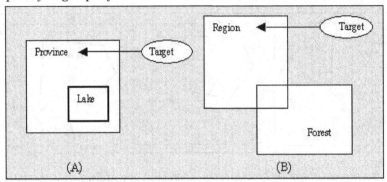

Figure 17. The same visual query represented with different languages

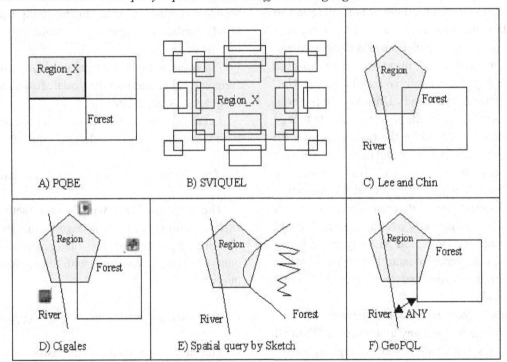

specify the feature (region or lake in the first case, region or forest in the second) that he or she has selected as the target.

Figure 17 shows the images associated with visual sentences according to different visual query languages for the following query:

Find all the regions passed through by a river and partially overlapping a forest

PQBE (Papadias & Sellis, 1995) expresses the query without any ambiguity, but reduces the possibility to formulate more complex queries involving topological relationships. SVIQUEL (Kaushik & Rundensteiner, 1998) avoids multiple interpretations by limiting the number of involved objects (to just two) and provides a tool with a low expressive power to specify the relative spatial positions.

The language defined by Lee and Chin (1995) gives a query expressed by an ambiguous visual sentence whose image is in Figure 17C. The undesired relationships among drawn characteristic structures are removed or an a priori restrictive interpretation is imposed using the foreground/background metaphor.

Cigales (Calcinelli & Mainguenaud, 1994), sketch (Meyer, 1993), and spatial query by sketch (Egenhofer, 1997) do not give a unique interpretation of the visual sentence for the query. The solutions proposed by Cigales to reduce ambiguity are: (1) introduce various interactions (feedback) with the user and (2) increase the complexity of the resolution model (see "The Management of Ambiguities"). Spatial query by sketch resolves the ambiguity problem by considering and proposing both (1) the exact solution and (2) approximate solutions obtained by relaxing some relationships. The need to relax relationships is due to the fact that interaction by sketching produces ambiguities caused by the imprecision of hand-drawn visual sentences in as well as interpretation (lexical) ambiguities. GeoPQL (Ferri & Rafanelli, 2004, 2005) introduces special operators to manage the lexical ambiguity connected to the need to express relationships between couples given by three different characteristic structures in a two-dimensional space, thus avoiding this ambiguity (see "The Management of Ambiguities").

DISCUSSION

This chapter provides a classification of ambiguities in visual languages from the perspective of human-computer interaction. When interpretation and materialization functions (Bottoni et al., 1995) are unable to univocally associate an image with its description and vice-versa, an ambiguity is intercepted. The classification presented here provides a coherent vision of ambiguities for different visual languages, combining ambiguities arising from the fact that a visual sentence can have a number of lexical and syntactic interpretations and ambiguities produced by imprecision in human-computer interaction behavior.

Different interaction behaviors can introduce imprecision in the image associated with the visual sentence expressing the query. In other words, a visual query language can combine all the ambiguities previously described. Some of the most significant examples for spatial query languages are discussed here.

REFERENCES

Bottoni, P., Costabile, M. F., & Mussio, P. (1999). Specification and dialogue control of visual interaction through visual rewriting systems. *ACM Transactions on Programming Languages and Systems, 21*(6), 1077-1136.

Bottoni, P., Costabile, M. F., Levialdi, S., & Mussio, P. (1995). Formalising visual languages. *Proceedings of the IEEE Symposium on Visual Languages* (pp. 45-52).

Calcinelli, D., & Mainguenaud, M. (1994). Cigales: A visual language for geographic information system: The user interface. *Journal of Visual Languages and Computing, 5*(2), 113-132.

Calcinelli, D., & Mainguenaud, M. (1991). The management of the ambiguities in a graphical query language for geographical information systems. In O. Günther & H. J. Schek (Eds.), *2°Large Spatial Database Symposium (SSD)* (Vol. 525, pp. 143-160). Zürich, Switzerland: Springer.

Carpentier, C., & Mainguenaud, M. (2002). Classifying ambiguities in a visual spatial language. *GeoInformatica Journal, 6*(3), 285-315.

Egenhofer, M. J. (1997). Query processing in spatial-query- by-sketch. *Journal of Visual Languages and Computing, 8*(4), 403-424.

Favetta, F., & Aufaure-Portier, M. A. (2000). About ambiguities in visual GIS query languages: A taxonomy and solutions. *Proceedings of the 4th International Conference on Advances in Visual Information Systems* (pp. 154-165). Springer-Verlag.

Ferri, F., & Rafanelli, M. (2005). GeoPQL: A geographical pictorial query language that resolves ambiguities in query interpretation. *Journal of Data Semantics*, (Vol III), 50-80.

Ferri, F., & Rafanelli, M. (2004). Resolution of ambiguities in query interpretation for geographical pictorial query languages. *Journal of Computing and Information Technology*, *12*(2), 119-126.

Futrelle, R. P. (1999). Ambiguity in visual language theory and its role in diagram parsing. *IEEE Symposium on Visual Languages* (pp. 172-175). Tokyo: IEEE Computer Soc.

Kaushik, S., & Rundensteiner, E. (1998). SVIQUEL: A spatial visual query and exploration language. *Database and Expert Systems Applications,* (*LNCS 1460*, 290-299.)

Lee, Y. C., & Chin, F. (1995). An iconic query language for topological relationship in GIS. *International Journal of Geographical Information Systems, 9*(1), 25-46.

Mankoff, J., Hudson, S. E., & Abowd, G. D. (2000). Providing integrated toolkit-level support for ambiguity in recognition-based interfaces. *CHI 2000* (pp. 368-375).

Meyer, B. (1993). Beyond icons: Towards new metaphors for visual query languages for spatial information systems. *Proceedings of the International Workshop on Interfaces to Database Systems* (pp. 113-135). Glasgow.

Papadias, D., & Sellis, T. (1995). A pictorial query-by-example language. *Journal of Visual Languages and Computing, 6*(1), 53-72.

Chapter VII
The Management of Ambiguities

Maria Chiara Caschera
IRPPS-CNR, Italy

Fernando Ferri
IRPPS-CNR, Italy

Patrizia Grifoni
IRPPS-CNR, Italy

ABSTRACT

This chapter introduces and discusses the classification of methods to resolve ambiguities that arise during the communication process using visual languages. Ambiguities arise when the user gives his or her own semantics to the information. Sometimes his or her actions do not represent his or her intentions, producing an ambiguous or incorrect interpretation by the system. This chapter deals with ambiguities related to the system's interpretation function and methods to resolve them, which can be grouped in three main classes: prevention, a-posteriori resolution, and approximation resolution methods of ambiguities. This chapter distinguishes among different prevention methods: the procedural method, the reduction, and the improvement of the expressive power of the visual languages. The most used method for the a-posteriori resolution of ambiguities is mediation, which consists of repetition and choice. Finally, approximation resolution methods are presented to resolve ambiguities caused by imprecision of the user's interaction.

INTRODUCTION

Ambiguity in the communication process is one of the main problems of human-human and human-computer interaction. Natural and flexible communication approaches such as visual languages are frequently the most ambiguous. This chapter

discusses the classes of methods for resolving ambiguities in visual languages. As defined in Bottoni, Costabile, Levialdi, and Mussio (1995) a visual language is a set of visual sentences, each consisting of an image, its description, its interpretation function (int), and its materialization function (mat). Ambiguities can arise from both materialization and interpretation functions. The functions int and mat link images with their descriptions and vice versa. Ambiguities arise when more than one image materializes the same description and/or the interpretation function associates an image with more than one description. One of the reasons for ambiguities is that a single space is used to represent different kinds of information. Another reason is that the user gives his or her own semantics to the information, but sometimes his or her actions do not represent his or her intentions, producing an ambiguous or incorrect interpretation by the system. The system can also represent information in different visual ways, one of which must be chosen. So ambiguities are found at different levels: the user's action and interpretation, and the system's interpretation and materialization.

This chapter deals with ambiguities related to the system's interpretation function and methods to resolve them. These methods can be grouped in three classes: prevention of ambiguities, a-posteriori resolution, and approximation resolution methods. Prevention methods consider only a predefined set of possible system configurations, avoiding ambiguous configurations. A-posteriori resolution methods are based on the mediation techniques introduced by Mankoff, Hudson, & Abowd (2000). These enable the user to disambiguate his or her intention by dialog. In contrast, approximation resolution methods are based on theories such as fuzzy logic, Markov Random Field, and Bayesian Networks and do not require user disambiguation.

AMBIGUITY RESOLUTION METHODS BY PREVENTION

The main methods to prevent interpretation ambiguities are:

• Procedural method

• Reduction of the expressive power of the visual language grammar
• Improvement of the expressive power of the visual language grammar

These methods are discussed next with descriptions of their main features and some examples.

The Procedural Method

Interpretation is a difficult task as it can introduce errors due to the gap between the user's intention, expressed according to his or her mental model, and the system's interpretation of the image associated with the visual sentence. This may lead to lexical and syntactic ambiguities (see the chapter titled "Classification of Ambiguities").

In the procedural method, the user's actions are aimed at (1) drawing the characteristic structures/images associated with the visual sentences and (2) controlling the state of the system in order to produce the correct interpretation of the image associated with the visual sentence according to the user's drawing process.

When considering how to resolve ambiguities produced by human-computer interaction, it must be specified that the user can visually interact with the system using (1) interfaces with predefined commands and their materialization according to a characteristic structure or an image or (2) interfaces enabling the user to draw the image associated with the visual sentence freehand directly on the screen, as if on a sheet of paper. We refer to the first class as command user interfaces, and to the second as sketch-based interfaces.

The procedural method can be adopted in both types of interfaces. Images associated with the visual sentences are correctly (syntactically and semantically) and unambiguously interpreted if and only if the user's actions develop according to the predefined sequence and/or state diagram that controls the system, and one and only one interpretation is produced for the image associated with each visual sentence. This method confines the human-computer interaction process within a closed procedure.

For example in the hand drawing process, some constraints to user drawing behavior are defined; a freehand sketching system could require that the user draws one sketch according to a predefined evolution of the system's state diagram.

Sketches can be interpreted according to a restricted set of characteristic structures, the spatial relationships among them, and the procedural (sequence) constraints followed in drawing the image associated with the visual sentence.

Let us consider a system with two possible states for editing an entity-relationship diagram using a sketch-based interaction approach. State 1 is associated with the entities and state 2 is associated with the relationship drawing. Our user has adopted a drawing sequence of strokes in which one characteristic structure must be completed before beginning a new one. At the beginning, our system is in the state 1. If the user draws the rectangle in Figure 1A containing the word professor and then the rectangle in Figure 1B containing the word course, the two rectangles are interpreted respectively as the entity professor and the entity course, due to the fact that a rectangle represents an entity. If the user's drawing produces an oval containing the word course (Figure 1C) then it will in any case be interpreted as a rectangle representing the

entity course, in accordance with the state of the system (state 1).

The procedural method can also be used to avoid ambiguities such as the segmentation ambiguity (see the chapter titled "Classification of Ambiguities"). Let us consider the image associated with the visual sentence in Figure 2.

This may give rise to a segmentation ambiguity because the short lines in the lower left corner of the diagram could represent tick marks or the ends of the x- and y-axis lines. The definition of constraints on the stroke drawing process can help to remove this ambiguity. Let us consider a constraint, which establishes that:

Each sequence of strokes must complete one characteristic structure before beginning a new one

Suppose that Figure 3 shows the user's sequence of actions made to obtain Figure 2.

The short lines in the lower left corner in Figure 2 are therefore the ends of the x- and y-axes as a single stroke has been made for each of the two axes.

Consider an example that uses the procedural approach, according to a given constraint in hu-

Figure 1. An example of procedural drawing of entities

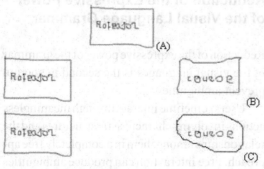

Figure 2. Segmentation ambiguity

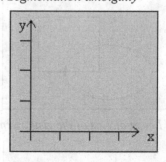

Figure 3. Procedural drawing to avoid segmentation ambiguity

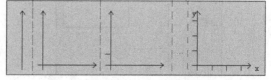

man-computer interaction, to reduce ambiguities due to not required spatial relationships between two of the three characteristic structures forced in a two-dimensional space.

A sentence containing this kind of ambiguity is given next:

Let there be a line that crosses a rectangle and a rectangle that overlaps an oval. No relationships are expressed between the oval and the line.

Three different objects in a bi-dimensional space have to be represented. This introduces an ambiguity as in the chapter titled "Classification of Ambiguities." The previously introduced description, for example, can be materialized using a unique bi-dimensional space for three objects as shown in Figure 4. The oval and the line in Figure 4 are in an undesired disjoint relationship that differs from the previously given description.

To resolve this ambiguity, the visual spatial query language proposed in Lee and Chin (1995) uses the foreground/background metaphor.

Figure 4. Ambiguity due to not required spatial relationships between two of the three characteristic structures forced in a two-dimensional space

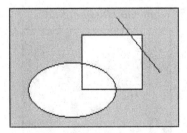

Figure 5. Lee et al.'s cs of the visual sentence

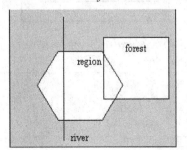

Figure 5 shows the shows the characteristic structures of the visual sentence using Lee et al.'s language to express the query:

Find all the regions, which are passed through by a river and partially overlap a forest

The user starts by drawing a line for the river and the area for the region in the foreground with a pass-through relationship (Figure 5). The river is then put in the background as it has no relationship with the forest. Finally, the user draws the forest area overlapped with the region area in the foreground.

In some visual spatial languages, including that of Lee et al. (1995), adopt a strategy of ambiguity prevention through a procedural method. Lee et al.'s language enables removal of unwanted relationships among drawn symbolic graphical objects or the imposition of an a priori restrictive interpretation using the foreground/background metaphor. The relationships of a new symbolic graphical object depend on the state (foreground or background) of those drawn previously. The parser must consider both the visual representation and the drawing process to interpret a query. In this manner, some procedural steps influence the query semantics but not its representation, and queries having the same materialization may have different semantics.

VISCO (Wessel & Haarslev, 1998) also uses a procedural method to prevent ambiguity.

Reduction of the Expressive Power of the Visual Language Grammar

Reduction of the expressive power of the grammar of the visual languages is the second method to prevent ambiguities.

Users sometime interact through meaningless actions involving characteristic structures and the relationships among them in a completely free approach. Free interaction can produce ambiguities in interpretation. A common method to resolve these ambiguities is the reduction of the visual language grammar's expressive power. A set of constraints can be established on the grammar of the visual language to limit the user's actions, the number of characteristic structures used, and their relationships. All meaningless commands and selections are disabled or ignored.

This method enables all commands and characteristic structures according to the syntactic and semantic constraints. It is adopted in the *command user interfaces* where all unusable or unselectable icons and characteristic structures can be disabled beforehand and/or the system can send the user a warning message on the interaction error.

Consider a system for editing an entity-relationship diagram. The system provides the user with the characteristic structures used for an entity and a relationship. When the user edits his or her entity-relationship diagram, the system enables all actions that cannot produce syntactic and semantic errors and ambiguities. The relationship definition therefore requires the preliminary identification of the entities that it connects. This approach can avoid errors and ambiguities in visual sentences that cannot be easily interpreted.

This solution method prevents the segmentation ambiguity and can also be used to avoid the occlusion ambiguity (see the chapter titled "Classification of Ambiguities"). It prevents segmentation ambiguity because each characteristic structure must be univocally intercepted by a command (user action) and unambiguously interpreted. It can also avoid occlusion ambiguity (see the chapter titled "Classification of Ambiguities") by splitting superposed characteristic structures. When the user edits the visual sentence, the system can impose that the characteristic structures must be spatially distinguishable.

For example, consider a system for entity-relationship diagram editing. To avoid segmentation ambiguities, the user is enabled to overlap two characteristic structures (entity, relationships) (Figure 6), and is disabled from editing isolated

Figure 6. Enabled (A) and disabled (B) configurations for characteristic structures

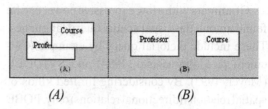

(A)   *(B)*

relationships (unless they are each connected with two entities).

The grammar's expressive power reduction can be meaningfully used in the case (see chapter titled "Classification of Ambiguities") of ambiguities due to not required spatial relationships between two of the three characteristic structures, forced in a bi-dimensional space (see The Procedural Method).

To go back to the previous description (The Procedural Method):

Let there be a line that crosses a rectangle and a rectangle that overlaps an oval. No relationships are expressed between the oval and the line.

To avoid the unwanted disjointed relationship (see Figure 4) between the line and the oval, the language can restrict the visual sentences to impose one spatial relationship between, at most, two characteristic structures at the same time.

This ambiguity may be resolved by reducing the grammar's expressive power. If three characteristic structures must be considered, as in the previous description, then the visual language

Figure 7. Unambiguous expression using a grammar with low expressive power

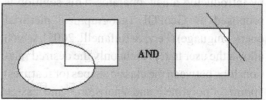

can be integrated with a textual part to represent the situation described in Figure 7.

Grammars with a low expressive power can be found among the visual spatial query languages. These include pictorial query by example (Calcinelli & Mainguenaud, 1994) and SVIQUEL (Meyer, 1993). By considering limited kinds of spatial relations (directional relations) only, PQBE avoids multiple query interpretations but reduces the possibility to formulate more complex queries involving topological relationships. SVIQUEL also includes topological operators, but avoids multiple interpretations by limiting the number of objects involved (to just two) and providing a tool with a low expressive power to specify the relative spatial positions.

Improvement of the Expressive Power of Visual Language Grammar

The improvement of the expressive power of the grammar of the visual languages is the last method to prevent ambiguities. In contrast with the reduction method, improving the grammar's expressive power produces the system that is closest to the user's intention. This approach enriches the visual language by defining new operators and/or new characteristic structures.

Consider this description:

Let there be a line that crosses a rectangle and a rectangle that overlaps an oval. No relationships are expressed between the oval and the line.

The ambiguity of expressing spatial relationships between two of three characteristic structures in a two-dimensional space can be resolved by introducing a new operator. This solution is proposed by GeoPQL (geographical pictorial query language) (Ferri & Rafanelli, 2005), which allows the user to represent only the desired relationships between the classic shapes (or features) "point," "polyline," and "polygon," and assign them a precise semantic (for example, "lake" to a

Figure 8. The image associated with the visual sentence using the any operator in GeoPQL

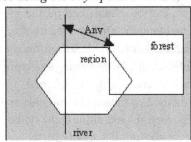

polygon, "river" to a polyline, etc.). For example, this language defines the *any* operator, which expresses all valid spatial relationships between two characteristic structures. Figure 8 shows the image associated with the visual sentence corresponding to the description next:

Find all the regions, which are passed through by a river and partially overlap a forest

The system can reduce interpretation ambiguities by taking into account of contextual information. The context is given by information about the application domain (language syntax and semantic), the interaction tool, and the user's skill.

The increasing tendency to use different devices for human computer-interaction activities and the pervasive use of mobile devices and PDAs (personal digital assistants) has led to the need for different characteristic structures depending on the different devices and users (for the same visual language) leading to the language's personalization. This produces the improvement in the grammar's expressive power.

A-POSTERIORI AMBIGUITY RESOLUTION METHODS

The main method for the a-posteriori resolution of ambiguities is mediation, which consists of:

- **Repetition:** The user repeats an action until the system is able to correctly interpret it.
- **Choice:** The system returns a candidate set of interpretations and the user selects the most appropriate.

These a-posteriori resolution methods are discussed next with descriptions of their main features and some examples.

Mediation

Mediation is the process that facilitates the correct interpretation of the user's actions according to the user's intention. It involves the user in the disambiguation activity, asking him or her for the correct interpretation of the ambiguity. These methods are particularly useful for the resolution of ambiguities caused by imprecision and noise in the human-computer interaction process.

Various mediation techniques exist: *repetition*, *choice*, and *automatic mediation*.

Repetition

This consists of the repetition of the user's action until the system is able to correctly interpret it.

Let us consider a user who adopts a freehand interaction approach. Suppose that he or she can draw a sketch or write a word. Due to the imprecision of the freehand interaction, it may be necessary to repeat the action.

If the user's intention is to draw a rectangle but he or she produces a sketch such as in Fig-

Figure 9. Uninterpretable sketch

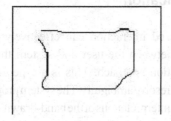

Figure 10. Imprecision in a sketched rectangle and its interpretation

ure 9, its imprecision is too high to produce any interpretation.

Repetition avoids cases of uninterpretable interactions—redrawing the sketch can help the interpretation. A different modality can also be used to support the interpretation. In the example in Figure 9, a speech modality could be used; the user can say the word *rectangle* after drawing the sketch.

If the user draws a rectangle (Figure 10A) whose imprecision is so high that it can be interpreted as both a rectangle (Figure 10B) and an oval (Figure 10C), the user can repeat the sketch in order to better specify his or her input.

In Mankoff et al. (2000), the different features of the repetition strategy are classified as:

- Modality,
- Granularity of Repair,
- Undo.

The *modality* feature stresses the repetition method from the perspective of the modality adopted for repetition. If the interaction modality used is mainly gesture (freehand sketching), then repetition using the same modality can be useful. However, repetition can be more effective if a different modality is used to resolve the introduced ambiguity, as use of the same modality frequently results in the same ambiguities. For example, to resolve the ambiguity in Figure 10A the user may suggest the correct interpretation by selecting the ambiguous sketch and typing or saying *rectangle* or *oval* as appropriate.

However, the use of a different modality can produce a potential conflict. If the sketch in Figure 10A is imprecisely drawn, then the interpretations

Figure 11. Repetition applied locally

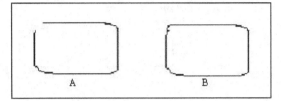

in Figures 10B and 10C are both possible (with a different score).

The repetition method can be applied locally to resolve a more general ambiguity. Suppose the user is sketching a freehand rectangle and does not close the shape, and the system is unable to provide any interpretation (Figure 11A). The user can then partially repeat the sketch by completing the edge of the rectangle (Figure 11B).

In this case, as introduced in Mankoff et al. (2000), the granularity of correction is different from the granularity of interpretation. In fact, correction is related only to a component part of the sketched object to be interpreted. This repetition strategy is known as *granularity of repair,* and is very frequently used for multimodal interaction approaches.

In the dictation system described in Spilker, Klarner, and Görz et al. (2000), the user can introduce or delete some characters in a sentence. Before repeating any action, the user can delete or undo the unwanted action. Undo or delete are necessary when the input represents a command (i.e., the repetition must undo this command before repeating the user's action). It should be noted that if no interpretation can be given to the user's action, then undo cannot be applied as there is nothing to undo.

Choice

An interesting method to resolve ambiguities is the *choice* method. Choice involves a dialog with the user to enable the system to correctly interpret each ambiguity. The system gives the user all candidate interpretations and the user

chooses the one which best fits his or her intention. User dialog can allow the system to take into account the user's interaction behavior and the preferences expressed by his or her choices, if feedback is considered in order to adapt the system to the context.

Let us consider the previous example in which the user draws a rectangle (Figure 10A) whose imprecision is so high that it can be interpreted as both a rectangle (Figure 10B) and an oval (Figure 10C). With the choice method, the system proposes the interpretations given in Figures 10B and 10C, and the user chooses the one best matching his or her intention.

This method is adopted in some visual spatial query languages including Sketch (Ferri et al., 2005), spatial query by sketch (Egenhofer, 1997), and Cigales (Calcinelli et al., 1994). Spatial query by sketch resolves the ambiguity problem by considering and proposing both the exact solution of the query, if possible, and other approximate solutions obtained by relaxing some relationships. In this manner, the language includes multiple interpretations in the result, and the user selects the representation that correctly interprets his or her query. Cigales is unable to give a unique interpretation of the visual query representation. Two possible solutions to reduce ambiguity in this language are the introduction of various interactions (feedback) with the user, and increased complexity of the resolution model. Ambiguities are resolved by detection, attempt at automatic solution and proposal of these solutions to the user.

To disambiguate visual sentences produced by sketch-based interaction using the choice method, the beautification approach can be useful.

Beautification

Sketch-based interaction can effectively support a dialog between the user and system through a beautification approach. This is a type of choice method to resolve ambiguity. The system proposes all candidate interpretations of the hand-drawn sketches

Figure 12. Constraint ambiguity

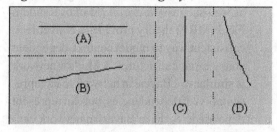

Figure 13. Hand drawn sketches and beautified candidates proposed by the system to the user

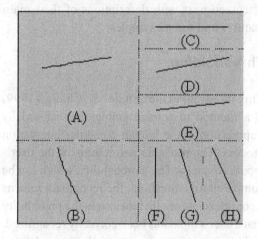

by using some beautification algorithms. The user then chooses the most correct interpretation.

Let us consider ambiguities in the constraint properties of characteristic structures. Consider whether the lines in Figure 12 should be classified as horizontal, vertical, or oblique.

Figures 12A and 12C are interpreted as a horizontal and a vertical line. Ambiguity usually involves oblique lines, as a line may be oblique due to sketching imprecision or because the user actually wished to draw an oblique line. Figure 12B could be interpreted as a horizontal or oblique line, while Figure 12D could be interpreted as a vertical or oblique line. After the user's freehand sketch, the system displays the beautified lines. The ambiguities lead the system to show more than one interpretation (candidate) for each sketched line, and the user must select the interpretation corresponding to his/her intention. Figures 13A

and Figure 13B represent the freehand sketch, while figures 13C, 13D, 13E, 13F, 13G, and 13H represent the beautified candidates among which the user selects the interpretation matching his or her intention.

APPROXIMATION RESOLUTION METHODS

Ambiguities caused by imprecision in human-computer interaction behavior can also be resolved using approximation resolution methods such as:

- Thresholding
- Historical statistics
- Rules

These methods do not require any user disambiguation process. They can all require the use of some theories such as fuzzy logic, Bayesian Networks, and Markov Random Field. The main features of these methods are briefly described next:

- **Fuzzy logic:** Fuzzy logic is widely used for imprecision and/or ambiguity problems due to its ability to describe classification uncertainty. It is based on the fuzzy set concept and was developed by Zadeh (1965) to provide a general representation of uncertainty considering different degrees of membership values.

  In general, when considering sets such as the set of natural numbers, the set of people, and so on, each object may or may not belong to this set. In contrast, the elements of a fuzzy set belong to the set with different graduations. The degree for each one of the elements of the set gives the degree of certainty that each element belongs to the set. "Fuzzy" therefore becomes synonymous with "imprecision."

Given the imprecision in human-computer interaction, fuzzy logic establishes the appropriate fuzzy set via membership functions, which are associated with each input in order to resolve the vagueness and ambiguities of the interaction behavior introduced by imprecision and noise.

CALI (Fonseca & Jorge, 2000) is a free-hand drawing information system, which uses fuzzy logic for sketch recognition. Its recognition method is based on three main ideas: extraction of the geometric properties from input shapes, enhancement of the recognition performance using a set of filters to either identify shapes or remove unwanted shapes and resolution of uncertainty, and imprecision in shape sketches by using fuzzy logic (Bezdek, 1992) to associate a degree of certainty to the recognized shapes.

The thresholding method can be used in combination with fuzzy logic; for example, fuzzy thresholding can use entropy as the measure for "fuzziness," or it can use a method that minimizes a "fuzziness" measure of the mean level of grayness in the object and background.

- **Bayesian networks:** A system, which uses Bayesian networks to deal with uncertainty and complexity can be helpful to manage ambiguities arising during the interpretation process. Bayesian networks give the set of interpretations that a system is considering. They consist of two parts: an acyclic direct graph and a set of probabilistic distributions. Each node of the graph represents one element to be interpreted and each arc gives the relationship between the two connected nodes. The different interpretations are related to different probabilities that can be influenced by factors such as context and stroke composition.
- **Markov random field:** Recognition of freehand sketches can depend strongly on the drawing's context. The spatial property

can be effectively modeled through different aspects such as *context, and* Markov Random Field (MRF) theory provides a convenient, consistent way to model context-dependent characteristic structures. A Markov network is similar to a Bayesian network in its representation of dependencies, but can represent dependencies that a Bayesian network cannot, such as cyclic dependencies.

Various approximation resolution methods are discussed next with descriptions of their main features and some examples.

Thresholding

Thresholding (MacKenzie & Chang, 1999) is a method to resolve ambiguities caused by imprecision in the human-computer interaction process. The probable correctness of the user's input is expressed by a probability, which can be compared to a threshold; the recognizer returns a confidence score that measures the probability that a user's input has been correctly recognized. If this confidence measure is below a predefined threshold, the system rejects the interpretation. Thresholding is used in Poon, Weber, and Cass (1995).

Historical Statistics

If the confidence score is not available or might be incorrect, probabilities can be generated by performing a statistical analysis of historical ambiguity data. Historical statistics may provide a default probability of correctness for a given interpretation when a recognizer is unable to do so. This approach may use a confusion matrix, whose values give an estimation of the number of times that the recognizer has confused the characteristic structure. So if thresholding is unable to disambiguate the freehand sketches, historical statistical data on correctly interpreted ambiguities can be used.

Figure 14. Procedural drawing of the E-R

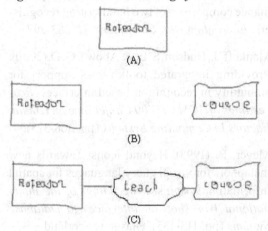

Rules

Freehand sketches are complex to recognize. In the absence of contextual information, their interpretation is often ambiguous. Their management may require the use of the context as thresholding and/or statistical approaches may not be sufficient for their resolution. An example of use of rules can be found in Baber and Hone (1993). The use of rules is more sophisticated than thresholding, as it allows the use of context. For example, a rule might use syntactic information to eliminate grammatically incorrect characteristic structures.

Let us consider the example of an E-R editor. If the user's intention is to draw the entity *professor* (Figure 14A), the entity *course* (Figure 14B), and the relationship *teach* between them, and the sketch is ambiguous due to ambiguity in the shape of the relationship (Figure 14C), then different strategies can be adopted to resolve the ambiguity.

In a *sketch-based interface* the interpretation of the image associated with a visual sentence requires that the sketch is matched to a set of characteristic structures and their spatial relationships. If the imprecision in drawing the *teach* relationship is so high that it could be interpreted as a rectangle or rhombus and the system has to resolve

this ambiguity, then thresholding and historical data could be used. However, if the thresholding value is low and historical data does not provide a solution on whether the shape is a rhombus or a rectangle, then contextual information and the use of rules may be a solution. In fact, given that a connection between two entities can be obtained only by considering relationships, and the characteristic structure for a relationship is a rhombus, then *teach* can be nothing other than a relationship according to the syntactic rules for entity-relationship diagrams (Figure 1C).

CONCLUSION

This chapter discusses methods to resolve ambiguities related to the interpretation function in visual sentences and groups them into three different classes. The first consists of ambiguity prevention methods, and considers the procedural method, reduction of the expressive power of the visual language grammar and improvement of the expressive power of the visual language grammar.

The second class considers a-posteriori resolution methods, mainly focused on mediation techniques. Finally, the third class considers approximation resolution methods based on thresholding, historical statistics, and rules underlying some theories such as fuzzy logic, Markov Random fields, and Bayesian Networks.

This chapter gives the main features of each method, providing examples of ambiguities and their resolution. It discusses some existing visual languages and their resolution of ambiguities through the solutions described.

These approaches can also be combined in each visual language, in order to specify the correct interpretation of each ambiguity according to the different context.

REFERENCES

Baber, C., & Hone, K. S. (1993). Modelling error recovery and repair in automatic speech recognition. *International Journal of Man-Machine Studies, 39*(3), 495-515.

Bezdek, J. C. (1992). Computing with uncertainty. *IEEE Communications Magazine, 30*(9), 24-36.

Bottoni, P., Costabile, M. F., Levialdi, S., & Mussio, P. (1995). Formalizing visual languages. *VL 1995* (pp. 45-52).

Calcinelli, D., & Mainguenaud, M. (1994). Cigales: A visual language for geographic information system: The user interface. *Journal of Visual Languages and Computing, 5*(2), 113-132.

Egenhofer, M. J. (1997). Query processing in spatial-query-by-sketch. *Journal of Visual Languages and Computing, 8*(4), 403-424.

Ferri, F., & Rafanelli, M. (2005). GeoPQL: A geographical pictorial query language that resolves ambiguities in query interpretation. *Journal of Data Semantics, III,* 50-80.

Fonseca, M. J., & Jorge J. A. (2000). *CALI : A software library for calligraphic interfaces. INESC-ID.* Retrieved from http://immi.inesc-id.pt/cali/

Lee, Y. C., & Chin, F. (1995). An iconic query language for topological relationship in GIS. *International Journal of geographical Information Systems, 9*(1), 25-46.

MacKenzie, I. S., & Chang, L. (1999). A performance comparison of two handwriting recognisers. *Interacting with Computers, 11,* 283-297.

Mankoff, J., Hudson, S. E., & Abowd, G. D. (2000). Providing integrated toolkit-level support for ambiguity in recognition-based interfaces. *Proceedings of ACM CHI'00 Conference on Human Factors in Computing Systems* (pp. 368-375).

Meyer, B. (1993). Beyond icons: Towards new metaphors for visual query languages for spatial information systems. *Proceedings of the International Workshop on Interfaces to Database Systems* (pp. 113-135). Glasgow, Scotland.

Poon, A., Weber, K., & Cass, T. (1995). Scribbler: A tool for searching digital ink. *Proceedings of ACM CHI'95 Conference on Human Factors in Computing Systems, Volume 2 of Short Papers: Pens and Touchpads* (pp. 252-253).

Spilker, J., Klarner, M., & Görz, G. (2000). Processing self corrections in a speech to speech system. *COLING 2000* (pp. 1116-1120).

Wessel, M., & Haarslev, V. (1998). VISCO: Bringing visual spatial querying to reality. *IEEE Symposium on Visual Languages* (pp. 170-177).

Zadeh, L. A. (1965). Fuzzy sets. *Information and Control, 8*(3), 338-353.

Section II
Approaches and Methods for Specific Domains

Chapter VIII
Visual Query Languages, Representation Techniques, and Data Models

Maria Chiara Caschera
IRPPS-CNR, Italy

Arianna D'Ulizia
IRPPS-CNR, Italy

Leonardo Tininini
IASI-CNR, Italy

ABSTRACT

An easy, efficient, and effective way to retrieve stored data is obviously one of the key issues of any information system. In the last few years, considerable effort has been devoted to the definition of more intuitive, visual-based querying paradigms, attempting to offer a good trade-off between expressiveness and intuitiveness. In this chapter, we analyze the main characteristics of visual languages specifically designed for querying information systems, concentrating on conventional relational databases, but also considering information systems with a less rigid structure such as Web resources storing XML documents. We consider two fundamental aspects of visual query languages: the adopted visual representation technique and the underlying data model, possibly specialized to specific application contexts.

INTRODUCTION

The retrieval of data from an information system requires specifically designed languages, enabling the user to extract the desired information by specifying properties on the structure and/or on the content of the information itself. These languages, commonly known as *query languages*, have been studied in detail in the literature and are one of the most important topics of database theory. Most query languages adopted in commercial database management systems (DBMSs) are of the *textual* type (i.e., the request consists of a sequence of words and textual symbols combined according to a well-defined syntax).

Although traditional textual query languages have been shown to enable the user to express complex requests and several techniques have been proposed for the efficient evaluation of the corresponding answers, their ease of use is very limited, particularly for non-expert users. In recent years, there has been a drive to define more intuitive, visual-based querying paradigms, attempting to offer a good trade-off between expressiveness and intuitiveness. In *visual query languages* (*VQLs*), words and textual symbols are replaced by graphical objects (e.g., arcs, geometric shapes, tables, icons), the spatial relationships among them (e.g., inclusion, connection, intersection), and some visual properties (e.g., the colour and line type: solid, thick, dotted, etc.).

In this chapter, we analyze the main characteristics of VQLs, mainly concentrating on languages to query conventional relational databases, but also examining information systems with a less rigid structure such as Web resources storing XML documents. We consider two main classifications of VQLs: the adopted visual representation technique (e.g., based on forms and tables, diagrams, icons, sketches, or on some combinations thereof) and the underlying data model (e.g., visual languages to query relational databases, object-oriented databases, collections of XML documents, as well as languages specifically designed for particular data such as geographical and multidimensional data).

BACKGROUND

In this section, we review some basic terms and concepts of database theory, especially those related to the area of query languages (see, for example, Abiteboul, Hull, and Vianu (1995) for a more comprehensive introduction). Given a database *D*, we distinguish the (database) *schema S* and the (database) *instance I*, representing the structure and the actual contents of the data stored in *D*. For example, in a relational database the schema is constituted by the relation (table) names, along with the corresponding attribute names (and possibly types), while the instance is constituted by the sets of tuples (records) having the structures specified by the single schemas.

A *query* is a syntactic object, typically constituted by a text string, a graph, a combination of shapes and icons, etc., constructed using ele-

ments of the schema *S* (the *input schema*), some specific symbols and according to the rules (the syntax) of a language. The query also describes the *output schema* (i.e., the structure of the data that will be produced by the query's interpretation). In visual queries, the elements of the input and output schema, the operations to combine them, and the constraints that must be satisfied by the required data are represented by visual metaphors, organized according to a visual syntax.

The interpretation of a query according to a predefined semantics determines a *query mapping* (see Figure 1) i.e., a function from the set of possible input instances (on the input schema) of a given database to the set of possible output instances (on the output schema). Given a certain input instance, the construction of the corresponding output instance is commonly known as *query evaluation*. In DBMSs, efficient query evaluation is obtained using a specifically designed component called the optimizer. Query optimization is often achieved by transforming the original query into another equivalent query, possibly expressed in a more suitable language. This is very common in VQLs where the original visual query is first transformed into a standard textual query (e.g., in SQL, datalog, XQuery) and then evaluated using a conventional text-based query engine.

The set of query mappings that can be expressed using a given query language defines the *expressive power* of the language itself. Although this aspect is fundamental for any query language, the expressive power of visual languages is a particularly delicate issue, as the adoption of visual constructs can make relatively simple queries

Figure 1. Query and query mapping

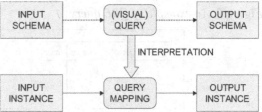

either very complex (hence compromising the benefit of the visual approach) or even impossible to express. The design of a VQL is therefore generally characterized by two opposite tendencies: on the one hand a growing attempt to increase the language's expressive power (introducing more complex, less intuitive visual constructs) and on the other the need to express simple, very common queries in a straightforward, user-friendly way. More details on the expressive power of VQLs can be found in Catarci, Costabile, Levialdi, and Batini (1997).

In the following sections, we illustrate some of the main characteristics of VQLs, namely the representation technique adopted (based on forms, diagrams, icons, etc.) and the underlying data model (relational, object-oriented, XML, etc.), with possible specialization to specific domains of interest (e.g., scientific databases and GISs). We also provide several examples of VQLs corresponding to the described characteristics.

REPRESENTATION TECHNIQUES FOR VQLS

As previously noted, a query is a syntactic object, which defines a mapping from the input to the output schema by using the language's specific syntax. Like any visual language, VQLs use visual representations and metaphors to achieve their aim, which is to describe this mapping (i.e., the input and output schema, the operations to combine the schema elements, and the constraints that must be satisfied by the required data). Despite the apparent differences between the visual and

textual approach, VQLs are often "inspired" in their structure by the most widespread textual query languages (e.g., datalog, XQuery, and some algebras). This is usually done to simplify the optimization process by transforming the visual query into an equivalent textual one and exploiting the efficient optimizers available for textual query languages. Depending on the set of visual techniques adopted to represent the concepts of interest (either directly available in the database or resulting from their manipulation), and the operators that can be used to manipulate them, VQLs can be broadly classified as form-based, diagrammatic, iconic, sketch-based, and hybrid.

Form-Based (Tabular) VQLs

In form-based VQLs (also called tabular VQLs), collections of objects sharing the same structure are visually represented by forms or tables. In these languages, queries are typically expressed by one or more prototype tables and the visually expressed constraints among them. Much like in an order form, the user can fill in some of the table fields with constant values or more complex expressions, corresponding to the desired data.

The most well-known and typical example of tabular VQL is without doubt QBE (Zloof, 1977), which has been implemented in several DBMSs, for example Microsoft Access. As with many other VQLs, QBE has many analogies with a textual language, especially the domain relational calculus. Each relation to be included in the query input schema is represented by a tabular skeleton and the user can specify conditions by filling in the skeleton columns with example values. These can

Figure 2. An example of QBE query

CHILDREN	cname	pname		PERSONNEL	pname	sex	airport
	P.*randy*	*ann*			*ann*	F	HOPKINS

act as variables (and in this case are underlined and written in lowercase) or as constants (written in uppercase). The output schema is specified by using the "P" prefix in front of variable example values. An example of a QBE query for the request "List the children of female personnel at Hopkins airport" is shown in Figure 2.

Tabular representations are quite obvious when the data has a rigid structure (as in the case of relational databases), but can also be used when dealing with the more complex structures of object databases. For example, Vadaparty, Aslandogan, and Ozsoyoglu (1993) propose a visual language inspired by the head-body structure of datalog queries, which uses nested tables to represent complex object-oriented structures, as well as limited forms of universal quantifications. To extend QBE to object databases, Staes, Tarantino, and Tiems (1991) propose the combination of conventional tabular forms with more complex display structures such as scrollable lists, pop-up menus, and stacks.

Diagrammatic VQLs

The importance of diagrams in supporting a large number of perceptual inferences has been extensively discussed by Larkin and Simon (1987), who assert that "a diagram is (sometimes) worth ten thousand words." *Diagrammatic* VQLs are usually based on models that represent objects and their relationships by simple geometric shapes

(e.g., rectangles, circles, and polygons) connected by (possibly oriented) arcs. Unlike iconic VQLs, the shapes manipulated by diagrammatic VQLs are simple and very abstract, and have no strict correspondence with the "real" visual appearance of the modelled objects.

Shapes typically correspond to concept types and arcs to the conceptual or logical relationships defined between two concepts. Shape interconnections can be exploited by the user during the query formulation process to navigate on the schema and identify the concepts of interest, thus expressing the desired result rather than the procedures to obtain it. A vast class of diagrammatic VQLs (e.g., those in Angelaccio, Catarci, and Santucci (1990), Czejdo, Embley, Reddy, and Rusinkiewicz (1989), and Rosengren (1994)) is based on the entity-relationship (E-R) model or on conceptually similar graph models (e.g., those in Papantonakis and King (1994) and Zhang, Chu, Meng, and Kong (1999)), where entities and classes are represented by variously shaped nodes and the relationships between concepts by (possibly oriented) edges.

Diagrammatic languages are usually based on fairly simple and straightforward structures (such as those of an E-R diagram), but can sometimes introduce more complex modular mechanisms, based on differently shaped elements and different types of oriented edges, and nesting mechanisms, based on containment relationships among visual components.

Figure 3. Quiver language diagrams with nested structures

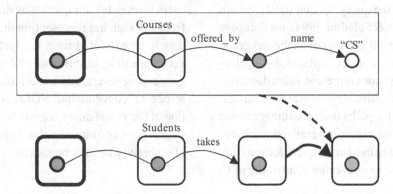

Figure 3 shows an example of a query in the Quiver language ("Find students who take only courses offered by the department named CS"), where graphs can be nested with subgraphs included in other nodes, various types of arrows, and bold nodes and arcs used to visually define the elements to be outputted by the query.

Iconic VQLs

Query languages based on iconic paradigms use sets of icons to represent both the concepts in the database and the operators to manipulate them. In other words, icons are used as visual metaphors for both the objects of interest and the ways to combine them. Queries are therefore expressed by selecting and combining icons, which are usually visualized as stylised images. Iconic VQLs have many similarities with diagrammatic ones, the fundamental difference lying in the abstraction level of the visual metaphors used. This difference is both the strong and the weak point of any iconic VQL, as poorly designed icons may not convey the expected meaning to users and can therefore be even less effective than a set of completely abstract geometric shapes (Blackwell & Green, 1999).

Despite the obvious differences, diagrammatic and iconic VQLs have several characteristics in common: both are often based on a semantic graph model, where the visual metaphors are used to visualize both the database schema with classes, relationships and database constraints, and the database instance (i.e., the specific contents). For example, in the query by icon (QBI) system (Massari, Pavani, & Saladini, 1994), the database schema is expressed in terms of a labelled graph of the graph model (Catarci, Santucci, & Angelaccio, 1993) where nodes represent value domains, classes of objects, and relationships among classes. Given a class *C,* the paths from *C* to other classes on the graph define a set of generalized attributes (GAs), which can be used in the query formulation process just like any conventional attribute of *C.*

Both classes and GAs are visually represented by icons and can be individually selected to define the desired output result.

Other iconic VQLs are more closely related to well-known textual query languages. For example in Keiron (Aversano, Canfora, De Lucia, & Stefanucci, 2002), icons are used to represent both entities and attributes of the database, but the sections of the graphical user interface are in obvious correspondence with the standard SQL select-from-where-order by/group by clauses and a textual SQL translation of the visual query is displayed in a specific section of the user interface. Similarly, the *query head* and *query body* sections of the VISUAL user interface (Balkir, Ozsoyoglu, & Ozsoyoglu, 2002) are clearly inspired by the rule head and body of datalog rules. Icons are mainly used in the query body to represent classes and objects, as well as methods, domains, and spatial relationships.

Spatial relationships can be very effectively represented by icons and consequently several VQLs for geographical information systems are iconic (e.g., Cigales (Aufaure-Portier, 1995) and Lvis (Aufaure-Portier & Bonhomme, 1999)). Icons can be effectively used to represent both spatial objects such as towns, forests, rivers, roads, etc., and the spatial relationships among objects such as intersection, inclusion, adjacency, etc.

Sketch-Based VQLs

Sketch-based querying systems are based on the metaphor of the virtual blackboard where the users formulate their queries by directly drawing freehand sketches representing the pattern of the data to be extracted from the system. Although very appealing in terms of usability, these languages pose several additional problems even with respect to "conventional" VQLs, as the interpretation of the visual query (constituted by the user's strokes) can be quite complex and relevant issues of ambiguity need to be tackled.

Most sketch-based VQLs are used to query geographic databases (Blaser & Egenhofer, 2000; Haarslev & Wessel, 1997) and the user normally formulates queries by combining topological and geometrical constraints defined by the sketch with additional meta-information representing user-defined relaxations and/or additional constraints. For example in Meyer (1994), propositional (non-spatial) constraints are expressed as object-graphs while spatial constraints are given in the form of sketches. The relaxation of some constraints is a typical problem of sketch-based techniques and is motivated by the unavoidable imprecision of freehand sketches, which in most cases do not exactly match the intended geometry of the target entities. Egenhofer (1997) suggests that this relaxation can be achieved by exploiting the *conceptual neighbourhood* (i.e., a measure of the similarity degree) among topological relations.

Hybrid VQLs

Although most VQLs have a clearly predominant tabular, diagrammatic, iconic, or sketch-based nature, in many cases the languages combine some aspects of the various approaches and are therefore defined as *hybrid*. In this type of language, tables and diagrams are often used to define the database schema and constraints, icons can represent specific prototypical objects and operations, and sketches can be useful to specify topological and geometrical constraints. This is particularly common when considering the implemented version of the languages; for example, even a purely tabular VQL like QBE has some diagrammatic features in the implemented version of the language provided by Microsoft Access.

An interesting example of hybrid VQL is Kaleidoquery (Murray, Paton, & Goble, 1998). This is based on a filter flow model, representing the successive filtering stages operated by the query from the initial mass of information to the required output result. In this language, classes of objects in the database are represented

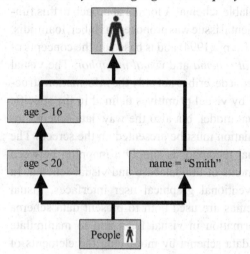

by icons and diagrams are used to depict the flow and refinement of information through the query (see Figure 4).

DATA MODELS AND VQLS

A data model is a combination of constructs used to organize data (Atzeni, Ceri, Paraboschi, & Torlone, 1999). This is strictly related to the concept of schema, as the adoption of a certain data model determines the way data are structured, and consequently the schema types present in the database. As previously noted, one of the key aspects in the formulation of a query is the specification of the input and output schemas. Since the schema types in a database are determined by the specific data model adopted, the model itself has a significant influence on the query language's characteristics: data models with more sophisticated, modular constructs require a corresponding higher level of complexity in the query language constructs, regardless of whether they are textual or visual. On the other hand, some data model constructs, such as hierarchical relationships, have a more straightforward, intuitive representation in visual languages.

A fundamental step in specifying the query input schema is the display of the database's available schema. A formal approach to this fundamental issue was proposed in Haber, Ioannidis, and Livny (1994) and is based on the concepts of *visual schema* and *visual metaphor*. The visual schema describes not only the information structure by visual primitives defined in the specific visual model, but also the way data schema information must be presented on the screen. The visual metaphor is simply a mapping between elements of the database and visual schema. In conventional graphical user interfaces, visual schemas are used both to present data schema information in visual form and to manipulate the data schema by modifying the elements of the visual schema.

The Impact of Model Abstraction

The effectiveness of a VQL is strongly influenced by the simplicity and intuitiveness of the visual model and hence, through the visual metaphor, of the data model. Complex, abstract, and semantically rich data models tend to produce complex visual models with a high *impedance mismatch* with the underlying data structures. However, elementary data models have necessarily limited representation capabilities and complex concepts need to be mapped to over-simplified visual constructs, far from the user's perception of the area of interest. Traditionally, data models are classified into three main categories each corresponding to a different abstraction level in the representation of the area of interest:

- **Conceptual models** (e.g., the entity-relationship data model) are the most abstract and describe concepts of the real world, rather than the data used to represent them. Due to their high level of abstraction they are commonly used in the first phases of the database design process, but the actual implementation of DBMSs (and consequently

of query languages) based on them can be quite problematic.

- **Logical models** (e.g., the relational, hierarchical, and object data model) reflect a particular organization (table, tree, object) of the data, facilitating the implementation of DBMSs based on them and query optimization, while maintaining a good level of abstraction expressed by the so-called property of *physical independence*. The interaction with the DBMS is independent of the data's physical aspects (files, storage systems, etc.). Most DBMSs and query languages (especially visual ones) are therefore based on logical models.

- **Physical models** are strictly related to the physical organization of data in the DBMS (storage techniques, access structures, etc.) and are therefore inappropriate for the definition of high-level, user-friendly query languages.

Even if most VQLs are based on logical models, there can be significant differences among them, mainly related to the particular data organization (e.g., table, tree, object) on which the model is based. In the following section, we classify VQLs according to their data model, focusing on languages based on (1) conceptual models; (2) the relational model; (3) the functional model; (4) the object model; (5) XML. Finally, we consider the case of VQLs specifically designed for particular types of data (e.g., geographical and multidimensional data).

VQLs Based on Conceptual Models

The entity-relationship (E-R) model was originally proposed in Chen (1976) and is commonly recognized as the standard conceptual model for database design. As such, it can be mapped to several different logical data models and consequently to DBMSs and storage techniques. It is also a graphical model based on fairly simple diagrams consisting of a few geometric elements connected by edges. In consequence, it could be considered an ideal starting point to define a visual query language. However, its high level of abstraction is also its main drawback for use in a real DBMS, as some transformations from the visual to the logical level can be particularly difficult and some manipulations that can be straightforwardly expressed at the logical level may be cumbersome to define at the conceptual level.

A VQL based on the E-R model is proposed in Czejdo et al. (1989). Queries are expressed by visually selecting the elements of interest (entities and relationships) in a database schema displayed as an E-R diagram. Conditions on the selected elements are expressed by a set C, initially empty, of *condition descriptors*, stating for example that the attribute of an entity must be equal to a given constant value. In Angelaccio et al. (1990), the QBD* system is described; this allows the user to interact with the conceptual (E-R) schema of the database at different abstraction levels through a top-down browsing mechanism. A set of graphical primitives can be used to extract the subschema containing the query concepts (i.e., the input schema) as well as to filter and transform the selected concepts, defining the desired output schema. SUPER (Dennebouy et al., 1995) is based on an object-based extension of the E-R model called ERC+ and designed to support complex objects and object identity. SUPER has a layered structure allowing the user to interact with the ERC+ elements independently of the actual underlying DBMS and comprising a specifically designed algebra in the intermediate layer. The construction of a query encompasses a sequence of activities performed through the visual interface: definition of the *query frame* (input schema), the specification of conditions on the database occurrences, and finally the output format. Another example of a "conceptual VQL" is ConQuer (Bloesch & Halpin, 1996), which is based on the object-role modelling (ORM) approach to conceptual modelling.

VQLs Based on the Relational Models

In the relational model (Codd, 1970), data are represented by collections of relations or, more intuitively, as collections of tables. Each table (relation) has a specific, well-defined structure (the *relation schema*) with a table name and a collection of column names called attributes, and consists of a collection of related rows (tuples) of data values (the *relation instance*). Queries can be expressed in a variety of textual languages (e.g., relational algebra, domain and tuple calculi, datalog and SQL.) *Integrity constraints* (i.e., properties that must be satisfied by relation instances representing semantically correct information in the domain of interest,) can also be defined. Integrity constraints, especially referential constraints, are often exploited by VQLs to highlight the semantic links existing among tables and to perform automatic *joins* between them.

The simplicity and strong mathematical foundations of the relational model are certainly two key factors for its great success. In fact, the vast majority of currently available DBMSs are relational and in consequence, many visual languages proposed in the literature are based on this model. Since relational data have a fairly simple structure, relational VQLs can usually achieve a good trade-off between expressive power and language complexity. In contrast, when dealing with more sophisticated data models (e.g., based on objects or semi-structured data) the higher complexity necessarily permeates the query language (even in the textual case) and this trade-off is much more difficult to achieve. The tabular structure underlying the model is well suited to VQLs based on tabular forms such as the query-by-example (QBE) language previously mentioned, originally proposed in Zloof (1977) and later implemented with some variations in several DBMSs.

Other approaches are based on the use of icons and attempt to exploit the additional information provided by the integrity constraints to guide the query's construction. For example, VISION-ARY (Benzi, Maio, & Rizzi, 1999) is based on a layered structure where the visual metaphor uses an intermediate graph model for the mapping between the internal relational schema and the external icon-based visual schema. A relational database is represented in the intermediate graph model by a non-directed graph where each vertex corresponds to a table and the edges represent potential links (i.e., relationships determined by referential integrity constraints). The basic primitives of the visual model are the *concepts* (represented by the combination of a text and an icon) and the *associations* between concepts (represented by labelled oriented edges). The user specifies the input schema starting from a primary concept, which determines a set of default joins, and then refines it up to the desired output with projection and selection operations by interacting with the visual schema displayed on the screen. A semantic graph model is also used in Zhang et al. (1999) where nodes represent tables and the edges correspond to joins between relations, which are used to support the user in the query formulation process.

The query-by-browsing (QBB) paradigm (Polyviou, Samaras, & Evripidou, 2005) proposes a quite different approach to visual querying based on the tuple relational calculus and folder hierarchies. Tables are represented as folders and the relationships between them (e.g., foreign key references) as folder/subfolder relationships, which can be "followed" by opening the table folder containing the reference. A table folder also contains attributes and records corresponding to the table schema and instance on which constraints can be defined. Figure 5 gives an example of a folder tree representing the schema of a relational database describing the relationships between students, professors, courses, classes, and rooms.

Folders can also act as operators to filter and combine the respective subfolders. To define the query output schema the concept of *document* is introduced. This is a materialized view over the

Figure 5. A folder tree in query by browsing

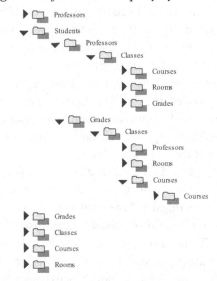

data contained in the document's parent folder and its subfolders. Although based on the relational model, QBB has also been shown to possibly accommodate more complex data models (e.g., based on objects or XML).

VQLs Based on the Functional Data Model

The functional data model (Sibley & Kerschberg, 1977) is basically a functional view of the binary relational model in which the area of interest is represented by entities and binary relations between pairs of entities. More precisely, each binary relation over domains A and B is equivalently defined by a pair of (possibly multi-valued) functions from A to B and from B to A, forming, together with the entities, the basic elements of the model. The main advantage of this simplified data model is that mapping between the data schema and the visual schema is generally more straightforward and the user's navigation among the schema elements can be guided by the functional links between concepts.

Gql (Papantonakis et al., 1994) is a VQL based on the functional data model. Similarly to

VISIONARY, the database schema is represented by a graph where nodes correspond to entities and labeled directed edges to functions. Entities can be either lexical (broadly corresponding to simple data types such as strings, numbers, etc.) or abstract (corresponding to real world concepts). Lexical entities are visualized as ovals and abstract entities as circle nodes. Queries are expressed by selecting elements on the input schema, specifying constraints on them (e.g., ="Rome," >10, etc.) and indicating the subset that will constitute the output schema. Various types of boxes can be used to enclose portions of the input schema and define nested queries, aggregations, negations, disjunctions, quantifications, etc.

VQLs Based on the Object Data Model

The object data model was developed to overcome some limitations of the relational model and is based on the extension of the object-oriented programming paradigm (specifically, the concepts of class, object identity, encapsulation, inheritance) to databases (Atkinson et al., 1989). Objects in an object database can have a much

more complex structure with respect to the rows (tuples) of a relational database, as the single object components may also contain references to other objects, as well as sets, bags (multisets), and lists of elementary values or even of other objects. Classes of objects can also be organized in generalization hierarchies where more specific classes "inherit" and typically specialize the schema of the more general ones. Since the elements of an object database usually have this fairly complex nested structure, the use of tabular metaphors is not as obvious or straightforward as in the relational case. In contrast, graph-based approaches are usually preferred where different edges are used to represent nesting and relationships among objects. Iconic approaches are also well suited to represent objects, classes, and the various relationships among them visually.

The visual query system for object databases of the integrated environment PROOVE (Doan, Paton, Kilgour, & al-Qaimari, 1995) supports two alternative (form- and graph-based) visualization metaphors. In the graph-based interface, the input and output schemas are visualized by directed graphs where double rectangles represent classes, single rectangles represent elementary

Figure 6. The visual definition of a query in the PROOVE environment

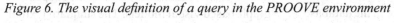

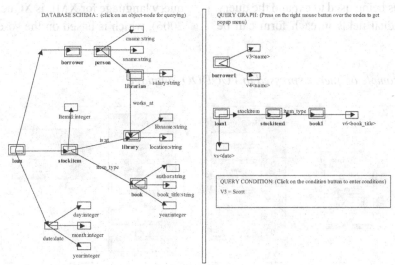

data types (e.g., integer, float, and string), and the edges describe the class structure. The two schemas are displayed in two separate frames of the user interface (see Figure 6). By selecting a node in the input schema, the user can include it in the output schema (*query graph*), which is displayed in the *query window*. The query can be further refined in this window by expressing conditions and/or extending the output schema by popup menus attached to the various nodes. The example query shown in Figure 6 is taken from Doan et al. (1995) and represents the retrieval of the details of all *books* borrowed by *borrowers* with a *cname* of Scott. A graph-based interface is also used in O_2Talk (Sentissi & Pichat, 1997). In this language, classes are depicted by rectangle nodes, attributes by continuous or discontinuous ovals (for atomic and complex attributes respectively), and the class-superclass relationships are represented by links between classes.

Queries in VOODOO (Fegaras, 1999) are represented by trees of forms, which have some analogies with QBB folder trees. The forms reflect the database schema and every class or type reference in the schema can be "expanded" by clicking on the corresponding form button in the visual interface, potentially leading to an infinite tree. Each tree node consists of a form and represents a class or structure in the database schema. Besides being used to expand the query tree, the individual fields in each form can be

filled in with constant values and expressions or be included in the output schema, similarly to QBE. Figure 7 represents the query "Find the name of the department whose head is Smith" in the VOODOO language.

Finally, Chavda and Wood (1997) propose the Quiver language with a fairly modular approach combining graphs with an iconic interface. Here, graphs are used not only to describe the database structure (as in many other VQLs), but also to represent the data flow to and from computations, for example the data flow corresponding to the application of a method to a class of objects. Furthermore, graphs are generally nested, as each node can include other nodes and possibly arcs and bold nodes and arcs are used to define the query output schema visually.

VQLs Based on the XML Data Model

The extensible markup language (XML) is a general-purpose textual language specifically designed to define various kinds of data structures (i.e., the database schema) as well as to store the data contents in XML documents (the database instance). The typical hierarchical structure of XML documents is reflected in the VQLs based on this language and naturally leads to the adoption of graph-based visual models. The standard textual query language for XML is XQuery (Boag et al., 2006), which is based on the so-called FLWOR

Figure 7. An example of query expressed in VOODOO language

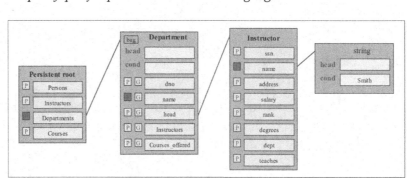

(for-let-where-order by-return) expressions and has some similarities with the SQL syntax.

XQBE (XQuery by example) was proposed by Braga, Campi, and Ceri (2005) to visually express a fairly large subset of XQuery and can be considered as an evolution of XML-GL (Comai, Damiani, & Fraternali, 2001). The main graphical element in XQBE is the tree, which is used to denote both the documents assumed as query input (the input schema) and the document produced by the query (the output schema). Tree nodes represent the various elements of the XML documents and are shaped in different ways according to the specific semantics. In particular: (1) root nodes are represented as grey squares labelled with the location (URI) of the corresponding XML document; (2) element nodes are shaped as rectangles labelled with the element name (or tagname); (3) PCDATA nodes are represented as empty circles, (4) attribute nodes are represented as filled black circles. Other node types and notations are introduced to express specific manipulations and selections. Finally, directed arcs are used to represent the containment relationship between two XML items. For example, Figure 8 shows the XQBE formulation of the query "Return all books in the source document, retaining for each book only the list of their authors and the title; change also the tagname to myBook."

Figure 8 shows that the query window is divided into two parts: the source (corresponding to the input schema) on the left and the construct (corresponding to the output schema) on the right. Obviously, the source part describes the structure to be matched against the set of input documents, while the construct part specifies which elements will be retained in the result, together with (optional) newly generated items. The two parts are linked by binding edges expressing the correspondence between the respective components.

Tree structures with variously shaped nodes are also used in the XQueryViz tool (Karam, Boulos, Ollaic, & Koteiche, 2006), which is strongly related to the XQuery syntax and whose interface is based on four interdependent windows displaying (1) the XML schemas and documents; (2) the for-let-where clause of the query in visual form; (3) the return clause of the query in visual form; (4) the textual XQuery representation of the query. During query formulation, the textual representation is continuously updated and the various parts are given different colors to reflect the correspondence between the visual and its textual counterpart.

The Xing language (Erwig, 2003) uses a completely different approach to the representation of the typical hierarchical structure of XML documents. Here, XML elements are represented by nested boxes/forms and the hierarchies between elements by relationships of visual inclusion. As in many other VQLs, the query is expressed by defining, in two separate sections of the visual interface, the input schema, through an *argument pattern*, which specifies the structural and content constraints, and the output schema, through a *result pattern*, which performs selection, and restructuring operations on the extracted data.

VQLs and Special Purpose Data

Several interesting applications of VQLs can be found in contexts where the data have some explicit geometric properties, describe some spatial relationships, or are commonly described by means of a geometric metaphor. This is obviously the case

Figure 8. Example of XQBE query

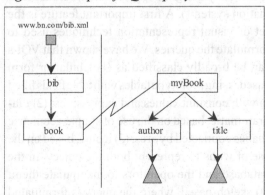

in geographical information systems (GISs), but also in data warehouses, which are based on the well-known metaphor of the multi-dimensional data cube and in scientific databases containing for instance scientific experimental data.

In geographic information systems (GISs), topological relationships between geographical entities can be expressed very intuitively in visual form. VQLs for this kind of data usually represent geographical entities with a very limited number of *symbolic graphical objects* (SGOs) namely point, polyline, and polygon. In several languages queries are expressed by drawing a geometric pattern (e.g., two intersecting polygons, a polygon including another polygon, a polyline adjacent to a polygon, etc.) corresponding to the desired result. For example in Cigales (Aufaure-Portier, 1995), queries are expressed using predefined *graphical forms* (icons) representing both the geographical entities and the topological relationships among them while in pictorial query-by-example (Papadias & Sellis, 1995) *skeleton arrays* are used to represent a set of objects and their spatial relationships. The inherent ambiguity of some geometric patterns has been studied by several authors and Ferri & Rafanelli (2005) propose the introduction of specific G-any and G-alias operators to cope with this issue. As previously discussed, an important family of VQLs for GISs is based on sketches (e.g., Sketch! (Meyer, 1992), spatial-query-by-sketch (Egenhofer, 1997), and VISCO (Haarslev et al., 1997)).

Data warehouses are traditionally described using the well-known metaphor of the multi-dimensional data cube and the concepts of dimensions and dimension hierarchies. A data cube is a collection of aggregate values (measures) classified according to several properties of interest (dimensions), each of which is possibly organized in hierarchies. Combinations of dimension values are used to identify the single aggregate values in the cube and querying is often an exploratory process, where the user "moves" along the dimension hierarchies by increasing or reducing the granularity of displayed data. A diagrammatic VQL for multidimensional data was proposed by Cabibbo and Torlone (1998) and is based on a graphical diagrammatic representation of the data warehouse schema where hierarchies are represented by directed arcs and dimensions by enclosing shapes. As in many other diagrammatic VQLs, the output data is selected by expressing constraints on the schema elements and highlighting the desired measures and dimension levels on the warehouse schema.

An example of VQL for the exploratory navigation of scientific data is VISUAL (Balkir et al., 2002), which was designed for the domain of materials engineers for use with scientific experimental data, in particular their spatial properties. VISUAL uses icons to represent both the objects of interest and their spatial relationships, and users can define their own graphical icons to recreate the environment that they are familiar with. Although graphical, the structure of a VISUAL query closely resembles datalog rules with a *body* section containing iconized objects, constraints, and references to other objects (i.e., the input schema) and a *head* section representing the various components of the query output.

CONCLUSION

In this chapter, we analyzed some fundamental characteristics of VQLs (i.e., visual languages specifically designed to retrieve data from information systems). A first important feature is the set of visual representation techniques used to formulate the queries. We have shown that VQLs can be broadly classified as (1) tabular or form based, using prototype tables with table fields filled in with constant values and expressions; (2) diagrammatic, based on the use of simple geometric shapes connected by arcs; (3) iconic, based on the use of icons to represent both the objects in the database and the operators to manipulate them; (4) sketch-based, where the query is formulated by freehand sketches on a virtual blackboard; and finally (5) hybrid, combining two or more of these approaches. Secondly, we have analyzed the relationships between VQLs and the features of the underlying data model, with a specific focus on the level of abstraction, the most commonly used data models (conceptual, relational, object, functional, XML) and information systems specifically designed for particular kinds of data such as GISs and data warehouses.

REFERENCES

Abiteboul, S., Hull, R., & Vianu, V. (1995). *Foundations of databases*. Addison-Wesley.

Angelaccio, M., Catarci, T., & Santucci, G. (1990). QBD*: A fully visual query system. *Journal of Visual Languages and Computing, 1*(2), 255-273.

Atkinson, M. P., Bancilhon, F., DeWitt, D. J., Dittrich, K. R., Maier, D., Zdonik, S. B. (1989). The object-oriented database system manifesto. The *1st International Conference on Deductive and Object-Oriented Databases (DOOD'89)* (pp. 223-240).

Atzeni, P., Ceri, S., Paraboschi, S., & Torlone, R. (1999). *Database systems: Concepts, languages, and architectures*. McGraw-Hill.

Aufaure-Portier, M. A. (1995). A high level interface language for GIS. *Journal of Visual Languages and Computing, 6*(2), 167-182.

Aufaure-Portier, M. A., & Bonhomme, C. (1999). A high-level visual language for spatial data management. The *3rd International Conference on Visual Information and Information Systems (VISUAL 1999)* (pp. 325-332).

Aversano, L., Canfora, G., De Lucia, A., & Stefanucci, S. (2002). Understanding SQL through iconic interfaces. The *International Computer Software and Applications Conference (COMPSAC 2002)* (pp. 703-710).

Balkir, N. H., Ozsoyoglu, G., & Ozsoyoglu, Z. M. (2002). A graphical query language: Visual and its query processing. *IEEE Transactions on Knowledge and Data Engineering, 14*(5), 955-978.

Benzi, F., Maio, D., & Rizzi, S. (1999). VISIONARY: A viewpoint-based visual language for querying relational databases. *Journal of Visual Languages Computing, 10*(2), 117-145.

Blackwell, A. F., & Green, T. R. G. (1999). Does metaphor increase visual language usability? *IEEE Symposium on Visual Languages (VL'99)* (pp. 246-253).

Blaser, A. D., & Egenhofer, M. J. (2000). A visual tool for querying geographic databases. *Working Conference on Advanced Visual Interfaces (AVI 2000)* (pp. 211-216).

Bloesch, A. C., & Halpin T. A. (1996). ConQuer: A conceptual query language. *International Conference on Conceptual Modeling (ER 1996)* (pp. 121-133).

Boag, S., Chamberlin, D., Fernandez, M. F., Florescu, D., Robie, J., & Simeon, J. (2006). *XQuery 1.0: An XML query language*. Retrieved October 13, 2006, from http://www.w3.org/TR/xquery/

Braga, D., Campi, A., & Ceri, S. (2005). XQBE (XQuery by example): A visual interface to the standard XML query language. *ACM Transactions on Database Systems, 30*(2), 398-443.

Cabibbo, L., & Torlone, R. (1998). From a procedural to a visual query language for OLAP. *International Conference on Scientific and Statistical Database Management (SSDBM'98)* (pp. 74-83).

Catarci, T., Costabile, M. F., Levialdi, S., & Batini, C. (1997). Visual query systems for databases: A survey. *Journal of Visual Languages and Computing, 8*(2), 215-260.

Catarci, T., Santucci, G., & Angelaccio, M. (1993). Fundamental graphical primitives for visual query languages. *Information Systems, 18*(3), 75-98.

Chavda, M., & Wood, P. T. (1997). Towards an ODMG-compliant visual object query language. *International Conference on Very Large Data Bases (VLDB'97)* (pp. 456-465).

Chen, P. P. (1976). The entity-relationship model: Towards a unified view of data. *ACM Transactions on Database Systems, 1*(1), 9-36.

Codd, E. F. (1970). A relational model of data for large shared databanks. *Communications of the ACM, 13*(6), 377-387.

Comai, S., Damiani, E., & Fraternali, P. (2001). Computing graphical queries over XML data. *ACM Transaction on Information Systems 19*(4), 371-430.

Czejdo, B., Embley, D., Reddy, V., & Rusinkiewicz, M. (1989). A visual query language for an ER data model. *IEEE Workshop on Visual Languages* (pp. 165-170).

Dennebouy, Y., Andersson, M., Auddino, A., Dupont, Y., Fontana, E., Gentile, M., & Spaccapietra, S. (1995). SUPER: Visual interfaces for object + relationships data models. *Journal of Visual Languages and Computing, 6*(1), 73-99.

Doan, D. K., Paton, N. W., Kilgour, A. C., & al-Qaimari, G. (1995). Multi-paradigm query interface to an object-oriented database. *Interacting with Computers, 7*(1), 25-47.

Egenhofer, M. J. (1997). Query processing in spatial-query-by-sketch. *Journal of Visual Languages and Computing, 8*(4), 403-424.

Erwig, M. (2003). Xing: A visual XML query language. *Journal of Visual Languages and Computing 14*(1), 5-45.

Fegaras, L. (1999). VOODOO: A visual object-oriented database language for ODMG OQL. *ECOOP Workshop on Object-Oriented Databases* (pp. 61-72).

Ferri, F., & Rafanelli, M. (2005). GeoPQL: A geographical pictorial query language that resolves ambiguities in query interpretation. *Journal on Data Semantics*, 50-80.

Haarslev, V., & Wessel, M. (1997). Querying GIS with animated spatial sketches. The *13th IEEE Symposium on Visual Languages 1997 (VL'97)* (pp. 201-208).

Haber, E. M., Ioannidis, Y. E., & Livny, M. (1994). Foundations of visual metaphors for schema display. *Journal of Intelligent Information Systems, 3*(3-4), 263-298.

Karam, M., Boulos, J., Ollaic, H., & Koteiche, Z. (2006). XQueryViz: A visual dataflow Xquery tool. *International Conference on Internet and Web Applications and Services (ICIW'06)*.

Larkin, J. H., & Simon, H. (1987). Why a diagram is (sometimes) worth ten thousand words. *Cognitive Science, 11*(1), 65-100.

Massari, A., Pavani, S., & Saladini, L. (1994). QBI: an iconic query system for inexpert users. *Working Conference on Advanced Visual Interfaces (AVI'94)* (pp. 240-242).

Meyer, B. (1994). Pictorial deduction in spatial information systems. *IEEE Symposium on Visual Languages (VL94)* (pp. 23-30).

Meyer, B. (1992). Beyond icons: Towards new metaphors for visual query languages for spatial information systems. *International Workshop on Interfaces to Database Systems (IDS'92)* (pp. 113-135).

Murray, N., Paton, N. W., & Goble, C. A. (1998). Kaleidoquery: A visual query language for object databases. *Working Conference on Advanced Visual Interfaces (AVI'98)* (pp. 247-257).

Papadias, D., & Sellis, T. K. (1995). A pictorial query-by-example language. *Journal of Visual Languages and Computing, 6*(1), 53-72.

Papantonakis, A., & King, P. J. H. (1994). Gql, a declarative graphical query language based on the functional data model. *Workshop on Advanced Visual Interfaces (AVI'94)* (pp. 113-122).

Polyviou, S., Samaras, G., & Evripidou, P. (2005). A relationally complete visual query language for heterogeneous data sources and pervasive querying. *International Conference on Data Engineering (ICDE'05)* (pp. 471-482).

Rosengren, P. (1994). Using visual ER query systems in real world applications. *Advanced Information Systems Engineering (CAiSE'94)* (pp. 394-405), LNCS 811.

Sentissi, T., & Pichat, E. (1997). A graphical user interface for object-oriented database. *International Conference of the Chilean Computer Science Society (SCCC'97)* (pp. 227-239).

Sibley, E. H., & Kerschberg, L. (1977). Data architecture and data model considerations. *AFIPS National Computer Conference.*

Staes, F., Tarantino, L., & Tiems, A. (1991). A graphical query language for object-oriented databases. *IEEE Symposium on Visual Languages (VL'91)* (pp. 205-210).

Vadaparty, K., Aslandogan, Y. A., & Ozsoyoglu, G. (1993). Towards a unified visual database access. In *ACM SIGMOD International Conference on Management of Data (SIGMOD'93)* (pp. 357-366).

Zhang, G., Chu, W. W., Meng, F., & Kong, G. (1999). Query formulation from high-level concepts for relational databases. *International Workshop on User Interfaces to Data Intensive Systems (UIDIS'99)* (pp. 64-75).

Zloof, M. M. (1977). Query-by-example: A database language. *IBM Systems Journal, 16*(4), 324-343.

Chapter IX
Toward a Visual Query System for Spatio-Temporal Databases

Valéria M. B. Cavalcanti
Federal University of Campina Grande, Brazil

Ulrich Schiel
Federal University of Campina Grande, Brazil

Claudio de Souza Baptista
Federal University of Campina Grande, Brazil

ABSTRACT

Visual query systems (VQS) for spatio-temporal databases, which enable formulation of queries involving both spatial and temporal dimensions, are an important research subject. Existing results treat these dimensions separately and there are only a few integrated proposals. This chapter presents a VQS called spatio-temporal visual query environment (S-TVQE), which allows the formulation of conventional, spatial, temporal, and spatio-temporal database queries in an integrated environment. With S-TVQE, the user, instead of querying the database by textual query languages will interact with the system by visual operators for the statement of the query conditions. The tool provides a visualization of the results in different formats such as maps, graphics, and tables.

INTRODUCTION

The growing significance of geographic information systems and other spatio-temporal information systems is unquestionable (Sellis, Frank, Grumbach, Guting, & Koubarakis, 2003). Decision-makers need to analyze data through thematic maps, timelines, search critical regions, and so on.

Therefore, it is mandatory to provide user-friendly tools, specially designed for these decision-makers so that they can express their needs adequately and explore the full potential of the underlying information systems. The visual specification of database queries enables an abstraction of the database schema and textual query languages, which makes user interaction easier.

A visual interface represents an additional layer (Shneiderman, 1998), which interacts between the user and a textual query language as, for instance, structured query language (SQL) (Silberschatz, Korth, & Sudarshan, 2005) in order to access a database. For instance, spatial constraints from the visual query are converted to SQL statements, which are executed on the underlined database management system (DBMS).

That task must be executed in a transparent way, in other words, no knowledge on database schema and language syntax is required (Snodgrass, 1999), which facilitates the usability of the database mainly for sporadic users, which are not familiar with technical details of the database.

The use of visual query interfaces is more significant for spatio-temporal databases as for conventional databases for two reasons: (1) spatial data are inherently visual and (2) textual query languages for those enhanced applications are more complicated since they must provide syntax to express temporal and spatial restrictions.

For textual database query languages such as SQL (Silberschatz, Korth & Sudarshan, 2005), there are extensions to access temporal data such as TSQL2 (Snodgrass 1995), and spatial data such as spatial-SQL (Egenhofer, 1994). These extensions are adequate for experienced database programmers and automatic data extraction tools. Many end users have no expertise on computer systems. For this group, visual query systems has proven to be the most adequate interface (Catarci et al., 1997).

This chapter presents a generic visual environment for the access to spatio-temporal database systems especially geographic information systems. The environment can be plugged into existing databases.

For the validation of the system, we used real data from geo-referenced health information of the Brazilian Health System (SUS). SUS is an institution responsible for collecting, processing, and disseminating health information of Brazilian government.

Information related to health is generated daily in the whole country, and is stored considering valid time and spatial parameters. The volume of information already existent is very large and increases every day. Seeking to improve the quality of investments of health resources, the administrators perform statistical analyses with this data.

The health information system divides the country into regions, states, regional health nucleus (NRS), and municipal districts. Data about hospitals, admissions, attendances, and so on are stored in the database. A simplified conceptual schema using UML notation for this system is shown in Figure 1. Note the following conventions: objects may be conventional, spatial, temporal, or combinations of them. These characteristics are stated at class level attached to the class name. For instance, HOSPITAL (S) is spatial and PATIENT (T) is temporal. This means that each instance of HOSPITAL has an implicit geometry and each

Figure 1. Class schema of the health information system

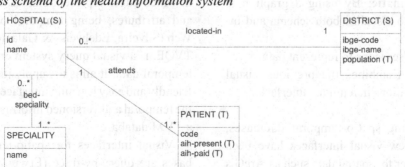

PATIENT has implicit valid-time attributes. Attributes may be either conventional or temporal. For instance, DISTRICT.population (T) is a temporal attribute. Note that in the class PATIENT we have the history of the patients and, for each patient, we have the history of their registration cards (aih), when they were admitted (aih-present) and when they were paid (aih-paid).

The remainder of this chapter is organized as follows. The next section addresses related work on visual query systems. After that, we review the limitations of current systems and present the S-TVQE environment. What is missing in order to get a completely satisfactory solution is discussed next, and the last section concludes the work.

RESEARCH BACKGROUND ON VISUAL QUERY SYSTEMS

A great effort in research has been spent to develop more user-friendly interaction paradigms, especially considering some kind of visual interaction, for both conventional and advanced databases (Bonhomme, Trépied, Aufaure, & Laurini, 1999; Morris, Abdelmoty, Tudhope, & El-Geresy, 2002; Shimabukuro, Branco, Oliveira, & Flores, 2003). According to the visual formalism adopted in the query, visual query systems may be classified into:

- **Table:** Data is organized and visualized as tables. Preview of table extension and intension may be available (e.g., QBE).
- **Diagrammatic:** By using a graph it is possible to visualize both schema and instances.
- **Iconic:** Uses icons to represent data.
- **Hybrid:** Combines the previous visual representations in a unique interface.

For accessing spatio-temporal databases, the most of new visual interfaces have been developed either for spatial data such as ArcGis

(2006), CIGALES (Calcinelli & Mainguenaud, 1994), Geomedia (2006), spatial query by sketch (Egenhofer, 1997), geovisual (Soares, 2002) or for temporal data as TVQE (Silva, Schiel, & Catarci 2002), and TVM-Web (Silveira, Edelweiss, & Galante, 2004).

Geomedia and ArcGis are commercial GIS, which provide visual interaction with limited support for temporal and spatio-temporal dimensions. CIGALES (cartographical interface generating and adapted language for extensible systems) (Calcinelli & Mainguenaud, 1994) supports visual queries to a geographical database. The user combines lines and areas with some spatial operators to build the query. Spatial query by sketch (Egenhofer, 1997) enables the definition of spatial queries through sketch, which represents the spatial relations between the schema elements. Apart from the spatial relation, other relations may be used. Ambiguities are solved through user interaction.

Morris et al. (2002) have developed a visual query environment for large spatial databases using a diagrammatic approach based on a data flow metaphor. They propose icons for the different spatial relations and use a hierarchy for the different granularities of these relations.

TVQE (temporal visual query environment) (Silva, Schiel & Catarci, 2002) is a visual query system for temporal databases. It is a hybrid system as it uses diagrammatic and iconic representations. It is based on the temporal graph model (TGM) (Silva, Schiel & Catarci, 2002), which specifies a conceptual database schema as a directed graph in which edges represent classes, relationships, and attributes, being temporal or not. TVM Web (Silveira, Edelweiss & Galante, 2004), like TVQE, is a visual query system on the Web for temporal data. It aims to supply the user with a friendly and easy learning interface that explores the temporal and versioned information stored in a TVM database.

Visual interfaces for spatio-temporal databases are query-by-trace (Erwig & Schneider,

2000) and the visual interactive query interface (Li & Chang, 2004). Query-by-trace (QBT) is a system that enables the definition of spatio-temporal queries through primitive graphics based on lines and areas that represent the space operations. The user inserts objects freely (line or area) in an area for definition of the moving trace of the object. Several such traces determine the spatial relations between the objects in the query. QBT realizes the mapping into primitive space operators for subsequent optimization. To represent the moving of objects through time they use a two-dimensional area, one axis representing the space and the other time. This system is specifically designed for describing and querying moving objects.

The visual interactive query interface (Li & Chang, 2004) proposes a visual query system based on an extension of SQL for spatio-temporal databases, called ΣQL. The system has been applied to movie databases and there is no evidence that it works properly on geographic information systems.

Lvis (Bonhomme et al., 1999) is a visual query language extended from the CIGALES project (Calcinelli & Mainguenaud, 1994), which provides support for conventional, spatial, temporal, and spatio-temporal queries, using the query-by-example metaphor. It uses topological and metric spatial relations and there is no evidence that the query results are spatial, temporal, or graphic.

THE SPATIO-TEMPORAL VISUAL QUERY ENVIRONMENT

As has been seen in the previous section, there are many approaches supporting the expression of visual queries for spatial database or for temporal databases. Integrated proposals for spatio-temporal databases concentrate on moving objects. One of the most significant data in geographic information systems are temporally

bounded maps. Therefore, in order to state queries adequately to their data structures, visual query systems integrating spatial and temporal constraints are mandatory. In this context, we present a spatio-temporal visual query environment called S-TVQE which achieves this integration.

S-TVQE is an extension of the temporal visual query environment (TVQE) (Silva, Schiel, & Catarci, 2002), which adds to conventional and temporal visual query operations, support for stating spatial and spatio-temporal queries. In this section, we address important issues on designing visual query system with spatio-temporal capabilities. Firstly, a methodology for the interface design is addressed, followed by the importance of providing a configurable interface. Then architectural issues are highlighted. Hence, we focus on the important aspects for non-spatial, spatial, temporal, and spatiotemporal visual query systems (VQS).

Interface Design Issues

There are many methodologies for designing a user-friendly interface (Hackos, 1998; Shneiderman, 1998). The task-oriented methodology such as ICM (interface conception method) (Scherer, 2003) is very appropriated for the development of visual query systems. This methodology is interactive, task oriented, and user-centered. ICM contains seven steps:

1. **Requirements analysis and specification:** Provides the requirement analysis for S-TVQE.
2. **Task modeling:** Determines the necessary actions to execute system tasks.
3. **Interaction modeling:** Associates task objects with interaction ones based on the task model giving an interaction model.
4. **Visual modeling:** Defines the objects presentation based on ergonomic issues, user profile, and task features.

5. **The establishment of navigation and help procedures:** Identifies and organizes the interface transition situations.

6. **Prototype construction:** Generates an interface prototype code, based on the previous artifacts.

7. **Prototype evaluation:** Interface validation through usability tests.

Flexible Configuration through XML

XML has been largely used for providing flexibility on system configuration. This flexibility avoids code recompilation, as only a new deployment is necessary. Therefore, we have followed this approach in the design of the S-TVQE, which enables it to work in different contexts, being necessary to just configure a XML file that determines the primitive operations and the schema of the database.

In order to define the current database, which determines the context to be configured in S-TVQE, an XML file is edited. This file represents a view of the underlying schema, which describes the tables, keys, and attributes.

For spatial objects there is an element called level with an id attribute, which indicates the "contains" spatial relationship. So that $level_{i+1}$ is spatially contained in $level_i$, each level element contains sub-elements, which indicate the geometric field, the table key, and attribute features such as column name, column type, table, and whether the attribute is conventional, spatial, or temporal. Finally, an element called *grouped* describes an optional aggregation function to be used. An example of such an XML configuration, describing the levels "state" and "district" of the health information system follows:

```
<stvqe>
  <level id = "1">
    <description>State</description>
    <geom>statemap</geom>
    <key>geom_id</key>
```

```
    <attribute field = "statename"
                     type = "string"
               table = "nrs"
               conventional = "true"
               spatial = "false"
               temporal = "false"
               grouped = "null" />
  </level>
  <level id = "2">
    <description>District</description>
    <geom>districtmap</geom>
    <key>geomid</key>
    <attribute field = "districtname"
               type = "string"
               table = "district"
               conventional = "true"
               spatial = "false"
               temporal = "false"
               grouped = "null" />
    <attribute field = "admission"
               type = "int"
               table = "admissions"
               conventional = "true"
               spatial = "false"
               temporal = "true"
               grouped = "sum" />
  </level>
</stvqe>
```

Architectural Issues

S-TVQE was developed to serve as a generic interface for spatio-temporal databases and could be connected easily to any relational database system with spatial capabilities such as PostgreSQL, Oracle, DB2, or MySQL. Nonetheless, there are many proposals of temporal query languages from which TSQL2 (Snodgrass, 1995) is the most representative. None of them have been incorporated in the SQL standard. Moreover, there is no SQL-like language combining spatial and temporal capabilities. Furthermore, there is no widely used temporal database management system. For this

Figure 2. The S-TVQE architecture

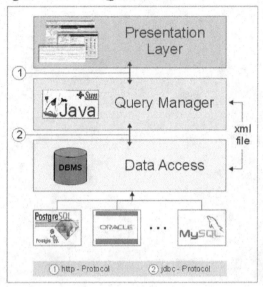

Query Interaction

In order to pose a query, users may follow several steps. The following algorithm presents the whole interaction process.

- Definition of the geographic area of interest: "*Visual Selection*";
- Chose the attributes, which will take part in the query: "*Searching Attributes*";
- Optionally, define restrictions on the chosen attributes: "*Query Item Edition*";
- Choose the operator (spatial, temporal, or relational) according to the dimension of the attribute: "*Operators*";
- Fill necessary fields: "*Query Item Edition*";
- Add the attribute to obtain the query: "*Current Query*";
- Query results.

In the following, we explain in detail each of these steps. As an example to illustrate the steps, we use the query "*show the neighbor districts of Campina Grande in the III NRS of the state of Paraíba, Brazil, which has an ambulatory and numbers of admission (aih) less than 50 during the year of 2002.*"

Step 1: The definition of the geographic area of interest is done through "*visual selection.*" The user visually chooses the region of interest by navigating in the map (Figure 3). Also, it is possible to enter the region of interest by name.

Step 2: Choice of the attributes, which will take part in the query: "*Searching Attributes.*" If the region of interest has been fixed, the attributes from the chosen geographical area are displayed. They may be conventional (non-spatial) (denoted by ▦), spatial (denoted by ◌), and temporal (denoted by ◔) as shown in Figure 4.

reason we considered that the underlying DBMS is relational with spatial capabilities. The valid-time temporal information is stored as explicit time attributes (*from, to*). In this environment, the temporal primitives must be converted to relational predicates concerning the attributes *from* and *to*. We have adapted the mapping of temporal queries of TVQE developed by Santos (2000), considering also spatial queries.

The S-TVQE architecture is distributed into three tiers as can be seen in Figure 2. S-TVQE is available on the Web through a browser and therefore can be used in different platforms.

After an interactive query statement has been produced, the interface (presentation layer) sends the query operators stored in an XML file to the query manager through an http protocol using JSP technology. These primitive graphical operations are converted into SQL commands running on the database via JDBC. The visual results are rendered using Java, XML, and SVG technologies.

Figure 3. Map navigation to define the region of interest—Brazil -> Northeast Brazil -> Paraiba State -> Campina Grande district

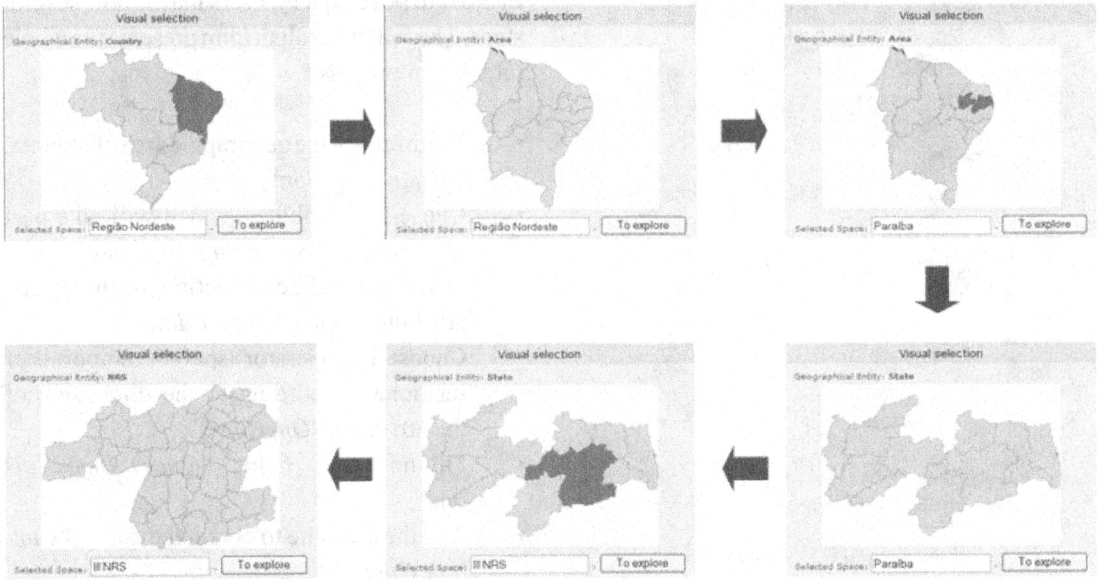

Figure 4. Attributes from the III NRS region

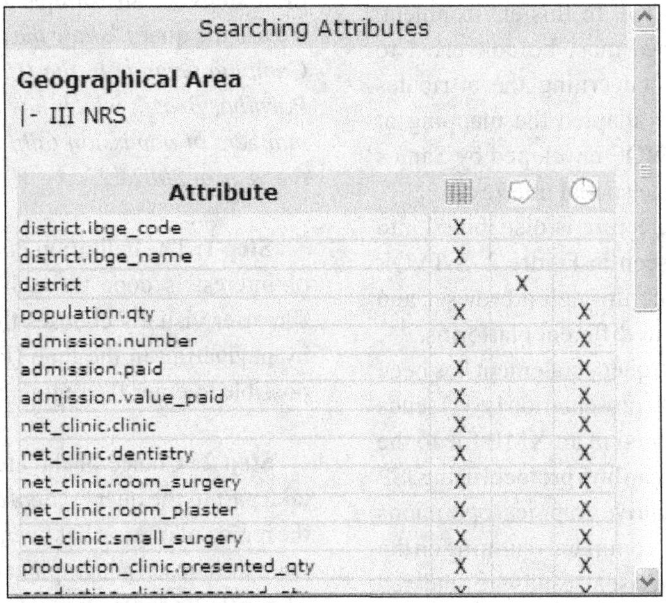

Searching Attributes

Geographical Area

|- III NRS

Attribute			
district.ibge_code	X		
district.ibge_name	X		
district		X	
population.qty	X		X
admission.number	X		X
admission.paid	X		X
admission.value_paid	X		X
net_clinic.clinic	X		X
net_clinic.dentistry	X		X
net_clinic.room_surgery	X		X
net_clinic.room_plaster	X		X
net_clinic.small_surgery	X		X
production_clinic.presented_qty	X		X

Figure 5. Example of a conventional attribute chosen

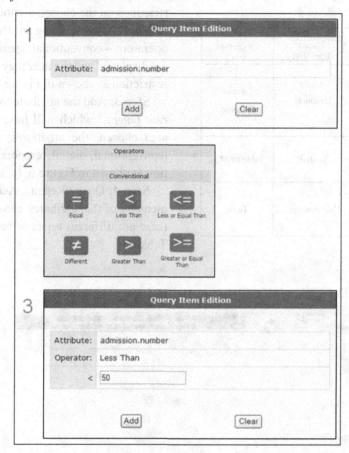

Figure 6. Example of a current query

Current Query				
Space	Attribute	Dimension	Operator	Restriction
III NRS	ibge_name	none	none	none
III NRS	geometry	Spatial	Adjacency	Campina Grande
III NRS	number	Conventional	Less Than	50
III NRS	number	Temporal	During	2002-01-01/2002-12-31
III NRS	clinic	Conventional	Greater Than	1

Table 1. Possible ways of exhibition in the projection of the results

Description	Supported dimension	Projection
Attributes with historical significance, in other words, associated to a valid time interval.	Temporal	Table or Graphic
Attributes related to a geographical location.	Spatial	Table or Map
Attributes without temporal or spatial reference.	Conventional	Table

Step 2.1: Definition of optional query restrictions on the chosen attributes: *"Query Item Edition."* After choosing an attribute, its possible operators—conventional, spatial, or temporal—are displayed and the user may specify the query restriction as shown in Figure 5.

Step 3: Add the attribute to the query: *"Current Query,"* which will have the geographical area chosen, the attributes, specific operator (conventional, spatial, temporal), and the restriction as shown in Figure 6.

Step 4: Query Results: According to the dimension of the attributes chosen for the query, there are different types of results as shown in Table 1.

Figure 7. Spatial query result

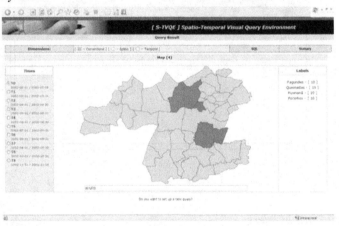

Figure 8. Temporal query result

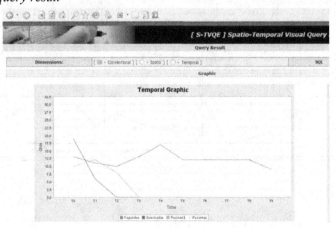

Spatio-temporal queries can use combinations of the previous formats. For instance, the result of a spatio-temporal query can show a sequence of maps, each one associated to a specific time. Figure 7 shows the map for February 2002 and Figure 8 displays a complete time-graph.

Query Translation

S-TVQE enables the definition of conventional, spatial, temporal, and spatio-temporal queries. The query translator is responsible for generating the SQL code of the visual query according to the underlying DBMS syntax.

Conventional Queries

Conventional queries are those that use neither spatial nor temporal dimensions. The operators allowed are the relational ones. Example of such query would be:

Retrieve the city names of the III NRS region, the population of which is greater than 10,000 inhabitants and net clinic is above 3.

Table 2. Relational operators mapping

Operator		SQL Mapping--Conventional
=	Equal	SELECT <attribute> FROM <table> WHERE table.attribute = value
<	Less Than	SELECT <attribute> FROM <table> WHERE table.attribute < value
<=	Less or Equal Than	SELECT <attribute> FROM <table> WHERE table.attribute <= value
≠	Different	SELECT <attribute> FROM <table> WHERE table.attribute <> value
>	Greater Than	SELECT <attribute> FROM <table> WHERE table.attribute > value
>=	Greater or Equal Than	SELECT <attribute> FROM <table> WHERE table.attribute >= value

Figure 9. Attributes and their restrictions

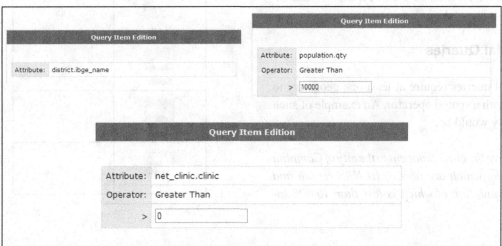

habitants.

Figure 9 shows the chosen attributes for this query.

Table 2 shows the relational operators for conventional queries and their equivalent SQL mapping.

The previous query is then translated into SQL as:

```
SELECT    district.ibge _
          name,sum(population.
          qty), sum(net _ clinic.
          clinic), nrs.ibge _ name

FROM      district, population,
          net _ clinic, nrs

WHERE     nrs.gid = district.nrs
          and upper(nrs.ibge _
          name) = upper('III NRS')
          and population.qty >
          10000 and district.gid
          = population.district
          and net _ clinic.clinic
          > 0 and district.gid =
          net _ clinic.district and
          population.until ISNULL
          and net _ clinic.until
          ISNULL

GROUP BY  district.ibge _ name,
          nrs.ibge _ name
```

Spatial Queries

Spatial queries require at least one geometry to deal with a spatial operator. An example of such a query would be:

Retrieve the cities adjacent to the city of Campina Grande, which are part of III NRS region and the population of which is less than 10,000 in-

Table 3. Mapping metric spatial operators into SQL

S-TVQE Operator	DBMS Operator
Area	AREA (GEOM)
Perimeter	PERIMETER (GEOM)
Distance	DISTANCE (geom1, geom2)

Table 4. Mapping directional spatial operators into SQL

S-TVQE Operator	PostgreSQL Operator
Top	|>>
Below	<<|
Left	<<
Right	>>
North	| &>
South	&<|
East	&>
West	&<

Table 5. Mapping topologic spatial operators into SQL

S-TVQE Operator	PostgreSQL + PostGis Operator
Adjacency	Touches (geom1, geom2)
Disjunction	Not touches (geom1, geom2)
Covered By	Contains (geom1, geom2)
Inside	Within (geom1, geom2)
Equals	Equals (geom1, geom2)
Overlap	Overlaps (geom1, geom2)
Union	GeomUnion (geom1, geom2)

Tables 3, 4, and 5 present the spatial operators and its mapping to SQL.

The previous query is translated into SQL as:

```
SELECT    district.ibge _ name,
          district.the _ geom,
          sum(population.qtdy),
          nrs.ibge _ name
FROM      district, population,
          nrs
WHERE     nrs.gid = district.nrs
          and  upper(nrs.ibge _
          name) = upper('III NRS')
          and  touches(district.
```
```
          the _ geom, (select the _
          geom from district where
          upper(ibge _ name)  =
          upper('Campina Grande')))
          and  population.qty  <
          10000 and district.gid =
          population.district and
          population.until ISNULL

GROUP BY  district.ibge_name,
          nrs.ibge_name, dis-
          trict.the_geom
```

Temporal Queries

Temporal queries deal with historical data, which have specific operators. An example of such query would be: "*Retrieve the cities, from III NRS region, which have the number of admissions(aih) less than 200, during the year 2002.*"

Tables 6, 7, and 8 present how temporal constraints are mapped into SQL clauses. The time of the query is given by the variable "p" and the valid-time of the objects in the database is "tv." The relation <table> is the corresponding table of the database. Note that for the operators of

Table 6. Mapping instant temporal operator into SQL

S-TVQE Operator	SQL Instant mapping
Begin	SELECT <attribute> FROM <table> WHERE tv.begin = p
At	SELECT <attribute> FROM <table> WHERE tv.begin <= p AND tv.end >= p
End	SELECT <attribute> FROM <table> WHERE tv.end = p

169

Table 7. Mapping interval temporal operator into SQL

S-TVQE Operator	SQL Interval selection
First Interval	SELECT <attribute> FROM <table> WHERE p >= (SELECT MIN(table.begin) FROM table) AND p <= (SELECT MIN(table.end) FROM table)
Last Interval	SELECT <attribute> FROM <table> WHERE p >= (SELECT MAX(tv.begin) FROM table) AND p <= (SELECT MAX(tv.end) FROM table)

Tables 6 and 7, "p" is an instant whereas in the other cases it represents a time period.

The previous query is translated into SQL as:

```
SELECT    district.ibge_name,
          sum(admission.present-
          ed), nrs.ibge_name, ad-
          mission.from, admission.
          until
FROM      district, admission,
          nrs
WHERE     nrs.gid = district.nrs
          and upper(nrs.ibge_
          name) = upper('III NRS')
          and admission.number <
          200 and district.gid =
          admission.district and
          admission.from>'2002-
          01-01' and admission.
          until<'2002-12-31'
GROUP BY  district.ibge_name,
          nrs.ibge_name, admis-
```

Table 8. Mapping period temporal operator into SQL

S-TVQE Operator	SQL Period mapping
Before	SELECT <attribute> FROM <table> WHERE tv.end < p.begin
Start	SELECT <attribute> FROM <table> WHERE tv.begin = p.begin AND tv.end < p.end
During	SELECT <attribute> FROM <table> WHERE tv.begin > p.begin AND tv.end < p.end
Cross 1	SELECT <attribute> FROM <table> WHERE p.begin > tv.begin AND tv.end > p.begin AND p.end > tv.end
Cross 2	SELECT <attribute> FROM <table> WHERE tv.begin > p.begin AND p.end > tv.begin AND tv.end > p.end
Precedes	SELECT <attribute> FROM <table> WHERE tv.end = p.begin
After	SELECT <attribute> FROM <table> WHERE p.end < tv.begin
Finish	SELECT <attribute> FROM <table> WHERE p.begin < tv.begin AND tv.end = p.end
Contain	SELECT <attribute> FROM <table> WHERE tv.begin < p.begin AND tv.end > p.end
Equals	SELECT <attribute> FROM <table> WHERE tv.begin = p.begin AND tv.end = p.end

```
            sion.from, admission.
            until
ORDER BY    admission.from, admis-
            sion.until
```

Spatio-Temporal Queries

Spatio-temporal queries deal with both spatial and temporal dimensions. An example of such query would be: *"Retrieve the cities adjacent to the city of Campina Grande, which are member of the III NRS region, and have the number of authorized admissions (AIH) lesser than 50, during the year 2002."*

This query is translated into SQL as:

```
SELECT    district.ibge _ name,
          district.the _ geom,
          sum(admission.present-
          ed), nrs.ibge _ name,
          aission.from, admission.
          until
FROM      district, admission,
          nrs
WHERE     Nrs.gid = district.nrs
          and upper(nrs.ibge _
          name) = upper('III NRS')
          and touches(district.
          the _ geom, (select the _
          geom from district where
          upper(ibge _ name) =
          upper('Campina Grande')))
          and admission.number <
          50 and district.gid =
          admission.district and
          admission.from>'2002-
          01-01' and admission.
          until<'2002-12-31'
GROUP BY  district.ibge _ name,
          nrs.ibge _ name, admis-
          sion.from, admission.
          until, district.the _
          geom
```

```
ORDER BY  admission.from, admis-
          sion.until
```

FUTURE TRENDS

The demand on visual interaction with spatio-temporal information sources applies not only to user-friendly statement of queries to databases. Also the visual presentation of the result is significant. Moreover, the user wants to interact dynamically with the system in order to satisfy its needs as stated by Shneiderman (1998), "overview-first, zoom and filter, details-on-demand." In this sense, we need more dynamic systems where the results of its initial statements are used to continuously restate and refine the query.

There are different techniques for information visualization such as scatterplot, table lens, choropleth maps, and other (Andrienko, Andrienko, & Gatalsky, 2002). For the visualization of spatio-temporal data, time-sliders may be appropriate to visualize the evolution of some region.

Some visualization can be considered as final, whereas others should be used as a starting point for the next step in the dialog with the system. This dynamic approach applies to several situations such as refinement of the result, temporal flow analysis, moving objects, zooming in and out, and so on. In most cases, multiple visualizations are more adequate, some may be only informative whereas others allow further interactions.

Another important issue is related to visual query systems for 3-D objects. The idea is to navigate in a 3-D environment. This has been done using virtual reality techniques, but the costs are very high. Querying objects in such environments is currently a very challenging research topic. We need new techniques for query formulation in 3-D models and new techniques for displaying results in 3-D, sometimes using simulation. More recently, with the advent of high-resolution satellite images, there are maps with less than one-meter resolution. Therefore, one can query, for instance, the evolution of deforestation in the Amazon rainforest during the last decade. This is obviously a spatio-temporal query, but the novelty here is that the objects are high-resolution spatial images, and the result might be a video, which shows the environmental degradation of the same region throw time. Commercially, there are projects like Google Earth (http://earth.google.com) and Microsoft Visual Earth (http://preview.local.live.com), which enable navigation on earth through high-resolution satellite images, although they are very timid on visual querying. Hence, there is a research gap on this theme.

Lastly, the routing map24.com site (http://www.map24.com/) provides a flight 3-D route option, which enables to simulate an end-to-end route with altitude and based on either shortest or fastest paths, velocity and so on.

CONCLUSION

The plethora of spatio-temporal data demands information systems, which deal with these dimensions efficiently. Most systems are supplied and updated continuously by thousands or millions of source data. These sources may be satellite images, educational information, health data, traffic flow, and so on. This data volume should be processed adequately and used adequately. Web information systems and decision support systems are typical application fields for those sources. The information manager wants tools for the expression of his or her needs, producing adequate information retrieval. Visual query systems (VQS) and information visualization are some of the most promising approaches to attend these requirements.

In this chapter, a visual query system for querying spatio-temporal databases has been presented. It can be improved if combined with more expressive information visualization and become a dynamic interaction environment between the user and the information base. It can be combined with data mining techniques, multimedia data processing, mobility of objects and sources, and others.

REFERENCES

Andrienko, N., Andrienko, G. & Gatalski, P. (2002). Data and Tasks Characteristics in Design of Spatio-Temporal Data Visualization Tools. In *Symposium on Geospatial Theory, Processing and Applications.*

ArcGis- The Complete Geographic Information System. (2006). ESRI GIS and mapping software. Retrieved April 28, 2006, from http://www.esri.com/software/arcgis/

Bonhomme, C., Trépied, C., Aufaure, M. A., & Laurini. R. (1999). A visual language for querying spatio-temporal databases. *Proceedings of the Workshop on Geographical Information Systems* (pp. 34-39). ACM Press.

Calcinelli, D., & Mainguenaud, M. (1994). CI-GALES: A visual query language for geographical information system: The user interface. *Journal of Visual Languages and Computing, 5*(2), 113-132. Academic Press.

Catarci, T., Costabile, M. F., Levialdi, S., & Batini, C. (1997). Visual query systems: Analysis and comparison. *Journal of Visual Languages and Computing, 8*(2), 215-260.

Egenhofer, M. J. (1997). Query processing in spatial-query-by-sketch. *Journal of Visual Languages and Computing, 8*(4), 403-427.

Egenhofer, M. J. (1994). Spatial SQL: A query and presentation language. *IEEE Transaction on Knowledge and Data Engineering, 6*(1), 86-95.

Erwig, M., & Schneider, M. (2000). Query-by-trace. Visual predicate specification in spatio-temporal databases. *Proceedings of the 5th IFIP Conference on Visual Databases* (pp. 199-218).

GeoMedia – About GeoMedia, Intergraph, http://imgs.intergraph.com/geomedia/

Hackos, J. T., & Redish, J. C. (1998). *User and task analysis for interface design*. New York: Wiley Computer Publishing.

Li, X., & Chang, S. K. (2004). An interactive visual query interface on spatial/temporal data. *Proceedings of the 10th International Conference on Distributed Multimedia Systems* (pp. 257-262).

Morris, A. J., Abdelmoty, A. I., Tudhope, D. S., & El-Geresy. B. (2002). A design and implementation of a visual query language for large spatial databases. *Proceedings of the 6th International Conference on Information Visualization* (pp. 226-233). IEEE Computer Society Press.

Santos, G. F. (2000). *Implementation of visual queries on temporal databases*. Master Thesis, Federal University of Campina Grande (in Portuguese).

Scherer, D. (2003). *Computer Support Proposal for ICM*. Master thesis. University of Campina Grande, Campina Grande. (in Portuguese).

Sellis, T., Frank, A., Grumbach, S., Guting, R., & Koubarakis, M. (2003). *Spatio-temporal da-tabases: The chorochronos approach*. Lecture Notes in Computer Science, Springer-Verlag.

Shimabukuro, M. H., Branco, V. M. A., Oliveira, M. C. F., & Flores. E. F. (2003). Visual exploration of spatio-temporal databases. *Proceedings of the GEOINFO.*

Shneiderman, B. (1998). *Designing the user interface—Strategies for effective human-computer interaction* (3rd ed.). Addison Wesley.

Silberschatz, A., Korth, H. F., & Sudarshan, S. (2005). *Database system concepts* (5th ed.). Mc-Graw Hill.

Silva, S. L. F., Schiel, U., & Catarci. T. (2002). Formalizing visual interaction with historical databases. *Information Systems, 27*(7), 487-521.

Silveira, V. N. K., Edelweiss, N., & Galante, R. M. (2004). TVM Web—A visual interface visual for the versioning temporal model. *Proceedings of the 19th Brazilian Symposium of Databases*, Brasília (in Portuguese).

Snodgrass, R. T. (1999). *Developing time-oriented database applications in SQL*. Morgan Kaufmann Publishers.

Snodgrass, R. T. (1995). *The TSQL2 temporal query language*. Springer Verlag.

Soares, V. G. (2002). *GeoVisual: A visual querying environment for geographic databases*. Ph.D. Thesis, Federal University of Pernambuco, Brazil (in Portuguese).

Chapter X
Multi–Facet Design of Interactive Systems through Visual Languages

Daniela Fogli
Università di Brescia, Italy

Andrea Marcante
CNR-ITC, Italy

Piero Mussio
Università di Milano, Italy

Loredana Parasiliti Provenza
Università di Milano, Italy

Antonio Piccinno
Università di Bari, Italy

ABSTRACT

In this chapter, it is recognized that the knowledge relevant to the design of an interactive system is distributed among several stakeholders: domain experts, software engineers, and human-computer interaction experts. Hence, the design of an interactive system is a multi-facet activity requiring the collaboration of experts from these communities. Each community describes an interactive system through visual sentences of a visual language (VL). A first VL allows domain experts to reason on the system usage in their specific activities. A second VL, the state-chart language, is used to specify the system behavior for software engineers' purposes. A communication gap exists among the two communities in that domain experts do not understand software engineers jargon and vice versa. To overcome this gap, a third VL permits human-computer interaction experts to translate the user view of the system embedded in their visual language into a specification in the software engineering visual language.

INTRODUCTION

In this chapter, "visual language" (VL) denotes a language whose alphabet consists of visual entities, which can be combined to be used in communications among humans and in human reasoning (Bianchi, Bottoni, Mussio, & Protti, 1993; Naranayan & Hubscher, 1998). Visual languages are seen as a means for communication, interaction, and reasoning in the design and use of *visual interactive systems* (VISs). VISs are designed to support users in performing their daily work and activities, not hindering them in doing their job and not requiring them to be aware of the complex hardware and software technology they are using (Buschmann, 2001). To reach this goal, the interaction style through which a VIS is used should fit the user culture and capabilities, the context of use, and the task being performed (Kuutti, 1995). Unluckily, a *communication gap* exists in that users do not understand designers and developers jargon and designers and developers in general do not understand the user jargon (Borchers, 2001; Lauesen, 2005; Majhew, 1992). Designers are often not aware of the gap and develop VIS interaction styles, which usually reflect their own culture, skills, and articulatory abilities rather than culture, skills, and articulatory abilities of the users. As a consequence, users are forced to adopt interaction styles that are different to their culture, and are often charged with housekeeping tasks in which they are not interested and divert their attention from the activity they are performing. The use of the VIS in the execution of real tasks may reveal difficult or impossible, and systems of great technological value have failed because of these hurdles (Carrara, Fogli, Fresta, & Mussio, 2002; Folmer, van Welie, & Bosch, 2005).

This chapter organizes some recent proposals to overcome the communication gap and to design usable interactive systems (Borchers, 2001; Costabile, Fogli, Mussio, & Piccinno, 2006a; Horrocks, 1998) into a unique frame. The frame explicitly recognizes the existence of different cultures and of the communication gap between the members of the communities of users and system designers. Moreover, it admits that the human-system interaction style must fit and enhance the user culture and capabilities. It also recognizes that to overcome the gap, the collaboration of experts of different cultures is necessary (Borchers, Fincher, Griffiths, Pemberton, & Siemon, 2001). Namely, software engineers have to collaborate with domain experts--representatives of the users--but in order to make it possible, the collaboration must be mediated by human-computer interaction (HCI) experts. The design and implementation of VISs is thus recognized as a complex activity, which requires collaborative and participatory approaches (Costabile et al., 2006a, Schuler & Namioka 1993). Being a complex activity, it requires more knowledge than any single member of the community of experts possesses because the knowledge relevant to the design problem is distributed among such experts (Arias, Eden, Fischer, Gorman, & Scharff, 2000). For this reason, design and implementation of a VIS have become a multi-facet activity, in that each expert is a stakeholder who evaluates the system and proposes solutions from his or her point of view, but discusses his or her insights with the other experts to reach a common agreed solution. This view results into an approach to VIS design based on the definition and use of three visual languages. Each VL permits to specify the process of user-system interaction from a different point of view and for a different audience. The pictorial parts of the three languages can be regarded as boundary objects (i.e., shared objects to talk about and to think with) (Arias et al., 2000, p. 87). Therefore, they are not independent: the system of three languages links the user views and jargons to the software engineer views and jargons and bridges the communication gap.

The first VL, the set VC of visual commands, is designed to specify the VIS to users and to allow them to reason on VIS usage. Its definition stems from the practical experience of tools used to present the VIS to users (Leach, 2006; Minami, 2000) and techniques described in the literature (Horrocks, 1998). Such language has to reflect the user community view of the interactive activity so that a novel user can derive a correct mental model of the system through its use and users in general express strategies to achieve their goals as sequences of visual commands meaningful to them.

On the other ridge of the gap, designers specify VIS behavior for software engineering (SE) purposes by finite state machines. The approach adopts the state-chart language (Harel, 1987; Horrocks, 1998) as the language for this specification.

The third VL, the set TR of transformation rules, bridges the two views. It is designed to translate the specification based on the visual language VC into a state-based description of the interaction process, which is expressive for designers still maintaining its expressiveness to users.

The chapter is organized as follows. In Section 2, the background and motivations of the work described here are presented, discussing the reasons for multi-facet design, introducing a concrete view of visual languages and their role in interaction processes, and presenting a model of HCI, which underlies the approach that was developed in recent years. In Section 3, the three VLs are defined to specify the interaction process from different points of views; their relations are also explored. Section 4 focuses on the use of the three languages in the development of a VIS. Last, conclusions are derived and future trends envisaged.

BACKGROUND AND MOTIVATION FOR A MULTI-FACET APPROACH TO VIS DESIGN

In this section, we outline a landscape of HCI and SE studies and experiences, which justify the need of a multi-facet design approach. We also argue that the VIS design must be framed in a model of HCI recently proposed, used as a compass to relate the different views.

Reasons for Multi-Facet Design

People facing real world problems act as *competent practitioners* in that "they exhibit a kind of knowing in practice, most of which is tacit", and they "reveal a capacity for reflection on their intuitive knowing in the midst of action and sometimes use this capacity to cope with the unique, uncertain, and conflicted situations of practice" (Schön, 1983, p. 8-9). Competent practitioners use their (tacit) knowledge to interpret documents that support their activity and understand the tools they use. In the case of VIS usage, a relevant part of the information carried by the system is "*implicit information*" (Costabile et al., 2006a) (i.e., embedded in the visual organization and shape materialization of the screen image and can only be understood by users who posses domain (tacit) knowledge). For example, sequences of images illustrating procedures or sequences of actions to be performed are organized according to the reading habits of the expected reader: from left to right for Western readers, from right to left for Eastern ones. Furthermore, some icons, textual words, or images may be meaningful only to the experts in some discipline: icons representing cells in a liver simulation may have a specific meaning only for hepatologists (Mussio, Pietrogrande, & Protti, 1991), while an x-ray may be meaningful to physicians but not to other experts (Costabile et al., 2006a). In a team of competent practitioners collaborating to solve a problem, each practitioner is a stakeholder, owner of a specific knowledge, a particular aspect of the knowledge crucial to the resolution of the problem, but not sufficient to solve it. Rittel (1984) defines this situation as the *symmetry of ignorance*: he suggests that, for overcoming the symmetry of ignorance, the knowledge owned by every stakeholder must be shared and integrated with the knowledge of the other stakeholders.

A competent practitioner interacting with a VIS needs to use it as a simple tool whenever it is possible and to use it as a powerful, programmable, and adaptable system whenever it is necessary (Costabile, Fogli, Fresta, Mussio, & Piccinno, 2004; Fischer, Giaccardi, Ye, Sutcliffe, & Mehandjiev, 2004). Let us restrict to WIMP interaction without loss of generality. Competent practitioners see their tools and data on the screen and need to understand and to directly manipulate them to achieve their goals. The tools and data on the screen are elements of a visual language, which assumes the central role of means of communication and interaction between humans and computers. Practitioners use the explicit and tacit knowledge gained in their traditional, concrete work environments, to understand the image on the screen and decide what to do next.

In designing a VIS, software engineers bring into design their tacit and explicit knowledge on software development and their own views of the activity to be performed. Users and designers adopt different approaches to abstraction, since, for instance, they have different notions about the details that can be abridged. Moreover, users reason heuristically rather than algorithmically, using examples and analogies rather than deductive abstract tools, documenting activities, prescriptions, and results through their own developed notations, articulating their activities according to their traditional tools rather than computerized ones (Majhew, 1992). Users and software designers possess distinct types of knowledge and follow different approaches and reasoning strategies to modelling, performing and documenting the tasks

to be carried out in a given application domain. Users do not understand designers and developers jargon and designers and developers in general do not understand the user jargon (Costabile et al., 2006a). It is important to notice that HCI experts often advocated to represent user views in the design, own a specific knowledge, which is not the one of the users neither that of software designers (Lauesen, 2005). Only users are able of reading the screen with user tacit knowledge and understanding what is misleading or difficult to interpret for them, but they are not able to think as HCI experts and propose adequate HCI solutions (Norman, 2005). Both users and HCI experts cannot evaluate the technical consequences of their proposals or the influence of the adopted technologies (i.e., they are not able to think as software engineers) (Majhew, 1992). The loop is closed by software engineers who know the technology, but in turn have difficulty thinking as users or HCI experts. As emphasized by activity theory studies, the implicit knowledge is embedded in tools and notations users adopt. Tools and notations depend on the context of activity and work organization (Kuutti, 1995).

SE and HCI experts are aware of the gaps existing among them and of the need of communicating and sharing their different points of view during the VIS design process. Lauesen (2005) proposes the *virtual window method*, an early graphical realization of the data presentation to bridge the gap between software engineers and HCI experts. Folmer et al. (2005) propose *bridging patterns,* which describe a usability design solution and consist of a user interface part and an architecture/implementation part. Borchers (2001) recognizes the necessity of capturing the knowledge of competent practitioners, together with HCI and SE expertise by forging a *lingua franca* that makes the design experience understandable by domain experts, HCI experts, and software engineers. He proposes a pattern framework in which three design pattern languages are used to bridge the gaps: the first describes the application domain, the second leads from domain and task analysis to interaction design, and the third is about software design solutions for the interactive system. The languages are formally structured in a hypertext graph notation, which underlies the definition and organization of the three pattern languages.

However, the problem is how to embed the user implicit information in these languages and how to make the stakeholders express their tacit knowledge. User-centered approaches adopt consultation of users as experts of the application domain to acquire knowledge about work activities, procedures, standards, users' habits, and needs (Norman & Draper, 1986). Participatory approaches include representatives of users, the domain experts, in the design team (Schuler et al., 1993). These approaches exploit techniques derived from social science that support communication and collaboration within the interdisciplinary team: these techniques move from system descriptions to collaborative construction of mockups to cooperative prototyping (Bødker & Grønbæk, 1991).

Meta-design (Fischer et al., 2004) goes beyond the user-centered and participatory design in that it allows users to act as designers and contribute to the co-evolution of the system. To support a meta-design approach, the seeding, evolutionary growth, and reseeding (SER) process model has been developed. In this model, designing systems is viewed as a three-phase activity: (1) seed creation, (2) a subsequent seed evolutionary growth, followed by (3) a reseeding phase (Fischer, 1998). The SER model is a process model for the development and evolution of the so-called DODEs (domain-oriented design environments), which are "software systems that support design activities within particular domains and that are built specifically to evolve" (Fischer, 1998). The software shaping workshop (SSW) methodology (Costabile et al., 2006a) shares with DODEs the meta-design approach and develops direct manipulation environments (system workshops)

to support software engineers, HCI experts, and end users representatives to create other end user environments (application workshops) customized to the considered domain, context of use, and end user.

Visual Languages Convey Domain Implicit Knowledge

Long before the computer age, people developed VLs for communication and reasoning on their experiences as competent practitioners in their daily activities performed in real environments with real entities and using real tools. According to written language scholars (Harris, 2000), written characters, being two dimensional representations perceived by the human visual system, are kinds of visual entities, which are combined to form words, paragraphs, and texts. A text is therefore an image built on an alphabet of written symbols, a sentence in a VL. Competent practitioners reason and communicate with each other through documents, expressed in specific domain notations—specialized VLs. These documents represent abstract or concrete concepts, prescriptions, or results of activities using texts, images, and graphics. Each document is an element of the specialized VL--an image--created and interpreted using (often informally defined) alphabets of letters, icons, and conventional symbols, and following the different sets of rules, which define the syntax of written, pictorial, and graphical expressions and of the combination of these expressions into a document. This document conveys explicit and implicit domain knowledge. These VLs emerge from people experience and evolve in time (Codognet, 1999; Jean, 1986). This chapter is an example of such a multimedia document, created following the rules of English language applied to a Latin alphabet, the rules of medical VL applied to medical images and icons, the rules of graphical representations applied to graphic signs used in the examples, and formatted following the editing rules of Idea Group Inc.

With the advent of computer-based systems, graphical interfaces, direct manipulation techniques, and the Web, the scenario changed. The new interaction, computation, and communication technologies transformed computers from technological artifacts, that are managed by programmers and must produce correct results, into ubiquitous cultural artifacts that, being embedded in nearly every tool people use, are managed by users and become inescapable to them even if not always usable (Carroll, 1995). The tools become virtual and their behavior differs from that of the real tools (Majhew, 1992). In this new scenario, VLs play a fundamental role providing elements that become interactive and sometimes proactive (Chang, Hou, & Hsu, 1992). In this perspective, graphical user interfaces for direct manipulation are seen as visual languages supporting the interaction between human and computer (Bottoni, Costabile, Levialdi, & Mussio, 1997; Naranayan et al., 1998). The novelty here is that this VL must not only fit its users' culture and capabilities, the context of use, and the task being performed, but it also must be amenable to efficient computer implementation. Its design is no more only a question of graphical and typographical design of its elements and of the rules for their combination, but also requires the definition of direct manipulation and of dynamic interaction processes. A VL design becomes the design of a VIS capable of supporting the desired visual interaction (Beaudouin-Lafon, 2004). Adopting the position of activity theory (Kuutti, 1995), VISs are seen as artifacts having a mediating role between objects and subjects of activities. The dynamics and evolution of user activities are considered as fundamental characteristics at all description levels (operations, actions, and activities themselves). In this line, domain-specific languages (Gray, Rossi, & Tolvanen, 2004) have been developed to define models that consist of elements representing things that are part of the considered domain. Domain-specific languages are defined focusing on concrete syntax and not on computer-based elements, allowing the design team (including software engineers, HCI experts, but also end user representatives) "to perceive themselves as working directly with domain concepts" (Gray et al., 2004, p. 207). In Sprinkle and Karsai (2004), the authors present domain-specific visual languages as special kinds of domain-specific languages that provide visual programming interfaces. Domain-specific visual languages whose abstract syntax is specified with a meta-modeling language based on UML class diagrams, permit to create models (called *domain models*) that can be represented using graph structures. Their evolution is specified through graph rewriting (Blostein & Schürr, 1997). This approach is amenable only to software engineers and theoretical computer scientists; therefore, a mapping is then needed from the abstract syntax elements to visual constructs.

The Two-Interpretation Model of HCI

A VIS should be cognitively usable, useful, and computationally efficient for users. To this aim, it is needed to model the HCI process in order to take into account both usability and computational features. The human side of the interaction has been explored in the seminal work of Hutchins, Hollan, and Norman (1986) in which the existence of semantic and articulatory distances in evaluation and execution of HCI activities are identified. More recently, the computer semiotics approach (Andersen, 2001; De Souza, 2005) brings us to the center of reasoning on HCI the system of signs--visual, but also haptic and audio--used by the human and the computer to communicate (the VCL elements in our language). These signs are interpreted both by the user and the system. Humans interpret the signs within the context of their activity and the whole interaction process depends on the pragmatic level of the communication.

On the machine side, the behavior of the computing system determined by the human activi-

Figure 1. An interaction trace: An annotation of a cs *(a medical structure in a MRI)*

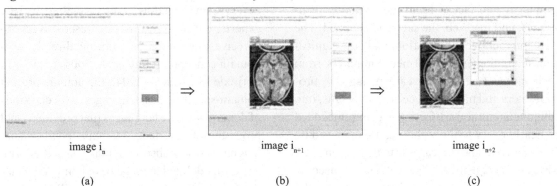

image i_n image i_{n+1} image i_{n+2}

(a)   (b)   (c)

ties must be modeled, highlighting the problems arising on the computer side in capturing and interpreting the human actions. This stance is clearly posed in Abowd and Beale (1991). However, the human and the system form a unique system, the *syndetic system*, whose dynamics are determined by the activities of the two subsystems of different nature, namely a cognitive system (the human) and a computing system (the computer) (Barnard, May, Duke, & Duce, 2000). Reaching the goals of the interaction process requires you to balance the requests of the two subsystems. To this end, a unified framework of the HCI process is required, which takes into account the cognitive system, the computational system, and the visual language allowing the communication between the two (Bottoni et al., 1997; Narayanan et al., 1998). The following section presents a model of HCI that evolves the model for WIMP interaction proposed in Bottoni, Costabile, and Mussio (1999) by the inclusion of some recent results on the dynamic and multimodal interactive aspects of the interaction and their links to the programmed implementation, following a state-based approach to system descriptions (Fogli et al., 2006).

The HCI process is a cyclic process in which the user and the interactive system communicate by materializing and interpreting in time sequences of messages (Figure 1). Users interpret the messages by applying human cognitive criteria, while the system applies criteria embedded in a program

P, which is being interpreted by the computer. P reflects the designer view of the user activity. In WIMP interaction, a message exchanged between the user and the system is the entire image i represented on the computer screen, formed by texts, pictures, icons, etc. Figure 1 shows three full screen images created in three steps in the interaction process of a radiologist with a VIS called B-radiologist. B-radiologist supports the radiologist in studying a magnetic resonance image (MRI) to derive a diagnosis (Costabile, Fogli, Lanzilotti, Mussio, & Piccinno, 2006b).

To this end, B-radiologist allows the physician to create multimedia documents called "annotations" that record the progressive findings of diagnostic activities. Since the diagnostic activity often requires different medical expertises, images and annotations can therefore be shared with other physicians accessing the Web with similar VISs.

Here the multimedia messages exchanged between the radiologist and the computer are the MRIs and the annotations. The program P is the set of programs that implement B-radiologist. Radiologists interpret icons and documents in the image on the screen using their explicit and tacit knowledge. In the example, a radiologist interprets the icons representing tools in i_n and acts to bring the data of a patient on the screen. Figure 1a shows the video screen at the beginning of this process. On the top of the screen, an

Figure 2. The workbench in the image i$_{n+2}$ enlarged and with some details emphasized

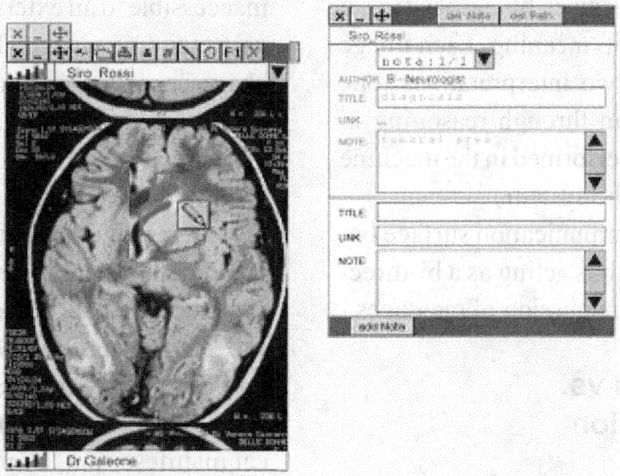

information space displays some data on the VIS. On the right side, three menus are available: the radiologist has opened the third and is selecting the item related to the data of the patient of interest. An empty workspace is present. The system reacts to the selection presenting a workbench in the workspace (image i$_{n+1}$). The workbench is composed by only one element, a bench, in turn formed by a *data space*, an *operator set,* and two *information space*s. The data space contains the data to be worked on, in this case, an MRI of interest. The operator set consists of a toolbar on the top of the bench, which provides the radiologist with all the tools required for his or her analysis. The two *information space*s present the name of the patient "Siro Rossi" and the name of the doctor "Dr. Galeone" performing the diagnosis. The radiologist recognizes a line in the MRI surrounding an area and a visual link—a pencil icon in this VL—denoting the presence of an annotation related to the area, which has been created by him or her or by another physician in a preceding occasion. The radiologist clicks on the pencil icon. The system reacts presenting i$_{n+2}$: an annotation manager is displayed on the screen showing the annotation to the radiologist (Figure 1c). Now the workbench is formed by two

elements: the bench and the annotation manger. The workbench provides the radiologist with the tools necessary to update the annotation, add a comment, or open a new annotation manager.

Figure 2 shows the *workbench* of the third image i$_{n+2}$ enlarged in Figure 1. This prototype provides a medical team—of which the radiologist is a member—with tools to create and exchange annotated MRI to derive a diagnosis. The radiologist can study the data—MRI and the annotation performed on it by other physicians—derive an opinion, and write it as a new annotation; a written sentence often complemented by graphics and explanatory drawings, which must be expressive to other physicians rather than to computer scientists.

The interaction process illustrated by the example is generalized in the HCI model. Users materialize their messages by using the input tools available in the computer at hand. The user materialization activity in general requires several user operations (e.g., typing of several characters, moving the cursor from a starting point to a final one). For each operation, the user receives a visual feedback, which permits the evaluation of the correctness of the action being performed. The image on the screen is the materialization of the meaning intended by the sender and must be interpreted by the receiver by associating it with a (possibly different) meaning. Each image is therefore subject to two interpretations: one performed by the human through reasoning in his or her head and one performed in the machine through computing by the system.

The screen is the communication surface between human and VIS, thus acting as a bi-directional channel in the transmission of messages.

User Interpretation vs. System Interpretation

Users interact with the VIS because they perceive and recognize the events generated by the system, thus interpreting the messages that it generates. Users perceive the system as a (virtual) environment, in which some activities can be performed and need to recognize in it the material and tools necessary to the performance. When users interact with a VIS, they interpret the meaning of the messages generated by the system because they perceive and recognize some subsets of pixels on the screen as functional or perceptual units called *user characteristic structures* (**css**) (Bottoni et al., 1997). Users perform each step in this process using their tacit knowledge. In Figure 1, buttons, letters, and words are css recognizable by a western observer, while the medical structure of interest within the MRI is recognizable only by a specialist. Users also perceive and recognize complex css formed by more simple ones (words formed by letters, the skull, and brain structures in the MRI etc.) and give them a meaning stemming from the meaning of each component cs. The whole image i_n is perceived by the user as a **cs** composed by all the other perceptible **css**. Users derive its meaning from the meaning of the set of **css** recognized in it. In other words, at step n of the interaction process, the user interprets the image on the screen to understand the state of the interaction process and the interpretation

occurs in the user's mind; such interpretation is inaccessible to an external observer and based on user tacit knowledge (Tondl, 1981). An external observer can understand the meaning associated by the user through inquires, interviews, and experiments.

When the user interacts with a VIS, he or she interacts with entities, which exist because a computer interprets a program P specifying their appearance and behavior. These entities are here called *virtual entities* (ves) in that they exist only until P is active (Costabile et al., 2004). Virtual entities react to the user by changing their physical manifestation, by modifying the appearance of other virtual entities, or by deleting existing virtual entities or creating new ones. Therefore, from the system point of view, a *system characteristic structure* cs is a physical manifestations of a ve (i.e., a set of pixels generated and managed by a computational process that is the result of the computer interpretation of the program P). (Note that words in bold italic *courier* denote entities perceived and interpreted by the human user, while those in arial denote entities perceived and computed by the system).

It is important to note that nowadays a program P is the result of a design and implementation activity performed by a team of designers. Therefore, computer interpretation of P is based on the team's view of the application domain: the team defines the program P that generates and maintains active virtual entities. By this definition, the team specifies the set of css that are the physical manifestations of P and the dynamics of the ves. The system knows, generates, and operates on the set of css defined by the designer's team. It interprets events generated by the users according to its own state (i.e., in relation to some css the system has generated). The whole image i on the screen is a cs generated by the program P.

Consequences of the Existence of Two Interpretations

The image i generated by P is the set of pixels presented to users and perceived by them as the image *i*. Users see an image on the screen, but not necessarily perceive and interpret it as it was devised by designers. The key point of the model is to highlight the existence of two interpretations of the image on the screen and to pose it as the starting point of the design of VISs, which must support users in their activities.

Misunderstandings may occur for different reasons. First, users may incorrectly perceive the image, for example if they are color blind or for other physical, cultural, or emotional reasons (Bianchi-Berthouze & Mussio, 2005). Second, they can organize the pixels on the screen differently from how it was devised in the design. In this case, the set *CS* of *cs*s a user recognizes in it is not the same set CS generated by P. Whatever the reasons are that can cause the user to see *cs*s different from those intended by the system, the consequence is that users try to use tools or to manipulate entities unknown to the system (Nielsen, 1993) with unpredictable consequences on the interaction process. Even when users correctly recognize the css on the screen, they can associate to some (or all) the css incorrect meanings, generating analogous usability problems.

Designers must take into account the existence of the two interpretations: in the design stage they must adopt symbols, icons, strategies from the user domain to define the VIS; then they must experimentally validate the VIS design by checking that users correctly perceive and interpret each cs (i.e., that each cs in CS coincides with *cs* in *CS*) (Nolan, 1989).

Niceties on the Interaction Process

A ve is a system because it reacts holistically to user actions, *virtual* in that it exists only as the result of the execution of the program p, a sub-program of the program P generating the VIS; *dynamic* in that its behavior evolves in time; *open* in that its evolution depends on its interaction with the user. A program p is organized in three modules <in, ap, out>, where in—input program acquires the input events generated by the user actions, ap—application program—computes the ve reactions to these events, out—output program—outputs the results of this computation.

At each instance, the state of a ve is specified by a *characteristic pattern* cp=<cs, d, <int, mat>>, where cs is the system characteristic structure (i.e., the set of pixels managed by in and out programs), d is a suitable description of the state of the program ap, int (interpretation) is a function, mapping the current cs onto d and mat (materialization) a function mapping d onto cs.

Each ve may be in a finite number of states (cps). We call CP_{ve} the finite set of cps of a ve. Each cp in CP_{ve} corresponds to a precise physical materialization of the ve (a characteristic structure). We denote by CS_{ve} the set of the characteristic structures of a ve. Being CP_{ve} finite, also CS_{ve} is finite.

Virtual entities can be composed to form complex ves by using composition rules. We call *atomic ve* a virtual entity that cannot be decomposed into other ves.

The workbench of Figure 2 is an example of composed ve. Its components are the bench and the annotation manager. The annotation manager can only exist associated to a bench. These two ves exchange messages during the use and therefore are two subsystems of one system, the workbench.

The buttons in the toolbar of the bench are the css associated to several operators. These operators are atomic ves. However, the user does not reason in terms of atomic ves, but rather in terms of sets of ves that are affected by a same user action. For this reason, in the following, we focus our attention on those sets of virtual entities that we call minimal virtual entities. Before providing a precise definition of minimal virtual entity, we refine the notions of operation, user action, and user activity. More details can be found in Fogli et al. (2006).

When interacting with the VIS, users operate on the devices made available by the system, say a mouse, a keyboard, and a video screen. A user looks at the screen, interprets the image on it, decides what to do, and manifests his or her intention to the VIS acting on the keyboard or the mouse. He or she performs an operation *op* on a recognized *cs*. The operation *op* results into a sequence of events generated by the operated device and called op, which are managed by the system. The system associates them with the cs being currently active and interprets the pair <op,cs> to decide which computation to perform next. Here the pair *a=<op,cs>* is called *user action* while a = <op,cs> perceived by the system is called *user activity* (*activity* in the following). The input device and the system software translate *a* into a.

Note that *cs*, the set of pixels recognized by the human, and cs, the set of pixels to which the system refers the captured events, not necessarily coincide. If the two sets are different, the system may execute a computation, which is not the one intended by the user (Nielsen, 1993). The fact that the user can correctly recognize the cs defined in the system and that therefore *cs* = cs can only be verified experimentally (Nolan, 1989).

Let us define the operation op more precisely in terms of the elementary events, which can be generated by the input devices. Let us denote with E the set of names of the elementary events. As an example, in a machine equipped with a mouse, a set of admissible elementary events the user may generate is the following: E={move_mouse, click_mouse, double_click_mouse}, where move_mouse denotes an event caused by a unitary movement of the mouse, click_mouse an event caused by a click on the mouse button, double_click_mouse denotes an event caused by a double click on the mouse button.

The possible sequences of events that result from user actions and whose descriptions can be built on E are infinite. As an example, to select a pixel on the screen, the user can follow an infinite set of paths from the current position to the pixel, resulting into an infinite number of sequences of elementary events. However, all these sequences of events are translated by the event handler into the (x,y) pair identifying the objective pixel, thus being equivalent from the point of view of the programs, which receive and manipulate this data. In general, given two sequences of events, we say that they are equivalent if and only if they are translated by the event handlers into data of the same type. Each name op denotes such an equivalence class of sequences of elementary events, and OP denotes the set of the names of such classes. Back to the example, sel and point are the names of two equivalence classes of sequences of elementary events, which are defined for sake of simplicity by the following regular expressions built on E (see Dix, Finlay, Abowd, & Beale, 2004) for a discussion of methods for textual dialog description):

point:=(move_mouse)*
sel:= point click_mouse

point denotes the equivalence class of sequences of elementary events generated by a movement of the mouse, which result into a pair of coordinates. An element of point ∈ OP is, for example in Figure 2, the sequence of move_mouse events the users must perform to bring the mouse cursor from a point on the screen over a pixel belonging to the pencil icon. Operation sel, instead, denotes the equivalence class of sequences of events generated by a point operation, followed by the event generated by a mouse button click, which results into the selection of the pixel. In the example of Figure 1, it may be the sequence of move_mouse events followed by a mouse_click event that determines the selection of the pencil icon.

Hence, an *activity*, as perceived by the system, is the pair <op, cs>, where op $\in$ OP, and cs $\in$ CS_{ve}.

Let us call A_{ve} the set of activities the user can perform on a virtual entity ve, A_{ve} ={a | a = <op, cs> where op $\in$ OP, and cs $\in$ CS_{ve}}. Since the event handler behaviors are finite, OP is finite. Being both OP and CS_{ve} finite then also A_{ve} is finite.

For example, let ⊙ and ⊙ be the two css in $CS_{\text{free-hand drawing}}$ of the button free-hand drawing allowing users to trace a boundary on the MRI in Figure 2. The input alphabet of free-hand drawing is $A_{\text{free-hand drawing}}$ = {<point, ⊙ >,<point, ⊙ >, <sel, ⊙ >, <sel, ⊙ >}, where OP = {point, sel}.

An important point to be noticed is that selecting the button free-hand drawing affects the behavior of a second ve, the data space in which the MRI is made available. Hence, to describe the effect the user sees when s/he selects the button free-hand drawing we must include the description of the change of states of both free-hand drawing and data space. From the point of view of the HCI process specification, to describe the reaction to a user activity a$\in$$A_{\text{free-hand drawing}}$, one must describe the output generated by the two ves. This case is common: therefore the notion of minimal ve is introduced in relation to user activities.

Def. 1: A *minimal* virtual entity ve in relation to a=<op,cs>$\in$$A_{ve}$ is the set of ves whose behavior is affected by the activity a. ◆

Adopting a state space approach to system description (Arbib and Padulo, 1974), the behavior of a ve, which is minimal with respect to a set of A_{ve} of user activities, may be specified by a 5-tuple ve = <S, O, f, η, s_0> on the input alphabet A_{ve}, where:

1. S is the set of admissible ve states (i.e., S = CP_{ve});
2. O is a finite set of outputs (i.e., the set CS_{ve} of possible characteristic structures that the ve may manifest);

3. f: A_{ve} × S→ S is the next state function;
4. η: A_{ve} × S→ O is the output function;
5. s_0 = cp_0 is the initial state of the ve.

The example of Figure 1 illustrates another important type of interaction, which is difficult to describe by the only specification of the program P, but which is easily specified taking into account the visual part of the specification. In Figure 1a the workspace is empty. Each activity on it is captured and managed by the ve workspace. In Figure 1b, in reaction to the user selection of a menu item, a bench, the cs of a ve bench, is superimposed to the workspace, the cs of workspace. Obviously in the second case, the 5-tuple defining workspace—and hence the program p describing its dynamics—is not changed: what is changed is the set of input activities $A_{\text{workspace}}$. In fact all the activities occurring on the bench cs are now reported to the bench ve, while they were previously reported to workspace ve. We say that bench cs is superimposed to the workspace cs. The two ves form a new composed ve obtained by superimposition. This is a common situation: for example whenever a menu is opened, its cs superimposes the adjacent css of other ves; in Figure 1c the annotation manager cs superimposes the workspace cs, but in general if a new annotation manager is opened its cs superimposes those of pre-existing ves.

To specify the composition by superimposition, let us recall here the formal definition of cs and kernel of cs as introduced in (Bottoni et al., 1997).

Let i be a digital image, i:$\{1,...,r_{max}\}$×$\{1,...,c_{max}\}$ → $V \cup \{\tau\}$, where r_{max} and c_{max} are two integers indicating the size of the image, V is an alphabet of pixel values, and τ is a special symbol (transparent symbol). A characteristic structure cs of i is an image on the same domain as i, defined as follows: cs: $\{1,...,r_{max}\}$×$\{1,...,c_{max}\}$ → $V \cup \{\tau\}$ s.t. if sel_{cs}(r,c)= 1 cs(r,c) = i(r,c), whereas if sel_{cs}(r,c) = 0 cs(r,c) =τ, where sel_{cs} is a selection function on i, sel_{cs}: $\{1,...,r_{max}\}$×$\{1,...,c_{max}\}$ → $\{0,1\}$.

The *kernel* of cs, denoted with ker(cs), is the set of pixels for which $sel_{cs}(r,c)=1$ in that those pixels over which the perceivable functional unit manifests itself to users.

Now we describe the composition among minimal virtual entities by superimposition of their characteristic structures. We start by defining the superimposition of two minimal virtual entities. Let ve_1 be a virtual entity and we denote with CP_{ve1} the set of its states (its characteristic patterns) $cp_{1k}=<cs_{1k},d_{1k},<int_{1k},mat_{1k}>>$ with $k=0,1,\ldots,m$. Let cp_{10} be its initial state and O_1, f_1, η_1 be, respectively, the set of outputs, the next state function and the output function. Similarly, consider the virtual entity $ve_2=<CP_{ve2}, O_2, f_2, \eta_2, cp_{20}>$, where $CP_{ve2} = \{cp_{2j}| cp_{2j} =<cs_{2j},d_{2j},<int_{2j},mat_{2j}>> j=1,2,\ldots,h\}$. In the following we briefly denote with cp_1 and cp_2 the characteristic patterns of ve_1 and ve_2, respectively, in a generic state. We define the *superimposition* of virtual entities ve_1, ve_2 as the virtual entity $ve_c = ve_1 \oplus_{ve} ve_2$ specified by the following tuple $< CP_{vec}, O_c, f_c, \eta_c, cp_{c0}>$ on A_{vec}, where (Box 1):

Then, ve_c is referred to as a *composed virtual entity* and ve_1,ve_2 as its *component entities*. Note that by definition, the superimposition is closed with respect to the minimality property of virtual entities (i.e., the superimposition of minimal **ves** is still a minimal virtual entity). The notion of composed **ve** by superimposition can be easily given for n virtual entities.

A VIS is a composed **ve**, which is not a component of any other **ve** in the process and characterized by **css**, which are the whole images i on the screen. Due to the first property, a VIS is generated by a program P=<In, Ap, Out>, which is not a subprogram of any other program.

The state of the VIS is a **cp** that has a special name: it is called *system visual sentence* $vs_n= <i_n,d_n,<int_n,mat_n>>$, and relates the description d_n of the state of Ap at instant n with the current image i_n on the screen, through int_n, a

Box 1.

$$CP_{vec} =\{ cp_{cz}| cp_{cz} = <cs_{cz},d_{cz},<int_c,mat_c>>\} \text{ where}$$

$$cs_{cz} : \{1,\ldots,r_{max}\}\times\{1,\ldots,c_{max}\} \to V\cup\{\tau\} \text{ s.t. } cs_{cz}(r,c) =$$

$$d_{cz} = <d_1,d_2> ;$$

$$int_c = int_1 \text{ if } cs_{cz} =cs_1, int_c = int_2 \text{ if } cs_{cz} =cs_2;$$

$$mat_c (d_{cz}) = <mat_1(d_1), mat_2(d_2)>.$$

$$A_{vec}= A_{ve1}\cup A_{ve2} -\{ <op,cs>\in A_{ve2}| ker(cs)\subseteq ker(cs_1)\cap ker(cs_2) \};$$

$$O_c = CS_{vec} = \{ cs_{cz} | cs_{cz} \ldots\ldots z=1,2,\ldots,m\cdot h\};$$

$$f_c: A_{vec} \times CP_{vec} \to CP_{vec} \text{ such that } f_c(a,cp_c) = \begin{cases} f_1(a,cp_1) \text{ if } a\in A_{ve1} \\ f_2(a,cp_2) \text{ if } a\in A_{ve2} \end{cases}$$

$$\eta_c: A_{vec} \times CP_{vec} \to O_c \text{ such that } \eta_c(a,cp_c) = \begin{cases} \eta_1(a,cp_1) \text{ if } a\in A_{ve1} \\ \eta_2(a,cp_2) \text{ if } a\in A_{ve2} \end{cases}$$

$$cp_{c0} = < cp_{10},cp_{20}>.$$

function, which maps css in i_n into elements of d_n and mat_n, which maps elements of d_n into css. When the state of the interaction process is $vs_1 = <i_1,d_1,<int_1,mat_1>>$, and the user generates activity a, the reaction of P will result into the creation of a new vs_2, whose image i_2 appears on the screen and whose d_2 describes the new state of the generating program P.

A VIS can be also defined as a 5-tuple $ve_{VIS} = <S_{VIS}, O_{VIS}, F, H, s_0>$ on A_{VIS} where A_{VIS} is a finite set of user activities, and:

1. S_{VIS} is the set of admissible vss (i.e., $S_{VIS} = \{vs \mid vs = <i, d_{VIS}, <int, mat>>, i \in O_{VIS}, d_{VIS} \in D_{VIS}\}$), where D_{VIS} is the set of the descriptions of admissible states of the programs Ap calculating the reactions of VIS in the current state vs to the user activities, $int(i) = d_{VIS}, mat(d_{VIS}) = i\}$;
2. O_{VIS} is a finite set of outputs, namely the set of possible images i on the screen that the VIS may manifest;
3. $F: A_{VIS} \times S_{VIS} \rightarrow S_{VIS}$ is the next state function;
4. $H: A_{VIS} \times S_{VIS} \rightarrow O_{VIS}$ is the output function;
5. $s_0 = vs_0$ an element in S_{VIS} is the initial state of VIS.

The design of a VIS consists in the definition of the 5-tuple on A_{VIS}, in validating it with respect to end users and verifying its computational properties. Section 3 and 4 of the chapter study how an I/O specification of a VIS usable by a specific community of end users can be designed and how to translate this specification into a SE specification suitable for developing the program P.

MULTI-FACET DESIGN OF VISUAL INTERACTIVE SYSTEMS FOR END USERS

Multi-facet design denotes a design activity in which the VIS is studied and specified from different points of view for different audiences. The different specification is not independent but allows different stakeholders to discuss, test, and use the VIS according to their specific cultures. The approach is aimed at overcoming the communication gap among end users and SE. The VIS specification for users is in the form of a visual command language (VCL). A VCL is defined specifying the image i_0 associated with the initial state of the system and a finite set of visual commands that can be used in the interaction. Visual commands constitute a visual language of multimedia expressions, built on an alphabet of visual entities derived from the end user traditional notations. VCL definition stems from the study of specifications used in practice to present interactive systems to users. Informal multimedia representations of visual commands are widely used in manuals—from those describing simple appliances to those describing complex systems such as GIS (Leach, 2006; Minami, 2000). Multimedia representations of visual commands are also documented in the literature, as for example the screen rules discussed in Horrocks (1998). The VCL definition given here capitalizes on the notion of minimal ve presented in Section 2 and describes the input-output behavior of the VIS in a form suitable to be used by end users, leaving implicit the concept of VIS state. On the other side, SE specification makes the state explicit and is expressed in a notation suitable to be used by computer experts. The technique adopts Harel (1987) state-charts as SE specification language. Carr (1997) suggested to extend state-charts by adding representation for the visual aspects of the user interface and a representation for data. But his usability results confirm that these notations are difficult for end users, and confirm the existence of a problem in creating a specification understandable both by software engineers and by end users. Here the proposal is to accept VCL as a language to specify the system to end users and state-charts—extended with visual specification of VIS states—as a language for software engineers.

To translate the VCL into a state-chart, an intermediate language is developed, the direct manipulation visual language (DMVL), which encompasses an event-state-action description of the VIS and of the interaction with it. DMVL is an intermediate language, in that it still maintains its expressiveness for domain and HCI experts and it is also expressive for software engineers. A DMVL exploits the concept of visual sentence (i.e., VIS state) to describe the dynamics of the VIS. The specification of such a language is based on the concept of transformation rule (Carrara et al., 2002), which describes, at a high level of abstraction, the process by which a visual sentence is transformed into another one as a reaction to a user activity. The set TR of transformation rules constitutes a visual language on which the specification of DMVL is based. This definition stems from the more formal models presented in Bottoni et al. (1999) and Bottoni et al. (1997). However, in this chapter we focus on the descriptions of the interaction process between end users and VIS rather then on the specification of VLs. Therefore, we adopt the definition of visual rewriting rule as the core of the definition of transformation used to describe the evolution of (minimal) virtual entities. These precise specifications of VCL, DMVL, and state-chart permit the definition of procedures for the translation among the three languages.

Visual Command Language

In this section, we provide the definition and specification of the visual command language (VCL). Its definition is based on the concept of visual command herewith introduced.

Def. 2: A *visual command* is a pair c = <activity description, reaction description>. Each description consists of a string of characters and icons. The activity description describes the operation on a characteristic structure on the

screen, as foreseen by the system. The reaction description describes the effects that can be observed by the user as system reaction to the user action. ♦

The activity description is the pair a=<op,cs> where op is the operation as defined in 2.4 performed on the characteristic structure cs. The reaction description is the set of css, outputted by the VIS on the screen.

A visual command is always associated with a text, which explains its meaning. Figure 3 shows the set of css associated with a visual command: some of them are characters or symbols, which appear on the screen during the interaction with the VIS being defined. sel denotes the operation performed by the user (i.e., the movement of the mouse in a chosen position followed by a click on the mouse button). The characteristic structure is a symbol ▨ that denotes the existence of an annotation. The pair <sel, ▨> denotes the activity of selecting the characteristic structure ▨. The reaction description provides information about the minimal set of css that are modified by the visual command. The rectangle labeled 'workspace' denotes the background area on which other css may be superimposed. The rectangle labeled 'data space' denotes an area in which a cs to be annotated exists. This cs can be a text, an image as in Figure 1, or a graphical representation. The complex cs on the right is an *annota-*

Figure 3. The pictorial part of a visual command showing how to open the annotation manager

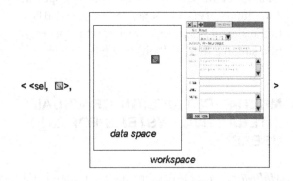

188

tion form, the cs of an annotation manager (i.e., a tool, which allows users to create and manage an annotation in the VIS being described). The introduction of workspace and data space css in the visual command is necessary to define the context in which activity and reaction occur.

The text associated with the command describes how to apply the visual command:

"Select ▨ and in the workspace an annotation form appears to be filled with annotation title and body."

The application of a command maps an image i_n into an image i_{n+1} in the following way:

1. Identify in $i_n \in O_{VIS}$ a cs, which can be mapped by a linear transformation into the cs appearing in the left part of the command;
2. Execute the required activity as explained by the text associated with the command;
3. let i_{n+1} be an image in O_{VIS} that differs from the image i_n only in the reaction description as explained by the text associated with the command.

The specification of a VCL requires the definition of the following sets:

1. A finite set OP of names of operations that the user may perform by acting on the input devices such as pointing or selecting a pixel of a cs on the screen;
2. A finite set CS_{VIS} of all the user characteristic structures of atomic and minimal virtual entities that compose the VIS. Note that $O_{VIS} \subset CS_{VIS}$.
3. A finite set of activities $A_{vis} = \{<op,cs> \mid op \in OP, cs \in CS_{VIS}\}$;
4. A finite set of visual commands VC = {c | c = <a,cs>, where a = <op_i,cs_j> ∈ A_{VIS}, cs_j ∈ CS_{VIS}, and cs∈CS_{VIS} is the characteristic structure of the minimal ve affected by the execution of the activity a}.

Note that statements 1-3 specify the lexicon of the interactive process, statement 4 specifies its syntax while the user interpretation establishes its semantics.

Def. 3: Let c_k = <a_k,cs_{k+1}> be a visual command at time k, where a_k = <op_j,cs_i> is the activity the user performs at time k on the characteristic structure cs_i through the operation op_j and cs_{k+1} is the characteristic structure of the minimal virtual entity (i.e., it includes all and only the visual structures on the screen affected by the command c_k after its execution). Additionally, let i_k be an image on the screen containing cs_i and i_{k+1} be the image derived from i_k where only cs_{k+1} is changed, then we refer to the pair <<c_k,i_k>,i_{k+1}> as *the application of the visual command c_k to the image i_k that gives as a result the image i_{k+1}*. ◆

Def. 4: A *visual command sequence* is a multimedia string s = <c_0,...,c_{n-1}> such that <<c_0,i_0>,i_1> is the application of the visual command c_0 ∈VC to the image i_0 that gives as a result the image. i_1, <<c_1,i_1>,i_2> is the application of the visual command c_1 ∈VC to the image i_1 that gives as a result the image i_2, and so on <<c_k,i_k>,i_{k+1}>, with k=2.. n-1, is the application of the visual command c_k∈VC to the image i_k that gives as a result the image i_{k+1}. ◆

Therefore, the application of the visual command sequence s = <c_0,...,c_{n-1}> to the image i_0 (the first image of the VIS) transforms i_0 into the image i_n. Each sequence of user activities is finite in time and results into an interaction trace of the performed HCI process defined as follows.

Def. 5: An *interaction trace* is a finite sequence it = < <<c_0,i_0>,i_1>, <<c_1,i_1>,i_2>, ..., <<c_{n-1},i_{n-1}>,i_n> >, where i_0,...,i_n are the images determined by the interactive system as a consequence of the application of the visual command sequence s = <c_0,...,c_{n-1}>. Each image i_k is the output of the reaction of the VIS. ◆

Figure 1 shows the sequence of images of an interaction trace. The set of all the interaction traces observed in a VIS constitutes a language (i.e., the visual command language, as specified by the following definition,) through which end users may describe the behavior of the VIS.

Def. 6: A *visual command language* is a set VCL = {it | it is an interaction trace}. ♦

A VCL is an infinite set. However, each trace starts from the common i_0 and develops because of the application of visual commands from the finite set VC. This observation suggests to adopt the ordered pair SVCL=$<i_0$,VC> as a finite specification of VCL. SVCL is an adequate specification of VCL as stated by the following:

Prop. 1: Given SVCL = $<i_0$,VC> where i_0 the first image of the VIS and VC a finite set of visual commands, for each it generated by SVCL then it∈VCL and for each it∈VCL then it is generated by SVCL.▲

Proof: See Appendix. □

Direct Manipulation Visual Language

The direct manipulation visual language (DMVL) describes the same interaction process described by the VCL maintaining the explicit visual part of the interaction process, and explicitly using VIS state (the visual sentence) and direct manipulation user activities. The DMVL definition is a refinement of the interaction visual language (IVL) definition provided in Carrara et al. (2002). With respect to that work, it exploits the concepts of minimal virtual entities to define the transformation rules and better characterize the elements of the language as interaction process instances. To specify DMVL, let us extend the definition of the rewriting rules introduced in Bottoni et al. (1999) to the rewriting of the characteristic patterns of minimal ve.

Def. 7: A visual *rewriting rule* is a triple <ant, cond, cons> where ant and cons are subsequent

states (cps) of a minimal virtual entity and cond is a condition on ant. ♦

In each state of the interaction, a finite number of user activities can be performed. As a consequence of an activity, a visual sentence vs_i is transformed into a visual sentence vs_j. The interaction process is specified as a sequence of such transformations. For example, the visual sentence whose image part is in Figure 1b is transformed into the visual sentence whose image part is in Figure 1c, as a consequence of the user selecting the pencil icon in the image.

Each step in the interaction process is thus described by a transformation that can be defined as follows:

Def. 8: A *transformation* is a triple $t=<<a,vs_i>,vs_{i+1}>$, where vs_i is the state of the VIS before the user activity is performed, vs_{i+1} is the new state computed as a reaction to a. ♦

In a transformation $t=<<a,vs_i>,vs_j>$, vs_i and vs_j share a common part, while the variable part of vs_i is transformed into the variable part of vs_j. A transformation t can be, thus, specified by providing the transformation rule tr=<a, r> that applies on the minimal ve involved in the transformation t. Therefore, we provide the following definition:

Def. 9: Let $t=<<a,vs_i>,vs_j>$ be a transformation from state vs_i to vs_j, due to the activity a=<op,cs>, the *transformation rule* determining t is defined as tr=<a, r>, where r=<ant,cond,cons> is a visual rewriting rule with ant e cons being the different states (cps) of the minimal ve involved in the transformation t, and cs in a also belonging to the characteristic structure of ant. ♦

Figure 4 shows the visual part of the transformation rule that fires when the user selects the pencil icon while interacting with the VIS shown in Figure 1. The visual part of the rewriting rule defines which cs is transformed from the state at time n+1 to the state at time n+2: in this case, it is the cs of the virtual entity workspace on which

Figure 4. The visual part of a transformation rule

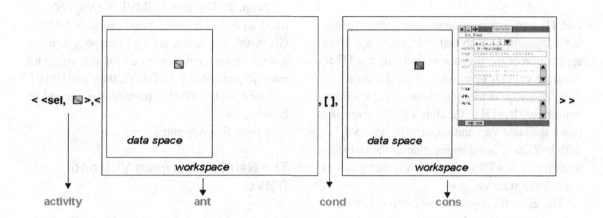

the cs of the virtual entity data space and the cs of the virtual entity annotation manager are superimposed forming the cs of a composed ve.

The computational part of this transformation rule can be specified by using an adequate description of the state of the programs generating the ve, which depends on the programming technique adopted. Being ant=<cs_{ant}, d_{ant}, <int, mat>> and cons = <cs_{cons}, d_{cons}, <int, mat>> two characteristic patterns, d_{ant} and d_{cons} are such suitable descriptions of the computational parts of ant and cons, respectively (i.e., of states of subprograms of P). Due to lack of space, we do not provide the details of such descriptions, which can be found in Fogli et al. (2006).

On the whole, the elements required to define a DMVL are:

1. A finite set OP of names of operations that the user may perform by acting on the input devices such as pointing or selecting a pixel of a cs on the screen;
2. A finite set CS_{VIS} of all the characteristic structures of atomic and minimal virtual entities that compose the VIS;
3. A finite set of activities A_{vis}={<op,cs> | op∈OP, cs∈ CS_{VIS} };

4. A finite set of transformation rules TR={tr| tr=<a,r>, where a=<op,cs>∈A_{VIS}, r=<ant, cond, cons> is a rewriting rule such that cs belongs to the characteristic structure of ant}.

Note that statements 1-3 specify the lexicon of the interactive process, statement 4 its syntax while the computational part of the transformation rules establishes the system semantics that reflects the designer interpretation.

Def. 10: Let tr_k=<a_k,r> be a transformation rule, where a_k=<op_j,cs_i> is the activity performed on cs_i by the user at time k and r=<ant,cond,cons> is a rewriting rule such that cs_i is a characteristic structure in the visual part of ant; additionally, let vs_k be the state of the VIS containing ant and vs_{k+1} be the state of the VIS derived from vs_k where ant is substituted by cons if the condition cond is true, then we refer to the pair <<tr_k,vs_k>,vs_{k+1}> as *the application of the transformation rule tr_k to the state vs_k that gives as a result the state vs_{k+1}* (See Bottoni et al., 1999) for formal details about the substitution of ant with cons in the rewriting process). ◆

Note that if condition cond is false, transformation rule tr_k cannot be applied; a different transformation rule with the same antecedent must be defined to manage this case.

Def. 11: A *transformation sequence* is a sequence $ts = <tr_0 \ldots tr_{n-1}>$ such that $<<tr_0, vs_0>, vs_1>$ is the application of the transformation rule $tr_0 \in TR$ to the state vs_0 that gives as a result the state vs_1, $<<tr_1, vs_1>, vs_2>$ is the application of the transformation rule $tr_1 \in TR$ to the state vs_1 that gives as a result the state vs_2, and so on $<<tr_k, vs_k>, vs_{k+1}>$, with $k=2 \ldots n-1$, is the application of the transformation rule $tr_k \in TR$ to the state vs_k that gives as a result the state vs_{k+1}. ◆

Therefore, the application of the transformation sequence $ts = <tr_0 \ldots tr_{n-1}>$ to the visual sentence vs_0 (the initial state of ve_{vis}) transforms vs_0 into vs_n. A transformation sequence thus determines a finite sequence of transformations that describes the process being determined by the activities performed by the user, as perceived by the system. More precisely, the following definition holds.

Def. 12: An *interaction process instance* is a finite sequence $ipi = < <<a_0, vs_0>, vs_1>, <<a_1, vs_1>, vs_2>, \ldots, <<a_{n-1}, vs_{n-1}>, vs_n>>$ determined by the application of the transformation sequence $ts = <tr_0 \ldots tr_{n-1}>$. Each visual sentence vs_k is the state reached by the VIS as a consequence of the application of transformation rule $tr_k = <a_k, r>$ in ts. ◆

A direct manipulation visual language (DMVL) is the set of all possible interaction process instances starting from vs_0.

Def. 13: A *direct manipulation visual language* (DMVL) is the set DMVL = {ipi | ipi is a interaction process instance}. ◆

The pair SDMVL = $<vs_0, TR>$ is a finite specification of DMVL, being TR a finite set of transformation rules defined on the set of activities A_{VIS}. It is easy to prove that each interaction process instance generated by SDMVL belongs to DMVL, and vice versa, that each interaction process instance belonging to DMVL can be generated by the pair SDMVL = $<vs_0, TR>$.

More precisely, the following proposition can be proved.

Prop. 2: The pair SDMVL = $<vs_0, TR>$ defined on A_{VIS} is a finite specification of DMVL. Given vs_0 the initial state of the ve_{VIS} and TR a set of transformation rules for the ve_{VIS}, for each ipi generated by SDMVL then ipi∈DMVL and for each ipi∈DMVL then ipi is generated by SDMVL. ♠

Proof: See Appendix. □

The Relation between VCL and DMVL

DMVL makes explicit the role of the set S_{VIS}—the VIS states—in the interaction process that VCL describes from the I/O point of view. A one-to-one correspondence exists among the VCL elements--the interaction traces--and the DMVL elements--the interaction process instances. The two languages must be defined on the sets CS_{VIS} and A_{VIS} defined in the VCL definition phase by domain and HCI experts to guarantee user acceptance. More precisely, given an interaction process instance in DMVL, a correspondent interaction trace exists in VCL, and, given an interaction trace in VCL a correspondent interaction process instance exists in DMVL. To guarantee this correspondence, the transformation rules in TR must be defined, so that the following condition holds:

$\forall c_i = <a_i, cs_{i+1}> \in VC \; \exists! tr_i = <a_i, r> \in TR$, s.t. $a_i = <op, cs>$, $r = <ant, cond, cons>$ and $cs \in ant$, cs_{i+1} in cons.

If the previous condition holds, it is easy to demonstrate the following propositions.

Prop. 3: Let it $= < <<c_0, i_0>, i_1>, <<c_1, i_1>, i_2>, \ldots, <<c_{n-1}, i_{n-1}>, i_n>>$ be an interaction trace in VCL and let i_0 be the characteristic structure of vs_0, then an interaction process instance ipi $= < <<a_0, vs_0>, vs_1>, <<a_1, vs_1>, vs_2>, \ldots, <<a_{n-1}, vs_{n-1}>, vs_n>> \in DMVL$ exists such that i_k is the characteristic structure of vs_k with $k \in \{1, \ldots, n\}$. ♠

Proof: See Appendix. □

Prop. 4: Let $ipi = <\ <<a_0,vs_0>,vs_1>, <<a_1,vs_1>,vs_2>, ..., <<a_{n-1},vs_{n-1}>,vs_n>>$ be an interaction process instance in DMVL and let $i_0 \in CS$, where i_0 is the characteristic structure of vs_0, then an interaction trace $it = <\ <<c_0, i_0>,i_1>, <\ c_1, i_1>,i_2>, ..., <<c_{n-1}, i_{n-1}>,i_n> > \in VCL$ exists corresponding to ipi, where i_k is the characteristic structure of vs_k, $k \in \{1,..,n\}$. ♠

Proof: See Appendix. □

The proof of proposition 3 suggests a procedure *VCL_to_DMVL* for the translation of visual commands specifying VCL in DMVL transformation rules. Such procedure is outlined in the following.

VCL_to_DMVL ($SVCL = <i_0,VC>$):

1. Given a visual command $c_k = <a_k, cs_{k+1}>$ in VC, where $a_k = <op, cs>$ determine the characteristic pattern cp_{k+1} whose visual part is the characteristic structure cs_{k+1}, the (visual) reaction description of the command c_k; such a characteristic pattern is the state of a minimal virtual entity at time $k+1$;

2. Next, determine the characteristic pattern cp_k of the same minimal virtual entity at time k and such that $cs \in cs_k$, being cs_k the characteristic structure of cp_k;

3. Construct $tr_k = <a_k, <ant, cond, cons>>$, where $ant = cp_k$, $cons = cp_{k+1}$ and cond is a condition on the applicability of a_k on cp_k, corresponding to the given visual command $c_k = <a_k, cs_{k+1}>$. ♣

Inconsistencies and ambiguities can be found in visual commands during the translation activity or in the interaction process. The design team can overcome such problems by modifying or extending the existing transformation rules or adding new ones. Then, they can refine the visual commands according to the DMVL refinement, by the procedure *DMVL_to_VCL* derived from the proof of proposition 4, herewith outlined.

DMVL_to_VCL ($DMVL = <vs_0, TR>$):

1. Given a rule $tr_k = <a_k, r>$, where $r = <ant, cond, cons>$, consider cs_{cons}, the visual part of cons;

2. Construct the visual command $c_k = <a_k, cs_{k+1}>$ with $cs_{k+1} = cs_{cons}$ corresponding to the rule tr_k. ♣

From DMVL to FSM Software Specification

In this section, a three stages procedure *Build_FSM*(vs_0, TR) is introduced which translates a DMVL specification $SDMVL = <vs_0, TR>$ of the VIS behavior into a finite state machine (FSM) that exhibits the same behavior. The FSM is specified as a state-chart (Harel, 1987) following the approach and notation described in Horrocks (1998). *Build_FSM*(vs_0, TR) requires designers to take some heuristic decisions. In its first stage, designers define the top level of the state-chart. Each state in the top level representation is characterized by a set of activities, heuristically identified by designers, equivalent with respect to the tasks to be performed using the VIS. In the second stage, the top-level states are refined by iterating the same process in which designers heuristically identify the refinement criteria. In the third stage, the state-chart graph is simplified reducing states and transitions by using Horrocks' heuristics (Horrocks, 1998).

Before detailing the procedure, let us introduce the input alphabet to the FSM.

Def. 14: Two activities $a_i = <op_i, cs_i>$ and $a_j = <op_j, cs_j>$ are *equivalent in behavior* if $op_i = op_j$ (i.e., they denote the same equivalence class of sequences of events and cs_j can be obtained by a linear transformation of cs_i) (Carrara et al., 2002). ♦

Behaviorally equivalent activities activate the same subprogram p of P causing the same effects on the VIS. Behavioral equivalence is an equiva-

Figure 5. The build_FSM procedure

Build_FSM(vs$_0$, TR):

STAGE 1: - Designers heuristically define an equivalence relation $\equiv_1$ on the set A_{VIS}

- Relation $\equiv_1$ groups elements of A_{VIS} into new classes and identifies a new partition A^1_{VIS} based

  on the task and the environment designers have to develop

- $S^1_{VIS} = \varnothing$, $G^1_{VIS} = \varnothing$

- For each element A^{1k}_{VIS} in A^1_{VIS} : Create a state in S^1_{VIS} and name it

- For each state $s_k \in S^1_{VIS}$
  Let TR^{1k} be the set of transformation rules in TR univocally identified by the activities in
  A^{1k}_{VIS} i.e., tr=<a,r> such that a is the name of a class of activities in A^{1k}_{VIS}
  For each transformation rule tr=< a,<ant,cond,cons>> in TR^{1k}
      If $cs_{cons} \notin cs$ of ant$_1$ of a rule tr$_1$=< a$_1$, <ant$_1$,cond$_1$, cons$_1$>> in TR then
      Go to the next transformation rule
      else
      If $\exists$ a rule tr$_2$=< a$_2$,<ant$_2$,cond$_2$,cons$_2$>>$\in$TR s.t. cs$_{cons1}$ of tr$_1$ is in ant$_2$ then
      If tr$_2 \in$ TR^{1k} then go to the next transformation rule
      else
        Let TR^{1h} be the set of transformation rules to which tr$_2$ belongs to
        Add to G^1_{VIS} an arrow from s_k to s_h labelled with (a$_2$,cond$_2$), where a$_2$
        denotes the activity causing the rule tr$_2$ whenever cond$_2$ is true

- endfor

STAGE 2: - $i = 2$, end_stage = false

- While not(end_stage) do
  For each state $s_k \in S^{i-1}_{VIS}$ denoting the set of all the (macro)states created at step i-1
  (corresponding to the class $A^{(i-1)k}_{VIS}$ in A^{i-1}_{VIS})
  Designers heuristically define an equivalence relation $\equiv_i$ on the set $A^{(i-1)k}_{VIS}$ (1)
  Relation $\equiv_i$ groups elements of $A^{(i-1)k}_{VIS}$ into new classes identifying a partition A^{ik}_{VIS}
  if $A^{(i-1)k}_{VIS} = A^{ik}_{VIS}$ then exit
  $S^{ik}_{VIS} = \varnothing$, $G^{ik}_{VIS} = \varnothing$
  For each element $A_j^{ik}_{VIS}$ in A^{ik}_{VIS} : Create a state in S^{ik}_{VIS} and name it
  For each state $s_j \in S^{ik}_{VIS}$ (corresponding to the class A_j^{ik} in A^{ik}_{VIS})
      Let TR_j^{ik} be the set of rules in TR univocally identified by the activities in
      $A_j^{ik}_{VIS}$, i.e., tr=<a,r> s. t. a denotes a class of activities in $A_j^{ik}_{VIS}$
      For each transformation rule tr=< a,<ant,cond,cons>> in TR_j^{ik}
      If $cs_{cons} \notin cs$ of ant$_1$ of a rule tr$_1$=< a$_1$, <ant$_1$, cond$_1$, cons$_1$>> in TR
      then Go to the next transformation rule
      else
        If $\exists$ tr$_2$=< a$_2$,<ant$_2$,cond$_2$,cons$_2$>>$\in$TR s.t. cs$_{const}$ of tr$_1$ is in ant$_2$ then
        If tr$_2 \in$ TR$_j^{ik}$ then Go to the next transformation rule
        else
          Let TR_w^{ik} be the set of transformation rules to which tr$_2$ belongs to
          Add to G^{ik}_{VIS} an arrow from s_j to s_w labelled with (a$_2$,cond$_2$), where
          a$_2$ is the name of the activity causing the rule tr$_2$ if cond$_2$ is true
  endfor
  if there exists a k s.t. $A^{(i-1)k}_{VIS} \neq A^{ik}_{VIS}$ then i = i+1 else end_stage = true

- enddo

STAGE 3: - Refine the state-charts taking into account the heuristics described in Horrocks (1998).
Concurrency can be exploited in case of independent separate behaviours, while clusters and
history symbols can be used to reduce the number of transitions. ♣

Figure 6. The state-chart specifying B-radiologist at the highest level of abstraction

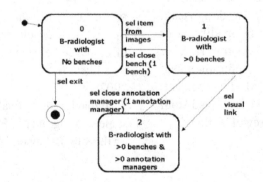

lence relation. Classes of behaviorally equivalent activities are denoted as $a = (a/\equiv)$.

Let $A_{VIS} = \{a = <op, cs> \mid op \in OP, cs \in CS_{VIS}\}$ be the set of user activities that can be performed with respect to the css of atomic and minimal ves composing the VIS, then the set of activity equivalence classes – *types of activities* – in a VIS is $A_{VIS} = (A_{VIS}/\equiv)$. Being OP finite and CS_{VIS} finite then also A_{VIS} is finite, and therefore A_{VIS} is finite. In the following, S^1_{VIS} and G^1_{VIS}, denote, respectively, the set of states and the set of transitions at the state-chart top level and S^{nk}_{VIS} and G^{nk}_{VIS} respectively, the set of states and the set of the transitions of the state-chart refining the macrostate s_k at n-th level of detail.

A state-chart on the input alphabet A_{VIS} specifying a finite state control machine of the VIS, which generates the set of the interaction process instances in DMVL, is derived by the *Build_FSM* procedure presented in Figure 5.

As an example, Figure 6 shows the top level state-chart specifying B-radiologist obtained by applying the first stage of procedure *Build_FSM*. The designer has identified three macro-states corresponding to three classes of tasks. State 0 is associated with all states of the virtual entity corresponding to the situation in which B-radiologist presents a workspace with no benches in it, and the set of admitted activities consists only in the use of the menu items and the exit button. Users can only perform the tasks of choosing the document to be worked out.

State 1 is associated with the situation in which one or more benches are present in the workspace, but no annotation manager is present. The set of admitted activities is now enriched by all the activities performable on benches. Users can thus perform the tasks of exploring data and starting the annotation process.

State 2 is associated with the situation in which at least one bench and one annotation manager are present. The set of admitted activities is now enriched by all the activities performable on annotation managers. Users can thus perform the annotation tasks. For sake of state-chart readability, the output function is not explicitly shown in Figure 6, but it is described in the associated input-output table (see Table 1) according to the technique adopted in Horrocks (1998). The visual parts of the states may be described referring to

Table 1. Input-output table of the state-chart shown in Figure 6

Current state	Input Event	Output computation	Next State
0	Selection of an item from menu "images"	Load selected image in a bench	1
0	Selection of the "exit" button		-
1	Selection of the button for closing the bench (only 1 bench open)	Save changes in the bench	0
1	Selection of a visual link	Load related annotations in an annotation manager	2
2	Selection of the button for closing the annotation manager (only 1 annotation manager open)	Save changes in the annotation manager	1

Figure 7. A portion of the state-chart specifying state 1 of Figure 6 at a lower level of abstraction

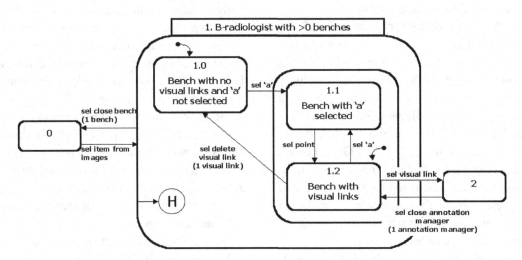

Figure 1: in particular, a representative visual part associated with state 0 is image i_n in Figure 1; a representative visual part associated with state 1 is image i_{n+1}; and a representative visual part associated with state 2 is image i_{n+2}.

Figure 7 shows a portion of the state-chart derived by applying stage 2 of the procedure *Build_FSM*, presented in Figure 5, still in the case of B-radiologist. It specifies state 1 in Figure 6 at a lower level of abstraction by considering the class of activities that can be performed with respect to a bench and partitioning it into further classes of activities that identify three significant sub-states of state 1 related with the creation of an annotation: sub-state 1.0 represents the situation in which no button in the bench is selected; sub-state 1.1 represents the situation in which button "a" in the bench has been selected to put an annotation; sub-state 1.2 represents the situation in which a point in the data space of the bench has been selected to add a visual link on the bench.

It is easy to prove that each interaction process instance belonging to DMVL corresponds to a path in the FSM, and that each path in the FSM corresponds to an interaction process instance

belonging to DMVL. More precisely, the following proposition can be proved.

Prop. 5: Let $SDMVL = <vs_0, TR>$ the specification of DMVL and $ipi \in DMVL$. Then $ipi \in DMVL$ corresponds to a path in the state-chart generated by SDMVL. Vice versa, each path in the state-chart generated by $SDMVL = <vs_0, TR>$ corresponds to an $ipi \in DMVL$. ♠

Proof: Trivial from procedure *Build_FSM*. □

THE VIS DEVELOPMENT: GUIDELINES FOR MULTI-FACET DESIGN AND VALIDATION

The framework of languages, language specifications, procedures, and algorithms developed so far are used here to steer the design and implementation of a VIS.

The goal of the design and implementation processes is to develop a VIS usable by end users in a specific environment and to develop activities whose results must be guaranteed. To this end, users must be able to exploit their tacit knowledge to evaluate the interaction process and

Figure 8. Relationships among VLs for VIS design--arrow labeled "VIS prototypes" identifies the feedback through prototypes

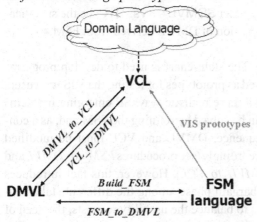

the intermediate and final results of every activity performed interacting with the VIS.

The set of characteristic structures, CS_{VIS}, of the operation set, OP, and of the user activities in A_{VIS} must be designed so that users correctly understand and articulates them (i.e., when users look at the system, they recognize the set of characteristic structures appearing on the screen and understand how to operate on them).

Let us denote with *CS* the set of characteristic structures recognized by the user and with *OP* and **A** respectively the set of operations and activities as perceived by the user, then the following conditions must be stated:

1. A one-to-one mapping δ exists between *CS* and CS_{VIS}. This implies that the cardinality of *CS* is equal to the cardinality of CS_{VIS}.
2. A one-to-one mapping μ exists between *OP* and OP and thus the cardinality of *OP* is equal to the cardinality of OP.
3. $\forall a = <op, cs> \in A \ \exists! a = <op, cs> \in A_{VIS}$ such that $\mu(op) = op$ and $\delta(cs) = cs$.

The three statements constrain the design activity of CS_{VIS}, OP and A_{VIS}. Their design is

also constrained by the fact that what users see and the way they operate depends on their interpretation of the system appearance, the context, and the activity performed. On the whole, the user understanding and use of the tools depends on their knowledge, both tacit and explicit. Therefore, CS_{VIS}, OP, and A_{VIS} must be designed taking into account the user domain language (see Figure 8). The design of VCL elements must therefore be based on:

- **The pragmatics of the activity:** For example, in the VIS supporting the management of automation systems (Costabile et al., 2004), which input tools are at user disposal—and hence, which are the admitted operations op;
- **The semantics of the activity:** It may concern, for example, the most frequent errors and slips that occur on the workplace, and hence, which procedures to recover from them;
- **The syntax of the activity:** The domain language notations used by users to document their activity, but also to give warnings on the workplace (e.g., how to express alarm signals).

It is not always possible to directly assume the domain language symbols and constructs as VCL elements. Computer graphics and efficiency reasons force us to approximate traditional symbols of the domain language, and often new symbols must be introduced. Moreover, the characteristics of the virtual visual interaction and world may differ from the real ones. Therefore, VCL symbols and procedure may be different from traditional ones and/or new for the users. They can only be validated through usability experiments (Majhew, 1992; Nolan, 1989). CS_{VIS}, OP, and A_{VIS} are designed by HCI experts and user representatives, which may go through several cycles of definition and usability experiments in a specification of VCL.

However, the problem remains to translate the VCL into an efficient implementation. To face this problem, first HCI experts and software engineers translate VCL specification into DMVL by following the track described by *VCL_to_DMVL*. In this activity, ambiguities and non-deterministic definitions of VCL can be found. Therefore, HCI experts may decide to go back to the VCL definition and, with the help of domain experts, revise it in order to remove these faults, following in this case *DMVL_to_VCL*. At the end of this activity, the DMVL specification SDMVL = <vs_0,TR> is obtained. Next designers can derive the control FSM applying *Build_FSM*. The resulting FSM together with DMVL constitute a specification for software implementers. The state-chart definition permits checking properties, which can be formally stated such as completeness, determinism, reachability, reversibility, and viability (Dix et al., 2004)--and for which therefore automatized checking tools can be and often have been developed. The use of these tools may put in light incompleteness or faults in VIS definition. In these cases, the current FSM definition must be revised, as well as the corresponding SDMVL. To this end, three guidelines can be dictated, organized in the procedure *FSM_to_DMVL* here outlined.

FSM_to_DMVL(FSM):

1. Consider state s_0 in FSM, then let vs_0 such that $(vs_0/\equiv_{vs}) = s_0$ be the initial visual sentence of the VIS;

2. Construct TR as follows:
    For each level i in the state-chart
    For each state s_k at level i
    Let G^{ik}_{VIS} be the set of transitions from s_k to another state in the state-chart at level i
    For each $g \in G^{ik}_{VIS}$ being a transition from s_k to s_h labelled with the name a_j of the
    activity and a possible condition condj
    find ant_j in s_k and $cons_j$ in s_h s.t. s_h is obtained from s_k substituting ant_j with $cons_j$

create tr = <a_j, <ant_j, $cond_j$, $cons_j$>>
add tr to TR
endfor

3. Let SDMVL = <vs_0, TR> be the specification of DMVL derived from FSM.♣

The state-chart is used to develop programs used as prototypes for testing the VIS with users in a more realistic way. SE emerging problems can be solved by refining the FSM and, as a consequence, DMVL and VCL must be modified accordingly (see procedures *FSM_to_DMVL* and *DMVL_to_VCL*). However, this fact introduces a bargain phase among the different stakeholders to balance the usability requests, the need of satisfying end user requests on the expressiveness of the messages against the technological constraints. Figure 8 illustrates all the previously mentioned relationships. Note that procedures *Build_FSM, VCL_to_DMVL, DMVL_to_VCL* and *FSM_to_DMVL* require a certain amount of human decision-making, therefore they are not rigorous algorithms and cannot be fully automatized. The process is iterative and the developed prototypes are evolutionary (Preece, 1994) in that they are constructed, evaluated, and evolved continually throughout the VIS life cycle. In this way, co-evolution is taken into account explicitly: each new evaluation-evolution cycle requires the revision of VLC, DMVL, state-chart, and the balancing of usability-efficiency-domain fitting aspects of the design.

CONCLUSION AND FUTURE TRENDS

Nowadays interactive systems are evolving to multimodal interactive systems in which several modes of interaction between user and system are available beyond the visual one such as gestures, sounds, vocal, and haptic commands. Actually, current computing technologies empowers new forms of communication, reflection, and decision-making (Fischer, 2006; Mynatt, 2006) arriving at using the body of the user as a primary interface (Rabagliati, 2006). Therefore, multi-facet approaches should be extended to consider these emerging multimodal languages, which still must be explored and properly understood for the multi-facet design of multimodal interactive systems. In general, the approach must be experimented in several application domains in order to analyze its appropriateness and effectiveness.

ACKNOWLEDGMENT

The present work is partially supported by the web indexing language (WIL) project, financed by the Italian Ministry of Education, University, and Research (MIUR).

REFERENCES

Arias, E., Eden, H., Fischer, G., Gorman, A., & Scharff, E. (2000). Transcending the individual human mind: Creating shared understanding through collaborative design. *ACM Trans on CHI, 7*(1), 84-113.

Abowd, G. D., & Beale, R. (1991). Users, systems, and interfaces: A unifying framework for interaction. In D. Diaper & N. Hammond (Eds.), *HCI'91: People and computers VI* (pp. 73-87). Cambridge: Cambridge University Press.

Andersen, P. B. (2001). What semiotics can and cannot do for HCI. *Knowledge Based Systems, 14*(8), 419-424.

Arbib, M. A., & Padulo, L. (1974). *Systems theory: A unified state space approach to continuous and discrete systems.* Philadelphia: W. B. Saunders.

Barnard, P., May, J., Duke, D., & Duce, D. (2000). Systems, interactions, and macrotheory. *ACM Transactions on HCI, 7*(2), 222-262.

Beaudouin-Lafon, M. (2004). Designing interaction, not interfaces. *Proceedings of the Working Conference on Advanced Visual Interfaces 2004* (pp. 15-22). Gallipoli, Italy.

Bianchi, N., Bottoni, P., Mussio, P., & Protti, M. (1993). Cooperative visual environments for the design of effective visual systems. *Journal of Visual Languages & Computing, 4*(4), 357-381.

Bianchi-Berthouze, N., & Mussio, P. (2005). Introduction to the special issue on context and emotion aware visual computing. *Journal of Visual Languages & Computing, 16*(5), 383-385.

Blostein, D., & Schürr, A. (1997). Computing with graphs and graph rewriting. *Software-Practice and Experience, The 6th Proceedings in Informatics* (pp. 1-21).

Bødker, S., & Grønbæk, K. (1991). Cooperative prototyping: Users and designers in mutual activity. *International Journal of Man-Machine Studies, 34*(3), 453-478.

Borchers, J. (2001). *A pattern approach to interactive design.* Chichester, UK: John Wiley & Sons.

Borchers, J., Fincher, S., Griffiths, R., Pemberton, L., & Siemon, E. (2001). Usability pattern language: Creating a community. *AI & Society Journal of Human-Centred Systems and Machine Intelligence, 15*(4), 377-385.

Bottoni, P., Costabile, M. F., Levialdi, S., & Mussio, P. (1997). Defining visual languages for interactive computing. *IEEE Trans. on Systems, Man, and Cybernetics. Part A, 27*(6), 773-783.

Bottoni, P., Costabile, M. F., & Mussio, P. (1999). Specification and dialogue control of visual interaction through visual rewriting systems. *ACM TOPLAS, 21*(6), 1077-1136.

Buschmann, F. (2001). *Series foreword, A pattern approach to interactive design.* Chichester, UK: John Wiley & Sons.

Carr, D. (1997). Interaction object graphs: An executable graphical notation for specifying user interfaces. In P. Palanque & F. Paternò (Eds.), *Formal methods in human-computer interaction* (pp. 141-155). Springer-Verlag.

Carrara, P., Fogli, D., Fresta, G., & Mussio, P. (2002). Toward overcoming culture, skill, and situation hurdles in human-computer interaction. *International Journal Universal Access in the Information Society, 1*(4), 288-304.

Carroll, J. M. (1995). *Scenario-based design.* John Wiley & Sons.

Chang, S. K., Hou, T. Y., & Hsu, A. (1992). Smart image design for large image databases. *Journal of Visual Languages & Computing, 3*(4), 323-342.

Codognet, P. (1999). An Historical account of indexical images: From Ancient Art to the Web. *Proceedings of the 1999 IEEE Symposium on Visual Languages* (pp. 104-110). Tokyo, Japan: IEEE Press.

Costabile, M. F., Fogli, D., Fresta, G., Mussio, P., & Piccinno, A. (2004). Software environments for end user development and tailoring. *Psychology, 2*(1), 99-122.

Costabile, M. F., Fogli, D., Mussio, P., & Piccinno, A. (2006a). End user development: The software shaping workshop approach. In H. Lieberman, F. Paternò, & V. Wulf (Eds.), *End user development* (pp. 183-205). Dordrecht, The Netherlands: Springer.

Costabile, M. F., Fogli, D., Lanzilotti, R., Mussio, P., & Piccinno, A. (2006b). Supporting work practice through end user development environments. *Journal of Organizational and End User Computing, 18*(6), 63-65.

De Souza, C. S. (2005). *The semiotic engineering of human computer interaction.* MIT Press.

Dix, A., Finlay, J., Abowd, G., & Beale, R. (2004). *Human computer interaction.* London: Prentice Hall.

Fischer, G. (1998). Seeding, evolutionary growth, and reseeding: Constructing, capturing, and evolving knowledge in domain-oriented design environments. *Automated Software Engineering, 5*(4), 447-468.

Fischer, G. (2006). Distributed intelligence: Extending the power of the unaided, individual human mind. *Proceedings of the International Conference on Advanced Visual Interfaces 2006* (pp. 7-14). Venezia, Italia: ACM Press.

Fischer, G., Giaccardi, E., Ye, Y., Sutcliffe, A. G., & Mehandjiev, N. (2004). Meta-design: A manifesto for end user development. *Communications of the ACM, 47*(9), 33-37.

Fogli, D., Marcante, A., Mussio, P., Parasiliti Provenza, L., & Piccinno, A. (2006). *Modelling visual interactive systems through virtual entities* (Tech. Rep. No. 03). Italy: University of Bari.

Folmer, E., van Welie, M., & Bosch, J. (2005). Bridging patterns: An approach to bridge gaps between SE and HCI. *Journal of Information and Software Technology, 48*(2), 69-89.

Gray, J., Rossi, M., & Tolvanen, J. P. (2004). Preface. *Journal of Visual Languages and Computing, 15*(3-4), 207-209.

Harel, D. (1987). Statecharts: A visual formalism for complex systems. *Science of Computer Programming, 8*(3), 23-274.

Harris, R. (2000). *Rethinking writing.* London, UK: The Athlone Press.

Horrocks, I. (1998). *Constructing the user interface with statecharts.* Addison-Wesley.

Jean, G. (1986). *L'écriture, mémoire des homes.* Paris: Gallimard.

Hutchins, E. L., Hollan, J. D., & Norman, D. (1986). Direct manipulation interfaces. In D. Norman & S. Draper (Eds.), *User centred system design* (pp. 87-124). Hillsdale, NJ: Lawrence Erlbaum Associates.

Kuutti, K. (1995). Activity theory as a potential framework for human-computer interaction. In B. Nardi (Ed.), *Context and consciousness: Activity theory and human computer interaction.* Cambridge, MA: MIT Press.

Lauesen, S. (2005). *User interface design: A software engineering perspective.* Addison-Wesley.

Leach, L. (2006). *AutoCAD 2006 Instructor.* McGraw-Hill.

Majhew, D. J. (1992). *Principles and guideline in software user interface design.* Prentice Hall.

Minami, M. (2000). *Using ArcMap.* Environmental Systems Research Institute.

Mussio, P., Pietrogrande, M., & Protti, M. (1991). Simulation of hepatological models: A study in visual interactive exploration of scientific problems. *Journal of Visual Languages and Computing, 2*(1), 75-95.

Mynatt, E. (2006). From mainframes to picture frames: Charting the rapid evolution of visual interfaces. *Proceedings of the International Conference on Advanced Visual Interfaces 2006* (15). Venezia, Italia: ACM Press.

Naranayan Hari, N., & Hubscher, R. (1998). Visual languages theory: Towards a human-computer interaction perspective. In K. Merriot & B. Meyer (Eds.), *Visual language theory.* New York: Springer.

Nielsen, J. (1993). *Usability engineering.* San Diego: Academic Press.

Nolan, P. R. (1989). Designing screen icons: Ranking and matching studies. *Proceedings of the Human Factors Society, 33rd Annual Meeting* (pp. 380-384). Santa Monica, CA: The Human Factors Society.

Norman, D. A., & Draper, S. W. (1986). *User-centered system design: New perspectives on human-computer interaction.* Hillsdale, NJ: Lawrence Erlbaum Associates.

Norman, D. A. (2005). Human-centered design considered harmful. *Interactions, 12*(4), 14-19.

Preece, J. (1994). *Human-computer interaction,* Addison-Wesley.

Rabagliati, R. (2006). AVI and the art system: Interactive works at the Venice Biennale. *Proceedings of the International Conference on Advanced Visual Interfaces 2006* (pp. 3-6) Venezia, Italia: ACM Press.

Rittel, H. (1984). Second-generation design methods. In N. Cross (Ed.), *Developments in design methodology* (pp. 317-327). New York: John Wiley & Sons.

Schön, D. (1983). *The reflective practitioner: How professionals think in action.* Basic Books.

Schuler, D., & Namioka, A. (1993). *Participatory design: Principles and Practices.* Hillsday, NJ: Lawrence Erlbaum Associates.

Sprinkle, J., & Karsai, G., (2004). A domain-specific visual language for domain model evolution. *Journal of Visual Languages and Computing, 15*(3-4), 291-307.

Tondl, L. (1981). *Problems of semantics.* Dordrecht, Boston: D. Reidel Publishing.

APPENDIX A

Here we demonstrate the propositions introduced throughout the chapter.

Prop. 1: The ordered pair SVCL = $\langle i_0, VC \rangle$ is a finite specification of VCL. Given i_0 the first image of the VIS and VC a set of commands, for each it generated by SVCL= $\langle i_0, VC \rangle$ then it$\in$VCL and for each it$\in$VCL then it is generated by SVCL= $\langle i_0, VC \rangle$. ♠

Proof:

We have to prove that for each it generated by SVCL=$\langle i_0, VC \rangle$ then it$\in$VCL and for each it$\in$VCL then it is generated by SVCL.

Let c_0 be a visual command in VC applying on a characteristic structure cs_0 within the first image i_0 on the screen. Let's say $c_0 = \langle a_0, cs_1 \rangle = \langle \langle op, cs_0 \rangle, cs_1 \rangle$ where cs_1 is the minimal characteristic structure in i_0 changed after the application of c_0 and $a_0 = \langle op, cs_0 \rangle$ is the user activity realized by executing with the available input devices the operation op on cs_0 in i_0. Let i_1 be the image of the VIS appearing on the screen as result of the application of c_0 on i_0, then $cs_1 \in i_1$. Therefore, by applying c_0 on i_0 we derive the interaction trace of length 1, $\langle \langle c_0, i_0 \rangle, i_1 \rangle$. Again, consider the command c_1 in VC applying on i_1, $c_1 = \langle a_1, cs_2 \rangle$. Then, the application of the visual commands c_0 and c_1 on i_0 generates the interaction trace of length 2, $\langle \langle c_0, i_0 \rangle, i_1 \rangle, \langle \langle c_1, i_1 \rangle, i_2 \rangle \rangle$. By iterating this method, we find that the initial image i_0, and the visual commands $c_0, c_1, \ldots, c_n$ in VC generate the interaction trace it $= \langle \langle c_0, i_0 \rangle, i_1 \rangle, \langle \langle c_1, i_1 \rangle, i_2 \rangle, \ldots, \langle \langle c_{n-1}, i_{n-1} \rangle, i_n \rangle \rangle \in$VCL.

Vice versa, let it $= \langle \langle \langle c_0, i_0 \rangle, i_1 \rangle, \langle \langle c_1, i_1 \rangle, i_2 \rangle, \ldots, \langle \langle c_{n-1}, i_{n-1} \rangle, i_n \rangle \rangle$ be an interaction trace in VCL. It is evident that it is generated by applying the visual command $c_0, c_1, \ldots, c_n$ on initial image i_0. □

Prop. 2: The ordered pair SDMVL = $\langle vs_0, TR \rangle$ is a finite specification of DMVL. Given vs_0 the initial state of the ve_{VIS} and TR a set of transformation rules for the ve_{VIS}, for each ipi generated by SDMVL then ipi$\in$DMVL and for each ipi$\in$DMVL then ipi is generated by SDMVL. ♠

Proof:

We have to prove that given vs_0 the initial state of the ve_{vis} and TR a set of transformation rules for the ve_{vis}, for each ipi generated by $\langle vs_0, TR \rangle$ then ipi$\in$DMVL and for each ipi$\in$DMVL then ipi is generated by $\langle vs_0, TR \rangle$.

Let $tr_0 = \langle a_0, \langle cp_0, cond, cp_1 \rangle \rangle$ be a transformation rule in TR applied at the initial state $vs_0 = \langle i_0, d_0, \langle int_0, mat_0 \rangle \rangle$, due to the user activity a_0, where $cp_0 = \langle cs_0, d_0, \langle int_0, mat_0 \rangle \rangle$ and $cp_1 = \langle cs_1, d_1, \langle int_1, mat_1 \rangle \rangle$ are two subsequent states of a minimal ve in ve_{vis} affected by the transformation. Transformation rule tr_0, thus, determines the transformation $t_0 = \langle \langle a_0, vs_0 \rangle, vs_1 \rangle$ of the VIS from the initial state vs_0 to the state $vs_1 = \langle i_1, d_1, \langle int_1, mat_1 \rangle \rangle$ s.t. $cs_1 \in i_1$, that is the interaction process instance ipi of length 1. Then, considering the transformation rule $tr_1 = \langle a_1, \langle cp'_1, cond', cp_2 \rangle \rangle$ specifying how the state of the ve' composing the ve_{vis} at the state vs_1 changes due to the user activity a_1, where $cp'_1 = \langle cs'_1, d'_1, \langle int_1, mat_1 \rangle \rangle$ and $cp_2 = \langle cs_2, d_2, \langle int_2, mat_2 \rangle \rangle$, we find that there exists a transformation $t_1 = \langle \langle a_1, vs_1 \rangle, vs_2 \rangle$ of the VIS from the state vs_1 to $vs_2 = \langle i_2, d_2, \langle int_2, mat_2 \rangle \rangle$ s.t. $cs_2 \in i_2$. Then, given the initial state and the transformation rules tr_0, tr_1 the interaction process instance ipi$= \langle \langle a_0, vs_0 \rangle, vs_1 \rangle$,

$<<a_1,vs_1>,vs_2>>$ in DMVL of length 2 is generated. By iterating this method, we find that the initial state vs_0 and the transformations tr_0, tr_1,..., tr_{n-1} generate the interaction process instance $ipi = <t_0, t_1,...,$ $t_{n-1}> \in$ DMVL. By contrast, let $ipi = < <<a_0,vs_0>,vs_1>$, $<<a_1,vs_1>,vs_2>$, ..., $<<a_{n-1},vs_{n-1}>,vs_n> >$ be an interaction process instance in DMVL. Firstly, we consider the transformation $t_0 = <<a_0,vs_0>,vs_1>$ of the VIS from the state vs_0 to vs_1. Let i_0 and i_1 be the materializations of the VIS corresponding to the states vs_0 and vs_1. Now, let cs_0 be the minimal characteristic structure in i_0 changing due to the transformation t_0 and cs_1 be its materialization in i_1 after t_0, if we denote with cp_0 and cp_1 the states of the minimal ve in ve_{VIS} changing due to t_0 then the transformation t_0 is generated by applying on vs_0 the transformation rule $tr_0 = <a_0, r_0>$, where $r_0 = < cp_0$, cond, $cp_1>$ and a_0 is an activity the user performs a $cs \in cs_0$. Similarly, given the transformation $t_{n-1} = <<a_{n-1},vs_{n-1}>,vs_n>$ of the VIS from the state vs_{n-1} to vs_n, it can be specified by the transformation rule $tr_{n-1} = <a_{n-1}, r_{n-1}>$, where $r_{n-1} = < cp_{n-1}$, cond', $cp_n>$ is the rewriting rule specifying the change of the minimal ve involved in the transformation t_{n-1} that, when applied, transform vs_{n-1} into vs_n. Thus, the thesis is proved.

Prop. 3: Let $it = < <<c_0, i_0>,i_1,>$, $<<c_1, i_1>,i_2>$, ..., $<<c_{n-1}, i_{n-1}>,i_n> >$ be an interaction trace in VCL and let i_0 be the characteristic structure of vs_0, then an interaction process instance $ipi = < <<a_0,vs_0>,vs_1>$, $<<a_1,vs_1>,vs_2>$, ..., $<<a_{n-1},vs_{n-1}>,vs_n> > \in$ DMVL exists such that i_k is the characteristic structure of vs_k with $k \in \{1,..,n\}$. ▲

Proof:

Let $it = < <<c_0, i_0>,i_1>$, $<<c_1, i_1>,i_2>$, ..., $<<c_{n-1}, i_{n-1}>,i_n> > \in$ VCL determined by the visual command sequence $s = <c_0, c_1, ..., c_{i-1}>$.

At first, we consider the application of the visual command c_0 in s to the first image on the screen i_0 producing the new image i_1, that is, $<<c_0 i_0>,i_1>$. From the hypothesis, the first image i_0 of the VIS is the visual part of the initial state $vs_0 = <i_0,d_0,<int_0,mat_0>>$ of the VIS. Let $c_0 = <a_0,cs_1>$ where $cs_1 \in i_1$ is the minimal characteristic structure included in i_1 modified by c_0 by means of the user activity $a_0 = <op,cs_0>$, with $op \in OP$ and $cs_0 \in i_0 \in CS_{VIS}$.

Let $cp_0 = <cs_0,d_0,<int,mat>>$ and $cp_1 = <cs_1,d_1,<int,mat>>$ be, respectively, the states of the minimal virtual entity whose visual components are cs_0 and cs_1. Then a transformation rule $tr_0 = <a_0,r>$ exists such that $r = < cp_0$, cond, $cp_1>$, that is, tr_0 changes the state of the minimal ve involved in the transformation from cp_0 into cp_1. Therefore, if we denote with vs_1 the state of the VIS whose visual part is i_1, we can conclude that, given the application of the visual command c_0 on i_0, $<<c_0,i_0>,i_1>$, there exists a transformation $t_0 = <<a_0,vs_0>,vs_1>$, foreseen by the system, changing the state of the VIS from vs_0 into vs_1.

Similarly, if we consider the application of visual command $c_{k-1} = <a_{k-1},cs_k>$ on image i_{k-1}, $<<c_{k-1}, i_{k-1}>,i_k>$, we find that there exists a transformation rule $tr_{k-1} = <a_{k-1},r_{k-1}>$ where $r_{k-1} = < cp_{k-1}$, cond', $cp_k>$ and thus a transformation $t_{k-1} = <<a_{k-1},vs_{k-1}>,vs_k>$ exists that transforms the VIS state from vs_{k-1} into vs_k, where i_k visual part of the VIS state vs_k. As a result, $\forall it = < <<c_0, i_0>,i_k>$, $<< c_1, i_1>,i_2>$, ..., $<<c_{n-1}, i_{n-1}>,i_n>> \in$ VCL an interaction process instance $ipi = <<a_0,vs_0>,vs_1>,..., <a_{i-1},vs_{i-1}>, vs_i>> \in$ DMVL exists corresponding to the execution of the visual command sequence $s = <c_0,c_1,...,c_{n-1}>$ on i_0 where i_K with $k \in \{1,..,n\}$ is the characteristic structure of vs_k. □

Prop. 4: Let $ipi = < <<a_0,vs_0>,vs_1>$, $<<a_1,vs_1>,vs_2>$, ..., $<<a_{n-1},vs_{n-1}>,vs_n> >$ be an interaction process instance in DMVL and let $i_0 \in CS$ where i_0 is the characteristic structure of vs_0, then an interaction trace it = $< \; <<c_0, \; i_0>, i_1>, \; << c_1, \; i_1>, i_2>, \; ..., \; <<c_{n-1}, \; i_{n-1}>, i_n> \; > \in$ VCL exists corresponding to ipi, where i_k is the characteristic structure of vs_k, $k \in \{1,..,n\}$. ♠

Proof:

Let ipi = $< \; <<a_0, vs_0>, vs_1>, \; <<a_1, vs_1>, vs_2>, \; ..., \; <<a_{n-1}, vs_{n-1}>, vs_n> \; >$ be an interaction process instance in DMVL. We show how to construct an interaction trace it corresponding to ipi. Consider the transformation $t_0 = <<a_0, vs_0>, vs_1>$ of the VIS from the state vs_0 to vs_1. Let i_0 and i_1 be the materializations of the VIS corresponding to the states vs_0 and vs_1. Now, let cs_0 be the minimal characteristic structure in i_0 changing due to the transformation t_0 and cs_1 be its transformation in i_1 after t_0. If we denote with cp_0 and cp_1 the states of the minimal ve whose materializations are cs_0 and cs_1, then the transformation rule tr_0 determining t_0 is the following: $tr_0 = <a_0, r_0>$, where $r_0 = < cp_0, cond, cp_1>$ and $a_0 = <op_j, cs_j>$ with $op_j \in OP$, $cs_j \in cs_0 \in CS_{VIS}$. The transformation rule tr_0 determining t_0 can thus be expressed as the visual command $c_0 = <a_0, cs_1>$. Then, let i_1 be the image on the screen containing cs_1, the transformation $t_0 = <<a_0, vs_0>, vs_1>$ can be expressed (from the point of view of the users) as the application of the visual command c_0 to i_0 producing the new image i_1, that is, $<<c_0, i_0>, i_1>$. In the same way, given the transformation $t_k = <<a_{k-1}, vs_{k-1}>, vs_k>$, there exists a visual command $c_{k-1} = <a_{k-1}, cs_k>$, which applied on i_{k-1} produces the image i_k, that is the pair $<<c_{k-1}, i_{k-1}>, i_k>$. Therefore, the thesis is proved. □

Chapter XI
Designing a Visual Language for Interaction Representation Based on Aspects of Human Movement

Kristine Deray
University of Technology – Sydney, Australia

Simeon J. Simoff
University of Technology – Sydney, Australia & University of Western Sydney, Australia

ABSTRACT

Interactions are a core part of interactive computing. However, their mechanisms remain poorly understood. The tendency has been to understand interactions in terms of the results they produce rather than to provide the mechanisms that explain "how" interactions unfold in time. In this chapter, we present a framework for creating visual languages for representing interactions, which uses human movement as a source for the core concepts of the visual language. Our approach is motivated and supported by the evidence coming from the research on kinaesthetic thinking that constructs based on human movement support higher-level cognitive processes and can be intuitively recognised by humans. We presented an overview of the framework, an instance of a visual language design using the proposed framework, and its application for representing and analysing interactions between patients and practitioners in the healthcare domain. Developed approach and the corresponding techniques target interactive computer systems for facilitating interaction-rich domains such as healthcare, in particular occupational therapy, collaborative design, and learning.

INTRODUCTION AND PROBLEM DEFINITION

Interactive computing infers that communication is based on *interactions* between parties and that these interactions construct a dialog of some kind. Though interactions are a core part of the activi-ties performed in many computerised domains, their mechanisms remain poorly understood. The tendency has been to understand interactions in terms of the results they produce rather than to provide the mechanisms that explain "how" interactions unfold in time. In the area of health, for example, interactions between medical practitioners and patients have been playing a key role in the delivery of healthcare services, for instance, in determining the accuracy of diagnosis, patients' commitment to treatment regimes, and the extent to which patients are satisfied with the service they receive (Korsch & Negrete, 1972; Pendleton, 1983; Peräkyla, 1998). The importance of interactions has been increasingly recognised with the development of relationship-centred healthcare (see Wylie & Wagenfeld-Heintz, 2004, for a comprehensive literature review). Contemporary healthcare researchers clearly formulate the *need to facilitate patient-practitioner interactions and provide a means for understanding and interpreting the anatomy of these interactions*, ideally, by both sides. This result is an acknowledgment that the success of the healthcare provision, to a larger extent, depends on the *quality of interactions* between health professionals and patients. A hot example is medication concordance—an approach to prescribing medicines and patients' commitment to treatment regimes, especially for diseases where medicines are being used to prevent rather than treat symptoms, for instance, in diabetes type 2 (Hayes, Bowman, Monahan, Marrero, & McHorney, 2006). The process is focused on "shared decision making" through "negotiation between a patient and a healthcare professional that respects the understandings, beliefs, and wishes of the patient in determining whether, when, and how medicines are to be taken" (Hayes et al., 2006). The practical importance in providing interactive computing means to facilitate patient-provider interactions is extremely high: approximately 50% of patients may be non-compliant in their medicine taking (Dunbar-Jacob & Schlenk, 2001). Overall, the ability to communicate effectively between patient and practitioner has been linked to enhanced health outcomes (Stewart, 1995). Interactive computing can provide the key to the success in addressing this problem by providing means for unfolding the anatomy and dynamics of interactions, and facilitating in understanding the impact on patient-practitioner interactions of the different communicative choices, made both by healthcare professionals and by patients during their sessions.

Similar problems, which require better understanding of interactions between the parties involved, are experienced in the area of occupational therapy. An example is the developmental screening of children to assess their current level of performance from observation of their interactions with specially designed tasks. The analysis of the results of such screening will benefit from having means that allow comparing patterns of such interactions. Later in the chapter, we consider, in detail, the analysis of patient-practitioner interactions in paediatrics.

Computer-mediated design and collaborative learning are other areas that require and rely on ways of representing and interpreting interactions. Compactly expressing and representing interactions, so that the parties involved can identify problems in the interactions and address them, is crucial for the operation of virtual design studios (Maher, Simoff, & Cicognani, 2000). Effective collaborative learning in online educational environments also relies on understanding of interactions (for example, see Simoff & Maher, 2000, for a visualisation of communication utterances that assists in monitoring collaboration within teams).

These sample problems represent a class of practical problems, which involve deep understanding of interactions. But, despite the acknowledgment of the importance of interactions (especially, those between patients and practitioners), they remain problematic to study and measure because of the following features:

- Parties involved in the interaction may use different languages (in broad sense, including many aspects of non-verbal behaviour that are considered to be performing social actions of various kinds);

- Interactions are situated and the actions that constitute them are generally bound up with the broader activities associated with tasks, for example, in medical consultation that could be finding out the reasons for the patient's visit, history taking, conducting an examination, etc. (see Robinson, 1998);
- Interactions unfold dynamically as the actions are linked in sequences of mutually dependent actions (i.e., the actions of one of the parties are in response to the actions of the other).

Further, we focus on patient-practitioner interactions, as this is the area where we currently apply proposed visual language. Overall interactions form a dialog that can be understood from a number of different perspectives as evidenced by the research in conversation analysis, discourse analysis, interaction analysis, and the theory of speech acts, to name the few. Dialog has structure, which may be implicit or explicit, and content of some nature. Dialog can be one to one, or may involve many parties. Its parts are structurally and thematically linked to form a composition. Lastly, dialog has a physical and emotional presence. Largely addressed by qualitative research, emotional and physical presence constitutes an integral part of communication in dialog. Dialog, then, can be modelled on three levels: content, structure, and presence. Each or all of these levels can be directed to support or nullify common ground between parties. Here common ground refers to the knowledge shared by two communicating parties (Berg, 1997, cited by Coiera, 2001, p. 282).

Communicative acts grounded in linguistics have been substantially studied in areas such as discourse analysis (Schiffrin, Tannen, & Hamilton, 2001) and conversational analysis (Drew, Chatwin, & Collins, 2001). Both methodologies and corresponding techniques have been used extensively in research in patient-practitioner interactions. Roberts and Sarangi (2005) ap-

proached the problem from a linguistic perspective. Domain-oriented conversation analysis methods like Roter's interaction analysis system (see Sandvik et al., 2002, for the analysis of the method, and Kindler, Szirt, Sommer, Hausler, and Langewitz, 2005, for a recent application to practitioner-patient communications) have been applied to the domain. Yet researchers' experience shows that in the healthcare domain, these analyses are not a straightforward exercise, as they have to cover many levels and types of language and knowledge.

In this chapter, we approach these issues as a problem for developing an interactive computing system that provides the means for representing interactions, monitoring and collecting data, analysis of the interactions, and representing the results of the analysis. One of the tasks of interactive computing is to facilitate human interactions. Our approach looks at the problem as a dialog system that requires the placement of suitable artefacts to express and unfold that dialog. Although much work has been done in identifying and investigating human-to-human interaction to enable and enhance successful communication, very little has been done on (i) how to explain the mechanisms of such interactions, comparing patterns across them, and (ii) how to evaluate their progression and present it to all parties involved so that they can interpret it. Part of the problem can be related to the lack of a common language that could provide suitable constructs for understandings across and between parties in interactions. For example, this is a common situation in patient-practitioner interactions in the healthcare domain, due to a number of factors including the different background of patients and practitioners.

We argue that the form of interaction being inherently dynamic requires suitable constructs to express such dynamic values. We take the language/action perspective where the *construction of form* to give meaning and the use of such meaning in communication is considered the area of understanding (Winograd & Flores, 1986). We propose that constructs, that is the pairing of form and meaning for describing interactions, can be derived from *human movement* and that such constructs will reference embodied knowledge embedded in the source domain. Such a semantic connection can be established through the parameterisation of interaction features that explain the dynamic nature of interactions. The chapter proposes a framework for developing visual languages based on human movement, commonly understood across people and cultures. The research argues that languages based on human movement provide benefits to interactive computing in cases where it is necessary to facilitate common ground between parties with diverse backgrounds as:

- *Humans can intuitively recognize constructs in interactions modelled on human movement.* Such constructs can communicate meaning to humans and, as such, can direct action, infer goals being sought, and cooperate in their achievement;
- *If the constructs embody meaning, then a visual language of forms and functions, derived from these constructs, can provide efficient means for representing interactions consistently at different levels of granularity.*

The design principles of such visual language take human movement constructs and position them as artefacts that can be personified by humans in their usage. Such designated artefacts are the *elements* derived from the domain of human movement. These elements and their visual representation are presented in Sections 3 and 4, respectively. To some extent, the role of these elements in our approach can be understood via an analogy with the role of the lexons in (Pretorius, 2005) framework for visual ontology engineering. Lexons are generic constructs that are used to model abstract concepts and relationship types

in a domain of interest. A set of lexons forms the ontology base. The visualisations of the lexons are then used in a second layer of the framework to specify application specific logic. In our work, the elements and their visualisations, derived from the elasticities of the human movement, provide the expression base of the language that supports communication between different parties and further provides machine interpretable semantic bases. The rules for combining these elements in productions that reflect interaction patterns are the second level of our framework, resulting in a logic that is accessible to all participants by referencing human movement. In the next section, we provide the background in support of our argument that human movement provides a consistent basis for representing aspects of interactions and reasoning about them.

BACKGROUND

We see that cognition is an interaction of mind and body, and that embodied knowledge, specifically knowledge that relates to kinetics, can be accessed to provide foundations for higher-level reasoning (Anderson, 2003; Wilson, 2002). Our motivation to use the domain of human movement as a source for the concepts of our system of reference follows the recognition that humans can intuitively recognise constructs based on human movement, evidenced from the research on kinaesthetic thinking/understanding and its ability to support higher-level cognitive processes (Dreyfus, 1972; Seitz, 1994). Nicoladis et al. (1999) have studied how children learn to use their gestural and postural abilities to express concepts and ideas through movement. Through the years, researchers have suggested that:

- Skilled movement is a form of thinking (e.g., Bartlett, 1958; Fischer & Bidell, 1998; Seitz, 1994, 1996; Sudnow, 1978)

- Movement is predominant in all forms of human intellectual activity (Laban, 1956; Laban & Lawrence, 1974; Seitz, 2000a, 2000b)
- Children learn to communicate with gestures before they learn to speak (Nicoladis et al., 1999; Seitz, 1996)

Consequently, some cognitive researchers have argued that language understanding and conceptualisation are not a result of pure symbolic manipulation, but a process grounded in bodily interaction with the environment. Glenberg and Kaschak (2003) and Zwaan (2004) provide comprehensive reviews of the works that explain language phenomena in line with the idea of cognition as body-based simulation. Some work in information spaces looked at bodily-kinaesthetic skills as a basis for the construction of meaning. For instance, Deray (2000), looked at the association between non-verbal movement behaviour and thought processes in the context of human-computer interaction in information search. In a similar simulation context, it is worth noting Bergen et al. (2004), whose approach to the design of a situated grammar references embodied knowledge of perceptual and motor systems that play an important role in higher cognitive functions. Specifically this is in relation to mental imagery, association, and memory.

Several researchers (Barsalou, 1999; Barsalou, Niedenthal, Barbey, & Ruppert, 2003; Glenberg & Robertson, 2000) note that it has been proposed that understanding a piece of language entails internal simulation and/or mental imagery that provides access to the same neural structures "that would be involved in perceiving the precepts or performing the mental actions described." This is in line with recent research in neuroscience that indicates a neural basis for embodied understandings. Neural embodiment characterizes the neural mechanisms that give rise to concepts. Earlier research in cognitive science (Leiner, Leiner, & Dowq, 1986) proposed an extensive information

processing system involved with movement in the brain. This system has bi-directional pathways to parallel systems in the brain that are involved in (higher) logical thought processes. For instance, there are accounts of how deaf individuals "talk" to themselves using signs while sleeping (Sacks, 1989). The inference is the possibility that we may "think" kinetically (Johnson, 1987). Seitz (1994), building on the earlier work of Gardner (1983), indicate bodily-kinaesthetic skills as a basis for the construction of meaning, giving some breadth to a hypothesis that non-verbal behaviour and thinking share a unique connection. Cohen, Morrison, and Cannon (2005) used visual representation of verb semantics, utilising aspects of human movement, to investigate whether dynamical aspects of movies predict the words used for their description.

The argument that kinaesthetic thinking, kinaesthetic logic, supported also by the linguistic view of the mechanisms behind metaphors (Lakoff, 1988; Lakoff & Johnson, 1980, 1999), is fundamental to human thinking, then, has value, inferring that the concepts of human movement could provide a consistent and sustainable basis for developing tools for communication and interactive computing, including languages for representing, expressing, and analysis of interactions. Further, in Section 3, we present the proposed framework for designing visual languages that utilised aspects of human movement.

FRAMEWORK FOR DESIGNING VISUAL LANGUAGES BASED ON HUMAN MOVEMENT

The derivation of our framework can be viewed as drawing an analogy from the domain of human movement into the domain of representation, description, and interpretation of interactions. The overall idea is illustrated in Figure 1. In the theory of metaphors in cognitive linguistics (Lakoff, 1993; Turner, 1994), the terms "source" and "target" refer to the conceptual spaces connected by the metaphor. The "target" is the conceptual space that is being described and the source is the space that is being used to describe the target. In this mapping, the structure of the source domain is projected onto the target domain in a way that is consistent with the inherent target domain structure. In our approach, the source provides the constructs and relations between them. The constructs then are used to create the means of the language that is used to represent meaning in the target domain. The relations between these constructs act as semantic constraints.

Our source domain and its constructs are well investigated in the domain of movement observation science. Practitioners in this area have derived movement notational systems, designed to record human movement in symbolic form. One of these systems—Labanotoation, developed in the 1920s by Rudolf Laban's team, and the subsequently developed Laban Movement Analysis with its effort and shape components—provide us with valuable formalisms for extracting our movement constructs. These models relate two components or frames of reference of human movement:

- **Body position:** The place of the body in space

- **Body dynamics:** The motion that causes and expresses change from one position of the body to another

These two frames of reference provide schemas that can be utilised to transfer constructs from the source domain to the target domain. Labanotation focuses on the structural aspects of movement while Laban Movement Analysis focuses on the *movement qualities*. The x, y, and z coordinates describe what has been called "the dimensional cross" and is Laban's construct for the three dimensions of the body (Hutchinson, 1977; Newlove, 2001; Newlove & Dalby, 2004). These dimensions intersect at the centre of the body and are at the heart of the kinesphere--an imaginary sphere that sets the limits on the demarcation of personal space, the limits being measured by the full extension of the length of the limbs. The anatomical actions along side of these dimensions are focused to three aspects of human movement "elasticity." We refer to these movement aspects as *elasticities*. In the dimensional cross

- The vertical dimension (y) is linked to *up* and *down* movement (i.e., the *rising* and *sinking* elasticity)

Figure 1. The main idea in designing visual languages based on human movement

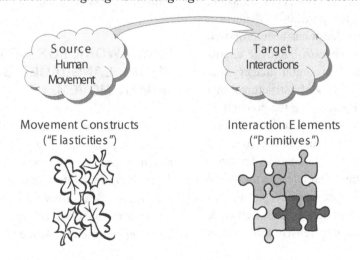

Table 1. Conceptualisation of interactions (target domain) through the elements of the Laban Movement Analysis and the effort shape conceptual framework of human movement (source domain)

Effort Shape element	Role of the concept in the source domain	Role of the concept in the target domain
Tension flow	Describes whether a movement is bound or relatively free with respect to the human body.	*Flow* as an interaction feature represents the amount of obstruction associated with an interaction. It ranges between bound and free.
Weight	Describes the "easiness" of movement, the quality of lightsomeness, or forcefulness of movement.	*Exertion* is the interaction feature associated with the amount of effort (force) required for the interaction to occur. Exertion ranges between light and strong.
Time	The length of a movement, or movement phrase, describes how the movement was communicated in, for instance, in a sudden or sustained manner.	*Transition time* is a combined measure of the time it takes to change from one action to another and the time it takes for a player to respond to an action from the other player. *Transition* (time) ranges between sudden and sustained.
Space	The spatial focus of movement describes spatial relatedness of movement elements to a single focus point or being divided amongst several foci.	*Control* is the factor that describes the interaction space. Control ranges between flexible and rigid.

- The horizontal dimension (x) to *side to side* movement (i.e., the *contraction* and *extension* elasticity)
- The saggital dimension (z) represents *rotational* forward and backward movement (i.e., the *rotate* and *tilt* elasticity)

This is facilitated by the degrees of freedom embedded in the architecture of body joints, giving three basic actions in the human body: *flex, extend,* and *rotate*. In Laban Movement Analysis, these concepts are linked through the notion of *effort,* which describes how the body concentrates its *exertion* while performing movements. Effort has been compared to dynamic terms in other domains such as music—and of note for our approach has been considered to explain how a piece of music is performed. Effort interpreted in this manner describes the unfolding of action in a particular

context. Some elements of the theory have been applied to clinical and physical therapy, verbal and nonverbal communication and management behaviour. Irmgard Bartenieff, founder of the Laban—Bartenieff Institute of movement studies—used understandings of movement placed as imagery to assist patients in hospitals to recover. She used concepts stemming from the effort shape analysis of Laban with polio patients who through imagery were led to experience the spatial shapes and dynamic qualities in their movement exercises. Bartenieff Fundamentals (Hackney, 2000) are an extension of Laban Movement Analysis.

The human movement conceptualisation, based on Laban Movement Analysis, specifically the effort shape framework, provides us with the conceptual basis for the mapping from the source to the target domain in our framework. In this chapter, we consider four basic effort shape elements—tension flow, weight, time, and space. The roles of each one in the source and target domains are summarised in Table 1. Further, we formalise these concepts and utilise them in our visual language, presented in the following sections.

DESIGNING VISUAL LANGUAGE BASED ON HUMAN MOVEMENT

In human movement, form and function are intrinsically coupled. For our methodology for designing the visual language, we have adapted:

- The "form-semantics-function" methodology for development of visualisation techniques for visual data mining (Simoff, 2001)
- The design principles for visual languages presented in Pretorius (2005)

The "form-semantics-function" methodology provides well-based approach for constructing consistent visual representations of concepts. The design principles for visual languages used by Pretorius (2005) follow the recommendations from the field of information visualisation and complement the "form-semantics-function" methodology.

Table 2 presents the formal derivation of the form constraints from the three elasticities, discussed in the previous section. The three form guides corresponding to these elasticities operate in one axis each. The form of "contraction and extension" does not carry any semantics in the vertical dimension. In the "rising and sinking" elasticity, the width on the horizontal axis does not carry any semantics.

This chapter considers only the elasticities of "contraction and extension" and "rising and sinking." Each of these elasticities may operate with one or more *qualities*. Further, we consider the "contraction and extension" elasticity operating with a single quality, and the "rising and sinking" elasticity—with four nominated qualities.

Table 2. Constructing the forms of the basic elasticities (based on the corresponding anatomical actions)

Elasticity	Contraction and Extension	Rising and Sinking	Rotate and Tilt
Form			
Semantics	The amplitude on the horizontal axis indicates the strength (weakness) of interaction. It models strength as states of attraction, repulsion, or stable behaviour.	The amplitude on the vertical axis indicates the elastcities that stretch up and sink down.	The angle of rotation on the sagittal axes. Measured by angle increment. Inference of causality.
Function	Describes the intensity of the interaction.	Describes flow and effort of the interaction.	Describes associations between interactions over time

THE "CONTRACTION AND EXTENSION" ELASTICITY

Each quality $q_{C-E}(i)$ of the "contraction and extension" elasticity is represented by a separate component. In this chapter, we consider only the quality, which indicates the strength of the interaction—the *intensity* of the interaction (by analogy with the intensity of movement). To measure the intensity of interaction, we look at the actions of individual parties during the interaction. Let consider an interaction j between two participants P_k and P_l. Let n_k and n_l be the number of actions in the interaction j for each participant, respectively. Then the intensity $Intensity_j(P_k, P_l)$ of the interaction j is defined as $Intensity_j(P_k, P_l) = 1 - \dfrac{|n_k - n_l|}{\max\{n_k, n_l\}}$. For instance if in an interaction between patient P and clinician C, the patient produces $n_P = 6$ actions and the clinician produces $n_C = 10$ actions, the intensity of the interaction between them $Intensity(P, C) = 1 - \dfrac{|6 - 10|}{\max\{6, 10\}} = 0.4$. The larger the difference between the number of

actions of the parties in an interaction the lower is the intensity of the interaction (i.e., the interaction "contracts") and vice versa the smaller the difference between the number of actions performed by the parties, the higher is the intensity of the interaction—the interaction "extends." An action is bounded by the so-called turn taking. An action can be either vocal, or non-vocal. Each participant performs a number of actions that contribute to

the interaction. In this context, we assume that repetitive actions by one of the partners indicate difficulties in the interaction. For example, in a message exchange, that can be a result of difficulties in the interpretation of the messages. In a treatment, that can be a result of an inappropriate dosage of the medicine. Such repetitions will lead to decrease of interaction intensity (as the difference in the number of interactions between the two parties increases).

Using the frequency of actions as a basis for measuring interaction intensity is a reasonable approximation. In general, interaction intensity may also depend on the length of actions. However, this analysis is beyond the scope of the chapter. Further we discuss the four qualities of the "rising and sinking" elasticity.

THE "RISING AND SINKING" ELASTICITY

Similar to the qualities of "contraction and extension" elasticity, each quality $q_{R-S}(i)$ of the "rising and sinking" elasticity is represented by a separate component. As in this chapter only this elasticity is considered with more than one quality, further we omit the "R-S" index in our notation whenever possible. In this chapter, we consider four qualities. We derive the measures for each of these qualities. In terms of interpretation, without loss of generality, we restrict each of the qualities to three ranges; "min," "mid," and "max" level ranges, each corresponding to

Table 3. Basic qualities, their value ranges, and relation to describing interaction

Quality	Min level	Mid level	Max level	Relation to describing interaction	No.
Flow	Bound	Neutral	Free	Value given to obstruction	1
Transition	Sustained	Neutral	Sudden	Value given to length of action	2
Exertion	Strong	Neutral	Light	Value given to number of goals or tasks	3
Control	Rigid	Neutral	Flexible	Value given to number of decision tree forks	4

a specific categorical value, derived in terms of human movement. In Table 3 we have specified the four nominated qualities of interactions—flow, transition, exertion, and control, their value ranges and relation to describing interaction. Further, we expand each quality in more details.

Flow, denoted as quality $q(1)$, indicates the obstruction (language/social/cultural, etc.). Currently, the categorical variables are assigned as:

- **Free:** Indicates that there is no obstruction (i.e., two players inferred common ground and this enhances communication)
- **Neutral:** Indicates that there is obstruction from one player (i.e., reduced common ground (the reasons may be manifold))
- **Bound:** Indicates that there is no flow (i.e., nil or minimal common ground)

At this stage the definition of the actual range for each category is defined by the modeller. The upper normalised (to 1) bound of the range for "free" is determined by the interaction with the lowest number of obstructions. The neutral value ranges around 0.5. The lower bound of the range for "bound" is defined by the interaction with the highest number of obstructions.

Transition, denoted as quality $q(2)$, characterises interaction in time. This quality is proportional to the length of the interaction. Each interaction happens in time, which can be viewed as the sum of the compound times of all individual actions. The compound time of an individual action includes the reaction time (the delay, before taking the action) and the actual action time. To measure the transition quality of an interaction, we look at the time length of the actions of individual parties during the interaction. Let consider an interaction j between two participants P_k and P_l. Let n_k and n_l be the number of actions in the interaction j for each participant, respectively. Let $T_j(P_k) = \sum_{i=1}^{n_k} t_{ij}(P_k)$ and $T_j(P_l) = \sum_{i=1}^{n_l} t_{ij}(P_l)$ be the compound times of all individual actions during the interaction j of the two participants P_k and P_l,

respectively. Then the normalised average action times for P_k and P_l are:

$$\overline{T}_j(P_k) = \frac{\frac{1}{n_k}\sum_{i=1}^{n_k} t_{ij}(P_k)}{\max_{i=1,\ldots,n_k}(t_{ij}(P_k))}$$

and

$$\overline{T}_j(P_l) = \frac{\frac{1}{n_l}\sum_{i=1}^{n_l} t_{ij}(P_l)}{\max_{i=1,\ldots,n_l}(t_{ij}(P_l))},$$

respectively, and the average normalised time length of an action for this interaction is $\overline{T}_j(P_k, P_l) = \overline{T}_j(P_k) + \overline{T}(P_l)$. Then the transition of the interaction j is computed as $Transition_j(P_k, P_l) = 1 - 0.5 * \overline{T}_j(P_k, P_l)$. The interaction with the shortest average time determines the upper bound of the value *sudden,* when the interaction with the longest average time determines the lower bound of the value *sustained* (see Table 3).

Exertion, denoted as quality $q(3)$, correlates to the amount of effort required for the interaction to proceed to some perceived position. For example, in the case of healthcare interactions, perceived position may refer the patient's progress—that is an identifiable landmark. This could be a test, a drug administration, a consultation, or part of a diagnosis, and so on. Exertion does not automatically correlate to values attributed to positive or negative outcomes. The measure of exertion relates the duration of the interaction to the maximum duration in the considered set of interactions. Following the same line of reasoning as for the transition quality, the length of the interaction j, is $Len_j(P_k, P_l) = T_j(P_k) + T_j(P_l)$, and the interaction with maximum length in the considered set of interactions is $\max_j\{Len_j(P_k, P_l)\}$. Exertion of the interaction j is computed as $Exertion_j(P_k, P_l) = 1 - \dfrac{Len_j(P_k, P_l)}{\max_j\{Len_j(P_k, P_l)\}}$. For example, if the $Len_j(P_k,$

Figure 2. A set of visual primitives for representing interactions

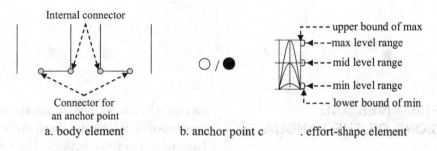

a. body element   b. anchor point c   . effort-shape element

P_l) = 40 secs and the longest interaction in the considered set of interactions $\max_{j}\{Len_j(P_k, P_l)\}$ = 60 secs, then $Exertion_j(P_k, P_l) = 1 - \frac{40}{60} = 0.33$. Is it closer to strong effort? To answer this question we need to find the interaction with the shortest length, which determines the upper bound of the value *light,* when the interaction with the longest length determines the lower bound of the value *strong* (see Table 3). This correlates with another way for defining these bounds through the content of the interaction: the interaction with the highest number of tasks/outcomes determines the lower bound of the value *strong* when interaction with lowest number of tasks/outcomes determines the upper bound of the value *light.*

Control, denoted as quality $q(4)$, refers to the amount of control applied in the interaction. The measure is derived from the analysis of the interaction content by evaluating how flexible is the context that the interaction is embedded into. This relates to the number of possible paths or decision forks the players have between them for progress to occur. In its simplest form, for a given interaction this can be derived from comparison between the number of iterations $Iterations_j(P_k, P_l)$

in the given interaction j compared to the largest number of iterations $\max_{j}\{Iterations_j(P_k, P_l)\}$ in the considered set of interactions, for example:

$$Control_j(P_k, P_l) = \frac{Iterations_j(P_k, P_l)}{\max_{j}\{Iterations_j(P_k, P_l)\}}.$$

The higher the number of iterations the more *flexible* the interaction (context) is. The lower the number of iterations, the more the interaction context moves to *rigid*. For example, if interaction j has $Iterations_j(P_k, P_l) = 3$ and the highest number of iterations in the considered set of interactions $\max_{j}\{Iterations_j(P_k, P_l)\} = 12$, the control value

$Control_j(P_k, P_l) = 0.25$, which tends towards a rigid control. In terms of decision-making, the number of iterations correlates with the number of options. For example, in patient-clinician interactions, the interaction with the lowest number of options in a patient decision tree determines the value *rigid* and the interaction with the highest number of options determines the value *flexible*.

In the next section, we introduce the visual primitives and how these primitives are used to construct visual expressions that that represent interactions at different levels of granularity.

Figure 3. Aspects of the body element design

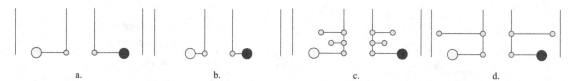

a.　　　　　　　b.　　　　　　　c.　　　　　　　d.

VISUAL PRIMITIVES AND EXPRESSIONS OF THE LANGUAGE

Following the guidelines on the forms and behaviour of the visual elements, formulated in Table 2, and the requirements and computational mechanisms specified in the previous section, we introduce the basic visual primitives of the language, illustrated in Figure 2.

Body Element

We label as a *body element* the element that visually represents the qualities of the "contraction and extension" elasticity. Recalling, that this elasticity operates in horizontal dimension and that the interactions that we consider are between pair of participants, the body element unit consists of two "track segments" (fields) of equal width, where each quality of the "contraction and extension" elasticity is represented as two horizontal "arms" (line segments)—one for each participant. As in this chapter, we consider only the quality of interaction intensity, the body element in Figure 2a includes only one pair of arms. As symmetry is one of the design principles that we follow, the two line segments are of the same length, defined by the value of the interaction intensity measure. The body element also has places for two connectors on each arm. The external connectors are where the anchor points are attached. An anchor point, shown in Figure 2b, represents a party involved in the interaction with static (passive) (O) or dynamic (pro-active) (●) behaviour. The internal connectors link the body element to the elements of the "rising and sinking" elasticity, which are discussed in the next section. The internal connectors are optional and may be omitted in the visualisation if we visualise large number of interactions. The visualisation algorithm of the body element satisfies the following composition rules:

- **Rule BE-1:** Each arm starts at the internal border of the respective track segment and expands towards the external border
- **Rule BE-2:** The arms that represent the first quality $q_{C-E}(1)$ are aligned with the lower end of the element; the anchor points are attached to the arms of $q_{C-E}(1)$
- **Rule BE-3:** The arms that represent each subsequent quality $q_{C-E}(1)$ of "contraction and extension" elasticity are positioned above the previous arm pair; the correspondence of position to the index number does not change

These rules enable consistency and comparability of visualisations generated from different data sets and with changes in the number of visualised qualities of the "contraction and extension" elasticity. Figure 3 illustrates current visualisation of the body element. Figure 3a and Figure 3b show the operation of the current body element with one quality. In particular, the interaction in Figure 3b indicates lower intensity of the interaction between the parties. Assuming that it follows a previous "measurement" of the same parties in Figure 3a, it illustrates contraction of the interaction.

Figure 3c and Figure 3d illustrate the way rule BE-3 works. The body element in Figure 3c is composed of three qualities of "contraction and extension" elasticity. The subsequent interaction data does not carry information about the second

Figure 4. Aspects of the design of the effort-shape element

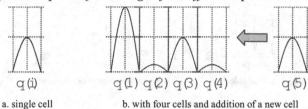 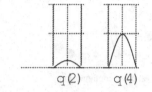

q (i)   q (1) q (2) q (3) q (4)   q (5)   q (2)   q (4)

a. single cell   b. with four cells and addition of a new cell   c. with two cells in a four cell element

quality; however, the third quality is present and visualised at the position assigned by the visualisation system for the third quality of "contraction and extension" elasticity for the considered set of interactions as shown in Figure 3d. Note that the anchor points can be in any combination (i.e., we can have an active and passive participants, two passive participants, or two active ones).

Effort-Shape Element

We label as an *effort-shape element* the element that visually represents the qualities of the "rising and sinking" elasticity. The visual representation of a quality in the "rising and sinking" elasticity fits in a cell a piece of basic trigonometric function (sin or cosine) with normalised amplitude coefficient $A_{q(i)}$, proportional to the value of the corresponding quality $q(i)$. The amplitude can change on a continuous scale or/and on a categorical scale. Without loss of generality, in this chapter we restrict each of the qualities to three discrete positions—"min," "mid," and "max" level ranges as shown in Figure 2c. The granularity of the representation is sufficient for illustrative purposes, preserving the attractive simplicity of the presentation. As in this chapter, we consider four qualities of the "rising and sinking" elasticity; our effort-shape elements are limited to four cells. As we mentioned earlier, the horizontal size of an element of "rising and sinking" elasticity does not carry any semantics. The horizontal and vertical sizes of the cells are scaled by the visualisation

system with respect to the display projection. The visualisation algorithm of the effort-shape element satisfies the following composition rules:

- **Rule ES-1:** Each curve representing the actual value of a quality of the "Rising and sinking" elasticity is symmetric with respect to the vertical access passing through the middle of the cell.
- **Rule ES-2:** The cell that represents the first quality $q_{R-S}(1)$ is aligned with the left end of the effort-shape element
- **Rule ES-3:** The cells that represent each subsequent quality $q_{R-S}(i)$ of the "rising and sinking" elasticity are positioned to the right of the previous cell; the correspondence of position to the index number does not change

Similar to the body element, these rules enable consistency and comparability of the effort-shape elements, generated from different data sets and with changes in the number of visualised qualities of the "rising and sinking" elasticity. If there is missing data on one or more qualities in some interactions than we won't be able to construct the four-position effort-shape element. However, for conducting proper analysis and interpretation of the interactions we need to be able to compare visually the qualities across different sets of interactions in consideration. Hence, we construct the effort-shape elements depending on the maximum number of different qualities measured across the set. Figure 4a shows a single cell element with a

Figure 5. Production element

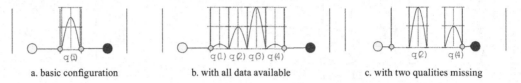

a. basic configuration   b. with all data available   c. with two qualities missing

neutral value of the corresponding quality. Figure 4b shows an effort-shape element with four cells. A new cell, representing quality $q(5)$ is attached to the right end of the existing effort-shape element. The element in Figure 4c operates with only two cells (qualities $q(2)$ and $q(4)$), assuming that the maximum number of qualities we want to display is four.

Production Element

The production element is a visual expression of an interaction. The body and effort-shape elements are then composed into a *production element* as shown in Figure 5a. The two internal borders of the body element are aligned, respectively, with left side of the first cell and the right side of the last cell in the effort-shape element, as shown in Figure 5b and Figure 5c.

Production

Each interaction in a session is represented by the corresponding production element. A set of interactions then is represented as a *production*. Here, we employ some analogy from the domain of music performance. The "interaction" of the musician with the musical instrument is encoded in a score (i.e., we can view a note as an action, a group of notes as the content of the interaction, and the way that these notes should be played indicates how the interaction with the instrument should proceed to achieve the goal. Groups of notes constitute musical scores. However, every musician has his or her own interpretation of these scores (which is the analogy of production in the proposed language) and if we could record his or her production precisely we can then compare the productions of different musicians

Figure 6. From actions to interactions and then productions

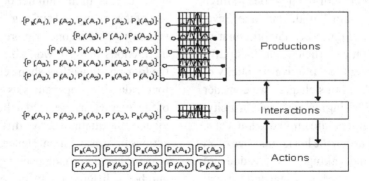

Figure 7. Productions of the interactions for each pair of designers working collaboratively

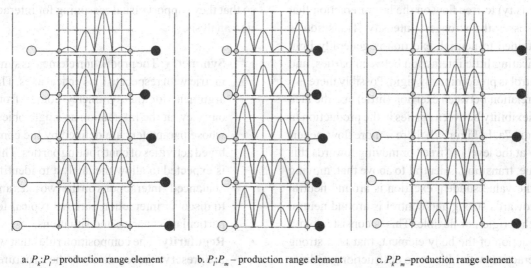

a. P_k:P_l – production range element   b. P_l:P_m – production range element   c. $P_k P_m$ –production range element

and elaborate on the deviation from the recorded score may even change the score. The relation between actions, interactions, and productions is illustrated in Figure 6. The order of production elements in a production with respect to time is as agreed within the study. By default, the time axis increases from top to bottom. Further, we also omit the labels of the qualities from the graphics of the production element as we have specified the position of each quality.

Productions are visual expressions. They provide rich and compact views of the different sets of interactions, allowing to grasp the macropicture of the interaction flow and to compare across different sets. For example, lets consider an experiment in collaborative design. We have three participating designers - P_k, P_l and P_m. The sessions are organised between pair of designers. Each pair is given the same tasks, which define the structure of the productions. Figure 7 shows a possible outcome from the representation of the interaction data collected in such experiment, which can be interpreted relative in terms of the variations of the body element and the effort shape element. The body element in Figure 7a, represents the variation of the interaction intensity between the two parties. The production shows

that there is no distinct level of intensity emerging. This indicates that the two designers varied the strength of the interaction relative to the task they were collaborating upon. The body element in Figure 7b consistently moves to the state of contraction, indicating that the intensity of the interaction between these designers is weak to very weak. If the production covers a synchronous collaborative design session this may indicate that the designers did not arrive at a level of common ground sufficient to support collaboration on design activities. If the production spans over a longer time (for example, over a project milestone) this may indicate that the designers have split the tasks and work on the project components individually. The timeframe over which the snapshot of the interaction is taken provides the background for the interpretation of productions. In Figure 7c, the body element's behaviour consistently indicates a state of extension, inferring that the designers had a strong interaction in their collaboration. This may indicate high level of common ground attained in this production.

If we look at the effort shape elements, the variation between the three productions is noticeable again. In Figure 7a flow registers as varied with neutral to bound obstruction, on the interactions where the interaction contracts (weak intensity) to free flow on the last interaction that expresses the strongest intensity. Transition is sustained to neutral, exertion is generally light indicating little interaction between parties, and control is predominately rigid. Possibly there is a correlation between exertion (little) and the lack of flexibility between parties in the production in Figure 7a. In Figure 7b there is more flow, generally at the level of "free" or moving towards this value, transition is neutral to above that, moving to the value sudden, exertion is around neutral or towards strong and control is around neutral neither rigid nor flexible. This is consistent with the action of the body element, that is, a strong interaction with little or no obstruction, medium control, medium exertion, and fairly quick transitions between turns. In Figure 7c we have very little obstruction, (common ground between parties is high), transition is generally sustained, exertion is varied indicating the task would have affected this quality and control is in the max level rang to mid level range indicating that these two parties were flexible in their approach to design solutions for the specified activities. In this manner the language represents in compact form significant amount of information about different aspects of the interactions. It can "tell" a lot about the type of interaction and if indexed to specific activities would provide some understanding of the performance of the designers in relation to the tasks.

DESIGN CONSIDERATIONS IN SUPPORTING VISUAL REASONING

The main thrust in the design of the visual components of the language and the way they constitute visual expressions has been derived from the principles of human movement. Our additional (and more general) design considerations are adapted from the requirements enlisted in Pretorius (2005). We follow them in order to develop our visual primitives and their behaviour, so that they support visual reasoning for interaction analysis.

- **Symmetry:** The production element is symmetric with respect to the vertical axes. The argument for the symmetry comes from our view at the interaction as single object whose parameters are defined by the combined activities of contributing parties. This is expected to allow the analyst to identify "balanced" interactions on the two axes and to discover interaction patterns typical for particular scenarios and situations.
- **Regularity:** The composition rules that we use preserve the regularity of the structures in the production element. The visual phrase (a collection of production elements, a whole production) constitutes a regular structure. These enable the comparison of individual production elements within and between productions, even when there is a missing data for their synthesis.
- **Similarity:** The constructs of our visual language have similar appearances in terms of colour and shape. Their size is normalised and the size is proportional to the corresponding elasticity quality.
- **Connectivity:** The visualisation markers that represent qualities of the different elasticities are connected within the respective (body and effort-shape) elements. The elements are connected in production elements, which, in turn, are connected through the production "score."
- **Legend:** If necessary, the qualities of the effort-shape element can be labelled at the bottom (similar to the way it is shown in Figure 5) and their values can be displayed appropriately above the visual markers. Similar algorithms position the labels for the qualities of the body element.
- **Containment and aggregation:** Membership to a production is represented by con-

Figure 8. Production range elements whose visual markers correspond to the range boundaries of the qualities in the corresponding productions in Figure 7

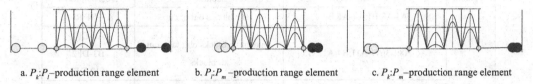

a. $P_k:P_l$–production range element b. $P_l:P_m$ –production range element c. $P_k:P_m$–production range element

tainment. The range of the qualities of the elasticities in all production elements can be aggregated visually into a *production range element*. For cognitive consistency, the production range element is visually similar to the production element. The visual markers are defined by values computed over the respective production set. Currently, for each quality this includes the average, the range, and the mode. Figure 8 illustrates production range elements that show the ranges of the qualities in the productions in Figure 7. The interaction in Figure 8c displays lower variations in its qualities. Overall, various aggregations provide means for analysis of interactions at different levels, though this feature is beyond the scope of this chapter.

For large amounts of interaction data, such aggregations also reduce the visual cluttering of the display.

- **Transparency:** This design principle is used for enabling analysis of productions by superimposing aligned productions. This allows the comparison across productions (for example, this can be a score that represents the same scenario in developmental screening, but obtained from different participants. As the time is framed around the developmental tasks (rather than the actual time scale) then the frames with the elements in them overlap and can be easily compared. Transparency is also used to emphasise the production in focus, or to reduce the visual cluttering when displaying many scores.

Figure 9. Computational processes that convert interaction data into productions

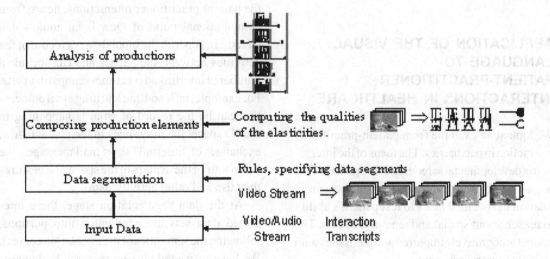

Table 4. The action sequences in the segments

Segment	Action sequences	Subtasks	Decision forks
1	A1-A3;B1;A4-A5;B2	Take blocks out of cup	A3-DF Root
	A6-A8;B3;A9-A11;B4;A12;B5	Take more blocks out; take out all blocks	A8-DF1 B3-DF2 A12-DF3
	A13-A15;B6	Put block on table	A15-DF4
	A16-A21	Take remaining blocks out of cup and put on table	A19-DF5
2	A1-A5;B1;A6-A7;B2;A8-A9;B3;A10-A11;B4	Put the blocks into the red box	A5-F Root
	A12-A13;B5;A14-A15;B6;A16-A17;B7	Put the block in the hand of practitioner	A13-DF1 A15-DF2
	A18-A19;B8	Put block into raised hand in air	A19-DF3
	A20-A21;B9	Get last block out of the box	A21-DF4
	A22-A23;B10;A24-A25	Put block into raised hand in air	A23-DF5
3	A1-A4;B1;A5-A7;B2;A8-A9;B3;A10;B4;A11-A14;B5;A15	Put the small blocks into the cup	A4-DF Root A11-DF1
4	A1-A6;B1-B2	Identify which cup the hidden block is under	A6-DF Root
5	A1-A11;B1;A12-A19;B2	Find the bunny inside the box	A11-DF Root
	A20-A23;B3;A24	Take the bunny out of the box	A20-DF1

In the next section, we demonstrate the application of our visual language for analysis of patient-practitioner interactions in healthcare.

APPLICATION OF THE VISUAL LANGUAGE TO PATIENT-PRACTITIONER INTERACTIONS IN HEALTHCARE

We look at an example from patient-practitioner interaction in paediatrics. The focus of the interaction is developmental screening of the patient. This is assessed by the performance of the patient in relation to specified tasks to test patient's ability to reason about spatial and temporal events. The patient is cognitively impaired and has issues with spatial temporal reasoning.

Figure 9 illustrates the computational processes that support the application of the language. The input data in this example is a video record of the patient-practitioner interactions, hence from computational point of view is an audio/video stream. In general, the input data is a record of the activities between the parties and can include a number of interlinked (via time-stamps) data sets. For example, in 3D online learning environments this can be the record of what is happening in the 3D space, the utterances in the chat window, exchanges of "internal" short mail messages, the behaviour of the avatars in the space, the gestures they use and other activity data.

At the data segmentation stage, these integrated data sets are segmented into portions, following the semantics of the interaction context. We have restricted current research to domains where the interaction scenarios are well structured. In our example, a segment corresponds to a specific (self-contained) scenario during which the patient attempts to complete a series of linked tasks. Within each segment then are identified sequences of actions. The length of these actions is used for computing the qualities of the elasticities. The values of these qualities are then used to compose production elements that express the interactions during the corresponding segment. The elements are integrated into productions that provide the "picture" of the interactions during the sessions.

The process structure in Figure 9, though focused on the video data source of our healthcare example, provides the general operational idea on how interaction data can be converted computationally into productions in our visual language, as after the segmentation stage the processing is independent of the data source. The input data is not limited to audio/video streams, but can be any form of action and utterance transcript. Currently segmentation is semi-automatic and requires human assistance. In our example, one of the bottle necks has been that some of the actions and vocal/non-vocal utterances are occurring in parallel and the current automatic segmentation procedure, based on the identification of turn-taking spots, can not handle correctly. We flagged the cases when the actions and/or utterances have been happening in parallel, but we count them as separate actions, introducing corrections (a number of extra actions) to the ones that have been derived automatically.

Further, we label the practitioner as Participant A and the patient as Participant B. The data in our example of screening of a patient to assess the current level of performance from observation of the fulfilment of specially designed tasks has been segmented into 5 segments labelled according to the tasks the patient needed to complete: Segment 1 – "Blocks into cup"; Segment 2 – "Blocks into large red box/hand"; Segment 3 – "Small blocks"; Segment 4 – "Identify which cup the block is under"; Segment 5 – "Where is

the bunny?" A summary of the segmented data including the action sequences (following the format in Figure 6), the subtasks, and the decision forks is presented in Table 4.

In the action sequences, actions labelled with "A" refer to the actions performed by Participant A – the practitioner; and actions labelled with "B" refer to the actions performed by Participant B – the patient. The decision forks are related to the last practitioner's action in the block when decisions were made. During the first segment, there were four subtasks with mixed correct and incorrect or missed responses by the patient to the designated tasks. At action B6 the patient looks away and no longer interacts with actions of the practitioner (actions A14-A19) until the practitioner modifies the task and then the patient at B8 actively engages again with task. In segment 2, the patient correctly responds to the given subtasks. In segment 3, the patient correctly completes the task after some incorrect responses and a series of additional cues provided by the practitioner. Segment 4 is an "atypical" segment with a single subtask and the patient correctly completes the task with little interaction with practitioner. In segment 5, the patient does not complete the complete task or the subtasks of the task at easier level.

Table 4 summarises the detailed protocols that are the output of the segmentation procedure. An instance of such protocol, representing the detailed content of the actions in segment too and their durations is presented in Table 5. The health practitioner generally does actions in parallel so they either partially or totally overlap. For instance in segment 5, the health practitioner explains the task with a series of coupled vocal and non-vocal actions. The patient, however, always responds with non-vocal actions. In all segments practitioner performs a higher number of actions then the patient, as shown in Table 6, and in most cases, these actions overlap to some extent. Practitioner's interaction style is either *sequential* or *parallel*. The patient interaction style, in contrast, is either sequential or *oppositional*.

Table 5. The protocol record of segment 2 "Blocks into large red box/hand"

Participant	Length (hrs/mins/secs)	Actions	Subtask	Decision forks
Participant A	00.01.16-00.01.25	Action A1: Puts blocks on table Action A2:Vocal Action A3: Puts large red box on table (in parallel) Action A4: Vocal "Put them in" Action A5: Demonstrates putting a block into box	Put the blocks into the red box	Decision fork (root)
Participant B	00.01.25-00.01.27	Action B1: Puts a block into box as demonstrated		
Participant A	00.01.27-00.01.30	Action A6: Vocal reinforcement and asking the child to put other blocks into box-tray as well Action A7: Non-vocal -spreads finger over blocks		
Participant B	00.01.30-00.01.35	Action B2: Takes block but pushes it off table		
Participant A	00.01.35-00.01.37	Action A8: Vocal reinforcement Action A9: Non-vocal hand in box to indicate place (in parallel)		
Participant B	00.01.37-00.01.39	Action B3: Puts a block into tray-box		
Participant A	00.01.30-00.01.42	Action A10: Vocal reinforcement Action A11: Non-vocal indicating the blocks to go into box		
Participant B	00.01.42-00.01. 48	Action B4: Pushes box away and starts to take blocks out again		
Participant A	00.01.48-00.01. 51	Action A12: Holds out her hand to child for block Action A13: Vocal "find the other ones too"	Put the block in the hand of practitioner	Decision fork (1)
Participant B	00.01.51-00.01.56	Action B5: Gives block to practitioner in her hand		
Participant A	00,01.56-00.02.00.	Action A14: Vocal--"Give them all to me now" Action A15: Non-vocal puts cup on table to put blocks into and re-holds out her hand		Decision fork (2)
Participant B	00,02.00-00.02.03	Action B6: Drops block on table		
Participant A	00.02.03-00.02.07	Action A16: Vocal "Give me the rest" Action A17: Non-vocal holds out hand again		
Participant B	00.02.07-00.02.11	Action B7: Gives block to practitioner		
Participant A	00.02.11-00.02. 14	Action A18: Non-vocal raises hand into air Action A19: Vocal "Can you give me the block right up here?"	Put block into raised hand in air	Decision fork (3)
Participant B	00.02.14-00.02,16	Action B8: Puts block in raised hand		

Table 5. continued

Participant A	00.02.16-00.02.20	Action A20: Vocal indicated one block left- asks the child to reach in and get that one. Action A21: Non-vocal. Tilts box up for child to reach into	Get last block out of the box	Decision fork (4)
Participant B	00.02.20-00.02. 23	Action B9: Reaches into box to get last block		
Participant A	00.02.23-00.02. 25	Action A22: Vocal--put block into raised hand Action A23: Non-vocal-raises hand into air (in parallel)	Put block into raised hand in air	Decision fork (5)
Participant B	00.02.25-00.02.28	Action B10: Puts block in practitioner's hand		
Participant A	00.02.28-00.02.33	Action A24: Vocal positive feedback Action A25: Pats child on head		

Table 6. Summary of the actions' parameters in the five segments in consideration

Segments	Length (in sec)	No. of Actions		Action length						No. of Iterations
				average		min		max		
		A	B	A	B	A	B	A	B	
1	49	21	6	4	5	2	1	7	6	6
2	77	25	10	4	4	2	2	12	6	11
3	28	15	5	4	4	2	3	6	6	6
4	20	6	2	11	9	11	9	11	9	2
5	51	24	3	7	5	3	3	11	6	4

Table 7. Parameters of the effort-shape elements of the five segments

Quality	Segment									
	1		2		3		4		5	
	Numeric	Categorical	Numeric	Categorical	Numeric	Categorical	Numeric	Categorical	Numeric	Categorical
Flow	0.5	neutral	0.5	neutral	0.5	neutral	1.0	free	0.5	neutral
Transition	0.34	sustained	0.52	neutral	0.41	neutral	0.00	sustained	0.30	Sustained
Exertion	0.30	strong	0.00	strong	0.54	neutral	0.76	light	0.51	Neutral
Control	0.55	neutral	1.00	flexible	0.55	neutral	0.18	rigid	0.36	Rigid
Intensity	0.29	contract	0.40	Mid	0.33	contract	0.33	contract	0.13	contract

Table 8. The production of the screening session, including the production elements of the corresponding segments and their brief descriptions/interpretations

Segment	Production element	Brief interpretation
Segment 1: Blocks into cup		The body element expresses relatively weak intensity (on the way to "contracting"). Effort shape qualities indicate some obstruction to flow, transition neutral, but close to sustained, exertion is just getting strong and control is neutral.
Segment 2: Blocks into hand/large red box		The body element expresses an increase of the intensity, though still in the area of contraction. Effort-shape qualities indicate still some obstruction to flow, neutral transition, exertion is clearly strong and control is flexible.
Segment 3: Little blocks into cup		The body element expresses stronger contraction. All effort-shape qualities indicate neutral values.
Segment 4: Identify which cup the block is under		The body element expresses stronger contraction. Effort-shape qualities indicate that the flow is free (no obstruction) with transition at sustained level, relatively light exertion (the lightest in the production set), and control at the level of rigid.
Segment 5: Where is the bunny		The body element has reached the highest contraction in the production. The effort shape qualities indicate neutral flow, transition is sustained (but moving towards neutral), exertion is neutral, and control is below neutral towards rigid.

Table 9. Ranges of the qualities of the elasticities in the production of the example and the corresponding production range element

Quality	Min	Max	Production range element
Flow	0.5	1.0	
Transition	0.0	0.52	
Exertion	0.0	0.76	
Control	0.18	1.00	
Intensity	0.13	0.40	

For instance in segment 2 the patient drops the block on the table rather then putting it into the practitioner' outstretched hand (see Participant B, Action B6 in Table 5).

The parameters of the production element (the qualities of the effort shape and body elements) are presented in Table 7. For each quality of the effort shape element, we present the numerical values and the corresponding categorical values, assigned according to Table 3. For the categorical values of the quality of the body element (the intensity) we use the labels "contract" to indicate values towards the lower end and "mid" for values close to 0.5. Though not used in this production, but label "expand" is reserved for the values of intensity close to 1.

The values of the qualities of the elasticities control the visual language primitives. The visual expressions of the interactions during the subtasks of the screening exercise are presented in Table 8. In the column "Segment" we have included a frame from the corresponding segment to provide an illustration of the type of data that is the input to the visual analysis process. Masking and blurring has been used for de-identification of the subjects in the frames.

As we mentioned in the introductory section, we view interactions as a sequence of actions where subsequent actions depend on the previous actions/behaviour of the interacting parties. In the scenario of this example, one possible

assumption is that the interactions in every subsequent task also depend on the interactions in the previous tasks. Exploring the behaviour of the body element, we can see that the intensity of the interactions is not high and across the whole session remain within the contraction range. The highest intensity of the interaction is observed in segment 2, with the contraction reaching its peak in segment 5. Variation is again noticeable between interaction elements with segment 5 having the least intense interaction and segments 1 and 2 having the strongest, most intense interaction between the parties.

These variations in the quality intensity are reflected in the behaviour of the arms of the body element. The low intensity of the interactions does not help in reaching common ground. This is indicated by the flow quality, which remains at the middle point through the session, and deviating from that only in the "atypical" segment 4. The patient has some obstruction with completing the designated task of putting the blocks back in the cup. Since it is only the patient, but not the practitioner, who expresses obstruction, the flow has a neutral value. Transition quality indicates that regardless of the low intensity, the interaction is more or less sustained in time. The initially strong exertion of the interaction in segments 1 and 2 may indicate the possible adaptation period between the communication styles of the patient and the practitioner. The exertion somewhat stabilises around the neutral level within the rest of the session, indicating decrease in the effort of both parties in their interaction during the remaining tasks. With respect to the control of the interaction and its context, through the production there seem to be an overall decrease in the flexibility towards a more rigid control, caused, perhaps, by the failures of the patient in achieving the task outcomes. Overall, the response from the patient varies, spanning from performing the task successfully as in segment 4, or being able to perform some parts of the task, as in segments 1, 2, and 3, to not being able to perform the task satisfactorily at all as in segment 5. This is reflected in the variation in the interaction between the patient and the practitioner, which is clearly reflected in the change of the shape of the production element through the production. The ranges of the qualities and the production range element for this production are presented in Table 9.

CONCLUSION AND FUTURE RESEARCH

In this chapter, we presented a framework for creating visual languages for representing interactions, which uses human movement as a source for the core concepts of the visual language. Our approach is based on the evidence that humans can intuitively recognise constructs based on human movement, coming from the research on kinaesthetic thinking/understanding and its ability to support higher-level cognitive processes. We presented an overview of the framework, an instance of a visual language design using the proposed framework and its application for representing and analysing interactions between patients and practitioners in the healthcare domain. Developed approach and the corresponding techniques target interactive computer systems for facilitating interaction-rich domains such as

healthcare, occupational therapy, collaborative design, and learning.

The current version of the language operates with a symmetric body element (i.e., the left and the right arm are of the same length) as it represents the intensity of the interaction resulting from the behaviour of both parties. However, as contributions to interactions may not be symmetric, there is a room for depicting and reflecting that in our language, if the analysis requires it. The further development of the language will be extending the body element semantics with a split representation of intensity, where the quantification of the contributions is attributed to the corresponding party. Secondly, we intend to extend the language by developing the third elasticity "rotate and tilt" (see Table 2). The visual elements derived from this elasticity will have the function of representing the relations between productions. The elasticity will be applied to the production element, that is, the composite structure (as described in Figure 5) supporting interpretations of association in different productions. The expression of this elasticity will assist in representing productions as patterns of changes, that is, paths. As a result, the analyst will be provided with means for visual reasoning about the evolution of the interactions between the parties, adding another layer of analysis.

ACKNOWLEDGMENT

This research has been supported by the University of Technology, Sydney, and the Gait Lab, Royal Children's Hospital, Herston, Brisbane. We would like to thank Dr Catherine Bridge, School of Health Sciences, University of Sydney, for her assistance in the interpretation of the developmental screening example in this chapter and persistent support of this research.

REFERENCES

Anderson, M. L. (2003). Embodied cognition: A field guide. *Artificial Intelligence, 149*(1), 91-130.

Barsalou, L. (1999). Perceptual symbol systems. *Behavioural and Brain Sciences, 22*(4), 577-609.

Barsalou, L. W., Niedenthal, P. M., Barbey, A. K., & Ruppert, J. M. (2003). Social embodiment. In B. H. Ross (Ed.), *The psychology of learning and motivation* (p. 43). San Diego: Academic Press.

Bartlett, F. C. (1958). *Thinking: An experimental and social study.* New York: Basic Books.

Bergen, B., Chang, N., & Narayanan, S. (2004). Simulated action in an embodied construction grammar. *Proceedings of the 26th Annual Meeting of the Cognitive Science Society*, Chicago.

Hackney, P. (2000). *Making connections: Total body integration through Bartenieff fundamentals.* Harwood Academic (Performing Arts).

Cohen, P. R., Morrison, C. T., & Cannon, E. (2005). Maps for verbs: The relation between interaction dynamics and verb use.

Coiera, E. (2001). Mediated agent interaction. *Proceedings of the 8th Conference on Artificial Intelligence in Medicine Europe*, AIME 2001.

Deray, K. (2000). Through plane: A kinetic model for information retrieval. *Proceedings of the 11th Australasian Conference on Information Systems ACIS 2000.*

Dreyfus, H. L. (1972). *What computers can't do: A critique of artificial reason.* NY: Harper and Row.

Drew, P., Chatwin, J., & Collins, S. (2001). Conversation analysis: A method for research into interactions between patients and healthcare professionals. *Health Expectations, 4*(1), 58-70.

Dunbar-Jacob, J., & Schlenk, E. (2001). Patient adherence to treatment regimens. In A. Baum, T. Revenson, & J. Singer (Eds.), *Handbook of health psychology.* Mahwah, NJ: Erlbaum.

Fischer, K. W., & Bidell, T. R. (1998). Dynamic development of psychological structures in action and thought. In T. R. Bidell & D. W. Damon (Eds), *Handbook of child psychology: Vol. 1: Theoretical models of human development* (pp. 467-561). NY: John Wiley & Sons.

Gardner, H. (1983). *Frames of mind: The theory of multiple intelligences.* NY: Basic Books.

Glenberg, A. M., & Kaschak, M. P. (2003). The body's contribution to language. In B. H. Ross (Ed.), *The psychology of learning and motivation* (p. 43). San Diego: Academic Press.

Glenberg, A. M., & Robertson, D. A. (2000). Symbol grounding and meaning. A comparison of high dimensional and embodied theories of meaning. *JML, 43*(3), 379-401.

Goldberg, A. (1995). *Constructions: A construction grammar approach to argument structure.* Chicago: University of Chicago Press.

Guest, A. H. (2005): *Labanotation: The system of analyzing and recording movement.* NY: Routledge.

Hayes, R. P., Bowman, L., Monahan, P. O., Marrero, D. G., & McHorney, C. A. (2006). Understanding diabetes medications from the perspective of patients with Type 2 diabetes: Prerequisite to medication concordance. *The Diabetes Educator, 32*(3), 404-414

Hutchinson, A. (1977). *Labanotation.* NY: Theatre Books.

Johnson, M. (1987). *The body in the mind: The bodily basis of cognition.* Chicago: University of Chicago Press.

Kindler, C. H., Szirt, L., Sommer, D., Hausler, R., & Langewitz, W. (2005). A quantitative analysis of anaesthetist-patient communication during the per-operative visit. *Anaesthesia, 60*(1), 53-59.

Korsch, B. M., & Negrete, V. F. (1972). Doctor-patient communication. *Scientific American, 227*(2), 66-74.

Laban, R. (1956). *Laban's principles of dance and movement notation* (2nd ed.). London: Macdonald & Evans.

Laban, R., & Lawrence, F. C. (1974). *Effort: Economy of human movement* (2nd ed.). Boston: Plays Inc.

Lakoff, G. (1993). The contemporary theory of metaphor. In A. Ortony (Ed.), *Metaphor and thought* (pp. 202-251). Cambridge: Cambridge University Press.

Lakoff, G. (1988). Cognitive semantics. In U. Eco et al. (Eds.), *Meaning and mental representations*. In G. Lakoff & M. Johnson (1999). *Philosophy in the flesh*. NY: Basic Books.

Lakoff, G., & Johnson, M. (1980). *Metaphors we live by*. Chicago: University of Chicago Press.

Leiner, H. C., Leiner, A. L., & Dowq, R. S. (1986). Does the cerebellum contribute to mental skills. *Behavioural Neuroscience, 100*(4), 443-454

Maher, M. L., Simoff, S. J., & Cicognani, A. (2000). *Understanding virtual design studios*. London: Springer.

Newlove, J. (2001). *Laban for actors and dancers*. NY: Routledge.

Newlove J., & Dalby, J. (2004). *Laban for all*. London: Nick Hern Publishers.

Nicoladis, E., Mayberry, R. L., & Genesee, F. (1999). Gesture and bilingual development. *Developmental Psychology, 35*(2), 163-174.

Pendleton, D. (1983). Doctor-patient communication: A review. In D. Pendleton & J. Hasler (Eds.), *Doctor-patient communication* (pp. 5-53). NY: Academic Press.

Peräkyla, A. (1998). Authority and accountability: The delivery of diagnosis in primary healthcare. *Social Psychology Quarterly, 61*, 301-320.

Pretorius, A. J. (2005). Visual analysis for ontology engineering. *Journal of Visual Languages and Computing, 16*(4), 359-381.

Roberts, C., & Sarangi, S. (2005): Theme-oriented discourse analysis of medical encounters. *Medical Education, 39*(6), 632-40.

Robinson, J. (1998). Getting down to business: Talk gaze and body orientation during openings of doctor-patient consultations. *Human Communication Research, 25*(1), 97-123.

Sacks, O. (1989). *Seeing voices*. NY: Harper Collins.

Sandvik, M., Eide, H., Lind, M., Graugaard, P. K., Torper, J., & Finset, A. (2002). Analyzing medical dialogues: Strength and weakness of Roter's interaction analysis system (RIAS). *Patient Education and Counselling, 46*(4), 235-241.

Schiffrin, D., Tannen, D., & Hamilton, H., (2001). *Handbook of discourse analysis*. Oxford: Blackwell.

Seitz, J. A. (2000a). The embodied self. *Proceedings of the 30th Annual Symposium of the Jean Piaget Society*, Montreal, Canada.

Seitz, J. A. (2000b). Embodied cognition. *Proceedings of the 12th Annual Convention of the American Psychological Society*, Miami, FL.

Seitz, J. A. (1996). Developmentally appropriate practice. *Journal of Education and Family Review, 3*(5), 7-9.

Seitz, J. A. (1994). Thinking kinesically: Theory and practice. *Proceedings of the 24ᵗʰ Annual Symposium of the Jean Piaget Society*, Chicago, Jean Piaget Society.

Simoff, S. J. (2001). Towards the development of environments for designing visualisation support for visual data mining. In S. J. Simoff, M. Noirhomme-Fraiture, & M. H. Bohlen (Eds.), *Proceedings the International Workshop on Visual Data Mining VDM@PKDD'01* (pp. 93-106). September 4, 2001, Freiburg, Germany.

Simoff, S. J., & Maher, M. L. (2000). Analysing participation in collaborative design environments. *Design Studies, 21*(2), 119-144.

Stewart, M. A. (1995): Effective physician-patient communication and health outcomes. *A review CMAJ, 152*(9), 1423-33.

Sudnow, D. W. (1978). *Ways of the hand: The organization of improvised conduct.* NY: Harper and Row.

Turner, M. (1994). Design for a theory of meaning. In W. Overton & D. Palermo (Eds.), *The nature and ontogenesis of meaning* (pp. 91-107). Lawrence Erlbaum Associates.

Winograd, T., & Flores, F. (1986). *Understanding computers and cognition.* Norwood, NJ: Ablex Publishing Corporation.

Wilson, M. (2002). Six views of embodied cognition. *Psychonomic Bulletin and Review, 9*(4), 625-636.

Wylie, J. L., & Wagenfeld-Heintz, E. (2004). Development of relationship-centered care. *Journal for Healthcare Quality, 26*(1), 14-21.

Zwaan, R. A. (2004). The immersed experiencer: Toward an embodied theory of language comprehension. In B. H. Ross (Ed.), *The psychology of learning and motivation* (p. 44). New York: Academic Press.

Chapter XII
Sketch Understanding:
Issues and State of the Art

Vincenzo Deufemia
Università di Salerno, Italy

ABSTRACT

Recognition of hand-drawn, diagrammatic sketches is a very active research field since it finds a natural application in a wide range of domains such as engineering, software design, and architecture. However, it is a particularly difficult task since the symbols of a sketched diagram can be drawn by using a different stroke-order, -number, and -direction. The difficulties in the recognition process are often made harder by the lack of precision and by the presence of ambiguities in messy hand-drawn sketches. In this article, we present a brief survey on sketch understanding techniques and tools. We first present major problems that should be considered in the construction of online sketch recognizers. We analyze representative works for the recognition of freehand shape and describe several shape description languages for the automatic construction of sketch recognizers.

INTRODUCTION

In the early creative phases of designing users prefer to use paper and pencil with respect to computers (Gross & Do, 1996). Indeed, when compared with pencil and paper, computer based tools require designers to specify ideas with unsuitable precision, and as a result are often tedious to use. On the contrary, paper and pencil allows people to formalize ideas in ambiguous, imprecise, and incremental way. As a consequence, in recent years, the growing availability of pen-based computing hardware, such as PDAs, electronic whiteboards and tablet computers, has increased the interest in the creation of computer software that works exclusively from freehand drawings, especially for the disciplines of engineering, software design, and architecture (Blostein & Haken, 1999; Caetano, Goulart, Fonseca, & Jorge, 2002; Gross, 1996; Hammond & Davis, 2002; Kara & Stahovich, 2004a; Stahovich, Davis, & Shrobe, 1998). These tools allow users to convey information efficiently releasing them from a maze of menus, toolbars, and many complicated commands.

The existing sketching systems provide good user interfaces but only have a limited recognition capability for the graphical input. This problem introduces redundancy and inefficiency when the systems are used as early phase design tools since they are not able to transform the edited sketches into input for more powerful design systems.

The sketchy graphic objects drawn using a digital pen are usually not easy for machines to understand and process. Sketch recognition algorithms can simply clean up roughly drawn strokes (Igarashi, Matsuoka, Kawachiya, & Tanaka, 1997); in this case, they are called *sketch beautification algorithms*, and/or solve the problem of recognizing the symbols in the hand-drawn user's diagrams. This problem is particularly difficult since the symbols of a sketched diagram can be drawn by using a different stroke-order, -number, and -direction. Several works concentrate on the recognition of symbols formed by a single-stroke gesture (Rubine, 1991) also named *glyph* and on the recognition of gestures formed by multiple strokes (Damm, Hansen, & Thomsen, 2000). The recognition of continuous sketches also involves the activities of segmentation and clustering of the user's strokes at the same time. This problem requires an exponential time complexity to be solved, as a consequence, the systems implementing such type of recognition work under some assumptions about how the sketches are drawn (Shilman, Pasula, Russell, & Newton, 2002; Wenyin, Qian, Xiao, & Jin, 2001). Moreover, the difficulties in the recognition process are increased by the lack of precision and the presence of ambiguities in messy hand-drawn sketches. Indeed, hand-sketched symbols are imprecise in nature such that the corners are not always sharp, lines are not perfectly straight, and curves are not necessarily smooth. As a consequence, accurate sketch recognition requires clever techniques for the resolution of these issues.

In this article, we discuss the main sketch understanding issues and then we survey recent techniques and tools proposed for their solution.

In particular, first we analyze several approaches for the recognition of freehand shape, then we survey experimental sketch-based interfaces integrating sketch recognizers developed for different discipline. Moreover, we describe the main formalisms and languages proposed for the description of symbol's shape and for the automatic construction of sketch recognizers.

BACKGROUND

By the term *sketch,* we mean an informal drawing created with pen strokes. By *understanding,* we mean having the computer reliably identify the objects suggested by the pen strokes, despite the inherent inaccuracies and ambiguities. Sketches are acquired initially in the format of point chains. The density of raw sampling points is relative to the sketching speed. When the user sketches slowly or rapidly, the distance between neighbor points can be small or large. Usually, the raw points are resampled for correct and effective recognition. The goal of resampling is to delete redundancy points for reducing calculation when raw points' density is high, and to add more points for reducing recognition error when the density is low.

In order to present the main sketch understanding issues clearly, we first define the following terms:

- **Stroke** is a unit of a user's original sketch input. It is the pen trajectory on the screen between each pair of pen-down and pen-up operations.
- **Breakpoint** is a point on a stroke where the stroke is split apart, which is also called splitting point.
- **Segment** is a primitive shape fitting a stroke.

The process of fitting user sketches using primitive shapes (such as elliptical arcs and straight lines) is usually referred to as *stroke segmentation* or *curve fitting.*

Diagrammatic notations are two-dimensional languages such as trees and graphs, characterized by notational conventions, which define a mapping between symbols and the information conveyed by a diagram. There is a many-to-one correspondence between images and information since the layout of a diagram can be changed in many ways without changing the conveyed information. Recognizing a diagram (like recognizing a sketch) is a matter of parsing the elements in the diagram according to a specified visual language. Given a set of hierarchical shape descriptions, the recognizers combine low-level shapes in a diagram according to the constraints given in the shape descriptions to produce higher-level descriptions for the diagram.

SKETCH UNDERSTANDING ISSUES

One of the most important parts of a natural sketching interface is the underlying recognition engine. Indeed, it should be accurate in order to reduce mistakes, but also flexible in order to not constrain users to a specific drawing style. In practice, we cannot build a system that makes no mistakes, but we endeavor to make as few as possible. In this section we discuss the sketch recognition problem and the main issues to be taken into account for the construction of sketch recognizers.

The sketch recognition process. In general, the problem of sketch recognition can be separated in the following three sequential processes:

1. **Primitive shape recognition:** While the user is drawing or immediately after he or she has drawn a freehand stroke, determine the type and parameters of its primitive shape (which can be line, triangle, rectangle, ellipse, and so on).

2. **Composite graphic object recognition:** After recognizing the current stroke, if possible, combine the current stroke (recognized primitive shape) with the ones previously drawn by the user based on their spatial relationship, determine, or predict the type and parameters of the composite graphic object that the user is intending to input.

3. **Document recognition and understanding:** After recognizing the graphical elements (primitive shapes and composite graphic objects), if possible, understand the connections and relationship among the elements and semantics in the current drawing.

However, the effectiveness of these processes constrain the user drawing style since they assume each pen stroke represents a single shape such as a single line segment or arc segment, which ever fits the stroke best. While this kind of approach facilitates shape recognition, it results in a less than natural user interface.

To support the recognition of composite objects drawn by varying the number of pen strokes, the sketch recognizer should also include a segmentation process of the pen strokes into individual primitive shapes that closely match the original

Figure 1. Segmentation of a square

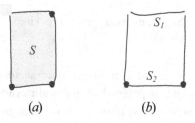

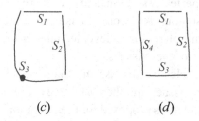

(a) (b) (c) (d)

ink. For example, a square can be drawn as a single pen stroke or as two separate strokes, or even as three or four strokes as shown in Figure 1(a)-(d), respectively, where the filled circles represent the breakpoints.

The segmentation process involves searching along each stroke the points that divide the stroke into different primitive shapes (i.e., the breakpoints). Usually, these points are points at which the pen speed is at a minimum, the ink exhibits high curvature, or the sign of the curvature changes (Calhoun, Stahovich, Kurtoglu, & Kara, 2002). Additional breakpoints occur at the start and end of each pen stroke. Once the breakpoints have been identified, primitive shape recognizers are used to fit the primitive shapes between the breakpoints.

Segmentation is a basic problem that has many applications for digital ink capture and manipulation, as well as higher-level symbolic and structural analyses. As an example, the structural information generated by the segmentation process can be useful for the beautification of the symbols (Igarashi et al., 1997), for developing a user interface with which to interact with sketched ink.

Issues

As opposed to traditional diagram editors where the domain specific symbols are provided in palettes, abstract shapes are imprecise and highly variable in hand-sketched diagrams. Thus, the first challenge in building a sketch-based system is recognizing the meaningful patterns implied by a user's pen stroke. This task is not trivial because pattern matching must be flexible enough to allow some tolerance in sketch recognition, but sufficiently constrained not to accept incorrect patterns. As an example, let us consider stroke 2 in Figure 2(a). It is an arc but in the recognition process, it should also be considered as a line segment since these two primitive elements are very similar.

Moreover, sketching, as well as all other natural ways of conveying information, is an intrinsically ambiguous process and varies greatly from person to person. As an example, a user-drawn square might easily be misinterpreted as a circle if it is drawn with rounded corners. Furthermore, semantically different objects might be graphically represented by identical or apparently similar symbols. As an example, an ellipse symbol in a use case diagram might be a use case symbol or the head of an actor symbol.

Sketch recognition systems should also not place constraints on how the users can draw a symbol. Indeed, they should be able to draw without having to worry about where to start a stroke, how many strokes to use, in what order to draw the strokes, etc. Thus, the recognition should be independent of stroke-order, stroke-number, and stroke-direction, as well as invariant to rotation, scaling, and reflection of symbols.

Another important issue in sketch is understanding concerns in *ink parsing* that establishes which strokes are part of which shapes by grouping and segmenting the user's strokes into clusters of intended symbols (Kara & Stahovich, 2004). This is a particularly challenging problem. For example, a use case symbol of a use case diagram can be drawn as a single pen stroke or as two or more separate strokes as shown in Figure 2(b). Alternatively, a single pen stroke can contain multiple shapes as in Figure 2(c) where a communication symbol (the line segment) and a use case are drawn. This variation in drawing style together with the inherent ambiguities increase the difficulties in the segmentation and clustering tasks because a recognizer cannot know a priori how many strokes will be used to draw each object, nor the order in which the parts of a shape will appear.

Based on these issues, accurate sketch recognition requires clever techniques for their resolution. As an example, sketch recognition merely based on shape has a number of serious drawbacks. Indeed, the recognition of a sketched symbol is

Figure 2. (a) A sketched actor symbol, (b) a use case symbol drawn with two strokes, (c) and two use case diagram symbols drawn with a single stroke

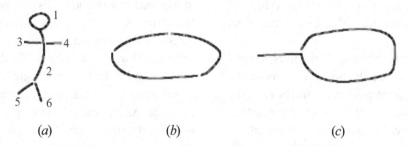

(a)   (b)   (c)

significantly influenced by the objects surrounding it. Thus, the ambiguities in the sketches can be correctly solved by analyzing the context around the ambiguous parts.

Another important issue that should be tackled by researchers is the construction process of a sketch recognizer. Currently, the implementation of sketch recognizers is quite time consuming since they are mostly based on specific techniques, as opposed to several other fields such as textual/visual languages and speech recognition, which benefit from the availability of compiler generation techniques and tools. Moreover, although some of the shapes and sketch recognition algorithms in different application domains are similar, distinct applications re-implement these similar sketching algorithms. A domain-independent recognition system would be able to recognize shapes from different domains by recognizing certain simple shapes and allowing users to use these shapes to hierarchically describe how to recognize other shapes. In this way programmers would be able to create new sketching interfaces simply by describing the domain specific information, including the shapes to be recognized in the domain without writing sketch recognition code.

SKETCH RECOGNITION

There has been a significant amount of research to date in various aspects of sketch-based user interfaces: interactive design tools (Landay & Myers, 2001), software toolkits (Hong & Landay, 2000), ink beautification (Igarashi et al., 1997), and sketch recognition (Alvarado & Davis, 2004; Gross, 1994; Kara & Stahovich, 2004b; Sezgin & Davis, 2005; Shilman et al., 2002). In the following sections, we provide a survey of shape recognition techniques and of sketch recognition systems, followed by a description of formalisms used for the construction of sketch recognizers.

Shape Recognition Techniques

In the last two decades, several approaches have been proposed for the recognition of freehand shapes. The techniques based on graphs decompose the input patterns into primitive shapes such as lines and curves, which are then assembled into a graph structure encoding both the intrinsic attributes of the primitives and their relationships (Calhoun et al., 2002; Lee, 1992). The problem of recognizing hand-drawn patterns is reduced to a graph/subgraph isomorphism problem. The main drawbacks of these approaches are the high computational complexity and the inefficiency of the segmentation process.

The Rubine recognition engine is a trainable, single-stroke gesture recognizer for direct manipulation interfaces (Rubine, 1991). A stroke is characterized by a set of 11 geometric and 2 dynamic attributes. Based on these attributes, a linear discriminant classifier is constructed whose weights are learned from the set of training examples. However, this method is sensitive to the drawing direction and orientation and does not scale well to complex sketches because they make the assumption that patterns in a domain can be represented and recognized in isolation. An efficient hand-coded recognizer based on filters has been introduced in Ajay, Van, and Takayuki (1993). The approach can handle six types of geometric shapes including triangles, rectangles, ellipses, circles, diamonds, and lines. However, these filters are sensitive to orientation of the geometric objects.

Fonseca, Pimentel, and Jorge have extended Ajay's work by providing more filters and using fuzzy logic (Fonseca et al., 2002). The recognizer of multi-stroke and single stroke shapes characterize each shape by a number of geometric features calculated from three special polygons: the smallest convex hull that can be circumscribed around the shape, the largest triangle that can be inscribed in the hull, and the largest quadrilateral that can be inscribed. Using the areas and perimeters of these polygons, a number of features such as thinness, hollowness, and openness are computed. The system is manually trained by identifying the right fuzzy feature sets to characterize a shape and distinguish it from the other shapes. The recognition of a scribble is performed by computing the degree of membership in the fuzzy set definitions of the various known shapes. However, the filters applied during the recognition are ineffective on ambiguous shapes such as pentagon and hexagon. Moreover, the method is unable to identify the constituent parts of a shape.

An approach for multi-stroke symbol recognition with arbitrary drawing orders and orientations has been presented in Kara, Gennari, and Stahovich (2004). The trainable recognizer uses nine geometric features to construct concise probabilistic models of input symbols. However, it is sensitive to the results of stroke segmentation, and additionally does not handle over stroking and different line styles.

Inspired by the success of Hidden Markov models (HMM's) in speech recognition, researches have considered these techniques as yet another approach to hand-drawn pattern recognition. In HMM's, the observed pattern is viewed as the result of a stochastic process that is governed by a hidden stochastic model. Each stochastic model represents a different class pattern capable of producing the observed output. The goal is to identify the model that has the highest probability of generating the output. One aspect that distinguishes HMM's is their strong temporal organization; processes are considered to be the result of time-sequenced state transitions in the hidden model and expectation of a particular observation is dictated by the current state in the model and (usually) the previous state. For sketch recognition, this ordering has limited HMM's to problems that exhibit strong temporal structure such as handwritten text recognition (Yasuda, Takahashi, & Matsumoto, 2000). One premise in these approaches is that users are not expected to go back and alter previously input text. In a general sketch-based system, however, one can, and typically does, go back to a previous spatial location and add new strokes. HMM-based methods become less appealing in such situations. Furthermore, the need for large training data sets may inhibit the use of HMM's when such data is scarce. By the observation that in certain domains people draw objects using consistent stroke orderings Sezgin and Davis have proposed a technique to model and recognize sketches using HMMs (Sezgin & Davis, 2005a). The approach exploits the regularities to perform very efficient segmentation and recognition. Recently, has been extended for recognizing sketches also drawn in an interspersed fashion (Sezgin & Davis, 2005b).

Kara et al. have introduced a domain-independent, multi-stroke, trainable symbol recognizer having the advantage of learning new definitions from single prototype examples (Kara et al., 2004b). Moreover, it includes a multi-level parsing scheme that allows users to continuously sketch.

The parser uses contextual knowledge to both improve accuracy and reduce recognition times. A trainable shape recognizer is used to find the best interpretations of the identified clusters (Kara & Stahovich, 2005). However, the recognition process is guided from "marker symbols," which are symbols easy to recognize, that they assume to exist always in the sketch. Moreover, the approach assumes that the hand-drawn diagram consists of shapes linked by arrows.

Regarding the segmentation techniques, different approaches have been proposed. Temporal information such as pen speed has been recently explored as a means to uncover users' intentions during sketching (Calhoun et al., 2002; Sezgin, Stahovich, & Davis, 2001). These methods focus on the detection of corner (segment) points, which usually help decompose the original ink into basic geometric components such as lines and arcs. Usually, curvature information alone is not a reliable way to determine such points. Instead, the speed-based methods have proven to be a much more reliable measure to determine the intended segment points. The observation is that the speed of the pen tip significantly reduces at the intended corner points (Kara et al., 2005).

Saund uses both local features (such as intersections and curvatures) and global features (such as closed paths) to locate breakpoints of a stroke (Saund, 2003); whereas Yu applied the mean shift procedure to approximate strokes (Yu, 2003). Hse, Shilman, and Newton have presented an optimal segmentation approach based on template that does not suffer of over- and under-segmentation of strokes (Hse et al., 2004). In particular, given a sketched symbol S and a template T, the algorithm finds a set of breakpoints in S such that the fitting performed according to T yields the minimum fit error. The templates T can be of two types, one specifies a sequence of lines and ellipses, and the other specifies the number of lines and ellipses.

Sketch Recognition Systems

Starting with Sutherland's sketchpad (Sutherland, 1963), there has been a considerable amount of work devoted to the creation of tools processing people's freehand drawings. Advances in machine intelligence, hardware technology, and computer graphics have accelerated this transition. Recent years have seen the development of experimental sketch-based interfaces for a number of different disciplines including engineering design, user interface design, and architecture.

ASSIST is a system that can interpret and simulate a variety of simple hand-drawn mechani-

Figure 3. A car on a hill, as drawn in ASSIST (a), and the simulation of the interpreted diagram (b), (Alvarado, 2000)

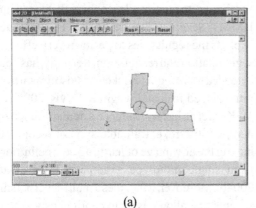

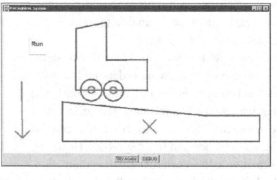

(a)   (b)

Figure 4. The sketch-based interfaces of SimuSketch (a) (Kara et al., 2004a); SILK (b) (Landay et al., 2001); JavaSketchIt (c) (Caetano et al., 2002); and Denim (d) (Newman et al. 2003)

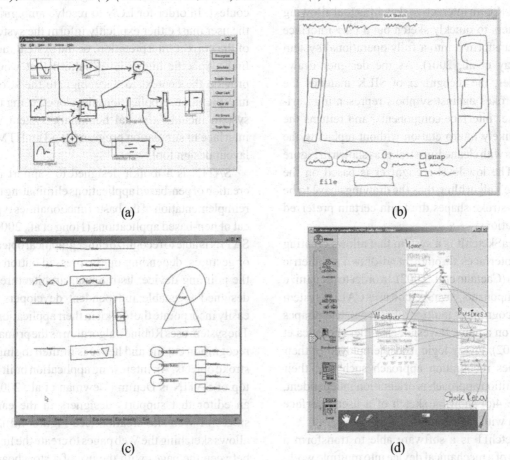

(a)

(b)

(c)

(d)

cal systems (Alvarado, 2000). Figure 3(a) shows a hand-drawn car on a hill using ASSIST. The arrow pointing down represents gravity. The drawing is interpreted by the recognition system and run using Working Model. The interpreted view is shown in Figure 3(b). The main strength of AS-SIST is that it presents a formalism for augmenting implicit and explicit feedback from the user with contextual information to disambiguate between multiple interpretations of a drawing. The main limitation, however, is that its shape recognizers are hand-coded and can recognize only a limited number of shapes specifically designed for the particular domain. Nevertheless, this work addresses a number of important issues in sketch-

based interface design including user involvement in recognition, ambiguity resolution and the level of software aggressiveness in recognition.

Sim-U-Sketch is a sketch-based interface for Simulink software package (Kara et al., 2004a). Once the user's sketch is interpreted by the system, it becomes a functional Simulink model that the user can interact with. In particular, after completing the sketch, the user can run a simulation of the system and view the results directly through the sketch-based interface as shown in Figure 4(a). The recognition algorithm used in the system is based on the recognizer proposed in Kara et al. (2004b) as a consequence users can customize the system to their own drawing styles by providing

239

a single prototype example of each object they would like to use.

SILK is an interactive sketching tool allowing designers to quickly sketch out a user interface and transform it into a fully operational system (Landay et al., 2001). As the designer draws sketches, the recognizer of SILK matches the pen strokes against symbols representing various user interface components, and returns the most likely interpretation without replacing the strokes with cleaned-up strokes as shown in Figure 4(b). The low-level recognizer is based on the Rubine's algorithm, thus the drawings have to be single-stroke shapes drawn in certain preferred orientations.

JavaSketchIt is a system that allows creating user interfaces through hand-drawn geometric shapes (Caetano et al., 2002). In order to recognize UI components, JavaSketchIt uses CALI, a system for recognizing multi-stroke geometric shapes based on a naïve Bayesian classifier (Fonseca et al., 2002). Fuzzy logic is also employed in their graphics recognition approach such that their recognition approach is orientation independent. Figure 4(c) shows a sketch of a user interface drawn with JavaSketchIt.

SketchIT is a software able to transform a sketch of a mechanical device into multiple working designs (Stahovich et al., 1998). To "interpret" a sketch, the system first identifies what behaviors the parts should provide, then derives constraints on the geometry to ensure it produces these behaviors. The desired behavior is specified by the user via a state transition diagram. SketchIT is concerned only with the high-level processing of the sketch; it assumes that the lines, arcs, and symbols contained in the sketch are extracted by another program.

The electronic cocktail napkin (ECN) is a pen interface for knowledge-based critiquing, simulation, and information retrieval (Gross, 1994, 1996). The system employs a bottom-up recognition method that also includes a method for representing ambiguities in the user's sketches,

and is capable of refining its early interpretations of user's strokes by analyzing the surrounding context. In order for ECN to resolve ambiguity, the user must either explicitly inform the system of the correct interpretation, or the system must find a specific higher-level pattern that would provide the context to disambiguate the stroke interpretation. Applications developed using the system include a visual bookmark system, an interface to simulation programs, and an HTML layout design tool.

SATIN is a toolkit designed to support the creation of pen-based applications eliminating the reimplementation of the basic functionalities typical of pen-based applications (Hong et al., 2000). SATIN is able to recognize either graphical objects or gestures, depending on the pressed button on the pointing device. Its modular architecture is designed to enable independent developers to easily incorporate the toolkit in their applications. The system uses Rubine's algorithm as the primary recognition engine and hence is limited to single stroke objects. An interesting application built on top of SATIN is Denim (Newman et al., 2003), an editor that supports designers in the early stages of Web site creation (see Figure 4(d)). It allows sketching the Web pages to create the links between the pages with the use of a storyboard, and to see the interaction in practice thanks to a run mode. However, the tool does not facilitate automatic transition from the early stage design to a more powerful design system.

SketchREAD (sketch recognition engine for any domain) is a system capable of understanding freely drawn, messy, two-dimensional diagrammatic sketches (Alvarado et al., 2004). The system can be applied to a variety of domains by providing structural descriptions of the shapes in that domain. The system uses context to solve the ambiguity and uncertainty inherent in complex, freely drawn sketches. The parsing approach is based on dynamically constructed Bayesian networks combining bottom-up and top-down recognition algorithm that generates the most likely interpretations first, then actively seeks out parts of those interpretations that are still missing. This process allows the system to recover from low-level recognition errors (e.g., a line misclassified as an arc) that would otherwise result in domain level recognition errors.

SketchBench is a tool supporting the specification and generation of a sketch recognizer (Costagliola et al., 2004). The recognition approach relies on an LR based parsing technique, which allows us to solve both the problem of stroke clustering and that of context based ambiguity resolution. The parser is then integrated into a sketch editor, where sketches are incrementally and unobtrusively interpreted as they are drawn. The use of well-known visual language parsing methodologies and powerful grammar formalisms enables the application of the approach to several application domains. In particular, the approach is well suited to applications requiring the parsing of user's strokes in real time, without limiting the designer's drawing freedom. Thus, such parser will enable the creation of powerful and natural early-stage computer aided design tools. Moreover, many of the results achieved in the visual language field such as flexible semantic interpretation and code generation can be inherited.

SPECIFICATION LANGUAGES

Shape grammars have been the first grammar formalism for describing shape languages (Stiny & Gips, 1972), and many systems have been built using this formalism (Gips, 1999). However, shape grammars have the drawback that do not provide several information about the strokes that may be helpful in their recognition, such as temporal information.

Mahoney & Fromherz (2002) uses a not hierarchical language to describe and recognize stick figures, which is not suitable to describe large shapes. Fuzzy relational grammars have been used by Caetano et al. (2002) for describing shapes. However, they do not take into account the possibility that a single pen stroke can contain multiple symbols.

The electronic cocktail napkin project (Gross, 1996) provides a way to construct a grammar for recognizing diagrams from basic shapes and relations. The recognition scheme is a series of graphical replacement rules similar to the shape grammars (Stiny et al., 1972).

The sketch recognition systems described in Landay (1996) and Shizuki, Yamada, Iizuka, and Tanala (2003) use variants of visual language grammars to provide contextual information in order to face the inherent ambiguity of sketched drawings. However, although these early efforts provide a context for resolving ambiguity, their use of grammars was not focused on ambiguity but to find a concise way to specify valid visual structures.

LADDER is a language that allows designers to specify how shapes are drawn, displayed, and edited in a certain domain (Hammond & Davis, 2005). The language consists of a set of predefined shapes, constraints, editing behaviors and a syntax for combining them. New domain objects are created by specifying the shape descriptions. They do not consider the problem of stroke segmentation in case of multi-symbol strokes.

A statistical visual language model for ink parsing has been introduced in (Shilman et al., 2002). A new recognizer is created by writing a declarative context-free grammar for the language, generating a model from the grammar, and training the model on drawing examples. The approach is designed to parse the single components of a composite symbol, rather than parsing entire sketches, and assumes that shapes are drawn in certain preferred orientations.

Inspired by the approaches used in visual language recognition and compiler compilers, grammar formalism, named *sketch grammars*, for specifying sketch languages and from which it is possible to automatically generate a parser for their recognition have been proposed in Costagliola, Deufemia, and Risi (2005). The grammar allows shapes to be defined hierarchically and to specify the syntax of the language by composing the defined shapes. Moreover, the actions associated to the productions allows to define editing gestures, to specify the display of the sketch after the strokes are recognized, to define semantic checks, and to realize code and report generation.

FUTURE TRENDS

Sketching understanding is a still challenging problem requiring integration of multidisciplinary technologies (e.g., both graphics recognition and imaginal thinking research). More research works should be done to achieve truly natural and practical pen-based computer interaction, such that reasoning and prediction of the user's intentions can be made from the sketches he or she draws in order to support and facilitate his or her conceptual design (e.g., in creative design tasks).

An interesting topic that should be analyzed regards adapting recognizers to an individual's use of the system. The system should be flexible and extendable, not only learning a specific user's drawing style, but also learning novel patterns that it had not seen before. Learning can also be applied at the reasoning level.

Finally, an interesting challenge that should be investigated is how to enter the knowledge into the recognition system. Indeed, the specification of shape and context information can be difficult to describe, and grammars are tedious to write. As a consequence, it should be useful to automatically generate shape descriptions from a drawn example. Similarly, it should be interesting to investigate ways to learn the grammars, as well as the temporal and spatial information, from examples.

CONCLUSION

The increasing diffusion of devices with pen-based interfaces has given rise to more and more interest into the problem of recognizing informal graphical input. The existing sketch recognizers perform only a limited drawing recognition since they process simple sketches, or rely on drawing style assumptions that reduce the recognition complexity, and in most cases, they require a substantial amount of training data. Moreover, their implementations are usually hand coded and then not efficient, as opposed to several other fields such as textual/visual languages and speech recognition, where the benefits of compiler generation techniques and tools are taken into account.

In this article, we have presented a brief survey of the state of the art of sketch recognition techniques and tools. We have examined representative works and related approaches to the problems of freehand shape recognition and of shape description for the automatic construction of sketch recognizers. Finally, we have described several open problems that should be investigated in the future.

REFERENCES

Ajay, A., Van V., & Takayuki, D. K. (1993). Recognizing multistroke geometric shapes: An experimental evaluation. *Proceedings of ACM Symposium on User Interfaces Software and Technology* (pp. 121-128). ACM Press.

Alvarado, C. (2000). *A natural sketching environment: Bringing the computer into early stages of mechanical design.* Unpublished master thesis, Massachusetts Institute of Technology, Cambridge, MA.

Alvarado, C., & Davis, R. (2004). SketchREAD: A multi-domain sketch recognition engine. *Proceedings of ACM Symposium on User In-*

terfaces Software and Technology (pp. 23-32). ACM Press.

Blostein, D., & Haken, L. (1999). Using diagram generation software to improve diagram recognition: A case study of music notation. *IEEE Transactions on Pattern Analysis and Machine Intelligence, 21*(11), 1121-1136.

Caetano, A., Goulart, N., Fonseca, M., & Jorge, J. (2002). JavaSketchIT: Issues in sketching the look of user interfaces. *Proceedings of AAAI Spring Symposium on Sketch Understanding* (pp. 9-14). AAAI Press.

Calhoun, C., Stahovich, T. F., Kurtoglu, T., & Kara, L. B. (2002). Recognizing multi-stroke symbols. *Proceedings of AAAI Spring Symposium on Sketch Understanding* (pp. 15-23). AAAI Press.

Costagliola, G., Deufemia, V., Polese, G., & Risi, M. (2004). A parsing technique for sketch recognition systems. *Proceedings of IEEE Symposium on Visual Languages and Human-Centric Computing* (pp. 19-26). IEEE Press.

Costagliola, G., Deufemia, V., & Risi, M. (2005). Sketch grammars: A formalism for describing and recognizing diagrammatic sketch languages. *Proceedings of ICDAR'05* (pp. 1226-1230). IEEE Press.

Damm, C., Hansen, K., & Thomsen, M. (2000). Tool support for cooperative object-oriented design: Gesture-based modeling on an electronic whiteboard. *CHI Letters, 2*(1), 518-525.

Fonseca, M. J., Pimentel, C., & Jorge, J. A. (2002). CALI: An online scribble recognizer for calligraphic interfaces. *Proceedings of AAAI Spring Symp. on Sketch Understanding* (pp. 51-58). AAAI Press.

Gips, J. (1999). Computer implementation of shape grammars. *NSF/MIT Workshop on Shape Computation.*

Gross, M. D. (1996). The electronic cocktail napkin: A computational environment for working with design diagrams. *Design Studies, 17*(1), 53-69.

Gross, M. D. (1994). Recognizing and interpreting diagrams in design. *Proceedings of Working Conference on Advanced Visual Interfaces* (pp. 88-94). ACM Press.

Gross, M. D., & Do, E. (1996). Ambiguous intentions: A paper-like interface for creative design. *Proceedings of ACM Symposium on User Interfaces Software and Technology* (pp. 183-192). ACM Press.

Hammond, T., & Davis, R. (2002). Tahuti: A geometrical sketch recognition system for UML class diagrams. *Proceedings of AAAI Symp. on Sketch Understanding* (pp. 51-58). AAAI Press.

Hammond, T., & Davis, R. (2005). LADDER, A sketching language for user interface developers. *Computers & Graphics, 29*(4), 518-532.

Hong, J. I., & Landay, J. A. (2000). SATIN: A toolkit for informal ink-based applications. *Proceedings of ACM Symposium on User Interfaces Software and Technology* (pp. 63-72). ACM Press.

Hse, H., Shilman, M., & Newton, A. R. (2004). Robust sketched symbol fragmentation using templates. *Proceedings of International Conference on Intelligent User Interfaces* (pp. 156-160). ACM Press.

Igarashi, T., Matsuoka, S., Kawachiya, S., & Tanaka, H. (1997). Interactive beautification: A technique for rapid geometric design. *Proceedings of ACM Symposium on User Interfaces Software and Technology* (pp. 105-114). ACM Press.

Kara, L. B., Gennari, L., & Stahovich, T. F. (2004). A sketch-based interface for the design and analysis of simple vibratory mechanical systems. *ASME International Design Engineering Technical Conferences.*

Kara, L. B., & Stahovich, T. F. (2004a). Sim-U-Sketch: A sketch-based interface for Simulink. *Proceedings of Working Conference on Advanced Visual Interfaces* (pp. 354-357). ACM Press.

Kara, L. B., & Stahovich, T. F. (2004b). Hierarchical parsing and recognition of hand-sketched diagrams. *Proceedings of ACM Symposium on User Interfaces Software and Technology* (pp. 13-22). ACM Press.

Kara, L. B., & Stahovich, T. F. (2005). An image-based, trainable symbol recognizer for hand-drawn sketches. *Computers & Graphics, 29*(4), 501-517.

Landay, J. (1996). *Interactive sketching for the early stages of user interface design.* Unpublished doctoral dissertation, Carnegie Mellon University, Pittsburgh, PA.

Landay, J. A., & Myers, B. A. (2001). Sketching interfaces: Toward more human interface design. *IEEE Computer, 34*(3), 56-64.

Lee, S. W. (1992). Recognizing hand-drawn electrical circuit symbols with attributed graph matching. *Structured Document Image Analysis* (pp. 340-358). Springer-Verlag.

Mahoney, J. V., & Fromherz, M. P. J. (2002). Three main concerns in sketch recognition and an approach to addressing them. *Proceedings of AAAI Symp. on Sketch Understanding* (pp. 105-112). AAAI Press.

Newman, M. W., Lin, J., Hong, J. I., & Landay, J. A. (2003). DENIM: An informal Web site design tool inspired by observations of practice. *Human-Computer Interaction, 18*(3), 259-324.

Rubine, D. (1991). Specifying gestures by example. *Computer Graphics, 25*(4), 329-337.

Saund, E. (2003). Finding perceptually closed paths in sketches and drawings. *IEEE Transactions on Pattern Analysis and Machine Intelligence, 25*(4), 475-491.

Sezgin, T. M., & Davis, R. (2005a). HMM-based efficient sketch recognition. *Proceedings of International Conference on Intelligent User Interfaces* (pp. 281-283). ACM Press.

Sezgin, T. M., & Davis, R. (2005b). Modeling sketching as a dynamic process. *Proceedings of CSW'05*, Gloucester, MA.

Sezgin, T. M., Stahovich, T., & Davis, R. (2001). Sketch-based interfaces: Early processing for sketch understanding. *Proceedings of Workshop on Perceptive User Interfaces*.

Shilman, M., Pasula, H., Russell, S., & Newton, R. (2002). Statistical visual language models for ink parsing. *Proceedings of AAAI Spring Symposium on Sketch Understanding* (pp. 126-132). AAAI Press.

Shizuki, B., Yamada, H., Iizuka, K., & Tanala, J. (2003). A unified approach for interpreting handwritten strokes. *Proceedings IEEE Symp. on Human-Centric Computing* (pp. 180-182). IEEE Press.

Stiny, G., & Gips, J. (1972). Shape grammars and the generative specification of painting and sculpture. *Information Processing, 71*, 1460-1465.

Stahovich, T. F., Davis, R., & Shrobe, H. (1998). Generating multiple new designs from a sketch. *Artificial Intelligence, 104*(1-2), 211-264.

Sutherland, I. E. (1963). *Sketchpad: A man-machine graphical communication system.* Unpublished doctoral dissertation, Massachusetts Institute of Technology, Cambridge.

Wenyin, L., Qian, W., Xiao, R., & Jin, X. (2001). Smart sketchpad: An online graphics recognition system. *Proceedings of ICDAR'01* (pp. 1050-1054). IEEE Press.

Yasuda, H., Takahashi, K., & Matsumoto. T. (2000). A discrete HMM for online handwriting recognition. *International Journal of Pattern*

Recognition and Artificial Intelligence, 14(5), 675-688.

Yu, B. (2003). Recognition of freehand sketches using mean shift. *Proceedings of International Conference on Intelligent User Interfaces* (pp. 204-210). ACM Press.

Section III
Visual Languages for the Semantic Web

Chapter XIII
User Interface Formalization in Visual Data Mining

Tiziana Catarci
University of Rome "La Sapienza", Italy

Stephen Kimani
University of Rome "La Sapienza", Italy

Stefano Lodi
University of Bologna, Italy

ABSTRACT

Despite the existence of various data mining efforts that deal with user interface aspects, very few provide a formal specification of the syntax of the interface and the corresponding semantics. A formal specification facilitates the description of the system properties without being concerned about implementation details and enables the detection of fundamental design issues before they manifest themselves in the implementation. In visual data mining, a formal specification can enable users to decide which interaction/ operation to apply to get a desired result; help users to predict the results of their interactions/operations with the system; and enable the development of a general interaction model that designers/developers can use to understand the relationships between user interactions and their compositions. In this work, we describe an approach for formalizing the visual interface of a core data mining system, which has been employed in the development of a visual data mining system named VidaMine.

INTRODUCTION

In this day and age, data still present formidable challenges to effective and efficient discovery of knowledge. It should be acknowledged that a lot of research work has been and is being done with respect to knowledge discovery (KD). Much of

the work has concentrated on the development and the optimization of data mining algorithms using techniques from other fields such as artificial intelligence, statistics, and high performance computing (Fayyad, Piatetsky-Shapiro, & Smyth, 1996b). Besides various glaring issues (such as the need to have an overall framework that can support the entire discovery process, supporting human involvement in the entire process, etc), Mannila observes that relatively little research work has been published on the theoretical foundations of data mining (Mannila, 2000). On the same note, although there are many data mining efforts that deal with user interface issues, very few efforts provide or give a precise definition of the syntax of the user interface and the corresponding semantics.

Formal specifications enable the description of the system properties without having to be concerned about implementation details. The system properties are often specified using a precise notation. The specification can be used to construct models of the system. Formal methods make the analyst think abstractly about the problem at hand and the corresponding system thereby exposing fundamental design decisions well in advance before they manifest themselves in the implementation of the system. While it is true that the formal specification should not determine the programming aspects (e.g., algorithms and data structures), it should describe the behavior of the system in a precise or rigorous manner. Moreover, with a formal specification it is possible to transform a system model while preserving important properties of the model. In practice, a formal approach in which each and every design decision is proven to be a correct refinement step is rarely performed due to the high costs involved. However, substantial application of refinement does considerably improve the understanding of the design process. A formal specification of the visual interface of a data mining system can facilitate the gathering of information about the most useful usage patterns, which can then be used to guide the design and layout of user interfaces for visual data mining. Moreover, a formal specification of the visual interface can facilitate automated (and/or objective) evaluation of the usability of the user interface of a visual data mining system.

In information visualization, various specifications/models for characterizing visualization aspects have been proposed such as (Baudel, 2004; Chi & Riedl, 1998; Chuah & Roth, 1996). In fact, it does turn out that most of the efforts that are related to our work are mainly found in information visualization and exploration efforts rather than in core data mining. Some of the benefits of specifications/models such as the foregoing do apply to visual data mining as well, where visualization tends to be a key ingredient. Consequently and borrowing from Chi et al. (1998), a similar formal specification in visual data mining can: enable users to decide which user interaction/operation to apply in order to get a desired result; help users to predict the results of their interactions/operations with the visual data mining system; and enable the development of a general interaction model that designers/developers can use to classify and understand the relationships between user interactions and the composition of interactions. In fact, such a model could help eliminate errors caused by other imprecise or incorrect models. In this work, we describe an approach for formalizing the visual interface of a core data mining system. The proposed approach has been employed in the development of a visual data mining system named VidaMine.

BACKGROUND

Knowledge Discovery

Knowledge discovery (KD) may be defined as the process of identifying valid, novel, potentially useful, and ultimately understandable models and/or patterns in data (Fayyad, Piatetsky-Shapiro, Smyth, & Uthurusamy, 1996a; Fayyad et al., 1996b). On the whole, the knowledge discovery process may be defined as an interactive and iterative non-trivial process that entails various phases as seen in Figure 1.

Figure 1. The knowledge discovery process

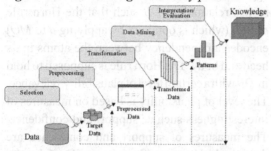

The KD phases include carrying out some initial planning (understanding the application domain, relevant prior knowledge, and goal/s of the user), data integration, selection of target data, data cleaning and pre-processing, data reduction and transformation, selection of suitable data mining techniques to support the discovery process, and evaluation, presentation, and interpretation of results. Through carrying out the phases, the KD process intends to find a subset of results that may be considered as new "knowledge" (Fayyad et al., 1996a, 1996b). KD is of interest to researchers in many research disciplines such as machine learning, pattern recognition, databases, statistics, artificial intelligence, expert systems, and information visualization.

Data Mining

Data mining is a core step in the knowledge discovery process that, under acceptable computational efficiency limitations, enumerates models and patterns over the data (Fayyad et al., 1996a, 1996b). It is worth recalling that the knowledge discovery process is as an interactive and iterative non-trivial process that entails: carrying out some initial planning (understanding the application domain, relevant prior knowledge, and goal/s of the user), data integration, selection of target data, data cleaning and pre-processing, data reduction and transformation, selection of suitable data mining techniques to support the discovery process, and evaluation, presentation,

and interpretation of results from which there exists a subset that may be considered as new "knowledge" (Fayyad et al., 1996a, 1996b). Data mining methods include clustering, classification, regression, characterization, dependency modeling change and deviation detection, and pattern-based similarity matching.

The primary goals of data mining are verification and discovery. The verification goal aims at validating some hypotheses based on specific user needs. The user generates a series of hypothetical patterns and relationships (assumptions or claims). The user then formulates and issues queries to the system (actually to the data itself) to verify (or disprove) the claims. The discovery goal involves finding "new" patterns or discovering new knowledge. Rather than verify hypothetical patterns, the goal here is to use the data itself to uncover or identify such patterns. Such methods of discovery may be initiated based on the guidance of a user to analyze a certain domain through a predetermined perspective or by automated learning. Discovery can be predictive or descriptive. Prediction entails "foretelling" unknown or future values of the same variables or other variables of interest whereas description involves getting an interpretation/understanding of the data. Classification, regression, and time series models are primarily useful for prediction. Clustering, association, and sequence discovery models are primarily useful for description of the behavior that is captured in the data.

Rules

Metaqueries

Metaquerying (Mitbander, Ong, Shen, & Zaniolo, 1996) is a data mining technique that is especially useful in mining relational and deductive databases. Metaqueries (or metapatterns) provide a generic description of a class of patterns that the user may want to discover from the underlying dataset. With metaqueries, it is possible to mine patterns that link several tables in the target dataset. Metaquery specification can be carried out manually (for instance by an expert user). Alternatively, the specification can be automated by exploiting the schema of the underlying dataset.

Let U be a countable domain of constants. A database DB is $(D, R_1, ..., R_n)$ where $D \subset U$ is finite, and each R_i is a relation of fixed arity $a(R_i)$ such that $R_i \subseteq D^{a(R_i)}$.

A metaquery is a second-order template of the form (Angiulli, Ben-Eliyahu-Zohary, Ianni, & Palopoli, 2000):

Equation 1

$$T \leftarrow L_1, ..., L_m$$

where T and L_i are literal schemes. Each literal scheme T or L_i is of the form $Q(Y_1, ..., Y_n)$ where Q is either a *predicate (second-order) variable* or a relation symbol, and each Y_j $(1 \leq j \leq n)$ is an ordinary (first-order) variable. If Q is a predicate variable, then $Q(Y_1, ..., Y_n)$ is called a *relation pattern* of arity n, otherwise it is called an *atom* of arity n. The left-hand side T is called the *consequent* or the *head* of the metaquery. The right-hand side $L_1, ..., L_m$ is called the *antecedent* or the *body* of the metaquery. Consider the relations *CustCent*, *ClustOut1* and *ServCent* with the following attributes: *CustCent.CustID, CustCent.CentID, ClustOut1.CustID, ClustOut1.ServID, ServCent. ServID* and *ServCent.CentID*. The following is an example of a corresponding metaquery:

Equation 2

CustCent(CustID, CentID) ← {ClustOut1 (Cus-tID, ServID), ServCent(ServID, CentID)}

Intuitively, given a database instance *DB*, answering a metaquery *MQ* on *DB* amounts to finding all substitutions σ of relation patterns

appearing in *MQ* by atoms having as predicate names relations in *DB* such that the Horn rule $\sigma(MQ)$ (which is obtained by applying σ to *MQ*) encodes a dependency between the atoms in its head and body. The Horn rule is supposed to hold in *DB* with a certain level of plausibility/relevance. The level of plausibility is based on measures of interestingness such as support and confidence. The measures of support and confidence are described in Section "Support and Confidence." Metaqueriers have been applied in the telecommunication industry, in a common-sense knowledge base, and in the chemical industry (Leng & Shen, 1996). Metaqueries have also been applied in analyzing time sequence data for semiconductor process control and fault-detection (Shen, Leng, & Chatterjee, 1995).

ASSOCIATION RULES

Association rules were introduced in Agrawal, Imielinski, and Swami (1993). Association rules represent a data mining technique that is used to discover implications between sets of items in the database.

Let $I = I_1, I_2, ..., I_m$ be a set of data items or literals and D a set (or database) of transactions, in which each transaction T is a set of items from I (i.e. $T \subseteq I$). Each transaction (T) is assigned some unique identifier, *TID*.

Let $X \subseteq I$ and $Y \subseteq I$. A transaction T is said to *contain X* if $X \subseteq T$. An association rule is an implication of the form:

Equation 3

$$Y \leftarrow X$$

where $X \cap Y = \emptyset$. The left-hand side, Y, is the consequent or the head of the association rule whereas the right-hand side, X, is the antecedent or the body of the association rule.

The problem of mining association rules is to generate all association rules with a degree of relevance/interestingness that is greater than a certain minimum (such as user-specified) value. The problem of discovering all association rules can be decomposed into two sub-problems (Agrawal et al., 1993):

1. Finding all sets of items (itemsets) that have support above the minimum support. The measure of support is described in Section "Support and Confidence." Itemsets with minimum support are called large itemsets and all others small itemsets.
2. Using the large itemsets to generate the desired rules. The desired rules are those whose confidence is greater or equal to the minimum confidence. The measure of confidence is described in Section "Support and Confidence."

Computing the solution to the first sub-problem naively is very expensive, and efficient techniques to reduce its complexity have been researched extensively (e.g., Agrawal et al., 1993; Agrawal & Srikant, 1994). Solving the second sub-problem is comparatively much easier, since it amounts to computing, for every frequent itemset, the confidence of the association rules obtained by picking one item as the consequent of the rule from the frequent itemset.

Association rules are valuable and readily applicable in many areas, including marketing, catalog design, business management, decision-making, add-on sales, mailing, customer segmentation, and store layout. For instance, a superstore dealing in clothing may find that customers who buy ties also tend to buy shirts at the same time (same "market basket"). Consequently, the following would be an association rule with fairly high measures of interestingness:

Equation 4

"shirt" ← *"tie"*

SUPPORT AND CONFIDENCE

The relevance of a rule may be determined by measures of interestingness. In general, measures of interestingness measure the overall value of a rule with respect to utility, novelty, certainty, and simplicity. In the mining of metaqueries and association rules, there are two common measures namely confidence and support.

Let D be the target dataset. The support of a rule in D is the fraction or percentage of tuples in D that contain the union of the antecedent and the consequent. For instance, the association rule in Equation 3 has support *supp* in D if *supp%* of transactions in D contain $X \cup Y$. The confidence of a rule in D is the fraction or percentage of tuples in D containing the antecedent, that also contain the consequent. For instance, the association rule in Equation 3 has confidence *conf* in D if *conf%* of transactions in D that contain X also contain Y. Intuitively, support indicates how frequently the items in the rule occur together in the transactions of the database, and therefore represents the utility of the rule, whereas confidence indicates the strength of the implication represented by the rule.

Clustering

Clustering is a process through which the target dataset is divided into groups of similar objects, such that the objects in a particular group are dissimilar to objects in other groups. Each such group is referred to as a cluster. Clustering is applicable in many arenas such as in analyzing astronomical data, in demographics, in insurance, urban planning, and Web applications.

Classification of Clustering Methods

Traditionally, clustering methods have been classified into a taxonomy having two broad groups: hierarchical and partitional (Jain, Murty, & Flynn, 1999).

Hierarchical Clustering

Hierarchical methods produce a sequence of nested partitions. A compact way to represent nested partitions is by a dendrogram, i.e., a tree having single objects as leaves, showing the hierarchical relationships among the clusters. It is therefore possible to explore the underlying dataset at various levels of granularity. Hierarchical methods are further subdivided into agglomerative and divisive (Jain & Dubes, 1988; Kaufman & Rousseeuw, 1990).

Agglomerative (bottom-up) clustering starts with singletons, i.e., with each cluster containing exactly one point. The clustering then recursively merges two or more most appropriate clusters. The process goes on until a stopping criterion is fulfilled (such as the number of clusters input by the user). Examples of agglomerative algorithms include CURE (clustering using representatives) (Guha, Rastogi, & Shim, 1998), and CHAMELEON (Karypis, Han, & Kumar, 1999).

Divisive (top-down) clustering starts with one single cluster of all objects, and recursively subdivides the most appropriate cluster. The process goes on until some criterion is met. The PDDP (principal direction divisive partitioning) (Boley, 1998) algorithm is an example of divisive algorithms. Also in this category of divisive clustering are approaches based on the k-means algorithm (Hartigan, 1975; Hartigan & Wong, 1979) such as the bisecting k-means algorithm (Steinbach, Karypis, & Kumar, 2000; Wang, Wiederhold, Firschein, & Wei, 1998).

Partitional Clustering

Partitional methods attempt to identify clusters directly either by iteratively relocating points between subsets, or by associating clusters with the areas that are densely populated with data. Consequently, partitional methods fall into two categories: relocation methods and density-based methods.

Relocation methods focus on how well points fit into their clusters. Such methods intend to ensure that the built clusters have the proper shapes. Relocation methods are further subdivided into probabilistic, k-medoids, and k-means. The probabilistic clustering model is based on the assumption that data has been independently drawn from a mixture model of several probability distributions. The results of probabilistic clustering are often easy to interpret. Probabilistic clustering algorithms include SNOB (Wallace & Dowe, 1994), AUTOCLASS (Cheeseman & Stutz, 1996), MCLUST (Fraley & Raftery, 1999). In clustering methods that adopt the k-medoids approach, a cluster is represented by one of its points. When the medoids are selected, clusters are considered to be subsets of points close to respective medoids. Algorithms based on the k-medoid approach include PAM (partitioning around medoids) and the algorithm CLARA (clustering large applications) (Kaufman et al, 1990), CLARANS (clustering large applications based upon randomized search) (Ng & Han, 1994). In k-means (Hartigan, 1975; Hartigan et al., 1979), a cluster is represented by its centroid, which is a componentwise arithmetic mean of points within a cluster. Although the k-means algorithm does not work well with a dataset that has categorical attributes, the algorithm is an appropriate choice for datasets with numerical attributes.

Density-based methods aim at identifying connected components/areas in the dataset that are dense with data. In this respect, a cluster therefore corresponds to a connected dense component. Density-based methods can be further divided into two main categories: density-based connectivity and density functions. Density-based connectivity approach reduces density to a training data point. Algorithms that use the approach include DBSCAN (Ester, Kriegel, Sander, & Xu, 1996), OPTICS (ordering points to identify the clustering structure) (Ankerst, Breunig, Kriegel, & Sander, 1999), DBCLASD (distribution based clustering of large spatial databases) (Xu, Ester, Kriegel, & Sander, 1998). Density functions approach reduces density to a point in the attribute space. DENCLUE (Hinneburg & Keim, 1998) is an example of an algorithm based on density functions. In fact, DENCLUE is a blend of density-based clustering and grid-based preprocessing.

Miscellaneous

There exist many other clustering techniques that do not fit well in one of the foregoing categories. For instance grid-based techniques, co-occurrence techniques, etc.

Grid-based techniques work indirectly with data by constructing summaries of data over the attribute space subsets. They segment the space and then aggregate appropriate segments. On the one hand, grid-based methods often use hierarchical agglomeration as a phase in their processing. Algorithms that use this approach include BANG (Schikuta & Erhart, 1997), STING (statistical information grid-based method) (Wang, Yang, & Muntz, 1997), and WaveCluster (Sheikholeslami, Chatterjee, & Zhang, 1998). On the other hand, the idea behind grid-based methods is exploited by other types of clustering algorithms (such as CLIQUE (clustering in quest) (Agrawal, Gehrke, Gunopulos, & Raghavan, 1998), MAFIA (merging of adaptive finite intervals) (Goil, Nagesh, & Choudhary, 1999; Nagesh, Goil, & Choudhary, 2001) as an intermediate phase in their processing.

Co-occurrence techniques are meant to handle special requirements when it comes to cluster-

ing categorical data. Algorithms ROCK (Guha, Rastogi, & Shim, 1999), SNN (shared nearest neighbors) (Ertöz, Steinbach, & Kumar, 2003), and CACTUS (clustering categorical data using summaries) (Ganti, Gehrke, & Ramakrishnan, 1999).

The Proposed Clustering Taxonomy and Framework

The foregoing traditional categorization of clustering methods into two broad groups—hierarchical and partitional (Jain et al., 1999)—is technically sound and relevant to various application domains. However, such categorization does not highlight similarities and differences between the various definitions of a cluster that are implicit in the methods. For instance, Ward's minimum-variance method (Ward, 1963) and the PAM method PAM (partitioning around medoids) (Kaufman et al., 1990) are similar. However, the former is hierarchical whereas the latter is partitional.

As an alternative to the foregoing traditional approach of categorizing clustering methods, clustering can be regarded as an optimization problem, in which the function to be optimized is a mathematical measure of homogeneity or separation (Hansen & Jaumard, 1997). Such a perspective enables one to categorize clustering methods according to a taxonomy of homogeneity or separation functions. Therefore, such a perspective provides recourse for categorizing clustering methods.

Moreover, such taxonomy expresses cluster definitions in an implicit manner. Such categorization is most likely more effective in capturing different behaviors in practice. It therefore provides a more natural avenue for the process of selecting a clustering algorithm, which is most suited to a particular application or domain.

In this research work, we therefore adopt this perspective and to the best of the research survey, this is actually the first effort that uses a uniform framework for selecting clustering algorithms.

More details about the same and how it has been applied in our design and implementation efforts will be discussed in Section "Formal Specification of the Visual Interface."

USER INTERFACE FORMALIZATION IN VISUAL DATA MINING

Introduction to VidaMine

VidaMine[1] is a visual data mining system that exploits various visual strategies thereby offering a consistent, uniform, flexible visual interface that allows or enables the user not only to process data, but also to steer, guide, or direct the entire process of data mining (DM) (Kimani, 2002). We adopted a user-centered user interface design, equipped with usability studies. As reported in Kimani, Catarci, & Santucci (2003), we employed various usability methods progressively in the development lifecycle. The visual interface of VidaMine offers visual interaction environments across different mining techniques and tasks. At present, the system offers visual environments for mining metaqueries, performing clustering, and mining association rules. Figure 2, which is for the metaquery environment, is an illustration that shows the overall outlook and feel of the visual interface.

Formal Specification of the Visual Interface

In developing a formal specification for the visual interface, we propose the provision of two specifications: an abstract formal specification that is defined for each of the mining methods currently supported by VidaMine and a corresponding operational specification that is defined and exploited for implementation purposes. The place of the two specifications with respect to the system can be seen in Figure 3.

Figure 2. An illustration of the overall outlook of the interface. Reproduced from Kimani, Lodi, Catarci, Santucci, and Sartori (2004) with the permission of Elsevier B. V.

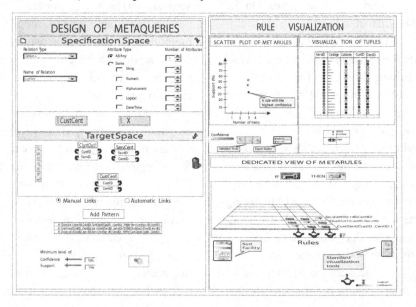

Figure 3. The place of the abstract and operational specifications in VidaMine

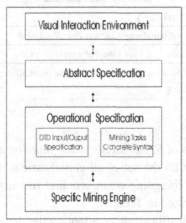

Abstract Formal Specification of the Visual Interface

In this area, we started by considering the definition an abstract syntax and a formal semantics for the visual interface. The abstract syntax is intended to provide a snapshot of the visual environment in terms of static and compact structures. This visual syntax reduces distance to mathematical objects (such as some specific data mining functions). We intend to describe an abstract formal specification of the visual interface for each of the visual interaction environments corresponding to each of the data mining methods currently supported by VidaMine *aka* metaqueries, clustering, and association rules.

In order to define a semantics for a supported data mining method, it is necessary to first define the visual language supported by the corresponding visual interaction environment (user interface). An *abstract syntax* for a visual language can be defined in terms of multi-graphs as follows (Erwig, 1998). Let α, β be sets representing label types. A *directed labeled multi-graph of type* (α, β) is a quintuple $G(V, E, l, v, \varepsilon)$ consisting of finite sets of nodes V and edges E where $l : E \rightarrow V \times V$ maps every edge to the pair of nodes it connects, $v: V \rightarrow$

α maps every node to its label, and $\varepsilon: E \rightarrow \beta$ maps every edge to its label. A *visual language of type* (α, β) is a set of directed labeled multi-graphs of type (α, β). Intuitively, visual controls are the nodes of the multi-graph, whereas the spatial relations between visual controls are the edges of the multi-graph. Since many of the visual controls appearing in the user interface are standard (such as check buttons, radio buttons, combo boxes, spin boxes, edit boxes, and sliders), their geometric properties will be ignored and simply use an abstract value to represent each visual control. Based on the foregoing notion of abstract syntax, we will define the visual language for each of the three visual interaction environments, and then describe the corresponding semantics.

Clustering

The clustering environment in VidaMine provides various visual widgets for specifying or selecting parameters characterizing a clustering task. The parameters include a fixed number of clusters or a measure (of homogeneity, separation, or density); attributes that will be directly involved in cluster analysis; and supplementary attributes (e.g., for labeling cases in the output). Specifying each such parameter may also involve more specific options/settings. The corresponding environment is seen in Figure 4.

In clustering, it is virtually impossible to apply uniformly a single technique to uncover the variety of structures present in multidimensional data sets (Jain et al., 1999). In most data mining applications, the user has to evaluate a set of techniques and then, based on experience and domain knowledge, select possibly more than one data mining technique to apply on the target dataset. A visual data mining system aimed at supporting the user during the entire mining process might be expected to provide support to the broadest range of clustering techniques possible. While it is true and commendable that VidaMine has an extensible framework, it is worth observing that

Figure 4. The clustering environment: Input. Reproduced from Kimani et al. (2004) with the permission of Elsevier B. V.

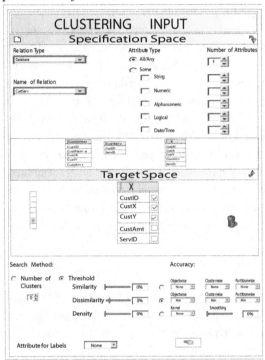

Table 1. Definitions of the main sets and functions

Main Sets and Functions
Dataset $S = \{O_i \mid i = 1, 2, \ldots, N\}$
Symmetric dissimilarity function $diss : S \times S \to R^+$
Classification C of S is a subset of a partition of S
Accuracy function m is a function on the set of all classifications of S to R^+

partition of S. Let an *accuracy function m* be a function on the set of all classifications of S to R^+. The foregoing main sets and functions are summarized in Table 1.

The justification for adopting the three clustering generalizations (or categorization) is highlighted in the descriptions of the generalizations. In the sequel are the descriptions of the clustering generalizations.

Clustering Based on Homogeneity or Separation

Traditionally, clustering methods have been classified into a taxonomy having two most general groups: hierarchical and partitional (Jain et al., 1999). Hierarchical methods produce a sequence of nested partitions, whereas partitional methods only produce one partition. Such distinction, although relevant for many application domains, does not highlight similarities and differences between the various definitions of a cluster that are implicit in the methods.

Alternatively, clustering can be regarded as an optimization problem, in which the function to be optimized is a mathematical measure of homogeneity or separation (Hansen et al., 1997). Homogeneity is a global measure of the similarity between points belonging to the same cluster, separation is a global measure of the dissimilarity between points belonging to different clusters. For instance, the maximum cluster diameter over all clusters is a measure of homogeneity, whereas the minimum distance between objects in different clusters is a measure of separation. In such a perspective, clustering methods are

adding one extension module for every clustering technique would render the system hard to utilize to anyone but the most informed practitioner, due to the variety of parameters and terminology. Therefore, in VidaMine, the approach is to provide and support three generalizations from the commonest types of clustering techniques. The three clustering generalizations are:

1. Clustering based on homogeneity.
2. Clustering based on separation.
3. Clustering based on density.

Here are some common terms that will be used while describing the foregoing clustering generalizations: Consider a dataset $S = \{O_i \mid i = 1, 2, \ldots, N\}$, and a symmetric dissimilarity function $diss : S \times S \to R^+$. It is worth noting that *classification C* of S refers to a subset of a classified according to a taxonomy of homogeneity or separation functions, which expresses implicitly cluster definitions. Such categorization is most likely more effective in capturing different behaviors in practice. It therefore provides a more natural avenue for the process of selecting a clustering algorithm, which is most suited to a particular application or domain.

It is worth noting that the actual implementation of the search for an optimal solution is left entirely unspecified. Therefore, a suitable uniform abstraction can be given for a broad class of methods, ranging from classical hierarchical methods, to approximation algorithms, and a consistent parametric user interface between the clustering engine and the graphical user interface can be designed.

Therefore and following up from Section "The Proposed Clustering Taxonomy and Framework," clustering can be formally defined as an optimization problem (Hansen et al., 1997) that takes one of the following forms:

Problem Π_1: Given an integer $K > 1$, find the partition P of S of size K such that $m(P)$ is optimal.

Problem Π_2: Given a threshold $\theta \in R^+$, find the partition P of S of minimum (maximum) cardinality such that $m(P) \leq \theta$ $(m(P) \geq \theta)$. In other words, sometimes $m(P)$ is optimal when large and at other times it is optimal when small.

In this research work, consideration is made only for functions m ranging over the union of two families H and S. The former family represents homogeneity functions and the latter represents separation functions. For a given data set S and dissimilarity *diss*, define H by:

Equation 5

$$H_o(P) = \{Q_{j \,:\, Oj \,\in\, C(O_i)} \; diss(O_i, O_j) \mid Q \in \{max, \Sigma, avg\}\}$$

Equation 6

$$H_c(P) = \{Q_{i:O_i \in C} \; h(O_i) \mid h \in H_o(P), Q \in \{min, max, \Sigma, avg\}\}$$

Equation 7

$$H = \{Q_c \in P \; h(C) \mid h \in H_c(P), Q \in \{max, \Sigma, avg\}\}$$

and S by

Equation 8

$$S_o(P) = \{Q_{j \,:\, Oj \,\notin\, C(O_i)} \; diss(O_i, O_j) \mid Q \in \{min, \Sigma, avg\}\}$$

Equation 9

$$S_c(P) = \{Q_{i \,:\, Oi \,\in\, C} \; s(Oi) \mid s \in S_o(P), Q \in \{min, max, \Sigma, avg\}\}$$

Equation 10

$$S = \{Q_{C \,\in\, P} \, s(C) \mid s \in S_c(P), Q \in \{min, max, \Sigma, avg\}\}$$

where $C(O_j)$ is the cluster containing object O_j.

Equation 5 defines a family of *pointwise* homogeneity functions, expressing that the homogeneity of object O_i can be defined as either the maximum (i.e., worst-case) dissimilarity to other objects in the same cluster, or the sum or average of all such dissimilarities. Likewise, Equation 6 defines a family of *clusterwise* homogeneity functions, expressing that the homogeneity of a cluster can be defined as the maximum, minimum, sum, or average of pointwise homogeneity of all its objects. Finally, Equation 7 defines a family of *partitionwise* homogeneity functions; the homogeneity of a partition can be defined as either the minimum (i.e., worst-case) clusterwise homogeneity over all its clusters, or the sum or average of all such homogeneities. Equation 8-Equation 10 provide analogous definitions for the separation function. Note, however, that the quantifier expressing worst-case pointwise or partitionwise separation is the minimum instead of the maximum, and that the quantifiers defining the separation of O_i extend to every object not in its cluster. Equation 5-Equation 10 induce a simple taxonomy with four levels into which functions m are classified. At the first level, homogeneity is separated from separation. Then, classes at lower levels in the taxonomy are separated according to the objectwise, clusterwise, or partitionwise quantifier.

Clustering Based on Density Estimation

In this section, *diss* is assumed to be a distance function and S to be a subset of a metric space $(X, diss)$. By elementary intuition, clusters can be regarded as regions of the object space where objects are located most frequently. Such simple analogy leads to approaches to clustering based on statistical techniques of *non-parametric density estimation* (Ankerst et al., 1999; Ester et al., 1996; Hinneburg et al., 1998; Schikuta, 1996; Silverman, 1986). The goal of density estimation is to fit to a data set S a density function of type $X \rightarrow R^+$. The implemented system supports clustering based on an important family of estimates, known as *kernel estimators* (Silverman, 1986). Functions in such family are defined modulo two parameters, the *window width h*, and the kernel function ψ. The value of the estimate at $x \in X$ is obtained by summing, over all data objects, a quantity modeling the influence of the object. Influence is computed by transforming distance, scaled by a factor $1/h$, using ψ:

Equation 11

$$\hat{\varphi}_{h,\psi}(x) = \frac{1}{Nh} \sum_{i=1}^{N} \psi\left(\frac{diss(O_i, x)}{h}\right)$$

Since the estimated density at x should be large when the number of data objects which are located near x is large, far data objects should have little influence. Thus ψ is usually a probability distribution function, which decreases monotonically with distance from zero. Commonly used kernel functions are the Gaussian kernel, $\frac{1}{\sqrt{2\pi}}\exp(-\frac{1}{2}x^2)$, and the Uniform kernel, $\frac{1}{2}$ (sign(x+1) – sign (x – 1).

The parameter h controls the amount of smoothing of the estimate, i.e. the sensitivity of the estimate to local structure in the data.

Once a density estimate is computed for a given kernel function, clusters can be defined in the following way. Let $A(O_i)$ be a neighborhood of O_i, and let $\alpha_{h,\psi}(O_i)$ be the data object (if it exists) nearest to O_i in $A(O_i)$ having density greater than O_i:

Equation 12

$$diss(\alpha_{h,\psi}(O_i), O_i) = \min_{O_j \in A(O_i)} \{diss(O_i, O_j) : \hat{\varphi}_{h,\psi}(O_j) > \hat{\varphi}_{h,\psi}(O_i)\}$$

The tree roots in the forest induced by α are objects whose neighborhood does not contain objects having greater density. Therefore, the tree roots may be considered as representatives of the modes of the density estimate, and the descendants of a root are part of a single cluster. Formally, α induces a forest whose connected components are clusters: If ~ is the equivalence relation generated by α, then the clustering P is the set of its equivalence classes:

Equation 13

$$P = \{C : (\exists x_o \in S)C = \{x \in S : x_o \sim x\}\}$$

The method can be further enhanced by introducing a notion of noise objects (Ester et al., 1996): Density at a noise object is less than a specified threshold parameter θ. Noise objects are not part of any cluster, thus the method generates a classification instead of a partition:

Equation 14

$$C = \{C : (\exists x_o \in S)C = \{x \in S : x_o \sim x \wedge \hat{\varphi}_{h,\psi}(x) \geq \theta\}\}$$

Problems Π_1 and Π_2 can be considered meaningful defining $m(C)$ as the minimum density of an object, over all objects in all clusters of C.

Abstract Syntax and Semantics of Clustering

The visual language is defined by the following:

Equation 15

$$\alpha = R^+ \cup \{min, max, \Sigma, avg\} \cup \{\pi_1, \pi_2\} \cup \{Homogeneity, Separation, Density\}$$

Equation 16

$$\beta = \phi$$

Equation 17

$V = \{ProbRad, NClusSpin, HomSlid, SepSlid, DenSlid, AccurRad, HomObjwQCom, HomCluswQCom, HomPartwQCom, SepObjwQCom, SepCluswQCom, SepPartwQCom, KernCom, SmoothSlid\}$

Finally, let for brevity $hpq = v(HomPartwQCom)$, $hcq = v(HomCluswQCom)$, $hoq = v(HomObjwQCom)$, $spq = v(SepPartwQCom)$, $scq = v(SepCluswQCom)$, $soq = v(SepObjwQCom)$. The classification C of the dataset S is defined by:

Equation 18

$C =$
$P_{hom}(S)$ if $v(accurRad) = Homogeneity$,
$P_{sep}(S)$ if $v(accurRad) = Separation$,
$C_{den}(S)$ if $v(accurRad) = Density$

and the following hold

Equation 19

$$|P_{hom}(S)| = v(NClusSpin)$$
$$|P_{sep}(S)| = v(NClusSpin)$$
$$|C_{den}(S)| = v(NClusSpin)$$

$if\ v(ProbRad) = \Pi_1$

Equation 20

$$m_{hom}(P_{hom}(S)) \leq v(HomSlid)$$
$$m_{sep}(P_{sep}(S)) \geq v(SepSlid)$$
$$m_{den}(C_{den}(S)) \geq v(DenSlid)$$

$if\ v(ProbRad) = \Pi_2$

Equation 21

$$\forall P : |P| = v(NClusSpin) \rightarrow m_{hom}(P) \geq m_{hom}(P_{hom}(S))$$
$$\forall P : |P| = v(NClusSpin) \rightarrow m_{sep}(P) \leq m_{sep}(P_{sep}(S))$$
$$\forall C : |C| = v(NClusSpin) \rightarrow m_{den}(C) \leq m_{den}(C_{den}(S))$$

$if\ v(ProbRad) = \Pi_1$

Equation 22

$$\forall P : m_{hom}(P) \leq v(HomSlid) \rightarrow |P| \geq |P_{hom}(S)|$$
$$\forall P : m_{sep}(P) \geq v(SepSlid) \rightarrow |P| \leq |P_{sep}(S)|$$
$$\forall C : m_{den}(C) \geq v(DenSlid) \rightarrow |C| \leq |C_{den}(S)|$$

$if\ v(ProbRad) = \Pi_2$

where

Equation 23

$$m_{hom}(P) = hpq_{\substack{C\in P}} \; hcq_{\substack{i:O_i\in C}} \; hoq_{\substack{j:O_j\notin C(O_i)}} \; diss(O_i,O_j)$$

Equation 24

$$m_{sep}(P) = spq_{\substack{C\in P}} \; scq_{\substack{i:O_i\in C}} \; soq_{\substack{j:O_j\notin C(O_i)}} \; diss(O_i,O_j)$$

Equation 25

$$m_{den}(C) = \min_{\substack{i:O_i\in \cup C}} \left\{ \hat{\phi}_{v(SmoothSlid),v(KernCom)}(O_i) \right\}$$

Metaqueries: In the metaquery environment of VidaMine, the user can specify patterns/relationships between or among data tables in an intuitive visual manner. The interface provides "hooks" and "chains" through which users can visually specify the relationships. By simply linking two attributes, the users indicate to the system that they are interested in metarules that have the two attributes related. Therefore, VidaMine enables users to visually construct metaqueries of interest. The left-hand side of Figure 2 shows the part of the metaquery environment that supports the foregoing specification.

Abstract Syntax and Semantics of Metaquerying

Here a simple abstract syntax for the metaquerying visual interaction environment is defined, together with its semantics, that is, the set of rules discovered by the system as instantiations of the metaqueries corresponding to the visual state of the interface when the "torch" icon is clicked (see Figure 2). For consistency with the visual interaction environments for the other mining techniques, the metaquerying visual environment represents metaqueries using relation schemes instead of literal schemes, that is, using named attributes to denote table columns, instead of the usual logical variables.

The metaqueries, which are added to the pool when the "add pattern" button is clicked, are all constructible metaqueries, given the named and unnamed relations (i.e., named "X") in the target space. Note that the links between handles which are represented in the target space do not have a counterpart in the "IF. . .THEN" expressions in the pool. In fact, such expressions only show the relation schemes, and not the literal schemes, that compose the head and body of a rule. Therefore, only the content of the target space defines multiple occurrences of variables in a rule. Since a user might click "add pattern" several times with different configurations of the target space, before clicking the "torch" button, for simplicity only one such configuration is considered in the semantics.

In the target space, rectangular frames enclosing attribute or relation names, and lines representing links connecting the frames (ignoring the handles) are nodes of the multi-graph. A node representing a frame is labeled by the relation name or attribute name it represents (i.e., the name appearing inside the frame). Attribute and relation frames may be adjacent, and attribute frames may be connected by lines. Therefore, for relations, attributes and links, two visual relations need to be represented: *adjacent* and *intersecting*. Adjacency will be assumed antisymmetric: A frame is adjacent to another if and only if the two frames share a horizontal edge, and the first frame is located above the second in the display.

In the following, let U and R be universes of attribute names and relation names, respectively, in the database. Let $V = \{X_1, \ldots, X_p, \ldots\}$ be a countably infinite set of variable symbols, and $W = \{P_1, \ldots, P_p, \ldots\}$ be a countably infinite set of predicate variable symbols. V and W are assumed disjoint and both disjoint from R. Let also $\zeta: V \rightarrow V$, $\lambda: V \rightarrow W$ be injective functions. In the sequel, ζ and λ will be used to construct the literals of the rules from the frames.

The language is defined by the following:

Equation 26

$\alpha = R^+ \cup U \cup R \cup \{"X"\}$

Equation 27

$\beta = \{adjacent, intersecting\}$

Equation 28

$V \supset \{ConfSlid, SuppSlid\}$

The set *IRS* of rules returned by metaquerying is defined as follows.

Equation 29

$IRS = \{r \in RS : conf(r) \geq v(ConfSlid) \wedge supp(r) \geq v(SuppSlid)\}$

Equation 30

$RS = \{r:(\exists\sigma)(\exists mq \in MQ)\ r = \sigma(mq)\}$

Equation 31

$MQ = \bigcup_{h \in L} \left\{ h \leftarrow \bigwedge_{b \in L-\{h\}} b \right\}$

Equation 32

$L = \{P(X_1, ..., X_m) : (\exists n)\ P = pred(n) \wedge isrel(n) \wedge (\forall i \leq m)(\exists n')X_i = \zeta(n') \wedge inschema\ (n', n)\}$

where

Equation 33

$isadj\ (n,n') \Leftrightarrow (\exists e)l(e) = (n,n') \wedge \varepsilon(e) = adjacent$

Equation 34

$intersects\ (n,n') \Leftrightarrow (\exists e)l(e) = (n,n') \wedge \varepsilon(e) = intersecting$

Equation 35

$pred(n) = \begin{cases} \lambda(n)\ if\ v(n) = "X", \\ v(n)\ otherwise \end{cases}$

Equation 36

$isconn = isadj^e$

Equation 37

$isrel(n) \Leftrightarrow (\nexists n')\ isadj\ (n', n)$

Equation 38

$islink\ (n) \Leftrightarrow (\exists n')(\exists n'')(\exists n_1)(\exists n_2)\ isrel(n_1) \wedge isrel\ (n_2) \wedge \neg\ isconn(n_1,n_2) \wedge isconn\ (n', n_1) \wedge isconn\ (n'', n_2)\ intersects\ (n, n') \wedge intersects\ (n, n'')$

Equation 39

$inschema\ (n,n') \Leftrightarrow (islink(n) \rightarrow (\exists n'')\ isconn\ (n',n'') \wedge intersects\ (n, n'') \wedge (\neg islink\ (n) \rightarrow isconn(n', n))$

and *isadj^e* is the equivalence relation generated by *isadj*, that is, the smallest equivalence relation containing *isadj*. Therefore, an equivalence class contains nodes corresponding to frames gathered in one relation scheme in the target space.

L is the set of literals defined by the visual configuration (Equation 32).

In each literal, *P* is the relation name enclosed in a frame, or a distinct predicate variable, if the name is "X" (Equation 35 and Equation 37). Every variable corresponds to an attribute frame that is connected to the relation frame, which names the literal, or corresponds to a link that intersects such an attribute frame (Equation 39). The set *MQ* of metaqueries is obtained from *L* by generating one metaquery for each literal, having the literal as head and the remaining literals as body. The rules *RS* instantiating *MQ* are defined by means of a class of substitutions. In Equation 30, σ is any substitution which, given a metaquery *mq*, consistently replaces exactly every predicate variable occurring in *mq* with a relation name. Finally, the rule set *IRS* is defined as the set of all rules in *RS* that satisfy the support and confidence specified by the sliders *SuppSlid* and *ConfSlid*.

Association Rules: Let Ω be a set of items, and *T* be a database of transactions, that is, a list of elements of 2^{Ω}. Association rules (Agrawal et al., 1993) are implications of the form:

Equation 40

$$I_{1}, ..., I_{m} \rightarrow I$$

where $\{I, I_{1}, \ldots, I_{m}\} \in \Omega$. If *r* is the foregoing association rule, and $t = \{I_{1}, \ldots, I_{m}\}$, then *r* has *confidence conf(r)* and *support supp(r)* in *T* defined by:

Figure 5. Association rule environment: Input. Reproduced from Kimani et al. (2004) with the permission of Elsevier B. V.

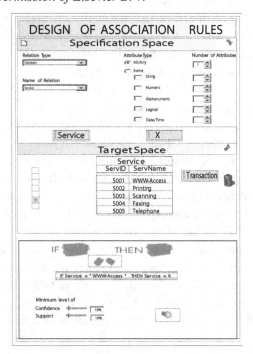

Equation 41

$$conf(r) = \frac{\left| \{t \in T : \{I\} \cup t' \subseteq t\} \right|}{\left| \{t \in T : t' \subseteq t\} \right|}$$

Equation 42

$$supp(r) = \frac{\left| \{t \in T : \{I\} \cup t' \subseteq t\} \right|}{|T|}$$

In the association rule environment of Vida-Mine, there is the provision of "market baskets." As seen in Figure 5, the association rule environment offers two baskets, the IF basket and the THEN basket. The IF basket represents items in the antecedent part of an association rule and the THEN basket represents items in the consequent part of the rule. Users may "drag and drop" items from the target dataset into the relevant baskets. When through with the visual construction of a particular association rule, the users may empty both baskets into a pool of association rules that are of interest to them, and may go ahead and construct another rule.

Abstract Syntax and Semantics of Association Rules

The VidaMine system's support for association rules permits the specification of *syntactic constraints* (Agrawal et al., 1993), that is, listing items, which must appear in the antecedent or the consequent. Such items are dragged from the target space to the "IF" or "THEN" basket, and later combined to form the rule and put into a "pool" (of rules). The reader may refer to the association rule visual environment in Figure 5, and where the "pool" of rules is formed below the baskets.

It is assumed that the abstract graph contains one "item" node for every item occurring in the "IF". . . "THEN" rule, labeled with the item's name.

Assuming also nodes representing confidence and support (see Section "Abstract Syntax and

Semantics of Metaquerying"), the set of association rules returned by the system is:

Equation 43

$$IAR = \{r \in AR : conf(r) \geq v(ConfSlid) \wedge supp(r) \geq v(SuppSlid)\}$$

Equation 44

$$AR = \{I_1, ..., I_m \rightarrow I : V_{THEN} = \{n\} \rightarrow I = v(n) \wedge (\forall n \in V_{IF})(\exists i \leq m)I_i = v(n)\}$$

where V_{IF} and V_{THEN} are the sets of "item" nodes in the rule's "IF" and "THEN" part, respectively.

Operational Specification of the Visual Interface

As part of implementation, our research effort also considers the provision of an operational specification. This specification entails defining a concrete syntax of mining tasks and an XML-based communication protocol. The concrete syntax of mining tasks is a high-level syntax of each of the tasks proposed in our task analysis and usability tests (Kimani et al., 2003). This syntax describes the click-streams that are allowed to occur during the user's interaction with the interface. The syntax reduces distance to the specification of procedural objects. The XML-based protocol serves as a two-way link for exchanging information between any applications that deal with mining aspects. It is interesting to note that the protocol idea can be exploited not only to import and incorporate new components into the system framework, but also to export the system's components to external systems.

We start by describing the syntax of mining tasks. We then use the clustering subtask to demonstrate how the communication protocol has been defined.

Figure 6. Mining task

> MiningTask → ClusteringTask | MQTask | ARTask
> Clustering Task → ClusteringInputTask "PerformClustering"
>   ClusteringOutputObservingInteracting
> MQTask → MQInputTask "PerformMQ" RuleOutputObservingInteracting
>
> ARTask →ARInputTask "PerformAR" RuleOutputObervingInteracting

Concrete Syntax of Tasks

Specifying a concrete, high-level syntax of mining tasks can serve at least three purposes. First, it highlights the most useful usage patterns, which guided the interface's layout and design. Second, it permits an objective evaluation of the results of usability tests. Finally, it provides a design specification, which can be refined to yield the complete parsing structure of the interface at the level of information passed to and returned by the mining engines. The abstraction level will be such that terminal symbols represent interactions that can be regarded as elementary in the current state of technology (e.g., clicking buttons, setting a slider's position, selecting an item in a combo box, setting the value of a spin box, etc.). The syntax will be defined using standard grammar notation, where terminal symbols are enclosed in double quotes. For brevity, only the first occurrence of every grammar rule, which is shared by two or more tasks has been written.

Figure 6 describes the mining task. Each subtask (clustering, metaquerying, association rules) comprises an input task, clicking the "torch" button to run the discovery algorithms, and an output task.

In the sequel we briefly describe the concrete syntax of clustering input and which can be seen in Figure 7. The task is divided into two consecutive parts, namely specifying target data and parameters, matching the upper and lower sections of the clustering interface. Specifying constraints means performing a sequence of manipulations of the controls in the top part of the specification phase, e.g., setting the number of attributes of a given type, choosing a relation, etc. (see Figure 4).

Figure 7. Syntax of clustering

```
ClusteringInputTask → ClusteringTargetDataSubTask
                      ClusteringParametersSubTask
ClusteringTargetDataSubTask→
        SpecifyConstraints AssignAttributes
        "ForwardingTargetRelation" |
        SpecifyConstraints AssignAttributes
        "ForwardingTargetRelation"
        ClusteringTargetDataSubTask
SpecifyConstraints → "SpecifyConstraint" |
            "SpecifyConstraint" SpecifyConstraints
AssignAttributes → "AssignAttribute"|
            "AssignAttribute" AssignAttributes
ClusteringParametersSubTask → Specify Parameter |
            Specify Parameter
            ClusteringParameterSubTask
SpecifyParameter → SelectAccuracyMeasure | "SelectCaseLabel" |
            "SelectMiningAttribute"
SelectAccuracyMeasure → SelectHomogeneity | SelectSeparation |
            SelectDensity
SelectHomogeneity → "PushHomogeneityRadioButton"
            SetHomogeneity
SelectSeparation → "PushSeparationRadioButton"SetSeparation
SelectDensity → "PushDensityRadioButton" SetDensity
SetHomogeneity → SetHomogQuantif | SelectHomFixedNum |
            SelectHomogThreshold |
            SetSeparQuantif SetSeparation |
            SelectSepFixedNum SetSeparation |
            SelectHomogThreshold SetHomogeneity
SetSeparation → SetSeparQuantif | SelectSepFixedNum |
            SelectSeparThreshold |
            SetSeparQuantif SetSeparation |
            SelectSepFixedNum SetSeparation |
            SelectSeparThreshold SetSeparation
SetDensity → "SetKernel" | SetSmoothing | SelectDenFixedNum
            | SelectensThreshold | "SetKernel" SetDensity |
            SetSmoothing SetDensity | SelectDenFixedNum SetDensity |
            SelectDensThreshold SetDensity
```

Assigning attributes corresponds to dragging and dropping attributes from the resource relations to the "X" relation, which is subsequently dragged into the target space. Selecting an accuracy measure leads to selecting either homogeneity, separation, or density, by pushing the respective radio buttons (see Figure 4). Subsequently (see Figure 7), the user may select quantifiers, or the kernel function and the amount of smoothing. Selecting the problem type gives access to setting the number of clusters or the threshold for the accuracy function.

An XML-Based Communication Protocol

The large amount of recently proposed mining techniques, and the need to easily select the most effective method for the multivariate data set at hand, calls for the design of extensible data mining systems. Exchanging XML documents allows for the addition of new mining engines

or new methods for existing engines as plug-ins. Such a protocol would serve as a two-way link for exchanging information between any applications that deal with mining aspects. It is interesting to realize that this idea can be exploited not only to import and incorporate new components into the system framework, but also to export the system's components to external systems. In the VidaMine system, communication between the GUI and the mining engines is established by means of XML document streams. The communication protocol is specified by XSchema for the selection of methods and passing parameters, and for passing output results to the GUI. Since PMML, the *predictive model markup language* (DMG), has already set an XML standard for representing mining results in the data mining community, our specification is based on, and in some parts extends, PMML.

Example of XML-Based Protocol for Clustering Task

Assuming the target dataset in Figure 4, the generated XML document for method selection is listed in Figure 8. Each attribute listed in the "X" relation matches exactly one corresponding "DataField" in "DataDictionary" and one "MiningField" in "MiningSchema." In this research work, "active" corresponds to the "checked" state whereas "supplementary" corresponds to the "unchecked" state of the attribute's check box in the target space. It is worth observing that "checked" attributes are those that have been chosen to directly participate in cluster analysis. "Unchecked" attributes are those that will not directly participate in cluster analysis but will be included in the results for other purposes (such as for labeling). "AccuracyFunction" allows for selecting one of "Homogeneity," "Separation," and "Density." Within each, the problem's form can be selected by "FixedNumberOfClusters" (problem Π_1 of Section "Clustering Based on Homogeneity or Separation") or "FixedThreshold" (problem Π_2 of Section "Clustering Based on Homogeneity or

Separation"). The "Density" element includes the type of density estimate used. Currently, the only allowed type is "Kernel." Other types can be easily added as alternatives to "Kernel." Figure 10 is a view of the XSchema, which specifies documents containing the selection of a method and parameters for clustering. It is worth noting that the XSchema in Figure 10 does not allow for specifying the algorithm used to solve the problem. Thus, for given problem definition and form of the accuracy function, the clustering engine may implement an exact or approximate algorithm. In the current example, the selection of min for objectwise, clusterwise, and partitionwise quantifiers is equivalent to the *worst-case split* clustering problem (Hansen et al., 1997). For such problem, an exact solution can be obtained applying the well-known single link hierarchical algorithm to the target dataset, halting at the topmost partition whose worst-case split value is less than the value of the split function (0.03 in the example). The document containing clustering result/output, whose view can be seen in Figure 9, represents the solution to the clustering problem in Figure 4. For brevity, the XSchema for the clustering output is omitted, which is an extension of the corresponding XSchema in PMML. The "Cluster" elements describe five clusters named 1, 2, 3, 4, and 5. Each "Cluster" element contains the clusterwise accuracy function that was selected for clustering, and its value at the cluster. (The split of the cluster, in the example.) The engine may include any other accuracy function in the result document, specifying its value at the cluster, and the clusterwise parameters defining it. (In the example, the engine returned the cluster's "Homogeneity" computed as its diameter.) Finally, "ClusteringArray" assigns each object in the target dataset to its cluster.

Mapping Between Clustering Task and XML Documents

It is important to define a mapping between the clustering and the XML-based communication

protocol that was just defined. When the formal specification of the interface is defined through an abstract syntax and semantics, a mapping between user actions and XML documents describing the actual parameters passed to the engines can be defined by means of a recursive function. In the VidaMine system, a mapping function M is defined by recursion on the grammar rules describing the clustering task of Figure 7 to XML documents conforming to the XSchema of Figure 10.

Although for brevity we have omitted its formalization, it should however be noted that M basically is a mapping satisfying a list of equalities of the forms:

Figure 8. An example XML document for clustering input

Figure 9. An example XML document for clustering output

Figure 10. XSchema for specifying clustering input

Equation 45

$$(term)^M - xml(value_1, ..., value_p)$$

Equation 46

$$(nt_1, nt_2)^M = (EXT(nt_1)^M(nt_2)^M)$$

In Equation 45, *term* is a terminal symbol, *xml* is a function constructing an appropriate XML element corresponding to *term, value* is the value of a visual control. In Equation 46, *nt* is a nonterminal symbol representing the manipulation of a visual control, *EXT* is a function that extends the XML tree in its second parameter using the elements in the first parameter. *EXT* also provides

appropriate defaults when the user's actions do not affect some of the controls.

Comparison with Data Mining Systems

SQL Server 2005, developed by Microsoft Corporation, includes several data mining tools: association rules, clustering, decision trees, linear and logistic regression, naive Bayes, and neural networks. Its interface is based on menus, panes, and tabs. Three panes present the user with an explorer tree of folders related to analytical tasks (data sources, multidimensional cubes, mining structures, etc.), a properties visualization tool, and tabs for model settings, visualization, evaluation, and for prediction. Parameters for the mining algorithms can be accessed from pop-up menus. The visualization tab supports all mining models with several types of visualization each, with some active graphical elements. Visual features, such as color, can be associated to quantitative features of models, such as relative frequency. Overall, the interface provides a powerful set of functionalities, but requires training to be used, in particular for structuring the mining task. No formal model is known for the graphical part of the interface.

Clementine was originally developed by Integral Solutions Ltd (ISL) and later distributed as a part of the SPSS system, after SPSS purchased ISL on December 31, 1998. Clementine supports many prominent mining techniques including clustering, association rules, sequential patterns, factor analysis, and neural networks. Users construct a map (a "stream") of their data mining project/model by selecting icons called "nodes" that represent steps in the data mining process. Clementine allows users to adjust/refine their "streams" and rerun the system on the refined model. Although its visual interface illustrates the flow of control and data, allowing the user to better understand and follow the mining process, no formal syntax and semantics of the interface as a whole is reported.

Enterprise Miner, developed by the SAS Institute, provides a large number of data mining algorithms, including decision trees, neural networks, regression, radial basis functions, self-organizing maps, and clustering. Enterprise Miner has an interesting visual interface, allowing for powerful support of data transformation, visualization tools for multidimensional analysis, and extensive parameter options for the algorithms. The user drags and drops icons from a task bar into a work area where the icons can be connected. Each connection represents the flow of information from one node to its successor, and

each icon type represents a type of processing (for example, imputation of missing data, declaration of variable types and target variables, regression, etc.) on the data from the predecessor node. Mining algorithms are viewed as a special type of processing. The visual metaphor of nodes and edges is intuitive; however, most of the complex settings of each node type cannot be operated upon graphically, but must be accessed through a type-specific tab-based interface. The effort does not report any formal description of the graphical interface available.

Intelligent Miner is a data mining software developed by IBM, supporting association rules, clustering, classification trees, and neural networks. There are two versions of Intelligent Miner, Intelligent Miner for Data and Intelligent Miner Modeling/Scoring/Visualization. Intelligent Miner for Data is a standalone program. Its interface is based on explorer-like panes and drop-down menus introducing the various data mining techniques, parameter settings, and visualization windows. Intelligent Miner Modeling/Scoring/Visualization is a suite of three distinct tools, for the extraction mining models, for prediction, and the visualization of models. The product is integrated into the IBM DB2 Universal Database, which provides all metadata support, for example by storing the mining models and their visualizations. The interface of the modeling component is textual and consists of stored procedures for data mining algorithms callable from DB2's command windows, whereas the visualization component has a graphical display with active elements and extensive sorting options. The interface of Intelligent Miner for Data has no known formal specification, as the interface of Intelligent Miner Modeling/Scoring/Visualization. (For the latter, a formal specification is relevant only to the visualization component, which is however, the same supplied with the standalone version.)

OPEN ISSUES AND FUTURE TRENDS

Despite the remarkable efforts and developments that have taken place in the field of visual data mining, the field still faces quite a number of challenges and also exhibits various issues as highlighted in the sequel:

- Data mining methods normally can handle or cope with large amounts of data. Since visual data mining systems integrate data mining techniques and visualization techniques, visualization techniques have to face up to the challenge regarding large quantities of data. Bearing in mind the limitations of the display space, visualizations have to seek effective mappings so as to display all relevant data. Moreover, visualizations have to use efficient techniques to load relevant data in the main memory.

- Most of the existing visual data mining systems have not been subjected to thorough usability evaluations. In order to determine the usefulness of visual data mining systems, the importance of usability studies cannot be overemphasized. On the same note, it is worth acknowledging that the lack of precise theory or a universal/standard framework for developing visual data mining systems may not only be partly responsible for the current situation, whereby each visual data mining system seems to be an ad-hoc development, but may also to some extent at least complicate the usability issue as far as the visual data mining field is concerned. In that respect, Grinstein, Hoffman, Laskowski, and Pickett's work on benchmarking and evaluation in visualizations for data mining (Grinstein et al., 2002) might be instructive.

- It is a challenging activity to find the methods, techniques, and corresponding tools that are suitable for a specific visual mining task, or a particular type of data. One way forward would be to evaluate the disparate frameworks to determine their effectiveness and to verify their applicability in different application domains (Simoff, 2001).

- Visual support often necessitates the usage of graphical elements. The user is expected to interact with these graphics in real time. When the user interacts with the visualization, there should be some kind of immediate feedback from the graphic. Bearing in mind the fact that the memory demands on the computer that are posed by graphics, may decrease the performance of the system. Consequently, changes introduced on the visual environment may not immediately reflect the changes occurring in the information realm in real time and vice versa. It is no trivial task determining a good balance between interactivity and performance.

In terms of our future research activities, we are planning to support the output of descriptive statistics, principally using pie charts and histograms, in the clustering environment. It also is worth noting that a set of the system features are under an engineering process in order to become part of the commercial suite D2I, distributed by *Inspiring Software* (http://www.cisat-group.com). The D2I (Data to Information) environment will serve as a generic suite for handling the data to be subjected to mining. Even as we consider the foregoing research directions, it is also important to be aware of various trends in data mining. One of the current trends is distributed data mining, where the target data is located in different places and/or in different physical locations. There is also a growing interest in ubiquitous data mining, where the user may carry out data mining from ubiquitous devices (such as PDAs, cellular phones, etc) rather than from the conventional computer. Another area that has been drawing a lot of attention is hypertext and hypermedia data mining. Efforts in the foregoing type of data mining would normally entail one or more of the following three aspects: content mining, structure mining, and usage mining. It is also interesting to observe a growing interest in audio data mining, where audio signals are used to represent data trends/patterns or other specific data features.

CONCLUSION

Despite the existence of many data mining efforts that deal with user interface aspects, there is relatively little work going on or that has been published on the specification of the syntax of such user interface and the corresponding semantics. In general, a formal specification can bring about many benefits such as facilitating the description of the system properties without having to be concerned about implementation details and enabling the detection of fundamental design issues before they manifest themselves in the implementation. In visual data mining, where visualization is often a key ingredient, a formal specification can be rewarding. For instance, it can enable users to decide which interaction/operation to apply to get a particular output, it can help users to predict the output of their interactions/operations with the system, and it can facilitate the development of interaction models. In this work, we have proposed and described an approach for specifying such a formal specification in the process of developing a visual data mining system, VidaMine.

REFERENCES

Agrawal, R., & Srikant, R. (1994). Fast algorithms for mining association rules in large databases. In J. B. Bocca, M. Jarke, & C. Zaniolo (Ed.), *Proceedings of the 20th International Conference on Very Large Data Bases (VLDB)*. San Francisco: Morgan Kaufmann Publishers.

Agrawal, R., Gehrke, J., Gunopulos, D., & Raghavan, P. (1998). Automatic subspace clustering of high dimensional data for data mining applications. In A. Tiwary & M. Franklin, (Ed.), *ACM SIGMOD Record, Proceedings of the 1998 ACM SIGMOD International Conference on Management of Data, 27*(2), 94-105. New York: ACM Press.

Agrawal, R., Imielinski, T., & Swami, A. N. (1993). Mining association rules between sets of items in large databases. In P. Buneman & S. Jajodia (Ed.), *ACM SIGMOD Record, Proceedings of the 1993 ACM SIGMOD International Conference on Management of Data, 22*(2), 207-216. New York: ACM Press.

Angiulli, F., Ben-Eliyahu-Zohary, R., Ianni, G., & Palopoli, L. (2000). Computational properties of metaquerying problems. *Proceedings of the 19th ACM SIGMOD-SIGACT-SIGART Symposium on Principles of Database Systems* (pp. 237-244). New York: ACM Press.

Ankerst, M., Breunig, M., Kriegel, H. P., & Sander, J. (1999). OPTICS: Ordering points to identify the clustering structure. *ACM SIGMOD Record, Proceedings of the 1999 ACM SIGMOD International Conference on Management of Data, 28*(2), 49-60. New York: ACM Press.

Baudel, T. (2004). Browsing through an information visualization design space. *Extended Abstracts on Human factors in Computing Systems (CHI04)* (pp. 765-766). New York: ACM Press.

Boley, D. L. (1998). Principal direction divisive partitioning. *Data Mining and Knowledge Discovery, 2*(4), 325-344.

Cheeseman, P., & Stutz, J. (1996). Bayesian classification (AutoClass): Theory and results. In U. Fayyad, G. Piatetsky-Shapiro, P. Smyth, & R. Uthurusamy (Ed.), *Advances in knowledge discovery and data mining.* Menlo Park, CA: AAAI Press/MIT Press.

Chi, E., & Riedl, J. (1998). An operator interaction framework for visualization systems. In G. Wills & J. Dill (Ed.), *Proceedings IEEE Symposium on Information Visualization (InfoVis 98)* (pp. 63-70). Los Alamitos, CA: IEEE Computer Society.

Chuah, M. C., & Roth, S. F. (1996). On the semantics of interactive visualizations. *Proceedings IEEE Symposium on Information Visualization 96* (pp. 29-36). Los Alamitos, CA: IEEE Computer Society.

DMG (The Data Mining Group). *PMML: Predictive Model Markup Language.* Retrieved March 15, 2006, from http://www.dmg.org

Ertöz, L., Steinbach, M., & Kumar, V. (2003). Finding clusters of different sizes, shapes, and densities in noisy, high dimensional data. In D. Barbará & C. Kamath (Ed.), *Proceedings of the 3rd SIAM International Conference on Data Mining.* SIAM. Retrieved from http://www.siam.org/meetings/sdm03/index.htm

Erwig, M. (1998). Abstract syntax and semantics of visual languages. *Journal of Visual Languages and Computing, 9*(5), 461-483.

Ester, M., Kriegel, H. P., Sander, J., & Xu, X. (1996). A density-based algorithm for discovering clusters in large spatial databases with noise. In E. Simoudis, J. Han, & U. M. Fayyad (Ed.), *Proceedings of the 2nd International Conference on Knowledge Discovery and Data Mining (KDD-96)* (pp. 226-231). AAAI Press.

Fayyad, U., Piatetsky-Shapiro, G., & Smyth, P. (1996b). Knowledge discovery and data mining: Towards a unifying framework. In E. Simoudis, J. Han, & U. M. Fayyad (Ed.), *Proceedings of the 2nd International Conference on Knowledge Discovery and Data Mining.* AAAI Press.

Fayyad, U., Piatetsky-Shapiro, G., Smyth, P., & Uthurusamy, R. (Ed.). (1996a). *Advances in knowledge discovery and data mining.* Menlo Park, CA: AAAI Press/MIT Press.

Fraley, C., & Raftery, A. (1999). *MCLUST: Software for model-based cluster and discriminant analysis* (Tech. Rep. 342). Department of Statistics, University of Washington.

Ganti, V., Gehrke, J., & Ramakrishnan, R. (1999). CACTUS: Clustering categorical data using summaries. In S. Chaudhuri & D. Madigan (Ed.), *Proceedings of the 5th ACM SIGKDD International Conference on Knowledge Discovery and Data Mining* (pp. 73-83). New York: ACM Press.

Goil, S., Nagesh, H., & Choudhary, A. (1999). *MAFIA: Efficient and scalable subspace clustering for very large data sets* (Tech. Rep. CPDC-TR-9906-010). Evanston, IL: Northwestern University.

Grinstein, G. G., Hoffman, P. E., Laskowski, S. J., & Pickett, R. M. (2002). Benchmark development for the evaluation of visualization for data mining. In U. Fayyad, G. G. Grinstein, & A. Wierse (Eds.), *Information visualization in data mining and knowledge discovery.* San Francisco: Morgan Kaufmann Publishers.

Guha, S., Rastogi, R., & Shim, K. (1999). ROCK: A robust clustering algorithm for categorical attributes. In M. Kitsuregawa, L. Maciaszek, M. Papazoglou, & C. Pu (Ed.), *Proceedings of the 15th International Conference on Data Engineering (ICDE)* (pp. 512-521). Los Alamitos, CA: IEEE Computer Society.

Guha, S., Rastogi, R., & Shim, K. (1998). CURE: An efficient clustering algorithm for large databases. *Proceedings of the 1998 ACM SIGMOD International Conference on Management of Data* (pp. 73-84). New York: ACM Press.

Hansen, P., & Jaumard, B. (1997). Cluster analysis and mathematical programming. *Mathematical Programming 79*, 191-215.

Hartigan, J. A. (1975). *Clustering algorithms.* New York: John Wiley & Sons.

Hartigan, J. A., & Wong, M. (1979). Algorithm AS136: A k-means clustering algorithm. *Applied Statistics 28*, 100-108.

Hinneburg, A., & Keim, D. A. (1998). An efficient approach to clustering in large multimedia databases with noise. In R. Agrawal, P. Stolorz, & G. Piatetsky-Shapiro (Ed.), *Proceedings of the 4th International Conference on Knowledge Discovery and Data Mining* (pp. 58-65). Menlo Park, CA: AAAI Press.

Jain, A. K., & Dubes, R. C. (1988). *Algorithms for clustering data*. Englewood Cliffs, NJ: Prentice-Hall.

Jain, A. K., Murty, M. N., & Flynn, P. J. (1999). Data clustering: A review. *ACM Computing Surveys, 31*(3), 264-323.

Karypis, G., Han, E. H., & Kumar, V. (1999). Chameleon: Hierarchical clustering using dynamic modeling. *IEEE Computer, 32*(8), 68-75.

Kaufman, L., & Rousseeuw, P. J. (1990). *Finding groups in data-introduction to cluster analysis*. New York: John Wiley & Sons.

Kimani, S. (2002). An effective visual data mining environment. *Doctoral Posters at the International Conference on Very Large Data Bases (VLDB)*.

Kimani, S., Catarci, T., & Santucci, G. (2003). Visual data mining: An experience with the users. In C. Stephanidis (Ed.), *Proceedings of HCI International: Universal Access in HCI: Inclusive Design in the Information Society*. Lawrence Erlbaum Associates.

Kimani, S., Lodi, S., Catarci, T., Santucci, G., & Sartori, C. (2004). VidaMine: A visual data mining environment. *Journal of Visual Languages and Computing, 15*(1), 37-67.

Leng, B., & Shen, W. M. (1996). A metapattern-based automated discovery loop for integrated data mining: Unsupervised learning of relational patterns. *IEEE Transactions on Knowledge and Data Engineering, 8*(6), 898-910.

Mannila, H. (2000). Theoretical frameworks for data mining. *SIGKDD Explorations Newsletter, 1*(2), 30-32. New York: ACM Press.

Mitbander, B., Ong, K., Shen, W. M., & Zaniolo, C. (1996). Metaqueries for data mining. In U. Fayyad, G. Piatetsky-Shapiro, P. Smyth, & R. Uthurusamy (Eds.), *Advances in knowledge discovery and data mining* (Ch. 15). Menlo Park, CA: AAAI Press/MIT Press.

Nagesh, H., Goil, S., & Choudhary, A. (2001). Adaptive grids for clustering massive data sets. *Proceedings of the SIAM International Conference on Data Mining*. Retrieved from http://www.siam.org/meetings/sdm01/pdf/sdm01_07.pdf

Ng, R. T., & Han, J. (1994). Efficient and effective clustering methods for spatial data mining. In J. B. Bocca, M. Jarke, & C. Zaniolo (Ed.), *Proceedings of the International Conference on Very Large Data Bases (VLDB)* (pp. 144-155). San Francisco: Morgan Kaufmann Publishers.

Schikuta, E. (1996). Grid-clustering: An efficient hierarchical clustering method for very large data sets. *Proceedings of the 13th International Conference on Pattern Recognition* (pp. 101-105). Los Alamitos, CA: IEEE Computer Society.

Schikuta, E., & Erhart, M. (1997). The BANG-clustering system: Grid-based data analysis. In X. Liu, P. Cohen, & M. Berthold (Ed.), *Advances in intelligent data analysis. Reasoning about Data: Second International Symposium, IDA-97, Proceedings, Lecture Notes in Computer Science, 1280.* Berlin; Heidelberg, Germany: Springer.

Sheikholeslami, G., Chatterjee, S., & Zhang, A. (1998). WaveCluster: A multi-resolution clustering approach for very large spatial databases. In A. Gupta, O. Shmueli, & J. Widom (Ed.), *Proceedings of the International Conference on Very*

Large Data Bases (VLDB) (pp. 428-439). Morgan Kaufmann Publishers.

Shen, W. M., Leng, B., & Chatterjee, A. (1995). *Applying the metapattern mechanism to time sequence analysis* (Tech. Rep. ISI/RR-95-398). USC Information Sciences Institute.

Silverman, B. W. (1986). *Density estimation for statistics and data analysis.* London: Chapman and Hall.

Simoff, S. J. (2001). Towards the development of environments for designing visualisation support for visual data mining. In S. J. Simoff, M. Noirhomme-Fraiture, & M. H. Böhlen (Eds.), *Proceedings of the ECML/PKDD Workshop on Visual Data Mining.* Retrieved from http://www-staff.it.uts.edu.au/~simeon/vdm_pkdd2001/

Steinbach, M., Karypis, G., & Kumar, V. (2000). A comparison of document clustering techniques. *Proceedings of the ACM SIGKDD Workshop on Text Mining.* Retrieved from http://www.cs.cmu.edu/~dunja/KDDpapers/

Wallace, C. S., & Dowe, D. L. (1994). Intrinsic classification by MML: The snob program. In C. Zhang, J. Debenham, & D. Lukose (Ed.), *Proceedings of the Australian Joint Conference on Artificial Intelligence* (pp. 37-44). World Scientific.

Wang, J. Z., Wiederhold, G., Firschein, O., & Wei, S. X. (1998). Content-based image indexing and searching using Daubechies' wavelets. *International Journal on Digital Libraries (IJODL), 1*(4), 311-328.

Wang, W., Yang, J., & Muntz, R. R. (1997). STING: A statistical information grid approach to spatial data mining. In M. Jarke, M. J. Carey, K. R. Dittrich, F. H. Lochovsky, P. Loucopoulos, & M. A. Jeusfeld (Ed.), *Proceedings of the 23rd International Conference on Very Large Data Bases (VLDB)* (pp. 186-195). San Francisco: Morgan Kaufmann Publishers.

Ward, J. H. (1963). Hierarchical grouping to optimize an objective function. *Journal of the American Statistical Association 58*(301), 236-244.

Xu, X., Ester, M., Kriegel, H. P., & Sander, J. (1998). A distribution-based clustering algorithm for mining in large spatial databases. *Proceedings of the International Conference on Data Engineering (ICDE)* (pp. 324-331). Los Alamitos, CA: IEEE Computer Society.

ENDNOTE

[1] VidaMine is an acronym for VIsual DAta MINing Environment.

Chapter XIV
Visual Development of Defeasible Logic Rules for the Semantic Web

Efstratios Kontopoulos
Aristotle University of Thessaloniki, Greece

Nick Bassiliades
Aristotle University of Thessaloniki, Greece

Grigoris Antoniou
Institute of Computer Science F.O.R.T.H., Greece

ABSTRACT

This chapter is concerned with the visualization of defeasible logic rules in the semantic Web domain. Logic plays an important role in the development of the semantic Web and defeasible reasoning seems to be a very suitable tool. However, it is too complex for an end-user who often needs graphical trace and explanation mechanisms for the derived conclusions. Directed graphs can assist in this affair by offering the notion of direction that appears to be extremely applicable for the representation of rule attacks and superiorities in defeasible reasoning. Their applicability, however, is balanced by the fact that it is difficult to associate data of a variety of types with the nodes and the connections between the nodes in the graph. In this chapter, we try to utilize digraphs in the graphical representation of defeasible rules by exploiting the expressiveness and comprehensibility they offer, but also trying to leverage their major disadvantages. Finally, the chapter briefly presents a tool that implements this representation methodology.

INTRODUCTION

The Semantic Web (Berners-Lee, Hendler, & Lassila, 2001) constitutes an effort to improve the current Web by adding metadata to Web pages and, thus, making the content of the Web accessible not only to humans as it is today, but to machines as well. The development of the Semantic Web proceeds in layers; each layer being on top of other layers. This architecture imposes the substantial evolvement of the previous layers before a specific layer can commence being developed. The upcoming efforts toward the development of the Semantic Web will be targeted at the logic and proof layers, which are believed to possess a key role in the eventual acceptance of the Semantic Web on behalf of the users.

Defeasible reasoning (Nute, 1987), a member of the non-monotonic reasoning family, represents a simple rule-based approach to reasoning not only with incomplete or changing but also with conflicting information. Defeasible reasoning can represent facts, rules and priorities, and conflicts among rules. Nevertheless, defeasible logic is based on solid mathematical formulations and is, thus, not fully comprehensible by end users who often need graphical trace and explanation mechanisms for the derived conclusions.

Directed graphs can assist in confronting this drawback. They are a powerful and flexible tool of information visualization, offering a convenient and comprehensible way of representing relationships between entities (Diestel, 2000). Their applicability, however, is balanced by the fact that it is difficult to associate data of a variety of types with the nodes and the connections between the nodes in the graph.

In this chapter, we try to utilize digraphs in the graphical representation of defeasible logic rules by exploiting the expressiveness and comprehensibility they offer, but also trying to leverage their major disadvantage by proposing a representation approach that features two distinct node types for rules and atomic formulas and four distinct connection types for each rule type in defeasible logic and for superiority relationships. The chapter also briefly presents a tool that implements this representation methodology.

The rest of the chapter is organized as follows: The next section presents the vision of the Semantic Web, reviewing the most important technologies for its development. Then the importance of logic in the Semantic Web domain is analyzed. The following two sections describe the key aspects of our approach, namely, the application of directed graphs in the representation of logic rules in general and of defeasible logic rules in particular. Then a system that implements this

approach, called VDR-DEVICE, is presented and the chapter ends with the conclusions and poses future research directions.

THE VISION OF THE SEMANTIC WEB

One of the most inspired definitions for the Semantic Web (SW) was given by the inventor of the current Web—and visionary of the SW—Tim Berners-Lee (2001), according to which *"the Semantic Web is an extension of the current Web, in which information is given well-defined meaning, better enabling computers and people to work in cooperation"* (p. 35). In other words, the Semantic Web is not a mere substitute but an important enhancement to the World Wide Web (WWW) and its primary goal is to make the content of the Web accessible not only to humans as it is today, but to machines as well. This way, software agents, for example, will have the capability to *"understand"* the meaning of the information available on the WWW and this will result in a better level of cooperation among agents as well as between agents and human users. The basic principle behind the SW initiative lies in organizing and inter-relating the available information so that it can be utilized more efficiently by a variety of distinct Web applications.

However, the SW has not yet acquired a concrete substance and still remains a vision to a great extend. Nevertheless, a significant number of researchers and companies are working toward this direction, developing technologies that will assist the SW initiative as well as applications specifically suitable for the SW environment. These efforts are also backed by generous funding from *DARPA* (Defense Advanced Research Projects Agency of the United States) and from the *EU* (European Union).

The development of the SW is based on technologies that form a hierarchy of layers; each layer is based on the layers and technologies below it. Every layer has to be widely approved by users, companies and trust groups, before the next technologies in the hierarchy can be further developed. One of the basic layers in this hierarchy deals with content representation, where *XML* (*extensible markup language*) is the dominant standard, allowing the representation of structured documents, using custom-defined vocabulary. However, although XML offers the capability of representing virtually any kind of information, it does not offer any further knowledge regarding the semantic meaning of the information described. Thus, it is not clear to the user what the nesting of tags, for example, means for each application. The need to represent meaning along with the content led to *RDF* (*resource description framework*), a statement model with XML syntax. RDF allows representation of data and *meta-data*, a term that refers to "data about data." Meta-data are important for the SW initiative since they also capture the meaning (or *semantics*) of the data. RDF does not supply, however, tools for structuring and organizing the data. The need for meta-data vocabularies was imperative and this was the role played by the *ontologies*. Ontology languages take representation a step further by allowing expression of high-level semantics. *RDF schema* and *OWL* (*Web ontology language*) are the main ontology-building tools in the SW. Furthermore, the *logic* layer, one of the top layers in the SW technologies hierarchy, is based on the previous layers and offers the representational capabilities of predicate logic as well as the possibility of correlating the data. The logic layer is accompanied by the *proof* layer that describes the inference mechanisms, which utilize the knowledge produced from the former layer. Finally, the *trust* layer offers trust mechanisms that allow the verification of the data exchanged in the SW.

The last layers of the SW hierarchy (i.e., the logic, proof, and trust layers) are not yet fully developed and, naturally, there exist almost no tools that perform such functionalities. Future attempts in the development of the SW will, nevertheless, be directed toward the evolution of these layers as well with a number of logic-based systems emerging to bridge the gap.

RDF: A Common Information Exchange Model in the Semantic Web

An important step toward augmenting the available information in the Web with semantic content involves the design and implementation of a common information exchange model that will be used by all the SW applications. The solution, as stated in the previous section as well, lies in the *resource description framework* (*RDF*), a generic model "*for supporting resource description, or metadata (data about data), for the Web*" (Powers, 2003, p. 20).

The basic idea behind RDF is a model comprised of a number of *statements* and connections between these statements. Thus, the statement is the basic building block of an RDF document and it consists of a resource-property-value triple:

- *Resources* are the objects we want to refer to or talk about. Every resource is uniquely identified by a uniform resource identifier (URI).
- *Properties* are used to describe relations between resources, but, in practice, they are a special kind of resources, being also identified by URIs.
- *Values* can either be resources or simply literals (strings).

An example of a statement that better illustrates the previous is:

The apartment `http://www.example.org/carlo_ex.rdf#ap01` *has a property* `http://www.example.org/carlo.rdf#pets` *whose value is "yes."*

Figure 1. Graph representation of an RDF statement

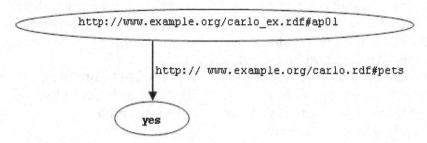

Figure 2. XML-based syntax of an RDF statement

```
<rdf:RDF
 xmlns:rdf="http://www.w3.org/1999/02/22-rdf-syntax-ns#"
 xmlns:carlo="http://www.example.org/carlo.rdf"
 xmlns:carlo_ex ="http://www.example.org/carlo_ex.rdf">
      <rdf:Description rdf:about="&carlo_ex;ap01">
      <carlo:pets> yes </carlo:pets>
      </rdf:Description>
<rdf:RDF>
```

This statement declares that pets are indeed allowed in a specific apartment with codename "ap01." Here "http://www.example.org/ carlo _ ex.rdf#ap01" is the resource (or *subject*), "http://http://www.example. org/carlo.rdf#pets" is the property (or *predicate*), and the value (or *object*) is "yes."

There are three ways to represent an RDF statement: The first one is also the simplest one and has to do with creating a subject-predicate-object triple from the statement. Thus, the previous statement would be represented by the triple: (http://www.example.org/carlo _ ex.rdf#ap01,http://www.example. org/carlo.rdf#pets, "yes"). Note here that the resource and property are uniquely identified by a URL (which is a kind of URI) and the value is simply a string (but could as well be a URI).

The second way of representing an RDF statement is graph-based, as can be seen in Figure 1. A directed graph is utilized with arcs directed from the resource to the value. Such graphs are more

often encountered with the name of *semantic nets* in the AI domain.

The third representation possibility, however, is probably the most important one, since it is based on XML and, thus, allows the re-usability of the various tools available for XML processing (*syntactic interoperability*). The XML fragment that expresses the above statement can be seen in Figure 2.

Every statement is represented by an rdf: Description element. The subject of the statement is being referred to in the rdf:about attribute, the predicate is used as a tag and the object is the content of the tag.

Finally, the important aspect of *namespaces* should be pointed out. Namespaces define a mechanism for resolving name clashes if more than one document is imported. According to namespaces, the names (actually URIs) of the elements in an XML/RDF document are defined using a combination of a base URL, using a prefix that is declared with the command: xmlns:

prefix="URL," and a local name that is unique within the base URL. This way the same local name can be used freely in many RDF/RDF Schema documents, since the existence of the prefix disambiguates things. The namespaces defined in an element can be used by that element and its descendants.

In RDF, external namespaces do not only offer disambiguation, as in XML, but they are also expected to be RDF documents defining resources, which are then used in the importing RDF document. This mechanism allows the reuse of resources by other people who may decide to insert additional features into these resources. The result is the emergence of large, distributed collections of knowledge.

In Figure 2, three namespaces are declared: rdf, carlo, and carlo_ex. The first one contains the necessary vocabulary for RDF statements, while the other two include vocabulary specific for the domain of apartment renting.

Ontologies in the Semantic Web

The main knowledge representation tool in the SW is the *ontology*, which is simply a structured representational formalism that shares a lot of common elements with the *frames* and the *semantic nets*. The ontologies are mainly used in defining common vocabularies used in the exchange of information among SW applications.

However, ontologies also offer interoperability among the available information and the various WWW applications like search engines, Web portals, intelligent agents, and Web services. For example, the major disadvantages of today's search engines are their low precision and high recall. If there existed the possibility to perform a search based on an ontology, then the input keywords would be associated with the intended meaning. The search results would not only be more accurate, but a number of results that would contain conceptual synonyms of the inserted keyword would also be returned.

The main ontology languages in the SW today, as mentioned earlier in this chapter, are RDF Schema and OWL. The former is a vocabulary description language for describing properties and classes of RDF resources, while the latter is a richer vocabulary description language that can also describe relations between classes, cardinality, equality etc. The system VDR-DEVICE, described later in this chapter, utilizes the RDF schema technology.

RDF Schema

Although RDF lets the user describe resources using a custom vocabulary, apparently the level of expressivity it offers is not sufficient. RDF Schema, RDF's *"semantic extension,"* equips users with mechanisms for describing domains and correlations among resources, namely the allowed vocabulary for resources and properties (i.e., resources types and property types).

Though there are significant differences between RDF schema and conventional object-oriented programming languages, the former is also based on classes and properties, similarly to the latter. Therefore, *classes* are sets of resources, while members of classes are called *instances*. On the other hand, users can also describe specific *properties* of class instances; properties impose a relation between subject and object resources and are characterized by their *domain* (the class of resources that may appear as subjects in a triple with the property as predicate); and *range* (the class of resources that may appear as values in a triple with the property as predicate).

Instances are associated to the corresponding classes by declaring their type using a statement like: carlo_ex:ap01 rdf:type carlo: apartment. This statement declares that instance ap01 belongs to the class apartment. However, this is indirectly extracted by the fact that rdf:type has rdfs:Class as range, which immediately results in apartment being a class, according to the descriptional nature of the RDF semantics.

Figure 3. Classes and properties in RDF schema

```
<rdfs:Class rdf:ID="house"/>

<rdfs:Class rdf:ID="apartment">
        <rdfs:subClassOf rdf:resource="#house"/>
</rdfs:Class>

<rdf:Property rdf:ID="size">
        <rdfs:domain rdf:resource="#house"/>
        <rdfs:range rdf:resource="&xsd;integer"/>
</rdf:Property>

<rdf:Property rdf:ID="gardenSize">
        <rdfs:subPropertyOf rdf:resource="#size"/>
</rdf:Property>
```

Naturally, the notions of hierarchy and inheritance are also applied in RDF Schema. However, they are not only applied in the case of classes but in the case of properties as well. Thus, there can be defined *super-* and *subclasses* of a specific class, but there can also exist *super-* and *subproperties* of a specific property.

An example of all the above can be seen in Fig. 3. Two classes are described: class "house" and its subclass "apartment." Similarly, two properties are also described: "size," which has class "house" as its domain and "gardenSize," which is a subproperty of "size" and, thus, inherits from the latter the domain and range. Note here that, contrary to object-oriented programming, properties are not part of a class description, but are "*globally*" visible in an RDF schema ontology. This not only imposes a different programming approach, but also offers flexibility in extending ontologies.

LOGIC IN THE SEMANTIC WEB

As stated in a previous section, the *logic* and *proof* layers of the Semantic Web architecture constitute the current targets of most development efforts toward the SW vision. Contrary to ontologies, logic can capture more complex semantic relationships between metadata and allow processing of the latter in various useful ways.

Rules usually arise naturally from the business logic of applications. Uses of logic and/or rules include the following:

- Logic (predicate logic) can capture some of the ontological knowledge expressed in description logics (e.g., OWL). For example, the fact that class lecturer is a subclass of faculty is represented as:

  lecturer(X) → faculty(X).

- Rules can be used to convert data and/or metadata documents from one format or type to another.
- Logic can be used to check the consistency of an ontology or a metadata document using the declarations and constraints of the ontology.
- Rules can be used to formulate questions in order to retrieve resources that belong to specified metadata terms or even to identify-classify unknown terms.
- Finally, intelligent Semantic Web agents can use logical rules for decision support and action selection among a number of possibilities, in a non-deterministic way.

One of the most important advantages of using logic is that it is easy for an agent to provide *explanations* to the user about its conclusions.

Simply, the explanations are formed by the sequence of inference steps that the agent's inference mechanism has followed. Explanations are very important for the adoption of Semantic Web, because they increase the confidence of users to agents' decisions.

Non-Monotonic and Defeasible Reasoning

Non-monotonic reasoning (Antoniou, 1997) constitutes an approach that allows reasoning with *incomplete* or *changing* information. More specifically, it provides mechanisms for retracting conclusions that, in the presence of new information, turn out to be wrong and for deriving new, alternative conclusions instead. Contrary to standard reasoning, which simply deals with universal statements, non-monotonic reasoning offers a significantly higher level of expressiveness.

Furthermore, *defeasible reasoning* (Nute, 1987), a member of the non-monotonic reasoning family, represents a simple rule-based approach to reasoning not only with incomplete or changing but also with *conflicting* information. When compared to mainstream non-monotonic reasoning, the main advantages of defeasible reasoning are enhanced representational capabilities coupled with low computational complexity.

Defeasible reasoning can represent facts, rules, priorities, and conflicts among rules. Such conflicts arise, among others, from rules with exceptions, which are a natural representation for policies and business rules (Antoniou, Billington, & Maher, 1999) and priority information is often available to resolve conflicts among rules.

Conflicting Rules in the Semantic Web

Conflicting rules might be applied in the Semantic Web in the following cases:

Reasoning with Incomplete Information

In Antoniou (2002), a scenario is described where business rules have to deal with incomplete information: in the absence of certain information, some assumptions have to be made that lead to conclusions not supported by typical predicate logic. In many applications on the Web, such assumptions must be made because other players may not be able (e.g., due to communication problems) or willing (e.g., because of privacy or security concerns) to provide information. This is the classical case for the use of non-monotonic knowledge representation and reasoning (Marek & Trusczynski, 1993).

Rules with Exceptions

As mentioned earlier, rules with exceptions are a natural way of representation for policies and business rules. And priority information is often implicitly or explicitly available to resolve conflicts among rules. Potential applications include security policies (Ashri, Payne, Marvin, Surridge, & Taylor, 2004), business rules (Antoniou & Arief, 2002), e-contracting (Governatori, 2005), brokering (Antoniou, Skylogiannis, Bikakis, & Bassiliades, 2005), and agent negotiations (Governatori, Dumas, Hofstede, & Oaks, 2001).

Default Inheritance in Ontologies

Default inheritance is a well-known feature of certain knowledge representation formalisms. Thus, it may play a role in ontology languages, which currently do not support this feature. In Grosof and Poon (2003), some ideas are presented for possible uses of default inheritance in ontologies. A natural way of representing default inheritance is rules with exceptions plus priority information. Thus, non-monotonic rule systems can be utilized in ontology languages.

Ontology Merging

When ontologies from different authors and/or sources are merged, contradictions arise naturally. Predicate logic based formalisms, including all current Semantic Web languages, cannot cope with inconsistencies. If rule-based ontology languages are used (e.g., DLP (Grosof, Gandhe, & Finin, 2002)) and if rules are interpreted as defeasible (that is, they may be prevented from being applied even if they can fire) then we arrive at non-monotonic rule systems. A skeptical approach, as adopted by defeasible reasoning, is sensible because it does not allow for contradictory conclusions to be drawn. Moreover, priorities may be used to resolve some conflicts among rules, based on knowledge about the reliability of sources or on user input). Thus, non-monotonic rule systems can support ontology integration.

LOGIC AND VISUAL REPRESENTATION

There exists a variety of systems that implement rule representation and visualization, although, to the best of our knowledge, no system exists yet that can visually represent defeasible logic rules.

WIN-PROLOG

WIN-PROLOG (Steel, 2005) is a well-known Prolog compiler system developed by LPA (Logic Programming Associates). It offers rule representation in the form of graphs as well as rule execution tracing (Figure 4). The graphs produced, however, feature an elementary level of detail, and therefore, do not assist significantly in the visualization of the rule bases developed.

Figure 4. Explanation trace produced by WIN-PROLOG

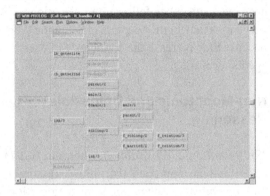

VisiRule

LPA is also the developer of *VisiRule*, a graphical tool for delivering business rule and decision support applications (Shalfield, 2005). All the user has to do is draw a flowchart that represents the decision logic and VisiRule will produce flex code from the flowchart and compile it. The system offers guidance during the construction process, constraining errors based on the semantic content of the emerging program. This reduces the potential for constructing invalid or meaningless links, improving productivity, and helping detect errors as early as possible within the design process (Figure 5).

Figure 5. Rule graph produced by VisiRule

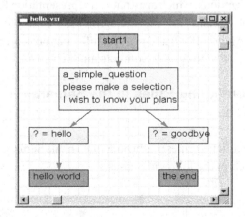

Figure 6. Screenshot of KEE illustrating the various tools of the system

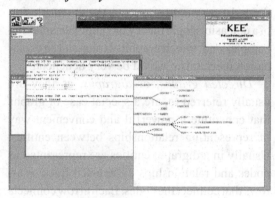

KEE

Certain knowledge-based system development tools also feature rule and execution graph drawing. An example is *KEE* (knowledge engineering environment) (Intellicorp, 1984) that offers several execution control mechanisms. The main features of the software include: (a) a knowledge base development tool, (b) utilities for the interface with the user, and (c) graph drawing tools for the knowledge base and execution. In this case, however, the visualizations offer little or no interaction with the user and simply offer an alternative view of the knowledge base (Figure 6).

Graphviz

Another example is *Graphviz*, an open-source graph visualization software with several main graph layout programs. Its applications are not limited to drawing rule graphs, but can also include other domains like software engineering, database, and Web design, networking and visual interfaces. As a general-purpose graph drawing utility, Graphviz can be applied in rule graph drawing since it offers variation in graph node types, but does not feature variety in the connection types in the graph and is, therefore, unsuitable for the representation of defeasible rules (Figure 7).

Figure 7. A simple graph produced with Graphviz

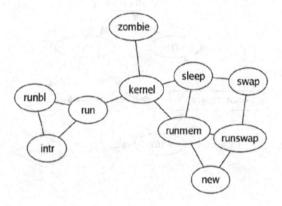

Spectacle

Another system that represents knowledge in a graphical context is *Spectacle*, one of Aidminis-trator's core products (Aidministrator is a software provider in the market of information and content management). As stated by Fluit, Sabou, and van Harmelen (2003), Spectacle *"facilitates the creation of information presentations that meet the needs of end users."* One of Spectacle's key components is the *cluster map*, used for visualizing ontological data. Actually, the cluster map is used to visualize RDFS-based *lightweight ontologies* that describe the domain through a set of classes and their hierarchical relationships

Figure 8. Screenshot of a Spectacle cluster map

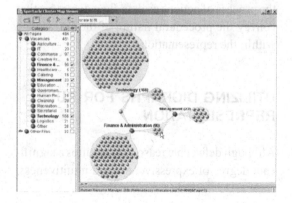

Figure 9. A simple program written in CPL

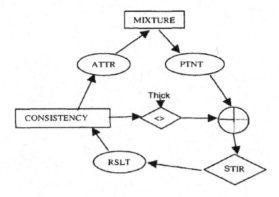

(Figure. 8). With Spectacle, users can efficiently perform analysis, search, and navigate, although the system's functionality is restricted to lightweight ontologies only.

CPL

CPL (conceptual programming language), introduced by Hartley and Pfeifer (2000), constitutes an effort to bridge the gap between knowledge representation (KR) and programming languages (PL). CPL is a visual language for expressing procedural knowledge explicitly as programs. The basic notion in CPL are *conceptual graphs* (CGs), which are connected multilabeled bipartite oriented graphs and can express declarative and/or procedural knowledge by defining object and action constructs (Figure 9). Particularly, the addition of visual language constructs (data-flow/flowchart) to conceptual programming allows the process of actions as data-flow diagrams that convey the procedural nature of the knowledge within the representation.

UTILIZING DIGRAPHS FOR RULE REPRESENTATION

Although defeasible reasoning features a significant degree of expressiveness and intuitiveness, it is based on a solid mathematical formulation, which, in many cases, may seem too complicated. So, end users might often consider the conclusion of a defeasible logic theory incomprehensible and complex and, thus, a graphical trace and an explanation mechanism would be very beneficial.

Directed graphs, or *digraphs*, as they are usually referred to, are a special case of graphs that constitute a powerful and convenient way of representing relationships between entities. Usually in a digraph, entities are represented as nodes and relationships as directed lines or arrows that connect the nodes. Each arrow connects only two entities at a time and there can be no two (or more) arrows that connect the same pair of nodes. The orientation of the arrows follows the flow of information in the digraph. Diestel (2000) offers a thorough mathematical definition of directed graphs as well as details on graph theory in general.

Digraphs offer a number of advantages to information visualization with the most important of them being:

- **Comprehensibility:** The information that a digraph contains can be easily and accurately understood by humans.
- **Expressiveness:** Although the appearance and structure of a digraph may seem simplistic, its topology bears non-trivial information.

There are, however, a couple of major disadvantages, not only of digraphs but of graphs in general, as described in Clarke (1982):

- It is difficult to associate data of a variety of types with the nodes and with the connections between the nodes in the graph.
- As the size and complexity of the graph grows, it becomes more and more difficult to search and modify the graph

Figure 10. Digraph displaying a simple rule base

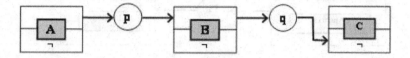

Figure 11. Digraph featuring a conjunction

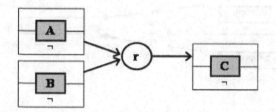

On the other hand, in the case of graphical representation of logic rules, digraphs seem to be extremely appropriate since they offer a number of extra advantages:

- Explanation of derived conclusions: The series of inference steps in the graph can be easily detected and retraced.
- Proof visualization and validation: By going backwards from the conclusion to the triggering conditions, one can validate the truth of the inference result.
- Especially in the case of defeasible logic rules, the notion of direction can assist in graphical representations of rule attacks, superiorities, etc.

Therefore, in this chapter we attempt to exploit the expressiveness and comprehensibility of directed graphs, as well as their suitability for rule representation, but also try to leverage the two aforementioned disadvantages by adopting a new, "enhanced" digraph approach. This visualization scheme was implemented as part of the VDR-DEVICE system, which is a visual integrated development environment for developing and using defeasible logic rule bases on top

of RDF ontologies (Bassiliades, Kontopoulos, & Antoniou, 2005) for the Semantic Web and is also briefly presented in this work.

Deductive Rules and Digraphs

In an attempt to leverage the first and most important disadvantage of graphs (inability to use a variety of distinct entity types), the digraphs in our approach will contain two kinds of nodes similarly to the methodology followed by Jantzen (1989). The two node types will be:

- Literals represented by rectangles, which we call "*literal boxes.*"
- Rules represented by circles.

Thus, according to this principle, the following rule base:

```
p: if A then B
q: if B then ¬C
```

can be represented by the directed graph in Figure 10.

Each literal box consists of two adjacent "*atomic formula boxes*" with the upper one rep-

Figure 12. Digraph displaying a strict rule

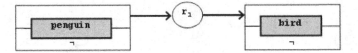

Figure 13. Digraph displaying two defeasible rules

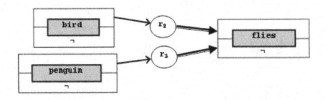

Figure 14. Digraph displaying a defeater

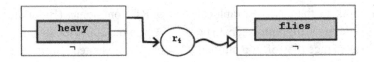

Figure 15. Digraph displaying a superiority relationship

resenting a positive atomic formula and the lower one representing a negated atomic formula. This way, the atomic formulas are depicted together clearly and separately maintaining their independence.

In the case of a rule body that consists of a conjunction of literals the representation is not profoundly affected, as illustrated in Figure 11.

```
r: if ¬A and B then C
```

As can be observed, digraphs, *"enhanced"* with the addition of distinct node types, offer a significant level of expressiveness in representing rules. The next step is to use directed graphs

in the representation of defeasible logic rules, which are more demanding in representational capabilities.

Defeasible Logics and Digraphs

A *defeasible theory D* (i.e., a knowledge base or a program in defeasible logic) consists of three basic ingredients: a set of facts (F), a set of rules (R), and a superiority relationship (>). Therefore, D can be represented by the triple (F, R, >).

In defeasible logic, there are three distinct types of rules: strict rules, defeasible rules, and defeaters. In our approach, each one of the three rule types will be mapped to one of three distinct

Figure 16. Digraph formed by the rules r1, r2, r3 and r4

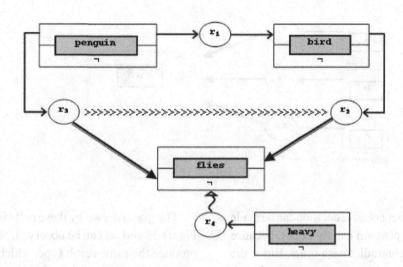

connection types (i.e., arrows) so that rules of different types can be represented clearly and distinctively.

The first rule type in defeasible reasoning is *strict rules*, which are denoted by $A \rightarrow p$ and are interpreted in the typical sense: whenever the premises are indisputable, then so is the conclusion. An example of a strict rule is: "*Penguins are birds*," which would become:

$$r_1: \text{penguin}(X) \rightarrow \text{bird}(X).$$

Figure 12 displays the corresponding digraph.

Notice that in the rule graph we only represent the predicate and not the literal (i.e., predicate plus all the arguments) because we are mainly interested in making clear to the reader the interrelationships between the concepts (through the rules) and not the complete details of the defeasible theory. The full representation schema is thoroughly described in a later section with the definition of *class boxes, class patterns,* and *slot patterns.*

Contrary to strict rules, *defeasible rules* can be defeated by contrary evidence and are denoted by $A \Rightarrow p$. Examples of defeasible rules are:

$$r_2: \text{bird}(X) \Rightarrow \text{flies}(X),$$

which reads as: "*Birds typically fly*" and

$$r_3: \text{penguin}(X) \Rightarrow \neg\text{flies}(X),$$

namely: "*Penguins typically do not fly.*" Rules r_2 and r_3 would be mapped to the directed graph in Figure 13.

Defeaters, denoted by $A \sim> p$, are rules that do not actively support conclusions, but can only prevent some of them. In other words, they are used to defeat some defeasible conclusions by producing evidence to the contrary. An example of such a defeater is:

$$r_4: \text{heavy}(X) \sim> \neg\text{flies}(X),$$

which reads as: "*Heavy things cannot fly.*" This defeater can defeat the (defeasible) rule r_2 mentioned above and it can be represented by the digraph in Figure 14.

Finally, the *superiority relationship* among the rule set R is an acyclic relation > on R, that is, the transitive closure of > is irreflexive. Superiority relationships are used, in order to resolve conflicts among rules. For example, given the defeasible

285

Figure 17. Representation of conflicting literals as a digraph

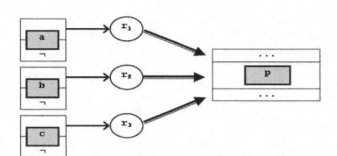

rules r_2 and r_3, no conclusive decision can be made about whether a penguin can fly or not, because rules r_2 and r_3 contradict each other. But if the superiority relationship $r_3 > r_2$ is introduced, then r_3 overrides r_2 and we can indeed conclude that the penguin cannot fly. In this case rule r_3 is called *superior* to r_2 and r_2 *inferior* to r_3. In the case of superiority relationships a fourth connection type is introduced. Thus, the aforementioned superiority relationship would be represented by Figure 15.

The set of rules mentioned in this section, namely rules r_1, r_2, r_3 and r_4, form a bigger directed rule graph, which is depicted in Figure 16.

Finally, another important type of conflicting evidence in defeasible reasoning is the notion of *conflicting literals*. In some applications (e.g., making an offer in a price negotiation setting), literals are often considered to be conflicting and at most one of a certain set should be derived. Consider the following three rules, which all produce the same literal type as a conclusion, and the constraint that requires at most one of the literals to be true:

```
r₁: a(X) ⇒ p(X)
r₂: b(X) ⇒ p(X)
r₃: c(X) ⇒ p(X)
p(X),p(Y),X≠Y -> ⊥
```

The graph drawn by these rules is depicted in Figure 17 and, as can be observed, all three rules produce the same result type, which is included in a *single literal truth box*. Of course, superiority relationships could still determine the priorities among the rules.

THE VDR-DEVICE SYSTEM

VDR-DEVICE is a visual, integrated development environment for developing and using defeasible logic rule bases on top of RDF ontologies (Bassiliades et al., 2005). It consists of two primary components:

1. *DR-DEVICE*, the reasoning system that performs the RDF processing and inference and produces the results, and
2. *DRREd* (defeasible reasoning rule editor), the rule editor, which serves both as a rule authoring tool and as a graphical shell for the core reasoning system.

Although the two subsystems utilize different technologies and were developed independently, they intercommunicate efficiently, forming a flexible and powerful integrated environment.

Figure 18. A strict rule written in the RuleML-compatible language of DR-DEVICE (this fragment displays rule r1 of section "Defeasible Logics and Digraphs")

```
<imp>
      <_rlab ruleID="r1" ruletype="strictrule">
            <ind>r1</ind>
      </_rlab>
      <_head>
            <atom>
                  <_opr>
                        <rel>bird</rel>
                  </_opr>
                  <_slot name="name">
                        <var>X</var>
                  </_slot>
            </atom>
      </_head>
      <_body>
            <atom>
                  <_opr>
                        <rel>penguin</rel>
                  </_opr>
                  <_slot name="name">
                        <var>X</var>
                  </_slot>
            </atom>
      </_body>
</imp>
```

The Reasoning System: Architecture and Functionality

The core reasoning system of VDR-DEVICE is DR-DEVICE (Bassiliades, Antoniou, & Vlahavas, 2004) and consists of two primary components (Figure 19): The *RDF loader/translator* and the *rule loader/translator*. The user can either develop a rule base (program, written in the RuleML-like syntax of VDR-DEVICE--see Figure 18 for a fragment) with the help of the rule editor described in the following sections, or he or she can load an already existing one, probably developed manually. The rule base contains: (a) a set of rules, (b) the URL(s) of the RDF input document(s), which is forwarded to the RDF loader, (c) the names of the derived classes to be exported as results, and (d) the name of the RDF output document.

The rule base is then submitted to the *rule loader,* which transforms it into the native CLIPS-like syntax through an XSLT stylesheet and the resulting program is then forwarded to the *rule translator,* where the defeasible logic rules are compiled into a set of CLIPS production rules. This is a two-step process: First, the defeasible logic rules are translated into sets of deductive, derived attribute and aggregate attribute rules of the basic deductive rule language using the translation scheme described in Bassiliades et al. (2004). Then, all these deductive rules are translated into CLIPS production rules according to the rule translation scheme in Bassiliades and Vlahavas (2004). All compiled rule formats are also kept in local files (structured in project workspaces) so that the next time they are needed they can be directly loaded, improving speed considerably (running a compiled project is up to 10 times faster).

Figure 19. The VDR-DEVICE system architecture

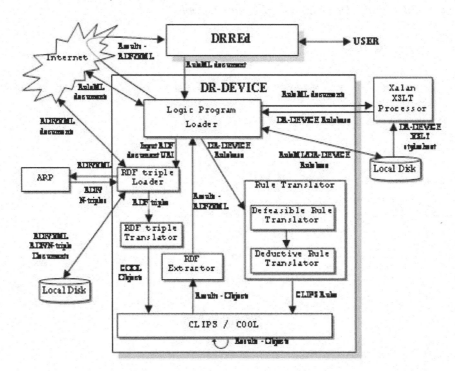

Meanwhile, the RDF loader downloads the input RDF documents including their schemas, and translates RDF descriptions into CLIPS objects according to the RDF-to-object translation scheme in (Bassiliades & Vlahavas, 2004), which is briefly described next.

The inference engine of CLIPS performs the reasoning by running the production rules and generates the objects that constitute the result of the initial rule program. The compilation phase guarantees correctness of the reasoning process according to the operational semantics of defeasible logic. Finally, the result-objects are exported to the user as an RDF/XML document through the RDF extractor. The RDF document includes the instances of the exported derived classes, which have been proved.

Rule Editor:Design and Functionality

VDR-DEVICE is equipped with DRREd, a visual rule editor that aims at enhancing user-friendliness and efficiency during the development of VDR-DEVICE RuleML documents. Key features of the software include: (a) functional flexibility-program utilities can be triggered via a variety of overhead menu actions, keyboard shortcuts, or popup menus, (b) improved development speed—rule bases can be developed in just a few steps, and (c) powerful safety mechanisms—the correct syntax is ensured and the user is protected from syntactic or RDF Schema related semantic errors.

The main window of the program (Figure 20) is composed of two major parts: (a) the upper part includes the menu bar, which contains the program menus, and the toolbar that includes icons, representing the most common utilities of the rule editor, and (b) the central and more "bulky" part is the primary frame of the main window and is in turn divided in two panels:

The left panel displays the rule base in XML tree-like format. The user can navigate through the tree and can add to or remove elements from the tree, obeying DTD constraints. Furthermore, the operations allowed on each element depend on the element's meaning within the rule tree.

The right panel shows a table, which contains the attributes that correspond to the selected tree node in the left panel. The user can also perform editing functions on the attributes, by altering the value for each attribute in the panel that appears in the bottom-right of the main window, below the attributes table. The values that the user can insert depend on the chosen attribute.

The development of a rule base using VDR-DEVICE is a process that depends heavily on

the context (i.e., the node being edited). Some examples follow:

- When a new element is added to the tree, all its mandatory sub-elements are also added. In cases where there are multiple alternative sub-elements, none is added. The user is responsible to manually add one of them by right clicking on the parent element and choosing a sub-element from the pop-up menu that appears (Figure 20).

- The atom element is treated in a specific manner since it can be either negated or not. The wrapping/unwrapping of an atom element within a neg element is performed via a toggle button on the overhead toolbar.

- The function names in a fun_call element are partially constrained by the list of CLIPS built-in function. However, the

Figure 20. The graphical rule editor main window

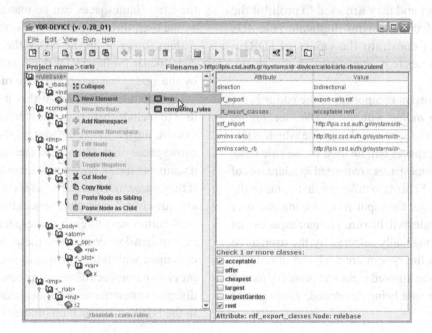

Figure 21. The namespace dialog window (NDW)

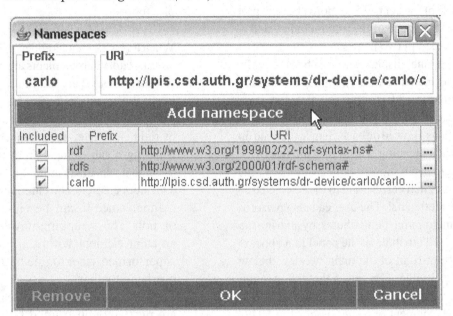

user can still use a user-defined function, which is unconstrained.

- Rule IDs uniquely represent a rule within the rule base; therefore, they are collected in a set and they are used to prohibit the user from entering duplicate rule IDs and to constrain the values of IDREF attributes (e.g., superior).

An important component of the editor is the *namespace dialog window* (NDW, see Figure 21), where the user can determine which RDF/XML namespaces will be used by the rule base. Actually, namespaces are treated as addresses of input RDF Schema ontologies that contain the vocabulary for the input RDF documents, over which the rules will be run. The namespaces that have been manually selected by the user to be included in the system are analyzed in order to extract all the allowed class and property names for the rule base being developed. These names

are then used throughout the authoring phase of the RuleML rule base, constraining the corresponding allowed names that can be applied and narrowing the possibility for errors on behalf of the user. Namespaces can be manually entered by the user, through the NDW. Furthermore, the system shows up in the NDW the namespaces contained in the input RDF documents (indicated by the `rdf _ import` attribute of the `rule-base` root element). Notice that it is up to the user to include them or not as ontologies into the system. Furthermore, the system shows up only namespaces that actually correspond to RDF documents (i.e., it downloads them and finds out if they parse to triples). The user can also manually "discover" more namespaces by pressing the "..." button next to each namespace entry. The system then downloads the namespace documents contained within this document and repeats the previous namespace discovery procedure. When it discovers a new namespace not already contained in the NDW, it shows it up (unchecked).

Figure 22. The trace window

Finally, users can examine all the exported results via an Internet Explorer window launched by the system (Figure 22). They can also examine the execution trace of compilation and running, both at run-time and also after the whole process has been terminated (Figure 23).

DRREd's Digraph Module

DRREd is equipped with a module that allows the creation of a directed rule graph from the defeasible rule base developed by the editor. This way, users are offered an extra means of visualizing the rule base besides XML-tree format and, thus, possess a better aspect of the rule base displayed and the inference results produced. This section describes thoroughly the steps towards the generation of the derived graph.

Collecting the Base and Derived Classes

The RDF schema documents contained in the namespace dialog window are being parsed, using the ARP parser of Jena (McBride, 2001). The names of the classes found are collected in the *base class vector* (CV_b), which already contains rdfs:Resource, the superclass of all RDF user classes. Therefore, the CV_b vector is constructed as follows:

$$rdfs:Resource \in CV_b \land (\forall C \, (C \, rdf:type \; rdfs:Class) \to C \in CV_b)$$

where $(X\,Y\,Z)$ represents an RDF triple found in the RDF schema documents.

Except from the base class vector, there also exists the *derived class vector* (CV_d), which contains the names of the derived classes (i.e., the classes, which lie at rule heads (*conclusions*)). CV_d is initially empty and is dynamically extended

Figure 23. The results window

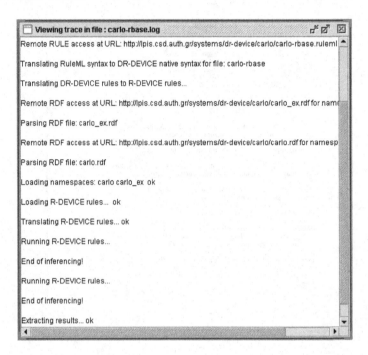

Figure 24. A class box example

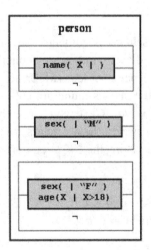

every time a new class name appears inside the `rel` element of the atom in a rule head. This vector is mainly used for loosely suggesting possible values for the `rel` elements in the rule head, but not constraining them, since rule heads can either introduce new derived classes or refer to already existing ones.

The union of the previous two vectors results in CV_f, which is the *full class vector* ($CV_f = CV_b \cup CV_d$) and it is used for constraining the allowed class names when editing the contents of the `rel` element inside atom elements of the rule body.

Elements of the Rule Graph

For each class that belongs to the full class vector CV_f, a *class box* is constructed, which apparently is simply a container. The class boxes are initially empty and are dynamically populated with one or more *class patterns*. For each `atom` element inside a rule head or body, a new class pattern is created and is inserted into (or, in a wider point

Figure 25. A code fragment for the third class pattern of Figure 24

```
<atom>
  <_opr>
    <rel href="person"/>
  </_opr>
  <_slot name="sex">
    <ind>"F"</ind>
  </_slot>
  <_slot name="age">
    <_and>
      <var>x</var>
      <function_call name="&gt;">
        <var>x</var>
        <ind>18</ind>
      </function_call>
    </_and>
  </_slot>
</atom>
```

of view, *associated with*) the class box, whose name matches the class name that appears inside the `rel` element of the specific atom. In practice, class patterns express conditions on instances of the specific class. Nevertheless, a class box could indeed remain empty, in the case when a base class is included in the loaded RDF Schema document(s), but is not being used in any rule during the development of the rule base. However, it is obvious that this does not apply for derived classes, since the latter are dynamically detected and added to/removed from the full class vector as mentioned in the previous section. Empty class boxes still appear in the rule graph, but naturally play a limited role.

Visually, class patterns appear as literal boxes, whose design was thoroughly described in a previous section of this chapter (see "*Deductive Rules and Digraphs*"). Similarly to class boxes, class patterns are empty, when they are initially created and are soon populated with one or more *slot patterns*. For each `_slot` element inside an atom, a slot pattern is created that consists of a slot name (contained inside the corresponding attribute) and, optionally, a variable and a list of value constraints. The variable is used in order for the slot value to be unified, with the latter having to satisfy the list of constraints. In other words, slot patterns represent conditions on slots (or *class properties*). Each of the slot pattern "ingredients" is being retrieved from the - direct and indirect - children of the `_slot` element in the XML tree representation of the rule base.

Since RuleML atoms are actually atomic formulas (i.e., they correspond to queries over RDF resources of a certain class with certain property values), the truth-value associated with each returned class instance will be either positive or negative. This justifies the mapping of class patterns to literal boxes.

An example of all the previous can be seen in Figure 24 and Figure 25. The figures illustrate a class box that contains three class patterns applied on the *person* class and a code fragment matching the third class pattern written in the RuleML-like syntax of VDR-DEVICE.

Figure 26. The rule stratification algorithm

```
1.Assign all class boxes contained in CBb to stratum 1
2.Assign all rules in R, whose bodies contain only
class patterns belonging to a base class box, to
stratum 2
3.Remove rules applied in STEP 2 from R
4.i = 3
WHILE R.size > 0 {
        5.Assign the class boxes contained in CBd that
        contain class patterns that act as heads for
        rules in stratum i - 1 to stratum i
        6.All rules in R with bodies in stratum i are
        assigned to stratum i + 1
        7.Remove rules applied in previous STEP from R
        8.i = i + 1 }
```

Table 1. Base classes, derived classes, and rules included in the rule base of the example

Base Classes	carlo:apartment
Derived Classes	acceptable offer cheapest largest largestGarden
Rules	$r_1 - r_{12}$ find _ cheapest find _ largest find _ largestGarden

Table 2. Stratum assignments for the classes and the rules in the example

stratum 1	carlo:apartment
stratum 2	r_1 to r_8
stratum 3	acceptable offer
stratum 4	r_9 find _ cheapest find _ largest find _ largestGarden
stratum 5	cheapest largest largestGarden
stratum 6	r_{10} r_{11} r_{12}

The first two class patterns contain one slot pattern each while the third one contains two slot patterns. As can be observed, the argument list of each slot pattern is divided into two parts, separated by "|"; on the left all the variables are placed and on the right all the corresponding ex-

pressions and conditions, regarding the variables on the left. In the case of constant values, only the right-hand side is utilized; thus, the second-class pattern of the box in Figure 24, for example, refers to all the *male* persons. This way the content of the slot arguments is clearly depicted and easily comprehended.

Besides class boxes and their "ingredients" (class patterns, slot patterns), a number of additional graph elements exist: circles that represent rules and arrows that connect the nodes in the graph. The graphical representation of rules in the digraph, using circles, was described in section "*Deductive Rules and Digraphs*." The circles in the graph include the rule name, which is equal to the value of the `ruleID` attribute in the _ `rlab` element of the corresponding rule. As for the arrows in the graph, there exist four types of them: three for the rule type and one for the superiority relationship, as explained in section "*Defeasible Logics And Digraphs*." The rule type is equal to the value of the `ruletype` attribute inside the _ `rlab` element of the respective rule and can only take three distinct values (`strictrule`, `defeasiblerule`, `defeater`). As for the superiority relationship, it is represented as attribute (`superior` attribute) inside the superior rule element.

Building the Rule Graph

After having collected all the necessary graph elements and having populated all the class boxes with the appropriate class and slot patterns, three new vectors are created:

- The *base class boxes* vector CB_b that contains the class boxes corresponding to base classes.
- The *derived class boxes* vector CB_d that contains the class boxes corresponding to derived classes.
- The vector R that includes all the rules of the rule base.

Figure 27. Rules r1-r4 expressed in the CLIPS-like syntax of VDR-DEVICE

```
(defeasiblerule r1
     (carlo:apartment (carlo:name ?x))
  =>
     (acceptable (apartment ?x))
)

(defeasiblerule r2
     (declare (superior r1))
     (carlo:apartment    (carlo:name ?x)
                         (carlo:bedrooms  ?y & :(<  ?y 2)))
  =>
     (not (acceptable (apartment ?x)))
)

(defeasiblerule r3
     (declare (superior r1))
     (carlo:apartment    (carlo:name ?x)
                         (carlo:size  ?y & :(<  ?y 45)))
  =>
     (not (acceptable (apartment ?x)))
)

(defeasiblerule r4
     (declare (superior r1))
     (carlo:apartment    (carlo:name ?x)
                         (carlo:pets "no"))
  =>
     (not (acceptable (apartment ?x)))
)
```

Figure 28. Rules r1-r4 expressed in defeasible syntax

```
r1 :  => acceptable(X)
r2 : bedrooms(X, Y), Y < 2 => ¬acceptable(X)
r3 : size(X, Y), Y < 45 => ¬acceptable(X)
r4 : ¬pets(X) => ¬acceptable(X)
```

Figure 29. The rule graph drawing module of DRREd

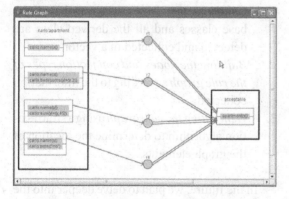

An important matter arises at this point regarding the placement of each element in the graph, namely, a plan has to be drawn concerning the location of the elements in the graph drawing panel of VDR-DEVICE. For this affair, a variation of the rule stratification algorithm found in Ullman (1988) was implemented. The algorithm aims at

giving a left-to-right orientation to the flow of information in the graph (i.e., the arcs in the digraph are directed from left to right) making the derived graph less complex, more comprehensible, and easily readable. The rule stratification algorithm implemented is displayed in Figure 26.

An example that could better illustrate the functionality of the algorithm is adopted from Antoniou and van Harmelen (2004, p. 161-165). The example deals with apartment renting; a number of available apartments reside in an RDF document along with the properties of each apartment and the potential renter expresses his or her requirements in defeasible logic regarding the apartment he or she wishes to rent. A defeasible rule base that contains the requirements of an imaginary renter is included in the example. The classes and the rules included in the rule base are displayed in Table 1.

Six strata are needed to display all the rules. Table 2 shows the stratum assignments according to the algorithm.

In our approach, each stratum is considered as a *column* in the graph drawing panel of the system. Thus, the first stratum is mapped to the first column on the left, the second stratum to the column on the right of the first one, and so on. Nodes in one column are never connected with nodes in the same column. Note also that no two nodes of the same type are ever connected with an arrow. As a result, the digraphs produced by our approach can be considered a type of *bipartite graphs*.

Obviously, the number of strata/columns can be too big to fit the screen. In this case, the user can traverse the graph, using the scroll bars located on the edges of the panel. Furthermore, similarly to the XML-tree format of the rule base, in the digraph there is also the possibility to collapse or expand certain parts of it. This way, a twofold advantage is offered: (a) the complexity of the digraph is minimized since only a limited number of graph parts are visible at a time and (b) the level of comprehensibility on behalf of the user is raised since he or she does not have to focus on the whole graph, but only a part of it.

The two aspects of the rule base, namely the XML-tree and the directed graph are interrelated, meaning that traversal and alterations in one will also be depicted in the other. So, if for example the user focuses on a specific element in the tree and then switches to the digraph view, the corresponding element in the digraph will also be selected and the data relevant to it displayed.

As mentioned in a previous section, the VDR-DEVICE system has a CLIPS-like syntax and a RuleML-compliant one. Figure 27 illustrates the first four rules of the above example expressed in the former syntax (the latter syntax can be found in APPENDIX A). Figure 28 displays the same rules in the typical defeasible syntax.

Figure 29 displays the output of the VDR-DE-VICE rule graph drawing module when a portion of the rule base of the example in Antoniou et al. (2004, p. 161-165) is loaded. For reasons of simplicity, only the first four rules are applied (rules r_1-r_4) and there exist only one base and one derived class. The total number of strata in *this* case is three (i.e., three columns).

CONCLUSION AND FUTURE WORK

This chapter presented the utilization of *directed graphs* (or *digraphs*) in the representation of defeasible logic rules, an affair where digraphs proved to be extremely suitable. It is, however, difficult to associate data of a variety of types with the nodes and with the connections between the nodes in the graph and this is probably the major disadvantage of graphs in information visualization.

In our approach we attempted to apply the use of digraphs in the representation of defeasible logic rules, exploiting the advantages they offer (comprehensibility, expressiveness), but also trying to leverage their primary disadvantage. We adopted a novel "*enhanced*" digraph approach

that features two types of nodes (one for rules and one for literals) and four connection types (one for each of the three distinct rule types in defeasible reasoning and a fourth for the representation of superiority relationships). It was observed that these enhanced directed graphs offer a significant level of expressiveness in representing defeasible logic rules.

A system that implements this digraph approach was briefly described. The system is called *VDR-DEVICE* and is a visual, integrated development environment for developing and using defeasible logic rule bases on top of RDF ontologies. VDR-DEVICE consists of two sub-components: *DR-DEVICE*, the reasoning system that performs the inference and produces the results and *DRREd*, the rule editor, which serves both as a rule authoring tool and as a graphical shell for DR-DEVICE. DRREd's graph drawing module that allows the creation of a directed rule graph from the defeasible rule base developed by the editor was also demonstrated. The steps towards the creation of a digraph from a rule base include:

1. *Collecting the classes*, meaning that all the base classes and all the derived class are detected and collected in a vector,
2. *Building the nodes and connection types of the rule graph* according to the information collected,
3. *Generating the rule graph* using a stratification algorithm to determine the location of the graph elements.

In the future, we plan to delve deeper into the proof layer of the Semantic Web architecture by further enhancing the rule representation utility demonstrated with rule execution tracing, explanation, proof exchange in an XML or RDF format, proof visualization and validation, etc. These facilities would be useful for increasing the trust of users for the Semantic Web agents and for automating proof exchange and trust among agents in the Semantic Web.

REFERENCES

Antoniou, G. (2002). Nonmonotonic Rule systems on top of ontology layers. *Proceedings of the 1ˢᵗ International Semantic Web Conference* (pp. 394-398). LNCS 2342. Springer-Verlag.

Antoniou, G. (1997). *Nonmonotonic reasoning*. MIT Press.

Antoniou, G., & Arief, M. (2002). Executable declarative business rules and their use in electronic commerce. *Proceedings of the ACM Symposium on Applied Computing* (pp. 6-10). ACM Press.

Antoniou, G., & van Harmelen, F. (2004). *A Semantic Web primer*. MIT Press.

Antoniou, G., Billington, D., & Maher, M. J. (1999). On the analysis of regulations using defeasible rules. *Proceedings of the 32ⁿᵈ Hawaii International Conference on Systems Science.* IEEE Press.

Antoniou, G., Skylogiannis, T., Bikakis, A., & Bassiliades, N. (2005). DR-BROKERING--A defeasible logic-based system for semantic brokering. *Proceedings of the IEEE International Conference on E-Technology, E-Commerce, and E-Service* (pp. 414-417). IEEE Computer Society.

Ashri, R., Payne, T., Marvin, D., Surridge, M., & Taylor, S. (2004). Towards a Semantic Web security infrastructure. *Proceedings of the Semantic Web Services 2004 Spring Symposium Series.* Stanford University, Stanford California.

Bassiliades, N., & Vlahavas, I. (2004). R-DEVICE: A deductive RDF rule language. *Proceedings of the RuleML 2004* (pp. 65-80). Springer-Verlag, LNCS 3323, Hiroshima, Japan.

Bassiliades, N., Antoniou, G., & Vlahavas, I. (2004). A defeasible logic reasoner for the Semantic Web. *Proceedings of the RuleML 2004* (pp. 49-64). Springer-Verlag, LNCS 3323, Hiroshima, Japan.

Bassiliades, N., Kontopoulos, E., & Antoniou, G. (2005). A visual environment for developing defeasible rule bases for the Semantic Web. In A. Adi, S. Stoutenburg, & S. Tabet (Eds.), *Proceedings of the International Conference on Rules and Rule Markup Languages for the Semantic Web (RuleML-2005)* (pp. 172-186). Springer-Verlag, LNCS 3791, Galway, Ireland.

Berners-Lee, T., Hendler, J., & Lassila, O. (2001). The Semantic Web. *Scientific American, 284*(5), 34-43.

Clarke, D. (1982). An augmented directed graph base for application development. *Proceedings of the 20ᵗʰ Annual Southeast Regional Conference* (pp. 155-159). Knoxville, Tennessee: ACM Press.

Diestel, R. (2000). *Graph theory (graduate texts in mathematics)* (2ⁿᵈ ed.). Springer.

Fluit, C., Sabou, M., & van Harmelen, F. (2003). Ontology-based information visualization. In V. Geroimenko & C. Chen (Ed.), *Visualizing the Semantic Web* (pp. 36-48). Springer-Verlag.

Governatori, G. (2005). Representing business contracts in RuleML. *International Journal of Cooperative Information Systems, 14*(2-3), 181-216.

Governatori, G., Dumas, M., Hofstede, A., & Oaks, P. (2001). A formal approach to protocols and strategies for (legal) negotiation. *Proceedings of the 8ᵗʰ International Conference of Artificial Intelligence and Law* (pp. 168-177). ACM Press.

Graphviz: Graph Visualization Software. Retrieved April 23, 2006, from http://www.graphviz.org

Grosof, B. N., & Poon, T. C. (2003). SweetDeal: Representing agent contracts with exceptions using XML rules, ontologies, and process descriptions. *Proceedings of the 12ᵗʰ International Conference on World Wide Web* (pp. 340-349). ACM Press.

Grosof, B. N., Gandhe, M. D., & Finin, T. W. (2002). SweetJess: Translating DAMLRuleML to JESS. *Proceedings of the International Workshop on Rule Markup Languages for Business Rules on the Semantic Web*. Held at 1st Int. Semantic Web Conference.

Hartley, R., & Pfeiffer, H. (2000). Visual representation of procedural knowledge. *Proceedings of the 2000 IEEE International Symposium on Visual Languages (Vl'00)*. VL. IEEE Computer Society, Washington, DC, 63.

Jantzen, J. (1989). Inference planning using digraphs and Boolean arrays. *Proceedings of the International Conference on APL* (pp. 200-204). ACM Press.

Kehler, T. P., & Clemenson G. D. (1984, January). KEE the knowledge engineering environment for industry. *Systems and Software, 3*(1), 212-224.

Marek, V. W., & Truszczynski, M. (1993). *Nonmonotonic logics; Context dependent reasoning*. Springer-Verlag.

McBride, B. (2001). Jena: Implementing the RDF model and syntax specification. *Proceedings of the 2nd International Workshop on the Semantic Web*.

Nute, D. (1987). Defeasible reasoning. *Proceedings of the 20th International Conference on Systems Science* (pp. 470-477). IEEE Press.

Powers, S. (2003). *Practical RDF*. Beijing; Cambridge: O'Reilly.

Shalfield, R. (2005). *VisiRule user guide*. Retrieved March 10, 2006, from http://www.lpa. co.uk/ftp/4600/vsr_ref.pdf

Steel, B. D. (2005). *WIN-PROLOG Technical Reference*. Retrieved April 23, 2006, from http://www.lpa.co.uk/ftp/4600/win_ref.pdf

Ullman, J. D. (1988). *Principles of database and knowledge-based systems* (Vol. 1). Computer Science Press.

APPENDIX A

Rules r_1 to r_4 expressed in the RuleML-compliant syntax of VDR-DEVICE:

```
<imp>
  <_rlab ruleID="r1" ruletype="defeasiblerule">
   <ind href="http://lpis.csd.auth.gr/systems/dr-device/carlo/carlo-rbase.ruleml#r1">r1</ind>
  </_rlab>
  <_head>
   <atom>
    <_opr>
     <rel href="acceptable"/>
    </_opr>
    <_slot name="apartment">
     <var>x</var>
    </_slot>
   </atom>
  </_head>
  <_body>
   <atom>
    <_opr>
     <rel href="carlo:apartment"/>
    </_opr>
    <_slot name="carlo:name">
     <var>x</var>
    </_slot>
   </atom>
  </_body>
</imp>
<imp>
  <_rlab ruleID="r2" ruletype="defeasiblerule" superior="r1">
   <ind href="http://lpis.csd.auth.gr/systems/dr-device/carlo/carlo-rbase.ruleml#r2">r2</ind>
  </_rlab>
  <_head>
   <neg>
    <atom>
     <_opr>
      <rel href="acceptable"/>
     </_opr>
     <_slot name="apartment">
      <var>x</var>
     </_slot>
    </atom>
   </neg>
```

```
</_head>
<_body>
 <atom>
  <_opr>
   <rel href="carlo:apartment"/>
  </_opr>
  <_slot name="carlo:name">
   <var>x</var>
  </_slot>
  <_slot name="carlo:bedrooms">
   <_and>
    <var>y</var>
    <function_call name="&lt;">
     <var>y</var>
     <ind>2</ind>
    </function_call>
   </_and>
  </_slot>
 </atom>
</_body>
</imp>
<imp>
 <_rlab ruleID="r3" ruletype="defeasiblerule" superior="r1">
  <ind href="http://lpis.csd.auth.gr/systems/dr-device/carlo/carlo-rbase.ruleml#r3">r3</ind>
 </_rlab>
 <_head>
  <neg>
   <atom>
    <_opr>
     <rel href="acceptable"/>
    </_opr>
    <_slot name="apartment">
     <var>x</var>
    </_slot>
   </atom>
  </neg>
 </_head>
 <_body>
  <atom>
   <_opr>
    <rel href="carlo:apartment"/>
   </_opr>
   <_slot name="carlo:name">
    <var>x</var>
```

```
      </_slot>
      <_slot name="carlo:size">
       <_and>
        <var>y</var>
        <function_call name="&lt;">
         <var>y</var>
         <ind>45</ind>
         </function_call>
        </_and>
       </_slot>
      </atom>
     </_body>
   </imp>
<imp>
   <_rlab ruleID="r4" ruletype="defeasiblerule" superior="r1">
    <ind href="http://lpis.csd.auth.gr/systems/dr-device/carlo/carlo-rbase.ruleml#r4">r4</ind>
    </_rlab>
   <_head>
    <neg>
     <atom>
      <_opr>
       <rel href="acceptable"/>
       </_opr>
      <_slot name="apartment">
       <var>x</var>
       </_slot>
      </atom>
     </neg>
    </_head>
   <_body>
    <atom>
     <_opr>
      <rel href="carlo:apartment"/>
      </_opr>
     <_slot name="carlo:name">
      <var>x</var>
      </_slot>
     <_slot name="carlo:pets">
      <ind>"no"</ind>
      </_slot>
     </atom>
    </_body>
   </imp>
```

Chapter XV
A Visual Programming Tool for Designing Planning Problems for Semantic Web Service Composition

Dimitris Vrakas
Aristotle University of Thessaloniki, Greece

Ourania Hatzi
Harokopio University of Athens, Greece

Nick Bassiliades
Aristotle University of Thessaloniki, Greece

Dimosthenis Anagnostopoulos
Harokopio University of Athens, Greece

Ioannis Vlahavas
Aristotle University of Thessaloniki, Greece

ABSTRACT

This chapter is concerned with the issue of knowledge representation for AI planning problems, especially those related to semantic Web service composition. It discusses current approaches in encoding planning problems using the PDDL formal language and it presents ViTAPlan, a user-friendly visual tool for planning. More than just being a user-friendly environment for executing the underlying planner, the tool serves as a unified planning environment for encoding a new problem, solving it, visualizing the solution, and monitoring its execution on a simulation of the problem's world. The tool consists of various sub-systems, each one accompanied by a graphical interface, which collaborate with each other and assist the user, either a knowledge engineer, a domain expert, an academic, or even an end-user in industry, to carry out complex planning tasks such as composing complex semantic Web services from simple ones in order to achieve complex tasks.

INTRODUCTION

Planning is the process of finding a sequence of actions (steps), which if executed by an agent (biological, software, or robotic), result in the achievement of a set of predefined goals. The sequence of actions previously mentioned is also referred to as plan.

The actions in a plan may be either specifically ordered and their execution should follow the defined sequence (linear plan), or the agent is free to decide the order of executions as long as a set of ordering constraints are met. For example, if someone wishes to travel by plane, there are three main actions that he or she has to take: (a) buy a ticket, (b) go to the airport, and (c) board on the plane. A plan for traveling by plane could contain these three actions in a strict sequence as the one defined previously (first do action a, then b, and finally c), or it could just define that action c (board on plane) should be executed after the first two actions. In the second case, the agent would be able to choose which plan to execute since both a→b→c and b→a→c sequences would be valid.

The process of planning is extremely useful when the agent acts in a dynamic environment (or world), which is continuously altered in an unpredictable way. For instance, the auto pilot of a plane should be capable of planning the trajectory that leads the plane to the desired location, but also be able to alter it in case of an unexpected event like an intense storm.

The software systems that automatically (or semi- automatically) produce plans are referred to as planners or planning systems. The task of drawing a plan is extremely complex and it requires sophisticated reasoning capabilities, which should be simulated by the software system. Therefore, planning systems make extensive use of artificial intelligence techniques and there is a dedicated area of AI called automated planning.

Automated planning has been an active research topic for almost 40 years and during this period a great number of papers describing new methods, techniques, and systems have been presented that mainly focus on ways to improve the efficiency of planning systems. However, there are not many successful examples of planning systems adapting to industrial use. From a technical point of view, this can be mainly explained by four reasons: (a) There is a general disbelief by managers and workers in industry that AI tools can really assist them, (b) There is a need for systems that combine methods from many areas of AI such as planning, scheduling, and optimization, (c) The industry needs more sophisticated algorithms than can scale up to solve real-world problems, and (d) in order for workers in industry to make use of these intelligent systems, they must be equipped with user friendly interfaces that: (i) allow the user to intervene in certain points and (ii) can reason about the provided solution.

The greatest problems that one faces when he or she tries to contact companies and organizations for installing a planning system come from the workers themselves. These problems concern two issues: (a) It has been noticed that people find it hard to trust automated systems when it comes to crucial processes. Many people still think that they can do better than machines. (b) There is a quite widespread phobia toward computers and automated machines due to the lack of information. A large number of people are afraid of being replaced or governed by machines and they try to defend their posts by rejecting everything new.

Although it is necessary for researchers to specialize in very specific parts of their research area, commercial systems, dealing with real time problems, have to combine techniques and methods from many areas. It has been shown that AI planning techniques for example, are inadequate to face with the complexity and the generality of real world problems. For example, it has been proven that scheduling and constraint-solving techniques can handle resources more efficiently. Commercial applications must combine methods from many areas of AI and probably from other areas of computer science as well.

Another issue that must be dealt with is the large gap between toy problems used by researchers for developing and testing their algorithms and the actual problems faced by people in industry. Researchers are usually unaware of the size of real world problems or they simplify these problems in order to cope with them. However, these algorithms prove themselves inadequate to be adopted by commercial software. So it is a general conclusion that researchers should start dealing with more realistic problems.

Last but certainly not least is the direct need of software based on AI tools to be accompanied with user-friendly interfaces. Since the user will be a manager or even a simple worker in a company and not a computer scientist, the software must be easy to use. Furthermore, it must enable the user to intervene in certain points for two reasons: (a) Mixed initiative systems can deal with real-world problems better and (b) people in companies do not like to take commands and therefore a black box, which can not reason about its output, will not do. So it is necessary for the software to cooperate with the user in the process of solving the problem in hand, since people have a more abstract model of the problem in their mind and are better in improvising, while computers can deal with lower levels of the problem more efficiently.

Semantic Web Service Composition

The Web is becoming more than just a collection of documents--applications and services are coming to the forefront. Web services will play a crucial role in this transformation, as they will become the basic components of Web-based applications (Leymann, 2003). A Web service is a software system identified by a URI (universal resource identifier), whose public interfaces and bindings are defined and described using XML (extensible markup language). Its definition can

be discovered by other software systems. These systems may then interact with the Web service in a manner prescribed by its definition, using XML based messages conveyed by internet protocols (Booth et al., 2003).

The use of the Web services paradigm is expanding rapidly to provide a systematic and extensible framework for application-to-application (A2A) interaction, built on top of existing Web protocols and based on open XML standards. Web services aim to simplify the process of distributed computing by defining a standardized mechanism to describe, locate, and communicate with online software systems. Essentially, each application becomes an accessible Web service component that is described using open standards.

When individual Web services are limited in their capabilities, they can be composed to create new functionality in the form of Web processes. Web service composition is the ability to take existing services (or building blocks) and combine them to form new services (Piccinelli, 1999) and is emerging as a new model for automated interactions among distributed and heterogeneous applications. To truly integrate application components on the Web across organization and platform boundaries, merely supporting simple interaction using standard messages and protocols is insufficient (Aalst, 2003) and Web services composition languages such as WSFL (Leymann, 2001), XLANG (Thatte, 2001) and BPEL4WS (Thatte, 2003) are needed to specify the order in which WSDL (Web service definition language) services and operations are executed.

Automatic application interoperability is hard to achieve with low cost without the existence of the *semantic Web*. semantic Web is the next big step of evolution in the Web (Berners-Lee, Hendler, & Lassila, 2001) that includes explicit representation of the meaning of information and document content (namely *semantics*), allowing the automatic and accurate location of information in the WWW as well as the development of intelligent Web-based agents that will facilitate cooperation among heterogeneous Web-based computer applications and electronic devices. The combination of the semantic Web with Web Services (namely *semantic Web Services*) will achieve the automatic discovery, execution, composition, and monitoring of Web services (McIlraith, Son, & Zeng, 2001) through the use of appropriate Web service descriptions such as OWL-S (OWL Services, 2003), that allow the semantics of the descriptions to become comprehensible by other agents-programs through *ontologies*.

Composing Web services will become harder as the available Web services increase. Therefore, automating Web service composition is important for the survival of Web services in the industrial world. One very promising technique to compose semantic Web services is to use planning techniques (Milani, 2003).

Using planning, the Web service composition problem can be described as a goal or a desired state to be achieved by the complex service and the planner will be responsible to find an appropriate plan (i.e., an appropriate sequence of simple Web service invocations) to achieve the desire state (Carman, Serafini, Traverso, 2003). In this way, not-predetermined Web services can exist on users demand. The abilities of simple Web services will be described in OWL-S and can be considered as planning operators.

Chapter Scope and Outline

This chapter describes ViTAPlan (Vrakas & Vlahavas, 2003a, 2003b, 2005), a visual tool for adaptive planning, which is equipped with a rule system able to automatically fine-tune the planner based on the morphology of the problem in hand. The tool has been developed for the HAP planning system, but it can be used as a graphical platform for any other modern planner that supports the PDDL (planning domain definition language) language (Ghallab et al., 1998). The tool consists of various sub-systems that collaborate in order to carry out several planning tasks and provides

the user with a large number of functionalities that are of interest to both industry and academia. ViTAPlan interfacing with the user and the rest of the world is currently extended in order to be used as a visual tool to aid the composition of complex semantic Web Services out of simpler ones by visually describing the composition problem as a planning problem.

The rest of the chapter is organized as follows: The next section presents an overview of the work related to automated planning systems, graphical environments for planning, semantic Web service composition approaches based on planning, and visual tools for Web service composition. Section 3 discusses certain representation issues concerning planning problems and presents the various versions of the PDDL definition language. Section 4 describes the architecture of the visual tool and briefly describes the contained sub-systems. Sections 5, 6, and 7 present the modules of ViTAPlan in more detail. More specifically, Section 5 analyzes the graphical tool for visualizing and designing problems and domains and illustrates the use of the sub-system with concrete examples. The next section presents the execution module that interfaces the visual tool with the planning system and the knowledge module that is responsible for the automatic configuration of the planning parameters. Section 7, finally, discusses certain issues concerning the sub-systems that visualize the plans and simulate their execution in virtual worlds. The last section concludes the chapter and poses future directions, including currently developing extensions to ViTAPlan to be used for semantic Web service composition.

RELATED WORK

Two of the most promising trends in building fast domain-independent planning systems were presented over the last few years.

The first one consists of the transformation of the classical search in the space of states to other kinds of problems, which can be solved more easily. Examples of this category are the SATPLAN (Kautz & Selman, 1996) and BLACKBOX (Kautz & Selman, 1998) planning system, the evolutionary GRAPHPLAN (Blum & Furst, 1995), and certain extensions of GRAPHPLAN as the famous STAN planner (Long & Fox, 1998).

SATPLAN and BLACKBOX transform the planning problem into a satisfiability problem, which consists of a number of Boolean variables and certain clauses between these variables. The goal of the problem is to assign values to the variables in such a way that all of the clauses are established.

GRAPHPLAN on the other hand creates a concrete structure called the planning graph where the nodes correspond to facts of the domain and edges to actions that either achieve or delete these facts. Then the planner searches for solutions in the planning graph. GRAPHPLAN has the ability to produce parallel plans where the number of steps is guaranteed to be minimum.

The second category is based on a relatively simple idea where a general domain independent heuristic function is embodied in a heuristic search algorithm such as Hill Climbing, Best-First Search, or A*. Examples of planning systems in this category are the ASP/HSP family (Bonet & Geffner, 2001), AltAlt (Nguyen, Kambhampati, & Nigenda, 2002), FF (Hoffmann & Nebel, 2001), YAHSP (Vidal, 2004), and Macro FF (Botea, Enzenberger, Müller, & Schaeffer, 2005).

The planners of the latter category rely on the same idea to construct their heuristic function. They relax the planning problem by ignoring the delete lists of the domain operators and starting either from the initial state or the goals they construct a leveled graph of facts, noting for every fact f the level at which it was achieved $L(f)$. In order to evaluate a state S, the heuristic function takes into account the values of $L(f)$ for each $f \in S$.

The systems presented above are examples of real fast planners that are able to scale up to quite difficult problems. However, there are still open issues to be addressed that are crucial to industry, such as temporal planning or efficient handling of resources. Although there has been an effort during the last few years to deal with these issues there is still only a small number of systems capable of solving near real world problems.

An example of this trend is the SGPlan system (Chen, Wah, & Hsu, 2005), which won the first prize in the suboptimal temporal metric track and a second prize in the suboptimal propositional track in the Fourth International Planning Competition (IPC4). The basic idea behind SGPlan is to partition problem constraints by their subgoals into multiple subsets, solve each subproblem individually, and resolve inconsistent global constraints across subproblems based on a penalty formulation.

Another system able to handle planning problems that incorporate the notion of time and consumable resources is the LPG-TD planner (Gerevini, Saetti, & Serina, 2004), which is an extension of the LPG planning system. Like the previous version of LPG, the new version is based on a stochastic local search in the space of particular "action graphs" derived from the planning problem specification. In LPG-TD, this graph representation has been extended to deal with the new features of PDDL 2 (Fox & Long, 2003), as well to improve the management of durative actions and of numerical expressions.

There are also some older systems that combine planning with constraint satisfaction techniques in order to deal with complex problems with time and constraints. Such systems include the Metric FF Planner (Hoffmann, 2003), the S-MEP (Sanchez & Mali, 2003), and the SPN Neural Planning Methodology (Bourbakis & Tascillo, 1997).

As far as user interfaces are concerned, there have been several approaches from institutes and researchers to create visual tools for defining problems and running planning systems such as the GIPO system (McCluskey, Liu, & Simpson, 2003) and the SIPE-2 (Wilkins, Lee, & Berry, 2003). Moreover, there is a number of approaches in building visual interfaces for specific applications of planning. The PacoPlan project (Vrakas et. al., 2002) aims at building a Web-based planning interface for specific domains. AsbruView (Kosara & Miksch, 2001) is a visual user interface for time-oriented skeletal plans representing complex medical procedures. Another example of visual interfaces for planning is the work of the MAPLE research group at the university of Maryland (Kundu, Sessions, DesJardins, & Rheingans, 2002), which concerns the implementations of a 3D graphical interface for representing hierarchical plans with many levels of abstractions and interactions among the parts of the plan. Although these approaches are very interesting and provide the community with useful tools for planning, there is still a lot of work to be done in order to create an integrated system that meets the needs of the potential users.

Various works (Marcugini & Milani, 2002; McIlraith & Fadel, 2002; Sheshagiri, des Jardins, & Finin, 2003; Sirin, Parsia, Wu, Hendler, & Nau, 2004; Thakkar, Knoblock, Ambite, & Shahabi, 2002; Wu, Sirin, Hendler, Nau, & Parsia, 2003) propose to use a planning model to give a semantics to the behaviour of Web services, and to use planners in order to generate compositions of them (i.e., plans) for reaching complex goals on the Web.

There are many issues to be tackled both from the planning community and the Web service community in order to handle Web service composition as a planning problem (Koehler & Srivastava, 2003). Some of them are the following:

- New expressive languages for representing Web service actions, unifying existing standards of PDLL (Ghallab et. al, 1998), and OWL-S (OWL Services, 2003).
- Efficient planners produce quality plans that synthesize complex Web services.
- Web Service plan verification (Berardi, Calvanese, De Giacomo, & Mecella, 2003).

- Efficient Web service plan execution (Varela, Aparicio, & do Carmo Silva, 2003).
- Monitoring Web service plan execution and repairing the plan in cases where Web service execution failed (Blythe & Deelman, 2003).
- Mixing information retrieval and plan execution (Kuter, Sirin, Parsia, Dana, & James, 2005; Thakkar, Knoblock, & Ambite, 2003.

An approach of using HTN (hierarchical task network) planning in the realm of Web Services was proposed in Sirin et al. (2004), facilitating the SHOP2 system (Nau et al., 2003), which belongs to the family of *ordered task decomposition* planners where tasks are planned in the same order that they will be executed, which reduces the complexity of the planning problem greatly. Planners based on that principle accept goals as task lists where compound tasks may consist of compound tasks or primitive tasks--goal tasks are not supported. Hence, ordered task decomposition system do not plan to achieve a defined (declarative) goal, but rather to carry out a given (complex or primitive) task.

Such a HTN based planning system decomposes the desired task into a set of sub-tasks and these tasks into another set of sub-tasks (and so forth), until the resulting set of tasks consists only of primitive tasks, which can be executed directly by invoking atomic operations. During each round of task decomposition, it is tested whether certain given conditions are violated. The planning problem is successfully solved if the desired complex task is decomposed into a set of primitive tasks without violating any of the given conditions.

In Sirin et al. (2004) and Wu et al. (2003), a transformation method of OWL-S processes into a hierarchical task network is presented. OWL-S processes are, like HTN task networks, pre-defined descriptions of actions to be carried out to get a certain task done, which makes the transformation rather natural. The advantage of the approach is its ability to deal with very large problem domains; however, the need to explicitly provide the planner with a task it needs to accomplish may be seen as a disadvantage, since this requires descriptions that may not always be available in dynamic environments.

Another approach in using planning techniques for semantic Web service composition is in Sheshagiri et al. (2003), where their planner uses STRIPS (Stanford Research Institute Planning System) style services to compose a plan, given the goal and a set of basic services. They have used the Java Expert Shell System (JESS) (Friedman-Hill, 2002) to implement the planner and a set of JESS rules that translate DAML-S (a precursor to OWL-S) descriptions of atomic services into planning operators.

In order to enable the construction of composite Web services, a number of composition languages have been proposed by the software industry. However, the handiwork of specifying a business process with these languages through simple text or XML editors is tough, complex, and error prone. Visual support can ease the definition of business processes.

In Martinez, Patinio-Martinez, Jimenez-Peris, and Perez-Sorrosal (2005), a visual composition tool for Web services written in BPEL4WS, called ZenFlow, is described. ZenFlow provides several visual facilities to ease the definition of a composite Web services such as multiple views of a process, syntactic and semantic awareness, filtering, logical zooming capabilities, and hierarchical representations.

In Pautasso and Alonso (2004-2005), the JOpera system is presented. JOpera tackles the problems of visual service composition and efficient and scalable execution of the resulting composite services by combining a visual programming environment for Web services with a flexible execution engine capable of interacting with Web services through the SOAP protocol,

described with WSDL, and registered with an UDDI (universal description, discovery, and integration) registry.

To the best of our knowledge, there is no visual tool that combines visual planning problem design with Web service composition.

PROBLEM REPRESENTATION

Planning systems usually adopt the STRIPS (Stanford Research Institute Planning System) notation for representing problems (Fikes & Nilsson, 1971). A planning problem in STRIPS is a tuple $<I,A,G>$ where I is the Initial state, A a set of available actions and G a set of goals.

States are represented as sets of atomic facts. All the aspects of the initial state of the world, which are of interest to the problem, must be explicitly defined in I. State I contains both static and dynamic information. For example, I may declare that object John is a truck driver, there is a road connecting cities A and B (static information), and also that John is initially located in city A (dynamic information). State G on the other hand, is not necessarily complete. G may not specify the final state of all problem objects either because these are implied by the context or because they are of no interest to the specific problem. For example, in the logistics domain the final location of means of transportation is usually omitted, since the only objective is to have the packages transported. Therefore, there are usually many states that contain the goals, so in general, G represents a set of states rather than a simple state.

Set A contains all the actions that can be used to modify states. Each action A_i has three lists of facts containing:

1. The preconditions of A_i (noted as $prec(A_i)$);
2. The facts that are added to the state (noted as add(Ai)); and

3.   The facts that are deleted from the state (noted as del(Ai)).

The following formulae hold for the states in the STRIPS notation:

- An action A_i is applicable to a state S if $prec(A_i) \subseteq S$.
- If A_i is applied to S, the successor state S' is calculated as: $S' = S \setminus del(A_i) \cup add(A_i)$.
- The solution to such a problem is a sequence of actions, which if applied to I leads to a state S' such as $S \supseteq G$.

Usually, in the description of domains, action schemas (also called operators) are used instead of actions. Action schemas contain variables that can be instantiated using the available objects and this makes the encoding of the domain easier.

The choice of the language in which the planning problem will be represented strongly affects the solving process. On one hand, there are languages that enable planning systems to solve the problems easier, but they make the encoding harder and pose many representation constraints. For example, propositional logic and first order predicate logic do not support complex aspects such as time or uncertainty. On the other hand, there are more expressive languages, such as natural language, but it is quite difficult to enhance planning systems with support for them.

The PDDL Definition Language

PDDL (Planning Domain Definition Language) focuses on expressing the physical properties of the domain that we consider in each planning problem such as the predicates and actions that exist. There are no structures to provide the planner with *advice*, that is, guidelines about how to search the solution space, although extended notation may be used depending on the planner. The features of the language have been divided into subsets referred to as requirements, and each

domain definition has to declare which requirements will put into effect. Moreover, unless stated otherwise, the closed-world assumption holds.

The domain definition in PDDL permits inheritance. Each definition consists of several declarations which include the aforementioned requirements, types of entities used, variables and constants used, literals that are true at all times called *timeless*, and predicates. Besides, there are declarations of actions, axioms, and safety constraints, which are explained in the following three paragraphs.

Actions enable transitions between successive situations. An action declaration mentions the parameters and variables involved, as well as the preconditions that must hold for the action to be applied. As a result of the action we can have either a list of effects or an expansion, but not both. The effects, which can be both conditional and universally quantified, express how the world situation changes after the action is applied. The expansion decomposes the action into simpler ones, which can be in a series-parallel combination, arbitrary partially ordered, or chosen among a set. It is used when the solution is specified by a series of actions rather than a goal state. Furthermore, several additional constructs can be used, which impose additional preconditions and maintenance conditions.

Axioms, in contrast to actions, state relationships among propositions that hold within the same situation. The necessity of axioms arises from the fact that the action definitions do not mention all the changes in all predicates that might be affected by an action. Therefore, additional predicates are concluded by axioms after the application of each action. These are called derived predicates, as opposed to primitive ones.

Safety constraints in PDDL are background goals, which may be broken during the planning process, but ultimately they must be restored. Constraint violations present in the initial situation do not require to be fulfilled by the planner.

In PDDL, we can add axioms and action expansions modularly using the construct *addendum*. In addition, there are build-in predicates, under certain requirements, for expression evaluation, often used with certain types of entities that may change values as a result of an action called *fluents*.

After having defined a planning domain, one can define problems with respect to it. A problem definition in PDDL must specify an initial situation and a final situation, referred to as goal. The initial situation can be specified either by name or as a list of literals assumed to be true, or both. In the last case, literals are treated as effects, therefore they are added to the initial situation stated by name. The goal can be either a goal description, using function-free first order predicate logic, including nested quantifiers, or an expansion of actions, or both. The solution given to a problem is a sequence of actions, which can be applied to the initial situation, eventually producing the situation stated by the goal description, and satisfying the expansion, if there is one.

PDDL 2.1 (Fox & Long, 2003) was designed to be backward compatible with PDDL and to preserve its basic principles. It was developed by the necessity for a language capable of expressing temporal and numeric properties of planning domains. The extensions introduced were numeric expressions, durative actions and a new optional field in the problem specification that allowed the definition of alternative plan metrics to estimate the value of a plan.

PDDL 2.2 (Edelkamp & Hoffmann, 2004) added derived predicates, which are an evolution of the axioms construct of the original PDDL. In addition, timed initial literals were introduced, which are facts that become true or false at certain time points known to the planner beforehand, independently of the actions chosen to be carried out by the planner.

In PDDL 3.0 (Gerevini & Long, 2005), the language was enhanced with constructs that increase its expressive power regarding the plan quality specification. The constraints and goals are divided into strong, which must be satisfied by the solution, and soft, which may not be satisfied, but are desired. Evidently, the more soft constraints and goals a plan satisfies, the better quality it possesses. Each soft constraint and goal may be associated with a certain importance which, when satisfied, contributes to the plan quality. Moreover, there are state trajectory constraints, which impose conditions on the entire sequence of situations visited and not only on the final situation. Finally, this version allows nesting of modal operators and preferences inside them.

THE VISUAL TOOL

ViTAPlan (visual tool for adaptive planning) is an integrated environment for designing new planning problems, solving them, and obtaining visual representations of the plans/solutions. The architecture of the visual tool, which is outlined in Figure 1, consists of the following sub-systems, which are discussed in more detail later in the chapter: (a) designing, (b) configuration, (c) solving, (d) visualizing, and (e) simulating.

The designing module provides visual representations of planning domains and problems through graphs that assist the user in comprehending their structure. Furthermore, the user is provided with graphical elements and tools for designing new domains and new problems over existing domains. This module communicates with the file system of the operating system in order to save the designs in a planner--readable format (i.e., PDDL planning language) and also load and visualize past domains and problems.

The configuration module of ViTAPlan deals with the automatic fine-tuning of the planning parameters. This task is performed through two steps that are implemented in different sub-systems. The first one, called problem analyzer, reads the description of the problem from the input files, analyzes it, and outputs a vector of numbers

Figure 1. ViTAPlan's architecture

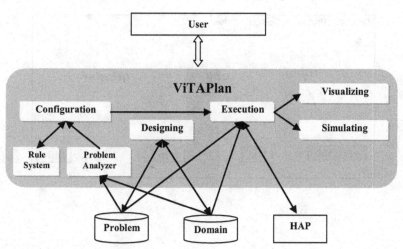

that correspond to the values of 35 measurable attributes that quantify the morphology of the problem in hand. The rule system, which is consulted after the analysis of the problem, contains a number of rules that associate specific values or value ranges of the problems' attributes with configurations of the planning parameters that guarantee good performance.

The execution module inputs the description of the problems (PDDL files of the domain and the problem) along with the values of the planner's parameters and executes the planner (HAP or any other system attached to ViTAPlan) in order to obtain a solution (plan) to the problem. The planner's parameters can be adjusted either by hand or automatically via the configuration module.

The last two sub-systems (visualization and simulation) present the plan that was inputted from the execution module in several forms. The visualization module presents the plan as a directed graph, through which the user can identify the positive and negative interactions among the actions and experiment with different orderings

in which the plan's steps should be executed. The second module simulates the problem's world presenting all the intermediate states that occur after the execution of each action.

VISUAL DESIGN OF PLANNING PROBLEMS

The design module of ViTAPlan serves as a tool for (a) visualizing the structure of planning domains and problems in order to get a better understanding of their nature and (b) designing new domains or new instances (problems) of existing domains with a user-friendly tool that can be used by non-PDDL experts. The steps that a typical user must go through in order to design a new problem through ViTAPlan are the following: (a) create the entity-relation model, (b) design the operators, (c) specify one or more problems, (d) check the validity of the designs, and (e) translate the visual representations in PDDL language in order to solve the problem(s).

Figure 2. Entities-relations diagram for gripper

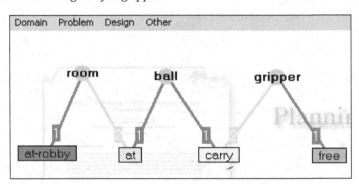

The Entity-Relation Model

The entities-relations diagram is a directed graph containing two types of nodes and one type of arcs connecting the nodes. The first type of nodes, called entity, is represented in the design as a circle, and corresponds to an object class of the domain. The second type is represented by the visual tool as a rectangle and is used to specify relations between the domain's classes. The edges connect rectangular with circular nodes and are used to specify which classes take part in each relation.

Consider the gripper domain for example, where there is a robot with *N* grippers that moves in a space, composed of *K* rooms that are all connected with each other. All the rooms are modeled as points and there are connections between each pair of points and therefore the robot is able to reach all rooms starting from any one of them with a simple movement. In the gripper domain there are *L* numbered balls, which the robot must carry from their initial position to their destination.

The diagram for the *gripper* domain, which was used in the AIPS-98 planning competition, is illustrated in Figure 2. There are three object classes in the domain, namely *room, ball,* and *gripper* that are represented with circles. There

is no class defined for the robot, since the domain assumes the presence of only one instance of it and therefore there is no need for an explicit definition.

The domain has four predicates: (a) *at-robby,* which specifies the position of the robot and it is connected only with one instance of *room,* (b) *at* which specifies the room in which each ball resides and therefore is connected with an instance of *ball* and an instance of *room,* (c) *carry,* which defines the alternative position of a ball (i.e., it is held by the robot and therefore it is connected with an instance of *ball* and an instance of *gripper*), and (d) *free,* which is connected only with an instance of *gripper* and states that the current gripper does not hold any ball.

Note here that although PDDL requires only the arity for each predicate and not the type of objects for the arguments, the interface obliges the user to connect each predicate with specific object classes and this is used for the consistency check of the domain design. According to the design of Figure 2, the arity of predicate *carry,* for example, is two and the specific predicate can only be connected with one object of class *ball* and one object of class *gripper.*

Representing Operators

The definition of operators in ViTAPlan follows a declarative schema, which is different from the classical STRIPS approach although there is a direct way to transform definitions from one approach to the other. More specifically, an operator in the visual environment is represented with two lists, namely *Pre* and *Post*, that contain the facts that must hold in a state S_1 in order to apply the operator and the facts that will be true in state S_2 that will result from the application of the operator on S_1 respectively. The relations between these lists and the three lists (*Prec, Add, Del*) of the STRIPS notation are the following:

From STRIPS to ViTAPlan:
$Pre(A) = Prec(A)$
$Post(A) = Add(A) \cup (Prec(A) - Del(A))$
From ViTAPlan to STRIPS:
$Prec(A) = Pre(A)$
$Add(A) = Post(A) - Pre(A)$
$Del(A) = Pre(A) - Post(A)$

Each operator in the interface is represented with a labeled frame, which contains a column of object classes in the middle, two columns of predicates on the two sides of it, and connections between the object classes and the predicates. The un-grounded facts that are generated by the classes and the predicates in the left column define the *Pre* list of the operator while the *Post* list is defined by the predicates in the right column.

For example, in the gripper domain there are three operators: (a) *move,* which allows the robot to move between rooms, (b) *pick,* which is used in order to lift a ball using a gripper, and (c) *drop,* which is the direct opposite of pick and is used to leave a ball on the ground.

The *move* operator is related with two instances of the room class (*room1* and *room2*), which correspond to the initial and the destination room of the robot's move. The *Pre* and *Post* lists of the operator contain only one instance of the *at-robby*

Figure 3. The move operator

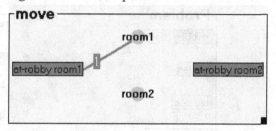

relation. In the *Pre* list, the at-robby is connected to *room1*, while the latter is replaced by *room2* in the *Post* list. The definition of the move operator is presented in Figure 3.

The second operator (*pick*), which is presented in Figure 4, contains one instance from three entities, namely *ball1, room1,* and *gripper1* that correspond to the ball that resided on the room and was picked by a robot's gripper. The *Pre* list defines that both the ball and the robot must be in the same room and that the gripper must be free. The new fact that is contained in the *Post* list is that the gripper holds the ball, while the freedom of the gripper and the fact that the ball resides on

Figure 4. The pick operator

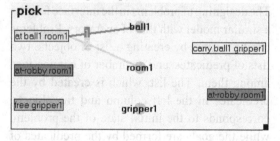

Figure 5. The drop operator

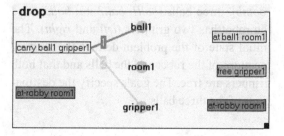

Figure 6. A problem of the gripper domain

Problem

at-robby rooma

free left

free right

at ball3 rooma

at ball2 rooma

at ball1 rooma

rooma

roomb

ball3

ball2

ball1

left

right

at ball3 roomb

at ball2 roomb

at ball1 roomb

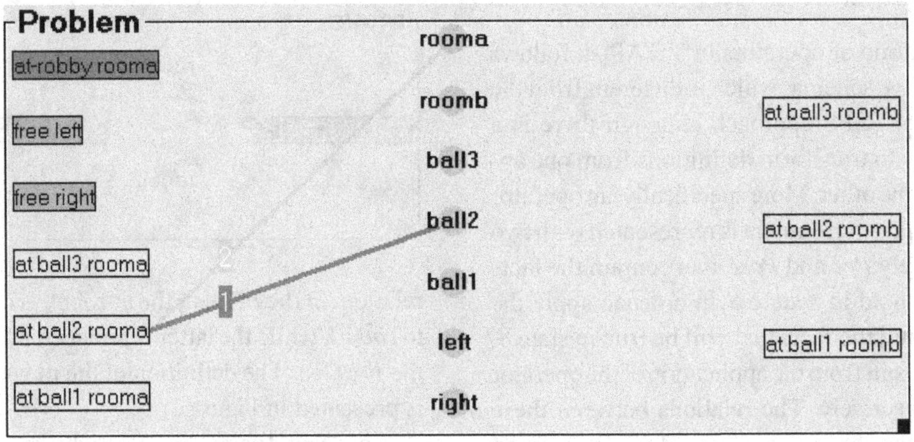

the room are deleted. The fact that the robot is in *room1* is contained in both lists (*Pre* and *Post*) since it is not deleted.

Similarly, we define the *drop* operator, which is presented in Figure 5. This operator is the direct opposite of the *pick* operator and in fact, it is produced by exchanging the *Prec* and *Post* lists of the latter.

Representing Problems

The designing of problems in the interface follows a similar model with that of operators. Problems can be formed by creating a list of objects, two lists of predicates, and a number of connections among them. The list, which is created by the predicates in the left column and the objects, corresponds to the initial state of the problem, while the goals are formed by the predicates of the right column.

Figure 6 presents a problem of the gripper domain, which contains two rooms (*rooma* and *roomb*), three balls (*ball1, ball2 και ball3*), and the robot has two grippers (*left* and *right*). The initial state of the problem defines the starting locations of the robot and the balls and that both grippers are free. The goals specify the destinations of the three balls.

Figure 7. A map for a gripper problem

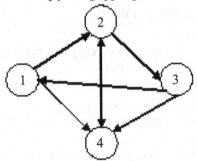

One of the key enhancements of ViTAPlan-2 over the past versions concerns the ability to use a predefined chain of objects that can be utilized for the definition of many kinds of facts. Consider, for example, the case where in gripper the moves of the robot are restricted by a relation (e.g., *connected*), which specifies which movements are feasible. If we suppose that the map of the rooms is the one presented in Figure 7, then this would require the user to add the *connected* relation seven times in the problem's definition and each time to make the appropriate connections (see Figure 8). This can become a severe problem for large and complex maps.

There are a number of cases where similar maps are required. For example in the *hanoi* domain, according to the definition adopted by

Figure 8. The connections between the rooms

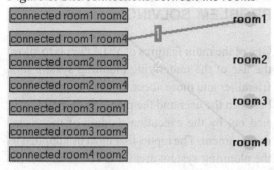

Figure 9. The map tool

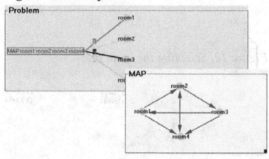

the planning community, the problem file must specify for each possible pair of pegs and discs which of the two is smaller. For a simple problem with three pegs and 5 discs, this yields 39 smaller relations.

In order to deal with this problem, ViTAPlan-2 contains a tool for building maps, which makes it easier for the user to define multiple relations between pairs of objects that belong to the same entity. The user can use simple drag 'n drop operations in order to define single and duplex connections between them. For example, the case described in Figure 8 can be easily encoded in ViTAPlan-2 using the map tool as shown in Figure 9.

Syntax and Validity Checking

The visual environment, besides the automation and the convenient way in which new domains and

problems are designed, also performs a number of validity checks in the definitions in order to assist the user in this really complex task. The entities-relations diagram, which is probably the most important part of the design of new domains, is further used by ViTAPlan-2 as a reference model for the checks.

Each time the user tries to connect an instance of an entity E to an instance of a relation R, the tool checks if:

1. This specific connection generates a fact that has already been defined in the same operator or in the problem. In this case, the connection is rejected since PDDL does not allow redefinitions of the same fact inside the same scope.
2. The definition of the relation in the entities-relations diagram contains a connection to the entity in which E belongs.
3. There is an empty slot in R, which according to the diagram should be connected to objects of the same class as that of E.

The checks previously listed are also performed dynamically at each attempted change in the entities-relations diagram. For example, if the user deletes a connection between an entity and a relation, ViTAPlan will automatically delete any instance of this connection from all the operators and the definition of the problem. A similar update will also take place in the definition of the operators and in the problem, if the user deletes an entire relation or an entity.

Finally, a number of checks are also performed during the compilation of the design in PDDL. More specifically these checks contain:

- The case where no operator is defined.
- The definition of empty operators .
- The definition of void operators (i.e., operators with empty *Pre* and *Post* lists).
- The definition of effectless operators (*Pre* ≡ *Post*).

Figure 10. The gripper domain in PDDL

Figure 11. The PDDL file of a gripper's problem

- The definition of empty problems.
- Semi-connected edges, which lead to incomplete facts.

Translation to PDDL

The domains and the problems that are designed in ViTAPlan are automatically compiled to the PDDL definition language in order to allow their solving using different planning systems. The environment contains a PDDL editor, which enables the user to see and even modify the PDDL files of his or her designs. For example, the gripper domain and the specific problem used in this section are presented in Figure 10 and Figure 11 respectively.

SYSTEM CONFIGURATION AND PROBLEM SOLVING

One of the main features of ViTAPlan is to allow the use of the underlying planning system in a friendlier and more accurate way. This interface between the user and the planning engine is carried out by the execution module of the visual environment. The inputs that must be supplied to the planning system are: (a) the domain file, (b) the problem file, and (c) the values of the planning parameters in case of adjustable planners.

Figure 12. Selecting the input files

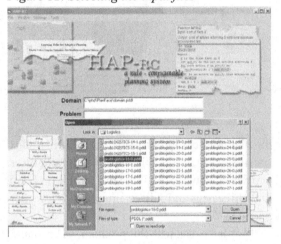

Figure 13. Solving the problem

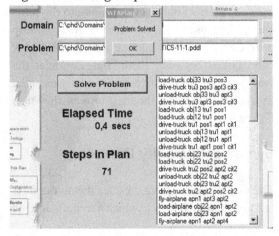

Figure 14. Setting the planning parameters

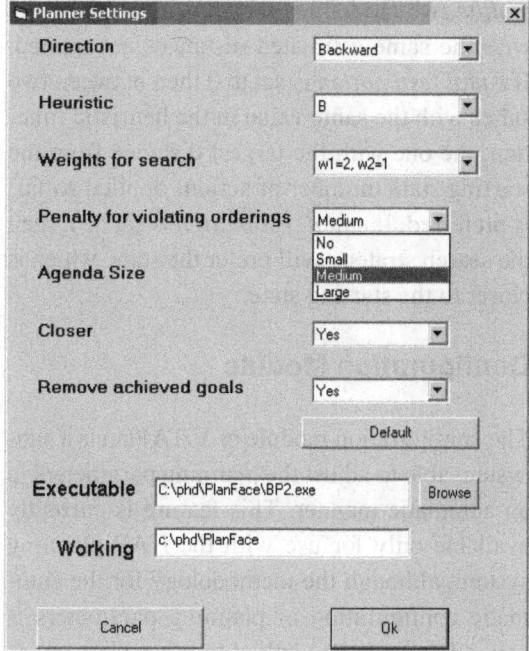

Hap Planner

HAP is a highly adjustable planning system that can be customized by the user through a number of parameters. These parameters concern the type of search, the quality of the heuristic, and several other features that affect the planning process. The HAP system is based on the BP (bi-directional planner) planning system (Vrakas & Vlahavas, 2002a) and uses an extended version of the ACE (Vrakas & Vlahavas, 2002b) heuristic.

HAP is capable of planning in both directions (progression and regression). The system is quite symmetric and for each critical part of the planner (e.g., calculation of mutexes, discovery of goal orderings, computation of the heuristic, search strategies etc.), there are implementations for both directions. The *direction* of search is the first adjustable parameter of HAP used in tests with the following values: (a) 0 (regression or backward chaining) and (b) 1 (progression or forward chaining).

As for the search itself, HAP adopts a weighted A* strategy with two independent weights: w_1 for the estimated cost for reaching the final state and w_2 for the accumulated cost of reaching the current state from the starting state (initial or goals depending on the selected direction). For the tests with HAP, we used four different assignments for the variable *weights*, which correspond to different assignments for w_1 and w_2: (a) 0 (w_1 =1, w_2 =0), (b) 1 (w_1 =3, w_2 =1), (c) 2 (w_1 =2, w_2 =1), and (d) 3 (w_1 =1, w_2 =1).

The size of the planning agenda (denoted as *sof_agenda*) of HAP also affects the search strategy and it can also be set by the user. For example, if we set *sof_agenda* to 1 and w_2 to 0, the search algorithm becomes pure Hill-Climbing, while by setting *sof_agenda* to 1, w_1 to 1 and w_2 to 1 the search algorithm becomes A*. Generally, by increasing the size of the agenda we reduce the risk of not finding a solution, even if at least one exists, while by reducing the size of the agenda the search algorithm becomes faster

From the initial screen of the interface, which is shown in Figure 12, the user uses common dialogues and graphical elements in order to browse for the domain and problem files that will be inputted to the planner. From the same screen, the user can also execute the planner and obtain the solution (plan) along with statistics concerning the execution, such as the planning time and the length of the plan. The way the results of the planner are presented to the user is shown in Figure 13.

There are three ways for tuning the planner's parameters in ViTAPlan: (a) using the default values provided by the system, (b) let the user assign the values by hand, or (c) use the configuration module in order to have the parameters set automatically. The user can select among the first two ways through the settings window presented in Figure 14. The parameters presented in this window correspond to the HAP planner, which is embodied in ViTAPlan.

and we ensure that the planner will not run out of memory. For the tests, we used three different settings for the size of the agenda: (a) 1, (b) 100, and (c) 1000.

The *OB* and *OB-R* functions introduced in BP and ACE respectively are also adopted by HAP in order to search the states of the search for violations of orderings between the facts of either the initial state or the goals, depending on the direction of the search. For each violation contained in a state, the estimated value of this state that is returned by the heuristic function, is increased by violation penalty, which is a constant number supplied by the user. For the experiments of this work, we tested the HAP system with three different values of *violation_penalty*: (a) 0, (b) 10, and (c) 100.

The HAP system employs the heuristic function of the ACE planner, plus two variations of it, which are in general more fine-grained. There are implementations of the heuristic functions for both planning directions. All the heuristic functions are constructed in a pre-planning phase by performing a relaxed search in the opposite direction of the one used in the search phase. During this relaxed search, the heuristic function computes estimations for the distances of all grounded actions of the problem.

The user may select the heuristic function by configuring the *heuristic_order* parameter. The three acceptable values are: (a) 1 for the initial heuristic, (b) 2 for the first variation, and (c) 3 for the second variation.

HAP also embodies a technique for simplifying the definition of the sub-problem in hand. This technique eliminates from the definition of the sub-problem (current state and goals) all the goals that have already been achieved in the current state and do not interfere in any way with the achievement of the remaining goals. In order to do this the technique performs, off-line before the search process, a dependency analysis on the goals of the problem. The parameter *remove_subgoals* is used to turn on (value 1) and off (value 0) this feature of the planning system.

The last parameter of HAP is *equal_estimation*, which defines the way in which states with the same estimated distances are treated. If *equal_estimation* is set to 0 then between two states with the same value in the heuristic function, the one with the largest distance from the starting state (number of actions applied so far) is preferred. If *equal_estimation* is set to 1, then the search strategy will prefer the state, which is closer to the starting state.

Configuration Module

The configuration module of ViTAPlan is a subsystem able to adjust the planning parameters in an automatic manner. This feature is currently available only for use with the HAP planning system, although the methodology for the automatic configuration of planning parameters is general and can be applied to other planners as well (Tsoumakas, Vrakas, Bassiliades, & Vlahavas, 2004).

The automatic configuration is based on HAP-RC (Vrakas et al., 2003), which uses a rule system in order to automatically select the best settings for each planning parameter, based on the morphology of the problem in hand. HAP-RC, whose architecture is outlined in Figure 15 is actually HAP with two additional modules (problem

Figure 15. HAP-RC architecture

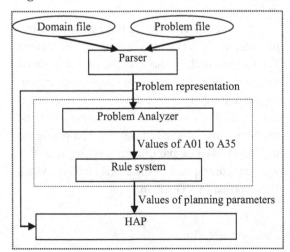

analyzer and rule system), which are utilized off-line just after reading the representation of the problem in order to fine tune the planning parameters of HAP.

The role of the problem analyzer is to identify the values of a specific set of 35 problem characteristics (noted as A1 to A35). These characteristics include measurable attributes of planning problems, such as number of facts per predicate and the branching factor of the problem, that present the internal structure of the problems in a quantified way. After the identification of the values of the attributes, which may require a limited search in the problem, the analyzer feeds the rule system with a vector containing the values for the 35 problem attributes.

The rule system contains a number of rules of the following format:

If preconditions list Then actions list

The preconditions of the rules check if the values of the problem's attributes comply with some constraints on them, while the actions set one or more planning parameters to specific values. For example, the rule:

If A24<1.8 and A17<9.7 Then direction=1 and closer=yes

will trigger in a given problem if the values of A24 (ratio between the branching factors of the two directions) and A17 (standard deviation of the average number of actions deleting a fact) are smaller than 1.8 and 9.7 respectively. If this rule is eventually fired, then the planning direction will be set to forward and the search algorithm will use the technique for overcoming plateaus.

What these rules actually do, is to propose setups for the planning parameters that worked efficiently in similar problems in the past. This knowledge has been extracted from machine learning techniques on data produced by thorough experiments with the HAP system. More specifically, we tested all the possible combinations of the parameters of HAP on a large set of problems

from various domains and for each run, we kept record of the values of the problem attributes, the specific setup for HAP, and the value of a metric combining planning time and plan length. The data set was then fed to a machine learning tool in order to learn a rule-based classification model that would discriminate between good and bad values of the metric based on the rest of the attributes.

The configuration module of ViTAPlan-2 also provides the user with the option to use the problem analyzer and the rule System of HAP-RC in order to automatically fine-tune the planning parameters of HAP. The relevant window of the interface is shown in Figure 16. This window is divided in three parts: (a) the first part shows the discretized values for the 35 problem characteristics as produced by the problem analyzer, (b) the second part provides the user with the list of the rules that comprise the core knowledge of the system, and (c) the last part provides the user with the proposed values for the planning parameters of HAP.

The values of the problem's attributes are presented in order to check for the triggered rules, but more importantly to assist the knowledge engineer or the domain expert in decoding the internal structure of the problem and extract useful insights from it. The tool presents the following information for each one of the 35 attributes: (a) the code name (e.g., *A07*), (b) a description of the attribute (e.g., *standard deviation of the number of facts per predicate*), (c) the arithmetic value, (d) a discretized value (e.g., *small*), and (e) the usual upper and lower limit for its value.

The rules are shown in the appropriate frame of the environment sorted by decreasing order of their confidence, as this was calculated by the learning algorithm. ViTAPlan presents all the rules, but the user is able to control the viewable part of the rules through two controls that select only the triggered rules or the rules that affect a specific parameter (e.g., heuristic function).

Figure 16. The rule system

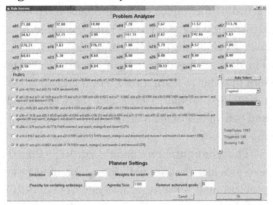

Figure 17. The initial firing set

Figure 18. The final firing set

From the set of triggered rules, ViTAPlan makes an initial choice, selecting the rules with the highest confidence factor that are not in conflict with any other already selected rule. We say that two rules are in conflict, if they propose different setups for the same parameter. The configuration module uses the initial subset of selected rules in order to calculate the values of the parameters and present them to the user, leaving each unset parameter to its default value.

Instead of just accepting or rejecting the proposed parameter setting, the user has the ability to interfere with the rule system, thus modifying the adopted conflict resolution strategy. More specifically, the user may either include a new rule in the firing set, or request the removal of a selected one and thus alter the firing set and therefore the setup of the parameters. Each time the user requests the firing of a new rule R_i, the module automatically checks the resulting firing set for conflicts and removes all the rules that propose contradictory values for the parameters affected by R_i.

Consider for example the case in Figure 17, which presents a portion of the triggered rules (i.e., those that require values for the attributes A01 to A35 that are compatible with the problem in hand). The initial selection contains rules 49, 74, and 154 that define the values 100, 2, 3, and 0 for the parameters *penalty, heuristic, search_strategy,* and *direction* respectively.

Lets also suppose that the user requests rule number 35 (the first rule in Figure 17) to be included in the firing set. Rule 35 is in contradiction with rule 49 since the first sets *penalty* to 500 while the second sets it to 100 and with rule 154 for the same reason. There is no contradiction with rule 74, since the only common parameter is *heuristic* and they propose the same value (2) for it. Therefore, after the inclusion of rule 35, rules 49 and 154 are removed from the firing set as shown in Figure 18. The proposed setup of the planner's parameters becomes the following: *closer=1, penalty=500, heuristic=2, search_strategy=3* and *direction=0.*

Embedding Other Planning Systems

The current version of ViTAPlan embodies the HAP system, but the environment is open and the

Figure 19. Communication with the planner

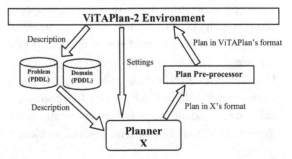

Table 1. Specification of LPG's parameters

Parameter	Option	Values
Heuristic identifier	-h	1,2
Max number of restarts	-restarts	1,2,3,4,5,6,7,8,9....
Noise added to Walksat	-noise	0,0.1,0.2,0.3....
...		

user can easily attach any other planner that reads the PDDL language. The communication protocol between the visual environment and the planner (including HAP) is outlined in Figure 19.

As already discussed, the data that should be transmitted between ViTAPlan and the planning system are: (a) the description of the domain and the problem, (b) optionally the settings for the planner's parameters, and (c) the plan that solves the problem.

Concerning the description of the problem, ViTAPlan is able to extract PDDL files, which is the standard definition language for all modern planners. Therefore, it is trivial to submit the problem to any new planning system.

For each configurable parameter, ViTAPlan needs a description, the option used to set this parameter in the planner and the domain of values. This information must be specified by the user in order to add a new planner in the environment. The current version of ViTAPlan supports only discrete values for the domains of the parameters, but this can very easily be extended to support continuous values or other data types (e.g., bool-

eans). For example, Table 1 presents part of the information that should be inputted to ViTAPlan-2 in order to connect it with the LPG planning system (Gerevini, Saetti, & Serina, 2003).

The output of any planner to a given problem is a sequence of actions that achieve the predefined goals. However, since there has not been a standard for describing plans yet, each planner may present the sequences of actions in a different way. Therefore a necessary step in order to attach a different planning system X on ViTAPlan, is to format its output, either by modifying the system, or by adding a pre-processor that reads the plan in X's format and transforms it. Figure 20 presents an example of a plan in ViTAPlan's format.

PLAN REPRESENTATIONS

There are two modules for visualizing the plans in ViTAPlan: the execution simulation, which simulates the execution of the plan in a virtual world and the steps visualization, which presents the plan as an action graph.

World Simulation

This module of ViTAPlan allows the user to execute the plan that was acquired from the execution sub system and trace the changes that occur to the world as the actions of the plan are sequentially applied. Figure 21 presents the simulation module, which consists of three parts. The first one is a scroll bar, through which the user can browse for a specific action of the plan. The other two parts

Figure 20. A plan's excerpt in ViTAPlan's format

```
Begin of Plan
1: (drive truck0 distributor1
distributor0)
2: (lift hoist1 crate0 pallet1
distributor0)
3: (load hoist1 crate0 truck0
distributor0)
...
11: (drop hoist1 crate1 pallet1
distributor0)
End of Plan
```

Figure 21. Execution simulation

present the states of the world before the application of the selected action (left part) and after it (right part) respectively.

In the example presented in Figure 21 the first action of the plan is selected and therefore the state presented in the left part is the initial one, while the one in the right part is the first intermediate state. The tool uses proper color-coding in order to discriminate the facts in four categories:

1. Facts of the preceding state that are deleted by the action.
2. New facts that are added to the new state.
3. Propagated facts.
4. Static facts.

Graph-Based Representations

The second option for the user is to view the actions of the plan on a timeline as shown in Figure 22. The timeline for the plan presents for each action the point in which it is scheduled to be executed and the facts in its precondition and add lists. Moreover, the visualization shows the interactions between the actions in the plan. More specifically, for each action A the user is able to see connections between:

1. Each precondition of A and the most recent action that achieved it.
2. Each fact that is deleted by A and the most recent action that established it.
3. Each fact that is added by A and the following actions that have it in their preconditions.

The connections represented by the arcs in the graph present in graphical way all the interactions (positive and negative) between the steps of the plan and therefore allow the user to:

1. Comprehend the specific sorting in which the steps have been ordered and why a specific

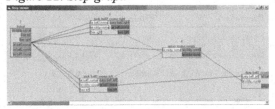

Figure 22. Step graph

action should be placed before (or after) another one.
2. Replace an action or a set of actions with another, taking care so as not to violate the interactions, and thus produce modified or alternative plans.
3. Find parallelizations in the plan execution and therefore reduce the total execution time and the cost of its application.

CONCLUSION AND FUTURE WORK

This chapter presented ViTAPlan, a unified environment for automated planning, which contains several modules with user-friendly interfaces. The main feature of the environment is the designing module, which saves the user from the strict syntax of the planning domain definition language (PDDL). The user is able to visualize and design new domains and problems in an easy-to-use graphical way and the tool is responsible for checking the validity of the designs and translating them in PDDL files.

The current version of the environment has four main functions: (a) using the planning system through a number of windows, controls, and common dialogues, which makes it much easier for a non-programmer to use the planner and experiment with different setups of the planning parameters, (b) use the problem analyzer and the rule system of HAP-RC in order to acquire useful knowledge about the morphology of each problem and automatically fine tune the planner with the most appropriate values for the planning parameters, (c) generating new domains and problems using a visual tool, and (d) produce visual representations of the plans found by the planning system, which enable the user to better understand each step in the plan and also intervene and alter the plan at will.

In the future, we plan to improve the interface in all functions of it and introduce others that will make it a complete tool for planning both for academic and industrial use. It is in our direct plans to enhance the tool for designing domains and problems with the ability to handle advanced aspects of the latest versions of PDDL such as treatment of numerical values, explicit representation of time and duration, conditional effects, etc.

In parallel, we are currently working on developing an interface for ViTAPlan in order to input OWL-S documents that describe simple or complex semantic Web services and automatically translate them to PDDL problem definitions. Then, our visual tool will enable authoring of appropriate service composition operators as planning operators that will solve the semantic Web service composition problem. The produced plan will constitute the complex Web service and it will be exported in an appropriate Web service choreography language or in OWL-S to a corresponding complex Web Service execution monitoring tool or it will be just published at a UDDI registry.

REFERENCES

Berardi, D., Calvanese, D., De Giacomo, G., & Mecella, M. (2003). Reasoning about actions for e-service composition. *ICAPS 2003 Workshop on Planning for Web Services*.

Berners-Lee, T., Hendler, J., & Lassila, O. (2001). The semantic Web. *Scientific American, 284*(5), 34-43.

Blum, A., & Furst, M. (1995). Fast planning through planning graph analysis. *Proceedings of the 14th International Conference on Artificial Intelligence* (pp. 636-642). Berlin, Germany.

Blythe, J., Deelman, E., & Gil, Y. (2003). Planning for workflow construction and maintenance on the Grid. *ICAPS 2003 Workshop on Planning for Web Services*.

Bonet, B., & Geffner, H. (2001). Planning a heuristic search. *Artificial Intelligence, Special issue on Heuristic Search, 129*(1-2), 5-33.

Booth, D., Haas, H., McCabe, F., Newcomer, E., Champion, M, Ferris, C., & Orchard, D. (2003). *Web services architecture*. W3C Working Draft, Aug. 2003. Retrieved from http://www.w3.org/TR/ws-arch/

Botea, A., Enzenberger, M., Müller, M., & Schaeffer, J. (2005), Macro-FF: Improving AI planning with automatically learned macro-operators, To appear in *Journal of Artificial Intelligence Research*.

Bourbakis, N., & Tascillo, A. (1997). An SPN-neural planning methodology for coordination of two robotic hands with constrained placement. *Journal of Intelligent and Robotic Systems archive, 19*(3), 321-337.

Carman, M., Serafini, L., & Traverso, P. (2003). Web service composition as planning. *ICAPS 2003 Workshop on Planning for Web Services*.

Chen, Y., Wah, B. W., & Hsu, C. (2005). Subgoal partitioning and resolution for temporal planning in SGPlan. *Journal of Artificial Intelligence Research, 26,* 323-369.

Edelkamp, S., & Hoffmann, J. (2004). PDDL 2.2: The language for the classical part of IPC-4. *Proceedings of the International Planning Competition International Conference on Automated Planning and Scheduling* (pp. 1-7).

Fikes, R., & Nilsson, N. J. (1971). STRIPS: A new approach to the application of theorem proving to problem solving. *Artificial Intelligence, 2*(3-4), 189-208.

Fox, M., & Long, D. (2003). PDDL2.1: An extension to PDDL for expressing temporal planning domains. *Journal of Artificial Intelligence Research, 20,* 61-124.

Friedman-Hill, E. J. (2002). *Jess, the expert system shell for the Java Platform.* Retrieved from http://herzberg.ca.sandia.gov/jess/

Gerevini, A., & Long, D. (2005). Plan constraints and preferences in PDDL3. *Technical Report R.T. 2005-08-47,* Dipartimento di Elettronica per l'Automazione, Università degli Studi di Brescia, via Branze 38, 25123 Brescia, Italy.

Gerevini, A., Saetti, A., & Serina, I. (2004). Planning in PDDL2.2 domains with LPG-TD. *International Planning Competition, 14th International Conference on Automated Planning and Scheduling (ICAPS-04), abstract booklet of the competing planners.*

Gerevini, A., Saetti, A., & Serina, I. (2003). Planning through stochastic local search and temporal action graphs. *Journal of Artificial Intelligence Research, 20,* 239-290.

Ghallab, M., Howe, A., Knoblock, C., McDermott, D., Ram, A., Veloso, M., Weld, D., & Wilkins, D. (1998). PDDL: The planning domain definition language. *Technical report, Yale University,* New Haven, CT.

Hoffmann, J., & Nebel, B. (2001). The FF planning system: Fast plan generation through heuristic search. *Journal of Artificial Intelligence Research, 14,* 253-302.

Hoffmann, J. (2003). The metric-FF planning system: Translating "ignoring delete lists" to Numeric State Variables. *Journal of Artificial Intelligence Research, 20,* 291-341.

Kautz, H., & Selman, B. (1996). Pushing the envelope: Planning, propositional logic, and stochastic search. *Proceedings of the 13th National Conference on Artificial Intelligence* (pp. 1194-1201). Portland, Oregon.

Kautz, H., & Selman, B. (1998). BLACKBOX: A new approach to the application of theorem proving to problem solving. *Proceedings of the AIPS-98 Workshop on Planning as Combinatorial Search* (pp. 58-60). Pittsburgh, Pennsylvania.

Koehler J., & Srivastava B. (2003). Web service composition: Current solutions and open problems. *ICAPS 2003 Workshop on Planning for Web Services* (pp. 28-35).

Kosara, R., & Miksch, S. (2001). Metaphors of movement: A visualization and user interface for time-oriented, skeletal plans. *Artificial Intelligence in Medicine, Special Issue: Information Visualization in Medicine, 22*(2), 111-131.

Kundu, K., Sessions, C., DesJardins, M., & Rheingans, P. (2002). Three-dimensional visualization of hierarchical task network plans. *Proceedings of the 3rd International NASA Workshop on Planning and Scheduling for Space,* Houston, Texas.

Kuter, U., Sirin, E., Parsia, B., Dana, N., & James, H. (2005). Information gathering during planning for Web service composition. *Web semantics: Science, services, and agents on the World Wide Web, 3*(2-3), 183-205.

Leymann, F. (2003). Web services: Distributed applications without limits: An outline. Proceedings of the Database Systems for Business, Technology and Web (BTW 2003). In G. Weikum, H. Schöning, & E. Rahm (Eds.), GI-Edition. Lecture Notes in Informatics (LNI) (pp. 26). Bonner Köllen Verlag.

Leymann, F. (2001, May). *Web services flow language* (WSFL 1.0). IBM. Retrieved from http://www-3.ibm.com/software/solutions/Webservices/pdf/WSFL.pdf

Long, D., & Fox, M. (1998). Efficient implementation of the plan graph in STAN. *Journal of Artificial Intelligence Research, 10,* 87-115.

Marcugini, S., & Milani, A. (2002). Automated planning of Web services. *Proceedings of the 3rd International Conference on Electronic Commerce, ICEC 2002,* Hong Kong.

Martinez, A., Patinio-Martinez, M., Jimenez-Peris, R., Perez-Sorrosal, F. (2005). ZenFlow: A visual Web service composition tool for BPEL4WS. *IEEE Symp. on Visual Languages and Human-Centric Computing,* Dallas, Texas.

McCluskey, T. L., Liu, D., & Simpson, R. (2003). gipo ii: htn planning in a tool-supported knowledge engineering environment. *Proceedings of the 13th International Conference on Automated Planning and Scheduling* (pp. 92-101). Trento, Italy.

McIlraith, S., & Fadel, R. (2002). Planning with complex actions. *Proceedings of the AIPS 2002 Workshop on Exploring Real World Planning,* Toulouse, France.

McIlraith, S., Son, T. C., & Zeng, H. (2001). Semantic Web services. *IEEE Intelligent Systems, Special Issue on the Semantic Web, 16*(2), 46-53.

Milani, A. (2003). Planning and scheduling for the Web roadmap. *Technical Coordination Unit for Planning and Scheduling for the Web, PLANET Network of Excellence,* March. Retrieved from http://www.dipmat.unipg.it/~milani/Webtcu/

Nau, D. S., Au, T. C., Ilghami, O., Kuter, U., Murdock, W., Wu, D., & Yaman, F. (2003). SHOP2: An HTN planning system. *Journal of Artificial Intelligence Research, 20,* 379-404.

Nguyen, X., Kambhampati, S., & Nigenda, R. (2002). AltAlt: Combining the advantages of graphplan and heuristics state search. *Proceedings of the 2000 International Conference on Knowledge-Based Computer Systems,* Bombay, India.

OWL Services Coalition (2003). *OWL-S: Semantic markup for Web services.* OWL-S 1.0 Release. Retrieved http://www.daml.org/services/owl-s/1.0/

Pautasso, C., & Alonso, G. (2004-2005). JOpera: A toolkit for efficient visual composition of Web services. *International Journal of Electronic Commerce, 9*(2), 107-141.

Piccinelli, G. (1999). Service provision and composition in virtual business communities. *Tech. Report HPL-1999-84,* Hewlett-Packard, Palo Alto, CA, 1999. Retrieved from http://www.hplhp.com/techreports/1999/HPL-1999-84.html

Sanchez, J., & Mali, A. D. (2003). S-MEP: A planner for numeric goals. *Proceedings of the 5th IEEE International Conference on Tools with Artificial Intelligence* (pp. 274-283). Sacramento.

Sheshagiri, M., des Jardins, M., & Finin, T. (2003). A planner for composing services described in DAML-S. *ICAPS 2003 Workshop on Planning for Web Services.*

Sirin, E., Parsia, B., Wu, D., Hendler, J., & Nau, D. (2004). HTN planning for Web service composition using SHOP2. *Web Semantics: Science, Services, and Agents on the World Wide Web, 1*(4), 377-396.

Thakkar, S., Knoblock, C., Ambite, J. L. (2003). A view integration approach to dynamic composition of Web services. *ICAPS 2003 Workshop on Planning for Web Services.*

Thakkar, S., Knoblock, G. A., Ambite, J. L., & Shahabi, C. (2002). Dynamically composing Web services from online source. *Workshop on Intelligent Service Integration, The 18th National Conference on Artificial Intelligence (AAAI),* Edmonton, Alberta, Canada. Retrieved from http://www.isi.edu/info-agents/dotnet/aaaiworkshop2002.pdf

Thatte S. (2003, May). *Business process execution language for Web services* (Version 1.1). Retrieved from http://www-106.ibm.com/developerworks/Webservices/library/ws-bpel

Thatte, S. (2001). *XLANG: Web services for business process design*. Microsoft. Retrieved from http://www.gotdotnet.com/team/xml_wsspecs/xlang-c/default.htm

Tsoumakas, G., Vrakas, D., Bassiliades, N., & Vlahavas, I. (2004). Lazy adaptive multicriteria planning. *Proceedings of the 16th European Conference on Artificial Intelligence* (pp. 693-697). Valencia, Spain.

Van der Aalst, W. (2003). Don't go with the flow: Web services composition standards exposed. *IEEE Intelligent Systems, 18*(1), 72-76.

Varela, M. L. R., Aparicio, J. N., & do Carmo Silva, S. (2003). A scheduling Web service based on XML-RPC. *ICAPS 2003 Workshop on Planning for Web Services.*

Vidal, V. (2004). A Look ahead strategy for heuristic search planning. *Proceedings of the 14th International Conference on Automated Planning and Scheduling* (pp. 3-7). Whistler, British Columbia, Canada.

Vrakas, D., & Vlahavas, I. (2005). A visualization environment for planning. *International Journal on Artificial Intelligence Tools, 14*(6), 975-998

Vrakas, D., & Vlahavas, I. (2003). A graphical interface for adaptive planning. *Proceedings of the Doctoral Consortium of the 13th International Conference on Automated Planning and Scheduling*, (pp. 137-141). Trento Italy.

Vrakas, D., & Vlahavas, I. (2002). A heuristic for planning based on action evaluation. *Proceedings of the 10th International Conference on Artificial Intelligence: Methodology, Systems, and Applications*, (pp. 61-70). Varna, Bulgaria.

Vrakas, D., & Vlahavas, I. (2002). Combining progression and regression in state-space heuristic planning. *Proceedings of the 6th European Conference on Planning*, (pp. 1-12). Toledo, Spain.

Vrakas, D., & Vlahavas, I. (2003). ViTAPlan: A visual tool for adaptive planning. *Proceedings of the 9th Panhellenic Conference on Informatics*, (pp. 167-177). Thessaloniki, Greece.

Vrakas, D., Gkioulekas, G., Refanidis, I., Sakellariou, I., & Vlahavas, I. (2002). *The PACOPLAN project: A parallel constraint planner with Java Interface*. Retrieved from http://lpis.csd.auth.gr/projects/pacoplan

Vrakas, D., Tsoumakas, G., Bassiliades, N., & Vlahavas, I. (2003). Learning rules for adaptive planning. *Proceedings of the 13th International Conference on Automated Planning and Scheduling*, (pp. 82-91). Trento, Italy.

Wilkins, D. E., Lee, T. J., & Berry, P. (2003). Interactive execution monitoring of agent teams. *Journal of Artificial Intelligence Research, 18*, 217-261.

Wu, D., Sirin, E., Hendler, J., Nau, D., & Parsia, B. (2003). Automatic Web services composition using SHOP2. *ICAPS 2003 Workshop on Planning for Web Services.*

Section IV
Visual Interfaces for Standard Languages

Chapter XVI
User Interaction and Interface Design with UML

Jesus M. Almendros-Jimenez
Universidad de Almeria, Spain

Luis Iribarne
Universidad de Almeria, Spain

ABSTRACT

This chapter will show you how to use and specialise UML diagrams for describing the user interfaces of a software system. In order to accomplish the description of user interfaces, the proposed technique considers three specialised UML diagrams called user-interaction, user-interface, and GUI-class diagrams, which will be built following a model-driven development (MDD) perspective. These diagrams can be seen as the UML-based UI models of the system. In addition, this chapter is concerned with code-generation to implement the user interfaces of the system by using GUI-class diagrams and user-interaction diagrams. A case study of an Internet book shopping system is introduced in this chapter to proof and illustrate the proposed user interaction and interface design technique.

INTRODUCTION

The emergence of the *unified modelling language* (UML) (OMG, 2005) as an industry standard for modelling systems has encouraged the use of automated software tools that facilitate the development process from analysis through coding. The *user interface (UI)*, as a significant part of most applications, should also be modelled using UML. UML diagrams could be used to model user interfaces, and automatic CASE tools could help to generate code for user interfaces from UML designs. In general terms, *visual modelling* allows the developers to visualize source code in a graphical form: graphical abstractions, such as flow charts to depict algorithmic control flows and structure charts or simple block diagrams with boxes representing functions and subprograms, and so on. UML provides system architects with a *visual language* for specifying, constructing, and documenting the artefacts of software systems. In particular, user interfaces should be visually modelled in order to describe the behaviour of the window system in response to *user interactions*.

This chapter is firstly devoted to show how to *use* and *specialise* UML diagrams in order to describe the user interface and user interactions of a software system, following a particular *model-driven development* (MDD) perspective. Model-driven development involves creating models through a methodological process that begins with requirements and looks into a high-level architectural design. Model-driven development facilitates and improves the software analysis and design and code generation facilities from models prevent the loss of substantial information during the transition of a model to its implementation.

In our MDD perspective, we consider the following steps for user interface design and modelling:

1. Firstly, we use a UML *use case diagram* for extracting the *main user interfaces*.
2. Secondly, we describe each use case by means of a special kind of *UML activity diagrams*, called *user-interaction diagrams*, whose states represent *data output actions* and transitions represent *data input events*. This perspective allows the designer to model the user interaction (i.e., input-output interaction) in each main user interface.
3. Thirdly, each input and output interaction of the *user-interaction diagrams* allows the designer to extract *GUI components* used in each user interface. Therefore, we can obtain a new and *specialized version of the use case diagram* representing the user interface design, and a class diagram for GUI components: *user-interface* and *GUI-class* diagrams, respectively.
4. The *user-interaction, user-interface,* and *GUI-class* diagrams can be seen as the *UML-based user interface models* of the system.

This chapter will also deal with *code generation* techniques. In our MDD perspective, the UML-based user interface models can be used

for generating *executable code* with the following advantages:

1. **Rapid prototyping of the developed software:** Software modellers would find it useful to quickly generate user interfaces from high-level descriptions of the system.
2. **Model validation and refinement:** Prototyping can detect fails in design and refinement and validation of model by testing user interfaces and user requirements.
3. **Model-based code generation:** Generated code would fit with developed models.
4. **Starting point for implementers:** Prototypes can be refined until final implementation.

BACKGROUND

In the literature there are some works dealing with the problem of user interfaces in UML.

Use Cases and UI Design

Some of these works (CommentEdition, 2000; Constantine & Lockwood, 2001; Nunes & Falcao, 2001; Paterno, 2001) are focused on the utilisation of UML *use case diagrams* as a "starting point" of the user interface design, or even as a "high-level description" of the structure of the user interface. However, there are some considerations about the use case diagram style. Following the UML philosophy, a use case diagram could not be suitable for extracting the user interfaces. Use case diagrams may include some use cases referred to parts of the system not related to user interfaces such as classes, human tasks, components of other systems interacting with us, and so on. Or even decomposing use cases by means of *include* and *extend* relationships, one could specify specific parts of the system, which are not related with the user interface. Therefore, in our opinion, a specialized version of the use case model could be required, or even some other UML diagrams could be used to complete the use case view.

Adapting UML to UI Design

Other works (Campos & Nunes, 2005; Conallen, 1999; Heumann, 2003; Lieberman, 2004; Nunes, 2003; Nunes et al., 2001; Pinheiro da Silva & Paton, 2000) propose the introduction of new UML elements in order to model user interfaces. In this case, the need of new stereotypes or classifiers in UML in order to distinguish GUI components from other system components is well known. In this case, there is a common point of view: classes should be stereotyped with <<screen>>, <<applet>>, and <<input form>>, to be distinguished from data classes.

In addition, there are some works (Anderson, 2000; Elkoutbi & Keller, 2000) (Elkoutbi, Khriss, & Keller, 1999) interested in the description of the logic of GUI components, using activity and state diagrams for that. In this case, user interaction can be specified by means of states, where the system shows output data and requests input data. It should be specified how the user can navigate through the user interface, opening, closing windows, picking up in links, and so on. The specified logic should describe the set of states (input, output, windows) in which the user can be found.

Code Generation and UML

With respect to code generation, unfortunately, the capabilities of code generator CASE tools to transform design to an implementation are often restricted to produce class definitions consisting of attributes and operation signatures captured in class diagrams, but not methods to implement the procedural flow within the operations. Existing approaches in this last sense turn statecharts into executable code. Statecharts are used as object controllers for specifying when an object is willing to accept request. CASE tools supporting code

generation from statecharts are Statemate (Ilogix, 2006a), Omate (Harel & Gery, 1997), Rhapsody (Ilogix, 2006b), and Fujaba (Schäfer, 2002).

MAIN THRUST OF THE CHAPTER

With regard to previous works on UML (use cases) and UI design, our contribution can be summarized as follows:

- Firstly, we consider use cases as a starting point of the user interface design. Here we define a new kind of diagram, *user-interface diagram*: a specialized version of the use case diagram as a high-level description of the user interface.
- In addition, following the MDD perspective, we integrate this system view with a set of specialized activity diagrams for user interaction design (*user-interaction diagrams*). One of the benefits of this integration is that each use case in the specialized use case diagram is described by means of a specialized activity diagram, and therefore interfaces can be analyzed and built from these two models.
- In addition, a class diagram is generated from the specialized activity diagrams. GUI components can also be built from both modelling techniques.

With regard to previous works on code generation, the UI models can get prototypes of the user interface of our application. Through mapping between UML and Java, we are able to generate low-level Java code directly from the user interaction diagram. This code generation is adapted to the special case of user interfaces, which is user event-based and handles input and output data by means of special kinds of UI components.

ORGANISATION OF THE CHAPTER

The next section describes our model-driven development technique for user interfaces. The chapter continues with the technique for the code generation by using user-interface models. This chapter finishes with some conclusions and future work.

MODEL-DRIVEN DEVELOPMENT FOR USER INTERFACES

Use Case Diagrams

Use case diagrams are used as starting point for user-interface design. Use cases are also a way of specifying required usages of a system, and they are typically used for capturing the requirements of a system (that is, what a system is supposed to do). The key concepts associated with the use-case model are *actors* and *use cases*. The users and systems that may interact with the system are represented by actors. Actors always model entities that are outside the system. Use cases represent the set of tasks that the actors carry out. In addition, the "use cases" can be decomposed by means of *include* relationships, and they can also be related by means of *generalisation/specialisation* relationships that compare more general and particular tasks.

In order to design a prototype of the user interface, the use case diagram should include the system actors and the set of (main) tasks for each one in which he or she takes part. From a point of view of user interface modelling, the use case diagram can be seen as a high-level description of the main windows of the system.

To illustrate the functionality of the MDD-based technique we will explain a simple Internet book shopping (IBS) model.

In the IBS example (Figure 1), three actors appear: the customer, the ordering manager, and the administrator. A customer directly makes

Figure 1. A preliminary use case description of the IBS example

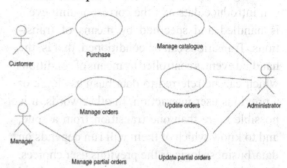

the purchases on the Internet, querying certain issues of the product in a catalogue of books before making the purchase. The manager deals with customer's orders (total or partially). And finally, the system's administrator can manage the catalogue of books by adding and eliminating books in the catalogue or modifying those already existing. The administrator can also update or cancel certain component characteristics of an order or those orders fulfilling certain searching criteria.

This information is described with a use case diagram containing the identified actors and main tasks of the system. In our case study (see Figure 1), the actors are the `customer`, the `manager`, and the `administrator`, and the main tasks are `purchase`, `manage orders`, `manage partial orders`, `manage catalogue`, `update orders`, and `update partial orders`.

From this use case diagram, one can identify the *future windows* of the system that will comply with the needs of the *presentation logic* (graphical user interfaces).

User Interaction Diagrams

The second modelling technique in our framework is the activity diagram. However, we need to specialise the activity diagram for user interface design in the following sense.

Our activity diagrams include states and transitions. The states represent data output actions, that is, how the system responds to user interactions showing data (or requesting them). Then the user can introduce data and the corresponding event is handled and specified by means of transitions. Transitions can be conditioned, that is, the handled event is controlled by means of condition, which can be referred to data/business logic or a previous user interaction. In other words, it is possible more than one transition from a state, and to know which of them will run depends on data/business logic or the previous user choices. We call *user-interaction diagrams* to this kind of activity diagrams used for user interaction description.

Now, it is supposed that each use case in the use case diagram is described by means a *user-interaction diagram*. However, from a practical point of view, it is convenient to use more than one *user-interaction diagram* for describing a use case. This is so because the logic of a use case is usually too complex. For this reason, a *user-interaction diagram* can be deployed in several *user-interaction diagrams*, where a part of the main logic is separately described. For this reason, user interaction diagrams can include states that do not correspond to data output, rather than representing subdiagrams. Now, it is desirable in some cases to be able to combine the logic of the subdiagrams and the main logic. For this reason, we will use in the main diagram transition conditions that can be referred to the logic of the subdiagrams.

Activity diagrams describe input and output user interactions. Given that we have decided to implement our user interface by means of Java swing package, we will consider the `JFrame` class as a container class that opens new frame windows (if needed). In addition, graphical components can be classified as input (a text field, a button, etc) and output components (a label, list, etc). Input/output components are associated with terminal states and transitions by using the appropriate stereotype. For instance, the stereotypes `JTextField, JList, JLabel` are associated

with states and the stereotype `JButton` with transitions. Since the graphical behaviour concerns with states and transitions, next we will describe them separately.

States can be stereotyped or not. Stereotyped states represent terminal states, which can be labelled by <<JTextField>>, <<JList>>, and <<JLabel>> stereotypes. For instance, let us focus our attention in the purchase use case. Figure 2 shows the whole user-interaction diagram modelled for the purchasing process. Initially, the behavioural description starts with an original user-interaction description (Figure 2a). The behaviour shows how the customer begins the purchasing process of querying, adding, or removing articles of the shopping cart. After a usual purchasing process, the shopping system requests the customer's card number and an address to carry out the shipment whenever the shopping cart is not empty. This diagram shows the graphical and behavioural content of the applet window where the purchases can be carried out.

The main *user-interaction diagram* (Figure 2a) is composed of three states (i.e., "query catalogue," "confirm proceed," and "shopping cart"). Two of them are terminal states (i.e., "confirm proceed" and "query catalogue"). A terminal state is described in a new diagram whose states correspond to graphical elements stereotyped (for instance <<JTextField>> or <<JList>>) and labelled by a text related to the graphical element. The name of a separate *user-interaction diagrams* should be the same as that of the state. A non-terminal state is also described in a separate user-interaction diagram containing one or more non-terminal states.

Transitions can be labelled by means of *stereotypes, conditions,* or both. For instance, a button is connected with a transition by using a <<JButton>> stereotype, and the name of the label is the name of the button. For example, a show cart transition stereotyped as <<JButton>> will correspond with a button component called "Show cart."

Figure 2. The whole user-interaction diagram of the purchase use case

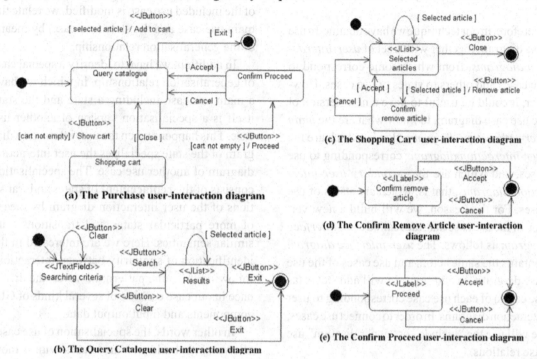

(a) The Purchase user-interaction diagram

(b) The Query Catalogue user-interaction diagram

(c) The Shopping Cart user-interaction diagram

(d) The Confirm Remove Article user-interaction diagram

(e) The Confirm Proceed user-interaction diagram

Conditions can represent *user choices* or *business/data logic*. The first one is a condition of the user's interaction with a graphical component (related to button or list states), and the second one is an internal checking condition (not related to the states, but to the internal process). For example, in our case study the selections from a list are modelled by conditions. Note in the query catalogue *user-interaction diagram* how the `results` list is modelled by a `<<JList>>` state and a `[Selected article]` condition.

Figure 2 shows some transitions (i.e., `[close]`, `[exit]`, or `[proceed]`) that correspond with conditions of the *user choice* type. The `[Exit]` output transition of the state `query catalogue` (Figure 2a) means that the user has pressed a button called `exit`, which has been defined in a separate

query catalogue *user-interaction diagram*. Nevertheless, conditions like the `[cart no empty]` condition are *business/data logic* conditions, in which the human factor does not take part.

Furthermore, stereotyped transitions (buttons in our example) and conditions connect (non) terminal states with (non) terminal states. A condition would be an output of a non-terminal state if the user interacted with a button or a list component inside the respective non-terminal state. The usual way of "condition/event" transition can connect (no)terminal states with (non) terminal states. A condition/event transition between states means which condition should be present to trigger the event. In our case study, an event can only be a button. For instance, to remove an article from the shopping cart, it must previously be selected from the cart list (Figure 2c).

User Interface Diagrams

Therefore, in our technique we have obtained a use case diagram together with a set of *user-interaction diagrams*, from which some correspond to use cases and others to states of use cases. However, it could be useful to have a new version of the use case diagram, to know what are the *main user-interaction diagrams*, that is, which are the *user-interaction diagrams* corresponding to use cases, and which are the *secondary user-interaction diagrams*, that is, which are states of use cases. For this reason, we will build a new version of the use case diagram called *user-interface diagram* as follows. The *user-interface diagram* contains the same actors and use cases of the use case diagram. In addition, we will add states (as use cases) of each use case corresponding to user interaction diagrams. In order to connect use cases, we will use the "include" or "generalisation" use case relations.

User Interface Relationships

Include and generalisation relationships have the following meaning in this *user-interface diagram*, similarly to the same relations in the use case diagram. If a use case contains in its user interaction diagram a state described by means of another user interaction diagram, the state is also considered as a use case, and the included state (use case) is related in the user interface diagram by the inclusion relationship with the main use case. However, this is achieved whenever the logic of the included use case is not modified by the main use case. The logic of an included use case is modified in the main use case whenever the user interaction diagram of the main use case includes transitions that are referred to internal states or conditions of the included use case. This typically happens when the main use case defines its own logic using the included use case as a piece of behaviour, but *access* to the included

use case. Otherwise, that is, whenever the logic of the included use case is modified, we relate the main use case and the state (use case) by means of the generalisation relationship.

In addition, we have to identify a special case of generalisation relationship, in which we have a main use case including a state and the state itself is a specialisation version of another use case. This happens when the user interaction diagram of the state specialises the user interaction diagram of another use case. The specialisation consists of the **replacement** of states and transitions of the user interaction diagram by means of more particular states and transitions with similar semantics. Here we are interested in the identification of similarity between interactions following the same pattern; however, the difference in our case consists of several kinds of GUI components and input/output data.

In other words, the specialisation of use cases allows us to build new use cases with a more complex logic containing the specialized use case, and adding transitions and states or modifying the existent ones. On the contrary, the inclusion allows us to build new use cases with a more complex logic without adding or modifying the states and transitions of the included use case.

Given that the user interface diagram is a kind of high-level description of the user interface, the developer still could decide not to include in it all the states representing user interaction diagrams. In other words, the user interface diagram represents the set of windows of the system by means of use cases. However, there could be more user interaction diagrams than windows. Usually, some user interaction diagrams can be built for deploying some states but they will not correspond to system windows.

Once *user-interaction diagrams* have been described, the designer proceeds to build the *user interface diagram*. It contains new use cases that are some of the non-terminal states of the user interaction diagrams. In addition, the developer has to identify use case relationships in the new user interface diagram as follows.

Include Relationships

Let us consider the purchasing process described in previous *user-interaction diagrams*.

purchase use case is a frame that includes (uses) three other frames (use cases): query

Figure 3. A user-interface diagram for the purchasing process

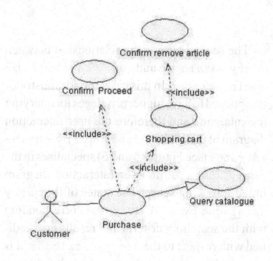

catalogue, shopping cart, and confirm proceed. These use cases are described by means of separate user interaction diagrams. In addition, the logic of the use cases is not modified in the purchase user interaction diagram. It integrates the logic query catalogue diagram by checking which buttons (i.e., exit) the user pressed when he or she exits from shopping cart.

The developer can also identify an inclusion relationship between manage catalogue and withdraw article, Modify article and add article use cases (Figure 4). In these cases, four windows can be optionally opened (depending on a menu) from the manage catalogue window. In addition, the administrator identification window is mandatory opened from the Manage catalogue window in order to achieve the system's administrator tasks.

Generalisation Relationships

In order to illustrate the generalisation/specialisation relationship, we will pay attention to three use cases: purchase, query catalogue, and query catalogue by administrator. In previous sections, we have identified two cases of generalisation/specialisation.

Figure 4. A piece of the user interface diagram of the administrator side

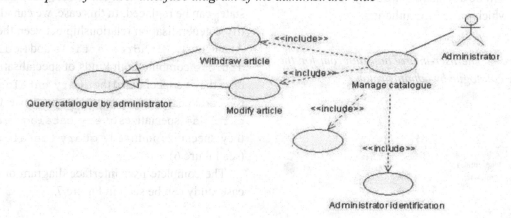

Figure 5. A piece of the user-interface diagram

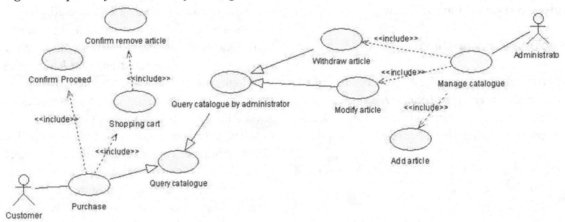

The first case is the `query catalogue` and `purchase` case. In this case, the `purchase` user-interaction diagram contains a state (use case) that specialises `query catalogue` in the following sense. The `query catalogue` user interaction diagram describes how to query the catalogue of the IBS by introducing the searching criteria and showing the results. However, the `purchase` user interaction diagram can interrupt the querying process by adding the searched items to the shopping cart. It is specified by adding the `Add to cart` button as transition from (and to) `query catalogue`. Therefore we can identify a specialisation relationship between `purchase` and `query catalogue`. It is also supposed that there will be a window for `query catalogue` from which `purchase` inherits.

Figure 6. The user-interaction diagram for the query catalogue by administrator

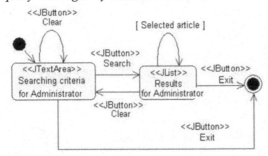

The second case is the relationship between `query catalogue` and `query catalogue by administrator`. In this case, the administrator is supposed to have higher privileges for querying the catalogue and therefore the user interaction diagram of the `query catalogue by administrator` (see Figures 5 and 6) specialises in the `query catalogue` user interaction diagram in the following sense. The states of the `query catalogue by administrator` corresponding with the searching criteria and results are modified with respect to the `query catalogue`. It is supposed that the searching and result fields are different but the logic is similar. In other words, the `query catalogue` can be replaced by `query catalogue by administrator` given that the states can be replaced. In this case, we can identify a generalisation relationship between them. Analogously, `Withdraw article` and `Modify article` combine both kinds of specialisation, once they've specialized the `query catalogue by administrator` in the same sense that `purchase` specializes `query catalogue`, and they specialize indirectly `query catalogue` (see Figure 6).

The complete user interface diagram of our case study can be seen in Figure 7.

Figure 7. The Internet shopping user-interface diagram

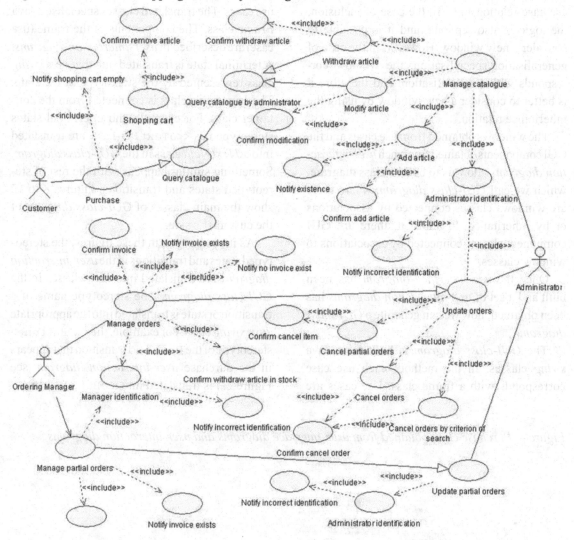

GUI Class Diagram

The next step of our model-driven technique consists of the building of a class diagram for GUI components. The *user-interface diagrams* obtained in the previous state give us the main windows. Each use case connected to an actor can be converted into a window, and if an actor is connected to more than one use case, it can be considered a window by the actor that invokes (or embeds) each window of each use case.

Therefore, the actor window can be a menu window. In addition, in the *user-interaction diagrams* obtained from use cases, we have also described input and output components for data output and request and user events. It gives us the GUI components for each window. If a *user-interaction diagram* has a state described by means of another *user-interaction diagram*, we can suppose that the window of the use case could also contain a separate window for this separate task. However, now, we have to take into account the *user-interface diagram* and the use case relationships. In the case of inclusion, the logic is also separate, and it is possible to consider a new window. However, in the case of generalisation/specialisation, the window corresponds with a specialisation, and therefore it is better to consider a new window by using the inheritance relation.

The windows obtained from use cases and the GUI components obtained from each *user-interaction diagrams* allow us to build a class diagram, which we call *GUI-class diagram*, where there are windows classes connected by associations or by inheritance. In addition, there are GUI component classes connected by associations to window classes.

Once the *user-interface diagram* has been built and a set of *user-interaction diagrams* has been obtained, now we can generate a *GUI-class diagram*.

The *GUI-class diagram* is built from Java *swing* classes. In the method, each use case corresponds with a frame class. Use cases are

translated into classes with the same name as these use cases. The translated classes specialise a Java *Frame* class. The components of the frame (use case) are described in *user-interaction diagrams*. A terminal state is translated into that Java *swing* class represented by the stereotype of the state. The Java *swing* class is connected from the container class. For example, those terminal states stereotyped as <<JTextField>> are translated into a *JTextField* class in the *GUI-class diagram*. Something similar happens with the rest of stereotyped states and transitions. Figures 8 to 12 show the main classes of *GUI-class diagram* of the customer's side.

As it can be seen in these figures, the stereotyped states and transitions in the *user-interaction diagrams* are translated into Java classes in the *GUI-class diagram*. The stereotype name of a transition or state is translated into the appropriate *Java swing* class. For example, the <<JButton>> stereotype of the Proceed transition that appears in the purchase *user-interaction diagram* (see Figure 2a) is translated into a JButton class.

Figure 8. Purchase class obtained from user-interface diagrams and user-interaction diagrams

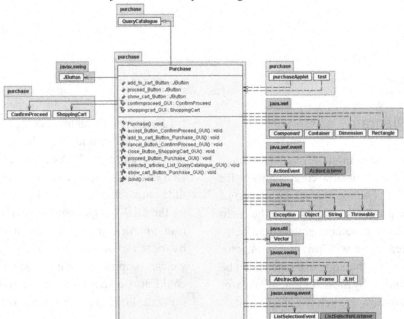

Figure 9. Query catalogue class obtained from user-interface diagrams and user-interaction diagrams

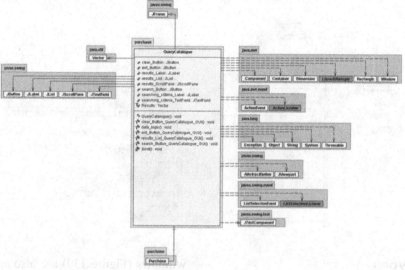

Figure 10. Shopping cart class obtained from user-interface diagrams and user-interaction diagrams

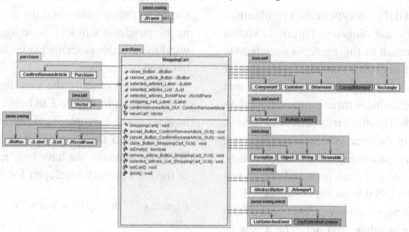

Figure 11. Confirm proceed class obtained from user-interface diagrams and user-interaction diagrams

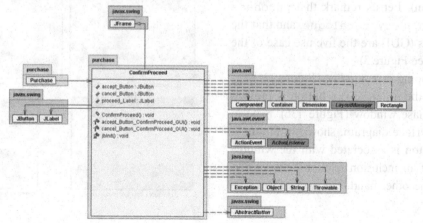

Figure 12. Confirm remove article class obtained from user-interface diagrams and user-interaction diagrams

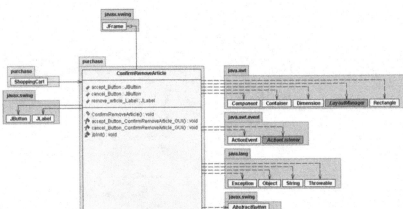

GUI Prototypes

Finally, rapid GUI prototypes could be obtained from the *GUI-class diagram*. Figure 13 shows a first visual result of the `purchase` window. Note how the `purchase` window is very similar to the `query catalogue` window, except that the second one includes three buttons more than the first window. This similarity between windows was revealed in the user interface diagram as a generalisation relationship between use cases: between the `query catalogue` and `purchase` use cases. In the IBS design, the customer will always work on a `purchase` window opened from the `Customer` window, and never on a `query catalogue` window, though the former inherits the behaviour of the latter (i.e., by the relation of generalisation). Let us remark that `purchase` inherits from `query catalogue`, and that the five windows (GUI) are the five use case of the client side (see Figure 3).

The shopping cart window (Figure 13c) appears when the `show cart` button is pressed on the purchase window (Figure 13b). Note in the user interface diagram, shown in Figure 7, how the button is associated with the window by means of an inclusion relation between use cases. On the other hand, the two information

windows (Figure 13d) are also associated with two buttons: the `remove article` button in the shopping cart window and the `proceed` button in the purchase window. Note again how these windows are also described as inclusion relations between use cases.

Moreover, observe the *user-interaction diagrams* shown in Figure 2 to better track the behaviour of the example. To develop the example, we have used the Rational Rose for Java tool. For space reasons, we have only included a part of the GUI project developed for the case study.

Figure 13. The applet windows of the customer's side

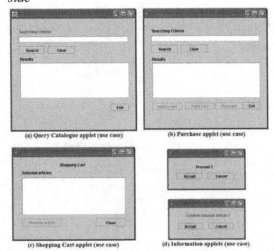

A complete version of the project is available at http://indalog.ual.es/mdd/purchase.

CODE GENERATION FOR USER INTERFACES

Finally, our model driven technique allows us to obtain code generation from the developed models. The user-interaction diagrams describe each user interaction of each use case by means of states representing data output and transitions representing data input and events.

Code generation consists of coding an event-based user interface. We have decided to implement our user interface by means of the *Java swing classes*, and therefore we will use *Applet* and *Frame* classes for window components, and *button*, *label*, *list*, etc., for other UI components. According to the Java swing package, events are

Figure 14. All complete sequence of the purchase interaction

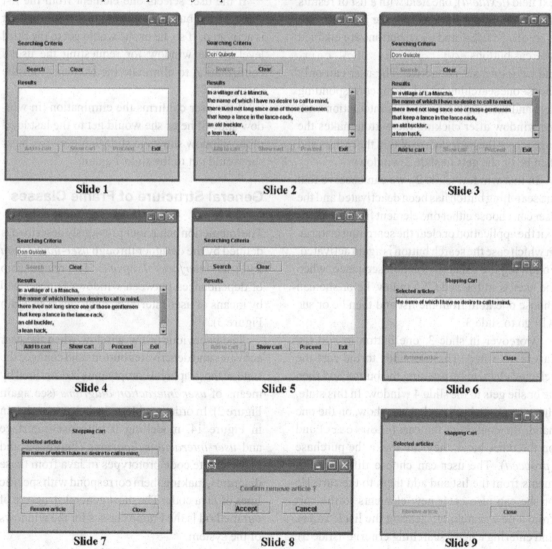

handled by means of *listeners* and *event handlers* in the corresponding window classes.

In order to explain the transition of the user interaction diagrams to code, we should first track a real interaction of the users with windows from the example: the purchase behaviour from the client side.

Here we can see the complete sequence of user/windows interaction. The first window (purchase, slide 1) shows ten graphical components: two labels (*searching criteria* and *results*), one text field (*textfield*), one field with a list of results (*results*), and six buttons. As we can see, the search, close and exit buttons are enabled whereas buttons add to cart, show cart, and proceed are not active. The user can only choose one searching criteria in the corresponding field and then click search. This interaction with the window after clicking the button makes the user access the logic data to obtain the results and then he or she gets to slide 2 window.

In that window (slide 2), we can observe that the searching button has been deactivated and the user can choose either one element from the list or exit the application or clear the searching criteria, in which case the search button is again activated. Following the usual interaction sequence, when the user is in the slide 2 window, he or she can choose one item from the list and then he or she will go to slide 3.

Moreover in slide 3, one button to add the cart is activated. The user adds to the cart the selected element by pressing the button and then he or she gets to the slide 4 window. In this state, there are some buttons that can show, on the one hand, the content of the cart (show cart) and on the other hand, they can make the purchase (*proceed*). The user can choose different elements from the list and add them to the cart. He or she can also enter new elements to the cart from a new searching, clearing the list (clear), and entering a new "searching criteria" (slide 5). In this state, we can observe that the searching button is activated and the adding to cart button is

deactivated. However, show cart and proceed buttons are not activated because the cart is not empty and the user at any time can see the cart or make the purchase. If the user wishes to see the content of the cart, he or she would get to the slide 6 window (shopping cart).

This new window (slide 6) has two labels, one list and two buttons; the first one is deactivated to avoid the removal of an element from a list until the user hasn't selected one of them and the second one allows us to close the window.

If the user selects one element from the list (slide 7), the button to eliminate it from the cart is activated. If so, he or she would get to the third level of the window for requesting the user's confirmation to eliminate the element from the cart (slide 8).

If the user confirms the elimination (in window slide 8) he or she would get to the last level of the window shown in slide 9; otherwise, he or she would get to the slide 7 again.

General Structure of Frame Classes

The interaction behaviour previously described is defined by the designer through *user-interaction* and *user-interfaces diagrams*. The relationship of dependences between windows is described by means of user-interfaces diagrams (see again Figure 3).

The behaviour of the window when the user activates and deactivates buttons and changes the state of the graphical components is described by means of *user-interaction diagrams* (see again Figure 2). In order to obtain the behaviour shown in Figure 14, modelling it with user-interface and *user-interaction diagrams* (Figures 2 and 3), we create code prototypes in Java from these diagrams, making them correspond with specific lines of Java code. The most general structure of our method is the Frame classes for the windows of the system.

To explain how to make this relationship between diagrams and code, we are focussing on the purchase *user-interaction diagram*. Figure 15 shows three perspectives of the purchase:

1. The user-interface perspective, where the designer studies the dependences between windows through use cases;
2. The user-interaction perspective, where the designer models the behaviour of the graphic components of the windows and their interaction with the user; and
3. The GUI perspective, where the user works with a rapid prototype of the windows through

a rapid generation of the code from both aforesaid perspectives (as previously seen).

In a symbolic way, we have represented in the picture the GUI perspective (of the windows) with its equivalent in the user-interface perspective, including the type of relationship between windows (in order to clarify the dependences between them).

In this example, these five use cases lead to five Java files of frame type. Their names are obtained from the use case name (which will be the

Figure 15. A summary for the user-interface and user-interaction diagram of the purchase function

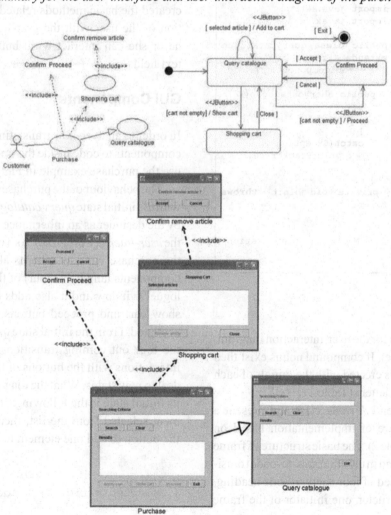

Table 1. Correspondence between diagram names and file names

User-interface & user-interaction name	File name
purchase	purchase.java
query catalogue	querycatalogue.java
shopping cart	shoppingcart.java
confirm proceed	confirmproceed
confirm remove article	confirmremovearticle.java

Table 2. General structure of querycatalogue (frame)

User-Interface Diagram	Code generation
| query catalogue | ```
import java.awt.*;
import javax.swing.*;

public class querycatalogue
extends JFrame {
   /** @GUIcomponents */
   ...
   public querycatalogue() {
     try {
        jbInit();
     }
     catch(Exception e) {
        e.printStackTrace();
     }
   }
   private void jbInit() throws
Exception {
        ...
   }
   // Methods implementation
   ...
}
``` |

same as the one for the user-interaction diagram, one per use case). If compound nouns exist then a simple name is created with the initials of each word in capital letters (Table 1).

Classes extend *JFrame* class and present a general structure of implementation based on frames (see Table 2). The basic structure of frame prototype created in the diagrams-to-code transition, is composed of four sections: one heading, one class constructor, one initiator of the frame

(*jbInit*) and one basic prototype of the implementation of the detected methods (related with the logic of presentation). In the heading (labelled with `/** @GUIcomponents */`) the attributes are considered to be graphical components that have been detected in the corresponding *user-interaction diagram*. The class constructor is the same for all code files created (except for the name of the constructor). In the initiator of the frame (*jbInit*) it is included the code lines that model the graphical content of the window. The designer should establish the position and size of the graphical components of the frame later on, as the code generated is just a prototype of the window. In the fourth section of the Frame, it is created the basic methods related to the interaction of the user with the graphic elements that he or she can interact with: buttons, lists, and text fields.

GUI Components

In order to analyze how translating the diagrams components to code inside the frame, we'll again use the purchase example in Figure 15.

The behaviour of the purchase window begins with the initial state *query catalogue* (represented by the designer as an inheritance of behaviour in the *user-interface diagram*). As it can be observed, the purchase window inherits all the graphical components (and behaviour) of the "query catalogue" window and it also adds the add to cart, show cart and proceed buttons, which are not activated. From the initial state *query catalogue*, the four out coming transitions correspond to interactions with the buttons of the window and deal to new states. What the diagram shows from its initial state is the following: If there is an element selected from the list, then it is activated the button to add one element to cart.

```
<<JButton>>
[ selected article ] / Add to cart
```
```

If the cart is not empty ([cart not empty]) it is activated the button to show the content of the cart and make the purchase of the products in the cart.

```
                 <<JButton>>
[ cart not empty ] / Shopping cart

                 <<JButton>>
[ cart not empty ] / Proceed
```

The transition [exit] in the initial *query catalogue* state, corresponds with the operation of clicking on the exit button inside the behaviour diagram of the window (frame): *query catalogue* (window inherited by purchase). The same happens with the other two transitions that reach this initial state from the state *Confirm proceed* (window to confirm the purchase).

For this example, there are four modelled graphical components: labels, text fields, lists, and buttons. In Table 3, it is shown the correspondence between graphic components of the *user-interaction diagram* (stereotypes) and the code generation.

In Table 3, column "stererotype" represents the stereotypes used in the states/transitions of the *user-interactions diagram.*

The columns "attribute" and "class" represent the name of the attribute and the base class instantiated in the code generated. The criterion followed to establish the name generated in the code is: *name_Type*. That is, as a name it is used the same name indicated in the interaction diagram in capital letters, followed by a hyphen (i.e., "_") and then finished by base type (label, button, list, etc.). If the original name has blanks in between, they are substituted by hyphens. For example, the label:

```
<<JLabel>>
Shopping cart
```

It is translated to the name of the attribute shopping cart button and then it is generated the following Java code:

```
public JLabel shopping_cart_
Button = new JLabel();
```

Table 3. Correspondence between user-interaction stereotypes and code generation

UI diagrams	Code generation					
Stereotype	Atribute	Class	In/Out	Listener	S/T	Markup
<<JLabel>> name	name _ Label	JLabel	Out	No	State	/** @Label */
<<JTextField>> name	name _ Label name _ TextField	JTextField	In/Out	No	State	/** @TextField */
<<JList>> name	name _ Label name _ List name _ ScrollPane	JList	In/Out	Maybe	State	/** @List */
<<JButton> name	name _ Label name _ Button	JButton	In	Yes	Trans.	/** @Button */
[condition]	None	None	In/Out	No	Trans.	None

the "in/out" column represents an exit from/to the user (or window). So, for example, one stereotype label will represent a text shown from the system towards the user (window) whereas the button (according to its graphic behaviour) represents an income action (interaction) from the user towards the system. The "textfields" and lists stereotypes represent both options: the system shows and modifies the content of these graphic components and at the same time, the user can either write (*textfield*) or choose (list) in these graphic components. The "out" components have no correspondence with the code, whereas the "in" components have correspondence with one listener class.

The "listener" column indicates whether a graphical component is moved by means of a listener class. This type of class allows the class creating it for listen the behaviour of the graphic component with the user. It is usual to use listener in buttons and lists (we'll study these later).

The "S/T" column is referred to whether the graphic component corresponds with a state or a transition in the user-interaction diagram.

Finally, "markup" column is referred to the mark prototype created before the translated code. This mark helps to identify the content of the text when the programmer has to rewrite or insert the new code to add and complete the functionality of the windows.

Mapping States into Code

As previously said, the states of a user-interaction diagram can be referred to terminal states (label, textfield, list) and non-terminal states

Non-Terminal States

Let us begin with the *user-interaction diagram* purchase (see Figure 15). The diagram is composed of three non-terminal states. We should remember that a non-terminal state is a state whose behaviour is defined separately from other

diagram of interaction. For example, the *query catalogue, confirm proceed,* and *shopping cart* states will be defined in independent user-interaction diagrams having the same name as the corresponding state. In the *user-interface diagram,* the *query catalogue* is established by the designer as an inheritance for purchase, whereas the other two states (which are "use cases" and therefore windows) are established as conclusions in the *user-interface diagram* (i.e., <<include>>). The translation is as follows:

```
public class purchase extends que-
rycatalogue {

    /** @GUI */
    ShoppingCart shoppingcart_ GUI =
new ShoppingCart();

    /** @GUI */
    ConfirmProceed confirmproceed_ GUI
= new ConfirmProceed();
    ...
```

Note that purchase class inherits querycatalogue in the code. The two "include" relationships are included in the code in the heading section (one of the four that frame has). On the code line a @ GUI mark is inserted to trace an inclusion of the window in the process of translation. Moreover, the criterion for the name of the GUI variable is considering the original name of the included window followed by "_GUI."

Terminal States

Terminal states (*label, list, textfield*) are translated into code lines in the heading, initiation of Frame (*jbInit*) and implementation of methods sections (only in list). Appendix A contains the Java code patterns translated from the graphical components of the *user-interaction diagram*. Let's see each of them separately.

Figure 16. The confirm remove article-label state in query catalogue

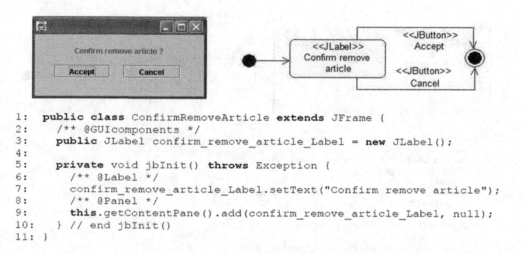

```
1:   public class ConfirmRemoveArticle extends JFrame {
2:     /** @GUIcomponents */
3:     public JLabel confirm_remove_article_Label = new JLabel();
4:
5:     private void jbInit() throws Exception {
6:       /** @Label */
7:       confirm_remove_article_Label.setText("Confirm remove article");
8:       /** @Panel */
9:       this.getContentPane().add(confirm_remove_article_Label, null);
10:   } // end jbInit()
11: }
```

Figure 17. The searching criteria text field state in query catalogue

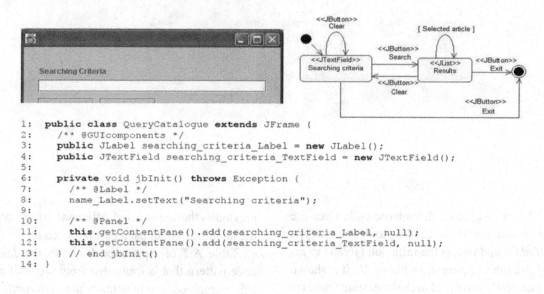

```
1:   public class QueryCatalogue extends JFrame {
2:     /** @GUIcomponents */
3:     public JLabel searching_criteria_Label = new JLabel();
4:     public JTextField searching_criteria_TextField = new JTextField();
5:
6:     private void jbInit() throws Exception {
7:       /** @Label */
8:       name_Label.setText("Searching criteria");
9:
10:      /** @Panel */
11:      this.getContentPane().add(searching_criteria_Label, null);
12:      this.getContentPane().add(searching_criteria_TextField, null);
13:   } // end jbInit()
14: }
```

Figure 18. The results list state in query catalogue

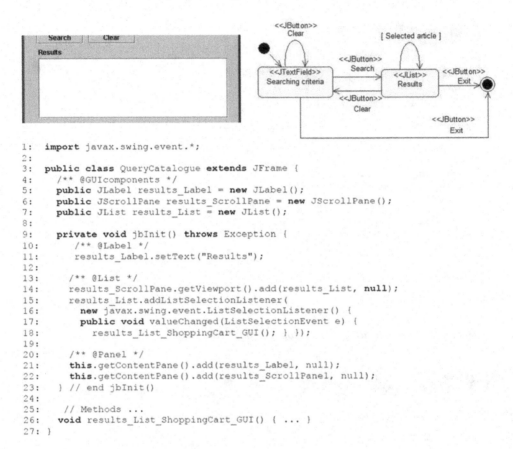

```
1:    import javax.swing.event.*;
2:
3:    public class QueryCatalogue extends JFrame {
4:      /** @GUIcomponents */
5:      public JLabel results_Label = new JLabel();
6:      public JScrollPane results_ScrollPane = new JScrollPane();
7:      public JList results_List = new JList();
8:
9:      private void jbInit() throws Exception {
10:       /** @Label */
11:       results_Label.setText("Results");
12:
13:       /** @List */
14:       results_ScrollPane.getViewport().add(results_List, null);
15:       results_List.addListSelectionListener(
16:         new javax.swing.event.ListSelectionListener() {
17:         public void valueChanged(ListSelectionEvent e) {
18:           results_List_ShoppingCart_GUI(); } });
19:
20:       /** @Panel */
21:       this.getContentPane().add(results_Label, null);
22:       this.getContentPane().add(results_ScrollPanel, null);
23:     } // end jbInit()
24:
25:       // Methods ...
26:       void results_List_ShoppingCart_GUI() { ... }
27:   }
```

For a label case, three basic code lines are generated: one in the heading to define the type (*JLabel*) and two in the initiation (*jbInit*) to establish the component. In Figure 16, it is shown a bit of code generated to the label state "confirm remove article." The code line 3 creates one variable of *JLabel* type. Note how the name of the variable is obtained from the name given to the <<JLabel>> state in the *user-interaction diagram*. The line 7 establishes the text that will appear in the window. Line 9 adds the label to the container. Lines 2, 6, and 9 are marks established

previously that are inserted in the code to facilitate the identification of each part of the code.

Table A.2 of Appendix A shows the Java code pattern that is translated from the <<JLabel>> graphical components of *user-interaction diagram*.

For the "text fields," five basic code lines are generated. Two of them are generated in the heading to define two graphical components in the heading: one JTextField and one Jlabel to name it in the window. The other three code lines are generated in the initiation section of frame (*jbInit*). For example, Figure 17 shows how translating the terminal state searching criteria (in the *user-interaction diagram* of frame *query catalogue*) into a code in two components (lines 2 and 3). It is created a "text field" area (`Jtext-Field`) and a text (`label`) which accompanies the text field. For the naming of the variables we use the same criterion established before: the same text that appears in the state followed by "label" or "textfield". In line 9, it is established the text in the window. Lines 11 and 12 add both graphical components to the container.

Table A.3 of Appendix A shows the Java code pattern that is translated from the `<<Jtext-Field>>` graphical components of the *user-interaction diagram*.

Finally, there are the terminal states of *list* type. Graphically these states are somehow special since—like a *textfield*—they can be translated into different ways: a label component, other list or even a scrollpane. The latter can be used as a container to show the elements from the corresponding list. Several lines are generated in the translation, in three sections (heading, initiation, and methods). For example, Figure 18 shows a translation of the results state.

Lines 5, 6, and 7 are generated in the heading (after `/** @GUIcomponents */`) defining the name of the variables of the three graphical components. Again the criterion used for the naming of the variables is the same as that one used in previous examples. In the initiation section (*jbInit*) the following code is created. Firstly, the label text is established in the panel (line 11). Then, an event of *listener* type is used to catch the interactions of the user with the list when he or she presses the elements of the list. Therefore, in line 14, there is the container *Scrollpane* type where the list is and from lines 15 to 18 there is the *listener* event on the list. To do so, the library `javax.swing.event.*` is imported (line 1). Lines 21 and 22 add graphical elements to the panel. Finally, the method implementation section (line 26) includes the prototype of the method

used each time the user presses on an element from the list. The implementation of the method is a later task of the programmer.

In table A.3 of Appendix A it is shown the Java code pattern translated from *JList* graphical components of *user-interaction diagram*.

Mapping Transitions into Code

Transitions correspond with buttons (`<<JBut-ton>>`) or changes in the internal state of the data logic. They are represented in the diagram as a condition markup (p.e., `[cart not empty]` o `[Close]`). Table A.1 (Apendix A) shows the Java code pattern for a graphical component `<<JButton>>` translated from the *user-interaction diagram*.

Transitions represent graphical components that generate code at several sections of the program. The translation into code is the more important issue in the code generation process, since it reveals the usefully of the user-interaction diagrams for the traceability of the interaction of the user with the graphical components of the window and also how that (window) responds to the user. To explain the translation of states to code, we will use again the purchase windows sample. In Figure 19, we show (at the right side) the two related *user-interaction diagrams* of the purchase window (showed at left side).

Remember that the system's designer has described the purchase window from the *query catalogue* window, which represents a state in the *user-interaction diagram* of the purchase window. This state inherits the inner behaviour of the *query catalogue* (whose behavioural interaction is shown at the right-lower side in Figure 19). It arrives at two possible states through four transitions from the state *query catalogue*: (a) see the state of the cart (*shopping cart* state); or (b) carry out the purchase of the products stored in the cart (*confirm proceed* state). Both states are reached from the purchase window through the buttons `show cart` and `proceed`. In the state,

Figure 19. The purchase window

a conditioned transition has been included for reaching these two windows from purchase: that the cart is no empty. In other words, a conditioned button-transition corresponds with an operation of activation/deactivation of buttons.

Since these three buttons are conditioned by a selection action in a list, a *listener* operation is generated on the list in the *purchase* class. Remember that both the list and the most of the graphical components of the purchase window are inherited from *query catalogue* window (i.e., **public class** purchase **extends** querycatalogue), and therefore the operation *listener* is done on the superclass, which contains the list.

```
/** @List */
super.results_List.addListSelectionListener(
    new javax.swing.event.ListSelectionListener() {
        public void valueChanged(ListSelectionEvent e) {

            selected_articles_List_querycatalogue_GUI(); } } );
```

In this way, whenever the user presses on the list, an event is captured, which calls to the function selected_articles_List_query-catalogue_GUI(). The name of the method is established by the text included in the condition

of the transition in the *user-interaction diagram*. For instance, a button-transition Add to cart containing a condition [selected articles] means that the class (frame) purchase enables the button Add to cart in the window if and only if an element of the list has been selected; in other case, the button will remain disabled (see Figure 19). In case of exist a selected element in the list, the button is activated and the transition leads again to the same state, to include the selected element (and others) to the list. This generates the following lines of code for the method on the listened element.

```
/** @List */
void selected_articles_List_querycatalogue_
GUI() {
    if (results_List.getSelectedIndex()==-1)
        add_to_cart_Button.setEnabled(false);
    else add_to_cart_Button.setEnabled(true);
}
```

The activation of the button (add_to_cart.Button.setEnabled) implies the button has been before declared in the panel, created and added.

```
public class purchase extends querycatalogue {
  /** @GUIcomponents */
  public JButton add _ to _ cart _ Button = new JBut-
ton();

  private void jbInit() throws Exception {
    /** @Button */
    name _ Button.setText("Add to cart");
    name _ Button.addActionListener(
      new java.awt.event.ActionListener() {
        public void actionPerformed(ActionEvent
e) {
          add _ to _ cart _ Button _ Purchase _ GUI();
} });

    /** @Panel */
    this.getContentPane().add(add _ to _ cart _ But-
ton, null);
  } // end jbInit()

    // Methods ...
    /** Button */
    void add _ to _ cart _ Button _ Purchase _ GUI()
{ ... }

  }
```

Following the trace of the example, the other two button-transitions that leave the state *query catalogue* remain disabled until the cart is not empty (button Add to cart):

```
/** @Button */
void add _ to _ cart _ Button _ purchase _ GUI() {
  show _ cart _ Button.setEnabled(true);
  proceed _ Button.setEnabled(true);
}
```

Once the buttons is activated, two other states can be reached from the state *query catalogue*: (a) the state *shopping cart*, whether the button show cart is pressed; or (b) the state *confirm proceed,* whether the button proceed is pressed. Since both states are not stereotyped, they are translated into two independent windows (frames) with independent behaviours in *user-interaction diagrams*, also independent (i.e., with an initial state and another end state).

Nevertheless, this encapsulated behaviour (i.e., a *user-interaction diagram*) can be interrupted by means of *conditioned simple transitions* (or simply "simple transitions"). Simple transitions are those transitions that are labelled only by a condition (p.e., [screen], [accept], [close], and [exit]). These transitions refer to an action of pressing a button that exists inside the

non-terminal state (a window). For instance, the button-transitions [accept] and [screen] refer that, being in the state (frame) *confirm proceed* the user presses one of these buttons, and one returns to the state (frame) *query catalogue*. The same for the transition [close].

Nevertheless, there is a special case of simple transition: that one that does not come from another state, but it departs from the target state. For example, the simple transition [exit] means that there has been pressed the button exit inside the frame *query catalogue*, whose behaviour is defined in another independent *user-interaction diagram* (in which the button is defined). In any case, both the simple-transitions of the type [accept] or of the type [exit] the interpretation in the code is reflected by means of a *listener* operation on those buttons of the window (class) containing the buttons, that interrupts the normal interaction sequence of the above mentioned class.

```
public class purchase extends querycatalogue {
  ...
  private void jbInit() throws Exception {
...

    // Listener on children

    /** @Button */
    shoppingcart _ GUI.close _ Button.addAction-
Listener(
      new java.awt.event.ActionListener() {
        public void actionPerformed(ActionEvent
e) {
          close _ Button _ ShoppingCart _ GUI();
} } );
    /** @Button */
    confirmproceed _ GUI.accept _ Button.addAction-
Listener( ... );
    /** @Button */
    confirmproceed _ GUI.cancel _ Button.addAction-
Listener( ... );
  }
  ...
}
```

Appendix B partially shows the java code of one of the five classes of the project example: the class *ShoppingCart*. This information is available in the following Web page: http://indalog.ual.es/mdd/purchase.

CONCLUSION AND FUTURE WORK

In this chapter, we have studied a model-driven development technique for GUI design. We have defined a new kind of UML diagram (i.e., the *user-interface diagram*), which specialises in the use case diagram for user interface design. In addition, we have shown how to describe use cases by means of specialized activity diagrams (*user-interaction diagrams*) in order to specify the user interface of each use case. Finally, we have shown how to generate class diagrams for GUI and how to build rapid prototypes for the user interface. As future work, we plan to study the following extensions of our work:

1. Integrate the user interface view with the data and business logic;
2. Incorporate our method in a CASE tool in order to automate it;
3. Integrate our technique in the whole development process.

ACKNOWLEDGMENT

This work has been partially supported by the Spanish project of the Ministry of Science and Technology TIN2005-09207-C03-02 and TIN2006-06698 under FEDER funds.

REFERENCES

Anderson, D. J. (2000). Extending UML for UI. *UML'2000 Workshop on Towards a UML Profile for Interactive Systems Development* (TUPIS2000), York, UK, October 2/3.

Campos, P. F., & Nunes, N. J. (2005). A UML-based tool for designing user interfaces. *UML 2004 Satellite Activities*, LNCS 3297 (pp. 273-276).

CommentEdition. (2000). *UIRupture* (Tech. Rep.).

UIDesign. http://www.uidesign.net

Conallen, J. (1999). Modelling Web application architectures with UML. *Communications of the ACM, 42*(10), 63-70.

Constantine, L. L., & Lockwood, L. A. D. (2001). Structure and style in use cases for user interface design. In M. van Harmelen (Ed.), *Object modelling and user interface design* (pp. 245-279). Addison-Wesley Longman Publishing.

Elkoutbi, M., & Keller, R. K. (2000). User interface prototyping based on UML scenarios and high level Petri nets. *International Conference on Application and Theory of Petri Nets (ICATPN 2000)*, LNCS 1825 (pp. 166-186).

Elkoutbi, M., Khriss, I., & Keller, R. K. (1999). Generating user interface prototypes from scenarios. *Requirements Engineering'99* (pp. 150-158). IEEE Computer Society.

Harel, D., & Gery, E. (1997). Executable object modelling with statecharts. *IEEE Computer, 30*(7), 31-42.

Heumann, J. (2003). User experience storyboards: Building better UIs with RUP, UML, and Use Cases (Tech. Rep.). Rational Software.

Ilogix. (2006a). *Rhapsody 6.2*. Iogix/Telelogic. Retrieved from http://www.ilogic.com

Ilogix. (2006b). *Statemare*. Iogix/Telelogic. Retrieved from http://www.ilogic.com

Kovacevic, S. (1998). UML and user interface modeling. *UML'98*, LNCS 1618 (pp. 253-266).

Lieberman, B. (2004). *UML activity diagrams: Detailing user interface navigation* (Tech. Rep. 29 April). Rational Software.

Nunes, N. J., & Falcao e Cunha, J. (2001). Wisdom a UML based architecture for interactive systems. *DSVIS 2000*, LNCS 1946 (pp. 191-205).

Nunes, N. J. (2003) Representing user interface patterns in UML. In In D. Konstantas, M. Leonard, Y. Pigneur & S. Patel (Eds.), *Object-oriented information systems*, LNCS 2817 (pp. 142-151).

OMG. (2005). *Unified modeling language specification* (Tech. Rep. No 2). Object Management Group.

Paterno, F. (2001). Towards a UML for interactive systems. *EHCI 2001*, LNCS 2254 (pp. 7-18).

Pinheiro da Silva, P., & Paton, N. W. (2000). User interface modelling with UML. *Information Modelling and Knowledge Bases XII* (pp. 203-217). IOS Press.

Schäfer, W. (2002). *Fujaba documentation* (Tech. Rep.). University of Paderborn.

APPENDIX A. GUI CODE PATTERNS

A.1. Mapping transitions (buttons) into code

User-Interaction stereotype	Code generation

<<JButton>>_ name	<pre>import java.awt.event.*;
	
	public class className extends JFrame {
	  /** @GUIcomponents */
	  public JButton name _ Button = new JButton();
	
	  private void jbInit() throws Exception {
	    /** @Button */
	    name _ Button.setText("name");
	    name _ Button.addActionListener(
	        new java.awt.event.ActionListener() {
	        public void actionPerformed(ActionEvent e) {
	          name _ Button _ nameClass _ GUI(); } });
	
	    /** @Panel */
	    this.getContentPane().add(name _ Button, null);
	  } // end jbInit()
	
	  /***
	   * Method THIS
	   */
	
	  /** Button */
	  void name _ Button _ className _ GUI() { ... }
	}</pre>

A.2. Mapping labels to code

User-Interaction stereotype	Code generation

<<JLabel>> name	<pre>public class className extends JFrame {
	  /** @GUIcomponents */
	  public JLabel name _ Label = new JLabel();
	
	  private void jbInit() throws Exception {
	    /** @Label */
	    name _ Label.setText("name");
	
	    /** @Panel */
	    this.getContentPane().add(name _ Label, null);
	  } // end jbInit()
	}</pre>

A.3. Mapping textfields to code

User-Interaction stereotype	Code generation

<<JTextField>>
 name
	``java
	public class className extends JFrame {
	  /** @GUIcomponents */
	  public JLabel name_Label = new JLabel();
	  public JTextField name_TextField = new JTextField();
	
	  private void jbInit() throws Exception {
	    /** @Label */
	    name_Label.setText("name");
	
	    /** @Panel */
	    this.getContentPane().add(name_Label, null);
	    this.getContentPane().add(name_TextField, null);
	  }// end jbInit()
	}
	``

A.4. Mapping lists to code

User-Interaction stereotype	Code generation

<<JList>>
 name
	``java
	import javax.swing.event.*;
	
	public class className extends JFrame {
	  /** @GUIcomponents */
	  public JLabel name_Label = new JLabel();
	  public JScrollPane name_ScrollPane = new JScrollPane();
	  public JList name_List = new JList();
	
	  private void jbInit() throws Exception {
	    /** @Label */
	    name_Label.setText("name");
	
	    /** @List */
	    name_ScrollPane.getViewport().add(name_List, null);
	    name_List.addListSelectionListener(
	      new javax.swing.event.ListSelectionListener() {
	      public void valueChanged(ListSelectionEvent e) {
	        selected_articles_List_ShoppingCart_GUI(); } });
	
	    /** @Panel */
	    this.getContentPane().add(name_Label, null);
	    this.getContentPane().add(name_ScrollPane, null);
	  } // end jbInit()
	
	  /***
	   * Method THIS
	   */
	
	  /** @List */
	  void selected_articles_List_ShoppingCart_GUI() { ... }
	}
	``

355

APPENDIX B. THE SHOPPING CART FRAME

```java
public class ShoppingCart extends JFrame {

  /** @GUIcomponents */
  public JLabel shopping_cart_Label = new JLabel();
  public JLabel selected_articles_Label = new JLabel();
  public JButton remove_article_Button = new JButton();
  public JButton close_Button = new JButton();
  public JScrollPane selected_articles_ScrollPane = new JScrollPane();
  public JList selected_articles_List = new JList();

  /** @GUI */
  ConfirmRemoveArticle confirmremovearticle_GUI = new ConfirmRemoveArticle();

  public ShoppingCart() { // Constructor }

  private void jbInit() throws Exception {
    /** @Label */
    shopping_cart_Label.setText("Shopping Cart");
    ...

    /** @Button */
    remove_article_Button.setText("Remove article");
    remove_article_Button.setEnabled(false);
    remove_article_Button.addActionListener(new java.awt.event.ActionListener() {
      public void actionPerformed(ActionEvent e) {
          remove_article_Button_ShoppingCart_GUI(); } });
    ...

    /** @List */
    selected_articles_ScrollPane.getViewport().add(selected_articles_List, null);
    selected_articles_List.addListSelectionListener( ... );

    /** @Panel */
    this.getContentPane().add(close_Button, null);
    ...

    /***
     *  Listener on children
     */
    confirmremovearticle_GUI.cancel_Button.addActionListener( ... );
    confirmremovearticle_GUI.accept_Button.addActionListener( ... );
  } // end jbInit()

  /***
   * Methods THIS
   */

  /** @Button */
  void remove_article_Button_ShoppingCart_GUI() {
    this.setEnabled(false); confirmremovearticle_GUI.setVisible(true);
  }

  /** @Button */
  void close_Button_ShoppingCart_GUI() { this.setVisible(false); }

  /** @List */
  void selected_articles_List_ShoppingCart_GUI() {
    remove_article_Button.setEnabled(true);
  }

  /***
   * Methods children
   */

  /** @Button */
  void cancel_Button_ConfirmRemoveArticle_GUI() { this.setEnabled(true); }

  /** @Button */
  void accept_Button_ConfirmRemoveArticle_GUI() { this.setEnabled(true); }
}
```

Chapter XVII
XQBE:
A Visual Language for XML Data Management

Alessandro Campi
Politecnico di Milano, Italy

Davide Martinenghi
Free University of Bozen/Bolzano, Italy

Alessandro Raffio
Politecnico di Milano, Italy

ABSTRACT

This chapter describes a visual framework called XQBE that covers the most important aspects of XML data management, spanning the visualisation of XML documents, the formulation of queries, the representation, and specification of document schemata, the definition of integrity constraints, the formulation of updates, and the expression of reactive behaviors in response to data modifications. All these features are strongly unified by a common visual abstraction and a few recurrent paradigms, so as to provide a homogeneous and comprehensive environment that allows even users without advanced programming skills to deal with nontrivial XML data management and transformation tasks. The intrinsic ambiguity inherent in any visual representation of richly expressive languages required a considerable effort of formalisation in the semantics of XQBE that eventually lead to a solution with major advantages in terms of intuitiveness. In other words, this means that the unique (and unambiguous) effect of a statement is the one the user would expect.

INTRODUCTION

The diffusion of XML in most applicative fields poses a pressing need for providing a wide spectrum of professionals with the ability to handle XML data, including users with minimal programming skills. The chapter describes a

visual environment called XQBE (XQuery By Example, Braga, Campi, & Ceri, 2005a), which we developed for this purpose, provided with a user friendly interface and based on an intuitive visual paradigm. The theoretical definition of the syntax and semantics of the language is accompanied by a full (albeit prototypal) implementation, which already proved effective also for didactical purposes.

The W3C (World Wide Web Consortium) promotes two textual languages to express XML document transformations and to query XML data: XSLT (W3C, 2001) and XQuery (W3C, 2003), respectively.

These languages, however, are far too complicated for occasional or unskilled users who might need to specify document mappings or transformations. Nevertheless, awareness of the basics of the XML data model and familiarity with the schema of the documents to be managed should be enough to allow such users to express their queries and transformations with the core primitives of a simple manipulation language.

Without this, XML will never step up to the status of a universally and successfully adopted data representation format.

XQBE was first designed as an interface for simple XQuery statements and has evolved to become a visual syntax also for XSLT transformations, XUpdate statements (Laux & Matin, 2000), and Active XQuery triggers (Bonifati, Braga, Campi, & Ceri, 2002). The language also supports schema-driven query formulation and schema definition. For each of these features the chapter describes theory and practice in terms of both formalisation and examples.

The main mission of the chapter is then to show a "best practice" case in which a visual language was tailored to the specificity of a data model—namely XML as the main representative for semi-structured data. In our opinion, the simplicity of the proposed visual data model, the intuitiveness of its fundamental paradigms, and the easiness of use of XQBE make it a good example of an elegant and effective visual language for XML data management.

In earlier times, the success of the QBE paradigm (query by example, Zloof, 1977) demonstrated that, in order for a visual query language to be effective and intuitive, the basic graphical constructs of the language need to be close to a

well-known and well-understood visual abstraction of the underlying data model. Accordingly, XQBE is based on annotated trees so as to adhere to the hierarchical nature of the XML data model, leveraging a common understood abstraction of XML data. Coherence between the data model and the visual language is the lesson that we have learned from the XQBE project and that this chapter witnesses.

In summary, it will be shown how it is possible for a visual language to reach a good trade-off between easiness of use, intuitiveness, and expressiveness, leveraging one simple visual abstraction. Of course, such goals cannot be fully achieved at the same time. Therefore, usability being the most critical success factor in order for XQBE to appeal to a wide audience has been given higher priority during the whole language design and implementation process.

The different features of XQBE are gradually introduced in order of complexity without separating the "theoretical" description from the "practical" aspects. We will therefore build an incremental and example-driven exposition that moves from the basic data model to the most advanced and specific features, such as visual triggers.

The rest of the chapter is organized as follows.

The "Related Work" Section shows the relationships and a brief comparison with other projects with similar purposes.

The objective of the section on "The XQBE visual data model and paradigm" is to describe the XQBE paradigm and to show to which extent it is easy to use, and yet highly expressive. There, we describe the basic visual paradigm of XQBE. We first present the basics of the language: the visual representation of XML documents in XQBE relies on a simplified XML data model, reduced to the notion of elements, attributes, and PCDATA content with containment hierarchies connecting such elements.

In the section on "XQBE as a query language," we discuss the visual *query* paradigm of XQBE and the translation algorithm from XQBE to XQuery: the query area is divided in two regions, one used to express data selection and one to express composition of selected data items. The section on "XQBE as a transformation language" describes how the same XQBE query paradigm can be used to describe XML-to-XML transformations (including XML-to-XHTML transformations, as a notable application). With a special eye on XHTML, we introduce a set of abbreviated constructs that allow one to insert in the resulting document the typical components of XHTML pages (lists, tables, etc.) with little effort. Such constructs are then expanded into regular XQBE structures at query compile time.

The section on "XQBE as a schema definition language" describes the schema definition and guided composition components of XQBE. Our visual language can be used to easily build DTDs for XML documents, by means of an extension of the data model that allows specifying sequences and mutually exclusive sets. Schemata, either created within XQBE or loaded from files, can then be used to guide the composition of queries and transformations by means of an intuitive paradigm.

In the section on "XQBE as an update language," we extend the query paradigm with a third region to support update operations. The XML fragments of an existing document, described in the new region, are updated with elements selected (and, if needed, manipulated) inside the first two regions, whose syntax and semantics remain unaltered.

In the section on "XQBE as a constraint and trigger definition language," ActiveXQBE, an extension of XQBE, is presented. ActiveXQBE can be used as a visual approach to the formulation of active rules. Our approach is motivated by the need to provide unskilled users with the capability of expressing business rules in an intuitive fashion. The ActiveXQBE paradigm makes use of three regions to model the triggering event and the compensating action, with an emphasis on usability and intuitiveness, yet without heavily sacrificing generality and expressiveness. Triggers visually designed with ActiveXQBE can then be translated into textual representations to be executed by rule engines.

We conclude our discussion in the section on "Enhancing users' experience" by pointing out that XQBE represents a stimulating example for both academic and industrial research in the field of visual XML languages and interfaces, which we deem fundamental to the spreading of XML to a wider audience.

RELATED WORK

Since the introduction of XML, several textual query languages were proposed and analyzed by the database community (Fernandez et al., 1999; Ives & Lu, 2000), far before the proposal of XQuery (W3C, 2003b).

XQBE, in turn, comes after a long stream of research on graph-based logical languages, started many years ago with QBE (Zloof, 1977), a user friendly query language for relational databases in which the user can formulate simple queries by filling in skeleton tables with an example of possible answers.

The first *object-oriented* graphical query languages were G (Cruz, Mendelzon, & Wood, 1987) and G+ (Cruz, Mendelzon, & Wood, 1988). In turn, graphlog (Consens & Mendelzon, 1990) and good (Paredaens et al., 1992) descend from G+; good offers a uniform notation for object databases where nodes represent objects and edges represent relationships. A good-like notation was used by G-Log (Paredaens, Peelman, & Tanca, 1995), a logic-based graphical language that makes it possible to represent and query complex objects by means of directed labeled graphs. An evolution of this language, WG-Log (Comai, Damiani, Posenato, & Tanca, 1998), was built to query Internet pages and semi-structured data adding to G-Log some hypermedia features. A direct descendent of WG-Log was XML-GL (Comai, Damiani, & Fraternali, 2001), an early, self-standing visual query language for XML, designed far before XQuery. XQBE can then be considered as an evolution of XML-GL; initially targeted to be a suitable visual interface for XQuery, XQBE has evolved to become a richer language for the definition, query, transformation, and update of XML data.

QSByE (Filha, Laender, & Da Silva, 2001) is a graphical interface that represents data as nested tables and extends the QBE paradigm to deal with semi-structured data. MiroWeb Tool (Bouganim et al., 1999) uses a visual paradigm based on trees that implements XML-QL. QBEN is a graphical interface to query data according to the nested relational model; the users specify their queries with the operations of the nested relational algebra (Jaeschke & Schek 1982).

Equix (Cohen et al., 1999) is a form-based query language for XML repositories based on a tree-like representation of the documents, automatically built from their schemas. Equix supports the visual construction of complex queries including quantification, negation, and aggregation; it has limited restructuring capabilities (the only restructuring primitive is the introduction of new nodes).

BBQ (Munroe & Papakonstantinou 2000)—Blended Browsing and Querying—is a front-end for XMAS (Ludaescher, Papakonstantinou, Velikhov, & Vianu, 1999), a query language for XML-based mediator systems (a simplification of XML-QL). In BBQ, XML elements and attributes are shown in a directory-like tree and the users specify possible conditions and relationships (as joins) among elements.

PESTO (Carey, Haas, Maganty, & Williams, 1996) is an integrated user interface that supports browsing and querying of object databases; PESTO allows users to navigate in a hypertext-like fashion, following the relationships that exist among objects. In addition, it allows users to formulate object queries through a unique, integrated query paradigm that presents querying as a natural extension of browsing. PESTO includes support for basic query operations (such as simple selections, value based joins, universal quantification, negation, and complex predicates).

VQBD (Chawathe, Baby, & Yeo, 2001) addresses the objective to explore an XML document of unknown structure. XQForms (Petropoulos, Vassalos, & Papakonstantinou, 2001) is a generator of Web-based query forms and reports for XML data. XQForms takes as input the XML schema, a declarative specification of the logic of the query and a set of template libraries. The use of these three different inputs allows a clear separation between data to be queried, query logic, and presentation of the results.

QURSED (Papakonstantinou, Petropoulos, & Vassalos, 2002) allows the development of Web-based query forms and reports for XML data. QURSED is based on the QSS formalism, a capability-description language (Levy, Rajaraman, & Ordille, 1996; Vassalos & Papakonstantinou, 2000), and produces XQuery-compliant queries. QURSED allows the user to use both conjunction and disjunction; disjunctive queries are pre-processed, and OR conditions are substituted by a forest of condition trees without OR nodes called *conjunctive condition trees*. The QURSED editor inputs the XML schema that describes the structure of XML data and an HTML query form page (that provides the visual part of the form page). The editor displays the XML Schema and the HTML pages to the developer, who uses them to visually build the query set specification and the query/visual association (that indicates how each parameter is associated to HTML form). Then a compiler generates Java Server Pages, which control the interaction with the end user.

GXQL (Quin, Yao, Liu, & McCool, 2004) is a graphical language that produces XQuery queries from nested windows. Windows with different borders and colors are used to represent different constructs, and the language takes advantage of layering to express nested queries.

XQueryViz (Karam, Boulos, Ollaic, & Koteiche, 2006) is a data-flow-like syntax for XQuery. Many different nodes are used to depict XQuery constructs, and three windows are present. The first one shows the schemas of the source documents from which *path expressions* are selected to generate variables. The second window contains a graph, which is translated into *for-let-where* clauses, while the last one is dedicated to the *return* clause. While the language covers a big subset of XQuery, sub-query nesting inside return clauses is not supported. Compared to XQBE, their visual approach does not seem flexible enough to support updates and active rules.

As will be shown in the next sections, the XQBE approach distinguishes itself from most other tools for its intuitiveness, simplicity, and flexibility.

THE XQBE VISUAL DATA MODEL AND PARADIGM

The visual representation of XML documents in XQBE relies on a simplified XML data model, basically reduced to the notion of elements, at-

tributes, and PCDATA content, with containment hierarchies connecting such elements. Data types as described in XML Schema are not supported, and ID/IDREF couples are treated just like all other attributes (thus, the underlying XML data model is even simpler than a DTD specification).

XQBE uses a tree structure whose nodes represent the elements, attributes, and PCDATA content of given XML documents.

Elements are shaped as labelled rectangles; their label represents the element name (or tagname). PCDATA nodes are represented as empty circles and denote the textual content of XML elements. Attributes are represented as filled (black) circles; the label on the incoming arc represents the attribute name. Nodes represented as circles can be referred as value nodes, as they represent the actual data content of the XML documents.

XQBE has no graphical constructs to represent different parts of the textual content of an element, nor parts of the textual value of an attribute. In the case of mixed elements, the value represented by a PCDATA node is the concatenation of all the text excerpts at the first level of nesting (a deep concatenation can be expressed by means of a Kleene cross on the arc going from the element to the PCDATA). This inability to distinguish substrings is a precise design choice, motivated

Figure 1. The XQBE data model

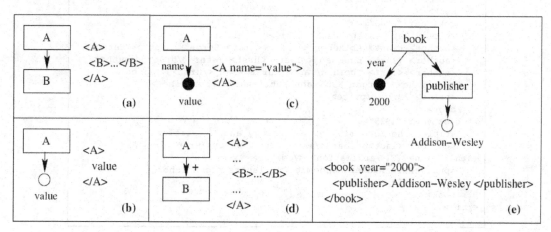

by the need for simplicity; we believe that a visual construct intended to cut a string in substrings would be rather confusing, and of marginal importance for most users.

The containment relationship between two XML items is represented by means of a directed arc from the container to the contained item. Arcs labelled with a cross (that reminds of the Kleene cross operator) express the ascendant-descendant relationship (i.e., the transitive closure of the relationship).

The aforementioned components combine into structures like those in Figure 1. The figure shows (a) a direct containment, (b) PCDATA content, (c) attributes, (d) and the transitive closure of the containment relationship. Finally, Figure 2 represents an element matching with **book** elements having as year of publication "2000" and as publisher "Addison-Wesley" and reports its XML counterpart.

XQBE AS A QUERY LANGUAGE

In order to introduce the basic features of XQBE, we show the XQBE version of some simple queries taken in the W3C XMP XML query use cases, based on the XML fragment of Figure 2.

In this section, we present XML data taken from the W3C "XML query use cases."

Query q1 below reads "List books published by Addison-Wesley after 1991, including their year and title":

```
<bib>
  {for $b in document("www.bn.com/bib.xml")/bib/book
  where $b/publisher="Addison-Wesley" and $b/@year>1991
  return <book year="{ $b/@year }">
          { $b/title }
          </book> }

</bib>
```

Its XQBE version is depicted in Figure 3. A query always has a vertical line in the middle that separates the *source* part (the one on the left) from the *construct* part (on the right, so that the query

Figure 2. Running example

```
<bib>
  <book year="1994">
    <title> TCP/IP Illustrated </title>
    <author> <last> Stevens </last> <first> W. </first> </author>
    <publisher> Addison-Wesley </publisher>
    <price> 65.95 </price>
  </book>
  <book year="1992">
    <title> Advanced Programming in the Unix...</title>
    <author> <last> Stevens </last> <first> W. </first> </author>
    <publisher> Addison-Wesley </publisher>
    <price> 65.95 </price>
  </book>
  <book year="2000">
    <title> Data on the Web </title>
    <author> <last> Abiteboul</last> <first> Serge </first> </author>
    <author> <last> Buneman </last> <first> Peter </first> </author>
    <author> <last> Suciu </last> <first> Dan </first> </author>
    <publisher> Morgan Kaufmann Publishers </publisher>
    <price> 39.95 </price>
  </book>
  <book year="1999">
    <title> The Economics of Technology and... </title>
    <editor> <last>Gerbarg</last> <first>Darcy</first>
<affiliation>CITI</affiliation> </editor>
    <publisher> Kluwer Academic Publishers </publisher>
    <price> 129.95 </price>
  </book>
</bib>
```

has a "natural" reading order from left to right). Both parts contain labelled graphs that represent XML fragments and express properties of such fragments (like conditions upon values, ordering properties, etc.). The source part describes the XML data to be matched in order to construct the query result, while the construct part specifies which parts are to be retained in the result and (optionally) which newly generated XML items are to be inserted.

The correspondence between the components of the two parts is expressed by explicit bindings across the vertical line that connects the nodes of the source part to the nodes that will take their place in the output document.

Elements, attributes, and PCDATA content are always depicted according to the data model presented in the previous section. Value nodes may be labelled so as to express conditions on the values they represent.

In Figure 3, we extract data from the document of the running example: the source part matches all the book elements with a year attribute whose value is greater than 1991 and publisher subelement whose PCDATA content equals "Addison-Wesley." The location of the XML document target of the query is indicated by the little grey square used as the root of the tree.

In the construct part, the paths that branch out of a bound node indicate which of its sub-items are to be retained, thus "projecting" the bound node (in Figure 3 only the title and publication

Figure 3. Query q1

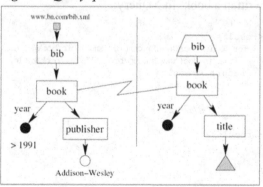

Figure 4. Query q2

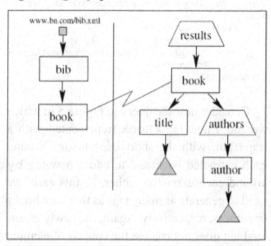

year of the selected books are retained). The binding edge between the book nodes states that the query result shall contain *as many* book elements *as* those matched in the source part.

The trapezoidal bib node above the book node means that all the generated books are to be contained into a single bib element. This node represents a newly generated element, and *new elements* are always depicted as trapezia in XQBE.

Trapezia can be depicted with their short edge on the upper side or on the bottom side. These two configurations impose different cardinality constraints on the newly generated elements, which we illustrate in Figures 4 and 5.

The **results** node of Figure 4 (a trapezium with the short edge above) placed above the **book** node means that all the generated **books** are to be contained into a single **results** element. Similarly, one **authors** tag is generated for all **author**s of each **book**. Note that the newly generated tag does not change the context of element names, therefore author in the construct part is considered as a subelement of **book** in the source part. In XQuery:

```
<results> {
  for  $b  in  doc("www.bn.com/bib.xml")/bib/
book
    return <book>
              { $b/title }
          <authors> { $b/author } </authors>
              </book>
} </results>
```

Consider now the query in Figure 5 in which we add a new tag **aBook** (represented with a trapezium with the short edge below) around each extracted book and to add a new tag **by** around each extracted author. In this case, we need to generate as many tags as there are books or authors, respectively. Again, the newly generated tag does not change the context of element names, therefore **author** in the construct part is considered as a subelement of **book** in the source part. In XQuery:

```
for $b in doc("www.bn.com/bib.xml")/bib/book
return <aBook>
          <book>
            { $b/title }
            { for $a in $b/author
              return <by> $a </by> }
          </book>
        </aBook>
```

XQBE allows one to express many kinds of document transformations. As an example, we show how to synthetically express the flattening

Figure 5. Query q3

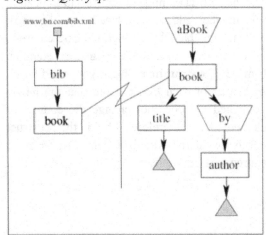

of hierarchical data structures. Consider the query in Figure 6(a) "Create a flat list of all the title-author pairs with each pair enclosed in **result** element." In XQuery:

```
<results>
  { for $b in doc("www.bn.com/bib.xml")/bib/book,
      $a in $b/author
      $t in $b/title,
      return <result>
                { $a }
                { $t }
              </result>
  }
</results>
```

Its XQBE version is in Figure 6(a). The **results** element in the construct part is a new tag enclosing the result document; then, several **result** elements are generated by means of a trapezium with the short edge below; the cardinality of these elements is determined by the number of book elements that are extracted by the source part of the query. Each such element has a pair of successors tagged **title** and **author**, and such pairs (with all the fragments underlying each of them) are enclosed within each generated **result** tag. Note that the book element in the source part provides a common context, enabling the pairing of authors and titles only when they have actually written a book.

Let us next consider a (rather unusual) query with two unrelated binding edges. Consider query in Figure 6(b) asking to build the Cartesian product of all possible pairs of authors and titles, regardless of the fact that the authors have indeed written a book. In XQuery:

```
<results>
  { for $a in doc("www.bn.com/bib.xml")/bib/book/author
      $t in doc("www.bn.com/bib.xml")/bib/book/title,
      return <result>
                { $a }
                { $t }
              </result>
  }
</results>
```

Figure 6. Queries q4 and q5

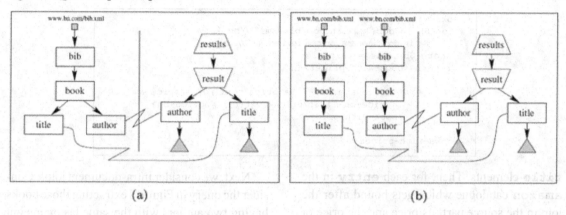

(a)   **(b)**

Its XQBE version is in Figure 6(b). Also in this case, several **result** elements are generated by means of a trapezium with the short edge below, but the cardinality of these elements is determined by the product of the number of different **title** and **author** elements, which are retrieved from two independent copies of the bibliography document. Thus, this query builds the Cartesian product of all titles and authors appearing in the source document.

We turn now to join queries and consider first the join between two documents (inter-document join). Consider the query in Figure 7 that constructs a joint book catalogue collecting information from different documents. It states, "For each book found at both **bn.com** and **amazon.com**, list the title of the book and its price from each source." In XQuery: (See Box 1).

Value-based equality is expressed by means of a join connection between the PCDATA of the

Figure 7. Query q8

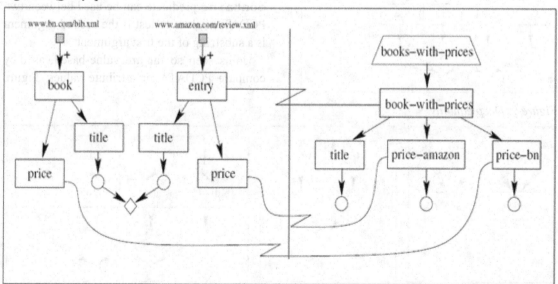

Box 1.

```
<books-with-prices>
 { for $b in doc("www.bn.com/bib.xml")//book,
       $a in doc("www.amazon.com/review.xml")//entry
   where $b/title = $a/title
   return <book-with-prices>
            { $a/title }
            <price-amazon> { $a/price/text() } </price-amazon>
            <price-bn> { $b/price/text() } </price-bn>
          </book-with-prices>
 }
</books-with-prices>
```

title elements. Then, for each **entry** in the **amazon** catalogue which gets bound after the join in the source part, its price and the price of the corresponding book in the **bn** catalogue are extracted from the two documents. Of course, a symmetric solution is possible, that binds the **book** elements instead. The **books-with-prices** element in the construct part is a new tag enclosing the result document.

Figure 8. Query q9

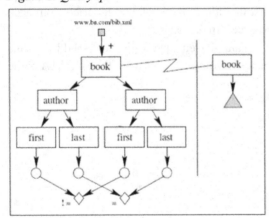

Figure 9. Deep equality

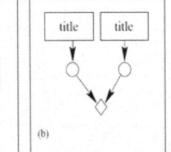
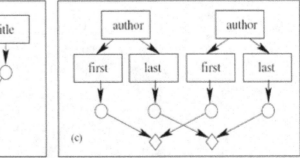

Next, we consider intra-document joins. Consider the query in Figure 8 extracting those books having two authors with the same last name but different first name. In XQuery:

```
for $b in doc("www.bn.com/bib.xml")/bib/book
where some $a1 in $b/author satisfies
     some $a2 in $b/author satisfies
     ( $a1/last = $a2/last and $a1/first != $a2/first )
return $b
```

Its XQBE version is based on the conjunction of two joins, having as arguments the PCDATA content of the **first** and the **last** elements, where elements of the first pair must be different, and elements of the second pair must be equal. All typical binary comparison predicates are allowed ($<, <=, !=, >, >=, =$); equality is assumed as default if the predicate is unspecified. The **contains** predicate can be used between two PCDATA values to test if the second argument is a substring of the first argument.

Joins seen so far are value-based, as they compare PCDATA or attribute values. Figure

366

Figure 10. Negation

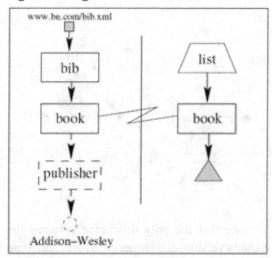

9(a) shows join connections that express the deep equality (i.e., confluences on the same element). Such join condition is satisfied when at least one fragment contained in the left structure is equal to at least one fragment contained into the right structure. Note that the confluence on a **title** element (a1) is equivalent to the join upon PC-DATA values (b), and similarly the confluence on the **author** element (a2) is equivalent to the conjunction of two joins upon the **first** and **last** PCDATA values (c).

XQBE allows one to express negative conditions by means of negation nodes and arcs. Negation nodes and arcs are represented in XQBE by means of dashed figures (nodes and lines). They represent conditions that *must not* hold. Negated elements and PCDATA nodes are dashed. All arcs incoming to, or outgoing from, a negation node must be dashed as well. Negated attribute nodes are represented just like other attributes (filled black circles), but they can be distinguished because of the incoming dashed arc. Negated nodes cannot be followed by "positive" (i.e., non negated) nodes and cannot be connected by binding edges.

The query shown in Figure 10, "List all the books not published by Addison-Wesley," exemplifies the use of negation. It translates to the following XQuery statement:

```
<list>
 { for $b in doc("www.bn.com/bib.xml")/bib/book
  where not(some $p in $b/publisher/text() satisfies
          ( $p = "Addison-Wesley" ) ) )
  return $b
 }
</list>
```

In this example, we ask for **book** elements inside which no **publisher** elements exist with a PCDATA content equal to "Addison-Wesley."

If no labels were specified on negation nodes, the global requirement would be stricter, discarding all books with a publisher (disregarding the PCDATA value). In the general case, as in the case of positive predicates, the negative predicates must hold in conjunction (the fragment must satisfy the negation of the conjunction of the predicates).

XQBE allows also the use of ghost elements. They are represented (as negated elements) by means of dashed rectangle nodes. They are used to explicitly mention an XML element that will not be included in the constructed result but contributes to the construction. Note that dashed rectangles represent a negated condition when included in the source part and represent elements that should not be retained in the result when included in the construct part. Although these two meanings are different, the use of dashed nodes in the two parts of XQBE queries was found very intuitive and natural by XQBE users - the meaning of a dashed node in either part can be summarized as "this node is not in the document."

This feature is exemplified by the query in Figure 11 that states, "For each book list only the title and the surnames of the authors (maintaining the books in the order of the original document)." In XQuery:

Figure 11. Ghost elements

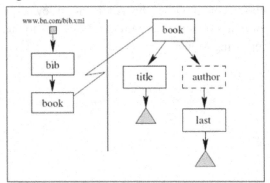

Figure 12. Sorting

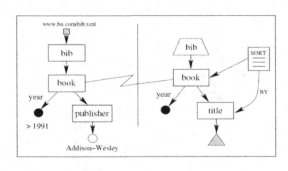

```
for $b in /bib/book
return <book>
        { $b/title }
        { $b/author/last }
        </book>
```

Sorting is expressed by means of sorting nodes. The nodes to be sorted are reached by the (only) unlabeled outgoing arc, while the sorting criteria are the nodes reached by the **BY** arcs; the optional **ASC** or **DESC** keywords can be added as well, with **ASC** used as the default. If there is more then one ordering, an optional number between brackets indicates the ordering priority, and if no order is specified the counter clockwise order from the unlabeled arc is assumed as default.

Consider the query in Figure 12, "List books published by Addison-Wesley after 1991 with their year and title, sorting the retrieved books in lexicographic order." This is a refinement of first query with the addition of a sorting criterion in the construction of the result. It translates to:

```
<bib>
 { for $b in doc("www.bn.com/bib.xml")/bib/book
   where $b/publisher="Addison-Wesley" and
$b/@year>1991
    order by $b/title
    return <book>
            { $b/@year }
            { $b/title }
            </book>
 }
</bib>
```

Note that the only difference between the XQuery versions of this query and the original one shown in Figure 3 is the addition of the **order by** clause. Accordingly, in the graphical representation we just need to add the node expressing the sorting condition to query in Figure 3.

Visual languages become difficult to use as the size of the query grows. However, complex queries can be decomposed by using views. XQBE provides a special node type to denote the result of a query within another query, as if it were a *virtual* XML document representing a *view* over the actual XML documents. As shown in Figure 12, XQBE allows one to include in the source part of a query a special node, named *View-Node*, represented as a grey rectangle marked with a darker grey triangle and labeled with a view name. The figure also shows that a view can in turn contain a reference to other views. This is not surprising, as *every* legal XQBE expression can be associated to a View-Node and reused within another XQBE query.

In principle, any available transformation that generates a well-formed XML document can be associated to a view-node. In saying that view-nodes represent the root of virtual documents (i.e., documents computed as the result of some manipulation), we state that the data extraction process associated to the view node is *totally in-*

Figure 13. View

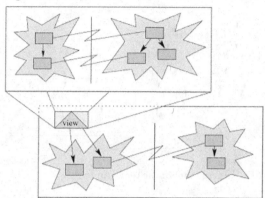

Figure 14. A query without views and with views

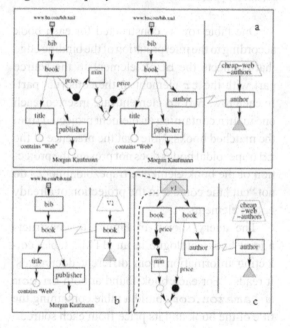

Box 2.

```
<cheap-web-authors>
{
    let $MKWeb := ( for $b in doc("www.bn.com/bib.xml")/bib/book
                    where $b/publisher = "Morgan Kaufmann"
                      and contains($b/title, "Web")
                    return $b )
    for $b in $MKWeb
    where $b/@price = min($MKWeb/@price)
    return $b/author
}
</cheap-web-authors>
```

dependent of the query in which it is embedded. This means that no parameter-passing mechanism is provided, and that the semantics is simply that of pre-computing all the embedded queries before computing the external query.

As an example, consider the query in Figure 14a, that extracts the authors of the cheapest books containing "Web" in their title and published by Morgan Kaufmann. In XQuery: (See Box 2).

Note that the XQuery statement conveniently defines the MKWeb variable and uses it twice: first to restrict the scope of $b and then to compute the minimum price.

In Figure 14b, *v1* represents an XQBE query that extracts all the books collected in the $MKWeb variable by the XQuery previous statement.

Query *v1* provides an intermediate step, which is useful for computing the final result. Here, the query in Figure 14c is an equivalent, yet much simpler formulation of the query depicted in Figure 14a.

XQBE AS A TRANSFORMATION LANGUAGE

Although XQBE was designed to be directly mappable to XQuery and to work as a GUI capable of running on top of any existing XQuery engine, it can also be used very easily to generate XSLT stylesheets performing XML-to-XML transformations, including XML-to-HTML transforma-

Figure 15. Transformation T1

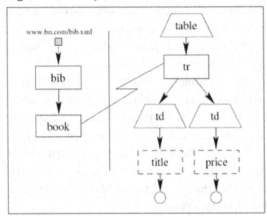

tions, as HTML can be regarded as one particular XML language.

For example, the first query shown in the previous section is translated to the following XSLT template:

```
<xsl:template match="/">
<bib>
 <xsl:for-each select="bib/book[@year>1991
           and publisher/text()='Addison-
Wesley']">
  <book> <xsl:copy-of select="@year"/>
        <xsl:copy-of select="title"/> </
book>
 </xsl:for-each>
</bib>

</xsl:template>
```

In order to better appreciate the use of XQBE for transformations we show a set of examples generating HTML components.

The query shown in Figure 15 constructs a table containing information about books. It reads "Build an HTML table with each book in a different row and with a column for the title and a column for the price." In XSLT:

```
<xsl:template match="/">
 <table>
  <xsl:for-each select="bib/book">
   <tr>
    <td>
     <xsl:value-of select="title"/>
    </td>
```

Figure 16. Transformation T2

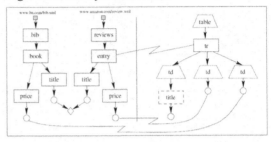

```
   <td>
    <xsl:value-of select="price"/>
   </td>
  </tr>
 </xsl:for-each>
 </table>
</xsl:template>
```

One table row is constructed for each book according to the interpretation of the binding edge that connects the **book** element in the source part with the **tr** element in the construct part. In each row, two **td** elements are inserted, each one in turn containing an element projected from the matched books. Note that the presence of the **td** trapezoidal nodes does not prevent the projection of the book elements: trapezoidal nodes do not "cut" the context in the projection of already bound elements.

The query shown in Figure 16 constructs a joint book catalogue in an HTML table, collecting information from different documents. It reads, "For each book found at both **bn.com** and **amazon.com**, build a table containing the title of the book and its price from each source." In XSLT: (See Box 3).

This query performs the "inner join" of the books of two documents based on their title. Note that the XSLT generated code considers both documents as external documents. The values to be inserted into the **td** elements cannot be automatically determined, so the user has to explicitly bind them to the appropriate PCDATA nodes in the match part.

Box 3.

```
<xsl:template match="/">
 <table>
  <xsl:for-each
       select="doc('www.amazon.com/review.xml')/reviews/entry">
   <xsl:variable name="price1" select="price"/>
   <xsl:variable name="title1" select="title/text()"/>
   <xsl:for-each
        select="doc('www.bn.com/bib.xml')/bib/book">
    <xsl:variable name="price2" select="price"/>
    <xsl:variable name="title2" select="title/text()"/>
    <xsl:if test="$title1=$title2">
     <tr>
      <td><xsl:value-of select="$title1"/></td>
      <td><xsl:value-of select="$price1/text()"/></td>
      <td><xsl:value-of select="$price2/text()"/></td>
     </tr>
    </xsl:if>
   </xsl:for-each>
  </xsl:for-each>
 </table>
</xsl:template>
```

XQBE AS A SCHEMA DEFINITION LANGUAGE

XQBE can be used to draw schemas of XML documents. The importance of defining schemas, even in a simple environment, is manifold; for example, it is often necessary to provide the definition of a structure for documents so that proper tools can validate them. Besides, the XQBE system can benefit from the presence of a schema to support users in building their queries as shown in the section on "Enhancing users' experience." Endowing users with a tool to visually define simple schemas can be useful, for instance, when the target user is unacquainted with textual schema languages, or to provide even expert users with a complete tool to quickly draft schemas and queries to be fine-tuned afterwards.

Data Model and Syntax

The XQBE data model is quite simple: it can predicate on tags, attributes, and text without information about the data type of contents. This is a precise design choice to keep the language as simple as possible, though expressive. The schema definition language is tailored to the need of simplicity so only a subset of the DTD language is supported. In particular, any element's content is considered as PCDATA, while attributes are always CDATA. Of course, as any DTD can be translated into an XML chema document, we could easily generate XML schemas from our graphical language; yet, we are not planning to introduce data types and more complex features available in this language, because we believe that simplicity and ease-of-use are key factors of XQBE.

XQBE schemas are expressed by means of the following elements:

Labeled rectangular nodes represent *XML elements*; the label is the tag name.

 Empty circles represent the *textual content* of elements.

Figure 17. Snapshot of DTD creation

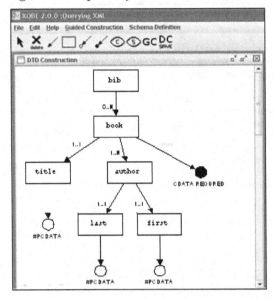

Filled circles represent *attributes* whose names are placed on the arc connecting the node to its parent. An optional label below the node can state whether the attribute is *REQUIRED* or *IMPLIED* (default).

Ellipses marked with a "**C**" represent *choices*: all their sub-elements are in mutual exclusion. The same node is used to define mixed elements.

Ellipses marked with an "**S**" represent *sequences*: all their sub-elements are to be considered as a sequence.

Nodes are connected through **arcs**, which describe *parent-child* relationships. Arcs can be labeled with additional information such as attribute names, minimum and maximum cardinality of elements, as described next.

Choice and *sequence* ellipses can only be parents of rectangles or empty circles (defin-

ing a sequence or a choice of attributes is not allowed).

Defining Schemas

As a first example, Figure 17 shows our tool used to define the schema of a simple bibliographical document in which a **bib** element contains an arbitrary number of **book**s. Each **book** is made of a single **title** and one or more **author**s, as well as a **year** attribute, which is required. **author**s are made of a **last** and a **first** elements. Note that each arc connecting two rectangular nodes is decorated with a label, describing the *cardinality* of the containment relationship. Labels can take any of the values (0..N, 0..1, 1..1, 1..N), stating the minimum and maximum number of children with the same tag under a given parent node.

Attributes are connected to their parent node by means of an arc, the label of which is used to specify the attribute name. The node is labeled with its type (**CDATA**) and constraint (**REQUIRED**). The type is optional, since any attribute is of type **CDATA** by default; if no constraint is specified, the attribute is meant as **implied**.

Text nodes are labeled with the (optional) **#PCDATA** tag, while no sign can appear next to the arc connecting them to their parent nodes.

The diagram depicted above is translated into the following DTD:

```
<!ELEMENT bib (book*)>
<!ELEMENT book (title,author+)>
```

Figure 18. XQBE version of a DTD schema

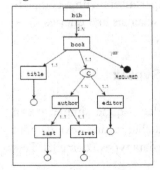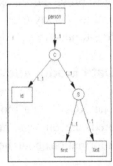

```
<!ATTLIST book year CDATA #REQUIRED>
<!ELEMENT title (#PCDATA)>
<!ELEMENT author (last,first)>
<!ELEMENT last (#PCDATA)>
<!ELEMENT first (#PCDATA)>
```

We now show an example that extends the previous one with the introduction of a choice element, to state that a **book** may have one or more **author**s, or one **editor** (but not both of them). The DTD becomes as follows:

```
<!ELEMENT bib (book*)>
<!ELEMENT book (title, (author+ | editor ))>
<!ATTLIST book
          year CDATA #REQUIRED>
<!ELEMENT title (#PCDATA)>
<!ELEMENT author (last,first)>
<!ELEMENT editor (#PCDATA)>
<!ELEMENT last (#PCDATA)>
```

Figure 19. Schema describing a recursive table

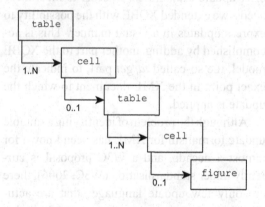

Figure 20. Recursive DTD schema

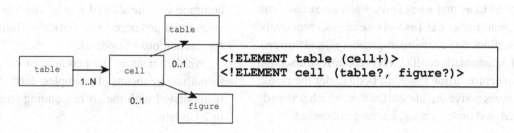

```
<!ELEMENT first (#PCDATA)>
```

This DTD is equivalent to the XQBE Schema of Figure 18a):

Sequences are usually rendered as a series of elements rooted in the same rectangular node. Elements inside a sequence are ordered according to the left-to-right order of nodes in the tree. For example, in Figure 18a an **author** contains a sequence of **last** and **first**, in this exact order. A sequence node is needed to disambiguate those situations where only some of the children of a node compose a sequence. For example, in Figure 18b a **person** contains either one **id** or a sequence of **first** and **last**; without the sequence node, the three elements would all be in mutual exclusion with one another (i.e., the corresponding DTD fragment would be **(id | first | last)** instead of **(id | (first, last))**.

Automatic Conflict Detection

Often, in particular with complex schemas, the user may introduce more than one node with the same label. This may happen because of an error, but more often it is due to partial views of the same, complex element. Another frequent situation is when the document structure is recursive: since XQBE doesn't allow for cyclic graphs, it is necessary to introduce the same element twice. The system must recognize these special cases and treat them properly.

As a first example, consider a schema, which describes a recursive table: a **table** is made of **cell**s; each **cell** can contain a **figure** and another **table**.

373

Figure 21. Automatic conflict resolution in DTD definition

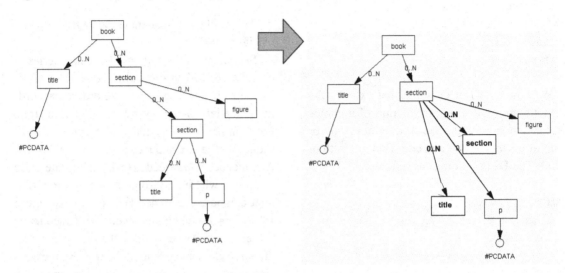

A naïve user could express this structure as seen in Figure 19.

Note that **table** and **cell** are repeated twice and the **figure** is shown in the last **cell** element only. Our system is capable of recognizing this conflict and to suggest a solution. To achieve this goal, it is necessary to detect duplicate elements and collapse all their contents into a single node (say, the first encountered). The collapse is realized by means of a mathematical union; cardinality conflicts are resolved by choosing the loosest available. All the occurrences, which are removed, are replaced with a reference, visually rendered by means of a green, dashed border. Figure 20 shows the proposed solution along with the final DTD schema.

The following figure shows a more complex example:

This particular example shows a **book** made of **title**s and **section**s. Each **section** can contain other **title**s and **section**s, recursively. Sections also contain paragraphs (**p**s) and **figure**s. The automatic conflict solver collapses the section structure inside the main node under the **book**; the recursive section and the title, which is already defined under a book, become references.

XQBE AS AN UPDATE LANGUAGE

Besides the need of querying XML documents, the XML user communities call for mechanisms that offer update capabilities. In order to meet these needs, we extended XQBE with the possibility to express updates in a visual manner. This is accomplished by adding another part to the XQBE model, the so-called *target* part, to indicate the exact point in the XML document to which the update is applied.

Although the problem of identifying a suitable update formalism for XML has been known for almost a decade, and a W3C proposal is currently under standardisation (W3, 2006), there are only few update languages that are actually implemented. Among these, we refer in this chapter to XUpdate (Laux et al., 2000) since it has a sufficient expressive power to satisfy all common user needs and it is adequately simple so as to be generated automatically from visual representations of updates.

We demonstrate the potential of our update formalism by means of examples, each of which is annotated with the corresponding translation in XUpdate.

Figure 22. Example of "append"

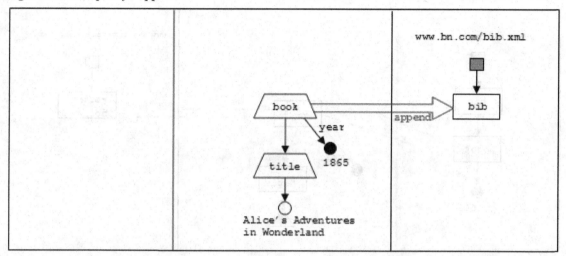

We start with a simple addition of a new fragment representing the book "Alice's Adventures in Wonderland" to the **bib** element (which is the root) of the **bib.xml** document. The new **book** element is created in the construct part, whereas the select part is not used here and can be left blank. The label on the double-lined arrow branching from the **book** element in the construct part to the **bib** element in the target part indicates that the operation is an append (i.e., the fragment will be placed after all **bib**'s sub-elements).

Note that, in general, the update may be a multi-update (i.e., it can cause the insertion of the constructed fragment into several parts of the document, namely, all those that are matched by the destination element of the arrow pointing to the target part). Here we know that the fragment will be inserted exactly once because of the uniqueness of the bib element, as required by the document's well-formedness. The XUpdate version of this update is[1]:

Figure 23. Example of "insert"

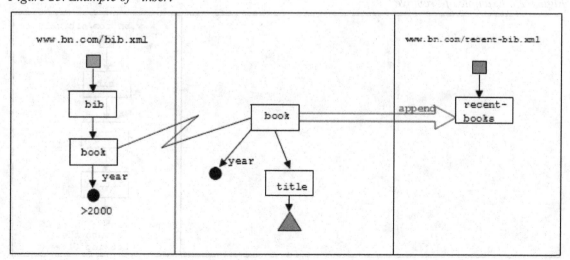

Figure 24. Example of "append" with a selection

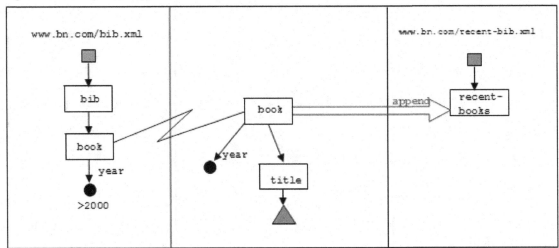

```
<xupdate:append select="/bib" child="last()">
  <xupdate:element name="book">
    <xupdate:attribute name="year">1865</xup-
date:attribute>
    <title>Alice's Adventures in Wonderland</title>
  </xupdate:element>

</xupdate:append>
```

Fragments can also be inserted in specific positions among the children of a given element. In this case the arrow points to a child element and is labeled with "insert after" or "insert before" to indicate that the fragment will be inserted imme-

diately after (resp., before) the element pointed at. Again, if the element is univocally identified via a key attribute, the insertion is unique; otherwise, there will be as many insertions, in the respective positions, as there are elements that match the element pointed at by the arrow. The example next shows an insertion of a book element immediately before *all* book elements whose title is "Through the Looking Glass" (which are guaranteed to be one if the title is a key). Its XUpdate version:

Figure 25. Example of "remove"

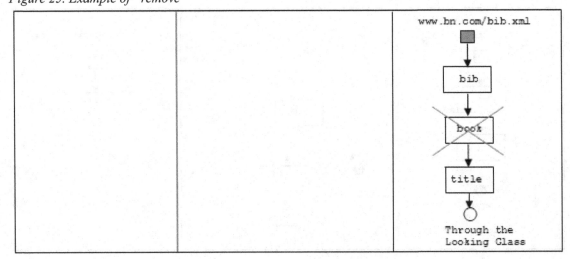

Figure 26. Example of "replace"

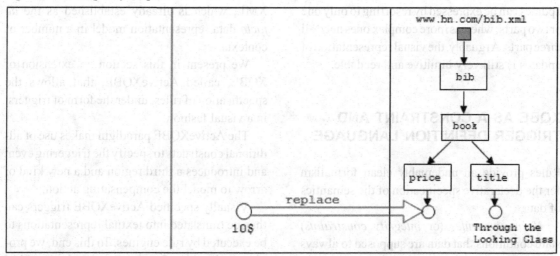

```
<xupdate:insert-before
      select="/bib/book[title="Through the
looking glass"]" >
    <xupdate:element name="book">
      <xupdate:attribute name="year">1865</
xupdate:attribute>
      <title>Alice's Adventures in Wonder-
land</title>
    </xupdate:element>
  </xupdate:insert-before>
```

Next, we show an update that inserts all books published after the year 2000, as children of a **recent-books** element in a different document called **recent-bib.xml**. Here all three parts are used: the select and the construct parts behave as usual, whereas the new target part is used to indicate the position at which the fragment constructed in the second part will be inserted. In this case the equivalent XUpdate statement has to be built in two steps: first we extract with an XQuery statement the data that are to be inserted, then we build the update statement by inserting the extracted elements as constant values in the XUpdate statement (note that XUpdate does not allow referring to XQuery statements for the selection of elements).

Deletions have a simpler visual representation than insertions, as we do not need to build new fragments and therefore we can simply tag, in the target part, the root of the fragment to be dropped with a red cross. The example next shows the deletion of all books with a given title.

In XUpdate:

```
<xupdate:remove  select="/bib/
book[title="Through the Looking Glass"]"/>
```

In the last example, we show the update of sub-elements: all **price** subelements within the **book** element corresponding to the title "Through the Looking Glass" are replaced by a **price** element with textual value **10$**. As usual, the new constituent is created in the construct part, whereas the position is indicated in the target part. In this case the arrow is tagged with the "replace" keyword to indicate that the **10$** value will overwrite the content of the **price** attribute in the book(s). The equivalent XUpdate statement is:

```
<xupdate:update
  select="/bib/book[title="Through the look-
ing glass"]/price">
    10$
</xupdate:update>
```

As shown in the previous examples, simple updates can be expressed by resorting to only one or two parts, whereas more complex ones need all three parts. Arguably, the visual representation of updates is still very intuitive and readable.

XQBE AS A CONSTRAINT AND TRIGGER DEFINITION LANGUAGE

Rules provide an undeniably clean formalism for the declarative specification of the semantics of data.

Normative rules (or *integrity constraints*) state conditions that data are supposed to always satisfy. *Active rules* indicate policies to be applied on data according to the current state of the store and, possibly, in response to events of different kinds.

Both kinds of rules, often collectively referred to as *business rules*, may describe the process flows or business level requirements that apply to organisations. As such, they should be business owned and oriented and should be specified in the most intuitive way. More so, users should ideally be able to define and maintain business rules without the intervention of an IT professional. Besides, complex rules are best specified by domain experts, who, however, may lack knowledge in data definition and manipulation languages. In this regard, an intuitive visual paradigm may prove very useful.

This is especially apparent in the context of XML, which is already established as the *de facto* data representation model in a number of contexts.

We present in this section an extension of XQBE, called ActiveXQBE, that allows the specification of rules, under the form of triggers, in a visual fashion.

The ActiveXQBE paradigm makes use of additional constructs to specify the triggering event and introduces a third region and a new kind of arrow to model the compensating action.

Visually specified ActiveXQBE triggers can then be translated into textual representations to be executed by rule engines. To this end, we provide an algorithm for transforming the graphical representation of a trigger into a trigger expressed in Active XQuery (W3C, 2003b), an extension of XQuery to define active rules for XML.

In this section, we first introduce ActiveXQBE, then we describe its formal semantics and, finally, exemplify the translation of ActiveXQBE graphs into Active XQuery expressions.

Introducing ActiveXQBE

ActiveXQBE extends XQBE in several ways; first of all, while XQBE uses two regions to extract data and construct results, ActiveXQBE uses three regions (cf. Figure 27a):

Figure 27. Active XQBE

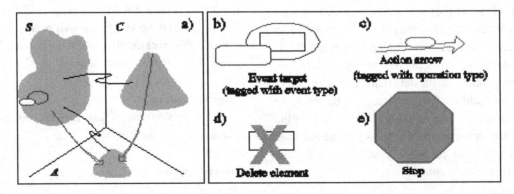

- The region on the left is the *Source Part* (S). The graph in S represents the XML nodes on which the triggering events are defined, as well as the conditions that apply to such nodes for the rule to be triggered. Any valid XQBE source graph is allowed in S; besides, exactly one node in this region must be tagged as the node on which the event occurs (the *event node*). Visually, the event node (an element, attribute, or PCDATA) is surrounded by a blue oval, and a tag specifies the type of event as shown in Figure 27b. One *action arrow* may optionally go out of a node and point to an element in the action part A described next.

- The region on the right is the *Construct Part* (C). The tree contained in this region, when present, defines new data structures to be inserted into suitable positions (as specified in the third region A); such insertions may implement the actions of the active rules. If C is not empty, an action arrow must connect the root of the tree in C and a node in A; in this case, no action arrow may be drawn from S to A. Any regular XQBE construction tree is allowed in C.

- A new region, the *Action Part* (A) is placed below S and C. This region specifies the compensating action of the trigger and supports insertion, update, and deletion operations, as well as the expression of denials (i.e., conditions that must never occur). In this last case, a red *stop sign* is placed in

this region (Figure 27e) to indicate that the event should be prevented (i.e., a rollback is needed if the trigger is evaluated *after* an event, or the action must be stopped if the trigger is evaluated *before* the event). For the other three kinds of action, a tree in A expresses the selection of the XML fragments on which the action must take place. Such tree can be either rooted in a *Root Element*, or in a *Rectangular Element* bound to a node in S. If the action is an update or an insertion, then the target of the action is the node reached by the action arrow (described below), which is tagged with the type of operation. If the action is a deletion, then a red cross marks the element to be deleted. As a design choice toward simplicity, ActiveXQBE triggers can only perform one compensating action, so at most one action arrow can reach A, either originating from S or C. Multiple compensating actions may, however, be obtained through multiple triggers and possibly specifying priorities.

The visual representation of compensating actions is shown in Figure 27c, d, and e. An *action arrow* is used to *update* or *insert* an element with data extracted from the original document (or built on the fly); the arrow starts from the element to be updated or inserted and reaches the element that will be updated (or, respectively, below which the new item will be inserted). The tag on the ar-

Figure 28. An XML document and its DTD schema

```
<dept>                        <!ELEMENT dept(budget, manager, emp*)>
  <budget>1000000</budget>    <!ELEMENT manager(name, salary, numOfEmps)>
  <manager>                   <!ELEMENT emp (name, salary)>
    <name>Smith</name>        <!ELEMENT name (#PCDATA)>
    <salary>10000</salary>    <!ELEMENT numOfEmps (#PCDATA)>
    <numOfEmps>9</numOfEmps>  <!ELEMENT salary (#PCDATA)>
  </manager>
  <emp>
    <name>Jones</name>
    <salary>8000</salary>
  </emp>
</dept>
```

Figure 29. Disallowing insertions

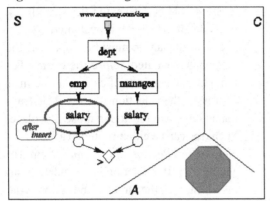

Figure 30. Updating budget

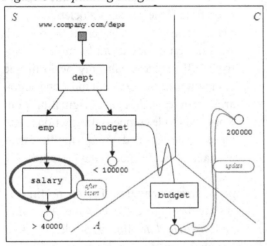

Figure 31. Updating salary

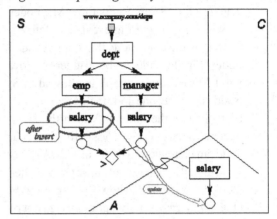

it, the trigger is evaluated *after* a **salary** node is inserted as a child of **emp**.

Coherently with the XQBE semantics, the compensating action (in this case, a rollback of the insertion) is performed only when all the conditions of the source graph apply (i.e., only when the value of the employee's **salary** is greater than the value of a manager's **salary**[3]). The small rhombus in the figure is the *join node* used to compare the salaries.

The example of Figure 30 shows a compensating action built in the construct part. In particular, when a salary greater than 40,000$ is inserted for an employee belonging to a department with low budget (say, less than 100,000$), this budget is updated to 200,000$.

Note that the **dept** element in the action part is bound to the **dept** element in S: the binding edge toward the action part transfers the context from S, so, when a high salary is set to an employee, only the budget of his department is updated. The construct part of this trigger is used to build a new **budget** element with constant value of 200,000$, that is used to update the budget of the department by means of an action arrow.

In Figure 31, we extend the example of Figure 29. We compare the newly inserted salary of an employee with the manager's salary. If the manager's salary is lower, then the employee's

row specifies the kind of action to be performed (insert-before, insert-after[2], update).

We now show some examples of ActiveXQBE triggers that apply to the XML data set and DTD schema of Figure 28.

As a first example, consider the trigger of Figure 29, which blocks insertion of salaries of employees that are greater than a salary of a manager in the same department. In this example the construct part is empty, since there is no need to build any new elements; the symbol in the action part states that the insertion is to be undone.

The **salary** node is the subject of the event: as stated by the label attached to the oval surrounding salary is updated to be the same as the manager's, as indicated by the action arrow coming from the source part. The construct part is unused.

Note that the compensating action updates the newly inserted salary (i.e., the salary is removed and inserted again). This causes the trigger to be evaluated again; however, the second time the comparison between salaries fails, since **emp/ salary** equals **manager/salary**.

From ActiveXQBE to Active XQuery

ActiveXQBE triggers are not directly interpreted by a specific engine, but translated into Active XQuery triggers and evaluated by existing rule engines. The syntax is as follows.

```
1.   CREATE TRIGGER Trigger-Name [WITH PRIOR-
     ITY Signed-Integer-Number]
2.   (BEFORE|AFTER) (INSERT|DELETE|REPLACE|RE
     NAME) OF XPathExpr (,XPathExpr)*
3.   [FOR EACH (NODE|STATEMENT)]
4.   [XQuery-Let-Clauses]
5.   [WHEN XQuery-Where-Clause]

6.   DO (XQuery-UpdateOp|ExternalOp)
```

Lines 1 and 3 are a sort of *header*, defining name, granularity, and priority (when the same

event fires multiple rules, their actions are executed in priority order; within the same priority level, an implicit creation order is followed). Line 2 describes the triggering *event*. Line 5 contains the trigger *conditions* and line 6 the *action* to be performed when the rule is triggered, possibly using *variables* defined in line 4.

Of course, there are several ways to express the same trigger in Active XQuery. We therefore first define a *canonical Active XQuery form* and that can then be used as a reference when translating an ActiveXQBE graph into Active XQuery. We say that a trigger is in *canonical form* when

1. The target nodes are identified by a *single path expression.*
2. The triggering conditions are expressed by stating the *non-emptiness* of *node sequences* defined by means of *XQuery let-clauses.*

Any Active XQuery trigger can be expressed in canonical form, by replacing the *when-clauses* with a conjunction of non-emptiness statements on sets extracted by proper *let-clauses*, which select elements using the conditions formerly expressed

Figure 32. An ActiveXQBE trigger and its Active XQuery translation

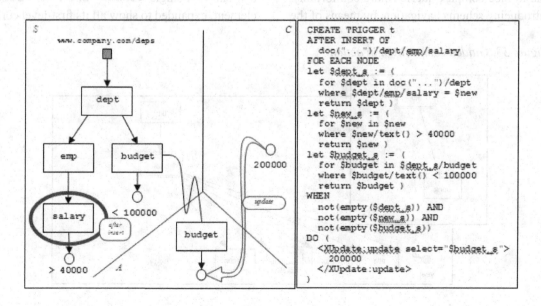

by the *when-clauses*. Then, a different copy of the same trigger must be produced for each *path expression* that describes the event.

We refrain from giving the details of the translation algorithm in this chapter and show instead how the trigger of Figure 30 is translated into ActiveXQuery in Figure 32.

While every well-formed ActiveXQBE graph can be translated into canonical Active XQuery, the reverse does not hold, since, in a way, ActiveXQBE captures a subset of Active XQuery as XQBE does for XQuery. Mainly, the limitations of ActiveXQBE, due to precise design choices toward visual intuitiveness, are the absence of RENAME events and the restriction to TPWJs in the specification of the WHEN condition, which are certainly less expressive than turing complete language as in Active XQuery. As for the action part, it roughly corresponds to the simplified version of XUpdate, as described in the section on updates.

ENHANCING USERS' EXPERIENCE

This section describes some advanced features that augment users experience with the XQBE system. In particular, these extensions allow one to face complex queries more comfortably, introducing schema navigation, by means of the guided composition facility, and pattern aggregation, by means of macro constructs.

Guided Composition

XQBE queries are expressed by means of predicates over XML documents. The user composes his or her query by inserting and connecting to other nodes, whose label is the element's tag name. So, of course, users should know the schema of their data in order to perform queries.

When a user is administering a collection of documents with many different schemas, or when schemas are huge and complex? In such cases, the XQBE system comes to help by means of a *guided composition* facility; this tool can load a DTD or XML schema (either from a local file or from a remote site), thus enabling the navigation through the document's structure.

Figure 33 shows the guided composition in action. One level at a time is expanded.

From the schema of our bibliographic document, the system knows that a **<bib>** element can contain **<book>**s, so a multiple selection node is shown (the grey, layered node in the first box). Clicking on this node adds a new **<book>** under the parent node. Another click on the newly inserted node removes it from the tree. The second box shows a single **<book>** under the **<bib>** element, expanded to show all its first-level con-

Figure 33. Guided composition in action

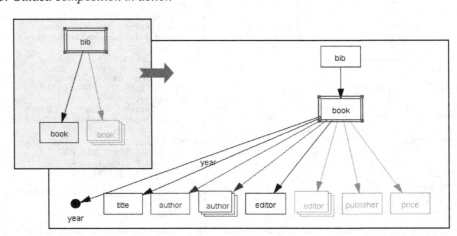

tents. In particular, note the year attribute on the left (conditions on its value can be specified after confirmation of the selection), and multiple nodes for **<author>** and **<editor>**. Other elements appear as simple grey rectangles, because of their **0..1** cardinality. Besides, **<author>**s selection is blocked (the nodes are red), because an editor is selected, and the document's schema contemplates these elements in mutual exclusion (to unblock the **<author>** node, unselect the **<editor>** by clicking on the black node).

The guided composition tool can also be loaded with schemas, which are inferred from the construct part of a view (see the section on "XQBE as a query language"); the tool will determine the necessary conditions to be met by the schema, such as cardinality constraints and the hierarchical structure of documents described by the tree.

Macros

The XQBE data model is straightforward: each rectangular (or trapezoidal) node is an XML ele-

ment, each filled circular node is an attribute, and each empty circular node is text. This approach is quite simple and well suited for simple queries or transformations, which involve few elements. In many situations, though, many nodes are needed even to perform conceptually simple queries, affecting negatively the graph readability. In every case where a common pattern can be found, the *macro* utility can be helpful. An XQBE macro is a special node (represented by a yellow curly rectangle), which is expanded into a set of base nodes before translation. Among the several possible scenarios, consider the query of RSS feeds coming from the Web or the composition of HTML pages from an XML document.

Figure 34 shows an HTML page with some text and a table reporting title and authors of books inside a table. The first box shows the transformation by means of macro nodes: an HTML header node is the root of the resulting document; a paragraph node contains some predefined text, entered inside a property field (see below), then a table is instantiated and a row is built for each book found

Figure 34. HTML formatting using macros

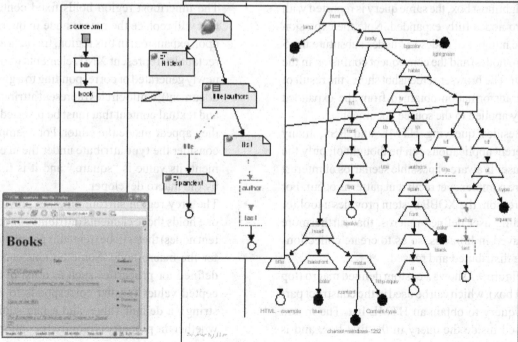

Figure 35. Custom macro

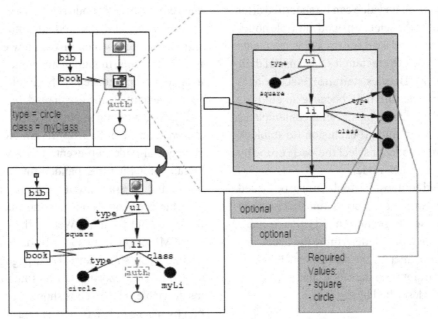

in the source document. The table is made of two columns: the book's title, formatted according to a paragraph node, and a list of authors (remember that dashed node in the construct part are XPath steps, which project sub-elements without tags). In the rightmost box, the same query is reported with macro nodes fully expanded. Note the explosion in the number of nodes (22 nodes substitute the 5 macro nodes) and the consequent confusion in the graph. The browser screenshot shows the result of the transformation obtained from the expanded query applied to the source document.

Besides querying HTML and RSS, many different applications can be thought of; only the end user is aware of possible scenarios of interest where complex, yet recurrent patterns occur. For this reason, the XQBE system provides a tool for building user defined macros, that furthermore be saved in libraries, so as to create collections to be distributed and reused.

Figure 9.3 shows a custom defined macro (top right box), which can be used in the construct part of a query to obtain an HTML list. The macro is used inside the query in the first box, and is expanded as in the bottom left box (the HTML header node was intentionally not expanded).

The macro editor is composed of three regions:

- The innermost region holds fixed content that will replace the macro node in queries upon expansion; in this region, trapezia and rectangles represent XML elements (either newly generated or corresponding to a given document), while circles represent attributes and textual content that must be inserted as they appear inside the editor. For example, consider the **type** attribute under the **ul** element: its value is "square," and it is fixed by the macro developer.

- The grey region surrounding the previous one holds those elements (attributes or content nodes) that will be treated as parameters for the macro node. Some options can be defined for properties such as a list of accepted values (no list corresponds to any string), a default value, and a flag stating whether the property is required or optional.

For example, the macro defined above will produce three properties (li/@type, li/@ class, li/@id--names can be personalized). Only the type property is required and a list of values is specified. Values specified for properties are used to label corresponding nodes upon macro expansion, as shown in Figure 9.3.

- The outermost region is a simple placeholder for stating the correspondence between arcs and binding edges reaching the macro node and their expanded version; for instance, each arc entering the macro node will be connected to the ul node, each node reached from the macro node will be connected to the li element, while each node reaching the macro by means of a binding edge will be connected to the li node. This binding causes the production of a <li> node for each node coming from the left, which in fact is renamed; thus, all <li> attributes and subelements will be a projection of the original element (so, in our example, each book is renamed as li, and is then projected to retain its /auth/text() children).

CONCLUSION

In this chapter, we presented a visual, general-purpose framework called XQBE for the design of semi-structured data and operations thereupon.

We have shown and exemplified the use of XQBE as a tool for expressing, in an intuitive way, queries to be executed by an XQuery engine. We then demonstrated the flexibility of the XQBE paradigm by applying its constructs to describe transformations from XML to possibly different target formats, namely HTML. Even more generally, XQBE has been shown to support the specification of document modifications in the form of update statements by adding a new area devoted to the identification of the update target position. To complete the scenario, we have brought forward

applications of XQBE to specify DTDs, help the user with macros and guided composition, and design active rules that capture the semantic requirements of an application domain.

Among the possible future directions of research, we are studying the creation of an XQBE-based tool to be integrated with ActiveXQBE for the automatic or semi-automatic generation of optimized versions of the visual triggers that respond to given events and integrity constraints. Such tool would be designed along the lines of optimisation frameworks for integrity constraints in deductive databases, but based on graph grammars to define rewrite rules for graphs. These techniques would prove useful in several contexts in which XML is already a *de facto* standard for data exchange, e.g., in the medical domain, not only because data integrity in this context is a strong requirement, but also because the presence of large quantities of data makes optimisation techniques indispensable.

Other possible directions of research include the extension to advanced tools for the interaction with XML data storage systems such as visual mining tasks and fuzzy queries.

We conclude our discussion by pointing out that XQBE represents a stimulating example for both academic and industrial research in the field of visual XML languages and interfaces, which we deem fundamental to the spreading of XML to a wider audience.

REFERENCES

Amer-Yahia, S., Cho, S., Lakshmanan, L. V., & Srivastava, D. (2001). Minimisation of tree pattern queries. In T. Sellis (Ed.), *Proceedings of the 2001 ACM SIGMOD International Conference on Management of Data* (pp. 497-508). SIGMOD '01. New York: ACM Press.

Atzeni, P., Mecca, G., & Merialdo, P. (1997). To weave the Web. *Proceedings of the 23rd International Conference on Very Large Databases (VLDB)* (pp. 206-215).

Bouganim, L., Chan-Sine-Ying, T., Dang-Ngoc, T. T., Darroux, J. L., Gardarin, G., & Sha, F. (1999). Miro Web: Integrating multiple data sources through semistructured data types. *Proceedings of the 25th International Conference on Very Large Data Bases (VLDB'99)* (pp. 750-753). Edinburgh, Scotland, UK.

Bonifati, A., Braga, D., Campi, A., & Ceri, S. (2002). Active XQuery. *Proceedings of ICDE 2002* (pp. 403-412). San Jose, CA, USA

Braga, D., Campi, A., & Ceri, S. (2005a). XQBE (XQuery By Example): A visual interface to the standard XML query language. *ACM Transactions on Database Systems, 30*(2), 398-443.

Braga, D., Campi, A., Ceri, S., & Raffio, A. (2005b). XQBE: A visual environment for learning XML query languages. *Proceedings of the 2005 ACM SIGMOD International Conference on Management of Data* (pp. 903-905). New York: ACM Press.

Carey, M., Haas, L., Maganty, V., & Williams, J. (1996). Pesto: An integrated query/browser for object databases. *Proceedings of the 22nd International Conference on Very Large Data Bases (VLDB'96)* (pp. 203-214). Mumbai, India.

Chawathe, S., Baby, T., & Yeo, J. (2001). VQBD: Exploring semistructured data (demonstration description). *Proceedings of the ACM SIGMOD* (p. 603).

Cohen, S., Kanza, Y., Kogan, Y. A., Nutt, W., Sagiv, Y., & Serebrenik, A. (1999). Equix easy querying in XML databases. *WebDB (Informal Proceedings)* (pp.43-48).

Comai, S., Damiani, E., & Fraternali, P. (2001). Computing graphical queries over XML data. *ACM TOIS 19*(4), 371-430.

Comai, S., Damiani, E., Posenato, R., & Tanca, L. (1998). A schema based approach to modeling and querying WWW data. *FQAS'98* (pp. 110-125).

Consens, M. P., & Mendelzon, A. O. (1990). The G+/GraphLog visual query system. *Proceedings of the 12th ACM SIGMOD* (p. 388). Atlantic City, NJ, USA.

Cruz, I. F., Mendelzon, A. O., & Wood, P. T. (1988). G+: Recursive queries without recursion. The *2nd International Conference on Expert Database Systems* (pp. 355–368).

Cruz, I. F., Mendelzon, A. O., & Wood, P. T. (1987). A graphical query language supporting recursion. *Proceedings of the 9th ACM SIGMOD Conference* (pp. 323-330). San Francisco, California, USA.

Fernandez, M., Siméon, J., Wadler, P., Cluet, S., Deutsch, A., Florescu, D., Levy, A., Maier, D., Mchugh, J., Robie, J., Suciu, D., & Widom, J. (1999). *XML query languages: Experiences and exemplars.* Retrieved April, 19, 2006 from http://www-db.research.bell-labs.com/user/simeon/xquery.html

Filha, I. M. R. E., Laender, A. H. F., & Da Silva, A. S. (2001). Querying semistructured data by example: The QSBYE interface. *Workshop on Information Integration on the Web* (pp. 156-163).

Ives, Z. G., & Lu, Y. (2000). XML query languages in practice: an evaluation. *Proceedings of WAIM'00* (pp. 29-40).

Jaeschke, G., & Schek, H. J. (1982). Remarks on the algebra on non first normal form relations. *Proceedings of 1st ACMSIGACT-SIGMOD Symposium on the Principles of Database Systems* (pp. 124-138).

Karam, M., Boulos, J., Ollaic, H., & Koteiche, Z. (2006). XQueryViz: A visual dataflow XQuery tool. *Advanced International Conference on Telecommunications and International Conference on Internet and Web Applications and Services (AICT-ICIW'06)* (p. 196).

Kepser, S. (2002). A proof of the Turing-completeness of XSLT and XQuery. *Technical report SFB*

441, Eberhard Karls Universitat Tubingen. May.

Lakshmanan, L. V. S., Ramesh, G.,Wang, H., & Zhao, Z. J. (2004). On testing satisfiability of tree pattern queries. *Proceedings of the 30th International Conference on Very Large Databases (VLDB)* (pp. 120-131).

Laux, A., & Martin, L. (2000). *XUpdate working draft.* Technical report. Retrieved October, 6, 2006 from *http://xmldb-org.sourceforge.net/xupdate/.*

Levy, A. Y., Rajaraman, A., & Ordille, J. J. (1996). Querying heterogeneous information sources using source descriptions. *Proceedings of the 22nd International Conference on Very Large Databases (VLDB)* (pp. 251-262).

Ludaescher, B., Papakonstantinou, Y., Velikhov, P., & Vianu, V. (1999). View definition and DTD inference for XML. *Proceedings of the Post-IDCT Workshop.*

Munroe, K., & Papakonstantinou, Y. (2000). BBQ: A visual interface for browsing and querying XML. *Proceedings of the 5th Working Conference on Visual Database Systems* (pp. 277-296).

Papakonstantinou, Y., Petropoulos, M., & Vassalos, V. (2002). QURSED: Querying and reporting semistructured data. *Proceedings of the ACM SIGMOD* (pp. 192-203).

Paredaens, J., Den Bussche, J. V., Andries, M., Gemis, M., Gyssens, M., Thyssens, I., Gucht, D. V., Sarathy, V., & Saxton, L. V. (1992). An overview of good. *SIGMOD Record 21*(1), 25-31.

Paredaens, J., Peelman, P., & Tanca, L. (1995). G-Log: A declarative graph-based language. *IEEE Trans. Knowl. Data Eng, 7*(3), 436-453

Petropoulos, M., Vassalos, V., & Papakonstantinou, Y. (2001). XML query forms (XQForms): Declarative specification of XML query interfaces. *Proceedings of the 10th WWW Conference.* (pp. 642-651)

Quin, Z., Yao, B. B., Liu, Y., & McCool, M. (2004). A graphical XQuery language using nested windows. *Lecture Notes in Computer Science, 3306* (pp. 681-687).

Vassalos, V., & Papakonstantinou, Y. (2000). Expressive capabilities description languages and query rewriting algorithms. *J. Logic Prog, 43*(1), 75-122.

W3C. (2006). *XQuery update facility.* Retrieved October 6, 2006 from http://www.w3.org/TR/2006/WD-xqupdate-20060127/

W3C. (2003a). *XML query use cases.* Retrieved October 6, 2006 from http://www.w3.org/TR/xmlquery-use-cases

W3C. (2003b). *XQuery: An XML query language.* Retrieved October 6, 2006 from http://www.w3.org/XML/Query

W3C. (2001). *Extensible stylesheet language (XSL).* Retrieved October 6, 2006 from http://www.w3c.org/TR/xsl/

Zloof, M. M. (1977). Query-by-example: A database language. *IBM System Journal, 16*(4), 324-343.

ENDNOTES

[1] Note that all XUpdate operations are to be wrapped into
```
<?xml version="1.0"?>
    <xupdate:modifications version="1.0"
            xmlns:xupdate="http://www.
xmldb.org/xupdate">
    ......

</xupdate:modifications>
```

[2] The "-before" and "-after" suffixes are to be interpreted with respect to the position of the pointed node.

[3] Note that the trigger would also be evaluated after the insertion, for instance, of an **emp** element, because a **salary** sub-element would be inserted too.

Section V
Visualization, Aesthetic Computing, and Usability

Chapter XVIII
GeoVisualization and GIS:
A Human Centered Approach

Vlasios Voudouris
Birkbeck University of London, UK

Stephanie Marsh
City University, London, UK

ABSTRACT

This chapter introduces the relationships among geovisualisation, human computer interaction (HCI), geographic information systems (GIS), and cartography as a means of supporting decision-making. It emphasizes the importance of the data modelling and the associated visualisations in terms of what we can do by way of analysis and the methods by which we can undertake the analysis. It also argues that concepts from usability evaluation methods (UEMs) and other HCI techniques offer a potentially more substantive approach to understanding the use of visualisations in collaborative decision-making. Furthermore, the authors hope that understanding the underlying assumptions and relations among geovisualisation, human computer interaction, geographic information systems, and cartography will inform researchers and decision makers of a better design for studying geovisualisation as enabling means of decision making.

INTRODUCTION

Geovisualization is regarded as a means of representing spatial information (where things are on the earth's surface) visually in a way that allows people to interact, explore, synthesize, refine, analyse, and communicate conclusions and ideas. It is, therefore, an interactive visual language that enables people to make sense of data archives and communicate this sense effectively. One characteristic of geovisualization is that it brings together knowledge and ideas from a variety of disciplines including but not limited to cartography, information visualization, visualization is scientific computing (ViSC), exploratory data analysis (EDA), geographic information science (GIS), and human computer interaction (HCI) (MacEachren & Kraak, 2001). HCI increasingly plays an important role as new variances of geo-ovialization such as collaborative geovisualization and geoanalytics, attack research attention.

In this chapter, we will briefly discuss how cartography, GIS, and HCI shape aspects of geovisualization that can support decision-making. We first discuss the interrelation of cartography and geovisualization and how this interrelation supports decision making by discussing the concepts such as choropleth, cartograms, spatial dimensionality, levels of measurement, graphic variables, and feature's continuity, and level of variation. Then we discuss the interrelation of GIS and geovisualization. This section presents three conceptual representation methods—the continuous-field, discrete-object, and object-field representations. It emphasizes the importance of the representations and the associated visualizations in terms of what we can do by way of analysis and the methods by which we can undertake the analysis. We then discuss the relationship between cartography and GIS. The aim of this section is to emphasize the importance of communicating the classification scheme and the number of classes (and any other individual and disciplinary axioms) used for the visualization of the data in order to support collaborative decision making. The final sections of this chapter introduce the relationship between HCI and geovisualization and outline future trends by acknowledging the needs to integrate data and knowledge and to combine visual or exploratory techniques with formal statistical modelling in terms of supporting collaborative decision-making. As the use of usability evaluation methods (UEMs) and other HCI techniques become more prevalent in geovisualization, these future trends can be realised.

CARTOGRAPHY AND GEOVISUALIZATION

Cartography has had a profound impact on digital map-based visual representations. It emphasizes the connection between map use and map users with symbolization. Therefore designing an appropriate and effective visual language is of critical importance when information is communicated using both spatial and aspatial visual metaphors. This importance is also emphasized when cartographic visualization is used to summarise complex spatial data. However, this technique can be subjective, as it is dependent not only on personal interpretations, but also on the cartographic techniques involved. This is especially true when minor variations in density are represented. Failing to visualize the distribution of features such as customers or stores results in a poor understanding of the phenomenon under question. The nature of the feature being visualized should drive the visualization techniques, often it is beneficial to provide the user with more than one representation of the same data, this could allow dynamic comparison. For example, Figure 1 uses a choropleth and cartogram to visualize the distribution of census data. In this case, the choropleth map may produce a more meaningful representation than the cartogram for the user. This is due to several reasons, including the fact that choropleth has been a dominant, though flawed, form of mapping in the last decade and because the lack of spatial location preservation in the cartogram, making it difficult to relate geographic areas. However, some users may prefer the cartograms as it provides an easier visual impact and more visualization space is used for larger volumes of data such as population totals per ward. In other words, the data drives the visualization and not the geography, which can be distorted. This can be important as people tend to estimate values better when sizes are compared rather than colour hues or values, as suggested by Cleveland and McGill (1984). We could also visualize census data using continuous surfaces rather that discrete choropleth or cartogram representations. MacEachren and DiBiase (1991) proposed a series of graphic models that exhibit a range of different types of spatial continuity

Figure 1. Visualization of census data using different cartographic techniques. Taken from Dykes (1995, 1998). Census Data Source: 1991 Census Area Statistics; 1991 Census, Output Area Boundaries. Crown copyright. Crown copyright material is reproduced with the permission of the Controller of HMSO.

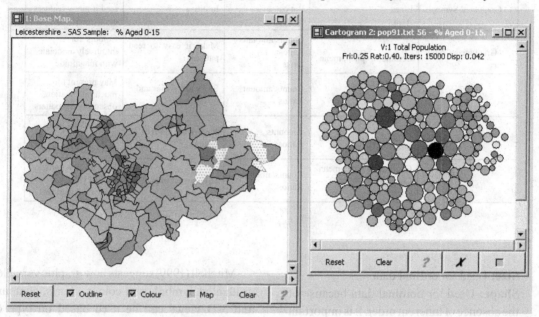

and statistical variation. These models can be used to visualize phenomena according to their continuity and levels of variation, which can help decision makers exploit the data representing a phenomenon better. In our view, the nature of the feature being visualized, the scale of analysis and the user should drive the visualization techniques. The latter is easily forgotten in practise.

DiBiase (1990) argues that visual thinking and communication of map use define a spectrum of design and symbolization goals. A problematic aspect of achieving the design and symbolization goals is the lack of general agreement on symbology. This means that different map users can interpret map symbols in different ways depending on a number of reasons such as lack of definitions, environmental context, level of knowledge about the phenomenon being visualised, as well as social and cultural backgrounds. This (multi-interpretation of symbols) is particularly important in collaborative decision-making as it may lead to semantic inaccuracies. In other words, developing cartographic language to sup-

port collaborative decision-making is not trivial and requires not just application of cartographic rules but also, thorough understanding of visual users and it will always involve personal creativity. MacEachren (1994) presents a typology for creating a cartographic language by elaborating ideas about spatial dimensionality, levels of measurement, and graphic variables.

Once we have determined the spatial dimensionality and the level of measurement of the data, an informed consideration of the available graphic variables is the next natural step. The aim here is how variations in graphic primitives are to be matched to the variations in the data that represent them. The aim of this step to show the data in a way that is useful to the decision maker. Bertin (1983) provides the first comprehensive attempt. MacEachren (1994) demonstrates how the graphics variables can be applied to dimensions of points (stores), lines (retail networks), and areas (London Boroughs) that represent the spatial dimension of the phenomenon.

391

Table 1. From Mitchell (1999)

		Which Features	Which Values	Advantages	Disadvantage
Graduated Symbols		Locations Lines Area	Counts/amounts Ratios ranks	Intuitive	May be difficult to read if many features on map
Graduated Colour		Area Continuous phenomena	Counts/amounts Ratios ranks	Make it easy to read patterns	Colours not intuitively associate with magnitude
Charts		Locations Area	Counts/amounts Ratios	Show categories and quantities	May present too much information, obscuring the patters
Contours		Continuous phenomena	Amounts Ratios	Easy to see rates of change	May make it hard to read patterns and individual features
3-D views		Continuous phenomena Locations Area	Counts/amounts Ratios	High visual impact	May make it hard to read values of individual features

- **Size:** Used for ordinal data.
- **Shape:** Used for nominal data because of the absence of inherent order. It is important to make shapes distinguishable by using additional graphic variables when numerous small shapes are used.
- **Colour Value:** Used for ordinal data because there is an inherent order.
- **Colour Hue:** Used for symbolising nominal data. Humans are less good at detecting hue applied to small symbols. This can be managed by stimulating human perception using colour value and colour hue simultaneously. The use of colour hue is unsuitable for ordinal data.
- **Colour Saturation:** Used with hue to apply ordering.
- **Texture:** Used to represent ordinal data but large symbols are required.
- **Arrangement:** Used to represent different categories with line symbols, but used less successfully for point and area symbols.
- **Orientation:** Used to represent nominal data and direction.
- **Focus:** Used to represent uncertainty in data (source: MacEachren, 1994).

Mitchell (1999) suggests how graphic variables graduated symbols and colour, charts, contours and 3-D views can be used based on type of feature and level of data measurement as show in Table 1.

It is therefore important to consider during the visualization process—spatial dimensionality, levels of measurement, graphic variables, and the appropriate graphic model. It is also important to focus on the need to direct attention to the purpose of the visual representation at the early stages. This is important because it determines the symbolization, degree of interactivity and graphic variables that can be used by decision makers. For example, if the purpose of a visual representation is to evaluate social policies over years, a discrete rather that continuous representation may be more appropriate as we tend to, rather arbitrarily, draw political boundaries, which partition space, as an expression of influence and power. In other words, a discrete visual language may provide us a more direct link between implementation and evaluation of social policies.

Cartographic visualization (as a variance of visual languages) has been extensively used by cartographers to convey/communicate a message to the public realm. Computing technologies has enabled us to extend the design and symbolization goals as there is a shift from *optimal visual representations* to *alternative visual representations*. This means that instead of allocating resources and time to identify the optimal visual language for visual users, computing technologies enable us to produce a number of visual representations, which can be selected by the users themselves. This is also consistent with the theory of choices, which is concerned with the theory of decision-making. Another advantage of the alternative visual representations is the use of a bottom-up design approach instead of a top-down. One of the enabling technologies that exploit the bottom-up approach is geographic information systems (GIS) which are a variance/specialization of information systems.

GIS AND GEOVISUALIZATION

One of the aims in GI science is to model spatial phenomena in a way that humans can understand and analyse. Representation is fundamental for one very good reason. How we represent things constrains not only what we can do by way of analysis but also the methods by which we undertake the analysis.

Over the past few decades, two main representations have been extensively used, namely continuous-field and discrete-object representations. Additionally, a new model, the object-field model, is being suggested by Voudouris, Wood, and Fisher (2005) elaborating that of Cova and Goodchild (2002). These three conceptual models attempt to represent the four dimensions (spatial, graphical, thematic, and temporal) of spatial phenomena in a way that enable us to conduct and share analysis (as already been mentioned dimensionality is one of the three main considerations in designing appropriate visual languages). Therefore, examining how these models store phenomena will enable us to investigate what

we can do with visual means operating on these models. And, in our view, this is a critical factor in our GIS's success or failure in terms of supporting spatial decision-making.

In the *discrete-object view*, the world is considered as a series of entities located in space. An object is a digital representation of these entities. Objects are classified into different object types such as point objects (stores), line objects (retail network), and area objects (London Boroughs). These objects are defined by their boundaries. In turn, we attach/associate one or more attributes with these objects to specify what is located at these places. These general classes are instantiated by specific objects and, we can attach behaviours to these objects. Any object can be represented by any number of object classes at different scales, which leads to a *multiple representation problem*. For example, we can represent a store as a point or area object. This constrains what we can do by way of analysis and also constrains the methods by which we undertake the analysis of stores. In short, the representation underlies almost all work with spatial data. However, there are a number of underlying assumptions here, such as the world is partitionable into discrete objects; for these discrete partitions, we can demarcate well-defined boundaries approximated with Euclidean geometry. The problematic aspects with the working assumptions are that many spatial phenomena do not have fixed boundaries and cannot be well approximated with Euclidean geometry. For example, how can we define the boundaries of town centres in a consistent way?

In terms of performing visual analysis, the ecological fallacy and modifiable area unit problem are also brought on board. For example in socioeconomic analysis, we aggregate data at the area level such as output areas—the smallest spatial unit for which the latest 2001 census data is available in Britain, while we discard variations within the areas and then we make inferences about points such as households, based on this aggregated data. In other words, we aggregate data at the object level while we discard variations within the object and then we apply this aggregated data to individuals living within the object. Suppose that Figure 2 represents economic activity in London. This object view implies that in many London boroughs the economic activity is uniform. It also states that changes in economic activities occur only between the boundaries of the London boroughs. Furthermore, these two maps represent the same data but communicate different results. For example, southwest boroughs are assigned to different economic classes represented by different colour value. This is because a different classification schemes have been used for the production of the maps. The different classification of the boroughs emphasizes the importance of uncertainty introduced through classification in decision-making. Most contemporary GIS enable us to visualize data using a number of different classification schemes. It is therefore important to understand how and why we use a particular classification scheme within a GIS during the visualization process. Otherwise, objects-based data can be misinterpreted leading to inappropriate conclusions and actions.

A complementary but not overlapping approach is the *continuous-field* representation. In the continuous-field view, the world is made up of properties varying continuously across space. The key factors of the field view are spatial continuity and self-definition. As the key characteristics of the field view is spatial continuity and self-definition we are not forced to identify objects and their boundaries. In other words, the field is a collection of a certain kind of measurements (such as consumer's spending behaviour) that are used to define a value everywhere in the field and it is the values themselves that define that field. In terms of visual analysis, the field view is particularly good in defining trends and patterns rather than the exact location of the phenomenon being investigated. One problematic aspect is that the local underling geography is not always represented appropriately. For example, objects within the field are not identified without extract processing. And because of that the analytical advantages offer by the object view is lost or are programmatically difficult and inefficient to achieve. Figure 3 uses continuous density representations of crime incidences and crime incidences relative to population risk. Langford and Unwin (1994) have shown that continuous surface representations of population have advantages in the visualization and analysis of population distributions. Wood, Fisher, Dykes, Unwin, and Stynes (1999) explored this idea further using concepts and techniques developed for the analysis of terrain surfaces and a relief metaphor.

Figure 2. Visualizing economic activity using object view with different classification schemes (Source: Borders-Crown copyright)

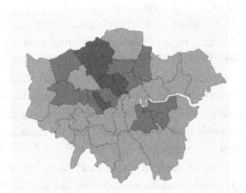
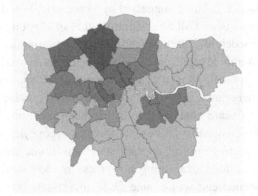

Figure 3. Kernel density representations of crime incidences and crime incidences relative to population risk (source: Levine, 2004)

**Single kernel density of crime incidences
(assualt & batter, Cologna 1999/2000)**

**Dual kernel density of crime incidences
relative to population at rish**

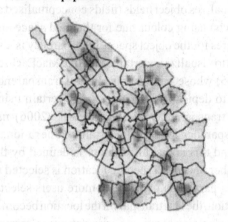

The *object-field* representation is considered to combine of both the discrete-object and continuous-field representations. The object-field model attempts to integrate the field and the object view in a single, combined, and integrated data model. This is achieved by mapping locations in a field to objects. Aggregating field locations forms the objects. A workable formalization of this model has been suggested by Voudouris et al. (2005). This model uses a single elementary spatial unit (hereafter object element) to exploit the benefits of continuous-field and discrete-object views. The object elements are associated with a field value and a variable number of object references. Semantic and uncertainty information is also associated with these object elements. The semantic dimension is used to communicate users' understanding about the phenomenon being represented. The uncertainty dimension is used to record internally variable levels of uncertainty associated with the underlying location in fields. In other words, the object-field model uses two spaces. One space is used to represent observational data and the other derived knowledge. We

believe that the integration of derived knowledge and data is a key research challenge in facilitating intelligence decision making. The derived knowledge is stored as uncertainty and semantic objects attached to object elements and objects (collection of object elements) and are treated as part of the 3D matrix of metadata proposed by Voudouris, Fisher, and Wood (2006). The object elements are grouped together explicitly to form objects that represent conceptualizations of the underlying local geography. In terms of visual analysis the advantages of the object-field model is that qualitative and quantitative information is stored together in one integrated data model. This means that with appropriate visual methods and tools users can explore, analyse, criticise, and share not only observational data but also derived knowledge. The potential disadvantage of this model is information overload. Both observational data and derived knowledge need to be interactively explored. Therefore, a combination of user-centred selection mechanisms and automatic algorithms is required. Voudouris et al. (2006) have suggested the sketching approach as an interactive human-centred visual mechanism, which emphasises the importance of human-computer interaction (HCI) in determining appropriate interaction mechanisms for visual decision-making. Figure 4 visualizes object fields (fields conceptualised as objects) using colour hue for the field space and squares for the object space. Transparency is also used to visualize uncertainty. Unlike MacEachren (2005) whose initial application of transparency was to depict areas that are fairly certain using less transparency, Voudouris et al. (2006) use transparency to depict uncertainty. The rationale behind this is that uncertainty is defined by the number of times a specific location is selected as being part of an object. The more users select a location, the less transparent the location becomes as the location acquires a crisp definition because of the number of people who conceptualize it as being part of the object. The uncertainty can be specified both at the object element level, along with the associated semantics, and at the object level. This enables the visualization of combined uncertainties.

Having discussed the three conceptual data representations and the associated visualization and analysis limitations, it is needless to say, that application mandates and priorities influence the selection of the data and graphic models, which, as has been already said, determines the enabling visual languages. In other words, how we represent things constrains what we can do by way of analysis and also constrains the methods by which we undertake the analysis. A careful consideration of the representation method can facilitate spatial decision-making.

The next section of this chapter discusses how classifications can be appropriately selected and how to make the classes easier to read within a GIS using cartographic principles. This discussion is based on Mitchell (1999).

CARTOGRAPHY AND GIS

The visual representation is largely determined by the classification scheme as how we define class ranges will determine which features fall into each class as much discussed in cartographic literature, often in association with choropleth mapping. By changing the classes, we can create very different representation (see Figure 2) and introduce uncertainty.

Figure 4. Object-field visualisation and visualisation of uncertainty using rough demarcation and transparency (source: Voudouris et al., 2006)

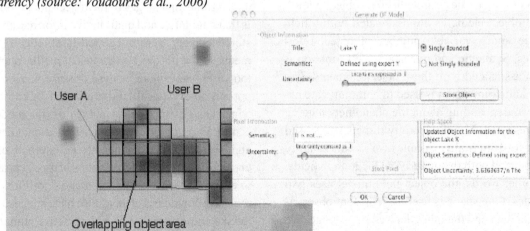

We can create classes manually or use a standard classification schemes such as natural breaks, quantiles, equal intervals, or standard deviation, which are available in current GI systems. We usually create classes manually when specific criteria or organization's standards are required or when we want to compare features using specific meaningful values. This is achieved by specifying the number and bounds of the class and the associated symbol. If, for example, we want to identify highly deprived areas, we could map areas with at least 25 percent of residents living below the poverty level. Or the classes might be based on standards in a particular discipline or industry. In collaborative decision making, it is increasingly important to communicate the individual standards or disciplinary axioms.

We tend use a standard classification scheme when we look for patterns in the data. By specifying the classification scheme and the number of classes and the GIS calculates the upper and lower limit for each class. The selection of classification scheme and the number of classes should be based on how the data values are distributed. Thus, it is important to visualize the data values using standard statistical means such as histograms.

For the selection of an appropriate *classification scheme,* it is essential to compare the various methods:

- *Natural breaks* is a classification scheme, which is based on natural groupings of data values. This is achieved by determining the high and low values for each class using a mathematical procedure to test different class breaks. The GIS picks the class breaks that maximize similar values and differences between classes. It is effective for unevenly distributed data. However, since the class ranges are specific to the individual dataset, comparing maps is problematic.
- *Quantile* is a classification scheme, which has an equal number of features in it. The GIS orders the features and sums the number of features. Next it divides the total with the number of classes we have specified (it is, therefore, important to make a sensible the number of classes as we shall see) to have a suitable number of features in each class. The first features in the order are assigned to the lowest class until that class is filled and the algorithm moves on. Quantiles are often used to map evenly distributed data, to compare areas that are roughly similar size and to emphasise the relative position of a feature among other features. However, features with similar values may end up in different classes and areas that vary greatly in size, skewing the patterns on the map.
- *Equal internals* is a classification scheme, which has an equal range of values. The GIS subtracts the lowest and the highest values in the dataset. It then divides this range with the specified number of classes. It then adds that number to the lowest value to form the first class. Then the algorithm moves on. It is effective to present information to nontechnical audiences because it is easier to interpret and to map continuous data. However, if the data is not evenly distributed there may be many features in some classes and no features in others.
- *Standard deviation* is a classification scheme, which is defined by its distance from the mean value of all features. The GIS calculates the mean and the standard deviation and then creates the class breaks above and below the mean based on the number of standard deviations we specify. This can be used for identifying which features are above or below an average value, and displaying data that has a normal distribution. However, the actual values of the features are not presented and outliers may skew the final result. (Mitchell, 1999)

Generally speaking, to decide which scheme to use, first plot the data in a bar chart using a statistical or GIS program that supports conventional statistical representations. If your data has many similar values and there are gaps between groups of values, it is appropriate to use natural breaks. If your data is evenly distributed and you want to emphasise differences between features use equal intervals or standard deviation. If your data is evenly distributed but you want to emphasise relative difference between features, use the quantile classification scheme. Again, in collaborative decision-making, it is increasingly important to communicate the rationale of the classification scheme as it provides the basis of our analysis.

Once we have made an informed decision on the appropriate classification scheme, the appropriate number of classes needs to be specified. Most map readers, including decision makers, can distinguish seven (minus/plus two) classes. Fewer than three classes do not show variations between features. If the map is for exploration (an early data analysis stage), a large number of classes can be used to reveal subtleties in the patterns.

However, the GIS may produce a classification scheme that hinders the purpose of the visual language by making it difficult to read. We can manage this by adjusting the classification scheme. For example, if we want to show the relative differences between visual features, we simulate actual ranked values by changing the numeric values to labels such as "high," "medium," and "low." Or we may want to round the low and high bounds for each class to make the legend easier. We may also need to adjust the bounds of the class to show the actual range. However, these adjustments should not change the patterns represented by the original visual representation.

We would like to point out that the guidelines outlined in these and the previous sections are general guidelines. These guidelines can be challenged. Nevertheless, it is important to remember them when we design visual languages for interactive decision making, especially when these languages use a spatial metaphor. Another important consideration is the types of interaction used to support the visual languages such as visualization. It is, therefore, important to discuss how HCI influences visualization and how we can evaluate this influence.

HCI AND GEOVISUALIZATION

The concept within HCI of interaction styles refers to ways in which the user can communicate with the computer system (Soegaard, 2004). In HCI there are five main interaction styles (Jakobsson, 2003):

- Command entry.
- Menus and navigation.
- Form-fills and spreadsheets.
- Natural language dialogue.
- Direct manipulation.

Most important to geovisualization are menus and navigation and direct manipulation. Direct manipulation is particularly relevant; direct and interactive manipulation of data may give users the experience of being in direct contact with the data (Ware, 2000), thus understanding it better. Brushing, dynamic querying, and multiples are principal methods. Dynamic querying (Williamson & Shneiderman, 1992) is a technique that allows users to perform SQL queries on the fly using graphic/visual devices such as scrollbars and slider bars. North and Schneiderman (1998) highlighted that multiple coordinated visualizations enable the rapid exploration of complex information and improve user performance, multiples representations of the same subset of data, brushing allows one (or several) data items to be highlighted in these multiple representations. An example of this can be seen in Figure 5:

pixelEx provides an interactive graphical interface for image analysis and the classification of multispectral data. True and false colour composites can be produced and investigated

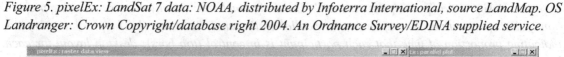

Figure 5. pixelEx: LandSat 7 data: NOAA, distributed by Infoterra International, source LandMap. OS Landranger: Crown Copyright/database right 2004. An Ordnance Survey/EDINA supplied service.

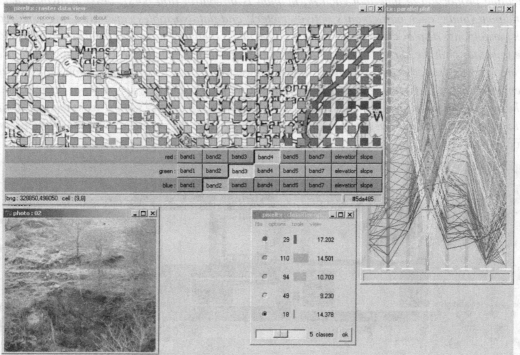

through dynamically linked spatial and statistical views of the data. The integration of spatial and statistical views is important in decision-making as the use can interact with quick overviews of the data and explore more precise and detailed statistical descriptions. Imagery (in pixelEx) can be classified using supervised and unsupervised per-pixel methods. Pixels can be selected in the software and associated locations loaded into GPS receivers to aid navigation in the field. Tracks recorded in the field by GPS receivers can be subsequently displayed on the interactive image and the routes taken compared with the environment experienced in the field to facilitate "ground truthing"—an important activity in the learning process (Gardiner & Unwin, 1986). This comparison is enhanced by functionality that al-

lows digital photographs collected in the field to be georeferenced using GPS waypoints (Marsh & Dykes, 2005). Such interactive software is used to reduce cognitive load when large amounts of complex structured data are being analysed (Marsh, Dykes, & Attilakou, 2006).

HCI can play an important role in defining appropriate visual languages/interaction styles. In a collaborative environment, for example, there is a clear need to define the appropriate flow of information among participants. In particular, for synchronous communication, the mode of interaction needs to be specified including sequential—one participant at a time—simultaneous—many participants at the same time—a mixed participation—one controls the object of discussion and the other can communicate (some-

Figure 6. Design for a "participant watcher": The design includes: activity meters indicating proportion of time spent with each component of the collaborative analysis system (left bars); activity meters indicating proportion of time that each participant is in control (top bars); desktop layout for each participant (under each participant's activity meter); and data variables currently being explored in each participant's display components (colour coded under their desktop displays). The snapshot shown here indicates both the current status of group work (e.g., User B is in control of the joint display and her map view is the active one; user b is exploring fewer variable in their parallel coordinate plot than other users) as well as some temporal characteristics of the session (e.g., User B has been in control of the joint display for the most time while User C has been in control for the least amount of time; the scatterplot has been the active view for less time than either the parallel coordinate plot). (Source: MacEachren, 2005)

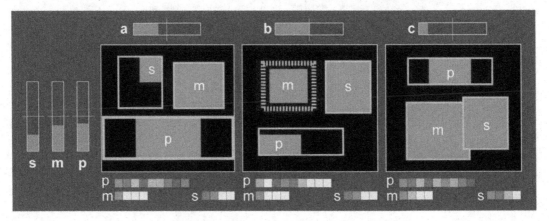

how). Furthermore, technology can offer new ways of collaboration rather than just simulating those that are face-to-face. For example, in face-to-face collaboration, one person talks and the other people are waiting for cues to take the control of the collaboration. Technology can extend this turn-talking approach by allowing, for example, multi-text based communication chat rooms. However, these new ways of collaboration have the disadvantage of increasing ways for the communication break down phenomenon, thus new recover mechanisms are required. Furthermore, as dynamic visual representations enable users to pose "what if" questions, users feel that they have a real "voice" in the data exploration and knowledge construction process. Thus the development of a framework for understanding both human-machine-human and human-machine interaction is essential for the implementation of interactive visual languages enabling advanced spatial analysis.

Designing collaborative environments is a complex process and we need to look to HCI for interaction styles that give the user both tools of exploration/visualization and presentation, in other words visual thinking and visual communication (as seen next and considered by MacEachren, 1994). It is not only interaction styles that need to be considered but the maps/graphics used within the interface or are used as the interface. *Maps suitable for visualization* should not communicate a single message…they should prompt insight, reveal patterns in data, and highlight anomalies (MacEachren, 1994). *Maps for communication* should have a clear message to communicate particular knowledge effectively (MacEachren, 1994). Thus, HCI cannot provide all the answers to a well-designed collaborative geovisualization application.

However, we suggest that HCI can give us the methods and tools to capture personal unquantifiable experience. This is important as it provides a context within which analysis can be shared, understood, and interpreted. For example, MacEachren's "participant watcher" (see Figure 6) can be regarded as a mechanism that can be used to capture unquantifiable experience using abstract symbols. These abstract symbols, for example, can answer questions such as "what kind of tools and variables user B uses to suggest solution X?" User B may use a specific subset of variables and visual tools (and the interaction between the tools) to address a problem based on his or her past experience. In other words, he or she uses a cognitive solution template (comprised by variables and associated visual tools) to address a problem. The communication of this unquantifiable experience is important in collaborative decision-making as it provides the context of the analysis.

User experience of interactive visual languages can also be captured and analysed through usability evaluation. HCI provides guidelines of how to develop tools appropriately but this does not guarantee successful and useful tools, thus, usability testing is required. This has become increasingly important in geovisualization over the last few years as hardware/software associated with novel methods are often expensive, thus, developers need to know before investing if these new methods are likely to provide advantage over old methods. Novel geovisualization methods will also require fundamentally different design approaches than existing methods. Knowledge discovery through geovisualization methods requires a high degree interactivity not characteristic of traditional software for spatial data processing; thus there is a need to define appropriate methods for handling this interactivity and how best to integrate them in a user interface. Usability offers a user-centred viewpoint through interaction design and user-centred design that counters the software engineering perspective, which can be described generally as a system-centred perspective (Preece, Rogers, & Sharp, 2002). Users may

find new methods of geovisualization difficult to apply, derive full benefit from, or not utilize them effectively, if cognitive and usability issues aren't considered (Slocum et al., 2001).

There are many contentions between HCI and geovisualzation practice, which pose many challenges for how to proceed with usability evaluation in geovisualization. Gabbard, Hix, and Swan (1999) suggested that usability engineering and user-centred design practice in virtual environments (and geovisualization) practice still lags behind what is needed and this is still true today. Established paradigms for conducting cognitive and usability research do not map well to highly interactive visual environments, particularly when these environments are designed to support ill-structured tasks such as knowledge construction or decision-making (MacEachren & Kraak, 2001). For example, usability testing often involves the quantification and measurement of the performance of typical users in completing typical and specific tasks (Preece et al., 2002). Such an approach has limited scope when applied to geovisualization, especially when considering the discovery of unknowns (during the knowledge construction or decision-making) where task and user goals are ill-defined.

Other contentions include the binary distinction between experts and users often employed in HCI evaluation paradigms. Studies reporting comparison between domain experts and users implies two distinct categories, but knowledge differences are more correctly considered as a continuum (McGuinness, 1994). The distinction between experts and users is also limiting when considering constructing a framework for usability evaluation of a system developed for (domain) expert users. An example of such a system would be that created by Koua and Kraak (2005). Through the analysis of two focus-group discussions, one between experts and one between novices, Harrower, MacEachren, and Griffin (2000) discovered that the ability to identify usability problems within their software (EarthSystemsVisualiser, ESV) was of a similar level, though experts had the ability to cite literature and case studies to back up their opinions. This is regarded as being due to the familiarity of the "Nintendo generation" with interactive graphics. In generic software domains there are seen to be two distinct domains that make up interactive system development—behavioural and constructional (Gabbard et al., 1999). The behavioural domain represents the user's view of and interaction with the application. The constructional domain represents the software developer and overall system. However, in many fields, the distinction between the constructional and behavioural again is not necessarily a binary one, and this is particularly true in geovisualization. For example, a scientist may be developing and using a range of tools and techniques for use in knowledge discovery by a variety of users including themselves and colleagues from different disciplines (with a range of skills, specialisms, and preferences), possibly in a collaborative environment. This adds further complexities to the ways in which users, interactive visual languages, and data come together to advance our knowledge.

There are many concerns relating to the user population used as subjects in usability evaluations. In traditional evaluations, subjects are gathered from the target user population of an application or from a similar representative group of people (Bowman, Gabbard, & Hix, 2002). The nature of geovisualization evaluation, however, does not always allow for such straightforward selection of users. It may be difficult to generalize performance results. Because these tools will be novel to many potential subjects, the results of an evaluation may exhibit high variability and differences among individuals (Bowman et al., 2002). The issue of generalizability is an important one.

Many usability tests use the technique of completing one task and then moving on to another. This is not necessarily representative of "free exploration" (usually conducted in the initial pe-

riod of using new data). A user may not even fully complete a (perhaps semi-defined) task before moving on to the next, if they suddenly have an idea that they want to follow, they are not necessarily doing anything wrong, they just want to do something different. Edwards (1987) supports this notion and describes this as insight; an exploratory stage involving searching out productive questions from intuitive leaps of awareness based on wide knowledge of a subject. It can relate to existing problems or involve problem solving.

Usability in the context of field and object representations is very limited. The object-field interface comparative and usability studies are non-existent. Davies and Medyckyj-Scott (1994) conducted a study of actual GIS users, some of their findings showed that Raster (a realization of the field representation) based GIS was significantly more likely to be used for complex analysis and modelling tasks. There was also a clear tendency for the use of more complex modular vector (a realization of the object representation) based systems for only relatively simple mapping and inventory storage. The longevity of Davies and Medyckyi-Scott's findings are questionable considering the rapid and immense changes GIS / geovisualization applications have been thorough in the last decade. However, the authors have found no other studies relating to this subject. How are users using their data? What data are they using? And how usable is this data? Which representation enhances users understanding?

Usability in collaborative geovisualization is also very limited, examples include Fuhrmann, MacEachren, Dou, Wang, and Cox (2005) who evaluated the DAVE_G prototype; a multimodal, dialog-assisted visual environment for geoinformation that will support a set of real-world scenarios that focus on collaborative domain-specific tasks of emergency management specialists (but novice GIS users) in response situations crisis management. With collaborative tools, usability becomes increasingly important, with the need to support a variety of users and the question of how to appropriately evaluate these tools becomes increasing complex.

FUTURE TRENDS

We discussed how cartography, GIS, and HCI shape aspects of geovisualization that can support decision-making. One of the future trends for geovisualization as an enabling means of decision-making is the integration of data and knowledge. This will open new ways of analysis and drive the development of new methods by which we can undertake the analysis. The object-field representation provides a potentially useful and usable approach in collaborative modelling and decision-making as it recognises the importance of storing and communicating individual preferences, concepts, interpretations, and knowledge. Another related future trend is the need for the development of new interaction styles such as sketching proposed by Voudouris et al. (2006) in exploring and interfacing with knowledge and data. This is becoming increasingly important as multimedia recording of knowledge is researched. It is also important to incorporate fundamentals principles of decision making from theories such as behaviour theory, theory of choices, learning theories and the theory of games with visual or exploratory techniques. For example, principles from the theory of statistical decision-making can be integrated with a mixture of informal, visual, or exploratory techniques to support collaborative decision making.

As the use of usability evaluation methods (UEMs) and other HCI techniques become more prevalent in geovisualization and GIScience in general, more consideration is being taken over the appropriate methods to be used. In time, usability research within geovisualization will move away from small-scale case-by-case reporting of usability evaluations to more generic studies of usability. Investigating how certain techniques affect outcomes in particular research situations.

To work towards a matrix of techniques that can be utilised in appropriate circumstances. For example, Marsh et al. (2006) reports not only the results of two evaluations of a geovisualization prototype, focusing on usability, interaction and ideation but also gives recommendations of appropriate data collection techniques to be utilised for exploratory geovisualization. Another trend that is slowly coming to light is the more extensive use of longitudinal studies, such as indepth ethnographic studies of small groups of experts with real research problems using geovisualization for the purposes of evaluation, as described in Robinson et al. 2005. Thus, not only relying on the traditional user testing with large numbers of novices (in academia generally students) for statistically significant results. But also, collecting comprehensive qualitative evidence of tool usability, how the tool is used to accomplish task and whether the tools support hypothesis generation and knowledge construction. Due to the expensive nature of such longitudinal studies, these are unlikely to become as commonplace as traditional user testing in geovisualization. As more knowledge is gained in using UEMs in geovisualization, techniques can be better tailored to suit the specific needs of geovisualization interfaces.

CONCLUSION

This chapter presented how cartography, GI science, and HCI influence the definition of geovisualization and, to some extent, collaborative geovisualization, which is regarded as a visual language that can support spatial decision-making. The concepts and ideas inherent to each of these disciplines are not always compatible. It is, therefore, important to explicitly identify how these components interact and what these interactions mean for the definition of geovisualization in terms of supporting data analysis and sharing. Fisher (1998) has already advocated the need for abounding the GIS from cartography to support new methods of analysis and visualization. These incompatibilities and the novelty of techniques being applied to new geovisualization applications can create hindrances to the users' progression in the visualization process. This discussion has shown that HCI, usability evaluation, and user-centred design have become increasingly prevalent in geovisualization because of these hindrances. However, HCI practice in such fields as geovisualization with its fast-paced development requires further research for effective and efficient evaluation and design. Evaluation is particularly needed in the niche area of object-field interfaces.

ACKNOWLEDGMENT

Thanks to Jason Dykes for permission to use screenshots from cdv and pixelEx.

REFERENCES

Bertin, J. (1983). *Semiology of graphics: Diagrams, networks, maps.* Madison, WI: University of Wisconsin Press.

Bowman, D., Gabbard, J. L., & Hix, D. (2002). A survey of usability evaluation in virtual environments: Classification and comparison of methods. *Presence: Teleperators and Virtual Environments, 11*(4), 404-424.

Cleveland, W. S., & McGill, R. (1984). Graphical perception: Theory, experimentation, and application of the development of graphical methods. *Journal of American Statistical Association, 79*(387), 531-554.

Cova, T. J., & Goodchild, M. F. (2002) Extending geographical representation to include fields of spatial objects.

Davies, C., & Medyckyj-Scott, D. (1994). GIS usability: Recommendations based on the user's view. *International Journal of Geographic Information Systems, 8*(2), 175-189.

DiBiase, D. (1990), Visualization in the Earth Sciences. Earth and Mineral Sciences, Bulletin of the College of Earth and Mineral Sciences, PSU 59(2). 13-18.

Dykes, J. A. (1998). Cartographic visualization: Exploratory spatial data analysis with local indicators of spatial association using Tcl/Tk and cdv. *The Statistician, 47*(3), 485-497.

Dykes, J. A. (1995). Cartographic visualization for spatial analysis. *Proceedings International Cartographic Conference* (pp. 1365-1370), ICA Barcelona.

Edwards, B. (1987) Drawing on the artist within: A guide to innovation, invention, imagination and creativity. Collins, London.

Fisher, P. F. (1998). Is GIS hidebound by the legacy of cartography? *Cartographic Journal, 35*(1), 5-9.

Fuhrmann, S., MacEachren, A. M., Dou, J., Wang, K., & Cox, A. (2005). Gesture and speech-based maps to support use of GIS for crisis management. In *AutoCarto* Las Vegas, NA.

Gabbard, J. L., Hix, D., & Swan, J. E. (1999). User-centred design and evaluation of virtual environments. *IEEE Computer Graphics and Applications, 19*(6), 51-59.

Gardiner, V., & Unwin, D. J. (1986). Computers and the field class. *Journal of Geography in Higher Education, 17*21-32.

Harrower, M., MacEachren, A., & Griffin, A. L. (2000). Developing a geographic visualization tool to support earth science learning. *Cartography and Geographic Information Science, 27*(4), 279-293. Retrieved April 21, 2006, from http://www.interaction-design.org/encyclopedia/interaction_styles.html

Jakobsson, M. (2003). *Interaction styles.* Retrieved April 21, 2006 from http://lipas.uwasa.fi/~mj

Koua, E. L., & Kraak, M. J. (2005). Evaluating self-organizing maps for geovisualization. In J. Dykes, A. M. MacEachren, & M. J. Kraak (Eds.), *Exploring geovisualization.* (Eds,) pp. 627-634). Oxford: Elsevier.

Langford, M., & Unwin, D. J. (1994). Generating and mapping population density surfaces within a geographical information system. *Cartographic Journal, 31*(1), 21-6.

MacEachren, A. (2005). Moving geovisualization toward support for group work. In J. Dykes, A. MacEachren, & M. J. Kraak (Eds), *Exploring geovisualization* (pp. 710). Amsterdam: Elsevier.

MacEachren, A. M., & Kraak, M. J. (2001). Research challenges in geovisualization. *Cartography and Geographic Information Science, 28*(1), 1-11.

MacEachren, A. M. (1994). *Some truth with maps: A primer on symbolization & design.*

MacEachren, A. M., & DiBiase, D. W (1991). Animated maps of aggregate data: Conceptual and practical problems. *Cartography and Geographic Information Systems, 18*(4), 221-29.

Marsh, S. L., & Dykes, J. A. (2005). Using usability techniques to evaluate geovisualization in learning and teaching In L. Zentai, J. J. R. Nunez, & D. Fraser (Eds.), *Joint ICA commissions seminar "Internet-based cartographic teaching and learning: Atlases, map use, and visual analytics."* (pp. 29-34). ICA, Madrid.

Marsh, S. L., Dykes, J. A., & Attilakou, F. (2006). Evaluating a geovisualization prototype with two approaches: Remote instructional vs. face-to-face exploratory. *The 10th International Conference on Information Visualization.* IEEE Computer Society, London.

McGuinness, C. (1994). Expert/novice use of visualization tools. In A. M. MacEachren, & D. R. F. Taylor (Eds.), *Visualization in modern cartography* (pp. 185-199). Pergamon.

Mitchell, A. (1999). *The ESRI guide to GIS analysis.* New York: Environmental Systems Research Institute.

North, C., & Shneiderman, B. (2000). Snap-together visualization: Can users construct and operate coordinated visualizations? *International Journal of Human-Computer Studies, 53,* 715-39.

Original Data Depositor. (1991). *Census: Digitised Boundary Data (England and Wales)* [computer file]. ESRC/JISC Census Programme, Census Geography Data Unit (UKBORDERS), EDINA (University of Edinburgh).

Original Data Depositor, *1991 Census : Small Area Statistics (England and Wales)* [computer file]. ESRC/JISC Census Programme, Census Dissemination Unit, MIMAS (University of Manchester).

Preece, J., Rogers, Y., & Sharp, H. (2002). *Interaction design: Beyond human-computer interaction.* New York: Wiley.

Robinson, A. C., Chen, J., Lengerich, E. J., Meyer, H. G., & MacEachren, A. M. (2005). Combining usability techniques to design geovisualization tools for epidemiology. *Cartography and Geographic Information Science, 32*(4), 243-255.

Shneiderman, B. (1998). *Designing the user interface: Strategies for effective human computer interaction.* Reading, MA: Addison-Wesley.

Slocum, T. A., Blok, C., Jiang, B., Koussoulakou, A., Montello, D. R., Fuhrmann, S., & Hedley, N. R. (2001). Cognitive and Usability Issues in Geovisualization. *Cartography and Geographic Information Science, 28*(1), 61-75.

Soegaard, M. (2004). Interaction Styles.

Voudouris, V., Fisher, P. F., & Wood, J., (2006). Capturing conceptualization uncertainty interactively using object-fields. In W. Kainz, A. Reid, & G. Elmes (Eds), The *12ᵗʰ International Symposium on Spatial Data Handling*. Springer-Verlag.

Voudouris, V., Wood, J., & Fisher, P. F. (2005). Collaborative geovisualization: Object-field representations with semantic and uncertainty information. In R. Meersman, Z. Tari, & P. Herrero et al. (Eds), *OTM Workshops 2005*, Vol. 3762 of Lecture Notes in Computer Science (LNCS), Springer, Berlin

Ware, C. (2000) *Information visualization: Perception for design*. Morgan Kaufmann.

Williamson, C., & Shneiderman, B. (1992). The dynamic homefinder: Evaluating dynamic queries in a real estate information exploration system. *SIGIR'92* (pp. 339-46). Copenhagen.

Wood, J. D., Fisher, P. F., Dykes, J. A., Unwin, D. J., & Stynes, K. (1999). The use of the landscape metaphor in understanding population data. *Environment and Planning B: Planning and Design, 26*, pp. 281-295.

Chapter IXX
A New Constraint-Based Compound Graph Layout Algorithm for Drawing Biochemical Networks

Sabri Skhiri dit Gabouje
Alcatel Bell, Belgium

Esteban Zimányi
Université Libre de Bruxelles, Belgium

ABSTRACT

Due to the huge amount of information available in biochemical databases, biologists need sophisticated tools to accurately extract the information from such databases and to interpret it correctly. Those tools must be able to dynamically generate any kind of biochemical subgraph (i.e., metabolic pathways, genetic regulation, signal transduction, etc.) in a single graph. The visualization tools must be able to cope with such graphs and to take into account the particular semantics of all kinds of biochemical subgraphs. Therefore, such tools need generic graph layout algorithms that adapt their behavior to the data semantics. In this chapter, we present the constrained compound graph layout (C^2GL) algorithm designed for the generic representation of biochemical graphs and in which users can represent knowledge about how to draw graphs in accordance with the biochemical semantics. We show how we implemented the C^2GL algorithm in the visual BioMaze framework, the visualization tool of the BioMaze project.[1]

INTRODUCTION

The advent of a new generation of biochemical databases (e.g., aMAZE) (Lemer, 2004), asks for more efficient and flexible visualization tools. Biochemical databases typically contain information about biochemical entities such as compounds, genes, and polypeptides, as well as the interactions between them. There are two categories of interactions: (1) *transformations*, such as reactions (between compounds), expressions (of a gene that lead to synthesis of polypeptides), assembly-disassembly (between biochemical entities) and (2) *control*, like catalysis (a polypeptide catalyzes or inhibits one or more biochemical reactions), or activation-deactivation (turning on or off the biochemical function of a polypeptide). The term *biochemical pathway* or *biochemical network* regroups different families of networks. *Metabolic pathways* are networks of biochemical reactions catalyzed by polypeptides resulting from the expression of a gene. This expression is controlled by a set of parameters like transcription factors, activation, inhibition, etc. For this reason, metabolic pathways are said to be genetically regulated. These regulatory actions are represented in *metabolic regulation networks*. Finally, *signal transduction networks* describe the information transfer from a cellular location, typically the extra-cellular medium, to another one, typically the cell nucleus.

Biochemical pathways are modeled in the aMAZE database as complex networks of interactions. A powerful extraction tool allows users to extract and generate a metabolic pathway on-demand as well as its genetic regulation, transduction signal information, or any other biological information. Such networks are called *heterogeneous biochemical graphs*, where nodes are biological elements such as compound, gene, polypeptide, and where interactions are arcs such as substrate, product, catalyze, inhibition, expression, etc. An example of such graphs arrives when a liver cell receives the signal that the sugar rate is increasing (signal transduction) and its response in which the insulin acts (metabolic pathway).

For many years, each subpart of such a graph has been drawn separately by hand in biochemistry books and have thus graphical conventions that graph layout algorithms must respect. Then, visualization tools coping with such graphs must be able to draw each biochemical subpart according to its particular semantics and representation rules in the same graph. This problem can be generalized as "how to draw a graph according to the particular semantics of its subgraphs?"

BACKGROUND

Graphs provide a way to structure the information presented to users by showing the relevant objects and the relations between them. Such a representation is used in a significant number of areas: software design, business processes, semantic Web, electrical design, bioinformatics, etc. Graph drawing has emerged in recent years as an important area in computer science. The aim of graph drawing algorithms is to compute the position of each node of a graph while optimizing several æsthetics and efficiency criteria, such as edge-crossing minimization, bend minimization, area minimization, symmetries, angle maximization, distance between nodes, etc. (Sugiyama & Eades, 1990; Sugiyama & Misue, 1995).

Usually the output of graph drawing algorithms can be improved manually. The reason is that most of graph drawing algorithms do not take into account domain semantics known by the persons working with the graph. For instance, in a graph representing a typical class diagram one could prefer to see the generalization or "is-a" relationship vertically forming tree-like hierarchies while the aggregation or "part-of" relationship shown horizontally. This constraint is impossible to express in layered graph layout algorithms. On the other hand, force-directed graph layout algorithms try to optimize a mathematical function, named *energy*, which satisfies æsthetic constraints such as in Simon, Steinbruckner, and Lewerentz (2000), Eades (1984), or Davidson and Harel (1996). This means that the semantics of the graph to draw must be expressed as a mathematical function and must be optimized against æsthetic criteria. One drawback of such algorithms is that each application domain should define its own mathematical criteria. In addition, the computation time may become important. In Kaufmann and Wagner (2001), the authors note that these æsthetics and efficiency criteria contrast with more intuitive criteria concerning the semantics and the intended meaning of graphs. Then, we should be able to separate the semantics of information conveyed by the graph and the graph layout algorithm. The questions we try to answer are then "how can we express the drawing knowledge of a particular application domain and how can the graph layout algorithm consider it?"

Drawing a biochemical pathway is such a typical graph drawing problem (van Helden et al., 2001). The traditional æsthetics and efficiency criteria are obviously important but do not take into account the semantics of biological pathways defined by biologists for many years. In addition, as already said, such graph layout algorithms must be able to cope with heterogeneous graphs and thus must take into account the semantics of each kind of subgraph involved. Most of the bioinformatics tools aiming to represent biochemical pathways on-demand such as BioPath (Schreiber, 2002), PathDB (Mendes et al., 2000), ISYS (Siepel et al., 2001), and BioCYc (Karp & Paley, 1994) are not able to draw heterogeneous graphs having in the same drawing a biochemical subpart, a transduction subpart, and a regulation subpart. The reason is that either they use force-directed algorithms or because the graph layout algorithm used has been customized for a specific type of subgraph, and thus cannot represent a heterogeneous graph according to the different semantics. As graphs to lay out are generated on demand as answers to queries addressed to the database, the processing time becomes a significant constraint. Thus, we must provide an efficient method that limits the computation time as well.

The CSCGL algorithm (Skhiri dit Gabouje & Zimányi, 2005) provides a first attempt to solve this problem. However, the algorithm suffers from the following drawbacks: (1) it can only place a subgraph horizontally and thus, it is unable to draw products and substrates in one side of biological reactions, (2) the layout of the genetic regulation of cycles is not in accordance with usual drawing conventions, (3) the available graphical constraints are too limited, and (4) the computing time is too high for graphs having more than 2000 nodes.

In this chapter, we present a generic algorithm that answers this problem more efficiency and in which users can introduce the knowledge about how to draw a graph more accurately and

in accordance with the particular semantics of biochemical pathways. This knowledge is introduced in the algorithm via graphical constraints. We have implemented our algorithm in the Visual BioMaze framework (Skhiri dit Gabouje, 2005; Zimányi & Skhiri dit Gabouje, 2004), a generic viewer of graphs developed in the BioMaze project (Dooms et al., 2004a; Dooms et al., 2004b; Zampeli et al., 2004).

THE BIOMAZE PROJECT

A major challenge of the post-genomic era is to determine the functions of all the genes and gene products at the genome level. In order to improve the prediction of such functions it is important to take in account the information about the different organization levels of the living cell. In particular, it is necessary to consider the set of physical and functional interactions between genes and proteins. Such interactions form networks of cellular processes, called *biochemical networks*, which include metabolic networks, regulatory networks for gene expression, and signal transduction.

The huge quantity of data available and its continuous growth, the need to integrate such information, as well as the necessity of sophisticated software tools for manipulating it, represent true challenges for research in bioinformatics. New tools for integrating, querying, extracting, analyzing, and visualizing biochemical databases are essential for the pharmaceutical and biotechnology industry, in particular for the design of new drugs and vaccines. Such highly sophisticated tools must be designed by multi-disciplinary teams, and require recent results in computer science in areas such as operational research (graph algorithms, constraint logic programming, automatic learning, form recognition, etc.), databases (huge schema management, object-oriented interfaces, evolution, metadata, etc.), and visualization (multi-resolution, multi-representation, complexity management, etc.).

The aim of the BioMaze project is to develop a set of tools including:

1. An information system allowing to represent information about biochemical networks, and including functions for evolution management, generation, and documentation;
2. An open system of specialized software components to exploit biochemical data including extraction, analysis, navigation, and visualization; and
3. A Web interface given access to the services providing by those specialized components.

BioMaze is implemented in the Eclipse platform. It uses the database of the aMAZE project (Lemer *et al.*, 2004).

Visual BioMaze (VBM) (Zimányi et al., 2004), is the visualization framework of the BioMaze project. Although it was developed in the context of BioMaze, the visualization framework can be used independently. The aim of the Visual BioMaze project is to provide a generic graph visualization tool (i.e., a framework able to show any kind of graph, with any kind of graphical representation and with any kind of graph layout algorithm).

When a graph has to be shown, the visualization framework uses two important parameters: the representation model and the graph layout algorithm. We call *representation model* the graphical semantics used to represent the data embedded in a graph (i.e., the graphics associated to each node type and each arc type). On the other hand, a *graph layout algorithm* computes the position of each node of the graph. A generic graph viewer must answer to two fundamental requirements: it must be able to associate to each node type a specific graphical representation and it must be able to dynamically load any graph layout algorithm. The Visual BioMaze framework fulfills these two requirements thanks to a modular architecture based on plug-ins.

As a result, the tool can cope with any kind of graph independently of its semantics and users can choose both a suited representation model and a suited graph layout algorithm. Concerning the BioMaze project, it means that VBM can cope with any kind of biochemical graph and it is able to represent them in the same drawing. An example of a network composed of a signal transduction part and a metabolic part arrives when a liver cell receives the signal that the sugar rate increases in the blood (transduction) and its response in which the insulin acts (metabolic pathway). Since users write a query in BioMaze that retrieves such a graph, the VBM framework is able to represent these two kinds of biochemical networks in the same drawing. Such a result is not yet available in other biochemical visualization software.

Therefore, a generic visualization framework requires algorithms that adapt themselves to the specific semantics of a domain, and that can draw graphs accordingly. The C²GL algorithm is one of such generic algorithms.

THE ALGORITHM

Graphs

The constrained compound graph layout (C²GL) algorithm takes general typed directed graphs as input $G(V, E, T_V, T_E)$, where V is the set of typed nodes, E is the set of typed arcs, and T_V (respectively, T_E) is the set of node (respectively, arc) types. However, the algorithm is suited for graphs outlining a particular information flow as in the case of metabolic pathways. Those pathways are a collection of interconnected biological reactions in which the main substrates and products constitute the backbone of the pathway. Figures 1 and 2 show, respectively, a graph and its backbone.

Our algorithm starts by extracting the backbone constituting the main direction of the graph. Then,

Figure 1. A part of the methionine biosynthesis pathway and its genetic regulation. The main direction (vertical) shows the sequence of biochemical reactions of the pathway. Each of them is regulated by a polypeptide resulting from the expression of a gene. This graph was automatically generated by the C2GL algorithm.

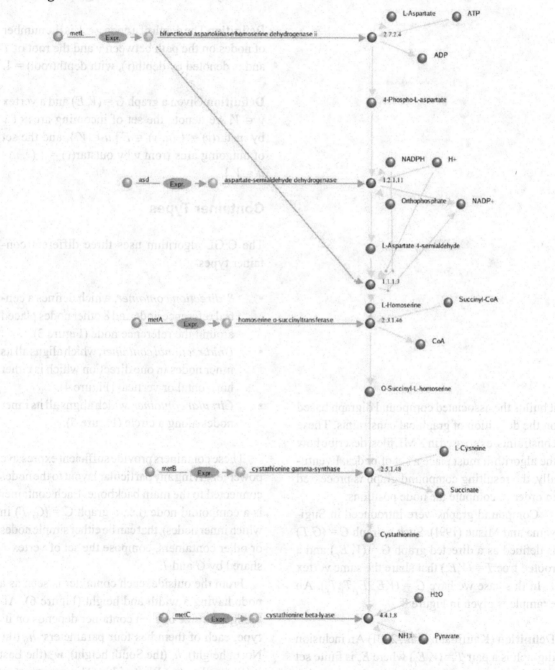

Figure 2. The backbone of the graph of Figure 1. The backbone is a subgraph representing the main direction of the information flow.

it builds the associated compound digraph based on the definition of graphical constraints. These constraints, expressed in XML files, describe how the algorithm must place a set of nodes. Eventually, the resulting compound graph is processed in order to compute the node positions.

Compound graphs were introduced in Sugiyama and Misue (1991). Such a graph $C = (G,T)$ is defined as a directed graph $G = (V, E_G)$ and a rooted tree $T = (V, E_T)$ that share the same vertex V. In this case we have $G = (V, E_G, E_T, T_V, T_E)$. An example is given in Figure 8.

Definition (Kaufmann et al., 2001) An inclusion digraph is a pair $T = (V, E_T)$ where E_T is finite set of inclusion edges such that $(u, v) \in E_T$ means that u includes v. T is required to be a rooted tree. An adjacency digraph is a pair $G = (V, E_G)$ where F

is a finite set of adjacency edges such that $(u, v) \in E_G$ means that u is adjacent to v. A compound digraph is defined as a triple $D = (V, E_T, E_G)$ obtained by composing these two graphs.

Definition The depth of a node $v \in V$ is the number of nodes on the path between v and the root of T and is denoted by depth(v), with depth(root) = 1.

Definition Given a graph $G = (V, E)$ and a vertex $v \in V$, we denote the set of incoming arcs of v by instar(v) = { $(u, v) \in E \mid u \in V$ }, and the set of outgoing arcs from v by outstar(v) = { $(v, u) \mid u \in V$ }.

Container Types

The C²GL algorithm uses three different container types.

- *8-direction container*, which defines a central reference node and 8 other nodes placed around the reference node (Figure 3).
- *Unidirectional container*, which aligns all its inner nodes in one direction which is either horizontal or vertical (Figure 4).
- *Circular container*, which aligns all its inner nodes along a circle (Figure 5).

These containers provide sufficient expressive power for giving any particular layout to the nodes connected to the main backbone. Each container is a compound node (i.e., a graph $C = (G, T)$ in which inner nodes), that can be either simple nodes or other containers, compose the set of vertex V shared by G and T.

From the outside, each container is seen as a node having a width and height (Figure 6). Although the size of each container depends on its type, each of them has four parameters: h_N (the North height), h_S (the South height), w_E (the East width), and w_W (the West width). These parameters are used in the coordinate assignment phase.

Figure 3. An 8-direction container defines a reference node and 8 other nodes around it. The other nodes can be simple nodes or other containers.

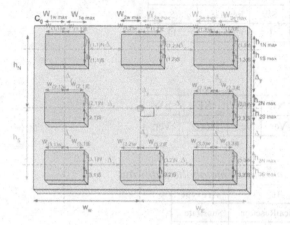

Figure 4. An unidirectional container

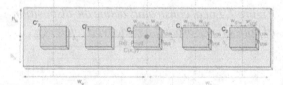

Figure 5. A circular container

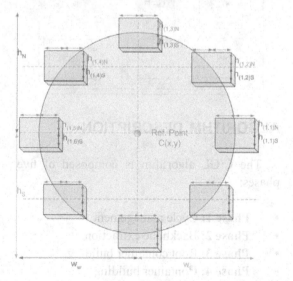

Figure 6. All containers, independently of their type, are seen as nodes having a certain width and height.

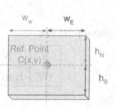

Graphical Constraints

We use graphical constraints to express the information about how to draw any information flow diagram according to specific domain semantics. These graphical constraints are expressed as a set of *local constraints*, *circular constraints*, and *backbone constraints* which are encoded in XML. These constraints are described next.

Local Constraints

A local constraint is defined by a set of tables as those shown by Tables 1 and 2. The first table defines for one reference node type, in this case *biologicalReaction*, the node types that must be placed around the reference node and their relative positions (Figure 7). The second table defines how to manage more than one constrained node in the same position. For each local constraint on a reference node (Table 1), we have to define one such a table.

Nodes involved in a local constraint can be the reference node for other constraints. A priority policy assigns higher priority to reference

Table 1. Local constraints around the reference type node

Node type	Arc type	Pos.	Dir.	D.ratio
Compound	Reaction.in	NW	Forward	5
Compound	Reaction.out	SW	Reverse	5
Catalysis	Catalysis.Reaction	E	Forward	10

Table 2. Alignment policies

S	N	E	W	NE	NW	SE	SW
Ver.	Horiz.	Ver.	Ver.	Ver.	Ver.	Horiz.	Ver.

Table 3. The set of nodes and arcs constituting the backbone of metabolic pathways

From	To	Arc type
Compound	BiologicalReaction	Substrate
BiologicalReaction	Compound	Product

nodes contained in the backbone. The priority processing will be explained in Section 4.4. The local constraints define also the kind of behavior to adopt if more than one node is matched in one constraint container. For instance, Table 2 states that if two nodes must be placed in NW of the reference node, those will be aligned vertically.

Circular Constraints

Circular constraints define whether a cycle must be drawn along a circle or must be drawn by inversing the minimal set of backward edges (Eades, Lin, & Smyth, 1993). They are constituted by a set C_T of arc types specifying the allowed types for a circle. For cycles having at least one arc which is not contained in C_T we inverse the backward edges, otherwise, we draw it along a circle.

Backbone Constraints

These constraints define the set of nodes and arcs that constitute the main direction flow of the graph (Table 3).

Figure 7. Local constraints define the disposition of nodes types around a node type reference

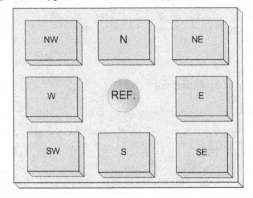

ALGORITHM DESCRIPTION

The C²GL algorithm is composed of five phases:

- **Phase 1:** Cycle management.
- **Phase 2:** Backbone extraction.
- **Phase 3:** Root container building.
- **Phase 4:** Container building.
- **Phase 5:** Coordinate assignment.

We describe these phases in more detail next.

Cycle Management

This phase isolates and enumerates all cycles. We first find the strongly connected components (Tarjan, 1972) of the graph, then, we apply a modified version of the depth-first search that uses backtracking in order to enumerate cycles. If more than one cycle is found in a strongly connected component, the outer cycle is called the *main cycle* and the others are called *inner cycles*. Each component is replaced by a *cycle node*, which is a special node representing a cycle and its inner cycles. Algorithm 1 returns all cycles of a strongly-connected component.

This algorithm marks recursively the nodes of the strongly connected components. If one marked node is found, we add the cycle to the list of cycles (variable cycles in the pseudo-code). If a node has more than one outgoing arc, we store the size of the current cycle, we copy its list of nodes, and we launch recursively the algorithm. When the algorithm returns, all cycles that can be reached from this node have already been discovered. Finally, we demark the nodes of the current cycle from index because they can be involved in other cycles.

Algorithm 1. Cycle search

```
procedure cycleSearch
    /* start is an arbitrary node of the component, cycles is the list of all cycles of
the  component initialized as empty, and currentCycles is a temporary list.*/
    Node current = start;
    Bool stop = false;
    while stop ≠ true
        if current is not marked
            mark(current)
            currentCycle.add(current)
            if current.outStar >1
                for i ← |current.outStar|
                    nexti = current.outStar[i]
                    int index = size(currentCycle)
                    List cyclei = copy(currentCycle)
                    cycleSearch(nexti, cycles, cyclei)
                    demark(cyclei, index)
                end for
            else
                current = current.outStar[0]
            end if
        else
            stop = true
            if current = currentCycle[0]
                cycles.add(currentCycle)
            end if
        end if
    end while
end procedure
```

Backbone Extraction

This phase extracts all nodes composing the backbone of the graph. These nodes represent the main direction from which the graph has to be drawn. Given a set of backbone constraints C, this phase is composed of four steps:

- **Step 1:** Removing all nodes u such that $u \notin C$.
- **Step 2:** Removing all nodes u such that $instar(u) = 0$.
- **Step 3:** Removing all nodes u such that $outstar(u) = 0$.
- **Step 4:** Backbone layers assignment.

Step 1 consists in removing nodes and arcs that are not involved in the backbone. Steps 2 and 3 process the backbone, and finally Step 4 assigns a layer to each node. If Step 4 finds a cycle node, it will investigate its content (i.e., the list of nodes composing the main cycle and the lists composing the inner cycles) in order to know if the cycle must be included in the backbone. In Step 4, layers cannot be assigned as in a traditional layered algorithm, since in this case the branches of a pathway will not appear correctly. Figure 8(a) shows several branch nodes (i.e., nodes having more than one successor). Our approach is as follows. For each successor node u of a branch node: (1) we launch the algorithm recursively with a new list of layers (newLayers) and with u as root, and (2) we build a container layer with the newLayers as content. Figure 8(b) shows such a result, the container layers are recursively built from a branch. If a node already belongs to another layer container, a bend point is taken instead of the node itself.

As a result, we obtain a set of layers constituting the backbone where layers contain either simple nodes or other container layers.

Figure 8. (a) Example of layer assignment in a branch case. (b) The algorithm builds recursively the container layers that will be transformed later in unidirectional containers.

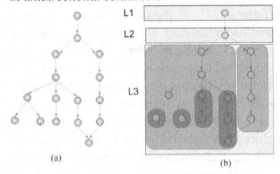

Root Container Building

This phase builds a unique container from the backbone extracted in the previous phase. The procedure is simple. The backbone is composed by layers. Each of them will be transformed into an unidirectional container as shown by Figure

Figure 9. (a) The extracted backbone. (b) The unique container that is the root of the new created compound graph built from the backbone.

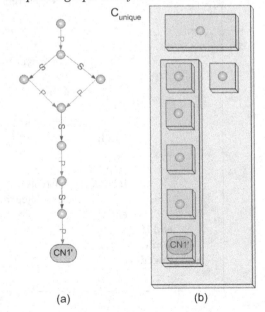

(a) (b)

Figure 10. (a) Building of constrained containers in a container CR. For the reference node R there are two nodes in NW, one node in SW, and two nodes in E. Further, in position E, there is a local constraint on the constrained nodes. We build two new containers, we add the nodes inside, and we replace the nodes by the container parent. We continue by applying recursively this phase. (b) The corresponding inclusion graph T before investigating nodes P1 and P2.

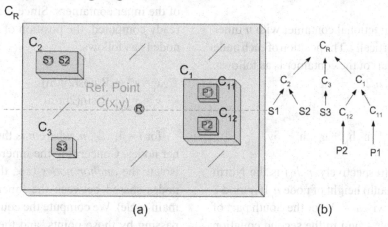

(a)   (b)

9, and all these containers will be included in a root container. If a layer contains a container layer instead of a simple node, we build recursively a unidirectional container corresponding to this container layer. As a result we obtain a root container which is the root of $T = (V, E_T)$, the inclusion graph of the general compound graph. After this phase, we must delete all arcs involved in the backbone, since they cannot participate into the next phase.

Container Building

This phase parses the backbone and for each node builds the associated compound node from local constraints. The input of this phase is the root container and the set of local constraints, and as output we obtain the root container enriched by new containers in which inner nodes are either simple or compound nodes. We denote by C_L the set of local constraints, where each $c_i \in C_L$ has all attributes defined by Table 1. Also C_B denotes the set of backbone nodes.

This phase parses recursively the *constrained nodes* of the root container (i.e., the set of nodes) $\{ u \mid u \in V, u \in C_B \}$ such that there is a constraint $c_i \in C_L$ involving u.type as reference. Given a reference node u for a constraint c_i:

1. For each position (E, W, NW, etc.) of the reference node we build a new container container$_i$ and we add the constrained nodes found for this position (Figure 10).
2. We replace the reference node u by the container$_i$.
3. We apply recursively the same procedure to the constrained nodes.

Coordinate Assignment

This phase computes the position of each inner node in all containers. First, the size of the root container will be computed, this includes the recursive computation of the size of all inner containers. Then, the position of each base node and container can be computed. We assign an initial position (0,0) to the reference position of the root container, and this position will be propagated to inner nodes and inner containers.

Unidirectional Container

Consider a unidirectional container with n inner nodes aligned vertically. The position of each node n_i in the North part of the container is as follows, where $i = 1, \ldots, n/2$:

$$x_i = x_{ref}$$
$$y_i = y_{ref} - \sum_{k=b}^{i-1} n_k.h_N + n_{k+1}.h_S + \delta y$$

where $n_i.h_N$ (respectively, $n_i.h_S$) is the North (respectively, South) height of node n_i If n mod 2 $= 0$, $b = 1$, otherwise $b = 0$. For the South part of the container, the $-$ sign in the second equation above is replaced by a $+$ sign.

8-Direction Container

The position of each node is computed from the size of its neighbors. 8-direction containers can be seen as a 3×3 matrix, each node being identified by $n_{j,k}$ where j is the row and k the column. For example, $n_{1,2}$ is the node in the north position (N). We define next the position of the last line of the container, the other lines are computed similarly. For node $n_{3,1}$:

$$x_{3,1} = x_{ref} - (n_{3,2}.w_W + \delta x + n_{3,1}.w_E)$$
$$y_{3,1} = y_{ref} + n_{2,1}.h_S + \delta y + n_{3,1}.h_N$$

where δx (respectively, δy) is the minimal distance between nodes along the y (respectively, x) direction. For the node $n_{3,2}$:

$$x_{3,2} = x_{ref}$$
$$y_{3,2} = y_{ref} + n_{2,2}.h_S + \delta y + n_{3,2}.h_N$$

And finally for the node $n_{3,3}$:

$$x_{3,3} = x_{ref} + n_{3,2}.w_E + \delta x + n_{3,3}.w_W$$

$$y_{3,3} = y_{ref} + n_{2,3}.h_S + \delta y + n_{3,3}.h_N$$

Circular Container

The size of the circle is computed from the size of the inner containers. Since the radius R is already computed, the position of each contained node is as follows:

$$x_i = x_{ref} + R.\cos(2i\pi/n)$$
$$y_i = y_{ref} + R.\sin(2i\pi/n)$$

for $i = 1, \ldots, n$, where n is the number of inner nodes. Concerning the inner cycles, we first isolate the *anchor nodes* (i.e., the first and last nodes shared between the inner cycle and the main cycle). We compute the equation of the line passing by those points, and then, we compute the position of each node of the inner cycle on this line.

RESULTS

The main characteristics of the C^{2}GL algorithm are as follows:

1. It emphasizes the hierarchical flow of biochemical networks due to the backbone extraction (Figure 11);
2. It can cope with any kind of biochemical network;
3. Users can customize the representation of subgraph types according to the graphical representation rules; and
4. Metabolic pathways are visualized as is usually done in biochemistry books.

Figure 12 shows the results of our algorithm on the proline biosynthesis pathway. We used graphical constraints stating the positions of substrate, product, and polypeptide for biological reactions as well as gene and gene expression for polypeptides.

Figure 11. The fuculose catabolism pathway. The drawing shows the backbone of the pathway given by our extraction algorithm. Notice that the branches are correctly drawn, in particular the left branch which is a cycle.

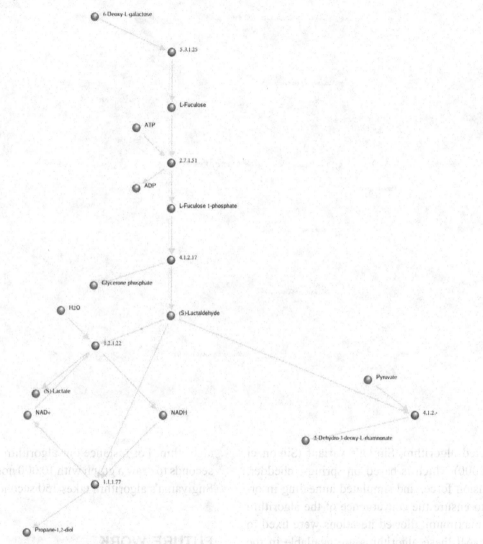

Figure 13 shows the results on a part of the glycolisys and the TCA cycle. In addition to the graphical constraints defined for the proline, cycle constraints allowed product and substrate in biochemical cycles. As can be seen, our algorithm allows to visualize metabolic pathways including cycles or branches, as well as other biological information such as genetic regulation, signal transduction, etc. Further, users can customize the representation of each kind of biological interaction.

The computing time of graph layout algorithms constitutes often a bottleneck, since users do not want to wait several minutes for visualizing the regulated metabolic pathway they have just extracted from a database. In order to test the robustness of our algorithm, we randomly generated 30 graphs from 5 to 10,000 nodes, and we successively applied the C²GL algorithm, the circular layout algorithm, Sugiyama's algorithm (Sugiyama et al., 1981), and a particular force-

Figure 12. The proline pathway and its genetic regulation

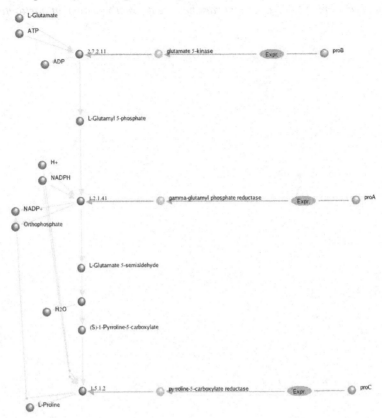

directed algorithm, Simon's variant (Simon et al., 2000) which is based on spring-embedder, repulsion force, and simulated annealing in order to ensure the convergence of the algorithm (the maximum allowed iterations were fixed to 150). All these algorithms are available in the Visual BioMaze framework. The circular layout algorithm is often used as a reference algorithm for measuring complexity since it has a linear complexity in O(*n*).

Figure 14 shows the results of the experiments. As can be seen, the C²GL algorithm is very efficient, the computing time is similar to that obtained by the circular layout algorithm (i.e., our algorithm behaves as having linear complexity). Further, the computing time is below that of Sugiyama's

algorithm. For instance our algorithm needs 40 seconds to draw a graph with 10,000 nodes while Sugiyama's algorithm takes 150 seconds.

FUTURE WORK

The current version of our algorithm applies a simple layout for the inner cycles of a cycle that has to be drawn along a circle. As already said in Section 4.1, a line is computed between the nodes belonging to the main cycle and the nodes of the inner cycle are placed along this line. However, this algorithm is too simple, for instance it cannot avoid the collision of nodes when two inner cycles cross over each other. This problem is not

Figure 13. The TCA cycle and its genetic regulation. The figure shows the topological arrangement of a biochemical cycle.

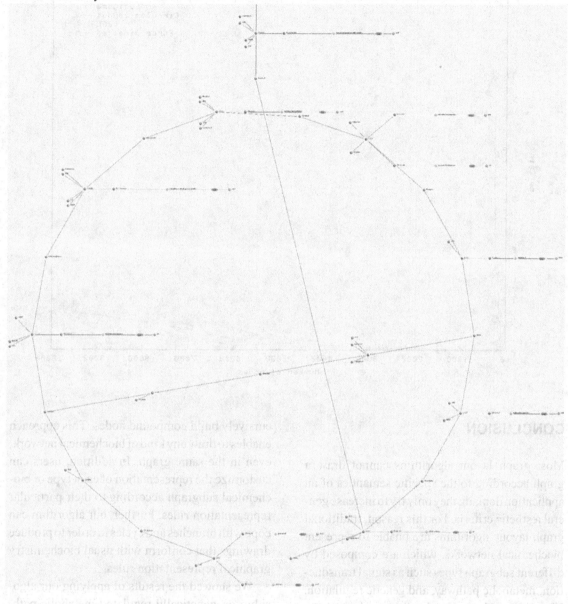

trivial. The next release will improve the layout of the interior of main cycles.

We will also introduce æsthetic criteria such as minimizing drawing area and minimizing edge crossing. In order to minimize the drawing area, we can apply a method proposed in Castello, Mili, and Tollis (2000), which consists in applying a technique similar to the one used for minimizing VLSI chip area.

Figure 14. Benchmarks of the C2GL algorithm

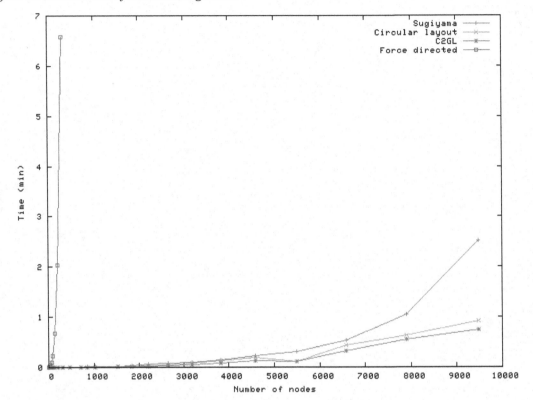

CONCLUSION

Most graph layout algorithms cannot draw a graph according to the specific semantics of an application domain; they only try to increase general æsthetic criteria. For this reason, traditional graph layout algorithms are unable to represent biochemical networks, which are composed by different subgraph types such as signal transduction, metabolic pathway, and genetic regulation. The reason is that each subgraph type has its own semantics and thus, its own drawing rules.

In this chapter, we described the C²GL algorithm, a constraint-based graph layout algorithm. The algorithm uses graphical constraints to re-cursively build compound nodes. This approach enables to draw any kind of biochemical network, even in the same graph. In addition, users can customize the representation of each type of biochemical subgraph according to their particular representation rules. Further, our algorithm can cope with branches and cycles in order to produce drawings that conform with usual biochemistry graphical representation rules.

We showed the results of applying our algorithm on genetically regulated metabolic pathways, such pathways being extracted typically from a database. In addition we evaluated the robustness of the C²GL on 30 random graphs from 5 to 10,000 nodes and we obtained computing times similar to those of an $O(n)$ algorithm.

REFERENCES

Castello, R., Mili, R., & Tollis, I. G. (2000). An algorithmic framework for visualizing statecharts. *Proceedings of the 8th International Symposium on Graph Drawing, GD 2000* (pp. 139-149).

Davidson, R., & Harel, D. (1996). Drawing graphs nicely using simulated annealing. *ACM Transaction on Graphics, 15*(4), 301-331.

Dooms, G., Deville, Y., & Dupont, P. (2004a). Constrained path finding in biochemical networks. *Proceedings of the 5th Open Days in Biology, Computer Science, and Mathematics, JOBIM 2004* (pp. J0-40).

Dooms, G., Deville, Y., & Dupont, P. (2004b). A Mozart implementation of CP(BioNet). *Proceedings of the 2nd International Conference on Multiparadigm Programming in Mozart/Oz, MOZ 2004* (pp. 237-250). LNCS 3389, Springer.

Eades, P. (1984). A heuristic for graph drawing. *Congressus Numerantium, 42,* 149-160.

Eades, P., Lin, X., & Smyth, W. F. (1993). A fast and effective heuristic for the feedback arc set problem. *Information Processing Letters, 47*(6), 319-323.

Karp, P. D., & Paley, S. M. (1994). Automated drawing of metabolic pathways. *Proceedings of the 3rd International Conference on Bioinformatics and Genome Research.*

Kaufmann, M., & Wagner, D. (2001). *Graph drawing: Methods and models.* Springer.

Lemer, C., Antezana, E., Couche, F., Fays, F., Santolaria, X., Janky, R., Deville, Y., Richelle, J., & Wodak, S. (2003). The aMaze lightBench: A Web interface to a relational database of cellular processes. *Nucleic Acids Research, 32,* 443-448. Retrieved from http://nar.oxfordjournals.org/cgi/content/full/32/suppl_1/D443

Mendes, P., Bulmore, D. L., Farmer, A. D., Steadman, P. A, Waught, M. E., & Wlodek, S. T. (2000). PathDB: A second generation metabolic database. *Animating the Cellular Map, Proceedings of the 9th International BioThermoKinetics Meeting* (pp. 207-212). Stellenbosch University Press.

Schreiber, F. (2002). High quality visualization of biochemical pathways in BioPath. *Silico Biology, 2*(0006).

Siepel, A., Farmer, A., Tolopko, A., Zhuang, M., Mendes, P., Beavis, W., & Sobral, B. (2001). ISYS: A decentralized, component-based approach to the integration of heterogeneous bioinformatics resources. *Bioinformatics, 17*(1), 83-94.

Simon, F., Steinbruckner, F., & Lewerentz, C. (2000). *3D-Spring embedder for complete graphs.* Technical report, Technical University Cottbus, Germany.

Skhiri dit Gabouje, S. (2005). *The Visual BioMaze Tutorial.* Retrieved from http://cs.ulb.ac.be/research/ biomaze

Skhiri dit Gabouje, S., & Zimányi, E. (2005). Generic visualization of biochemical networks: A new compound graph layout algorithm. *Poster Proceedings of the 4th International Workshop on Efficient and Experimental Algorithms, WEA 05.*

Sugiyama, K., & Eades, P. (1990). How to draw a directed graph. *Journal of Information Processing, 13*(4), 424-437.

Sugiyama, K., & Misue, K. (1991). Visualization of structural information: Automatic drawing of compound digraphs. *IEEE Transactions on Systems, Man, and Cybernetics, 21*(4), 876-893.

Sugiyama, K., & Misue, K. (1995). A simple and unified method for drawing graphs: Magnetic-spring algorithm. *Proceedings of the DIMACS International Workshop on Graph Drawing, GD'94* (pp. 364-375). LNCS 894, Springer.

Sugiyama, K., Tagawa, S., & Toda, M. (1981). Methods for visual understanding of hierarchical system structures. *IEEE Transactions on Systems, Man, and Cybernetics, 11*(2), 109-125.

Tarjan, R. (1972). Depth-first search and linear graph algorithms. *SIAM Journal of Computing, 1*(2), 146-160.

van Helden, J., Naim, A., Lemer, C., Mancuso, R., Eldridge, M., Wodak, S., & Gilbert, D. (2001). Representing and analyzing molecular and cellular function in the computer. *Biological Chemistry, 381*(9-10), 921-935.

Zampelli, S., Deville, Y., & Dupont, P. (2004). Finding patterns in biochemical networks: A constraint programming approach. *Proceedings of the 5th Open Days in Biology, Computer Science, and Mathematics, JOBIM 2004* (pp. J0-85).

Zimányi, E., & Skhiri dit Gabouje, S. (2004). Semantic visualization of biochemical databases. *Semantic for GRID Databases: Proceedings of the International Conference on Semantics for a Networked World, ICSNW04* (pp. 199-214). LNCS 3226, Springer.

ENDNOTE

[1]   The partners of the Biomaze project (http://biomaze.info.ucl.ac.be) are Université Libre de Bruxelles, Université Catholique de Louvain-la-neuve, and Facultés Universitaires Notre-Dame de la Paix de Namur.

Chapter XX
Customized Visual Computing:
The Aesthetic
Computing Method

Paul Fishwick
University of Florida, USA

ABSTRACT

Aesthetic computing is defined as the application of art theory and practice toward the field of computing. This chapter introduces aesthetic computing and its approach for the task of multimedia representation of formal structures. We chose the structure of a simple computer program to illustrate the method. Examples used to represent the program illustrate how we may customize formal structures such as programs to allow users to employ visualization and human interaction as means to achieve a variety of diverse presentation artifacts. To date, the method has been used in education to promote creativity in computing and model building, and as a technique for bridging the arts with computer science.

INTRODUCTION

The purpose of *aesthetic computing* is to apply the theory and practice of art and design to the field of computing. The range of aesthetics within the arts is broader than those in mathematics and computing where aesthetics is often synonymous with *optimality criteria* (i.e., elegant proof, minimal line crossings). Therefore, the new field encourages applying an artistically-based *expanded range* of

"aesthetic" to basic elements of computing such as programs, models, and data.

A Dagstuhl workshop in 2002 surfaced the core areas of aesthetic computing, culminating in a recently published edited volume (Fishwick, 2006). Aesthetic computing is associated with three levels of art-computing integration: *cultural, implementation*, and *representation*. The *cultural level* is one where computing artifacts (i.e., structures) or process (i.e., collaboration) are affected by an introduction of the expanding role of aesthetics or contact with designers and artists. The *processing* language (Greenberg, 2006) is a good example of this level, where a strong community is sustained by people who are programmers, designers, or both. Other examples of cultural infusion are the collaborations of artists with scientists (Cox, 2006; Prophet & d'Inverno, 2006,). In this level, the practice of computing is modified through a cultural form of integration: artists and computer scientists working together in teams.

The *implementation level* creates a situation where computing artifacts have a tight *behavioral coupling* with design and art artifacts. Each computing artifact, when executed, exhibits an artistic consequence. Processing also reflects this level through its extensive documentation where concise code fragments that demonstrate a specific Java method have corresponding design equivalents. For example, the "while statement" in the online reference manual is specified through a five-line Java program. Thus, there is a tight coupling between code and design: for any piece of code, there is a commensurate, behaviorally generated, visual design. This creates a strong bond to where the visual pattern becomes partially synonymous with the *concept of conditional iteration* associated with the computing artifact. Another system that exhibits aesthetic computing via the implementation level is Alice (Dann, Cooper, & Pausch, 2006) since every programming fragment can have audio or visual consequence in the 3D display space.

The final *representation level* is an extension of the implementation level since the coupling between design and computing artifacts occurs at a structural, as well as behavioral, level. The artifacts reflect each other to the extent that they can be used interchangeably, suggesting a strong level of one artifact *structurally representing* the other. Moreover, the artifact and the behavior may occupy the same human interface space, allowing one to be juxtaposed with the other, or otherwise connected through morphing or transitioning. Information visualization (Ware,

2004), if expanded, as done by the Processing community to span the range from pure utility to artistic freedom, is one example of the representation level. The computing artifact for information visualization is generally a simple data structure such as an array or tree; however, other possibilities emerge in representing formulae, code, and model structures. In our work, we attempt to embrace all three of these levels:

- **Cultural:** artists and computer scientists take the same classes as part of the Digital Arts and Sciences degree programs.
- **Implementation:** Mathematical and computing elements are taught within the context of design and art, forming new bonds between both.
- **Representation:** The aesthetic computing class emphasizes a process where student create different types of representations of formal structures using a variety of styles and metaphors.

Four years ago, we created the aesthetic computing class at the University of Florida with the goal of exploring the third level of art-computing integration as previously specified. The class is organized with lecture, invited speakers, student team speakers, and projects. The projects are divided into four categories: 1D, 2D, 3D, and Physical. The 1D project is one where a student takes a text-based structure and represents it in text, but perhaps with embedded interaction. The 2D and 3D projects are similar, except that the visual represents are similarly limited to those dimensions. The physical project involves a juried exhibition of sculptures and prototypes. For Spring 2006, we had an exhibition in a refurbished warehouse called *WARPhaus* (Warphaus, 2006). The process of representation involves a careful study of semiotics, a brief introduction to categories, basic parsing, and computational manipulation methods from analogy to simple graph transformation. Figure 1 illustrates the process.

Figure 1. A simplified process flow of beginning with a source structure and applying a wide range of aesthetics to create a target structure

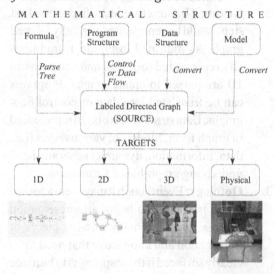

RELATED WORK

The use of aesthetics and artistic design as a motivator for the creative representation of discrete structures finds a locus in aesthetic computing (Fishwick, 2006). The purpose of aesthetic computing is to explore the application of aesthetics, in all of its diversity, to the field of computing. While the overall effect of aesthetic computing covers many sub-areas, our work interprets aesthetic computing as artistic exploration of representation of discrete structures such as equations, trees, graphs, and the more complex structures built upon these: program and data structures. While many researchers in visual languages employ aesthetics, the definition is one generally limited to quantitatively defined metrics (Battista, Eades, Tamassia, & Tollis, 1999; Purchase, 2002) often defined as optima: *minimizing* line crossings and *maximizing* symmetry. However, when we peruse a comprehensive resource on aesthetics (Kelly, 1998), we find that aesthetics is much broader than quantitatively defined optimality criteria. Aesthetics also connotes exploring form and

beauty for the sake of the potential in visual and artistic design.

The need to apply this expanded role of aesthetics in visual languages is based in several areas. First, implementations in visual software and algorithms come with the aesthetics of their designers. For example, Lieberman's 3D code representation (Lieberman, 1991) and Najork's CUBE (Najoork, 1996) present a primitive block environment that has its own visual simplicity and elegance. Diehl (2001) emphasizes *cross-cutting* and interdisciplinary approaches for future software visualization research. To a great extent, diversity of presentation is at the heart of aesthetics, which is frequently catalogued by genre, or indeed by the artist whose design aesthetic is under consideration. Gardner (1984) reinforces the strong relationship between the creative act and art.

A balance between form and function is necessary if all aspects of aesthetics are to be employed in visual language development. The HCI community speaks to this in ways that emotion (i.e., frequently associated with artistic practice) plays a significant role in the interface (Norman, 2004, Tractinsky, 1997; Tractinsky, Shoval-Katz, & Ikar, 2000). Moreover, this balance is viewed as fundamental in design with all interfaces vacillating between transparency and reflectivity, or seeing through the interface to complete utility vs. reflecting on its visual or aural structure (Bolter & Gromala, 2003). In a recent study by Lavie and Tractinsky (2004), this duality between focus on function vs. form, or transparency vs. reflectivity, might be interpreted along the two chronologically demarcated approaches to aesthetics: *classical* vs. *expressive*. The classical definition of aesthetics was prevalent prior to Baumgarten (1750) and Kant (1790), where aesthetics—and what we would term *usability* in today's parlance—were tightly coupled. Then, in the latter half of the seventeenth century until the present day, aesthetics can be viewed on a more diverse scale as evidenced in (Kelly, 1998), allowing for artistic expression, creativity, and pleasure.

The arts have historically defined modern aesthetics as capturing the philosophy of art and perhaps extending the definition. Within the arts, one finds all aspects of aesthetics. Certainly, expression and creativity are to be found in any museum or magazine devoted to art and design. However, we also find what the artists term *formal* aspects, which correlate well with the previously described optimality conditions in computer science. Arnheim (1954, 1966) defines a number of abstractions necessary to view art from a formal perspective. Concepts such as balance, dynamics, perspective, and symmetry would fit easily into the lexicon of the visual language or mathematics aesthete. The challenge is for visual languages to explore the remainder of the arts, outside of pure formalism, to where the totality of aesthetics is considered. Aesthetics in visual languages needs to be more than usability and the establishment of optimal metrics--there is a need to bring in the *artistic half*, which naturally promotes creativity and personal expression.

A SIX-STEP PROCESS

Encouraging artists, computer scientists, and mathematicians to collaborate is a good way to initiate any task involving representation (i.e., cultural level). Having tools that help forge connections (i.e., implementation level) between art and mathematical structures provides additional assistance. However, we wish to focus on the representation level where the potential for representing structure is given a framework for creative exploration. This framework is defined in six steps:

1. **Identification:** One needs a source structure to represent. The following are the sorts of structures that are presented as possibilities in the class: number, variable, formula, function, program, data, and model. The first four are commonly found in K-12 mathemat-

ics, whereas program and data structures are often not introduced to students until university computing classes.

2. **Graph:** The structure identified in the first step should be represented as a fully labeled graph. As indicated in Figure 1, traditionally represented formulas and functions in 1D are parsed to create graphs. Programs can be translated into data or control flow graphs. Data structures are often represented in graph form. Models of various sorts (i.e., data, information, dynamic) generally have underlying graph-based formalisms.

3. **Ontology:** Even though it may seem a source graph is enough to begin a representation process, there are many missing pieces of information and knowledge that need to be clearly surfaced if the mapping is to be made clear, complete, and consistent. Semantic networks should be created to describe the ontological foundation for the source item to be represented.

4. **Map:** How does one take a source graph and an ontological framework and actually craft a representation? A mapping must occur from source to target. This mapping begins with a determination of the sort of target to forge. Are we to transform a structure into a dance, a song, a landscape, or a cityscape? The use of metaphor is warranted, but even before specific metaphors, we employ the use of a simple table that provides ideas as to how the key parts of a graph (i.e., relations) can be mapped to concepts in *spacetime*.

5. **Representation:** The final stage is the actual representation with the assistance of the table in step 4. This is where the designer employs the most creativity.

6. **Assessment:** After creating a representation, it should be critiqued through peer evaluation or heuristics.

It is certainly possible to skip one or more steps. One might immediately envision the Pythagorean theorem as a tree, the tree as a set of enclosed rings, and then go about sketching the rings or producing them from a rapid prototyping machine. However, having the steps allows us to capture a guiding *method* even if all steps are not rigorously followed.

We will use several examples to illustrate the first five steps and then provide assessment criteria for the final step. In general, like most processes for creating large products (i.e., software engineering), there is a significant iterative component where steps are revisited as required.

Step 1: Identification

Consider the code-design coupling similar to the original presentation depicted within the processing reference guide (Processing, 2006) for the *while statement* shown in Figure 2.

This example is typical of the tight relationship promoted between text-based code and a visual behavior in Processing. One can imagine a number of creative representations of the behavior from using other iconic and geometric forms in the iteration to using sound and music.

Figure 2. The while statement code-design coupling (created after the processing reference guidelines (Processing, 2006)

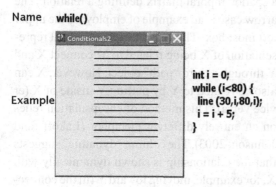

Step 2: Graph

Our source structure is a textual computer program in Figure 2, and so our first goal is to represent this as a graph of some sort. Figures 3 and 4 illustrate control and data flow representations of the program. Other type of graphs, especially "models" used to encode process, are possible; however, data and control flow diagrams are two of the most common generic graphs.

Graph nodes in both Figures 3 and 4 are shown as boxes. The control flow diagram is often termed a *flowchart*. The edges labeled 0 and 1 represent false and true, respectively. Figure 4 shows the corresponding data flow diagram, which emphasizes the flow of data rather than of control. A key difference between these models is that the control flow is sequential, while the data flow is parallel: all nodes in the data flow graph execute simultaneously.

Figure 3. Control flow diagram for the code in Figure 2

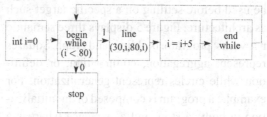

Figure 4. Data flow diagram for the code in Figure 2

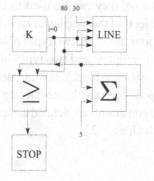

Now that we have the core program in Figure 2 in terms of data and control flow graphs, or models, we can proceed with the semantic networks needed to capture the ontological level.

Step 3: Ontology

A semantic network is a labeled graph of nodes defining concepts. An ontology is based on a semantic network and usually includes additional arithmetic or logical-based constraints; for example, mammals have four legs or a transport vehicle may have one more wheels. Semantic networks and ontologies are important not only for representing what we know about a source structure, but also, what we know about the chosen target domain identified in the subsequent step. For the computer program, we need to define what it means *to be* a program, and then similarly, what it means to be a product of architecture if architecture captures our target domain. In this example, we are going to mix concepts of steps 3 and 4 together and then use our definition of step 4 to illustrate a higher level approach to mapping that would normally be used before settling on a specific target such as architecture. Figure 5 displays three semantic networks: program, building, and graph. Squares represent aggregation, composition, or definition while circles represent generalization. For example, a program is composed of an initialization, a body, a stop, and a sequence whereas a building contains a portico, a primary structure, an exit, and portal. These are concepts that are to be viewed in the same light as classes in Java or C++, and so, they can be used to instantiate multiple objects of that particular *type*. As for the circle relations, there are two types of statements (simple and complex) and two types of areas for buildings (room and block). The numbers that appear as superscripts are defined in step 4. Simple ontological constraints are defined using relational operators such as "=2."

Figure 5. A simple ontology containing knowledge of what it means to be a program (upper left), building (upper right), and graph (bottom)

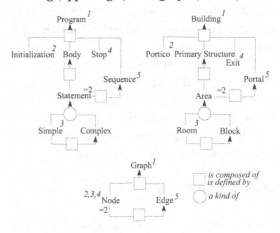

Step 4: Map

Given that we have source structures as graphs and that graphs are composed of multiple relations (i.e., on edges), how can a relation be reified? Let's take an example of two elements X and Y. We can show a relationship between X and Y by drawing an arrow between them. This is conventional and requires knowledge of what an "arrow" is, and yet this is an effective method for capturing a directional relationship of X to Y.

Figure 6 is a general method for this approach: a spatiotemporal matrix defining a relation. The arrow case is an example of employing the upper left most box. The target is a static visual representation of X being related to Y: connect X and Y through a third "path" object. However, X can also be related to Y by putting Y inside of X (or vice versa). This method of encapsulation relies on an entirely different metaphor (Lakoff and Johnson, 2003). The column "dynamic" suggests that the relationship is shown dynamically with X, for example, moving toward Y (in the connection row), X turning into Y upon magnification (encapsulation row), or X morphing "in place" to Y over some period of time.

Figure 6. A matrix capturing different ways of reifying the concept of a relation in spacetime

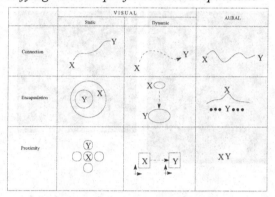

Figure 7. Architectural 2D floor plan target for the control flow model in Figure 3

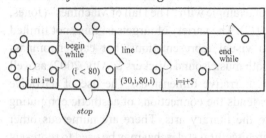

The column labeled "aural" is also dynamic, yet non-visual: the connection-type is where there exists a musical or sonic passage that separates X from Y, thus identifying X as being related to Y. For the encapsulation row of aural, X "contains" Y as a subcomponent musical element. For the proximity row, X is followed by Y.

For our program representation, we will use the static/visual column and "connection" row by way of portals (i.e., doorways) from one area into another. We further refine our mapping by revisiting Figure 5, and noting the correspondence between the concepts in the top two ontologies as indicated by the superscript identifiers. A program is a building (using superscript 1) and a stop is an exit (using superscript 4.

Step 5: Representation

For architecture, one may use a spatial data structure that captures *adjacency*, which means that the originally embedded, implicit semantics of "next" for the edge between the nodes labeled "int i=0" and "begin while (i<80)" maps to "adjacent to" in the target adjacency graph that must be created to eventually yield an architectural schematic. The original style of "square box" for each node in Figure 3 will map to "room" in the target. The graph edges themselves will map to "portals" in the target. The detailed mapping,

along these lines, uses semantic networks and simple ontology construction (i.e., Figure 5 superscript identifiers) to map from source to target. Then, the representation step yields one of many possible interpretations of the target graph such as the one shown in Figure 7. This is a top-down floor layout (i.e., plan view) for a large building with an entrance portico on the left, denoting the place where an imaginary person enters to begin the computation. The small circles represent columns and the diagonal lines with circular arcs represent doorways. For the "while" box, all doorways leading in the linear direction are associated with a condition of true, whereas a false condition indicates an exit through the other doorway to the semi-circular "stop" room.

In two recent aesthetic computing classes, students were not only taught how to represent formal structures along the lines of Figure 7, but they also created narrative *targets*. Often, the narrative was made consistent with a 2D or 3D representation. For example, the floor plan in Figure 6 can serve as the basis for an accompanying narrative:

... as Shelly returned through the door at the end of the room containing the metallic switch machine, she noticed that a new silver bar had been positioned next to the previous one. This cast an eerie array of shadows against the far wall. It seemed as if by running through the outer corridor she returned to find the number of bars growing—perhaps to eventually create a jail-like barrier to leaving the room...

This particular type of narrative is consistent with elements from science fiction and fantasy, for example with "The Hall of Machines" (Jones, 1972). The variety of targets is, thus, not limited to visual representations, but can encompass both music/sound (Vickers & Alty, 2002) as well as narrative dimensions. The use of narrative extends the connections of aesthetic computing to the literary arts. There are numerous other architectural styles that may be used to represent the original program, but there are also many other possibilities such as the abstract model depicted in Figure 8.

The first step in realizing the model in Figure 8 is aggregating the control flow diagram into a three-block linear graph: initialization→ iteration→ stop, with this graph being shown as the left-most circle. The original control semantics of "next" is translated to "contains," so that the original initialization step of resetting variable *i* is a circle that contains a loop designated as shaded ring. The dashed arcs represent the interaction of touching with an input device such as the mouse. So when the ring is touched, the right-most circle appears to show what is inside of the iteration block. The small circle with the horizontal black bar is an icon representing "drawing a line." As a final example, Figure 9 shows a 3D representation of the dataflow in Figure 4. A fluid metaphor is used so that constants in Figure 4 are captures with valves that set flow rate and the output of each block in Figure 4 becomes a copper pipe exiting from a liquid-filled container.

Figure 8. Using a 2D container metaphor to represent the control flow

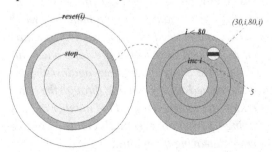

Figure 9. A 3D fluid metaphor representation of the dataflow (Figure 4) with two views

 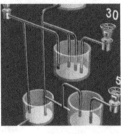

Step 6: Assessment

We have used the following criteria in the aesthetic computing class:

- **Syntax:** It is necessary for the visual and aural constructs to be complete: there needs to be an isomorphic mapping between source and target syntactical structures. This can sometimes be made difficult because even with mathematically rigorous source structures, there is often an abundance of external natural language text necessary for one to understand the formalism. So, in some sense, natural language undergirds the most formal of structures. Still, it is common to forget to map certain source elements, and this is problematic from a utilitarian perspective.

- **Metaphor:** The chosen analogy or metaphor needs to be consistently applied from source to target, with similar source components being respectively mapped to similar target structures. For example, mapping two different variables to two types of fruit in a target scenario is counterproductive since the fruit are far more different than the original two variables in both semantic and presentational context.

- **Scalability:** Does the target scale well with a commensurate increase in components in the source structure? The students must analyze the scalability of their products.

- **Semantics:** Models are executed using Java for processing. Students write their own code, and must convince the assessor that their code accurately relates to the syntactical components.

- **Communication:** The student must fully document the mapping so that the average reader may fully understand the isomorphism. This is the task of effective communication on the part of the creator. Each creator must make the target comprehensible. The task is to avoid mixed metaphors in the target.

- **Utility:** What are the actual and perceived utilities of the target structure? An actual utility estimates the usability of the target model with today's software and hardware technology, whereas perceived utility assumes an advanced technology where the 2D and 3D models are easy to construct, manipulate and interact-with. The actual utility is often fairly low in the case of 3D for reasons of that area still being nascent in terms of ease-of-use given our current state of technology. In the spirit of modeling research, students are encouraged to create designs, which may be usable in the future when interaction technology has improved to support their modeling technique. In some cases, a student might take a source component such as a function and map this to a temporal component--a sound or motion, so the user would have to experience and re-experience this component instead of being able to see the model *all at once*. This approach must be carefully weighed against usability requirements.

- **Aesthetics:** All aspects of aesthetics are covered, with a focus on effective and pleasing design. Naturally, there is a great deal of subjectivity, and yet other students can assist in providing a *juried evaluation*.

FUTURE TRENDS

The field of human-computer interaction has witnessed dramatic shifts away from a strictly textual interface to interfaces on a high-resolution color, graphics-intensive computer monitor. Furthermore, there has been increasing use of alternate modes of interaction including Web cameras, position and orientation tracking, voice input, and wearable computing peripherals. These shifts underscore the importance of developing interaction and visualization approaches that are customized and personalized, rather than adopting a "one size fits all" approach. Customization is a natural component of aesthetics since it drives *variety* within the interface. While some customization approaches exist in the form of *themes* and *application skinning*, we project that future computing platforms will go further and allow for other computing artifacts to take advantage of personalized interfaces. These artifacts include computer programs, data structures, models, and perhaps mathematical structures normally communicated via text. The field of aesthetic computing will assist in exploring these alternative interfaces. Customization tends to be naturally limited by the state of technology, which is why text was originally the only effective medium for interaction for human-computer interaction. Technological advance provides the seeds for customization (Pine 1993).

CONCLUSION

The goal of aesthetic computing is to apply elements of art and design to the field of computing.

We have defined the overall goals of aesthetic computing by creating three levels: cultural, implementation, and representation. The cultural level is achieved by social interaction--having artists and computer scientists work together in groups either in close collaboration or through Web-based interaction. The implementation level results from computing artifacts such as programs creating artistic behaviors. This level differs from the overall field of digital art in terms of *scale*: each small-scale programming element creates an artistic behavior. The representation level includes both structure and behavior so that computing artifacts are represented by artistic artifacts.

The goal of these representations is not to determine an optimal configuration or even to ensure that every mapping is completely isomorphic from source to target, but instead to leverage the creative and customizable aspects of art and design in learning about mathematically-based structures such as computer programs. We have had significant success in applying these goals within the aesthetic computing class itself (Fishwick, Davis, & Douglas, 2005). The procedure for applying the concept of multiple representations has played a significant and similar role in mathematics education (Kaput, 1985). Our work extends that tradition in two ways: leveraging design and art and applying the concept at the university level in computer science.

Aesthetic computing, in terms of the third level of understanding, is all about *representation as a field of study*. There is tension at meeting point between mathematics and computing on one hand and art and design on the other. Artists may feel inordinately constrained by the rules of representation, and computing professionals may be put off by the expanded role of "aesthetic." However, given that formation of media has in general followed the current state of technology, we are in a position to explore different ways of achieving representations, and to encourage students to design entirely new human-computer interfaces for formal structures.

ACKNOWLEDGMENT

The author would like to thank all students of past aesthetic computing classes as well as partial support from the National Science Foundation under grant EIA-0119532 entitled "An Investigation into Aesthetic Computing within the Digital Arts and Sciences Curricula" (with co-PIs Tim Davis and Jane Douglas). In particular, many thanks to Salam Daher and Hyunju Shim for their 3D representations, and to Yuna Park for the WARPhaus Web page design.

REFERENCES

Arnheim, R. (1966). *Toward a psychology of art: Collected essays*. University of California Press.

Arnheim, R. (1954). *Art and visual perception: A psychology of the creative eye*. University of California Press.

Battista, G. D., Eades, P., Tamassia, R., & Tollis, I. G. (1999). *Graph drawing: Algorithms for the visualization of graphs*. Prentice Hall.

Baumgarten, A. G. (1750). *Aesthetica*, Hildesheim, translated by G. Olms 1968.

Bolter, J. D., & Gromala, D. (2003). *Windows and mirrors: Interaction design, digital art, and the myth of transparency*. MIT Press.

Cox, D. (2006). Metaphoric mappings: The art of visualization. In P. Fishwick (Ed.), *Aesthetic computing* (pp. 89-114). MIT Press.

Dann, W. P., Cooper, S., & Pausch, R. (2006). *Learning to program in Alice*. Pearson Custom Publishing.

Diehl, S. (2001). *Software visualization*. Springer Verlag, May 2001, LLCS 2269.

Fishwick, P., Davis, T., & Douglas, J. (2005, July). An empirical study of aesthetic computing. *ACM Transactions on Modeling and Computer Simulation, 18*(3), 254-279.

Fishwick, P. (2006). *Aesthetic computing*. MIT Press.

Gardner, H. E. (1984). *Art, mind, and brain: A cognitive approach to creativity*. Basic Books.

Greenberg, I. (2006). *Foundation processing*. Friends of ED.

Jones, L (1972). *The Hall of Machines* In The Eye of the Lens, The MacMillan Company.

Kant, I. (1790). *The critique of judgment*. Oxford: Clarendon Press, translated by James Creed Meredith (1952).

Kaput, J. (1985). Representation and problem solving: Some methodological issues. In E. Silver (Ed.), *Teaching and learning problem solving: Multiple research perspectives* (pp. 381-398). Hillsdale.

Kelly, M. (1998). *Encyclopedia of Aesthetics (4 Volumes)*. Oxford University Press.

Lakoff, G., & Johnson, M. (2003). *Metaphors we live by* (2nd ed.). University of Chicago Press.

Lavie, T., & Tractinsky, N. (2004). Assessing dimensions of perceived visual aesthetics of Web sites. *International Journal of Human-Computer Studies, 60*(3), 269-298.

Lieberman, H. (1991). A three-dimensional representation of program execution. In E. P. Glinert (Ed.), *Visual programming environments: Applications and issues*. IEEE Press.

Najoork, M. (1996). Programming in three dimensions. *Journal of Visual Languages and Computing, 7*(2), 219-242.

Norman, D. A. (2004). *Emotional design: Why we love (or hate) everyday things*. Basic Books.

Pine, B. J. (1993). *Mass customization: A new frontier in business competition*. Harvard Business School Press.

Processing Reference Guide (2006). http://www.processing.org/reference/index.html

Prophet, J., & d'Inverno, M. (2006). Transdisciplinary collaboration in "cell." In P. Fishwick (Ed.), *Aesthetic computing* (pp. 185-196). MIT Press.

Purchase, H. C. (2002). Metrics for graph drawing aesthetics. *Journal of Visual Languages and Computing, 13*(5), 501-516.

Tractinsky, N. (1997). Aesthetics and apparent usability: Empirically assessing cultural and methodological issues. *1997 Proceedings of the Conference on Human Factors in Computing Systems, Association of Computing Machinery (ACM)* (pp. 115-122).

Tractinsky, N., Shoval-Katz, A., & Ikar, D. (2000). *What is beautiful is usable: Interacting with computers*, 13, pp. 127-145.

Vickers, P., & Alty, J. (2002). Using music to communicate computing information. *Interacting with Computers, 14*(5), 435-456.

Ware, C. (2004). *Information visualization: Perception for design* (2nd ed.). Morgan Kaufman.

Warphaus. (2006). *WARPhaus exhibition*. Retrieved from http://www.cise.ufl.edu/class/cap-4403sp06/Gallery/WARPhaus_exhibition/index.html

Chapter XXI
Documentation Methods for Visual Languages

Eduardo Costa
Uberlandia Federal University, Brazil

Alexandre Grings
Uberlandia Federal University, Brazil

Marcus Vinicius Santos
Ryerson University, Canada

ABSTRACT

Many people argue that Visual Programming languages are self-documenting. This article points out that there is no such thing as a self-documenting language. Besides this, many popular methods used to document programs written in other languages do not suit Visual Languages perfectly, and need some tailoring. Therefore, the authors propose a visual adaptation of the dataflow method of documentation. They also present versions of instantiated documentation and denotational semantics applied to visual languages. Finally, they present a Prolog based complete example of documentation.

INTRODUCTION

In this chapter, we analyze the use of visual programming languages (VPL) for the design and documentation of real world applications. We first characterize the life cycle of software from its initial requirements specification to its deployment and maintenance, and we analyze the role of VPL in the life cycle of software development. Then we show that in well-designed systems, there is a clear separation between requisite list, data flow, control design, and function description. This separation has its roots based upon the way a Von Newman computer operates, and a tradition of specifying formal systems that dates back to Aristotle. We compare the software development method with Von Newman's computer architecture, we discuss tools for specifying data flow, and we show that VPL facilitate the design and documentation of data flow. Finally, we propose new tools and approaches for the documentation of data flow for VPL.

BACKGROUND

The first programming language that one can call visual was designed by Ivan Sutherland in the sixties, and was called Sketchpad. Its concepts lead straight to the graphical user interface now manifest in Windows and the Apple Macintosh. Sketchpad treated the computer screen as a window on which the user could move around freely, unlike the command line interfaces that were popular at the time. It represented a variety of user modules as images or objects on the screen, which could be selected with a pointing device, and combined into more complex structures of shapes and behaviors. Smalltalk was the first visual language that achieved popularity. Although heavily influenced by Sketchpad, Smalltalk received strong support from Xerox, which explains its relative success when compared to Sketchpad.

Both Smalltalk and Sketchpad required more resources than one could afford at the time that these languages were created. Therefore, resourceful language designers started to popularize visual languages that required less machine power. Basically, they limited the visual aspects to the design and implementation of graphic user interfaces. They left out the complex Smalltalk browser and Sketchpad's sophisticated graphic constraint mechanism. The first simplified visual language to achieve commercial success was Delphi, a follow up of Turbo Pascal. To pay honor to priority, it is necessary to state that many LISP dialects presented sophisticated visual tools for source navigation, debugging, and designing graphic user interface. However, LISP never attained the popularity of Delphi.

Before going ahead with this discussion, it would be a good idea to clarify what is a visual language. A language can be called visual if human beings can understand its semantics from visual components, like layout, and syntactic constraints. This means that even a language based on text can be visual, if one can understand a program from layout and syntactic analysis only.

On the other hand, a language that requires the programmer to know the history and context of program execution to figure out what a snippet of code does is not a visual language. One could say that this definition rules out Delphi as a strict visual language, since Pascal is not a visual language, and Delphi is based on Pascal. However, Delphi can be considered visual in a broader sense; in fact, it can be taken as two languages, a visual language for GUI, and Pascal for the algorithmic part of the project.

Later on, we will see that a program has two organic components, a dataflow, and a controller. The dataflow specifies paths and operations for the data that will be processed, and the controller uses switches to redirect the data through the paths to devices that will perform the necessary operations. As one can infer, dataflow is well suited to visual design; in fact, when one talks about flows, one thinks of visual diagrams for plumbing, electric circuits, production control and planning, etc. Controllers, which turn on and off switches, redirecting the flow according to a temporal schedule are not visual at all; they are often likened to things as contingent plans, recipes, and to-do lists. Since programs must have these two organic components, one of them being of algorithmic nature, how can they be made visual? There are three ways of dealing with the problem, to wit:

1. Leaving the controller, or algorithmic part of the program, outside the scope of the visual paradigm. In general, languages that adopt this approach restrict the scope of the visual paradigm to the design of GUI (graphic user interface). Delphi is a well-known member of this group. Visual Eiffel also belongs to this group since it requires control written in Eiffel. However, Visual Eiffel has an interesting feature: It generates visual documentation for the algorithmic controllers.

2. Writing languages for applications that, by nature, are well suited to visual design since they do not have a controller of open nature. For instance, query languages for databases are a good example of systems that restrict themselves to visual applications, which is possible because they have a fixed, although complex, algorithm component. This explains the immense success of visual query languages, like SQL, that although based on text, satisfies our criteria for being visual. Another visual language that adopts this approach is LabVIEW. LabVIEW facilitates the creation of user interfaces, offering to the designer components that are similar to lab instruments, and a set of routines limited to tasks like data acquisition and control. A better language to illustrate this approach is PQL (pictorial query language) since it keeps user interaction compliant to the visual paradigm, as one can see from Ferri, Massari, and Rafanelli (1999). In PQL, one can make complex queries in geographical databases by manipulating pictorial objects representing geographic classes and objects.

3. Choosing a computational model with automatic control insertion. This is the only means of getting a general purpose visual language. The possibilities of automatic control insertions are many: Purely functional programming based on graphic reduction, logic programming, based on automated theorem proving (ATP), and constraint programming (CP). By the way, Sketchpad was based on a primitive form of constraint programming. The most popular language based on ATP is Visual Prolog, which we will discuss in some depth at the end of this chapter. All languages in this group require that the design of the dataflow component be such that it can be handled efficiently by the control insertion mechanism. For instance, Prolog requires that clauses are ordered according to execution priority. Clean and Haskell, that are purely functional languages, require that their clauses fit in a reduction graph. Constraint languages have similar requisites. Therefore, it is necessary to recognize that programming in a visual language of this group is not as easy as one would expect. In fact, the only group that produces languages really easy to work with and keep with the promises of visual languages is the second group.

THE SOFTWARE DEVELOPMENT LIFE CYCLE

Software development life cycle is a sequence of activities, which characterizes the development of a computer system. It includes five processes, to wit:

- **Specification:** Where one states the functionality and security concerns.
- **Development:** Refers the design and implementation of the system.
- **Correctness:** Construction of proofs that the system meets its specification.
- **Validation:** Where one verifies whether the system meets user needs.
- **Deployment and maintenance:** Concerns modifications to deal with changes in user needs, new technologies, hardware obsolescence, and applications to other fields of expertise.

The horizon of developers, no matter which language they use, often stop at the validation stage. They seldom leave suitable documentation for people who will be around during the last stage of the life cycle. However, a program, both conventional and visual, is likely to be used a long time after its creation. After all, the rationale of writing programs is to have an information processing tool that can be used again and again.

This is particularly true for programs dealing with Space Science Models, Weather Forecasting, Finance Engineering, Air Traffic Control, etc. Many programs survive by many years the languages, which their developers used to compile them. For instance, Astronomers still deploy the cleanest Fourier transform to filter observations of variable stars, although the compiler that Foster (1995) used is no longer available. Moreover, many mathematical programs are highly reusable, after small adaptations. For instance, Foster's software for time series analysis was intended for astronomical applications, but people are still using it in weather forecasting, portfolio design, risk evaluation, stock analysis, etc. Therefore, lack of documentation can cause serious economic hazards, since it hinders the evolution, deployment, and adaptation of software.

Let us take a look at the air traffic control situation. According to Perry (1997), the U.S. air traffic control system is organized around three types of facilities: airport towers, which give take-off and landing clearances; terminal radar approach control facilities (Tracon), which handle aircraft ascending and descending to and from airports; and en route centers, which handle aircraft flying between airports and use large computers that drive plan view displays (PVDs). Tracons use a computer system called automated radar terminal system (ARTS); most facilities still cling to old analogical data entry and display subsystems (DEDSs), which feature 1960s-designed displays. Few airports have switched to the newer full digital ARTS displays (FDADs). The FDAD, in use at some of the busiest Tracons, is an 80s microprocessor-based system, if we are to believe Perry (1995).

Air traffic control programs are relatively complex applications. Let us assume that it was written in a visual language whose compiler and IDE were obsolete. Let us also assume that one could not find people with hands on experience in developing the programs. In this case, the only documentation available would be the project

tree that would give access to packages, classes, and forms. The programmers who would try to maintain these visual applications would navigate blindly through the trees, trying to figure out the function of each node, and interface. This picture, and some imagination, will help us convince the reader that a text-based language, where the programs can be scrutinized with a text editor, would be better than a poorly designed visual documentation tool.

The authors have used the previous examples to argue for the need of well designed visual documentation and project managing tools. One could even dare to say that there is no need for arguing for documentation and good managerial methods. They are obviously necessary, and many software maturity models and quality control methods put strong emphasis on them (see Land & Waltz, 2005). Next, we further elaborate on the role of VPL in the software development life cycle, underlining their use in documentation and project management tools.

WHY VISUAL LANGUAGES MATTER

In 1990, Hughes wrote a very famous paper, whose title was *Why Functional Programming Matters?* In this section, the authors give their opinion on why visual programming matters. One obvious answer is that designers have a long tradition reporting to the ancient Greeks of designing things using diagrams, maps, drawings, drafts, and so on. From its inception, digital electronics relied heavily on circuit diagrams. Therefore, why programs should be different from other human endeavors? Visual languages provide the programmers with the tools they need to design software in a way that is more natural and resembles the methods used by electronic engineers to design circuits. Visual tools improve programmer productivity and allow an intuitive examination of the project by the customer, leading to a better specification of the main goals. On the other hand, one must remember that modern circuit design strongly relies on programming languages like VHDL and Verilog that are not visual. If one needs to design a really large circuit, one will end up using a textual programming language, like Verilog. Therefore, even if visual languages provide tools for coding through diagrams that may be useful for small projects, they must have another appeal, since they are used also in large projects, where pure diagrammatic programs are unfeasible.

The authors believe that visual languages are useful even in large projects where pure diagrammatic programming are not possible, because they provide documentation and road maps to navigate through the documentation, and through the implementation steps. If one holds this view, then the project tree is more important than the control components of the visual language. This said, one must decide what kind of diagram provides the best documentation for both the navigation tool and the implementation steps. Let us discuss this topic in the next section.

ON THE NATURE OF DOCUMENTATION

According to the Greek philosopher Aristotle (384-322 BC), an object (i.e., a "thing," abstract or not) has four possible explanations, or explanation factors (traditionally, the Greek term "*aitia,*" explanations, has been translated as *causes*). In modern terminology, the four explanations are:

1. **Material explanation:** "That out of which a thing comes to be, and which persists."
2. **Formal explanation:** "The account of what-it-is- to-be, and the parts of the account."
3. **Efficient explanation:** "The primary source of change."
4. **Final explanation:** "The end, that for the sake of which a thing is done."

In this section, we look at the technologies used in the documentation (i.e., explanation) of programs and position them in the context of Aristotle's theory. Such analysis is important because an explanation (for a given program) that includes all four causes completely captures the significance and reality of the program itself. Hence, it fully specifies the program.

We start our analysis by first looking at how developers design programs. Then we analyze the four causes (i.e., explanations for a program and discuss the technologies used in documenting each of these causes).

Controllers and Data Paths

The Von Newman computer is the architecture that most developers have in mind when they design programs. This computer has two sections: The controller and the data paths. Therefore, the most successful diagrams both for documentation and user feedback mirror these two sections. For instance, data flow diagrams is a documentation tool that mirrors the data paths of programs. They were invented by Constantine, based on data flow graph model of computation. Millet (1999) claims that, although 30 years old, DFDs are the most popular tool taught in design courses: 597 out of 647 schools (92%) indicated that they teach

Figure 1. Data flow path for the GCD

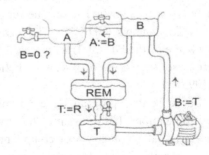

DFDs. Before taking a quick look at DFDs, let us examine what are data paths. We illustrate the concept of data paths by means of an example, namely, Euclid's Algorithm for computing the greatest common divisor (GCD) of two integers, which we explain next.

Euclid's Algorithm: Euclid introduced the method for computing the GCD in his manuscript Elements, Book VII. First, we will describe the method by means of the following example: to find the GCD of, say, 36 and 15, we divide 36 by 15 (the greater by the smaller), getting 2 with a remainder of 6. Then we divide 15 by 6 (the previous remainder) and we get 2 and a remainder of 3. Then we divide 6 by 3 (the previous remainder) and we get 2 with no remainder. The last non-zero remainder (3) is our GCD. Now let us present the algorithm:

Let A and B be positive integers, B smaller than A, and let R and T be auxiliary variables.

While B is not zero
- R becomes the remainder of A divided by B.
- T becomes R.
- A becomes B.
- B becomes T.

Figure 1 shows the data paths for the computation of the GCD, and Figure 2 shows the corresponding controller. In Figure 1, A, B, and T are memory storages, and R is the information process that calculates the remainder. For the computation to be performed correctly, the data must flow between these storages and the operation labeled REM (remainder). Arrows point the direction of flow. Overall, the data-flow diagram shows storages and operations that are required in the computation, how they are connected, and the switches to control the flow. The switches A:=B, T:=R, and B:=T must be closed in the correct sequence for the computation to be performed. Abelson and Sussman (1996) point out that this kind of diagram is not very different from a wiring

Figure 2. Controller

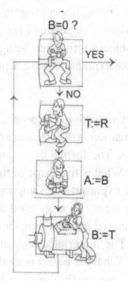

diagram for a machine that could be constructed from electronic components.

If you want to actually compute the GCD, you must provide for a device that closes the switches in the correct sequence. This device is called the controller (see Figure 2). One could use a diagram to describe the controller. One could even generate the controller automatically from constraints. For an automatically generated controller from constraints, see Carvalho (1999). The authors would like to point out that the first constraint language was, in fact, a visual language. In 1963, Ivan Sutherland presented his PhD thesis at the MIT, where he describes Sketchpad, A Man-Machine Graphical Communication System. As mentioned before, Sketchpad was a visual language, where the designer used a light pen to specify constraints that could determine geometrical figures.

The Four Explanations for a Program

Most visual documentation tools provide means for documenting data flow paths and controllers.

However, as seen previously, Aristotle concluded that an abstract object, like a program, has four explanations where explanations are necessary things for the object coming into being. Next are the four possible explanations for a program to come into being:

- **Formal explanation.** In a program, the formal explanation is the structure of the data flow paths. The formal cause answers the question: What is the shape of the object?
- **Material explanation.** Languages, hardware resources, libraries, and algorithms are the material explanations for a software product. The material cause answers the question: What the object is made of?
- **Efficient explanation,** also called *motor cause*. In software development, the controller provides the efficient cause. The efficient cause answers the questions: What drives the object? In what order the driver's operations are taking place?
- **Final explanation** is the function of the object. What is the use of this program?

We have said that most visual systems provide tools like DFD in the documentation of the formal cause. A few of them also have Petri nets and other tools for documenting the controller. There are also tools for documenting the final cause. In fact, annotated DFD documents—both the form and the function of a software product. Very few people document the material cause. This is a pity because one of the hardest maintenance problems is figuring out the workings of obsolete languages and algorithms. One could say that this is not a problem at all because there are manuals, even for dated compilers. The problem is that only a small part of the language is actually used in software development. A good material documentation must be concise, giving *instantiated documentation* for languages and algorithms. Let us explain the term *instantiated documentation*. The vendor of a compiler should cover all aspects

of the language. For instance, the vendor of Clean should discuss things like computer graphics, game programming, numerical analysis, generics, parser combinators, etc. It is unlikely that I will use all of these features. Thus, the vendor provides a general documentation and one must particularize it for his or her project. The material documentation must include also hardware specifics and instantiation of algorithms. Yes! Algorithms also become obsolete. For instance, since the appearance of B-trees, nobody uses quick sort any more. There are quite a few tools for documenting the material cause. The most popular ones are syntactic diagrams and denotational semantics.

Now we have a fairly complete overview of product documentation. However, product documentation is not enough. French engineer Eiffel is often used as a model for software development because he used to prepare careful designs of all his projects, finish them on time, and his products are so reliable that they are around a century after the inauguration. The Eiffel tower is an example.

"Few people know that Eiffel also made major contributions to aeronautical research. There was a long dispute about who made the first successful airplane flight. It seems, however, that aviation pioneer was the German-American engineer Gustav Albin Weißkopf (Whitehead, in English). On August 14, 1901 in Connecticut, Whitehead flew his Number 21 800m at 15m height, according to articles in the Bridgeport Herald, the New York Herald, and the Boston Transcript. Soon after that, the Wright brothers visited Whitehead to discuss the purchase of one of his engines and exchanged ideas and discoveries regarding flight. Whitehead also sold motors to Glenn Curtiss. However, it seems that Whitehead did not sell state of the art motors to his competitors, because when the Wrights flew two years later, they needed a catapult and strong head wind to take off. Even the replica of the Wright's plane was not able to

Figure 3. Whitehead's plane

fly in the commemoration of the 1903 flight. Of course, Whitehead's design flew spectacularly in the commemoration of the 1901 flight (Figure 3). Whitehead plane was pretty advanced when compared to the Wright's plane. Its use of powered wheels means that Whitehead did not have to use catapults or strong head winds like the Wright brothers. In fact, the plane started from a flat surface and landed in a nearby lake. Since the motor was not powerful enough, Whitehead was forced to leave the wheels behind at take off. Thus, the only solution was to land on water. During flight, he controlled roll by shifting his weight, and wing warping, much as on a glider. Pitch was controlled by a tail wing and yaw by differing the thrust of the two propellers.

From the previous discussion, you can figure out how primitive the controls used by Whitehead were. Of course, he would not be able to control a modern airbus shifting the weight of his body. The Wright brothers used exactly the same control methods pioneered by Whitehead. They also warped the wings of their airplanes! It was Eiffel who brought an engineer's discipline to aeronautics. He published accurate aeronautical data and discovered many well-known facts about fluid flow."

From the previous comments you can see that it was a well deserved tribute to Eiffel that Visual Eiffel, one of the most exciting visual programming languages, was named after him. Like software, airplanes also have form design. The plane architect makes careful drafts of the shape that his product will show, but it is not enough to design the airplane. One must also design and build the factory that will produce it. Boeing's assembly building at Everett, Washington, has a footprint that covers 98.3 acres. It was necessary to design paths to parts and subassemblies, which come to the plant from all over the globe. For instance, the largest parts are received at the Port of Everett, and then are loaded onto railcars that climb the steepest active gauge in the United States. For unloading, rail cars rolls into a yard containing 3 kilometers of track. Inside the factory, overhead bridge cranes cruise 27 meters above the floor on 50 kilometers of crane network, supported by the roof trusses of the factory building. As you can see, there is no question that airplane manufacturers need a good design in the layout of their factories. The question is whether software engineers also need to design their production lines. The answer is yes.

Even if you have a good design for your software product, a design that covers the four Aristotelic causes, you will not be able to maintain and assembly the final product if you do not have a good documentation of your *plant*. You need tools that will help you to find where your libraries are, which code produced this or that behavior, in which file you will find a given class, etc. Therefore, the development facility needs documentation even more than the product. Happily enough, most visual languages provide excellent facilities to browse code, libraries, etc. In the next sections, we examine a popular visual language, evaluating its tools for documenting the aspects of software creation depicted in Table 1.

VISUAL PROLOG

If you do not know anything about Prolog, it is wonderful because you will fully understand the necessity of instantiated language documentation.

Table 1. Aspects of software creation

Cause	Aspect of software creation
Material	Instantiation of language documentation.
Form	Tools for specifying data flow diagrams.
Plant form	Tools for navigating and browsing code, algorithms, libraries, and logic specifications. Tools for finding code that produces a given behavior.
Efficient	Tools like Petri Network to describe the behavior of the product. Tools for describing the control flux in the product. Usually one does not describe the control flux of the plant.
Final	Tools for describing the functional aspect of the product.

You are in the same situation of a programmer that will take a Visual Prolog project after the language becomes obsolete and try and figure out what the code means. This is likely to happen quite often because Visual Prolog is famed for its backwards incompatible releases. Thus, let us document a Visual Prolog project to implement Euclid's algorithm.

Description of the Project Components (DPC)

Before starting the documentation of the software, let us document the project components and the assembling steps of the foresaid components. This part of the documentation is equivalent to design an aeronautical plant, and to describe how it works. It covers Aristotle's Formal Cause and Motor Cause of the plant; for the time being, we are not talking about the product yet.

In a visual language, the resources used to develop and document a project is called integrated development environment (IDE). The first step of the documentation is the description of IDE components necessary to create the project.

1. Project settings (Figure 4). In the project settings, you will describe the storage location of your project, the basic tools, and libraries that you will use, the build options, the run options, and the workspace. Visual prolog,

for reasons that are hard to fathom, requires that libraries written in Visual Prolog itself be listed elsewhere. Most information required in the project settings is automatically provided by the IDE. For instance, the system fills out the build options for you. All you need to do is fill out the *general* folder, shown in Figure 4.

2. If you choose the option file/new from VIP IDE main menu, you will see a dialog box with quite a few item choices. Since we are using instantiated documentation, let us discuss only the ones necessary to design the

Figure 4. Project settings dialog

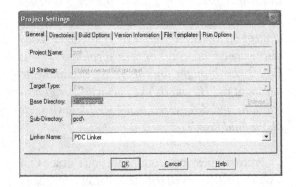

GCD project. We are going to use the create menu item to create an input output form and a class. Do not worry, we will discuss what a class is later on. As you can see in Figure 5, the form creation has a name, a package, and a public/private radio button choice.

When you choose the class option in the create project item, you will get the dialog shown in Figure 6. You must give the class name, the package name, say whether it is public or private, and specify whether you want it to create objects or not. Do not worry about names like package, class, objects, etc. Everything necessary to create a GCD program will be explained.

3. The form editor (Figure 7) is a tool that allows you to design a form or a window. A form is a window with buttons and edit-fields, and is used primarily for input/output. To design a form, all you need to do is to

Figure 5. Create project item dialog

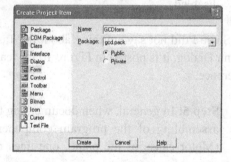

Figure 6. Create project item dialog after the class option

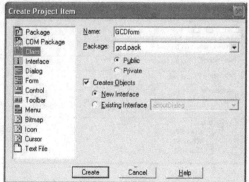

Figure 7. Form editor

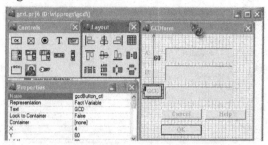

choose and drag components from a pool. For instance, if you need a button, choose it from the component pool whose title is controls and drag it to your form.

4. The form properties are a visual tool that you may need to prepare a custom style for your form. In this project, we will not worry about custom style. Therefore, if you come across a custom form, just close it by pressing OK.

5. The project tree (Figure 8) describes how the components of your project are linked together. It is a succinct documentation of the form of your project and also of your product. The project tree is a kind of map of the plant where you will build your software. You will use it to navigate through the places where one builds your software. The project tree appears on the left hand side of a window, whose right hand side is occupied by the program tree.

The program tree specifies the components of your program and how they are linked together. You use the program tree to browse programs and classes that are a kind of module, with storages and methods to process information. Programs appear both at the project tree, and at the program tree. They are similar to airplanes that appear both at the map of the construction plant and at the architect design.

When describing the steps for building a program, we are not supposed to describe these tools every time. Instead, we will say only what to do with them, like the controller described before,

Figure 8. Project Tree

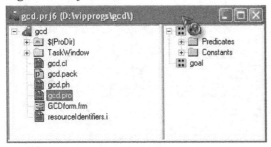

Figure 9. GCDform

that describes what to do with the components of the data flow.

Building the GCD Program

- **Step 1:** Project/new project opens project settings dialog.
  - **Project Name:** GCD
  - **UI Strategy:** Object-Oriented GUI
  - **Target Type:** Exe
  - **Base Directory:** D:\Vipprogs\
  - **Sub-Directory:** gcd\
  - **Liker Name:** PDC Linker

That is all that we are going to say about filling the project settings. Go to the appropriate dialog (Figure 4), and fill it as required.

- **Step 2:** On the project tree (Figure 8) select the root node, which is GCD. A package is a set of components that meets some criteria. You are going to insert a form into the GCD package. Choose the option project/new. fill the create project item dialog (Figure 5) as shown next:
  - Select Form
  - Name: gcdForm
  - Package: gcd.pack
  - Public

Press the create button. Drag and resize components to create the form of Figure 9:

- **Step 3:** Accept the default form properties.
- **Step 4:** In the project tree, open the task window folder. Click twice in the TaskMenu. mnu branch to open the TaskMenu Dialog. Open the file menu option of the menu tree and select &New/tF7. Uncheck the option disabled.

Since I did not say anything about the Task-Menu Dialog, it is posted in Figure 10 for ready reference.

- **Step 5:** In general, when documenting the assembling of the program components (Motor cause of the plant), one does not

Figure 10. TaskMenu dialog

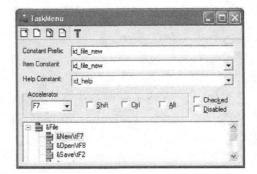

Figure 11. Entering the code expert

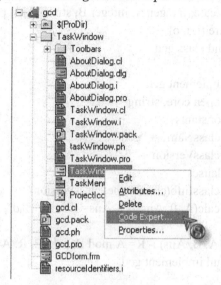

Figure 12. Dialog and window expert

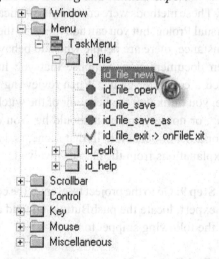

describe the project tree since it has already been described in the form cause. However, we will repeat it here, since this is a tutorial about documentation. In the project tree, right click the branch TaskWindow. On the floating menu, choose the option code expert, as shown in Figure 11.

- **Step 6:** Another tool that we have not seen is the dialog and window expert. Since this is an informal documentation, we are mix-

ing somewhat the form cause and the motor cause; when working with the real thing, this should not happen. Anyway, dialog and window expert are shown in Figure 12.

Open the necessary branches of the tree and double click the *id_file_new*. Modify the onFile-New prototype thus:

```
predicates
  onFileNew : window::menuItemListener.
clauses
  onFileNew(Parent, _MenuTag) :-
    F= gcdForm::new(Parent),
    F:show().
```

Let us say a few words about this snippet. You certainly have heard about object-oriented programming. In this paradigm, there are classes of objects. Let us compare computer classes with Linean biological classification. According to Linée, there are species that define classes of animals. For instance, the class *Canis Familiaris* defines the class of dogs. In our program, gcdform defines the class of all forms that calculate the GCD. When you call

Gcdform::new(Parent)

you will create an instance of this class that inherit a lot of properties of its parent window. In the example, you will store the instance into a variable F. Finally, you send a message to F, such that it shows the window. This kind of message activates methods inside the Motor Cause class. The class also has variables determining its shape. For instance, the gcdform has variables specifying its size.

You can already run the program. If you compile and run it, you will get the result shown in Figure 13. You certainly noticed that I am mixing the project, and the product documentation. However, the mixing is not complete. You can say that

Figure 13. Program execution

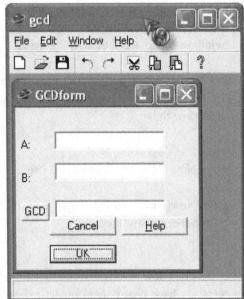

the two documentations are kept separate, with some overlapping for the sake of clarity.

- **Step 7:** Class GCD. To create a new class, choose the option File/New from the IDE main menu, and fill the class attributes.
  - Name: gcdclass
  - Package: gcd.pack
  - Public
  - Uncheck Create Objects
- **Step 8:** Define the new class. The GCD class has two parts, an interface, that shows how to use it inside a greater project, and an implementation module. Create the GCD class as described in Item 2 of description of the project components (DPC). Use the editor to enter the Class interface and the Class implementation. Do not worry about the code for the time being. We are going to discuss it later on.

```
class gcd
  open core
predicates
```

```
  classInfo : core::classInfo.
    calc:(integer A, integer B, string Ans) procedure (i, i, o).
  end class gcd

implement gcd
  open core, string
constants
  className = "gcd".
  classVersion = "".
clauses
  classInfo(className, classVersion).
  calc(A, 0, Ans) :- !, Ans= format("%d", A).

calc(A, B, Ans) :- R= A mod B, calc(B, R, Ans).
  end implement gcd
```

Even without understanding the code, you have noticed that the class has methods for describing itself. These methods were created automatically by Visual Prolog, but you can add things to them. For instance, there are people who add behavior driven documentation. Suppose that you have created a computer game. When reviewing the game, you think that the behavior of the witch is wrong, or not as good as it should be. You can ask for a list of behaviors in that scene, and ask for explanations from the classes involved.

- **Step 9:** Go to the project tree, enter the code expert, locate the pushButton_ctl, and add the following snippet to it:

```
onPushButton(_Source) = button::defaultAction() :-
    SA= edit_ctl:getText(),
    SB= edit1_ctl:getText(),
    A= toterm(SA),
    B= toterm(SB),
    gcd::calc(A, B, Ans),
    edit2_ctl:setText(Ans).
```

The entity **edit_ctl** is an object from one of the classes that Visual Prolog creates automatically.

To understand what an object is, let us go back to Linné. *Canis Famili*aris is a class in Baron Linné's classification. Your little puppy is an instance (or object) of that class. Visual Prolog editor class can create as many edit fields as necessary; in fact, it can create as many types of editors you may need and quite a few that you do not even dream of using. The entities edit1_ctl, and edit2_ctl are edit field objects too. The edit fields objects have methods like getText that extract typed in texts and setText that insert results into the field.

DATA FLOW DIAGRAMS

Figure 1 shows the data flow path for the GCD algorithm. In fact, Figure 1 shows a visual documentation tool called DFD or data flow diagrams. That data flow path, drawn by Priscila Melo, our artist, is somewhat fancy, but in essence, is a true DFD.

As you can see in Figure 1, the DFD has storages and processes. Each storage and process has input and outputs. For instance, process REM has two inputs (connected with A and B) and one output into storage T.

In most languages, transforming DFDs into code can be a difficult endeavor. DFD specification has a declarative nature, and the implementation is purely procedural. Lazarev (1989) demonstrated a method to map DFDs directly into code using Prolog. Prolog's declarative nature is ideal for the analysis phase, while Prolog's procedural interpretation is convenient for adding control to the DFD. Lazarev uses four major steps to accomplish the mapping. Let us tailor his method to better suit Visual Prolog.+

a. Each DFD process (transformation) generates a Prolog predicate with the same name.

Input and output flows are represented by typed variables, plus a mode list. The mode list specifies whether the variable is input or output. Here is the representation of the GCD predicate:

- *calc:(integer A, integer B, string Ans) procedure (i, i, o).*

b. A condition splits the flows, creating one Horn clause for each mutually exclusive case of the DFD OR-correlation. In the GCD algorithm, one has:

- *calc(A, 0, Ans) :- !, Ans= format("%d", A).*
- *(A, B, Ans) :- T= A mod B, calc(B, T, Ans)*

The predicate T= A mod B represents the REM process shown in Figure 1. It has two inputs, and one output. The inputs are A and B, and the output is R. The predicate

- *Ans= format("%d",A)*

has an input A, and one output Ans. The input is an integer, and the output is a string.

Since we assume the reader of the documentation is a novice in Visual Prolog, let us then explain what a horn clause is. Consider the rule below:

- *calc(A, B, Ans) :- T= A mod B, calc(B, T, Ans).*

It says: The GCD of A and B is Ans, if T= A mod B, and the GCD of B and T is Ans. Let us consider another example.

- *grandfather(Gf, Gc) :- father(Gf, F), father(F, Gc).*

This new clause can be read thus: Gf is the grandfather of Gc if Gf is the father of F, and F is the father of Gc. Let us see whether this clause is correct. Let us assume that Gf= 'Zeus,' and Gc= 'Esculapius.' Then, grandfather ('Zeus,' 'Esculapius') is true if there is an F such that father ('Zeus,' F) is true, and father (F, 'Esculapius') is true. This predicate can be satisfied if F= 'Apollo.' Then, one can have a new reading of the predicate: 'Zeus' is the grandfather of 'Esculapius' if 'Zeus' is the father of 'Apollo,' and 'Apollo' is the father of 'Esculapius.'

---

c. Mark all groups that form mutually exclusive sets.

d. Horn clauses are constructed from the predicates obtained in the steps a, b, and c above. Prolog programmers are able to write code using exclusively horn clauses. You can infer that this is possible because horn clauses match DFDs so well. A Visual Prolog program has two sections: (1) The predicate declaration, which is equivalent to a DFD diagram, and shows what the inputs and outputs are so that one can know how to connect the GCD program into another DFD, (2) and a set of horn clauses, that provides the control of the algorithm. If you take a look at the right hand side of the project tree below, you will see a visual tool that is equivalent to a DFD of the GCD class. It is not as fancy as Priscila's, but has the advantage of being succinct.

If you right click the *calc/3* branch of the tree (Figure 14), VIP IDE will give you two options. The first option is the predicate declaration that provides the input/output structure of *calc*. The second one is the set of horn clauses that the system will use as controller.

When a process in a DFD is exploded into several subprocesses, the head of the prolog horn clause represents the (upper-level) process, and the predicates in the tail represent DFD subprocesses.

By the way, a horn clause has the shape:

H :- T1, T2, T3...

where H is the head, and T1,T2,T3...is the tail. In the grandfather example,

grandfather(Gf, Gc)

is the head, and

father(Gf, F), father(F, Gc)

is the tail. Each component of the tail is called a subgoal, and the head is called the proof goal.

The rules for constructing horn clauses are the following:

*   d.1. Each group marked in (c) can provide, at most, one subgoal in a clause.
*   d.2. Each input of each subgoal must be matched with some input of the goal or with an output of some previous subgoal (a balanced input).
*   d.3. Each output of each subgoal must be matched with some output of the goal or with an input of some later subgoal (a balanced output).
*   d.4. If (d.2) or (d.3) fails, then unmatched inputs (outputs) of a subgoal are replaced by a nil atom. At least one input and one output of each subgoal must be non-nil.
*   d.5. Unmatched arguments of the goal (inputs and outputs) are replaced by the atom nil.

Figure 14. Program tree (calc/3 branch)

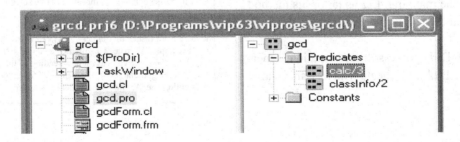

450

Let us try to apply this mapping of DFD into Prolog. The data flow diagram of the GCD algorithm has only three transforms (processes): the global transform, defining the whole algorithm, the outFormat transform, that converts integer to a formatted string, and the remainder (rem) bubble. The rest of the flows takes place between data storages. Also, the flow defines a recursive structure with a stop condition tied to the value of B. Lazarev's mapping algorithm does not cope with these situations. Nonetheless, the mapping for the GCD dataflow can be quite straightforward. Assuming that flows between data storages are simply assignments, and making a little effort to divise a circular call structure in the DFD we will be able to map it into horn clauses.

Figure 15 shows the DFD Level 1.

Step *a* for the GCD algorithm must be performed in a top-down way. Level 1 for our DFD yields the following clause:

Figure 15. DFD Level 1

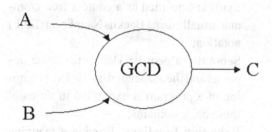

Figure 16. DFD Level 2

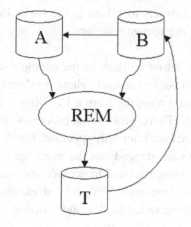

gcd(A,B, C).

Figure 16 shows the DFD Level 2.

The two transforms in level 2 are the *rem* operation, which generates the predicate and the outFormat operation, which generates the output.

rem:(integer A, integer B, integer T) procedure (i,i,o).

outFormat:(integer R, string S) procedure (i, o).

In step *b*, the test *B=0* splits the level 1 predicate in two horn clauses:

gcd(A,0,Ans)
gcd(A,B, Ans)

In step *d*, Lazarev explains that one must know the correct sequence of flux activation in order to get the code. In our example, the sequence in the body of the clause is given by the control diagram (Figure 2). As explained, fluxes between storages are represented as assignments. In the end, step *d* generates:

predicates
    gcd:(integer A, integer B, integer Answer) procedure (i, i, o).
    rem:(integer X, integer Y, integer R) procedure (i, i, o).
outFormat:(integer N, string Ans) procedure (i, o).
clauses
    gcd(A,0, A).
    gcd(A,B, C):- rem(A,B, T),
        A1 = B,
        B1 = T,
        gcd(A1,B1, C).

rem(X,Y, R):- R= X mod Y.
outFormat(N, Ans) :- Ans= string:: format("%d", N).

The processes *rem* and *outFormat* are not described in the DFD diagrams; therefore, their implementation depends on the developer's knowledge of the semantics of Visual Prolog.

For this and other reasons, the description of the semantic of the implementation language is so important. In the next section, you will learn how to describe the semantics of a computer language. One last thing: It is obvious that this program could be represented in a simpler manner, *viz.*:

calc(A, 0, Ans) :- !, Ans= format("%d", A).
calc(A, B, Ans) :- R= A mod B, calc(B, R, Ans).

You may be happy to know that there are people who study this kind of simplification, which is called partial evaluation. However, this theme is not in the scope of this chapter.

DENOTATIONAL SEMANTICS

Earlier in this chapter, when we discussed the four causes for a program, we mentioned that to provide a complete documentation of a computer system, we should include documentation of the programming language used to develop the system. In this section we analyze one semantic framework commonly used for documenting (specifying) programming languages, *viz.* the denotational semantics framework. We also show, by means of examples, that this work naturally captures the idea of instantiated documentation, a topic discussed earlier in this chapter.

In general, approaches to formally document the semantics of a programming language fall into one of the following three classes: operational, axiomatic, or denotational. In the operational approach, a program is interpreted as sequences of computational steps. These sequences are the meaning of the program. In the axiomatic approach, the semantics of a program is obtained by describing properties of statements in the program and how they affect the execution of

the program. In the denotational approach, (Stoy, 1981), the denotation (meaning) of a computer program is a function that maps the input of the program into its output.

Denotational semantics has some features, which make it especially convenient for providing user-friendly documentation for a programming language: it is not so low level as operational semantics, and not so high level as axiomatic semantics. The latter is more appropriate for analyzing particular properties of given statements in the language. The former provides lower level details which are useful for the implementor of the interpreter or compiler of the language. Denotational approaches on the other hand, provide the necessary level of abstraction for the user to quickly understand specific portions of the language, thus facilitating fast instantiation of documentation. The example shown in this section should suffice to drive this point home.

Denotational semantics framework for a language consists of three components:

- **Syntax:** Specified as a context free grammar, usually using Backus Naur Form (BNF) notation;
- **Semantic algebras:** Define the basic domains and the associated operations; meaning of a program is expressed in terms of these basic domains;
- **Valuation functions:** Provide a mapping from abstract syntax trees of language constructs to values in the basic domains of the semantic algebra.

Now let us go back to the example studied in the end of last section, where we showed how to obtain a mapping from a DFD into a Prolog program. There we saw that processes rem and outFormat were not fully specified. Process rem, for instance, depends on the mod function. To specify rem, we need to provide the meaning, formally, form mod. Next, we provide the denotational semantics for the mod function.

Following the BNF notation to write grammars, below, nonterminal symbols of a grammar are delimited by < >s; the other symbols are terminals, expect the meta-symbols '::=' and '|'. The latter denotes choice; the former means "consists of". For example: the rule <a> ::= <b> | <c> means: "<a> consists of <b> or <c>". Denotational Semantics for mod:

Syntax:
Let *Expressions* denote the set of all sentences one can derive from rule (1) below; and *Numbers* the set of all sentences one can derive from rule (2)
<remainder> is an element of *Expressions*
<number> is an element of *Numbers*
Grammar rules:
<remainder> ::= <number> mod <number > (1)
<number> ::= <digit> | <number> <digit> (2)
<digit> ::= 0 | 1 |2 | ...| 9 (3)

Semantic Algebras:
Domain: Natural numbers, *Nat*
Operations:
0, 1, 2,,...: Nat
+, -, *, \: Nat x Nat -> Nat
where +, -, * and \ denote addition, subtraction, multiplication and integer division, respectively.

Valuation functions:
E: a function from *Expressions* to *Nat*
E[<number$_1$>mod<number$_2$>] =
N[<number$_1$>]-N[<number$_2$>]*(N[<number$_1$>]\ N[<number$_2$>])
N: a function from *Numbers* to *Nat*
N[<number><digit>]=N[<number>]*10+N[<digit>]
N[0] = 0   N[1] = 1 .... N[9] = 9

An example is now in order. Based on the semantic description above, let us obtain the semantics for the following expression: *41 mod 3*

E[41 mod 3] = N[41]-N[3]*(N[41]\N[3])
= (N[4]*10+N[1])-N[3]*((N[4]*10+N[1])\N[3])
= (4*10+1)-3*((4*10+1)\3) = 41-3*(41\3)
= 41-3*13 = 41-39
E[41 mod 3] = 2
Therefore, the meaning of *41 mod 3* is 2.

REFERENCES

Abelson, H., & Sussman, G. J. (1996). *Structure and interpretation of computer programs* (Chapter 5). Cambridge, MA: The MIT Press.

Aristotle. (1996). *Metaphysics*. Loeb Classical Library. Original and translation by Hugh Tredennick. Harvard University Press. Reprinted 1996.

Carvalho, C. L., Costa Pereira, A. E., & da Silva Julia, R. M. (1999). *Data-flow synthesis for logic programs. System Analysis Modeling Simulation, 36*(3), 349-366.

Ferri, F., Massari, F., & Rafanelli, M. (1999). *A pictorial query language for geographic features in an object-oriented environment. Journal of Visual Languages and Computing, 10*(6), 641-671.

Foster, G. (1995, April). *The cleanest Fourier spectrum. Astronomical Journal, 109*(4), 1889-1902.

Hughes, J. (1989). *Why functional programming matters. The Computer Journal, 32*(2), 98-107.

Land, S. K., & J. Waltz, J. W. (2005). *Practical support for CMMI-SW software project documentation*. Wiley-IEEE Computer Society.

Lazarev, G. L. (1989). *Executable specifications with prolog. Dr. Dobb's Journal, 14*(10), 61-68.

Millet, I. (1999). *A proposal to simplify data flow diagrams. IBM Systems Journal, 38*(1), Retrieved March 2, 2006, from http://www.research.ibm.com/journal/sj/381/millet.html

O'Dwyer, M. W. J. (1998). The "Who flew first" debate. *Flight Journal*. October, 4-10.

Perry, T. S. (1997, August). In search of the future of air traffic control. *IEEE Spectrum, 34*(8) 18-35.

Scott, D. S. (1997) Logic and programming languages. *Communications of the ACM, 20*(9), 634-641.

Stoy, J. E. (1981) *Denotational Semantics: The Scott-Strachey approach to programming language theory.* Cambridge MA: MIT Press

Sutherland, I. E., Sketchpad: A Man Machine Graphical Communication System, dissertation submitted on January 1963 by the author for the degree of Doctor of Philosophy to the Massachussetts Institute of Technology.

Chapter XXII
Questioning Usability

Marco Padula
ITC-CNR Unità Staccata di Milano, Italy

Amanda Reggiori
FSLLS Università Cattolica del Sacro Cuore sedi di Brescia, Italy

ABSTRACT

This chapter is intended to question what usability is, or should be, in the field of computer science. We focus the design of information systems meant as systems enabling large virtual communities to access information and communications; systems aimed to support the working activities of a restricted team, but also to offer services accessible and usable in the perspective of global digital inclusion. We shall not propose a specific viewpoint to usability, but a focus to many concepts, aspects, potentialities, which have to be nowadays considered to detail the idea of usability, and design suited systems. Systems must be used by a community of users in their complex working activity to process material or information; to modify rough material but also the working environment and methods. This requires us to consider them as tools in a social context of use, which has expectations from the technological progress.

INTRODUCTION

The community of users, target for a system's release, the environment where they operate, and their expectations and requirements are usually simplified in the system design phase; the result is a product whose actual target is the community of those people, which are capable of adopting it notwithstanding the drawbacks they meet, and the constraints due to the aspects and functionalities, which were disregarded in the design phase even if they were already available or potential, and

which could have been fruitfully explored to give rise to novelties.

The relevance of the technological systems and their ability to fit the historical and socio-cultural context emerges from the social determinism; according to this approach, technological innovation can be perceived and exploited only if its motivations and roots spring from the cultural and social habits, conventions, and needs of the target community.

A technological product brings real effective innovation if it is the result of a process open to and influenced by the candidate context of use;

in fact, its use cannot be foreseen on the base of pre-defined exploitation plans or schema, but it depends on the socio-cultural context where it will be received (Preston, 2001).

As a consequence, technical design is conceived as a social process, which determines the technical specifications; namely it is the result of a social process for making technical definitions and choices according to criteria specific for each case and context of use. In real life, each attitude and meaning is directed toward technical objects to influence their development. Different social communities develop and adopt different methods to interpret and use the objects; this modifies the objects' nature. That is why social determinism believes that technology cannot follow a predetermined development path; the different ways adopted for artefact interpretation bring toward development paths, which differ for the problem faced and the solutions reached.

This social process concerns the definition of the needs and problems, of the ways to face them and, therefore, the search of possible solutions (Feenberg, 1999).

An information system is a complex of elements, which can be supported by an ICT (Information and Communication Technology) infrastructure, which constitutes the technological system composed of telecommunication devices, computers, which are connected to their peripherals and among them, and which are used for acquisition, storing, processing, transfer, control, visualization, exchange, transmission, and receiving of data. A technological infrastructure is only one of the possible results of the closure of a negotiation process. It cannot be shared from the target context of use, which sprang the evolutive dynamism, which produced it and will determine its life cycle.

Continuous and careful observation of the context of use allows us to focus and define the problems and the possible solutions, which must be precisely specified with no ambiguity and suggestively so they could be easily communicated and processed to reach effective results. Only a part of such solutions will require the installation of a technological tool (e.g., a computing system, a software application). In this case, a sub-model of the solution will be described so to be automatically executed (i.e., implemented on a computer).

The availability of synthetic and expressive models facilitate the job of the teams, which coordinate the negotiation process (i.e., lead the development of the information system). These teams need suited working methods, tools of thought, ways of reasoning, ways for documenting the work done, and to improve the interactivity among all the actors involved.

These teams are responsible for the assessment of the feasibility and the effectiveness of the solutions conceived and possibly implemented, of their usability in the context of use, and of the possibility to assimilate them. Assimilation means that the proposed solutions are accepted and they are fitted to the conventions and methods until now adopted. Furthermore, it requires that the users and all the people involved are suitably educated.

Sometimes the solutions will be actualized into technological systems to support information management, communication, or knowledge management services; other times they will be reached either updating or modifying the working procedures or supplying educational programs. For the design choices and the proposed solutions are fully assimilated, the negotiation process will possibly require lifelong updating and improvement. In this case, a solution, previously oriented toward a technological tool, may be later oriented toward education programs or modifications of the working methods or organization (Padula & Reggiori, 2006).

BACKGROUND

What characterizes a technological tool is its relationship with the social environment: what it represents for the target user groups determines what it will become (Feenberg, 1999).

This subjective interpretation of a technological object is made possible by the creative flexibility of the technology itself. As a technological object, a device could be used with aims, which were not foreseen during design. Today nobody would describe the main functionalities of a computer without outlining those concerning the communication medium even if, only twenty years ago, they were considered of minor relevance by many computer scientists.

The constructivism identifies the codes of the technology, which define the object with technical terms conforming to its social meaning. These codes, which could be consolidated into standards, are not autonomous from the context where they are formulated; on the contrary, they result from social negotiation whose tracks disappear when the technological objects are accepted in the culture and the habits of every day life. Technological innovation springs from a decoding process of the reality, which was already coded by a community of people according to their social and cultural criteria. The decoding process is then followed by a new coding process, which is guided by technological criteria.

A definition of usability, which in some respects takes into account social aspects, considers it as "the ease of use and acceptability of a system for a particular class of users carrying out specific tasks in a specific environment. Ease of use affects the users' performance and their satisfaction, while acceptability affects whether the product is used" (Holzinger, 2005).

Usability has to be considered before tools design and it is generally accepted that five characteristics have to be considered. Depending on the different situations, some of them are considered more important than others:

- Learnability, to enable the user rapid assimilation of the system;
- Efficiency, to increase the productivity in the working activity;
- Memorability, so that usability do not decrease after a period of inactivity of the user;
- Low error rate, and possibility to control and correct them;
- Satisfaction, as the system must be pleasant to use.

To generalize, we assume that a technological and a methodological progress, as soon as they are known, shift the users' expectations with respect to the desired support to their working activity. The tools used since then become to be considered old and limited. We do not mean that a single system have to necessarily include all the available functionalities and lean toward all the potentialities but we believe that the five usability's characteristics should be extended to suggest that a system be designed to foreseen its own immersion in a working context which possibly offers or give access to them. And the related standards, which consolidate the agreed characteristics should give the tools to verify that.

Usability is a topic which is today widely discussed in the field of human computer interaction as it is intended as an aspect largely dependent on the user interface.

"In computer science and human-computer interaction, the user interface (of a computer program) refers to the graphical, textual, and auditory information the program presents to the user, and the control sequences (such as keystrokes with the computer keyboard, movements of the computer mouse, and selections with the touch-screen) the user employs to control the program" (Wikipedia, 2006).

Interface design has been dominated by computer experts and psychologists. Computer technologists have conceived and produced advanced devices; psychologists have proposed new interaction metaphors and programmers have implemented them.

This has brought to a spread range of interfaces focusing on the way data could be entered into or received from a system—graphical user interfaces, Web-based user interfaces, command-line interfaces, tactile interfaces, touch interfaces, batch interfaces, crossing-based interfaces, gesture interfaces, noncommand user interfaces, reflexive user interfaces, tangible user interfaces, telephone user interfaces, text user interfaces, and zooming user interfaces.

As a consequence of such a technological view, a structured set of standards for usability has been released by ISO (International Organization for Standardization) in the document ISO 9241 (ISO, 1992; Travis, 2006).

The document titled "Ergonomic requirements for office work with visual display terminals (VDTs): Guidance on Usability" makes the standard seem out of date and reveals the limit of the view, which disregards many aspects that are nowadays recognized as fundamental for usability.

The document includes topics such as task requirements, visual displays, keyboards and non-keyboard input devices, workstation layout and postures, work environment, dialogues, information presentation, user guidance, menu, command, and direct manipulation dialogues. These topics do not exhaustively cover the aspects relevant for a tool to perform or support an activity. Anyway, we should consider that the document ISO 9241-11 gives a quite generic but open definition of usability as "The extent to which a product can be used by specified users to achieve specified goals with effectiveness, efficiency, and satisfaction in a specified context of use."

The term specified in the ISO definition of usability leaves the freedom to address to the generalization, internationalization, localization, and translation approach to tools development.

The globalization is (Cadieux & Esselink, 2002) the process to develop, adapt to different languages, cultures, and conventions, and to realize a product with the aim to satisfy the requirements and needs of different target communities.

The internationalization of a product (Esselink, 2000) is the approach to its development, which requires that the product designed in such a general version to allow it to adapt to very different realities with no need to re-design it. Software internationalization requires separating the source code from the texts and the icons, which have to be translated, and from the layouts, which have to be re-structured.

Localization (Esselink, 2000) is the process of adapting a product (which has possibly been internationalized) to the language, conventions, and culture of a specific community of target users.

These are relevant topics (personalization and user profiling could be added) related to market globalization, multiculture, multidisciplinarity, eterogeneity of the working groups, which are often decentralized both in the cyberspace, and in the physical space, unfortunately they are not regulated by any standard.

USABILITY IN INTERACTIVE ARTEFACTS MAKING

A main aspect to be deepened is the reply to questions like usability of what, to manipulate what, with what aim, during what activity, in which way. In other terms, if the material (i.e., the object of manipulation) is not clear, neither can be the tools for its manipulation or management. That is why we have to pay attention to the document as track of a human activity.

People with different skills use different vocabularies, rigorously defined in some cases but often subject to different interpretations. They use a variety of terms such as information, data, resource, file, written material, text, image, paper, article, work, book, journal, sheet, page, etc., which are not synonymous, but have a strict relation with the concept of document, which remains intuitive with no need to be clarified. But the electronic form of documents is revolutionizing its concept.

In the highly networked contexts of today's working realities, a document is produced, processed, managed, and used as a medium for communication in social relations. A community of users (which could be partially related face to face and partially virtual, therefore contacted through the Net) is responsible for the evolution of the document, which now resembles a channel of communication and becomes the concrete realization of a semantic emergence. Its singularity disappears, its outline is not precise, it has a transitory appearance, what matters in a document is the management in time (and time in virtual space is measured in acts of communication) of its successive versions (Musella & Padula, 1997; Padula & Reggiori, 1999;).

The polycephalus author Roger T. Pédauque (Pédauque, 2003) has deeply faced, and therefore reformulated, the concept of document immerged into a semiotic context where computational (i.e., computers or computer networks) and humans (i.e., people or social networks) interact for communication. He has proposed a three faceted definition:

- As form (i.e., object of communication structured according to agreed rules) with an identified boundary: "an electronic document is a data set organized in a stable structure associated with formatting rules to allow it to be read both by its designer and its readers";
- As sign, primarily perceived as meaningful and intentional, tightly connected to the subject in its context, which constructs or reconstructs it and gives it meaning, witness of local knowledge, and therefore, culture and experience: "An electronic document is a text whose elements can potentially be analyzed by a knowledge system in view of its exploitation by a competent reader";

- As medium, finally raises the question of the documents status in social relations as a trace of an actual communication: "An electronic document is a trace of social relations reconstructed by computer systems."

For a system to support human understanding and signification, a reference to consolidated knowledge has to be managed called ontologies.

The arrival of the new generation of markup languages allows the dissociation among the appearance, syntactics, and semantics of the document to manage them autonomously. On the other side, new methods for semantics and knowledge management in the Web have stressed the efforts for indexing them to emphasize the concepts they refer and to dissociate the consolidated knowledge from the representation and use of documents in the working contexts of a specific application domain, so to be able to refer, process, and update it autonomously and to reuse it by computer applications.

This has led to the definition and application of documentary languages to build the ontologies which, in schematic but practical terms, are structures extending the thesauruses or lexicons (which has a consolidated use in the domain of automatic information retrieval) in that they stress the semantic dimension. The meaning conveyed by ontologies is twofold: "that understood by human beings, which is interpretative semantics, and that 'understood' by machines, which is the formal semantics of ontology."

Jacob Nielsen observed that "using the system changes the users, and as they change they will use the system in new ways" (Nielsen, 1994). Assuming this as a principle, in Costabile, Fogli, Fresta, Mussio, and Piccinno (2004), interactive systems are analysed as syndetic systems (Barnard, May, Duke, & Duce, 2000) composed by humans and a computing system in interaction. Thanks to user capability in activating consolidated interaction strategies and in conceiving new paths to satisfy his or her needs, all the components of the syndetic system co-evolve on one side, updating users' culture, models, and working procedures; on the other, accessing new technological support to the interaction.

The attention to users responsible of a working activity, and therefore to possible errors and mistakes, leads to focus on a particular class of end-users, domain experts, which are experts in a specific domain, not necessarily in computer science. Consequently, to be accepted by their users, systems might offer "different levels of complexities, going from simply setting parameters to integrating existing components, up to extending the system by programming new components. To feel comfortable, users should work at any time with a system suitable to their specific needs, knowledge, and task to perform" (Costabile et al., 2004).

The holistic view suggested by the syndetic systems approach is framing the user-system interaction process into a semiotic schema, where the interface appearance is a complex of visual signs resulting from a system interpretation process, which, in its turn, is influenced by user interaction as sequences of communication acts and is supposed to be the kernel, which manages pragmatic. The idea of plastic systems, which can be easily moulded to user working needs on one side and the reality of e-documents as dynamic, evolving, reacting entities on the other, have shadowed the difference between them. The interactive visual system becomes an e-document, which can be annotated to comment browsed information, intervention requests, interface modification requests, to be forwarded to colleagues or designers with the same or different responsibilities in the working team (Costabile, Fogli, Mussio, & Piccinno, 2005; Fogli et al., 2004).

USABILITY IN SOCIAL COMMUNICATION

The computer has evolved from computing tool to communication medium among humans. Consequently, the notion of communicability has to be used as a practical guideline for interface design: "the relations between elements in a screen image must be describable in a few simple sentences. If you have to write a whole novel to capture the meaning of a screen, something is wrong" (Andersen, 2001).

The interface must be redefined in a semiotic context to take into account human comprehension and signification. Consequently, after Bodker (1987), who describes the user interface as the preconditions for operations given by the computer application for the way actions can be done by the users, Andersen (1997) adopts this shift of meaning and proposes to consider an interface as a collection of computer-based signs that are seen or heard, used, and interpreted by a community of users and whose expression is manifested changing the substance of the input and output media of the computer (screen, loudspeaker, keyboard, mouse, printer, etc.).

The interface emerges during user's activity. They focus on different system components, which can be interpreted differently due to the different languages adopted and originate different interfaces for a same system.

Let us go a bit further. Andersen proposes a semiological interpretation of computer systems as a processor of empty expression units, partially composing a sign system that emerges during human use and interpretation. Coherently with this view, what can be designed for a computing system is only its substance, the set of processes,

Figure 1. Development scheme for a semiotic system supported by a computing system

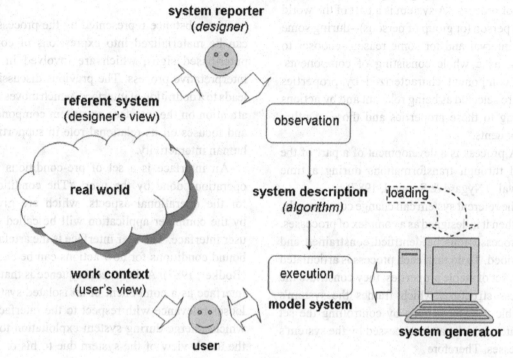

which give support to this sign system, not the sign system itself. The substance of a symbolic act can then be made to appear in different ways materializing it in a form, be it a gesture, a movement, a sketch, a set of pixels on a screen, etc..

We can start discussing this view from a sketch (Figure 1) of the development of a semiotic system supported by a computing system (Holbaek-Hannsen, Haandlykken, & Nygaard, 1973; Tondl, 1981). The referent system is a part of the world that the system reporter (designer) has chosen to view as a system; therefore, following an analysis and design phase, it is expressed into the system description. In the computer science domain it is a set of algorithms as computers need a formal and executable description of any activity they have to do. On the other side, people can be involved in a communication process without explicit description of the language scheme or linguistic usage guidelines or conventions. His or her view

of the real world, called work context, is implicit in his or her habits, knowledge, culture, experience, which he or she wants to be supported by an interactive technological environment.

The system description expresses in a programming language (i.e., implements), the substance of the system and it is used (i.e., interpreted and executed by the system generator) to make a model system, which simulates the referent system; in other terms, the system description describes a semiotic schema in which content and expression planes are homomorphic.

When the user's and designer's views overlap, that is they understand each other, proportionally the user feels directness in his or her engagement with the model system and in the manipulation he or she performs by means of the virtual tools it offers.

Let us now assume two definitions: the earlier definition approaches the concept of system to the concept of model, the latter proposes a dynamic view of process. "A system is a part of the world that a person (or group of persons)--during some time interval and for some reason--chooses to regard as a whole consisting of components, each component characterized by properties that are selected as being relevant and by actions relating to these properties and those of other components."

"A process is a development of a part of the world through transformations during a time interval" (Nygard & Sorgard, 1987).

The referent system can change continuously, but when it is designed as a complex of processes, the processes must be identified, constrained, and described. To do that, each process is articulated into a set of stable properties; they constitute the process structure, which frames the system's possible transformations by controlling the set of states, which can be accessed by the system's processes. Therefore

system = processes it undergoes + structure framing them

The substance represented by the processes can be materialized into expressions of computer-based signs, which are involved in an interpretative process. The previous discussion leads to a definition of interface, which moves the attention on the interface as system component and focuses on its relational role in supporting human interactivity.

An interface is a set of pre-conditions for operations done by the user: "The conditions for the operational aspects, which are given by the computer application will be called the user interface. The user interface is the artefact-bound conditions for how actions can be done" (Bodker, 1987). A direct consequence is that an interface as a component of an isolated system looses relevance with respect to the interfaces, which emerge during system exploitation to fit the user's view of the system due to his or her interpretation (Figure 2).

Figure 2. The interfaces with their relational role in supporting human interactivity

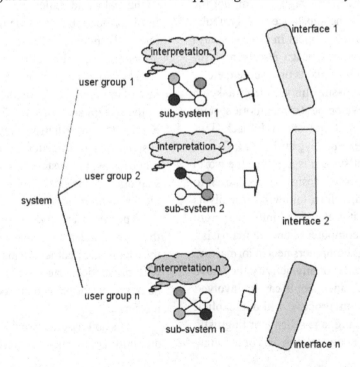

According to de Souza (2005), HCI should turn the attention to semiotic engineering as it could help in framing all the stages of software development in a unique homogeneous communicative space. In a way, which we consider complementary to the Andersen's view, she focuses basic semiotic concepts to define a theoretic perspective from which HCI designers and users are observed as interlocutors having a same role in a communicative process achieved by means of messages encoded in words, graphics, behaviour, help, and explanations.

The relevance of engineering comes from the need to extend and support a theory so that it is capable to spring ideas and abstractions, but also to concretize them into the design and construction of artefacts. We agree that "semiotics and engineering become tightly coupled when we think that HCI artefacts are intellectual constructs, namely, the result of choices and decisions guided by reasoning, sense making, and technical skills, rather than predictable natural laws. Like all other intellectual products, HCI artefacts are communicated as signs, in a particular kind of discourse that we must be able to interpret, learn, use, and adapt to various contexts of need and opportunity" (de Souza, 2005).

An artefact is defined as a product of a human activity with a concrete role in relation to a purpose or function. An intellectual artefact can be characterized by the following features:

- It results from a negotiation carried on to handle a problematic situation;
- It encodes the interpretation and the understanding agreed on the situation;
- It also encodes the design choices and the possible solutions, which have been conceived and could be possibly planned;
- It has to be brought into a communication process (e.g., for cooperating, teaching, updating, etc.); as a corollary it comes that the encoding of the situation, of the choices, and of the related solutions is fundamentally linguistic problem, managed by means of verbal, visual, aural, or other types of symbols;
- The target context of use of the artefact adopts a linguistic system, which is coherent with the one adopted during the negotiation for the artefact development, and can include the partial system, which is necessary to understand the function of the artifact, the possibilities and the solutions offered, and the strategies to follow to understand and reach the purpose of the artefact so to exhaustively and fruitfully exploit its potential.

Assuming a general semiotic point of view, semiotic engineering assigns a unique role to all the human interlocutors who are involved into an intellectual or communication process; in particular, designers and users of an HCI system have to be considered interlocutors in a same communicative process. During the system lifecycle, the two actors should remain in continuous communicative contact so that the designer could clarify the strategies that the users may adopt to exploit the available functionalities (i.e., what they mean by the artefact they have conceived). That is why interactive systems have to support these processes supplying epistemic tools that can benefit both designers and users, which are involved in the same dialog about and by means of the same system. Tools for online help must constitute both an operational guide, as usually happen, and also give hints and suggestions to define problem-solving strategies, which agree with the choices done by the designer during the system development.

Designers have to understand user's needs and requirements with the aim to communicate to them the design vision in development, not just to build a satisfying system image.

Conversely, the designers, which adopted a consolidated user centered design (UCD) methodology, have to precisely identify the users' needs and requirements to formulate a fitting design model, which is then projected by the system image with which users interact. Consequently, the system image will remain the only trace of all the intellectual negotiation that has been carried on. When the semiotic engineering perspective has been adopted, the designer is virtually present at interaction time, "telling the user about his or her design vision, to which the user will respond in various ways (including unexpected and creative ways). The ideal of UCD is that the user model captures the essence of the design model, projected in the system image. The ideal of semiotic engineering is that designer and user understand each other, and that users find the designer's vision useful and enjoyable" (de Souza, 2005).

The expression plane can be complex as it often offers different forms for a same substance or similar forms for different substances. This can create ambiguity and confusion if there is no reason behind the differences, or the reason is not immediately comprehensible. The rational, which motivated the design formalized into the description of the system have to be communicated to the user to avoid that content and expression planes are perceived by the user as not homomorphic.

THE USERS' FEELINGS

A digital gulf divides the human user and the computing system in the HCI process, as the first one is used to communicate by means of a natural language, the latter executes descriptions expressed in machine languages, which are not comprehensible to humans. Therefore, the interface should avoid the natural gap between man and computer, but it can introduce distance to the extent that the person's goals and knowledge and the expression plane provided by the systems are not homomorphic.

An important concept in interaction analysis is direct manipulation, which was introduced by (Shneiderman, 1983). A detailed frame, which is useful to deeply observe the relation between user and system mediated by interfaces, is discussed in

Hutchins, Hollan, and Norman (1985). The work discusses the concept of direct manipulation where directness is intended as the feeling of the user enabled to carry on his or her activities, having to commit few cognitive resources; directness increases when the cognitive effort decreases, but it has to be considered a feeling or an impression, influenced by a number of variables, not a feature or a parameter, which can be quantified or measured.

At the operative level, you can observe a gulf of execution, which is shortened by a precise and exhaustive satisfaction of the user requirements by means of powerful and useful functionalities, commands, and mechanisms. At the conceptual level, a gulf of evaluation is manifested when the output displays present conceptual representation, which is not quickly perceived, easily interpreted, suggestive, mnemonic, synthetic.

"The analysis of the execution and evaluation process explains why there is difficulty in using a system, and it says something about what must be done to minimize the mental effort required to use a system....The systems that best exemplify direct manipulation all give the qualitative feeling that one is directly engaged with control of the objects, not with the programs, not with the computer,..." (Hutchins et al., 1985).

In some respect, orthogonal to the concept of gulf are the notion of engagement and distance. Engagement depends on the metaphor adopted. You can roughly distinguish two main metaphors: the model world and the conversation metaphor. The model world metaphor is a form of the model system; therefore, it must be a simulation of the work context of the user (Figure 1). In this case, the interface offers the user the tools to operate as in his or her real working context it represents and is homomorphic to the working context; it reacts to user actions changing its state. In this situation, the user is directly engaged as the interface does not appear as an intermediary between himself and the model system. Conversely, the conversation metaphor offers the user a language medium to talk to the system. Even if in many situations the two metaphors are fruitfully intermingled, there is no doubt that directness in engaging the user decreases in a mediated conversation.

"Direct engagement occurs when a user experiences direct interaction with the objects in a domain. Here there is a feeling of involvement directly with a world of objects rather than of communication with an intermediary. The interactions are much like interacting with objects in the physical world" (Hutchins et al., 1985).

A system, which allows a feeling of direct engagement, must be designed paying attention to (Laurel, 1986):

- Both execution and evaluation gulfs must be bridged by directness;
- The interaction languages used by the user to act and by the system to react should overlap (i.e., be inter-referential allowing input expressions to be incorporated or referred by output expressions and vice versa);
- The system must be efficient leaving no delay between user's action and system's reply;
- The interface should be not interfering or intruding (i.e., model world metaphor has to be adopted).

Another underlying aspect of directness is called distance to emphasize that directness is referred to a relationship between the work context (i.e., the task the user has in mind and the way he or she would like to carry it on), and the expression plane of the model system (Figure 1) (i.e., the tools and the work strategies, which can be effectively accomplished via the interface). Short distance requires easy, straightforward, and therefore immediate translation of user's intentions into actions; ready comprehension of the system's reactions.

Semantic distance concerns the relation between what is the intention of the user (i.e., what is in his or her mind) and the meaning of the expressions he or she can effectively formulate

and receive as a system's reaction in the interface. In other words, it relates the work context and the substance represented by the processes of the model system. The substance is materialized into the expression plane by means of computer-based signs: this mapping is reflected by the articulatory distance.

The relationship between the user's intention and the effective possibilities available in the expression plane could be complex and hard to follow. "Where the machine is of minimal complexity, as is the case with the Turing machine example, the wide gulf between user intention and machine instructions must be filled by the user's extensive planning and translation activities" (Hutchins et al., 1985). On the other side, user's specific experience and skill can bridge this gulf. This is the case, for example, of the system administrators and the programmers that, being accustomed with the direct use of programming languages and command scripts, often prefer the character interaction offered by a command shell, or the plain text manipulation mode offered by a Web editor, or the traditional source code editing then the WYSIWYG metaphor offered by a "friendly" mediator.

FUTURE TRENDS AND CONCLUSION

Going a step further, we could schematically conclude indicating three directions we should focus on to increase the energy towards usability:

- The definition of working procedures to continuously update the technological standards, progress, and innovation;
- The disciplines, which have their foundation on the computer still considered as a computing system, which is now evolved and become a mediator for human to human communication. These disciplines should by newly structured and generated updating

consequently all their basic definitions and the logical processes which have framed and sustained them;

- The design of interactive systems for communication among workers, which could improve their usability if, besides functionalities to comment the information gathered by means of annotations, would also include services to allow to react and debate about news like it happens on the blog; and also services to understand during message exchanging with the computer or other humans, supported by ontologies; to store documents on the wiki, after they are debated on the blog to search continuously updated consensus and to collaboratively generate an online corporate encyclopaedia (Passant, Laublet, & Testard-Vaillant, 2005).

REFERENCES

Andersen, P. B. (2001). What semiotics can and cannot do for HCI. *Knowledge-Based Systems*, *14*(8), 419-424.

Andersen, P. B. (1997). *A theory of computer semiotics*. Cambridge, MA: Cambridge University Press.

Barnard, P., May, J., Duke, D., & Duce, D. (2000). Systems, interactions, and macrotheory. *ACM Trans. on HCI*, *7*(2), 222-262.

Bodker, S. (1987). *Through the interface--A human activity approach to user interface design*. PhD dissertation, Computer Science Dept., University of Aarhus, DK.

Cadieux, P., & Esselink B. (2002). GILT: Globalization, Internationalization, localization, translation. *Globalization Insider - LISA*, XI(1.5), 1-5.

Costabile, M. F., Fogli, D., Fresta, G., Mussio, P., & Piccinno, A. (2004). Software environments for end-user development and tailoring. *PsychNology Journal*, *2*(1), 99-122.

Costabile, M. F., Fogli, D., Mussio, P., & Piccinno, A. (2005). End-user development: The software shaping workshop approach. In H. Lieberman, F. Paternò, & V. Wulf (Eds), *End user development: Empowering people to flexibly employ advanced information and communication technology*. Dordrecht, The Netherlands: Kluwer Academic Publishers.

de Souza, C. S. (2005). *The semiotic engineering of human-computer interaction*. Cambridge, MA: The MIT Press.

Esselink, B. (2000). *A practical guide to localization*. Amsterdam, The Netherlands: John Benjamins Publishing Co.

Feenberg, A. (1999). *Questioning technology*. London, UK: Routledge.

Fogli, D., Fresta, G., Marcante, A., & Mussio, P. (2004). IM2L: A user interface description language supporting electronic annotation. *Proceedings of Workshop on Developing User Interface with XML: Advances on User Interface Description Languages* (pp. 135-142), Gallipoli, Italy.

Holbaek-Hannsen, E., Haandlykken, P., & Nygaard, K. (1973). *System description and the delta language* (Publ. no 523). Oslo, NO: Norwegian Computing Center.

Holzinger, A. (2005). Usability engineering methods for software developers. *CACM*, *48*(1), 71-74.

Hutchins, E. L., Hollan, J. D., & Norman, D. A. (1985). Direct manipulation interfaces. *Human-Computer Interaction*, *1*(4), 311-338.

ISO. (1992). *ISO 9241, Ergonomic requirements for office work with visual display terminals (VDTs)*. Retrieved November 3, 2006, from http://www.iso.org/iso/en/CombinedQueryResult.CombinedQueryResult?queryString=9241

Laurel, B. K. (1986). Interface as mimesis. In D. A. Norman, & S. W. Draper (Eds.), *User centred system design: New perspectives on human-computer interaction*. Hillsdale, NJ: Lawrence Erlbaum Associates Inc.

Musella, D., & Padula, M. (1997). Seeking emergences from digital documents in large repositories. *Sémiotiques, 12*(1), 129-150.

Nielsen, J. (1994), *Usability engineering*. San Diego, CA: Academic Press.

Nygaard, K., & Sorgarrd, P. (1987) The Perspective Concept in Informatics. In G. Bjerknes, P. Ehn, & M. Kyng (Eds.), *Compters and Democracy*. Aldershot, UK: Avebury

Padula, M., & Reggiori, A. (2006). *Fondamenti di informatica per la progettazione multimediale. Dai linguaggi formali all'inclusione digitale*. Milano, IT: FrancoAngeli.

Padula, M., & Reggiori, A. (1999). Art teams up with technology through the Net. *ACM Interactions, 6*(4), 40-50.

Passant, A., Laublet, P., & Testard-Vaillant, F. X. (2005). Annotations and collaborative work: a corporate approach. *Proceedings of International Workshop on Annotation for Collaboration*, (pp. 133-142). Paris: La Sorbonne.

Preston, P. (2001). *Reshaping communications*. London, UK: Sage.

Pédauque, R. T. (2003). Document: Form, sign and medium. As Reformulated for Electronic Documents, *Working paper STIC-CNRS*, September 12, 2003, from http://archivesic.ccsd.cnrs.fr/sic_00000594.html, original French version: http://archivesic.ccsd.cnrs.fr/documents/archives0/00/00/05/11/index_fr.html.

Shneiderman, B. (1983). Direct manipulation: A step beyond programming languages. *IEEE Computer, 16*(8), 57-69.

Travis, D. (2006). *Bluffers' guide to usability standards*. London, UK: Userfocus ltd.

Tondl, L. (1981). *Problems of semantics*. Boston: Reidel Publishing Company.

Wikipedia. (2006). *User interface*. Wikipedia, the free encyclopedia. Retrieved November 3, 2006, from http://en.wikipedia.org/wiki/User_interface

Compilation of References

Abelson, H., & Sussman, G. J. (1996). *Structure and interpretation of computer programs* (Chapter 5). Cambridge, MA: The MIT Press.

Abiteboul, S., Hull, R., & Vianu, V. (1995). *Foundations of databases*. Addison-Wesley.

Abowd, G. D., & Beale, R. (1991). Users, systems, and interfaces: A unifying framework for interaction. In D. Diaper & N. Hammond (Eds.), *HCI'91: People and computers VI* (pp. 73-87). Cambridge: Cambridge University Press.

Agrawal, R., & Srikant, R. (1994). Fast algorithms for mining association rules in large databases. In J. B. Bocca, M. Jarke, & C. Zaniolo (Ed.), *Proceedings of the 20th International Conference on Very Large Data Bases (VLDB)*. San Francisco: Morgan Kaufmann Publishers.

Agrawal, R., Gehrke, J., Gunopulos, D., & Raghavan, P. (1998). Automatic subspace clustering of high dimensional data for data mining applications. In A. Tiwary & M. Franklin, (Ed.), *ACM SIGMOD Record, Proceedings of the 1998 ACM SIGMOD International Conference on Management of Data, 27*(2), 94-105. New York: ACM Press.

Agrawal, R., Imielinski, T., & Swami, A. N. (1993). Mining association rules between sets of items in large databases. In P. Buneman & S. Jajodia (Ed.), *ACM SIGMOD Record, Proceedings of the 1993 ACM SIGMOD International Conference on Management of Data, 22*(2), 207-216. New York: ACM Press.

Aho, A. V., Sethi, R., & Ullman, J. D. (1985). *Compilers, principles, techniques, and tools*. New York: Addison-Wesley.

Ajay, A., Van V., & Takayuki, D. K. (1993). Recognizing multistroke geometric shapes: An experimental evaluation. *Proceedings of ACM Symposium on User Interfaces Software and Technology* (pp. 121-128). ACM Press.

Alvarado, C. (2000). *A natural sketching environment: Bringing the computer into early stages of mechanical design*. Unpublished master thesis, Massachusetts Institute of Technology, Cambridge, MA.

Alvarado, C., & Davis, R. (2004). SketchREAD: A multi-domain sketch recognition engine. *Proceedings of ACM Symposium on User Interfaces Software and Technology* (pp. 23-32). ACM Press.

Amer-Yahia, S., Cho, S., Lakshmanan, L. V., & Srivastava, D. (2001). Minimisation of tree pattern queries. In T. Sellis (Ed.), *Proceedings of the 2001 ACM SIGMOD International Conference on Management of Data* (pp. 497-508). SIGMOD '01. New York: ACM Press.

Andersen, P. B. (1997). *A theory of computer semiotics*. Cambridge, MA: Cambridge University Press.

Andersen, P. B. (2001). What semiotics can and cannot do for HCI. *Knowledge Based Systems, 14*(8), 419-424.

Anderson, D. J. (2000). Extending UML for UI. *UML'2000 Workshop on Towards a UML Profile for Interactive Systems Development* (TUPIS2000), York, UK, October 2/3.

Anderson, M. L. (2003). Embodied cognition: A field guide. *Artificial Intelligence, 149*(1), 91-130.

Andreoli, J. M. (1992). Logic programming with focusing proofs in linear logic. *Journal of Logic and Computation, 2*(3), 297-347.

Andreoli, J. M., & Pareschi, R. (1991). Linear objects: Logical processes with built-in inheritance. *New Generation Computing, 9,* 445-473.

Andrienko, N., Andrienko, G. & Gatalski, P. (2002). Data and Tasks Characteristics in Design of Spatio-Temporal Data Visualization Tools. In *Symposium on Geospatial Theory, Processing and Applications.*

Angelaccio, M., Catarci, T., & Santucci, G. (1990). QBD*: A fully visual query system. *Journal of Visual Languages and Computing, 1*(2), 255-273.

Angiulli, F., Ben-Eliyahu-Zohary, R., Ianni, G., & Palopoli, L. (2000). Computational properties of metaquerying problems. *Proceedings of the 19th ACM SIGMOD-SIGACT-SIGART Symposium on Principles of Database Systems* (pp. 237-244). New York: ACM Press.

Ankerst, M., Breunig, M., Kriegel, H. P., & Sander, J. (1999). OPTICS: Ordering points to identify the clustering structure. *ACM SIGMOD Record, Proceedings of the 1999 ACM SIGMOD International Conference on Management of Data, 28*(2), 49-60. New York: ACM Press.

Antoniou, G. (1997). *Nonmonotonic reasoning.* MIT Press.

Antoniou, G. (2002). Nonmonotonic Rule systems on top of ontology layers. *Proceedings of the 1st International Semantic Web Conference* (pp. 394-398). LNCS 2342. Springer-Verlag.

Antoniou, G., & Arief, M. (2002). Executable declarative business rules and their use in electronic commerce. *Proceedings of the ACM Symposium on Applied Computing* (pp. 6-10). ACM Press.

Antoniou, G., & van Harmelen, F. (2004). *A Semantic Web primer.* MIT Press.

Antoniou, G., Billington, D., & Maher, M. J. (1999). On the analysis of regulations using defeasible rules. *Proceedings of the 32nd Hawaii International Conference on Systems Science.* IEEE Press.

Antoniou, G., Skylogiannis, T., Bikakis, A., & Bassiliades, N. (2005). DR-BROKERING—A defeasible logic-based system for semantic brokering. *Proceedings of the IEEE International Conference on E-Technology, E-Commerce, and E-Service* (pp. 414-417). IEEE Computer Society.

Arbib, M. A., & Padulo, L. (1974). *Systems theory: A unified state space approach to continuous and discrete systems.* Philadelphia: W. B. Saunders.

ArcGis- The Complete Geographic Information System. (2006). ESRI GIS and mapping software. Retrieved April 28, 2006, from http://www.esri.com/software/arcgis/

Arias, E., Eden, H., Fischer, G., Gorman, A., & Scharff, E. (2000). Transcending the individual human mind--creative shared understanding through collaborative design. *ACM Trans on CHI, 7*(1), 84-113.

Arias, E., Eden, H., Fischer, G., Gorman, A., & Scharff, E. (2000). Transcending the individual human mind: Creating shared understanding through collaborative design. *ACM Trans on CHI, 7*(1), 84-113.

Aristotle. (1996). *Metaphysics.* Loeb Classical Library. Original and translation by Hugh Tredennick. Harvard University Press. Reprinted 1996.

Arnheim, R. (1954). *Art and visual perception: A psychology of the creative eye.* University of California Press.

Arnheim, R. (1966). *Toward a psychology of art: Collected essays.* University of California Press.

Arondi, S., Baroni, P., Fogli, D., & Mussio, P. (2002). Supporting co-evolution of users and systems by the recognition of Interaction Patterns. *Proceedings of the International Conference on Advanced Visual Interfaces (AVI 2002)* (pp. 177-189). Trento, Italy: ACM Press.

Ashri, R., Payne, T., Marvin, D., Surridge, M., & Taylor, S. (2004). Towards a Semantic Web security infrastructure. *Proceedings of the Semantic Web Services 2004*

Spring Symposium Series. Stanford University, Stanford California.

Atkinson, C., & Kühne, T. (2002). Rearchitecting the UML infrastructure. *ACM Transactions on Modeling and Computer Simulation, 12*(4), 290-321.

Atkinson, M. P., Bancilhon, F., DeWitt, D. J., Dittrich, K. R., Maier, D., Zdonik, S. B. (1989). The object-oriented database system manifesto. The *1st International Conference on Deductive and Object-Oriented Databases (DOOD'89)* (pp. 223-240).

Atzeni, P., Ceri, S., Paraboschi, S., & Torlone, R. (1999). *Database systems: Concepts, languages, and architectures*. McGraw-Hill.

Atzeni, P., Mecca, G., & Merialdo, P. (1997). To weave the Web. *Proceedings of the 23rd International Conference on Very Large Databases (VLDB)* (pp. 206-215).

Aufaure-Portier, M. A. (1995). A high level interface language for GIS. *Journal of Visual Languages and Computing, 6*(2), 167-182.

Aufaure-Portier, M. A., & Bonhomme, C. (1999). A high-level visual language for spatial data management. The *3rd International Conference on Visual Information and Information Systems (VISUAL 1999)* (pp. 325-332).

Aversano, L., Canfora, G., De Lucia, A., & Stefanucci, S. (2002). Understanding SQL through iconic interfaces. The *International Computer Software and Applications Conference (COMPSAC 2002)* (pp. 703-710).

Baber, C., & Hone, K. S. (1993). Modelling error recovery and repair in automatic speech recognition. *International Journal of Man-Machine Studies, 39*(3), 495-515.

Balkir, N. H., Ozsoyoglu, G., & Ozsoyoglu, Z. M. (2002). A graphical query language: Visual and its query processing. *IEEE Transactions on Knowledge and Data Engineering, 14*(5), 955-978.

Bardhol, R. (2002). A visual environment for visual languages. *Science of Computer Programming, 44*(2), 181-203.

Bardohl, B., Ehrig, H., de Lara, J., & Taentzer, G. (2004). Integrating meta modelling with graph transformation for efficient visual language definition and model manipulation. *Proceedings of Fundamental Approaches to Software Engineering 7th International Conference, held as part of the Joint European Conferences on Theory and Practice of Software, Barcelona, Spain. Lecture Notes in Computer Science 2984* (pp. 214-228). Springer-Verlag.

Bardohl, R. (2002). A visual environment for visual languages. *Science of Computer Programming, 44*(2), 181-203.

Bardohl, R., Minas, M., Schürr, A., & Taentzer, G. (1999). Application of graph transformation to visual languages. In H. Ehrig, G. Engels, H. J. Kreowski, & G. Rozenberg (Eds.), *Handbook of graph grammars and computing by graph transformation* (Vol. 2, pp. 105-18). Singapore: World Scientific.

Barnard, P., May, J., Duke, D., & Duce, D. (2000). Systems, interactions, and macrotheory. *ACM Transactions on HCI, 7*(2), 222-262.

Barsalou, L. (1999). Perceptual symbol systems. *Behavioural and Brain Sciences, 22*(4), 577-609.

Barsalou, L. W., Niedenthal, P. M., Barbey, A. K., & Ruppert, J. M. (2003). Social embodiment. In B. H. Ross (Ed.), *The psychology of learning and motivation* (p. 43). San Diego: Academic Press.

Bartlett, F. C. (1958). *Thinking: An experimental and social study*. New York: Basic Books.

Bassiliades, N., & Vlahavas, I. (2004). R-DEVICE: A deductive RDF rule language. *Proceedings of the RuleML 2004* (pp. 65-80). Springer-Verlag, LNCS 3323, Hiroshima, Japan.

Bassiliades, N., Antoniou, G., & Vlahavas, I. (2004). A defeasible logic reasoner for the Semantic Web. *Proceedings of the RuleML 2004* (pp. 49-64). Springer-Verlag, LNCS 3323, Hiroshima, Japan.

Bassiliades, N., Kontopoulos, E., & Antoniou, G. (2005). A visual environment for developing defeasible rule bases for the Semantic Web. In A. Adi, S. Stoutenburg, & S. Tabet (Eds.), *Proceedings of the International Conference on Rules and Rule Markup Languages for the Semantic Web (RuleML-2005)* (pp. 172-186). Springer-Verlag, LNCS 3791, Galway, Ireland.

Battista, G. D., Eades, P., Tamassia, R., & Tollis, I. G. (1999). *Graph drawing: Algorithms for the visualization of graphs.* Prentice Hall.

Baudel, T. (2004). Browsing through an information visualization design space. *Extended Abstracts on Human factors in Computing Systems (CHI04)* (pp. 765-766). New York: ACM Press.

Baumgarten, A. G. (1750). *Aesthetica*, Hildesheim, translated by G. Olms 1968.

Beaudouin-Lafon, M. (2004). Designing interaction, not interfaces. *Proceedings of the Working Conference on Advanced Visual Interfaces 2004* (pp. 15-22). Gallipoli, Italy.

Becker, S., & Westfechtel, B. (2003). Incremental integration tools for chemical engineering: An industrial application of triple graph grammars. *Proceedings of 29th International Workshop on Graph-Theoretic Concepts in Computer Science, Elspeet, the Netherlands. Lecture Notes in Computer Science 2880* (pp. 46-57). Springer-Verlag.

Benzi, F., Maio, D., & Rizzi, S. (1999). VISIONARY: A viewpoint-based visual language for querying relational databases. *Journal of Visual Languages Computing, 10*(2), 117-145.

Berardi, D., Calvanese, D., De Giacomo, G., & Mecella, M. (2003). Reasoning about actions for e-service composition. *ICAPS 2003 Workshop on Planning for Web Services.*

Bergen, B., Chang, N., & Narayanan, S. (2004). Simulated action in an embodied construction grammar. *Proceedings of the 26th Annual Meeting of the Cognitive Science Society*, Chicago.

Berners-Lee, T., Hendler, J., & Lassila, O. (2001). The semantic Web. *Scientific American, 284*(5), 34-43.

Berstel, J., Crespi-Reghizzi, S., Roussel, G., & San Pietro, P. (2005). A scalable formal method for design and automatic checking of user interfaces. *ACM Transaction on Software Engineering and Methodology, 14*(2), 124-167.

Bertin, J. (1983). *Semiology of graphics: Diagrams, networks, maps.* Madison, WI: University of Wisconsin Press.

Betz, H., & Frühwirth, T. (2005). A linear-logic semantics for constraint handling rules. *International Conference on Principles and Practice of Constraint Programming* (pp. 137-151). Barcelona, Spain.

Bezdek, J. C. (1992). Computing with uncertainty. *IEEE Communications Magazine, 30*(9), 24-36.

Bianchi, N., Bottoni, P., Mussio, P., & Protti, M. (1993). Cooperative visual environments for the design of effective visual systems. *Journal of Visual Languages and Computing, 4*(4), 357-381.

Bianchi-Berthouze, N., & Mussio, P. (2005). Introduction to the special issue on context and emotion aware visual computing. *Journal of Visual Languages & Computing, 16*(5), 383-385.

Billington, J., Soren, C., van Hee, K., Kindler, E., Kummer, O., Petrucci, L., Post, R., Stehno, C., & Weber, M. (2003). The Petri net markup language: Concepts, technology, and tools. *Proceedings of the 24th International Conference on Applications and Theory of Petri Nets, Eindhoven, The Netherlands. Lecture Notes in Computer Science 2679* (pp. 483-505). Springer-Verlag.

Blackwell, A. F., & Green, T. R. G. (1999). Does metaphor increase visual language usability? *IEEE Symposium on Visual Languages (VL'99)* (pp. 246-253).

Blanch, R., Conversy, S., Baudel, T., Zhao, Y., Jestin, Y., & Beaudouin-Lafon, M. (2005). Indigo: une architecture pour la conception d'applications graphiques interactives distribuées. In *Actes des dix-septièmes journées francophones sur l'Interaction Homme-Machine (IHM 2005)*, 139–146.

Blaser, A. D., & Egenhofer, M. J. (2000). A visual tool for querying geographic databases. *Working Conference on Advanced Visual Interfaces (AVI 2000)* (pp. 211-216).

Bloesch, A. C., & Halpin T. A. (1996). ConQuer: A conceptual query language. *International Conference on Conceptual Modeling (ER 1996)* (pp. 121-133).

Blostein, D., & Haken, L. (1999). Using diagram generation software to improve diagram recognition: A case study of music notation. *IEEE Transactions on Pattern Analysis and Machine Intelligence, 21*(11), 1121-1136.

Blostein, D., & Schürr, A. (1997). Computing with graphs and graph rewriting. *Software-Practice and Experience, The 6th Proceedings in Informatics* (pp. 1-21).

Blum, A., & Furst, M. (1995). Fast planning through planning graph analysis. *Proceedings of the 14th International Conference on Artificial Intelligence* (pp. 636-642). Berlin, Germany.

Blythe, J., Deelman, E., & Gil, Y. (2003). Planning for workflow construction and maintenance on the Grid. *ICAPS 2003 Workshop on Planning for Web Services*.

Boag, S., Chamberlin, D., Fernandez, M. F., Florescu, D., Robie, J., & Simeon, J. (2006). *XQuery 1.0: An XML query language*. Retrieved October 13, 2006, from http://www.w3.org/TR/xquery/

Bodker, S. (1987). *Through the interface--A human activity approach to user interface design*. PhD dissertation, Computer Science Dept., University of Aarhus, DK.

Bødker, S., & Grønbæk, K. (1991). Cooperative prototyping: Users and designers in mutual activity. *International Journal of Man-Machine Studies, 34*(3), 453-478.

Boley, D. L. (1998). Principal direction divisive partitioning. *Data Mining and Knowledge Discovery, 2*(4), 325-344.

Bolter, J. D., & Gromala, D. (2003). *Windows and mirrors: Interaction design, digital art, and the myth of transparency*. MIT Press.

Bonet, B., & Geffner, H. (2001). Planning a heuristic search. *Artificial Intelligence, Special issue on Heuristic Search, 129*(1-2), 5-33.

Bonhomme, C., Trépied, C., Aufaure, M. A., & Laurini. R. (1999). A visual language for querying spatio-temporal databases. *Proceedings of the Workshop on Geographical Information Systems* (pp. 34-39). ACM Press.

Bonifati, A., Braga, D., Campi, A., & Ceri, S. (2002). Active XQuery. *Proceedings of ICDE 2002* (pp. 403-412). San Jose, CA, USA

Booth, D., Haas, H., McCabe, F., Newcomer, E., Champion, M, Ferris, C., & Orchard, D. (2003). *Web services architecture*. W3C Working Draft, Aug. 2003. Retrieved from http://www.w3.org/TR/ws-arch/

Borchers, J. (2001). *A pattern approach to interactive design*. Chichester, UK: John Wiley & Sons.

Borchers, J., Fincher, S., Griffiths, R., Pemberton, L., & Siemon, E. (2001). Usability pattern language: Creating a community. *AI & Society Journal of Human-Centred Systems and Machine Intelligence, 15*(4), 377-385.

Botea, A., Enzenberger, M., Müller, M., & Schaeffer, J. (2005), Macro-FF: Improving AI planning with automatically learned macro-operators, To appear in *Journal of Artificial Intelligence Research*.

Bottoni, P. (2003). Dynamic aspects of visual modelling languages. In R. Bardohl & H. Ehrig (Eds.), UNIGRA 2003, *Electronic Notes on Theoretical Computer Science, 7*(82), 131-145.

Bottoni, P., & Costagliola, G. (2002). On the definition of visual languages and their editors. In M. Hegarty, B. Meyer, & N. Hari Narayanan (Eds.), *Diagrammatic representation and inference: Second International Conference, Diagrams 2002, Proceedings, LNAI 2317* (pp. 305-319). Berlin, Germany: Springer.

Bottoni, P., & Grau, A. (2004a). A suite of metamodels as a basis for a classification of visual languages. In P. Bottoni, C. Hundhausen, S. Levialdi, & G. Tortora (Eds.), *Proceedings of Visual Languages/Human Centric Computing 2004* (pp. 83-90). IEEE CS Press.

Bottoni, P., & Levialdi, S. (2005). Resource-based models of visual interaction: Learning from errors. *Proceedings of the VL/HCC 2005* (pp. 137-144). Dallas, USA: IEEE Computer Society Press.

Bottoni, P., Chang, S. K., Costabile, M. F., Levialdi, S., & Mussio, P. (1998b). On the specification of dynamic visual languages. In *Proceedings of IEEE Symposium Visual Languages* (pp. 14-21). Halifax, Canada: IEEE Computer Society Press.

Bottoni, P., Chang, S. K., Costabile, M. F., Levialdi, S., & Mussio, P. (2002). Modeling visual interactive systems through dynamic visual languages. *IEEE Trans. on Systems, Man, and Cybernetics--Part A, 32*(6), 654-669.

Bottoni, P., Costabile, M. F., & Mussio, P. (1999). Specification and dialogue control of visual interaction through visual rewriting systems. *ACM Trans. on Programming Languages and Systems (TOPLAS), 21*(6), 1077-1136.

Bottoni, P., Costabile, M. F., Fogli, D., Levialdi, S., & Mussio, P. (2001). Multilevel modeling and design of visual interactive systems. In *Proceedings of HCC 2001* (pp. 256-263). Stresa, Italy: IEEE Computer Society Press.

Bottoni, P., Costabile, M. F., Levialdi, S., & Mussio, P. (1995). Formalising visual languages. *Proceedings of the IEEE Symposium on Visual Languages* (pp. 45-52).

Bottoni, P., Costabile, M. F., Levialdi, S., & Mussio, P. (1996). Visual conditional attributed rewriting systems in visual language specification. *Proceedings of VL 1996* (pp. 156-163). Boulder: IEEE Computer Society Press.

Bottoni, P., Costabile, M. F., Levialdi, S., & Mussio, P. (1997). Defining visual languages for interactive computing. *IEEE Trans. on Systems, Man, and Cybernetics. Part A, 27*(6), 773-783.

Bottoni, P., Costabile, M. F., Levialdi, S., & Mussio, P. (1998). Specifying dialog control in visual interactive systems. *Journal of Visual Languages and Computing, 9*(5), 535-564.

Bottoni, P., de Lara, J., & Guerra, E. (2006c). Metamodel-based definition of interaction with visual environments. *Proceedings of MDDAUI 2006.* In press.

Bottoni, P., De Marsico, M., Di Tommaso, P., Levialdi, S., & Ventriglia, D. (2004). Definition of visual processes in a language for expressing transitions. *Journal of Visual Languages and Computing, 15*(3), 211-242.

Bottoni, P., Frediani, D., Quattrocchi, P., Rende, L., Sarajlic, G., & Ventriglia, D. (2006a). A transformation-based metamodel approach to the definition of syntax and semantics of diagrammatic languages. *In this volume.*

Bottoni, P., Mariotto, M., Mussio, P., & Biella, G. (1995). The design of anthropocentric cooperative visual environments. *Proceedings of VL 1995* (pp. 334-341). Darmstadt, Germany: IEEE Computer Society Press.

Bottoni, P., Mauri, G., & Mussio, P. (1998a). Coordination through group rewriting. In A. Salomaa & G. Paun (Eds.), *Grammatical models of multi agent systems* (pp. 226-246). IEEE Computer Society Press: Gordon & Breach.

Bottoni, P., Mussio, P., Olivieri, B., & Protti, M. (1998). A completely visual environment for agent-based computing. In T. Catarci, M. F. Costabile, G. Santucci, & L. Tarantino (Eds.), *Proceedings of AVI'98* (pp. 261-263). L'Aquila, Italy: ACM Press.

Bottoni, P., Quattrocchi, P., & Ventriglia, D. (2006b). Constraining concrete syntax via metamodel information. *Proceedings of VL/HCC 2006* (pp. 85-88). Città, stato: IEEE Computer Society Press.

Bouganim, L., Chan-Sine-Ying, T., Dang-Ngoc, T. T., Darroux, J. L., Gardarin, G., & Sha, F. (1999). Miro Web: Integrating multiple data sources through semistructured data types. *Proceedings of the 25th International Conference on Very Large Data Bases (VLDB'99)* (pp. 750-753). Edinburgh, Scotland, UK.

Bourbakis, N., & Tascillo, A. (1997). An SPN-neural planning methodology for coordination of two robotic hands with constrained placement. *Journal of Intelligent and Robotic Systems archive, 19*(3), 321-337.

Bourguin, G., Derycke, A., & Tarby, J. C. (2001). Beyond the interface: Co-evolution inside interactive systems: A proposal founded on the Activity theory. In Blandford, A., Vanderdonckt, J., & Gray, P.H. (Eds), *Proceedings of the of IHM-HCI 2001 Conference* (pp. 297-310). Lille, France, People and computer XV – Interactions without Frontiers: Springer Verlag.

Bowman, D., Gabbard, J. L., & Hix, D. (2002). A survey of usability evaluation in virtual environments: Classification and comparison of methods. *Presence: Teleperators and Virtual Environments, 11*(4), 404-424.

Braga, D., Campi, A., & Ceri, S. (2005). XQBE (XQuery by example): A visual interface to the standard XML query language. *ACM Transactions on Database Systems, 30*(2), 398-443.

Braga, D., Campi, A., Ceri, S., & Raffio, A. (2005b). XQBE: A visual environment for learning XML query languages. *Proceedings of the 2005 ACM SIGMOD International Conference on Management of Data* (pp. 903-905). New York: ACM Press.

Buschmann, F. (2001). *Series foreword, A pattern approach to interactive design.* Chichester, UK: John Wiley & Sons.

Cabibbo, L., & Torlone, R. (1998). From a procedural to a visual query language for OLAP. *International Conference on Scientific and Statistical Database Management (SSDBM'98)* (pp. 74-83).

Cadieux, P., & Esselink B. (2002). GILT: Globalization, Internationalization, localization, translation. *Globalization Insider - LISA*, XI(1.5), 1-5.

Caetano, A., Goulart, N., Fonseca, M., & Jorge, J. (2002). JavaSketchIT: Issues in sketching the look of user interfaces. *Proceedings of AAAI Spring Symposium on Sketch Understanding* (pp. 9-14). AAAI Press.

Calcinelli, D., & Mainguenaud, M. (1991). The management of the ambiguities in a graphical query language for geographical information systems. In O. Günther & H. J. Schek (Eds.), *2° Large Spatial Database Symposium (SSD)* (Vol. 525, pp. 143-160). Zürich, Switzerland: Springer.

Calcinelli, D., & Mainguenaud, M. (1994). Cigales: A visual language for geographic information system: The user interface. *Journal of Visual Languages and Computing, 5*(2), 113-132.

Calhoun, C., Stahovich, T. F., Kurtoglu, T., & Kara, L. B. (2002). Recognizing multi-stroke symbols. *Proceedings of AAAI Spring Symposium on Sketch Understanding* (pp. 15-23). AAAI Press.

Campos, P. F., & Nunes, N. J. (2005). A UML-based tool for designing user interfaces. *UML 2004 Satellite Activities*, LNCS 3297 (pp. 273-276).

Carey, M., Haas, L., Maganty, V., & Williams, J. (1996). Pesto: An integrated query/browser for object databases. *Proceedings of the 22nd International Conference on Very Large Data Bases (VLDB'96)* (pp. 203-214). Mumbai, India.

Carman, M., Serafini, L., & Traverso, P. (2003). Web service composition as planning. *ICAPS 2003 Workshop on Planning for Web Services.*

Carpentier, C., & Mainguenaud, M. (2002). Classifying ambiguities in a visual spatial language. *GeoInformatica Journal, 6*(3), 285-315.

Carr, D. (1997). Interaction object graphs: An executable graphical notation for specifying user interfaces. In P. Palanque & F. Paternò (Eds.), *Formal methods in human-computer interaction* (pp. 141-155). Springer-Verlag.

Carrara, P., Fogli, D., Fresta, G., & Mussio, P. (2002). Toward overcoming culture, skill, and situation hurdles in human-computer interaction. *International Journal Universal Access in the Information Society, 1*(4), 288-304.

Carroll, J. M. (1995). *Scenario-based design.* John Wiley & Sons.

Carroll, J. M., & Rosson, M. B. (1992). Deliberated evolution: Stalking the view matcher in design space. *Human-Computer Interaction, 6*(3 and 4), 281-318.

Carvalho, C. L., Costa Pereira, A. E., & da Silva Julia, R. M. (1999). *Data-flow synthesis for logic programs. System Analysis Modeling Simulation, 36*(3), 349-366.

Castello, R., Mili, R., & Tollis, I. G. (2000). An algorithmic framework for visualizing statecharts. *Proceedings of the 8th International Symposium on Graph Drawing, GD 2000* (pp. 139-149).

Catarci, T., Costabile, M. F., Levialdi, S., & Batini, C. (1997). Visual query systems for databases: A survey. *Journal of Visual Languages and Computing, 8*(2), 215-260.

Catarci, T., Santucci, G., & Angelaccio, M. (1993). Fundamental graphical primitives for visual query languages. *Information Systems, 18*(3), 75-98.

Celms, E., Kalnins, A., & Lace, L. (2003). Diagram definition facilities based on metamodel mappings. *Proceedings OOPSLA2003 Workshop on Domain Specific Modeling.*

Chang, S. K., & Mussio, P. (1996). Customized visual language design. *Proceedings of International Conference on Software Engineering and Knowledge Engineering (SEKE 96)* (pp. 553-562). Lake Tahoe, NV: IEEE Computer Society Press.

Chang, S. K., Hou, T. Y., & Hsu, A. (1992). Smart image design for large image databases. *Journal of Visual Languages & Computing, 3*(4), 323-342.

Chavda, M., & Wood, P. T. (1997). Towards an ODMG-compliant visual object query language. *International Conference on Very Large Data Bases (VLDB'97)* (pp. 456-465).

Chawathe, S., Baby, T., & Yeo, J. (2001). VQBD: Exploring semistructured data (demonstration description). *Proceedings of the ACM SIGMOD* (p. 603).

Cheeseman, P., & Stutz, J. (1996). Bayesian classification (AutoClass): Theory and results. In U. Fayyad, G. Piatetsky-Shapiro, P. Smyth, & R. Uthurusamy (Ed.), *Advances in knowledge discovery and data mining.* Menlo Park, CA: AAAI Press/MIT Press.

Chen, P. P. (1976). The entity-relationship model: Towards a unified view of data. *ACM Transactions on Database Systems, 1*(1), 9-36.

Chen, Y., Wah, B. W., & Hsu, C. (2005). Subgoal partitioning and resolution for temporal planning in SGPlan. *Journal of Artificial Intelligence Research, 26,* 323-369.

Chi, E., & Riedl, J. (1998). An operator interaction framework for visualization systems. In G. Wills & J. Dill (Ed.), *Proceedings IEEE Symposium on Information Visualization (InfoVis 98)* (pp. 63-70). Los Alamitos, CA: IEEE Computer Society.

Chok, S. S., & Marriott, K. (2003). Automatic generation of intelligent diagram editors. *ACM Transactions on Computer-Human Interaction, 10*(3), 244-276.

Christiansen, H. (2005). CHR grammars. *Theory and Practice of Logic Programming, 5,* 467-501.

Chuah, M. C., & Roth, S. F. (1996). On the semantics of interactive visualizations. *Proceedings IEEE Symposium on Information Visualization 96* (pp. 29-36). Los Alamitos, CA: IEEE Computer Society.

Clarke, D. (1982). An augmented directed graph base for application development. *Proceedings of the 20th Annual Southeast Regional Conference* (pp. 155-159). Knoxville, TN: ACM Press.

Cleveland, W. S., & McGill, R. (1984). Graphical perception: Theory, experimentation, and application of the development of graphical methods. *Journal of American Statistical Association, 79*(387), 531-554.

Codd, E. F. (1970). A relational model of data for large shared databanks. *Communications of the ACM, 13*(6), 377-387.

Codognet, P. (1999). An Historical account of indexical images: From Ancient Art to the Web. *Proceedings of the 1999 IEEE Symposium on Visual Languages* (pp. 104-110). Tokyo, Japan: IEEE Press.

Cohen, P. R., Morrison, C. T., & Cannon, E. (2005). Maps for verbs: The relation between interaction dynamics and verb use.

Cohen, S., Kanza, Y., Kogan, Y. A., Nutt, W., Sagiv, Y., & Serebrenik, A. (1999). Equix easy querying in XML databases. *WebDB (Informal Proceedings)* (pp.43-48).

Coiera, E. (2001). Mediated agent interaction. *Proceedings of the 8th Conference on Artificial Intelligence in Medicine Europe*, AIME 2001.

Comai, S., Damiani, E., & Fraternali, P. (2001). Computing graphical queries over XML data. *ACM Transaction on Information Systems 19*(4), 371-430.

Comai, S., Damiani, E., Posenato, R., & Tanca, L. (1998). A schema based approach to modeling and querying WWW data. *FQAS'98* (pp. 110-125).

CommentEdition. (2000). *UIRupture* (Tech. Rep.). UIDesign. http://www.uidesign.net

Conallen, J. (1999). Modelling Web application architectures with UML. *Communications of the ACM, 42*(10), 63-70.

Consens, M. P., & Mendelzon, A. O. (1990). The G+/GraphLog visual query system. *Proceedings of the 12th ACM SIGMOD* (p. 388). Atlantic City, NJ, USA.

Constantine, L. L., & Lockwood, L. A. D. (2001). Structure and style in use cases for user interface design. In M. van Harmelen (Ed.), *Object modelling and user interface design* (pp. 245-279). Addison-Wesley Longman Publishing.

Costabile, M. F., Esposito, F., Semeraro, G., & Fanizzi, N. (1999). An adaptive visual environment for digital libraries. *International Journal on Digital Libraries, 2*(2 and 3), 124-143.

Costabile, M. F., Fogli, D., Fresta, G., Mussio, P., & Piccinno, A. (2003). Building environments for end-user development and tailoring. In *Proceedings of the 2003 IEEE Symposia on Human Centric Computing Languages and Environments (HCC'03)* (pp. 31-38). Auckland, New Zealand: IEEE Computer Society Press.

Costabile, M. F., Fogli, D., Fresta, G., Mussio, P., & Piccinno, A. (2004). Software environments for end user development and tailoring. *Psychology, 2*(1), 99-122.

Costabile, M. F., Fogli, D., Lanzilotti, R., Mussio, P., & Piccinno, A. (2006b). Supporting work practice through end user development environments. *Journal of Organizational and End User Computing, 18*(6), 63-65.

Costabile, M. F., Fogli, D., Marcante, A., & Piccinno, A. (2006b). Supporting interaction and co-evolution of users and systems. *Proceedings of AVI 2006* (pp. 143-150). Venezia, Italy: ACM Press.

Costabile, M. F., Fogli, D., Marcante, A., Mussio, P., & Piccinno, A. (2006d). Interactive environments supporting user and system co-evolution. In C. Hochberger & R. Liskowsky (Eds.), *Lecture Notes in Informatics (LNI). Proceedings of Informatik 2006: Vol. P93* (pp. 588-591). Dresden, Germany: Köllen Druck+Verlag GmbH.

Costabile, M. F., Fogli, D., Mussio, P., & Piccinno, A. (2005). End-user development: The software shaping workshop approach. In H. Lieberman, F. Paternò, & V. Wulf (Eds), *End user development: Empowering people to flexibly employ advanced information and communication technology*. Dordrecht, The Netherlands: Kluwer Academic Publishers.

Costagliola, G., & Deufemia, V. (2003). Visual language editors based on LR parsing techniques. *Proceeding of SIGPARSE/ACL 8th International Workshop in Parsing Technologies* (pp. 79-90).

Costagliola, G., De Lucia, A., Orefice, S., & Polese, G. (2002). A classification framework to support the design of visual languages. *Journal of Visual Languages and Computing, 13*(6), 573-600.

Costagliola, G., Deufemia, V., & Polese, G. (2004). A framework for modeling and implementing visual notations with applications to software engineering. *ACM Transactions on Software Engineering and Methodology, 13*(4), 431-487.

Costagliola, G., Deufemia, V., & Risi, M. (2005). Sketch grammars: A formalism for describing and recognizing diagrammatic sketch languages. *Proceedings of ICDAR'05* (pp. 1226-1230). IEEE Press.

Costagliola, G., Deufemia, V., Polese, G., & Risi, M. (2004). A parsing technique for sketch recognition systems. *Proceedings of IEEE Symposium on Visual Languages and Human-Centric Computing* (pp. 19-26). IEEE Press.

Cova, T. J., & Goodchild, M. F. (2002). Extending geographical representation to include fields of spatial objects.

Cox, D. (2006). Metaphoric mappings: The art of visualization. In P. Fishwick (Ed.), *Aesthetic computing* (pp. 89-114). MIT Press.

Crimi, C., Guercio, A., Nota, G., Pacini, G., Tortora, G., & Tucci, M. (1990). Relation grammars for modelling multi-dimensional structures. *IEEE Symposium on Visual Languages* (pp. 168-173). IEEE Computer Society Press.

Cruz, I. F., Mendelzon, A. O., & Wood, P. T. (1987). A graphical query language supporting recursion. *Proceedings of the 9th ACM SIGMOD Conference* (pp. 323-330). San Francisco, California, USA.

Cruz, I. F., Mendelzon, A. O., & Wood, P. T. (1988). G+: Recursive queries without recursion. The *2nd International Conference on Expert Database Systems* (pp. 355–368).

Czejdo, B., Embley, D., Reddy, V., & Rusinkiewicz, M. (1989). A visual query language for an ER data model. *IEEE Workshop on Visual Languages* (pp. 165-170).

Damm, C., Hansen, K., & Thomsen, M. (2000). Tool support for cooperative object-oriented design: Gesture-based modeling on an electronic whiteboard. *CHI Letters, 2*(1), 518-525.

Dann, W. P., Cooper, S., & Pausch, R. (2006). *Learning to program in Alice*. Pearson Custom Publishing.

Davidson, R., & Harel, D. (1996). Drawing graphs nicely using simulated annealing. *ACM Transaction on Graphics, 15*(4), 301-331.

Davies, C., & Medyckyj-Scott, D. (1994). GIS usability: Recommendations based on the user's view. *International Journal of Geographic Information Systems, 8*(2), 175-189.

de Lara, J. (2002). Simulación Educativa mediante Meta-Modelado y Gramáticas de Grafos. *Revista de Enseñanza y Tecnología* nº 23, Mayo-Agosto 2002.

de Lara, J., & Taentzer, G. (2004). Automated model transformation and its validation using AToM³ and AGG. *Proceedings Diagrams 2004* (pp. 182-198). Berlin: Springer.

de Lara, J., & Vangheluwe, H. (2002). AToM³: Atool for multi-formalism modelling and meta-modelling. *Proceedings of Fundamental Approaches to Software Engineering 5th International Conference, held as part of the Joint European Conferences on Theory and Practice of Software, Grenoble, France. Lecture Notes in Computer Science 2306* (pp. 174-188). Springer-Verlag. Retrieved from http://atom3.cs.mcgill.ca

de Lara, J., & Vangheluwe, H. (2004). Defining visual notations and their manipulation through meta-modelling and graph transformation. *Journal of Visual Languages and Computing, 15*(3-4), 309-330.

De Souza, C. S. (2005). *The semiotic engineering of human computer interaction*. MIT Press.

Dennebouy, Y., Andersson, M., Auddino, A., Dupont, Y., Fontana, E., Gentile, M., & Spaccapietra, S. (1995). SUPER: Visual interfaces for object + relationships data models. *Journal of Visual Languages and Computing, 6*(1), 73-99.

Deray, K. (2000). Through plane: A kinetic model for information retrieval. *Proceedings of the 11th Australasian Conference on Information Systems ACIS 2000.*

DiBiase, D. (1990), Visualization in the Earth Sciences. Earth and Mineral Sciences, Bulletin of the College of Earth and Mineral Sciences, PSU 59(2). 13-18.

Diehl, S. (2001). *Software visualization*. Springer Verlag, May 2001, LLCS 2269.

Diestel, R. (2000). *Graph theory (graduate texts in mathematics)* (2nd ed.). Springer.

Dix, A., Finlay, J., Abowd, G., & Beale, R. (2004). *Human computer interaction*. London: Prentice Hall.

DMG (The Data Mining Group). *PMML: Predictive Model Markup Language*. Retrieved March 15, 2006, from http://www.dmg.org

Doan, D. K., Paton, N. W., Kilgour, A. C., & al-Qa-imari, G. (1995). Multi-paradigm query interface to an object-oriented database. *Interacting with Computers, 7*(1), 25-47.

Dooms, G., Deville, Y., & Dupont, P. (2004). Constrained path finding in biochemical networks. *Proceedings of the 5th Open Days in Biology, Computer Science, and Mathematics, JOBIM 2004* (pp. J0-40).

Dooms, G., Deville, Y., & Dupont, P. (2004). A Mozart implementation of CP(BioNet). *Proceedings of the 2nd International Conference on Multiparadigm Programming in Mozart/Oz, MOZ 2004* (pp. 237-250). LNCS 3389, Springer.

Drew, P., Chatwin, J., & Collins, S. (2001). Conversation analysis: A method for research into interactions between patients and healthcare professionals. *Health Expectations, 4*(1), 58-70.

Dreyfus, H. L. (1972). *What computers can't do: A critique of artificial reason.* NY: Harper and Row.

Dunbar-Jacob, J., & Schlenk, E. (2001). Patient adherence to treatment regimens. In A. Baum, T. Revenson, & J. Singer (Eds.), *Handbook of health psychology.* Mahwah, NJ: Erlbaum.

Dykes, J. A. (1995). Cartographic visualization for spatial analysis. *Proceedings International Cartographic Conference* (pp. 1365-1370), ICA Barcelona.

Dykes, J. A. (1998). Cartographic visualization: Exploratory spatial data analysis with local indicators of spatial association using Tcl/Tk and cdv. *The Statistician, 47*(3), 485-497.

Eades, P. (1984). A heuristic for graph drawing. *Congressus Numerantium, 42,* 149-160.

Eades, P., Lin, X., & Smyth, W. F. (1993). A fast and effective heuristic for the feedback arc set problem. *Information Processing Letters, 47*(6), 319-323.

Edelkamp, S., & Hoffmann, J. (2004). PDDL 2.2: The language for the classical part of IPC-4. *Proceedings of the International Planning Competition International Conference on Automated Planning and Scheduling* (pp. 1-7).

Edwards, B. (1987). Drawing on the artist within: A guide to innovation, invention, imagination and creativity. Collins, London.

Egenhofer, M. J. (1994). Spatial SQL: A query and presentation language. *IEEE Transaction on Knowledge and Data Engineering, 6*(1), 86-95.

Egenhofer, M. J. (1997). Query processing in spatial-query- by-sketch. *Journal of Visual Languages and Computing, 8*(4), 403-424.

Ehrig, H., Ehrig, K., de Lara, J., Taentzer, G., Varró, D., & Varró-Gyapay, S. (2005). Termination criteria for model transformation. *Proceedings of Fundamental Approaches to Software Engineering 8th International Conference, held as part of the Joint European Conferences on Theory and Practice of Software,* Edinburgh, Scotland. LNCS 3442 (pp. 49-63). Springer-Verlag.

Ehrig, H., Ehrig, K., Habel, A., & Penemann, K.-H. (2004). Constraints and application conditions: From graphs to high-level structures. *Proceedings of 2nd International Conference on Graph Transformation,* Rome, Italy. LNCS 3256 (pp. 287-303). Springer-Verlag.

Ehrig, H., Ehrig, K., Prange, U., & Taentzer, G. (2005a). Formal integration of inheritance with typed attributed graph transformation for efficient VL definition and model manipulation. *Proceedings of Visual Languages/Human Centric Computing 2005* (pp. 71-78).

Ehrig, H., Ehrig, K., Prange, U., & Taentzer, G. (2006). *Fundamentals of Algebraic graph transformation.* Monographs in Theoretical Computer Science. Springer.

Ehrig, H., Engels, G., Kreowski, H. J., & Rozenberg, G. (1997). *Handbook of graph grammars and computing by graph transformation. Vol 1.* World Scientific.

Ehrig, H., Heckel, R., Korff, M., Löwe, M., Ribeiro, L., Wagner, A., & Corradini, A. (1997). Algebraic approaches to graph transformation II: Single pushout approach and comparison with double pushout approach. In G. Rozenberg (Ed.), *Handbook of graph grammars and computing by graph transformation* (Vol. 1: Foundations, Chapter 4, pp. 247-312). Singapore: World Scientific.

Ehrig, K., Küster, J., Taentzer, G., & Winkelmann, J. (2005b). *Automatically generating instances of meta models* (Tech. Rep. No. 2005-09). Berlin, Germany: Technische Universität Berlin.

Elkoutbi, M., & Keller, R. K. (2000). User interface prototyping based on UML scenarios and high level Petri nets. *International Conference on Application and Theory of Petri Nets (ICATPN 2000)*, LNCS 1825 (pp. 166-186).

Elkoutbi, M., Khriss, I., & Keller, R. K. (1999). Generating user interface prototypes from scenarios. *Requirements Engineering'99* (pp. 150-158). IEEE Computer Society.

Ermel, C., & Bardohl, R. (2004). Scenario animation for visual behavior models: A generic approach. *Journal of Software and Systems Modeling, 3*(2), 164-177.

Ermel, C., Hölscher, K., Kuske, S., & Ziemann, P. (2005). Animated simulation of integrated UML behavioural models based on graph transformation. *Proceedings of the 2005 IEEE Symposium on Visual Languages and Human-Centric Computing* (pp. 125-133). Dallas, Texas, USA.

Ertöz, L., Steinbach, M., & Kumar, V. (2003). Finding clusters of different sizes, shapes, and densities in noisy, high dimensional data. In D. Barbará & C. Kamath (Ed.), *Proceedings of the 3rd SIAM International Conference on Data Mining*. SIAM. Retrieved from http://www.siam.org/meetings/sdm03/index.htm

Erwig, M. (1998). Abstract syntax and semantics of visual languages. *Journal of Visual Languages and Computing, 9*(5), 461-483.

Erwig, M. (2003). Xing: A visual XML query language. *Journal of Visual Languages and Computing 14*(1), 5-45.

Erwig, M., & Meyer, B. (1995). Heterogeneous visual languages—integrating textual and visual programming.

International IEEE Workshop on Visual Languages (VL'95) (pp. 318-325). Darmstadt, Germany.

Erwig, M., & Schneider, M. (2000). Query-by-trace. Visual predicate specification in spatio-temporal databases. *Proceedings of the 5th IFIP Conference on Visual Databases* (pp. 199-218).

Esselink, B. (2000). *A practical guide to localization.* Amsterdam, The Netherlands: John Benjamins Publishing Co.

Ester, M., Kriegel, H. P., Sander, J., & Xu, X. (1996). A density-based algorithm for discovering clusters in large spatial databases with noise. In E. Simoudis, J. Han, & U. M. Fayyad (Ed.), *Proceedings of the 2nd International Conference on Knowledge Discovery and Data Mining (KDD-96)* (pp. 226-231). AAAI Press.

Fahmy, H., & Holt, R. C. (2000). Software architecture transformations. *Proceedings of the 16th IEEE International Conference on Software Maintenance* (pp. 88-96).

Favetta, F., & Aufaure-Portier, M. A. (2000). About ambiguities in visual GIS query languages: A taxonomy and solutions. *Proceedings of the 4th International Conference on Advances in Visual Information Systems* (pp. 154-165). Springer-Verlag.

Fayyad, U., Piatetsky-Shapiro, G., & Smyth, P. (1996b). Knowledge discovery and data mining: Towards a unifying framework. In E. Simoudis, J. Han, & U. M. Fayyad (Ed.), *Proceedings of the 2nd International Conference on Knowledge Discovery and Data Mining*. AAAI Press.

Fayyad, U., Piatetsky-Shapiro, G., Smyth, P., & Uthurusamy, R. (Ed.). (1996a). *Advances in knowledge discovery and data mining.* Menlo Park, CA: AAAI Press/MIT Press.

Feder, J. (1971). Plex languages. *Information Science, 3*, 225-241.

Feenberg, A. (1999). *Questioning technology.* London, UK: Routledge.

Fegaras, L. (1999). VOODOO: A visual object-oriented database language for ODMG OQL. *ECOOP Workshop on Object-Oriented Databases* (pp. 61-72).

Fernandez, M., Siméon, J., Wadler, P., Cluet, S., Deutsch, A., Florescu, D., Levy, A., Maier, D., Mchugh, J., Robie, J., Suciu, D., & Widom, J. (1999). *XML query languages: Experiences and exemplars*. Retrieved April, 19, 2006 from http://www-db.research.bell-labs.com/user/simeon/xquery.html

Ferri, F., & Rafanelli, M. (2004). Resolution of ambiguities in query interpretation for geographical pictorial query languages. *Journal of Computing and Information Technology, 12*(2), 119-126.

Ferri, F., & Rafanelli, M. (2005). GeoPQL: A geographical pictorial query language that resolves ambiguities in query interpretation. *Journal of Data Semantics*, (Vol III), 50-80.

Ferri, F., Massari, F., & Rafanelli, M. (1999). *A pictorial query language for geographic features in an object-oriented environment. Journal of Visual Languages and Computing, 10*(6), 641-671.

Fikes, R., & Nilsson, N. J. (1971). STRIPS: A new approach to the application of theorem proving to problem solving. *Artificial Intelligence, 2*(3-4), 189-208.

Filha, I. M. R. E., Laender, A. H. F., & Da Silva, A. S. (2001). Querying semistructured data by example: The QSBYE interface. *Workshop on Information Integration on the Web* (pp. 156-163).

Finkelstein, A., Kramer, J., Nuseibeh, B., Finkelstein, L., & Goedicke, M. (1992). ViewPoints: A framework for integrating multiple perspectives in system development. *International Journal of Software Engineering and Knowledge Engineering, 2*(1), 31-57.

Fischer, G. (1998). Seeding, evolutionary growth, and reseeding: Constructing, capturing, and evolving knowledge in domain-oriented design environments. *Automated Software Engineering, 5*(4), 447-468.

Fischer, G. (2006). Distributed intelligence: Extending the power of the unaided, individual human mind. *Proceedings of the International Conference on Advanced Visual Interfaces 2006* (pp. 7-14). Venezia, Italia: ACM Press.

Fischer, G., Giaccardi, E., Ye, Y., Sutcliffe, A. G., & Mehandjiev, N. (2004). Meta-design: A manifesto for end user development. *Communications of the ACM, 47*(9), 33-37.

Fischer, K. W., & Bidell, T. R. (1998). Dynamic development of psychological structures in action and thought. In T. R. Bidell & D. W. Damon (Eds), *Handbook of child psychology: Vol. 1: Theoretical models of human development* (pp. 467-561). NY: John Wiley & Sons.

Fischer, T., Niere, J., Torunski, L., & Zuendorf, A. (1998). Story diagrams: A new graph rewrite language based on the unified modeling language. *Proceedings of Theory and Application of Graph Transformations 6th International Workshop,* Paderborn, Germany. LNCS1764 (pp. 296-309). Springer-Verlag. Retrieved from http://www.fuiaba.de

Fisher, P. F. (1998). Is GIS hidebound by the legacy of cartography? *Cartographic Journal, 35*(1), 5-9.

Fishwick, P. (2006). *Aesthetic computing.* MIT Press.

Fishwick, P., Davis, T., & Douglas, J. (2005, July). An empirical study of aesthetic computing. *ACM Transactions on Modeling and Computer Simulation, 18*(3), 254-279.

Fluit, C., Sabou, M., & van Harmelen, F. (2003). Ontology-based information visualization. In V. Geroimenko & C. Chen (Ed.), *Visualizing the Semantic Web* (pp. 36-48). Springer-Verlag.

Fogli, D., Fresta, G., Marcante, A., & Mussio, P. (2004). IM2L: A user interface description language supporting electronic annotation. *Proceedings of Workshop on Developing User Interface with XML: Advances on User Interface Description Languages* (pp. 135-142), Gallipoli, Italy.

Fogli, D., Marcante, A., Mussio, P., Parasiliti Provenza, L., & Piccinno, A. (2006). *Modelling visual interactive systems through virtual entities* (Tech. Rep. No. 03). Italy: University of Bari.

Fogli, D., Mussio, P., Celentano, A., & Pittarello, F. (2002). Toward a model-based approach to the specification of virtual reality environments. *Proceedings of the Multimedia Software Engineering (MSE2002)* (pp. 148-155). Newport Beach, CA: IEEE Computer Society Press.

Folmer, E., van Welie, M., & Bosch, J. (2005). Bridging patterns: An approach to bridge gaps between SE and HCI. *Journal of Information and Software Technology, 48*(2), 69-89.

Fonseca, M. J., & Jorge J. A. (2000). *CALI : A software library for calligraphic interfaces. INESC-ID*. Retrieved from http://immi.inesc-id.pt/cali/

Fonseca, M. J., Pimentel, C., & Jorge, J. A. (2002). CALI: An online scribble recognizer for calligraphic interfaces. *Proceedings of AAAI Spring Symp. on Sketch Understanding* (pp. 51-58). AAAI Press.

Foster, G. (1995, April). *The cleanest Fourier spectrum. Astronomical Journal, 109*(4), 1889-1902.

Fowler, M. (1999). *Refactoring: Improving the design of existing code*. Addison Wesley.

Fox, M., & Long, D. (2003). PDDL2.1: An extension to PDDL for expressing temporal planning domains. *Journal of Artificial Intelligence Research, 20*, 61-124.

Fraley, C., & Raftery, A. (1999). *MCLUST: Software for model-based cluster and discriminant analysis* (Tech. Rep. 342). Department of Statistics, University of Washington.

Friedman-Hill, E. J. (2002). *Jess, the expert system shell for the Java Platform*. Retrieved from http://herzberg.ca.sandia.gov/jess/

Frühwirth, T. (1998). Theory and practice of constraint handling rules. *Journal of Logic Programming, 37*, 95-138.

Fuhrmann, S., MacEachren, A. M., Dou, J., Wang, K., & Cox, A. (2005). Gesture and speech-based maps to support use of GIS for crisis management. In *AutoCarto* Las Vegas, NA.

Futrelle, R. P. (1999). Ambiguity in visual language theory and its role in diagram parsing. *IEEE Symposium on Visual Languages* (pp. 172-175). Tokyo: IEEE Computer Soc.

Gabbard, J. L., Hix, D., & Swan, J. E. (1999). User-centred design and evaluation of virtual environments. *IEEE Computer Graphics and Applications, 19*(6), 51-59.

Ganti, V., Gehrke, J., & Ramakrishnan, R. (1999). CACTUS: Clustering categorical data using summaries. In S. Chaudhuri & D. Madigan (Ed.), *Proceedings of the 5th ACM SIGKDD International Conference on Knowledge Discovery and Data Mining* (pp. 73-83). New York: ACM Press.

Gardiner, V., & Unwin, D. J. (1986). Computers and the field class. *Journal of Geography in Higher Education*, 1721-32.

Gardner, H. (1983). *Frames of mind: The theory of multiple intelligences*. NY: Basic Books.

Gardner, H. E. (1984). *Art, mind, and brain: A cognitive approach to creativity*. Basic Books.

GeoMedia – About GeoMedia, Intergraph, http://imgs.intergraph.com/geomedia/

Gerevini, A., & Long, D. (2005). Plan constraints and preferences in PDDL3. *Technical Report R.T. 2005-08-47*, Dipartimento di Elettronica per l'Automazione, Università degli Studi di Brescia, via Branze 38, 25123 Brescia, Italy.

Gerevini, A., Saetti, A., & Serina, I. (2003). Planning through stochastic local search and temporal action graphs. *Journal of Artificial Intelligence Research, 20*, 239-290.

Gerevini, A., Saetti, A., & Serina, I. (2004). Planning in PDDL2.2 domains with LPG-TD. *International Planning Competition, 14th International Conference on Automated Planning and Scheduling (ICAPS-04), abstract booklet of the competing planners*.

Ghallab, M., Howe, A., Knoblock, C., McDermott, D., Ram, A., Veloso, M., Weld, D., & Wilkins, D. (1998).

PDDL: The planning domain definition language. *Technical report, Yale University*, New Haven, CT.

Gips, J. (1999). Computer implementation of shape grammars. *NSF/MIT Workshop on Shape Computation.*

Girard, J. Y. (1987). Linear logic. *Theoretical Computer Science, 50,* 1-102.

Girard, J. Y. (1995). Linear logic, its syntax, and semantics. In Girard & R. Lafont (Ed.), *Advances in linear logic, London Mathematical Society Lecture Notes Series 222.* Cambridge University Press.

Glenberg, A. M., & Kaschak, M. P. (2003). The body's contribution to language. In B. H. Ross (Ed.), *The psychology of learning and motivation* (p. 43). San Diego: Academic Press.

Glenberg, A. M., & Robertson, D. A. (2000). Symbol grounding and meaning. A comparison of high dimensional and embodied theories of meaning. *JML, 43*(3), 379-401.

Goedicke, M., Enders, B. E., Meyer, T., & Taentzer, G. (1999). Towards integrating multiple perspectives by distributed graph transformation. *Proceedings of the 1st International Workshop on Applications of Graph Transformation with Industrial Relevance.* LNCS 1779 (pp. 369-377). Springer-Verlag.

Goil, S., Nagesh, H., & Choudhary, A. (1999). *MAFIA: Efficient and scalable subspace clustering for very large data sets* (Tech. Rep. CPDC-TR-9906-010). Evanston, IL: Northwestern University.

Goldberg, A. (1995). *Constructions: A construction grammar approach to argument structure.* Chicago: University of Chicago Press.

Goldberg, A., Burnett, M., & Lewis, T. (1995). What is visual object-oriented programming? In M. M. Burnett, A. Goldberg, & T. G. Lewis (Eds.), *Visual object-oriented programming: Concepts and environments* (pp. 3-20). Greenwich, CT: Manning Publications Co.

Golin, E. J. (1991). Parsing visual languages with picture layout grammars. *Journal of Visual Languages and Computing, 2*(4), 1-23.

Göttler, H. (1986). Graph grammars, a new paradigm for implementing visual languages. EUROGRAPHICS, 89, 505-516. Elsevier Science publishers (North-Holland).

Göttler, H. (1986). Graph grammars and diagram editing. *Graph-Grammars and Their Application to Computer Science,* LNCS 291 (pp. 211-231). New York: Springer-Verlag.

Governatori, G. (2005). Representing business contracts in RuleML. *International Journal of Cooperative Information Systems, 14*(2-3), 181-216.

Governatori, G., Dumas, M., Hofstede, A., & Oaks, P. (2001). A formal approach to protocols and strategies for (legal) negotiation. *Proceedings of the 8th International Conference of Artificial Intelligence and Law* (pp. 168-177). ACM Press.

Graphviz: Graph Visualization Software. Retrieved April 23, 2006, from http://www.graphviz.org

Gray, J., Rossi, M., & Tolvanen, J. P. (2004). Preface. *Journal of Visual Languages and Computing, 15*(3-4), 207-209.

Greenberg, I. (2006). *Foundation processing.* Friends of ED.

Grinstein, G. G., Hoffman, P. E., Laskowski, S. J., & Pickett, R. M. (2002). Benchmark development for the evaluation of visualization for data mining. In U. Fayyad, G. G. Grinstein, & A. Wierse (Eds.), *Information visualization in data mining and knowledge discovery.* San Francisco: Morgan Kaufmann Publishers.

Grosof, B. N., & Poon, T. C. (2003). SweetDeal: Representing agent contracts with exceptions using XML rules, ontologies, and process descriptions. *Proceedings of the 12th International Conference on World Wide Web* (pp. 340-349). ACM Press.

Grosof, B. N., Gandhe, M. D., & Finin, T. W. (2002). SweetJess: Translating DAMLRuleML to JESS. *Proceedings of the International Workshop on Rule Markup Languages for Business Rules on the Semantic Web.* Held at 1st Int. Semantic Web Conference.

Gross, M. D. (1994). Recognizing and interpreting diagrams in design. *Proceedings of Working Conference on Advanced Visual Interfaces* (pp. 88-94). ACM Press.

Gross, M. D. (1996). The electronic cocktail napkin: A computational environment for working with design diagrams. *Design Studies, 17*(1), 53-69.

Gross, M. D., & Do, E. (1996). Ambiguous intentions: A paper-like interface for creative design. *Proceedings of ACM Symposium on User Interfaces Software and Technology* (pp. 183-192). ACM Press.

Grundy, J. C., Mugridge, W. B., & Hosking, J. G. (1998). Visual specification of multiview visual environments. *Proceedings of the 1998 IEEE Symposium on Visual Languages* (pp. 236-243).Nova Scotia, Canada.

Guerra, E., & de Lara, J. (2004). Event-driven grammars: Towards the integration of meta-modelling and graph transformation. *Proceedings International Conference on Graph Transformation 2004* (pp. 54-69). Berlin: Springer.

Guerra, E., & de Lara, J. (2006a). *Typed attributed triple graph trasformation with inheritance in the double pushout approach* (Tech. Rep. UC3M-TR-CS-06-01). Madrid, Spain: Universidad Carlos III. Retrieved from http://www.ii.uam.es/~ilara/articles

Guerra, E., & de Lara, J. (2006b). Graph transformation vs. OCL for view definition. *Proceedings of the 1st International Workshop on Algebraic Foundations for OCL and Applications*, Valencia, Spain.

Guerra, E., Díaz, P., & de Lara, J. (2005). A formal approach to the generation of visual language environments supporting multiple views. *Proceedings of the 2005 IEEE Symposium on Visual Languages and Human-Centric Computing* (pp. 284-286). Dallas, Texas, USA.

Guest, A. H. (2005): *Labanotation: The system of analyzing and recording movement*. NY: Routledge.

Guha, S., Rastogi, R., & Shim, K. (1998). CURE: An efficient clustering algorithm for large databases. *Proceedings of the 1998 ACM SIGMOD International Conference on Management of Data* (pp. 73-84). New York: ACM Press.

Guha, S., Rastogi, R., & Shim, K. (1999). ROCK: A robust clustering algorithm for categorical attributes. In M. Kitsuregawa, L. Maciaszek, M. Papazoglou, & C. Pu (Ed.), *Proceedings of the 15th International Conference on Data Engineering (ICDE)* (pp. 512-521). Los Alamitos, CA: IEEE Computer Society.

Haarslev, V. (1994). Personal communication.

Haarslev, V. (1998). A fully formalized theory for describing visual notations. In K. Marriott, & B. Meyer (Eds.), *Visual language theory* (pp. 261-292). New York: Springer.

Haarslev, V., & Wessel, M. (1997). Querying GIS with animated spatial sketches. The *13th IEEE Symposium on Visual Languages 1997 (VL'97)* (pp. 201-208).

Haber, E. M., Ioannidis, Y. E., & Livny, M. (1994). Foundations of visual metaphors for schema display. *Journal of Intelligent Information Systems, 3*(3-4), 263-298.

Hackney, P. (2000). *Making connections: Total body integration through Bartenieff fundamentals*. Harwood Academic (Performing Arts).

Hackos, J. T., & Redish, J. C. (1998). *User and task analysis for interface design*. New York: Wiley Computer Publishing.

Hammer, E. (1996). Representing relations diagrammatically. In G. Allwein & J. Barwise (Eds.), *Logical reasoning with diagrams*. New York: Oxford University Press.

Hammond, T., & Davis, R. (2002). Tahuti: A geometrical sketch recognition system for UML class diagrams. *Proceedings of AAAI Symp. on Sketch Understanding* (pp. 51-58). AAAI Press.

Hammond, T., & Davis, R. (2005). LADDER, A sketching language for user interface developers. *Computers & Graphics, 29*(4), 518-532.

Hansen, P., & Jaumard, B. (1997). Cluster analysis and mathematical programming. *Mathematical Programming 79*, 191-215.

Harel, D. (1987). Statecharts: A visual formalism for complex systems. *Science of Computer. Programming, 8*(3), 231-274.

Harel, D. (1988). On visual formalisms. *Communications of the ACM, 31*(5), 514-530.

Harel, D., & Gery, E. (1997). Executable object modelling with statecharts. *IEEE Computer, 30*(7), 31-42.

Harland, J., & Pym, D. (1994). A uniform proof-theoretic investigation of linear logic programming. *Journal of Logic and Computation, 4*(2), 175-207.

Harland, J., Pym, D., & Winikoff, M. (1996). Programming in Lygon: An overview. *Algebraic methodology and software technology, LNCS 1101* (pp. 391-405). Springer.

Harris, R. (2000). *Rethinking writing.* London, UK: The Athlone Press.

Harrower, M., MacEachren, A., & Griffin, A. L. (2000). Developing a geographic visualization tool to support earth science learning. *Cartography and Geographic Information Science, 27*(4), 279-293. Retrieved April 21, 2006, from http://www.interaction-design.org/encyclopedia/interaction_styles.html

Hartigan, J. A. (1975). *Clustering algorithms.* New York: John Wiley & Sons.

Hartigan, J. A., & Wong, M. (1979). Algorithm AS136: A k-means clustering algorithm. *Applied Statistics 28,* 100-108.

Hartley, R., & Pfeiffer, H. (2000). Visual representation of procedural knowledge. *Proceedings of the 2000 IEEE International Symposium on Visual Languages (Vl'00).* VL. IEEE Computer Society, Washington, DC, 63.

Hayes, R. P., Bowman, L., Monahan, P. O., Marrero, D. G., & McHorney, C. A. (2006). Understanding diabetes medications from the perspective of patients with Type 2 diabetes: Prerequisite to medication concordance. *The Diabetes Educator, 32*(3), 404-414

Helm, R., & Marriott, K. (1990). Declarative specification of visual languages. *Proceedings of the IEEE Workshop on Visual Languages* (pp. 98-103). IEEE Press.

Helm, R., & Marriott, K. (1991). A declarative specification and semantics for visual languages. *Journal of Visual Languages and Computing, 2,* 311-331.

Helm, R., Marriott, K., & Odersky, M. (1991). Building visual language parsers. *ACM Conference Human Factors in Computing* (pp. 118-125).

Heumann, J. (2003). User experience storyboards: Building better UIs with RUP, UML, and Use Cases (Tech. Rep.). Rational Software.

Hinneburg, A., & Keim, D. A. (1998). An efficient approach to clustering in large multimedia databases with noise. In R. Agrawal, P. Stolorz, & G. Piatetsky-Shapiro (Ed.), *Proceedings of the 4th International Conference on Knowledge Discovery and Data Mining* (pp. 58-65). Menlo Park, CA: AAAI Press.

Hoffmann, J. (2003). The metric-FF planning system: Translating "ignoring delete lists" to Numeric State Variables. *Journal of Artificial Intelligence Research, 20,* 291-341.

Hoffmann, J., & Nebel, B. (2001). The FF planning system: Fast plan generation through heuristic search. *Journal of Artificial Intelligence Research, 14,* 253-302.

Holbaek-Hannsen, E., Haandlykken, P., & Nygaard, K. (1973). *System description and the delta language* (Publ. no 523). Oslo, NO: Norwegian Computing Center.

Holzinger, A. (2005). Usability engineering methods for software developers. *CACM, 48*(1), 71-74.

Hong, J. I., & Landay, J. A. (2000). SATIN: A toolkit for informal ink-based applications. *Proceedings of ACM Symposium on User Interfaces Software and Technology* (pp. 63-72). ACM Press.

Horrocks, I. (1998). *Constructing the user interface with statecharts.* Addison-Wesley.

Howes, A., & Young, R. M. (1991). Predicting the learnability of task-action mappings. *Proceedings SIGCHI Conference on Human Factors in Computing Systems* (pp. 113-118). New York: ACM Press.

Howse, J., Molina, F., Taylor, J., Kent, S., & Gil, J. (2001). Spider diagrams: A diagrammatic reasoning system. *Journal of Visual Languages and Computing, 12*(3), 299-324.

Hse, H., Shilman, M., & Newton, A. R. (2004). Robust sketched symbol fragmentation using templates. *Proceedings of International Conference on Intelligent User Interfaces* (pp. 156-160). ACM Press.

Hughes, J. (1989). *Why functional programming matters. The Computer Journal, 32*(2), 98-107.

Hutchins, E. L., Hollan, J. D., & Norman, D. (1986). Direct manipulation interfaces. In D. Norman & S. Draper (Eds.), *User centred system design* (pp. 87-124). Hillsdale, NJ: Lawrence Erlbaum Associates.

Hutchins, E. L., Hollan, J. D., & Norman, D. A. (1985). Direct manipulation interfaces. *Human-Computer Interaction, 1*(4), 311-338.

Hutchinson, A. (1977). *Labanotation*. NY: Theatre Books.

Ichikawa, T., Chang, S.K. (eds.) (1984). IEEE Computer Society Workshop on Visual Languages. Hiroshima, Silver Spring, USA: IEEE Computer Society Press.

Igarashi, T., Matsuoka, S., Kawachiya, S., & Tanaka, H. (1997). Interactive beautification: A technique for rapid geometric design. *Proceedings of ACM Symposium on User Interfaces Software and Technology* (pp. 105-114). ACM Press.

Ilogix. (2006a). *Rhapsody 6.2*. Iogix/Telelogic. Retrieved from http://www.ilogic.com

Ilogix. (2006b). *Statemare*. Iogix/Telelogic. Retrieved from http://www.ilogic.com

ISO. (1992). *ISO 9241, Ergonomic requirements for office work with visual display terminals (VDTs)*. Retrieved November 3, 2006, from http://www.iso.org/iso/en/CombinedQueryResult.CombinedQueryResult?queryString=9241

Ives, Z. G., & Lu, Y. (2000). XML query languages in practice: an evaluation. *Proceedings of WAIM'00* (pp. 29-40).

Jaeschke, G., & Schek, H. J. (1982). Remarks on the algebra on non first normal form relations. *Proceedings of 1ˢᵗ ACMSIGACT-SIGMOD Symposium on the Principles of Database Systems* (pp. 124-138).

Jain, A. K., & Dubes, R. C. (1988). *Algorithms for clustering data*. Englewood Cliffs, NJ: Prentice-Hall.

Jain, A. K., Murty, M. N., & Flynn, P. J. (1999). Data clustering: A review. *ACM Computing Surveys, 31*(3), 264-323.

Jakob, J., & Schürr, A. (2006). Creation of meta models by using modified triple graph grammars. *Proceedings of the 5ᵗʰ International Workshop on Graph Transformation and Visual Modelling Techniques. To appear in Electronic Notes in Theoretical Computer Science* (Elsevier).

Jakobsson, M. (2003). *Interaction styles*. Retrieved April 21, 2006 from http://lipas.uwasa.fi/~mj

Janneck, J., & Esser, R. (2001). A predicate-based approach to defining visual language syntax. *IEEE Symposium on Visual Languages and Formal Methods* (pp. 40-47). IEEE Computer Society.

Jansen, A. R., Marriott, K., & Meyer, B. (2004). Cider: A component-based toolkit for creating smart diagram environments. *Diagrams 2004* (pp. 415-419). Berlin: Springer.

Jansen, A., Marriott, K., & Meyer, B. (2003). CIDER: A component-based toolkit for creating smart diagram environments. The *9ᵗʰ International Conference on Distributed Multimedia Systems (DMS 2003)*, Miami, Florida.

Jantzen, J. (1989). Inference planning using digraphs and Boolean arrays. *Proceedings of the International Conference on APL* (pp. 200-204). ACM Press.

Jean, G. (1986). *L'écriture, mémoire des homes*. Paris: Gallimard.

Jensen, K. (1992). *Coloured Petri nets. Basic concepts, analysis methods, and practical use* (Vol. 1). EATCS Monographs in Theoretical Computer Science. Springer-Verlag.

Johnson, M. (1987). *The body in the mind: The bodily basis of cognition.* Chicago: University of Chicago Press.

Johnson, S. C. (1978). *YACC: Yet another compiler compiler.* Murray Hills, NJ: Bell Laboratories.

Jones, L (1972). *The Hall of Machines* In The Eye of the Lens, The MacMillan Company.

Kant, I. (1790). *The critique of judgment.* Oxford: Clarendon Press, translated by James Creed Meredith (1952).

Kaput, J. (1985). Representation and problem solving: Some methodological issues. In E. Silver (Ed.), *Teaching and learning problem solving: Multiple research perspectives* (pp. 381-398). Hillsdale.

Kara, L. B., & Stahovich, T. F. (2004). Sim-U-Sketch: A sketch-based interface for Simulink. *Proceedings of Working Conference on Advanced Visual Interfaces* (pp. 354-357). ACM Press.

Kara, L. B., & Stahovich, T. F. (2004). Hierarchical parsing and recognition of hand-sketched diagrams. *Proceedings of ACM Symposium on User Interfaces Software and Technology* (pp. 13-22). ACM Press.

Kara, L. B., & Stahovich, T. F. (2005). An image-based, trainable symbol recognizer for hand-drawn sketches. *Computers & Graphics, 29*(4), 501-517.

Kara, L. B., Gennari, L., & Stahovich, T. F. (2004). A sketch-based interface for the design and analysis of simple vibratory mechanical systems. *ASME International Design Engineering Technical Conferences.*

Karam, M., Boulos, J., Ollaic, H., & Koteiche, Z. (2006). XQueryViz: A visual dataflow XQuery tool. *Advanced International Conference on Telecommunications and International Conference on Internet and Web Applications and Services (AICT-ICIW'06)* (p. 196).

Karp, P. D., & Paley, S. M. (1994). Automated drawing of metabolic pathways. *Proceedings of the 3rd International Conference on Bioinformatics and Genome Research.*

Karsai, G., Agrawal, A., Shi, F., & Sprinkle, J. (2003). On the use of graph transformation in the formal specification of model interpreters. *Journal of Universal Computer Science 9*(11), 1296-1321.

Karypis, G., Han, E. H., & Kumar, V. (1999). Chameleon: Hierarchical clustering using dynamic modeling. *IEEE Computer, 32*(8), 68-75.

Kaufman, L., & Rousseeuw, P. J. (1990). *Finding groups in data-introduction to cluster analysis.* New York: John Wiley & Sons.

Kaufmann, M., & Wagner, D. (2001). *Graph drawing: Methods and models.* Springer.

Kaushik, S., & Rundensteiner, E. (1998). SVIQUEL: A spatial visual query and exploration language. *Database and Expert Systems Applications, (LNCS 1460, 290-299.)*

Kautz, H., & Selman, B. (1996). Pushing the envelope: Planning, propositional logic, and stochastic search. *Proceedings of the 13th National Conference on Artificial Intelligence* (pp. 1194-1201). Portland, Oregon.

Kautz, H., & Selman, B. (1998). BLACKBOX: A new approach to the application of theorem proving to problem solving. *Proceedings of the AIPS-98 Workshop on Planning as Combinatorial Search* (pp. 58-60). Pittsburgh, Pennsylvania.

Kehler, T. P., & Clemenson G. D. (1984, January). KEE the knowledge engineering environment for industry. *Systems and Software, 3*(1), 212-224.

Kelly, M. (1998). *Encyclopedia of Aesthetics (4 Volumes).* Oxford University Press.

Kepser, S. (2002). A proof of the Turing-completeness of XSLT and XQuery. *Technical report SFB 441, Eberhard Karls Universitat Tubingen. May.*

Kimani, S. (2002). An effective visual data mining environment. *Doctoral Posters at the International Conference on Very Large Data Bases (VLDB).*

Kimani, S., Catarci, T., & Santucci, G. (2003). Visual data mining: An experience with the users. In C. Stephanidis (Ed.), *Proceedings of HCI International: Universal Ac-*

cess in HCI: Inclusive Design in the Information Society. Lawrence Erlbaum Associates.

Kimani, S., Lodi, S., Catarci, T., Santucci, G., & Sartori, C. (2004). VidaMine: A visual data mining environment. *Journal of Visual Languages and Computing, 15*(1), 37-67.

Kindler, C. H., Szirt, L., Sommer, D., Hausler, R., & Langewitz, W. (2005). A quantitative analysis of anaesthetist-patient communication during the per-operative visit. *Anaesthesia, 60*(1), 53-59.

Koehler J., & Srivastava B. (2003). Web service composition: Current solutions and open problems. *ICAPS 2003 Workshop on Planning for Web Services* (pp. 28-35).

Königs, A. (2005). Model transformation with triple graph grammars. *Proceedings of the International Workshop on Model Transformation in Practice, satellite event of the ACM/IEEE 8th International Conference on Model Driven Engineering Languages and Systems*, Montego Bay, Jamaica.

Korsch, B. M., & Negrete, V. F. (1972). Doctor-patient communication. *Scientific American, 227*(2), 66-74.

Kosara, R., & Miksch, S. (2001). Metaphors of movement: A visualization and user interface for time-oriented, skeletal plans. *Artificial Intelligence in Medicine, Special Issue: Information Visualization in Medicine, 22*(2), 111-131.

Koua, E. L., & Kraak, M. J. (2005). Evaluating self-organizing maps for geovisualization. In J. Dykes, A. M. MacEachren, & M. J. Kraak (Eds.), *Exploring geovisualization.* (Eds,) pp. 627-634). Oxford: Elsevier.

Kovacevic, S. (1998). UML and user interface modeling. *UML'98*, LNCS 1618 (pp. 253-266).

Kreowski, H. J., & Kuske, S. (1999). *Graph transformation units and modules.* Handbook of graph grammars and computing by graph transformation: Vol. 2: Applications, languages, and tools (pp. 607-63). River Edge, NJ: World Scientific Publishing Co.

Kundu, K., Sessions, C., DesJardins, M., & Rheingans, P. (2002). Three-dimensional visualization of hierarchical

task network plans. *Proceedings of the 3rd International NASA Workshop on Planning and Scheduling for Space*, Houston, Texas.

Kuter, U., Sirin, E., Parsia, B., Dana, N., & James, H. (2005). Information gathering during planning for Web service composition. *Web semantics: Science, services, and agents on the World Wide Web, 3*(2-3), 183-205.

Kuutti, K. (1995). Activity theory as a potential framework for human-computer interaction. In B. Nardi (Ed.), *Context and consciousness: Activity theory and human computer interaction.* Cambridge, MA: MIT Press.

Laban, R. (1956). *Laban's principles of dance and movement notation* (2nd ed.). London: Macdonald & Evans.

Laban, R., & Lawrence, F. C. (1974). *Effort: Economy of human movement* (2nd ed.). Boston: Plays Inc.

Lakin, F. (1986). Spatial parsing for visual languages. In S. K. Chang, T. Ichikawa, & P. A. Ligomenides (Eds.), *Visual languages* (pp. 35-85). New York: Plenum Press.

Lakoff, G. (1988). Cognitive semantics. In U. Eco et al. (Eds.), *Meaning and mental representations.* In G. Lakoff & M. Johnson (1999). *Philosophy in the flesh.* NY: Basic Books.

Lakoff, G. (1993). The contemporary theory of metaphor. In A. Ortony (Ed.), *Metaphor and thought* (pp. 202-251). Cambridge: Cambridge University Press.

Lakoff, G., & Johnson, M. (1980). *Metaphors we live by.* Chicago: University of Chicago Press.

Lakoff, G., & Johnson, M. (2003). *Metaphors we live by* (2nd ed.). University of Chicago Press.

Lakshmanan, L. V. S., Ramesh, G.,Wang, H., & Zhao, Z. J. (2004). On testing satisfiability of tree pattern queries. *Proceedings of the 30th International Conference on Very Large Databases (VLDB)* (pp. 120-131).

Lambers, L. (2004). *A new version of GTXL: An exchange format for graph transformation systems.* Paper presented at the International Workshop on Graph-Based Tools, a Satellite Event of the 2nd International Conference on Graph Transformation, Rome, Italy.

Land, S. K., & J. Waltz, J. W. (2005). *Practical support for CMMI-SW software project documentation.* Wiley-IEEE Computer Society.

Landay, J. (1996). *Interactive sketching for the early stages of user interface design.* Unpublished doctoral dissertation, Carnegie Mellon University, Pittsburgh, PA.

Landay, J. A., & Myers, B. A. (2001). Sketching interfaces: Toward more human interface design. *IEEE Computer, 34*(3), 56-64.

Langford, M., & Unwin, D. J. (1994). Generating and mapping population density surfaces within a geographical information system. *Cartographic Journal, 31*(1), 21-6.

Larkin, J. H., & Simon, H. (1987). Why a diagram is (sometimes) worth ten thousand words. *Cognitive Science, 11*(1), 65-100.

Lauesen, S. (2005). *User interface design: A software engineering perspective.* Addison-Wesley.

Laurel, B. K. (1986). Interface as mimesis. In D. A. Norman, & S. W. Draper (Eds.), *User centred system design: New perspectives on human-computer interaction.* Hillsdale, NJ: Lawrence Erlbaum Associates Inc.

Laux, A., & Martin, L. (2000). *XUpdate working draft.* Technical report. Retrieved October, 6, 2006 from *http://xmldb-org.sourceforge.net/xupdate/.*

Lavie, T., & Tractinsky, N. (2004). Assessing dimensions of perceived visual aesthetics of Web sites. *International Journal of Human-Computer Studies, 60*(3), 269-298.

Lazarev, G. L. (1989). *Executable specifications with prolog. Dr. Dobb's Journal, 14*(10), 61-68.

Leach, L. (2006). *AutoCAD 2006 Instructor.* McGraw-Hill.

Lèdczi, A., Bakay, A., Maròi, M., Vögyesi, P., Nordstrom, G., Sprinkle, J., & Karsai, G. (2001). Composing domain-specific design environments. *IEEE Computer,* Nov. 2001 (pp. 44-51). Retrieved from http://www.isis.vanderbilt.edu/Projects/gme/default.html

Lédeczi, A., Bakay, A., Maróti, M., Vülgyesi, P., Nordstrom, G., Sprinkle, J., & Karsai, G. (2001). Composing domain-specific design environments. *IEEE Computer, 34*(11), 44-51.

Lee, S. W. (1992). Recognizing hand-drawn electrical circuit symbols with attributed graph matching. *Structured Document Image Analysis* (pp. 340-358). Springer-Verlag.

Lee, Y. C., & Chin, F. (1995). An iconic query language for topological relationship in GIS. *International Journal of geographical Information Systems, 9*(1), 25-46.

Leiner, H. C., Leiner, A. L., & Dowq, R. S. (1986). Does the cerebellum contribute to mental skills. *Behavioural Neuroscience, 100*(4), 443-454

Lemer, C., Antezana, E., Couche, F., Fays, F., Santolaria, X., Janky, R., Deville, Y., Richelle, J., & Wodak, S. (2003). The aMaze lightBench: A Web interface to a relational database of cellular processes. *Nucleic Acids Research, 32,* 443-448. Retrieved from http://nar.oxfordjournals.org/cgi/content/full/32/suppl_1/D443

Leng, B., & Shen, W. M. (1996). A metapattern-based automated discovery loop for integrated data mining: Unsupervised learning of relational patterns. *IEEE Transactions on Knowledge and Data Engineering, 8*(6), 898-910.

Levy, A. Y., Rajaraman, A., & Ordille, J. J. (1996). Querying heterogeneous information sources using source descriptions. *Proceedings of the 22nd International Conference on Very Large Databases (VLDB)* (pp. 251-262).

Leymann, F. (2001, May). *Web services flow language (WSFL 1.0).* IBM. Retrieved from http://www-3.ibm.com/software/solutions/Webservices/pdf/WSFL.pdf

Leymann, F. (2003). Web services: Distributed applications without limits: An outline. Proceedings of the Database Systems for Business, Technology and Web (BTW 2003). In G. Weikum, H. Schöning, & E. Rahm (Eds.), GI-Edition. Lecture Notes in Informatics (LNI) (pp. 26). Bonner Köllen Verlag.

Li, X., & Chang, S. K. (2004). An interactive visual query interface on spatial/temporal data. *Proceedings of the 10th International Conference on Distributed Multimedia Systems* (pp. 257-262).

Lieberman, B. (2004). *UML activity diagrams: Detailing user interface navigation* (Tech. Rep. 29 April). Rational Software.

Lieberman, H. (1991). A three-dimensional representation of program execution. In E. P. Glinert (Ed.), *Visual programming environments: Applications and issues.* IEEE Press.

Long, D., & Fox, M. (1998). Efficient implementation of the plan graph in STAN. *Journal of Artificial Intelligence Research, 10,* 87-115.

Ludaescher, B., Papakonstantinou, Y., Velikhov, P., & Vianu, V. (1999). View definition and DTD inference for XML. *Proceedings of the Post-IDCT Workshop.*

Mac Lane, S. (1972). *Categories for the working mathematician.* Volume 5 of Graduate Texts in Mathematics. Springer-Verlag, Berlin, 2nd. Edition (1st ed., 1971).

MacEachren, A. (2005). Moving geovisualization toward support for group work. In J. Dykes, A. MacEachren, & M. J. Kraak (Eds), *Exploring geovisualization* (pp. 710). Amsterdam: Elsevier.

MacEachren, A. M. (1994). *Some truth with maps: A primer on symbolization & design.*

MacEachren, A. M., & DiBiase, D. W (1991). Animated maps of aggregate data: Conceptual and practical problems. *Cartography and Geographic Information Systems, 18*(4), 221-29.

MacEachren, A. M., & Kraak, M. J. (2001). Research challenges in geovisualization. *Cartography and Geographic Information Science, 28*(1), 1-11.

MacKenzie, I. S., & Chang, L. (1999). A performance comparison of two handwriting recognisers. *Interacting with Computers, 11,* 283-297.

Magyari, E., Bakay, A., Lang, A., Paka, T., Vizhanyo, A., Agarwal, A., & Karsai, G. (2003). UDM: An infra-structure for implementing domain-specific modeling languages. *Proceedings OOPSLA2003 Workshop on Domain Specific Modeling.*

Maher, M. L., Simoff, S. J., & Cicognani, A. (2000). *Understanding virtual design studios.* London: Springer.

Mahoney, J. V., & Fromherz, M. P. J. (2002). Three main concerns in sketch recognition and an approach to addressing them. *Proceedings of AAAI Symp. on Sketch Understanding* (pp. 105-112). AAAI Press.

Majhew, D. J. (1992). *Principles and guideline in software user interface design.* Prentice Hall.

Mankoff, J., Hudson, S. E., & Abowd, G. D. (2000). Providing integrated toolkit-level support for ambiguity in recognition-based interfaces. *Proceedings of ACM CHI'00 Conference on Human Factors in Computing Systems* (pp. 368-375).

Mannila, H. (2000). Theoretical frameworks for data mining. *SIGKDD Explorations Newsletter, 1*(2), 30-32. New York: ACM Press.

Marcugini, S., & Milani, A. (2002). Automated planning of Web services. *Proceedings of the 3rd International Conference on Electronic Commerce, ICEC 2002,* Hong Kong.

Marek, V. W., & Truszczynski, M. (1993). *Nonmonotonic logics; Context dependent reasoning.* Springer-Verlag.

Marriott, K. (1994). Constraint multiset grammars. *IEEE Symposium on Visual Languages* (pp. 118-125). IEEE Computer Society Press.

Marriott, K., & Meyer, B. (1997). On the classification of visual languages by grammar hierarchies. *Journal of Visual Languages and Computing, 8*(4), 374-402.

Marriott, K., & Meyer, B. (1998). The CCMG visual language hierarchy. In K. Marriott & B. Meyer (Eds.), *Visual language theory* (pp. 129-169). New York: Springer.

Marriott, K., & Meyer, B. (1998). *Visual language theory.* Springer-Verlag.

Marriott, K., Meyer, B., & Wittenburg, K. (1998). A survey of visual language specification and recognition. In

K. Marriott & B. Meyer (Eds.), *Visual language theory* (pp. 5-85). New York: Springer.

Marsh, S. L., & Dykes, J. A. (2005). Using usability techniques to evaluate geovisualization in learning and teaching In L. Zentai, J. J. R. Nunez, & D. Fraser (Eds.), *Joint ICA commissions seminar "Internet-based cartographic teaching and learning: Atlases, map use, and visual analytics."* (pp. 29-34). ICA, Madrid.

Marsh, S. L., Dykes, J. A., & Attilakou, F. (2006). Evaluating a geovisualization prototype with two approaches: Remote instructional vs. face-to-face exploratory. *The 10ᵗʰ International Conference on Information Visualization.* IEEE Computer Society, London.

Martinez, A., Patinio-Martinez, M., Jimenez-Peris, R., Perez-Sorrosal, F. (2005). ZenFlow: A visual Web service composition tool for BPEL4WS. *IEEE Symp. on Visual Languages and Human-Centric Computing,* Dallas, Texas.

Massari, A., Pavani, S., & Saladini, L. (1994). QBI: an iconic query system for inexpert users. *Working Conference on Advanced Visual Interfaces (AVI'94)* (pp. 240-242).

McBride, B. (2001). Jena: Implementing the RDF model and syntax specification. *Proceedings of the 2ⁿᵈ International Workshop on the Semantic Web.*

McCluskey, T. L., Liu, D., & Simpson, R. (2003). gipo ii: htn planning in a tool-supported knowledge engineering environment. *Proceedings of the 13ᵗʰ International Conference on Automated Planning and Scheduling* (pp. 92-101). Trento, Italy.

McGuinness, C. (1994). Expert/novice use of visualization tools. In A. M. MacEachren, & D. R. F. Taylor (Eds.), *Visualization in modern cartography* (pp. 185-199). Pergamon.

McIlraith, S., & Fadel, R. (2002). Planning with complex actions. *Proceedings of the AIPS 2002 Workshop on Exploring Real World Planning,* Toulouse, France.

McIlraith, S., Son, T. C., & Zeng, H. (2001). Semantic Web services. *IEEE Intelligent Systems, Special Issue on the Semantic Web, 16*(2), 46-53.

Mendes, P., Bulmore, D. L., Farmer, A. D., Steadman, P. A, Waught, M. E., & Wlodek, S. T. (2000). PathDB: A second generation metabolic database. *Animating the Cellular Map, Proceedings of the 9ᵗʰ International BioThermoKinetics Meeting* (pp. 207-212). Stellenbosch University Press.

Mens, T., Demeyer, S., & Janssens, D. (2002). Formalising behaviour preserving program transformation. *Proceedings of the 1ˢᵗ International Conference on Graph Transformation.* LNCS 2505 (pp. 286-301). Barcelona, Spain: Springer-Verlag.

Meyer, B. (1992). Beyond icons: Towards new metaphors for visual query languages for spatial information systems. *International Workshop on Interfaces to Database Systems (IDS'92)* (pp. 113-135).

Meyer, B. (1992). Pictures depicting pictures: On the specification of visual languages by visual grammars. *IEEE Symposium on Visual Languages (VL'92)* (pp. 41-47). Seattle, WA.

Meyer, B. (1993). Beyond icons: Towards new metaphors for visual query languages for spatial information systems. *Proceedings of the International Workshop on Interfaces to Database Systems* (pp. 113-135). Glasgow.

Meyer, B. (1994). Pictorial deduction in spatial information systems. *IEEE Symposium on Visual Languages (VL94)* (pp. 23-30).

Meyer, B. (1997). Formalization of visual mathematical notations. In M. Anderson (Ed.), *AAAI Symposium on Diagrammatic Reasoning (DR-II)* (pp. 58-68). Boston: AAAI Press.

Meyer, B. (1999). Constraint diagram reasoning. *CP'99: Principles and Practice of Constraint Programming,* LNCS 1713. Alexandria, VA: Springer.

Meyer, B. (2000). A constraint-based framework for diagrammatic reasoning. *Applied Artificial Intelligence.*

Special Issue on Constraint Handling Rules, 4(14), 327-344.

Meyer, B., Bottoni, P., & Marriott, K. (2006). Formalizing interpretation of and reasoning with diagrams using linear logic. *Language and Computation.* submitted.

Meyer, B., Marriott, K., & Allwein, G. (2002). Intelligent diagrammatic interfaces: State of the art. In P. Olivier, M. Anderson, & B. Meyer (Eds.), *Diagrammatic representation and reasoning.* London: Springer.

Milani, A. (2003). Planning and scheduling for the Web roadmap. *Technical Coordination Unit for Planning and Scheduling for the Web, PLANET Network of Excellence,* March. Retrieved from http://www.dipmat.unipg.it/~milani/Webtcu/

Miller, D. (1995). A survey of linear logic programming. *Computational Logic, 2*(2), 63-67.

Millet, I. (1999). *A proposal to simplify data flow diagrams. IBM Systems Journal, 38*(1), Retrieved March 2, 2006, from http://www.research.ibm.com/journal/si/381/millet.html

Minami, M. (2000). *Using ArcMap.* Environmental Systems Research Institute.

Minas, M. (2002). Concepts and realization of a diagram editor generator based on hypergraph transformation. *Science of Computer Programming, 44*(2), 157-180.

Minas, M. (2003). Syntax definition with graphs. In Proceedings of the School on Foundations of Visual Modelling Techniques (FoVMT 2004) (ENTCS 148-1, pp. 19-40).

Minas, M. (2003). VisualDiaGen: A tool for visually specifying and generating visual editors. *Proceedings of the 2nd International Workshop on Applications of Graph Transformation with Industrial Relevance.* LNCS 3062 (pp. 398-412). Charlottesville, VA: Springer-Verlag. Retrieved from http://www2.informatik.uni-erlangen.de/DiaGen/

Minas, M. (2006). VisualDiaGen--A tool for visually specifying and generating visual editors. *In Proceedings of Application of Graph Transformations with Industrial Relevance 2003* (pp. 398-412). Berlin: Springer.

Mitbander, B., Ong, K., Shen, W. M., & Zaniolo, C. (1996). Metaqueries for data mining. In U. Fayyad, G. Piatetsky-Shapiro, P. Smyth, & R. Uthurusamy (Eds.), *Advances in knowledge discovery and data mining* (Ch. 15). Menlo Park, CA: AAAI Press/MIT Press.

Mitchell, A. (1999). *The ESRI guide to GIS analysis.* New York: Environmental Systems Research Institute.

MOF 2.0 specification at the OMG home page (2006). http://www.omg.org/docs/formal/06-01-01.pdf.

Mori, G., Paternò, F., & Santoro, C. (2002). CTTE: Support for developing and analyzing task models for interactive system design. *IEEE Transactions on Software Engineering, 28*(8), 797-813.

Morris, A. J., Abdelmoty, A. I., Tudhope, D. S., & El-Geresy. B. (2002). A design and implementation of a visual query language for large spatial databases. *Proceedings of the 6th International Conference on Information Visualization* (pp. 226-233). IEEE Computer Society Press.

Munroe, K., & Papakonstantinou, Y. (2000). BBQ: A visual interface for browsing and querying XML. *Proceedings of the 5th Working Conference on Visual Database Systems* (pp. 277-296).

Murray, N., Paton, N. W., & Goble, C. A. (1998). Kaleidoquery: A visual query language for object databases. *Working Conference on Advanced Visual Interfaces (AVI'98)* (pp. 247-257).

Musella, D., & Padula, M. (1997). Seeking emergences from digital documents in large repositories. *Sémiotiques, 12*(1), 129-150.

Mussio, P. (2003). E-documents as tools for the humanized management of community knowledge. In H. Linger et al. (Eds.), *Constructing the infrastructure for the knowledge economy: Methods and tools; theory and practice. Keynote Address, ISD 2003.* Melbourne, Australia: Kluwer.

Mussio, P., Pietrogrande, M., & Protti, M. (1991). Simulation of hepatological models: A study in visual interactive exploration of scientific problems. *Journal of Visual Languages and Computing, 2*(1), 75-95.

Mynatt, E. (2006). From mainframes to picture frames: Charting the rapid evolution of visual interfaces. *Proceedings of the International Conference on Advanced Visual Interfaces 2006* (15). Venezia, Italia: ACM Press.

Nagesh, H., Goil, S., & Choudhary, A. (2001). Adaptive grids for clustering massive data sets. *Proceedings of the SIAM International Conference on Data Mining.* Retrieved from http://www.siam.org/meetings/sdm01/pdf/sdm01_07.pdf

Najoork, M. (1996). Programming in three dimensions. *Journal of Visual Languages and Computing, 7*(2), 219-242.

Najork, M., & Kaplan, S. M. (1993). Specifying visual languages with conditional set rewrite systems. *Proceedings of the 1993 IEEE Workshop on Visual Languages* (pp. 12-18). Bergen, Norway: IEEE Computer Society Press.

Naranayan Hari, N., & Hubscher, R. (1998). Visual languages theory: Towards a human-computer interaction perspective. In K. Merriot & B. Meyer (Eds.), *Visual language theory.* New York: Springer.

Nau, D. S., Au, T. C., Ilghami, O., Kuter, U., Murdock, W., Wu, D., & Yaman, F. (2003). SHOP2: An HTN planning system. *Journal of Artificial Intelligence Research, 20,* 379-404.

Nelsen, R. (1993). *Proofs without words.* The Mathematical Association of America, Washington, DC.

Newlove J., & Dalby, J. (2004). *Laban for all.* London: Nick Hern Publishers.

Newlove, J. (2001). *Laban for actors and dancers.* NY: Routledge.

Newman, M. W., Lin, J., Hong, J. I., & Landay, J. A. (2003). DENIM: An informal Web site design tool inspired by observations of practice. *Human-Computer Interaction, 18*(3), 259-324.

Ng, R. T., & Han, J. (1994). Efficient and effective clustering methods for spatial data mining. In J. B. Bocca, M. Jarke, & C. Zaniolo (Ed.), *Proceedings of the International Conference on Very Large Data Bases (VLDB)* (pp. 144-155). San Francisco: Morgan Kaufmann Publishers.

Nguyen, X., Kambhampati, S., & Nigenda, R. (2002). AltAlt: Combining the advantages of graphplan and heuristics state search. *Proceedings of the 2000 International Conference on Knowledge-Based Computer Systems,* Bombay, India.

Nianping, Z., Grundy, J., & Hosking, J. (2004). Pounamu: A meta-tool for multi-view visual language environment construction. In *VL/HCC 2004* (pp. 254-256).

Nicoladis, E., Mayberry, R. L., & Genesee, F. (1999). Gesture and bilingual development. *Developmental Psychology, 35*(2), 163-174.

Nielsen, J. (1993). *Usability engineering.* San Diego: Academic Press.

Nolan, P. R. (1989). Designing screen icons: Ranking and matching studies. *Proceedings of the Human Factors Society, 33rd Annual Meeting* (pp. 380-384). Santa Monica, CA: The Human Factors Society.

Norman, D. A. (2004). *Emotional design: Why we love (or hate) everyday things.* Basic Books.

Norman, D. A. (2005). Human-centered design considered harmful. *Interactions of ACM, 12*(4), 14-19.

Norman, D. A., & Draper, S. W. (1986). *User-centered system design: New perspectives on human-computer interaction.* Hillsdale, NJ: Lawrence Erlbaum Associates.

North, C., & Shneiderman, B. (2000). Snap-together visualization: Can users construct and operate coordinated visualizations? *International Journal of Human-Computer Studies, 53,* 715-39.

Nunes, N. J. (2003) Representing user interface patterns in UML. In In D. Konstantas, M. Leonard, Y. Pigneur & S. Patel (Eds.), *Object-oriented information systems,* LNCS 2817 (pp. 142-151).

Nunes, N. J., & Falcao e Cunha, J. (2001). Wisdom a UML based architecture for interactive systems. *DSVIS 2000*, LNCS 1946 (pp. 191-205).

Nute, D. (1987). Defeasible reasoning. *Proceedings of the 20ᵗʰ International Conference on Systems Science* (pp. 470-477). IEEE Press.

Nygaard, K., & Sorgarrd, P. (1987) The Perspective Concept in Informatics. In G. Bjerknes, P. Ehn, & M. Kyng (Eds.), *Compters and Democracy*. Aldershot, UK: Avebury

O'Dwyer, M. W. J. (1998). The "Who flew first" debate. *Flight Journal*. October, 4-10.

OMG. (2005). *Unified modeling language specification* (Tech. Rep. No 2). Object Management Group.

Original Data Depositor, *1991 Census : Small Area Statistics (England and Wales)* [computer file]. ESRC/JISC Census Programme, Census Dissemination Unit, MIMAS (University of Manchester).

Original Data Depositor. (1991). *Census: Digitised Boundary Data (England and Wales)* [computer file]. ESRC/JISC Census Programme, Census Geography Data Unit (UKBORDERS), EDINA (University of Edinburgh).

OWL Services Coalition (2003). *OWL-S: Semantic markup for Web services*. OWL-S 1.0 Release. Retrieved http://www.daml.org/services/owl-s/1.0/

Padula, M., & Reggiori, A. (1999). Art teams up with technology through the Net. *ACM Interactions, 6*(4), 40-50.

Padula, M., & Reggiori, A. (2006). *Fondamenti di informatica per la progettazione multimediale. Dai linguaggi formali all'inclusione digitale*. Milano, IT: FrancoAngeli.

Papadias, D., & Sellis, T. K. (1995). A pictorial query-by-example language. *Journal of Visual Languages and Computing, 6*(1), 53-72.

Papakonstantinou, Y., Petropoulos, M., & Vassalos, V. (2002). QURSED: Querying and reporting semis-

tructured data. *Proceedings of the ACM SIGMOD* (pp. 192-203).

Papantonakis, A., & King, P. J. H. (1994). Gql, a declarative graphical query language based on the functional data model. *Workshop on Advanced Visual Interfaces (AVI'94)* (pp. 113-122).

Paredaens, J., Den Bussche, J. V., Andries, M., Gemis, M., Gyssens, M., Thyssens, I., Gucht, D. V., Sarathy, V., & Saxton, L. V. (1992). An overview of good. *SIGMOD Record 21*(1), 25-31.

Paredaens, J., Peelman, P., & Tanca, L. (1995). G-Log: A declarative graph-based language. *IEEE Trans. Knowl. Data Eng, 7*(3), 436-453

Passant, A., Laublet, P., & Testard-Vaillant, F. X. (2005). Annotations and collaborative work: a corporate approach. *Proceedings of International Workshop on Annotation for Collaboration*, (pp. 133-142). Paris: La Sorbonne.

Paterno, F. (2001). Towards a UML for interactive systems. *EHCI 2001*, LNCS 2254 (pp. 7-18).

Paulson, L. (1994). *Isabelle*. London: Springer Verlag.

Pautasso, C., & Alonso, G. (2004-2005). JOpera: A toolkit for efficient visual composition of Web services. *International Journal of Electronic Commerce, 9*(2), 107-141.

Pédauque, R. T. (2003). Document: Form, sign and medium. As Reformulated for Electronic Documents, *Working paper STIC-CNRS*, September 12, 2003, from http://archivesic.ccsd.cnrs.fr/sic_00000594.html, original French version: http://archivesic.ccsd.cnrs.fr/documents/archives0/00/00/05/11/index_fr.html.

Pendleton, D. (1983). Doctor-patient communication: A review. In D. Pendleton & J. Hasler (Eds.), *Doctor-patient communication* (pp. 5-53). NY: Academic Press.

Penna, G. D., Intrigila, B., & Orefice, S. (2004). An environment for the design and implementation of visual applications. *Journal of Visual Languages and Computing, 15*(6), 439-461.

Peräkyla, A. (1998). Authority and accountability: The delivery of diagnosis in primary healthcare. *Social Psychology Quarterly, 61*, 301-320.

Pereira, F., & Warren, D. H. (1980). Definite clause grammars for language analysis: A survey of the formalism and a comparison with augmented transition networks. *Artificial Intelligence, 13*, 231-278.

Perry, T. S. (1997, August). In search of the future of air traffic control. *IEEE Spectrum, 34*(8) 18-35.

Petropoulos, M., Vassalos, V., & Papakonstantinou, Y. (2001). XML query forms (XQForms): Declarative specification of XML query interfaces. *Proceedings of the 10ᵗʰ WWW Conference.* (pp. 642-651)

Piccinelli, G. (1999). Service provision and composition in virtual business communities. *Tech. Report HPL-1999-84,* Hewlett-Packard, Palo Alto, CA, 1999. Retrieved from http://www.hplhp.com/techreports/1999/HPL-1999-84.html

Pine, B. J. (1993). *Mass customization: A new frontier in business competition.* Harvard Business School Press.

Pinheiro da Silva, P., & Paton, N. W. (2000). User interface modelling with UML. *Information Modelling and Knowledge Bases XII* (pp. 203-217). IOS Press.

Pohjonen, R., & Tolvanen, J. P. (2002). Automated production of family members: Lessons learned. *Proceedings of the International Workshop on Product Line Engineering the Early Steps: Planning, Modeling, and Managing* (pp. 49-57), Seattle, USA.

Polyviou, S., Samaras, G., & Evripidou, P. (2005). A relationally complete visual query language for heterogeneous data sources and pervasive querying. *International Conference on Data Engineering (ICDE'05)* (pp. 471-482).

Poon, A., Weber, K., & Cass, T. (1995). Scribbler: A tool for searching digital ink. *Proceedings of ACM CHI'95 Conference on Human Factors in Computing Systems, Volume 2 of Short Papers: Pens and Touchpads* (pp. 252-253).

Powers, S. (2003). *Practical RDF.* Beijing; Cambridge: O'Reilly.

Preece, J. (1994). *Human-computer interaction,* Addison-Wesley.

Preece, J., Rogers, Y., & Sharp, H. (2002). *Interaction design: Beyond human-computer interaction.* New York: Wiley.

Preston, P. (2001). *Reshaping communications.* London, UK: Sage.

Pretorius, A. J. (2005). Visual analysis for ontology engineering. *Journal of Visual Languages and Computing, 16*(4), 359-381.

Processing Reference Guide (2006). http://www.processing.org/reference/index.html

Prophet, J., & d'Inverno, M. (2006). Transdisciplinary collaboration in "cell." In P. Fishwick (Ed.), *Aesthetic computing* (pp. 185-196). MIT Press.

Purchase, H. C. (2002). Metrics for graph drawing aesthetics. *Journal of Visual Languages and Computing, 13*(5), 501-516.

Quin, Z., Yao, B. B., Liu, Y., & McCool, M. (2004). A graphical XQuery language using nested windows. *Lecture Notes in Computer Science, 3306* (pp. 681-687).

QVT specification at the OMG home page (2006). http://www.omg.org/docs/ptc/05-11-01.pdf

Rabagliati, R. (2006). AVI and the art system: Interactive works at the Venice Biennale. *Proceedings of the International Conference on Advanced Visual Interfaces 2006* (pp. 3-6) Venezia, Italia: ACM Press.

Rekers, J., & Schürr, A. (1997). Defining and parsing visual languages with layered graph grammars. *Journal of Visual Languages and Computing, 8*(1), 27-55.

Rittel, H. (1984). Second-generation design methods. In N. Cross (Ed.), *Developments in design methodology* (pp. 317-327). New York: John Wiley & Sons.

Roberts, C., & Sarangi, S. (2005): Theme-oriented discourse analysis of medical encounters. *Medical Education, 39*(6), 632-40.

Robinson, A. C., Chen, J., Lengerich, E. J., Meyer, H. G., & MacEachren, A. M. (2005). Combining usability techniques to design geovisualization tools for epidemiology. *Cartography and Geographic Information Science, 32*(4), 243-255.

Robinson, J. (1998). Getting down to business: Talk gaze and body orientation during openings of doctor-patient consultations. *Human Communication Research, 25*(1), 97-123.

Rosengren, P. (1994). Using visual ER query systems in real world applications. *Advanced Information Systems Engineering (CAiSE'94)* (pp. 394-405), LNCS 811.

Rubine, D. (1991). Specifying gestures by example. *Computer Graphics, 25*(4), 329-337.

Sacks, O. (1989). *Seeing voices*. NY: Harper Collins.

Sanchez, J., & Mali, A. D. (2003). S-MEP: A planner for numeric goals. *Proceedings of the 5th IEEE International Conference on Tools with Artificial Intelligence* (pp. 274-283). Sacramento.

Sandvik, M., Eide, H., Lind, M., Graugaard, P. K., Torper, J., & Finset, A. (2002). Analyzing medical dialogues: Strength and weakness of Roter's interaction analysis system (RIAS). *Patient Education and Counselling, 46*(4), 235-241.

Santos, G. F. (2000). *Implementation of visual queries on temporal databases*. Master Thesis, Federal University of Campina Grande (in Portuguese).

Saund, E. (2003). Finding perceptually closed paths in sketches and drawings. *IEEE Transactions on Pattern Analysis and Machine Intelligence, 25*(4), 475-491.

Schäfer, W. (2002). *Fujaba documentation* (Tech. Rep.). University of Paderborn.

Scherer, D. (2003). *Computer Support Proposal for ICM*. Master thesis. University of Campina Grande, Campina Grande. (in Portuguese).

Schiffrin, D., Tannen, D., & Hamilton, H., (2001). *Handbook of discourse analysis*. Oxford: Blackwell.

Schikuta, E. (1996). Grid-clustering: An efficient hierarchical clustering method for very large data sets. *Proceedings of the 13th International Conference on Pattern Recognition* (pp. 101-105). Los Alamitos, CA: IEEE Computer Society.

Schikuta, E., & Erhart, M. (1997). The BANG-clustering system: Grid-based data analysis. In X. Liu, P. Cohen, & M. Berthold (Ed.), *Advances in intelligent data analysis. Reasoning about Data: Second International Symposium, IDA-97, Proceedings, Lecture Notes in Computer Science, 1280*. Berlin; Heidelberg, Germany: Springer.

Schön, D. (1983). *The reflective practitioner: How professionals think in action*. Basic Books.

Schreiber, F. (2002). High quality visualization of biochemical pathways in BioPath. *Silico Biology, 2*(0006).

Schuler, D., & Namioka, A. (1993). *Participatory design: Principles and Practices*. Hillsday, NJ: Lawrence Erlbaum Associates.

Schürr, A. (1994). *Specification of graph translators with triple graph grammars*. LNCS 903 (pp. 151-163). Springer-Verlag.

Schürr, A., Winter, A., & Zundorf, A. (1995). Graph grammar engineering with PROGRES. *Proceedings of the 5th European Software Engineering Conference ESEC*, LNCS 989 (pp. 219-234). Springer.

Scott, D. S. (1997) Logic and programming languages. *Communications of the ACM, 20*(9), 634-641.

Seitz, J. A. (1994). Thinking kinesically: Theory and practice. *Proceedings of the 24th Annual Symposium of the Jean Piaget Society*, Chicago, Jean Piaget Society.

Seitz, J. A. (1996). Developmentally appropriate practice. *Journal of Education and Family Review, 3*(5), 7-9.

Seitz, J. A. (2000). The embodied self. *Proceedings of the 30th Annual Symposium of the Jean Piaget Society*, Montreal, Canada.

Seitz, J. A. (2000). Embodied cognition. *Proceedings of the 12th Annual Convention of the American Psychological Society*, Miami, FL.

Sellis, T., Frank, A., Grumbach, S., Guting, R., & Koubarakis, M. (2003). *Spatio-temporal databases: The chorochronos approach*. Lecture Notes in Computer Science, Springer-Verlag.

Sentissi, T., & Pichat, E. (1997). A graphical user interface for object-oriented database. *International Conference of the Chilean Computer Science Society (SCCC'97)* (pp. 227-239).

Sezgin, T. M., & Davis, R. (2005). HMM-based efficient sketch recognition. *Proceedings of International Conference on Intelligent User Interfaces* (pp. 281-283). ACM Press.

Sezgin, T. M., & Davis, R. (2005). Modeling sketching as a dynamic process. *Proceedings of CSW'05*, Gloucester, MA.

Sezgin, T. M., Stahovich, T., & Davis, R. (2001). Sketch-based interfaces: Early processing for sketch understanding. *Proceedings of Workshop on Perceptive User Interfaces*.

Shalfield, R. (2005). *VisiRule user guide*. Retrieved March 10, 2006, from http://www.lpa.co.uk/ftp/4600/vsr_ref.pdf

Sheikholeslami, G., Chatterjee, S., & Zhang, A. (1998). WaveCluster: A multi-resolution clustering approach for very large spatial databases. In A. Gupta, O. Shmueli, & J. Widom (Ed.), *Proceedings of the International Conference on Very Large Data Bases (VLDB)* (pp. 428-439). Morgan Kaufmann Publishers.

Shen, W. M., Leng, B., & Chatterjee, A. (1995). *Applying the metapattern mechanism to time sequence analysis* (Tech. Rep. ISI/RR-95-398). USC Information Sciences Institute.

Sheshagiri, M., des Jardins, M., & Finin, T. (2003). A planner for composing services described in DAML-S. *ICAPS 2003 Workshop on Planning for Web Services*.

Shilman, M., Pasula, H., Russell, S., & Newton, R. (2002). Statistical visual language models for ink parsing. *Proceedings of AAAI Spring Symposium on Sketch Understanding* (pp. 126-132). AAAI Press.

Shimabukuro, M. H., Branco, V. M. A., Oliveira, M. C. F., & Flores. E. F. (2003). Visual exploration of spatio-temporal databases. *Proceedings of the GEOINFO*.

Shin, S. J. (1995). *The logical status of diagrams*. Cambridge: Cambridge University Press.

Shin, S. J. (1996). A situation theoretic account of valid reasoning with Venn diagrams. In G. Allwein & J. Barwise (Eds.), *Logical reasoning with diagrams* (pp. 81-108). New York: Oxford University Press.

Shizuki, B., Yamada, H., Iizuka, K., & Tanala, J. (2003). A unified approach for interpreting handwritten strokes. *Proceedings IEEE Symp. on Human-Centric Computing* (pp. 180-182). IEEE Press.

Shneiderman, B. (1983). Direct manipulation: A step beyond programming languages. *IEEE Computer, 16*(8), 57-69.

Shneiderman, B. (1992). Direct manipulation. In *Designing the User Interface*. Reading, MA: Addison-Wesley.

Shneiderman, B. (1998). *Designing the user interface: Strategies for effective human computer interaction*. Reading, MA: Addison-Wesley.

Sibley, E. H., & Kerschberg, L. (1977). Data architecture and data model considerations. *AFIPS National Computer Conference*.

Siepel, A., Farmer, A., Tolopko, A., Zhuang, M., Mendes, P., Beavis, W., & Sobral, B. (2001). ISYS: A decentralized, component-based approach to the integration of heterogeneous bioinformatics resources. *Bioinformatics, 17*(1), 83-94.

Silberschatz, A., Korth, H. F., & Sudarshan, S. (2005). *Database system concepts* (5th ed.). McGraw Hill.

Silva, S. L. F., Schiel, U., & Catarci. T. (2002). Formalizing visual interaction with historical databases. *Information Systems, 27*(7), 487-521.

Silveira, V. N. K., Edelweiss, N., & Galante, R. M. (2004). TVM Web—A visual interface visual for the versioning temporal model. *Proceedings of the 19ᵗʰ Brazilian Symposium of Databases*, Brasília (in Portuguese).

Silverman, B. W. (1986). *Density estimation for statistics and data analysis*. London: Chapman and Hall.

Simoff, S. J. (2001). Towards the development of environments for designing visualisation support for visual data mining. In S. J. Simoff, M. Noirhomme-Fraiture, & M. H. Bohlen (Eds.), *Proceedings the International Workshop on Visual Data Mining VDM@PKDD'01* (pp. 93-106). September 4, 2001, Freiburg, Germany.

Simoff, S. J., & Maher, M. L. (2000). Analysing participation in collaborative design environments. *Design Studies, 21*(2), 119-144.

Simon, F., Steinbruckner, F., & Lewerentz, C. (2000). *3D-Spring embedder for complete graphs*. Technical report, Technical University Cottbus, Germany.

Sirin, E., Parsia, B., Wu, D., Hendler, J., & Nau, D. (2004). HTN planning for Web service composition using SHOP2. *Web Semantics: Science, Services, and Agents on the World Wide Web, 1*(4), 377-396.

Skhiri dit Gabouje, S. (2005). *The Visual BioMaze Tutorial*. Retrieved from http://cs.ulb.ac.be/research/biomaze

Skhiri dit Gabouje, S., & Zimányi, E. (2005). Generic visualization of biochemical networks: A new compound graph layout algorithm. *Poster Proceedings of the 4ᵗʰ International Workshop on Efficient and Experimental Algorithms, WEA 05*.

Slocum, T. A., Blok, C., Jiang, B., Koussoulakou, A., Montello, D. R., Fuhrmann, S., & Hedley, N. R. (2001). Cognitive and Usability Issues in Geovisualization. *Cartography and Geographic Information Science, 28*(1), 61-75.

Snodgrass, R. T. (1995). *The TSQL2 temporal query language*. Springer Verlag.

Snodgrass, R. T. (1999). *Developing time-oriented database applications in SQL*. Morgan Kaufmann Publishers.

Soares, V. G. (2002). *GeoVisual: A visual querying environment for geographic databases*. Ph.D. Thesis, Federal University of Pernambuco, Brazil (in Portuguese).

Soegaard, M. (2004). Interaction Styles.

Spilker, J., Klarner, M., & Görz, G. (2000). Processing self corrections in a speech to speech system. *COLING 2000* (pp. 1116-1120).

Sprinkle, J., & Karsai, G., (2004). A domain-specific visual language for domain model evolution. *Journal of Visual Languages and Computing, 15*(3-4), 291-307.

Staes, F., Tarantino, L., & Tiems, A. (1991). A graphical query language for object-oriented databases. *IEEE Symposium on Visual Languages (VL'91)* (pp. 205-210).

Stahovich, T. F., Davis, R., & Shrobe, H. (1998). Generating multiple new designs from a sketch. *Artificial Intelligence, 104*(1-2), 211-264.

Steel, B. D. (2005). *WIN-PROLOG Technical Reference*. Retrieved April 23, 2006, from http://www.lpa.co.uk/ftp/4600/win_ref.pdf

Steinbach, M., Karypis, G., & Kumar, V. (2000). A comparison of document clustering techniques. *Proceedings of the ACM SIGKDD Workshop on Text Mining*. Retrieved from http://www.cs.cmu.edu/~dunia/KDDpapers

Stewart, M. A. (1995): Effective physician-patient communication and health outcomes. *A review CMAJ, 152*(9), 1423-33.

Stiny, G., & Gips, J. (1972). Shape grammars and the generative specification of painting and sculpture. *Information Processing, 71*, 1460-1465.

Stoy, J. E. (1981) *Denotational Semantics: The Scott-Strachey approach to programming language theory*. Cambridge MA: MIT Press

Sudnow, D. W. (1978). *Ways of the hand: The organization of improvised conduct*. NY: Harper and Row.

Sugiyama, K., & Eades, P. (1990). How to draw a directed graph. *Journal of Information Processing, 13*(4), 424-437.

Sugiyama, K., & Misue, K. (1991). Visualization of structural information: Automatic drawing of compound digraphs. *IEEE Transactions on Systems, Man, and Cybernetics, 21*(4), 876-893.

Sugiyama, K., & Misue, K. (1995). A simple and unified method for drawing graphs: Magnetic-spring algorithm. *Proceedings of the DIMACS International Workshop on Graph Drawing, GD'94* (pp. 364-375). LNCS 894, Springer.

Sugiyama, K., Tagawa, S., & Toda, M. (1981). Methods for visual understanding of hierarchical system structures. *IEEE Transactions on Systems, Man, and Cybernetics, 11*(2), 109-125.

Sutcliffe, A., & Mehandjiev, M. (2004). End-user development. *Communications of the ACM, 47*(9), 31-32.

Sutherland, I. E. (1963). *Sketchpad: A man-machine graphical communication system.* Unpublished doctoral dissertation, Massachusetts Institute of Technology, Cambridge.

Sutherland, I. E., Sketchpad: A Man Machine Graphical Communication System, dissertation submitted on January 1963 by the author for the degree of Doctor of Philosophy to the Massachussetts Institute of Technology.

Swoboda, N. (2002). Implementing Euler/Venn reasoning systems. In P. Olivier, M. Anderson, & B. Meyer (Eds.), *Diagrammatic representation and reasoning.* London: Springer.

Taentzer, G. (1999). AGG: A tool environment for algebraic graph transformation. *Proceedings of Application of Graph Transformations with Industrial Relevance 1999* (pp. 481-488). Berlin: Springer.

Taentzer, G., Ehrig, K., Guerra, E., de Lara, J., Lengyel, L., Levendovszky, T., Prange, U., Varro, D., & Varro-Gyapay, S. (2005). Model transformation by graph transformation: A comparative study. *Proceedings of the International Workshop on Model Transformation in Practice, satellite event of the ACM/IEEE 8ᵗʰ International Conference on Model Driven Engineering Languages and Systems,* Montego Bay, Jamaica.

Tanaka, T. (1991). Definite clause set grammars: A formalism for problem solving. *Journal of Logic Programming, 10*, 1-17.

Tarjan, R. (1972). Depth-first search and linear graph algorithms. *SIAM Journal of Computing, 1*(2), 146-160.

Thakkar, S., Knoblock, C., Ambite, J. L. (2003). A view integration approach to dynamic composition of Web services. *ICAPS 2003 Workshop on Planning for Web Services.*

Thakkar, S., Knoblock, G. A., Ambite, J. L., & Shahabi, C. (2002). Dynamically composing Web services from online source. *Workshop on Intelligent Service Integration, The 18ᵗʰ National Conference on Artificial Intelligence (AAAI),* Edmonton, Alberta, Canada. Retrieved from http://www.isi.edu/info-agents/dotnet/aaaiworkshop2002.pdf

Thatte S. (2003, May). *Business process execution language for Web services* (Version 1.1). Retrieved from http://www-106.ibm.com/developerworks/Webservices/library/ws-bpel

Thatte, S. (2001). *XLANG: Web services for business process design.* Microsoft. Retrieved from http://www.gotdotnet.com/team/xml_wsspecs/xlang-c/default.htm

Tiwari, A., Shankar, N., & Rushby, J. (2003). Invisible formal methods for embedded control systems, In *Proceedings of the IEEE, 91*(1), 29-39.

Tomita, M. (1991). *Generalized LR parsing.* Kluwer Academic Publishers.

Tondl, L. (1981). *Problems of semantics.* Boston: Reidel Publishing Company.

Tondl, L. (1981). *Problems of semantics.* Dordrecht, Boston: D. Reidel Publishing.

Tractinsky, N. (1997). Aesthetics and apparent usability: Empirically assessing cultural and methodological issues. *1997 Proceedings of the Conference on Human Factors in Computing Systems, Association of Computing Machinery (ACM)* (pp. 115-122).

Tractinsky, N., Shoval-Katz, A., & Ikar, D. (2000). *What is beautiful is usable: Interacting with computers*, 13, pp. 127-145.

Travis, D. (2006). *Bluffers' guide to usability standards*. London, UK: Userfocus ltd.

Tsai, W. H., & Fu, K. S. (1980). Attributed grammar: A tool for combining syntatic and statistical approaches to pattern recognition. *IEEE Trans. on Systems, Man, and Cybernetics, 10*(12), 873-885.

Tsoumakas, G., Vrakas, D., Bassiliades, N., & Vlahavas, I. (2004). Lazy adaptive multicriteria planning. *Proceedings of the 16th European Conference on Artificial Intelligence* (pp. 693-697).Valencia, Spain.

Tucci, M., Vitiello, G., & Costagliola, G. (1994). Parsing nonlinear languages. *IEEE Transactions on Software Engineering, 20*, 720-739.

Tucci, M., Vitiello, G., Pacini, G., & Tortora, G. (1992). Graphs and visual languages for visual interface. *Avanced Visual Interfaces (AVI 92)* (pp. 304-318). Singapore: World Scientific.

Turner, M. (1994). Design for a theory of meaning. In W. Overton & D. Palermo (Eds.), *The nature and ontogenesis of meaning* (pp. 91-107). Lawrence Erlbaum Associates.

Ullman, J. D. (1988). *Principles of database and knowledge-based systems* (Vol. 1). Computer Science Press.

UML 2.0 specification at the OMG home page (2006). http://www.omg.org/UML

Uskudarli, S. M., & Dinesh, T. B. (1995). Towards a visual programming environment generator for algebraic specifications. *Proceedings of the IEEE Symp. Visual Languages* (pp. 234-241). IEEE Press.

Vadaparty, K., Aslandogan, Y. A., & Ozsoyoglu, G. (1993). Towards a unified visual database access. In *ACM SIGMOD International Conference on Management of Data (SIGMOD'93)* (pp. 357-366).

Van der Aalst, W. (2003). Don't go with the flow: Web services composition standards exposed. *IEEE Intelligent Systems, 18*(1), 72-76.

van Helden, J., Naim, A., Lemer, C., Mancuso, R., Eldridge, M., Wodak, S., & Gilbert, D. (2001). Representing and analyzing molecular and cellular function in the computer. *Biological Chemistry, 381*(9-10), 921-935.

Varela, M. L. R., Aparicio, J. N., & do Carmo Silva, S. (2003). A scheduling Web service based on XML-RPC. *ICAPS 2003 Workshop on Planning for Web Services*.

Vassalos, V., & Papakonstantinou, Y. (2000). Expressive capabilities description languages and query rewriting algorithms. *J. Logic Prog, 43*(1), 75-122.

Vickers, P., & Alty, J. (2002). Using music to communicate computing information. *Interacting with Computers, 14*(5), 435-456.

Vidal, V. (2004). A Look ahead strategy for heuristic search planning. *Proceedings of the 14th International Conference on Automated Planning and Scheduling* (pp. 3-7). Whistler, British Columbia, Canada.

Voudouris, V., Fisher, P. F., & Wood, J., (2006). Capturing conceptualization uncertainty interactively using object-fields. In W. Kainz, A. Reid, & G. Elmes (Eds), The *12th International Symposium on Spatial Data Handling*. Springer-Verlag.

Voudouris, V., Wood, J., & Fisher, P. F. (2005). Collaborative geovisualization: Object-field representations with semantic and uncertainty information. In R. Meersman, Z. Tari, & P. Herrero et al. (Eds), *OTM Workshops 2005*, Vol. 3762 of Lecture Notes in Computer Science (LNCS), Springer, Berlin

Vrakas, D., & Vlahavas, I. (2002). A heuristic for planning based on action evaluation. *Proceedings of the 10th International Conference on Artificial Intelligence: Methodology, Systems, and Applications*, (pp. 61-70). Varna, Bulgaria.

Vrakas, D., & Vlahavas, I. (2002). Combining progression and regression in state-space heuristic planning. *Proceedings of the 6th European Conference on Planning*, (pp. 1-12). Toledo, Spain.

Vrakas, D., & Vlahavas, I. (2003). A graphical interface for adaptive planning. *Proceedings of the Doctoral Con-*

sortium of the 13th International Conference on Automated Planning and Scheduling, (pp. 137-141). Trento Italy.

Vrakas, D., & Vlahavas, I. (2003). ViTAPlan: A visual tool for adaptive planning. *Proceedings of the 9th Panhellenic Conference on Informatics,* (pp. 167-177). Thessaloniki, Greece.

Vrakas, D., & Vlahavas, I. (2005). A visualization environment for planning. *International Journal on Artificial Intelligence Tools, 14*(6), 975-998

Vrakas, D., Gkioulekas, G., Refanidis, I., Sakellariou, I., & Vlahavas, I. (2002). *The PACOPLAN project: A parallel constraint planner with Java Interface.* Retrieved from http://lpis.csd.auth.gr/projects/pacoplan

Vrakas, D., Tsoumakas, G., Bassiliades, N., & Vlahavas, I. (2003). Learning rules for adaptive planning. *Proceedings of the 13th International Conference on Automated Planning and Scheduling,* (pp. 82-91). Trento, Italy.

W3C. (2001). *Extensible stylesheet language* (XSL). Retrieved October 6, 2006 from http://www.w3c.org/TR/xsl/

W3C. (2003). *XML query use cases.* Retrieved October 6, 2006 from http://www.w3.org/TR/xmlquery-use-cases

W3C. (2003). *XQuery: An XML query language.* Retrieved October 6, 2006 from http://www.w3.org/XML/Query

W3C. (2006). *XQuery update facility.* Retrieved October 6, 2006 from http://www.w3.org/TR/2006/WD-xqupdate-20060127/

Wallace, C. S., & Dowe, D. L. (1994). Intrinsic classification by MML: The snob program. In C. Zhang, J. Debenham, & D. Lukose (Ed.), *Proceedings of the Australian Joint Conference on Artificial Intelligence* (pp. 37-44). World Scientific.

Wang, J. Z., Wiederhold, G., Firschein, O., & Wei, S. X. (1998). Content-based image indexing and searching using Daubechies' wavelets. *International Journal on Digital Libraries (IJODL), 1*(4), 311-328.

Wang, W., Yang, J., & Muntz, R. R. (1997). STING: A statistical information grid approach to spatial data mining. In M. Jarke, M. J. Carey, K. R. Dittrich, F. H. Lochovsky, P. Loucopoulos, & M. A. Jeusfeld (Ed.), *Proceedings of the 23rd International Conference on Very Large Data Bases (VLDB)* (pp. 186-195). San Francisco: Morgan Kaufmann Publishers.

Ward, J. H. (1963). Hierarchical grouping to optimize an objective function. *Journal of the American Statistical Association 58*(301), 236-244.

Ware, C. (2000) *Information visualization: Perception for design.* Morgan Kaufmann.

Warmer, J., & Kleppe, A. (2003). *The object constraint language: Getting your models ready for MDA* (2nd ed.). Boston: Pearson Education.

Warphaus. (2006). *WARPhaus exhibition.* Retrieved from http://www.cise.ufl.edu/class/cap4403sp06/Gallery/WARPhaus.exhibition/index.html

Wenyin, L., Qian, W., Xiao, R., & Jin, X. (2001). Smart sketchpad: An online graphics recognition system. *Proceedings of ICDAR'01* (pp. 1050-1054). IEEE Press.

Wessel, M., & Haarslev, V. (1998). VISCO: Bringing visual spatial querying to reality. *IEEE Symposium on Visual Languages* (pp. 170-177).

Wikipedia. (2006). *User interface.* Wikipedia, the free encyclopedia. Retrieved November 3, 2006, from http://en.wikipedia.org/wiki/ User_interface

Wilkins, D. E., Lee, T. J., & Berry, P. (2003). Interactive execution monitoring of agent teams. *Journal of Artificial Intelligence Research, 18*, 217-261.

Williamson, C., & Shneiderman, B. (1992). The dynamic homefinder: Evaluating dynamic queries in a real estate information exploration system. *SIGIR'92* (pp. 339-46). Copenhagen.

Wilson, M. (2002). Six views of embodied cognition. *Psychonomic Bulletin and Review, 9*(4), 625-636.

Winikoff, M. (1996). Hitch Hiker's Guide to Lygon 0.7. Technical Report TR 96/36, University of Melbourne, Dept. of Computer Science.

Winograd, T., & Flores, F. (1986). *Understanding computers and cognition.* Norwood, NJ: Ablex Publishing Corporation.

Wood, J. D., Fisher, P. F., Dykes, J. A., Unwin, D. J., & Stynes, K. (1999). The use of the landscape metaphor in understanding population data. *Environment and Planning B: Planning and Design, 26,* pp. 281-295.

Wu, D., Sirin, E., Hendler, J., Nau, D., & Parsia, B. (2003). Automatic Web services composition using SHOP2. *ICAPS 2003 Workshop on Planning for Web Services.*

Wylie, J. L., & Wagenfeld-Heintz, E. (2004). Development of relationship-centered care. *Journal for Healthcare Quality, 26*(1), 14-21.

XMI specification at the OMG home page (2006). http://www.omg.org/docs/formal/05-09-01.pdf

Xu, X., Ester, M., Kriegel, H. P., & Sander, J. (1998). A distribution-based clustering algorithm for mining in large spatial databases. *Proceedings of the International Conference on Data Engineering (ICDE)* (pp. 324-331). Los Alamitos, CA: IEEE Computer Society.

Yasuda, H., Takahashi, K., & Matsumoto. T. (2000). A discrete HMM for online handwriting recognition. *International Journal of Pattern Recognition and Artificial Intelligence, 14*(5), 675-688.

Yu, B. (2003). Recognition of freehand sketches using mean shift. *Proceedings of International Conference on Intelligent User Interfaces* (pp. 204-210). ACM Press.

Zadeh, L. A. (1965). Fuzzy sets. *Information and Control, 8*(3), 338-353.

Zampelli, S., Deville, Y., & Dupont, P. (2004). Finding patterns in biochemical networks: A constraint programming approach. *Proceedings of the 5th Open Days in Biology, Computer Science, and Mathematics, JOBIM 2004* (pp. J0-85).

Zhang, G., Chu, W. W., Meng, F., & Kong, G. (1999). Query formulation from high-level concepts for relational databases. *International Workshop on User Interfaces to Data Intensive Systems (UIDIS'99)* (pp. 64-75).

Zhang, K., Zhang, D. Q., & Cao, J. (2001). Design, construction, and application of a generic visual language generation environment. *IEEE Transactions on Software Engineering, 27*(4), 289-307.

Zhu, N., Grundy, J. C., & Hosking, J. G. (2004). Pounamu: A meta-tool for multi-view visual language environment construction. *Proceedings of the 2005 IEEE Symposium on Visual Languages and Human-Centric Computing* (pp. 254-256). Dallas, Texas, USA.

Zimányi, E., & Skhiri dit Gabouje, S. (2004). Semantic visualization of biochemical databases. *Semantic for GRID Databases: Proceedings of the International Conference on Semantics for a Networked World, ICSNW04* (pp. 199-214). LNCS 3226, Springer.

Zloof, M. M. (1977). Query-by-example: A data base language. *IBM System Journal, 16*(4), 324-343.

Zwaan, R. A. (2004). The immersed experiencer: Toward an embodied theory of language comprehension. In B. H. Ross (Ed.), *The psychology of learning and motivation* (p. 44). New York: Academic Press.

About the Contributors

Fernando Ferri received his degrees in electronics engineering and a PhD in medical informatics at the University of Rome "La Sapienza." Starting as a researcher at the National Research Council of Italy, he was a contract professor at the Sistemi di Elaborazione at the University of Macerata (1993-2000). He is the author of more than 90 papers in international journals, books, and conferences. His main methodological areas of interest are human-computer interaction visual languages, visual interfaces, sketch-based interfaces, and multimodal interfaces, data and knowledge bases, and geographic information systems.

* * *

Jesus M. Almendros-Jimenez received his MS and PhD degrees from the Complutense University of Madrid, Spain (1992, 1999). From 1992 to 1999, he was associate professor at the Complutense University of Madrid. Since 1999, he has been associate professor at the University of Almeria. His research interest has been on software engineering, especially on UML, model driven development, and user interface design. He is also interested in programming languages: declarative and database programming languages.

Dimosthenis Anagnostopoulos is associate professor at Harokopio University of Athens. He received a degree and a doctorate degree both in computer science from the University of Athens (1991, 1996). He has published more than 50 papers in refereed journals and conference proceedings. His research interests include modeling and simulation, business process modeling, object-oriented systems, and distributed systems and networks, as well as modeling and performance evaluation of transportation systems.

Grigoris Antoniou is professor of computer science at the University of Crete, and head of the Information Systems Laboratory at FORTH, Greece. Previously he held professorial appointments at Griffith University, Australia, and the University of Bremen, Germany. His research interests lie in knowledge representation and reasoning, and its application to Web information systems. He has published more than 150 technical papers and is co-author of *A Semantic Web Primer*, the standard textbook on the semantic Web, published by the MIT Press. He participates, among other projects, in the REWERSE Network of Excellence.

Nick Bassiliades received a BSc degree in physics from the Aristotle University of Thessaloniki, Greece (1991), an MSc degree in applied artificial intelligence from the University of Aberdeen, Scotland (1992), and a PhD degree in parallel knowledge base systems from the Department of Informatics, Aristotle University, Thessaloniki, Greece (1998), where he is currently an assistant professor. His research interests include knowledge base systems, rule systems, and the semantic Web. He has published more than 60 papers and articles in international journals, conferences, and books, and co-authored an international book on parallel, object-oriented, and active knowledge base systems and a Greek book on artificial intelligence. He has been involved in Greek and European projects concerning knowledge based systems, intelligent agents, e-learning, Web services, the semantic Web, etc. He is a member of the Greek Computer and Artificial Intelligence Societies and a member of the IEEE and the ACM.

Paolo Bottoni graduated in physics in 1988 and obtained his doctoral degree in computer science in 1995. Since 1994, he has been with the Department of Computer Science of the University "La Sapienza" of Rome, first as a researcher, and since 2000 as an associate professor. His research interests are mainly in the area of interactive computing, and include definition of pictorial and visual languages, visual simulation, formal models of visual interactive computing, agent-based computing, and multimedia applications for creative processes and fruition of cultural heritage. On these topics, he has published 120 scientific papers in international journals, contributed volumes, and conference proceedings.

Alessandro Campi received his PhD in computer science from Politecnico di Milano, Italy (2004) with a dissertation on extensions of XQuery, the query language for XML. He is now assistant professor at Politecnico di Milano, Italy. His main interests are query languages, software engineering, and data intensive Web site generation. He is also interested in Semantic Web and information retrieval.

Maria Chiara Caschera received her degree in informatic engineering at the University of Rome "La Sapienza" (2005). Since 2005, she has been a PhD student in computer science at the Roma Tre University sponsored by the Multi Media & Modal Laboratory (M3L) of the National Research Council of Italy. She is the author of eight international papers. She is mainly interested in human-computer interaction, multimodal interaction, visual languages, visual interfaces, and sketch-based interfaces.

Tiziana Catarci received her PhD in computer science from the University of Rome, where she is currently a full professor. She has published more than 100 papers and 10 books in a variety of subjects comprising user interfaces for databases, 2D and 3D data visualization, adaptive interfaces, visual metaphors, usability testing, data quality, cooperative database systems, database integration, and Web access.

Valéria M. B. Cavalcanti graduated in computer science at UNIPÊ-University Center of João Pessoa, João Pessoa-Brazil (2002) and received a masters in computer science at Federal at University of Campina Grande, Campina Grande-Brazil (2005). Research interests are geographic information systems and visual query systems.

Eduardo Costa has a PhD from Cornell University (1979). After his PhD, he worked for the Danske Meteorologiske Institut under I. S. Mikkelsen, and at the Brasilian Institute of Space Research. At different times, he has been professor at Sao Paulo University (USP), Sao Paulo State University (UNESP), Federal University of Uberlandia, and Utah State University. He also worked as visiting researcher at Université Paul Sabatier, Toulouse, France. His main interests are in computer languages, artificial intelligence, and computer modeling of geophysical phenomena, like Aurora Borealis and Ionospheric Ion Drift.

Maria F. Costabile has been a full professor since 2000 in the Department of Computer Science at the University of Bari, Italy, where she teaches human-computer interaction for the computer science curriculum. Formerly, she worked as assistant professor at the University of Calabria, Italy (1981-1988), and as associate professor at the University of Bari (1989-1999). She is currently the coordinator of the computer science curriculum at the University of Bari. She has been visiting scientist in several foreign universities, primarily in USA and Germany. Her current research interests are in human-computer interaction, visual system design, multimodal and multimedia interaction, usability engineering, adaptive interfaces, user models, information visualizations, and visual data mining. She has published more than 100 papers in scientific journals, books, and proceedings of international conferences, and edited six books, published by ACM Press and Springer. She has received several grants from national and international organizations for research on the previous topics. Costabile is regularly in the program committees of international conferences and workshops including IEEE Symposium of Visual Languages and the IEEE Human Centric Computing. She is in the steering committee of the International Working Conference on Advanced Visual Interfaces (AVI), which is in cooperation with ACM SIGCHI. She has been program chair of AVI 2004 and program co-chair of Interact 2005. She is a member of ACM and senior member of IEEE; she is a founding member of the Italian Chapter of ACM SIGCHI, and served as chair from 1996 to 2000.

Gennaro Costagliola received a Laurea degree *cum laude* in computer science from the University of Salerno, Italy (1987) and an MS degree in computer science from the University of Pittsburgh (1991). From 1991 to 1993, he was a visiting researcher at the University of Pittsburgh. He is currently a professor and director of the Laurea degree courses in computer science at the University of Salerno. His research interests include software engineering, visual languages, parsing technologies, multimedia databases, Web technologies, and e-learning.

Juan de Lara is an associate professor at the Universidad Autonóma (UAM) de Madrid in Spain, where he teaches software engineering, automata theory as well as modelling and simulation. His research interests include Web-based simulation, meta-modelling, graph transformation, distance learning, and agent-based simulation. He received his PhD at UAM in computer science (2000). During 2001, as a post-doctoral researcher at McGill University, he created the AToM3 prototype. Later, he also spent several periods at TU Berlin and the University of Rome "La Sapienza" working on graph transformation.

Kristine Deray is a senior lecturer in design at the University of Technology, Sydney. Her research is focused on human centered design with an emphasis upon intuitive human computer interface/interaction design in information technologies for consumer/patient empowerment and facilitation of communication in health care. Deray's unique scholarship is based on her interdisciplinary background in design computing, human movement studies and dance, and visual representation in plastic arts. She was a visiting artist to the School for New Dance Development in Amsterdam and has exhibited her work both locally and internationally, including the National Gallery of Australia. Kristine is the leader of the governmental community health project with Health Services Network, Australia, focused on the social construction of knowledge and community participation in health services. Currently she is completing her PhD on "human movement as a framework for representation of interactions"

Cláudio de Souza Baptista graduated in computer science from the Federal University of Paraíba-Campina Grande, Brazil (1989), received a masters in computer science at Federal University of Paraíba-Campina Grande, Brazil (2001), and a doctorate degree in computer science at University of Kent at Canterbury, Great-Britain. He is full professor at Federla Unviersity of Campina Grande, Campina Grande – Brazil. At present, he is coordinating a project called iGIS-Internet geographic information system. Main research interests are geographic information systems, multimedia databases, and digital libraries.

Vincenzo Deufemia graduated in computer science (cum laude) (1999). He received a PhD degree in computer science from the University of Salerno (2003). He is currently an assistant professor in computer science at Salerno University. His main research focuses on grammar formalisms and parsing techniques for visual languages, software-development environments, recovery of design patterns in object-oriented code, and sketch understanding. He published several peer-reviewed articles on these topics in international journals, books, conferences, and workshops. He has served as a program committee member for several international conferences.

Arianna D'Ulizia received her degree in informatic engineering at the University of Rome "La Sapienza" (2005). Since 2005, she has been a PhD student in computer science at the Roma Tre University sponsored by the Multi Media & Modal Laboratory (M3L) of the National Research Council of Italy. She is the author of eight international papers. She is mainly interested in human computer interaction, multimodal interaction, visual languages, visual interfaces, and geographical query languages.

Paul A. Fishwick is professor of computer and information science and engineering at the University of Florida in Gainesville, Florida. His primary areas of research interest are in computer simulation modeling methodology, aesthetic computing, and visualization. He obtained the PhD in computer science from the University of Pennsylvania (1986), has published more than 180 technical publications, and has served on editorial boards for transactions of SCS, ACM, and IEEE.

Daniela Fogli received the Laurea degree in computer science from the University of Bologna, Italy (1994) and a PhD degree in information engineering from the University of Brescia, Italy (1998). Since 2000, she has been assistant professor at the University of Brescia, Department of Electronics for Automation. In 2005, she has been visiting scholar at the Center for LifeLong Learning & Design (L3D), University of Colorado at Boulder, USA. Her current research interests are concerned with specification and design of visual interactive systems, W3C technologies supporting the implementation of visual interactive systems, meta-design, and end-user development techniques.

Dino Frediani received his degree in computer science at the University "La Sapienza" of Rome, Italy (2006), with a thesis on interactive definition of communication semantics for visual languages," from which the SemM tool is based. Since then he has been working on network and security projects.

Patrizia Grifoni received her degree in electronics engineering at the University of Rome "La Sapienza." She is a researcher of the National Research Council of Italy. From 1994 to 1999, she was a contract professor of "Elaborazione digitale delle immagini" at the University of Macerata. She is the author of more than 70 papers in journals, books, and conferences. Her scientific interests have evolved from query languages for statistical and geographic databases to the focal topics related to human-computer interaction, multimodal interaction, visual languages, visual interfaces, sketch-based interfaces, and accessing Web information.

Alexandre Grings got a BASc and MASc in computer science from the Federal University of Uberlandia, Brazil. Today he is PhD student working on computer modeling of geophysical phenomena. He has been working for 10 years as a consultant in computer science, network management, and support for Unix systems. His current research interests include artificial intelligence, functional languages, metaheuristics, mathematical modeling, distributed computing, and computer simulation.

Esther Guerra works as an assistant professor in the DEI lab (Interactive Systems Research group) at the Universidad Carlos III de Madrid, in Spain. Her research interests mainly concern topics such as meta-modelling, graph transformation, and their application for the automatic generation of environments for domain specific visual languages. In fact, these are the topics of her ongoing PhD thesis on computer science. She has spent some time at TU Berlin and the University of Rome "La Sapienza" working on graph transformation.

Ourania Hatzi received a degree in computer science from the Aristotle University of Thessaloniki, Greece (2004).

She is currently a PhD candidate in the area of intelligent systems for managing Web services in the semantic Web at the Department of Geography, Harokopio University, Athens, Greece. Her research interests are primarily focused on the semantic Web, Web service composition, and AI planning.

Luis Iribarne received a BSc degree in computer science from the University of Granada, and MSc and PhD degrees in computer science from the University of Almería, Spain. From 1991 to 1993, he worked as a lecturer at the University of Granada. In 1993, he collaborated as IT service analyst at the University School of Almería, and he served for nine years as a lecturer in the Polytechnic School at the University of Almería. Since 1991, he worked in several national and international research projects and contributions on distributed simulation, modeling of information systems, and geographic information systems (GIS). In 2001, he joined Information Systems Group and then became associate professor, University of Almería (2002). His research interests include component-based software development, modeling of complex systems, UML design, model driven development and user interface design, and 3D graphical computing.

Stephen Kimani is currently an academic and research member of Jomo Kenyatta University of Agriculture and Technology (Kenya) and is affiliated with the University of Rome "La Sapienza." He has been a post-doctoral researcher with the University of Rome "La Sapienza" (2004-2006). He holds a PhD in computer engineering (University of Rome "La Sapienza," Italy) and an MSc in advanced computing (University of Bristol, UK). His main research interest is in human-computer interaction (HCI). In particular, as HCI relates to areas/aspects such as user interfaces, usability, accessibility, visualization, visual information access, visual data mining, digital libraries, and ubiquitous computing.

Efstratios Kontopoulos holds a BSc in mathematics from the Aristotle University of Thessaloniki, Greece and an MSc in computer studies from the University of Essex, UK. He is currently pursuing a PhD in the area of inferencing systems for the semantic Web at the Department of Informatics, Aristotle University, Thessaloniki, Greece. His research interests are primarily focused on the semantic Web, defeasible reasoning, and intelligent agents. He is a member of the Intelligent Systems and Knowledge Processing group (http://iskp.csd.auth.gr) at the same university.

Stefano Levialdi finished high school at St Andrews' Scots School, Buenos Aires (1953) and obtained a degree in telecommunications engineering at the University of Buenos Aires, Argentina (1959). He won a scholarship at Marconi Wireless (Chelmsford, UK) (1960), and was next appointed as a lecturer in electronics at the University of Genoa, Italy (1961). After working for the Italian National Council for Research (CNR) for 13 years and leading a research group working on Parallel Image Processing, he became full professor of computer science (1981) at the University of Bari moving to Rome University "La Sapienza" (1983). In 1984, he shifted his research interests to visual interaction, interface design, and usability evaluation within the larger area of human-computer interaction together with a small group of researchers in Hiroshima (Japan). Levialdi has published more than 235 papers (on journals and in proceedings) co-authored more than 150 different researches, has edited more than 20 books, and is associate editor of journals devoted to pattern recognition and image processing. He is founder and co-editor of the *Journal of Visual Languages and Computing* (Elsevier Press) together with Prof. Shi-Kuo Chang, since 1990. He has taught computer programming, computer architectures, image processing, and presently two courses on human-computer interaction. He became IEEE fellow in 1988 and IEEE life fellow 2001 and is actively engaged in the organization of a variety of scientific meetings (IEEE Visual Language Symposia and ACM Advanced Visual Interfaces Working Conferences) since 1979. He was general chairman of the IEEE Symposia on human-centric computing held in Stresa on September 2001 and was the general chairman of the ACM Working Conference on Advanced Visual Interfaces that took place in Trento on May 2002. He was general chairman of Interact '05, an IFIPS conference held in Rome on September

2005. He is the panel chairman for Interact 2007 to be held in Rio de Janeiro in September 2007 and general chairman of Advanced Visual Interfaces (co-sponsored by ACM) to be held in Naples in 2008. Levialdi is the director of the Pictorial Computing Laboratory at the Department of Informatics, University of Rome and also is the head of the Laboratory for Usability and Accessibility studies at the main campus of the same University of Rome, "La Sapienza." Levialdi has given lectures and seminars in over 30 countries and has strong links with Universities from United States, Japan, Costa Rica, and Argentina.

Stefano Lodi received his PhD in electronic engineering from the University of Bologna, where he is currently associate professor. His research interests include knowledge representation, biomedical data analysis, knowledge discovery, and data mining. In particular, he has published papers in agent-based and peer-to-peer distributed data mining, visual data mining, and stream data mining.

Andrea Marcante received a Laurea degree in philosophy (1999) and master degree in computer science and communication for humanities (2000), at the University of Milano (UniMI), Italy. He is achieving a PhD in information society at University of Milano-Bicocca, Italy. He works in the ITIM group of ITC-CNR, in Milano, Italy. Since 2003, he is a tutor in the human-computer interaction courses and responsible of the Computer Semiotics Lab at Dept. of Information and Communication – UniMI. His main interests are computer semiotics, focusing on problems of human-computer interaction and management of electronic documents in the Web.

Stephanie Larissa Marsh is a PhD candidate in the School of Informatics, City University. Her research focuses on investigating the use of usability in geovisualization and how usability can most effectively support the development of geovisualization tools. She has a BSc in environmental geoscience from University College London and an MSc in geographic information from City University, her masters dissertation relating to the modification of OS MasterMap for specialist users.

Davide Martinenghi received his PhD in computer science from Roskilde University, Denmark, in 2005 with a dissertation on integrity checking for deductive databases, and is now assistant professor at the Free University of Bozen-Bolzano, Italy. His main interests are data integrity maintenance, data integration, logic programming, knowledge representation, and, in a broad sense, applications of logic to database systems. Recently he focused on the development of visual paradigms for the representation of data and actions in XML. He is also interested in software engineering and object-oriented programming and design.

Bernd Meyer is a senior lecturer in computer science at Monash University, Melbourne, Australia. He received his doctoral degree in 1994 for a thesis on "visual logic languages for spatial information handling" and has since been working on visual language specification, diagrammatic reasoning, and smart diagrammatic environments. His work on these and related topics is published in more than 50 papers.

Piero Mussio is full professor of computer science at the University of Milano (Italy), where he is the head of the Computer Semiotic Laboratory. His research interests include human computer interaction, visual communication, and interaction design. He published more than 150 scientific papers in international journal and conference proceedings. He served as scientific coordinator and principal investigator of national, regional and local research units in several international and national projects and industrial contracts. He is fellow IAPR, member of the ACM, member of the Pictorial Computing Laboratory; associate editor of the *Journal of Visual Languages and Computing*.

Marco Padula is senior researcher in information technology at the Institute for Construction Technologies – CNR, Milan. He is professor of system usability design at the Faculty of Language sciences and foreign literature of the

Catholic University of Brescia. He co-authored more then 40 contributions to international journals and conferences. His research interests include social informatics, distributed databases, Web-based services, and Web-based interaction.

Loredana Parasiliti Provenza received a Laurea degree in mathematics from the University of Messina, Italy (2001) and a masters degree in information and communication security from the University of Milano, Italy (2002). She took the PhD degree in computer science at the University of Milano (2006). Since May 2002, she is a research grant holder at the University of Milano, Department of Information and Communication. Her current research interests include specification, design, and development of visual interactive systems, theory of visual languages, W3C technologies, XML security, and privacy preserving data mining.

Antonio Piccinno received a Laurea degree with full marks and honors in computer science from the University of Bari (2001). In 2001, he worked as research collaborator of the Department of Computer Science. In March 2005, he got a PhD. Since April 15, 2005, he is assistant researcher at the Computer Science Department of the University of Bari. His research interests focus on human-computer interaction, visual interactive systems, theory of visual languages, end-user development, meta-design and multimodal and multimedia interaction. He was in the scientific secretariat of the International Conference AVI 2004 (advanced visual interfaces). He is member of ACM, ACM SIGCHI, and SIGCHI Italy.

Giuseppe Polese is an associate professor in the Department of Mathematics and Computer Science at the University of Salerno, Italy. His research interests include visual languages, multimedia databases, e-learning, and multimedia software engineering. He received a Laurea degree in computer science from the University of Salerno, an MS in computer science from the University of Pittsburgh, and a PhD in computer science and applied mathematics from the University of Salerno.

Paolo Quattrocchi received his degree in computer science at the University of Rome "La Sapienza" (2005), with a thesis on metamodels and rewriting systems in visual languages definition, an excerpt of which was published in the IEEE Symposium on Visual Languages and Human-Centric Computing 2006, presentino the foundations of the SynM. Since 2006, he has been a software developer of the Intecs s.p.a. company in Rome.

Maurizio Rafanelli received a degree in mathematics at the University of Rome "La Sapienza." (1976) Senior scientist at the Italian National Research Council, (Istituto di Analisi dei Sistemi ed Informatica "A.Ruberti") and in charge of the research area "methods and systems for information and knowledge." He is the general chairman of the 4th International Conference on Statistical and Scientific Database Management (SSDBM) (Roma June 1988-LNCS N.339) and of the 10th SSDBM (Capri July 1998). He is a contract professor at the Universities of Roma ("La Sapienza" and Tor-Vergata) (1980-1995). Rafanelli is a fellowship senior at the Lawrence Berkeley Laboratory-University of California (October 1988-January 1989). Organizing and teacher of an international school "GIS and DATABASES" (Rome June 1997). He is author of more than 130 papers on international conferences and journal, of different entries in various technical encyclopedias, of the book *Multidimensional Databases: Problems and Solutions*. His current professional interests include human-computer interaction, advanced query languages, geographical information systems, and multidimensional databases.

Alessandro Raffio is a PhD student at Politecnico di Milano, Italy since 2005. His main research field is about structured data schema transformations. His research interests include search engines composition, visual query languages, and other topics concerned with XML as a data storage format. He is also working on dynamic process modeling in cooperative environments.

Amanda Reggiori is an architect and journalist and specialised in social communications. She is professor of system usability design and multimedia design at the Faculty of Language sciences and foreign literature of the Catholic University of Brescia. She cooperates to different research projects and coauthored different papers on international scientific journals.

Luigi Rende received his degree in computer science at the University of Rome "La Sapienza," (2005) with a thesis on generation and execution of visual sentences, where the foundations of the GEVS tool were layed. Since 2006, he has been working at Etnoteam as technical leader.

Marcus Santos got a BASc and MASc in computer engineering from the Federal University of Uberlandia, Brazil (1990, 1993). From 1989 to 1998, he worked as a software engineer in the development of interactive multimedia systems for training security personnel. From 1997 to 2000, he worked as a visiting researcher at the department of computer science of the University of Toronto. He got a PhD in computer engineering from the University of Sao Paulo, Brazil (2000), and since 1999, he has been at Ryerson University where he is an assistant professor of computer science. His current research interests include logic programming technologies, functional programming, visual languages, distance learning, and interactive, distributed environments.

Goran Sarajlic attended the "Werner von Siemens" high school in Bad Neustadt,Germany from December 1995 to February 1998, and then got his high school graduation in Sarajevoa. After starting the computer science studies at "Johannes Kepler" University, Linz, Austria, following participation in the ERASMUS program from September 2000-September 2001 at "La Sapienza" University, Rome, Italy, he transferred to this university where he graduated in 2005. Currently he is working for a consulting company, Araneum Srl, as software developer for the Italian Ministry of Finance.

Ulrich Schiel graduated in mathematics at the Univeristy Mackenzie-São Paulo, Brazil (1971), received a masters in computer science from PUC-Rio, Brazil (1977), and Dr.rer.nat. in computer science from University of Stuttgart, Germany. He is a visiting researcher at GMD-IPSI, Darmstadt-Germany (1988-1999). He is a full professor of Federal University of Campina Grande, Campina Grande-Brazil. At present, he is coordinating a project called "SEI-Tur: A system supporting the creation of tourist and business trips using composed Web services." Main research interests are digital libraries, temporal databases, and Web information systems.

Simeon Simoff is associate professor in the Faculty of Information Technology, University of Technology, Sydney and leader of the e-Markets Research Group—a reference lab in the area of intelligent trading technology. His internationally renowned blend of interdisciplinary scholarship integrates data mining and visual analytics, multimedia virtual worlds, and design computing. He has published extensively and developed professionally renowned educational programmes in computational analytics. Simoff has initiated and co-chaired ACM conference series in visual, multimedia, and network data mining. He is a founding director of the Institute of Analytics Professionals of Australia and Editor of the ACS Series on Conferences in Research and Practice in Information Technology.

Sabri Skhiri dit Gabouje started his career as a researcher at the Engineering Faculty of the Université Libre de Bruxelles. He published several articles on generic algorithms for drawing graphs according to the semantics of the application domain. At Alcatel Sabri, he has been working on the JAIN SLEE (JAVA API for Integrated Networks) container. He has developed the J2EE and the JAIN SIP resource adaptors and has participated to the architecture of the container. Now, he is responsible for the evolution of the Alcatel SDK towards JAIN SLEE.

Leonardo Tininini is a researcher at the CNR Institute of Systems Analysis and Computer Science. He is the author of numerous scientific papers on statistical databases, aggregate data, query languages, spatio-temporal databases, and has been referee for prestigious international conferences and journals. He is lecturer at the "Campus Bio-medico" University in Rome. He has also been collaborating with the Italian National Institute of Statistics (ISTAT) for the design of the institute's statistical dissemination system on the Web and with the French research institute INRIA.

Domenico Ventriglia received his degree in computer science at the University of Rome "La Sapienza" (1999). Since then, he has been collaborating with Computer Science Department and written several articles on visual languages and Web programming. From 1999 to 2005, he has worked in the telecommunication and publishing areas. At present, he works for KataWeb Company and he manages a publishing and technology project in Internet context.

Ioannis Vlahavas is a professor at the Department of Informatics at the Aristotle University of Thessaloniki, Greece. He received his PhD degree in logic programming systems from the same University in 1988. During the first half of 1997, he was a visiting scholar at the Department of CS at Purdue University. He specializes in logic programming, machine learning, automated planning, knowledge based, and AI systems and he has published more than140 papers in scientific journals, conference proceedings, and book chapters in international edited volumes and 6 books in these areas. He has been involved in more than 25 research and development projects, leading most of them. He was the chairman of the 2nd Hellenic Conference on AI and the host of the 2nd International Summer School on AI Planning. He is leading the Programming Languages and Software Engineering Laboratory (PLASE Lab, http://plase.csd.auth.gr/) and the Logic Programming and Intelli-gent Systems Group (LPIS Group, http://lpis.csd.auth.gr) (more information at www.csd.auth.gr/~vlahavas).

Vlasios Voudouris is a senior lecturer in business analysis/quantitative analysis at London Metropolitan University. He was a lecturer and course director in applied GIS at Birkbeck University of London. He has also worked as senior consultant in a number of private and public organizations. His research work is related to human-centred visualization, data and knowledge modeling, decision making, and applied statistics and mathematics.

Dimitris Vrakas is a post-doctoral researcher at the Department of Informatics at the Aristotle University of Thessaloniki, Greece. He has worked as an adjunct lecturer at the Departments of Informatics, Aristotle University of Thessaloniki and the Computer & Communication Engineering of the University of Thessaly. He has also taught at post-graduate courses in the Aristotle University and the University of Macedonia during the last two years. He specializes in automated planning, heuristic search, search strategies, distributed problem solving, and parallel algorithms and he has published 25 papers, one book chapter, and co-authored two books (1 in progress) in the previous areas. He has been involved in seven European and National research projects and he is a member of the American Association for Artificial Intelligence, the Association of Greek Informaticians and the Hellenic Society for Artificial Intelligence.

Esteban Zimányi is a professor at the Engineering Faculty of the Université Libre de Bruxelles (ULB). He started his studies at the Universidad Autónoma de Centro América, Costa Rica. He received a BSc (1988) and a doctorate (1992) in computer science from the Faculté des Sciences at the ULB. During 1997, he was a visiting researcher at the Database Laboratory of the Swiss Federal Institute of Technology in Lausanne, Switzerland. His current research interests include bio-informatics, spatio-temporal databases, data warehouses, and Semantic Web.

Index